Software Engineering for Variability Intensive Systems

Software Engineering for Variability Intensive Systems

Foundations and Applications

Edited by Ivan Mistrik, Matthias Galster, and Bruce R. Maxim

CRC Press
Taylor & Francis Group
Boca Raton London New York

CRC Press is an imprint of the
Taylor & Francis Group, an **Informa** business

CRC Press
Taylor & Francis Group
6000 Broken Sound Parkway NW, Suite 300
Boca Raton, FL 33487-2742

Library of Congress Cataloging-in-Publication Data

Names: Mistrik, Ivan, author. | Galster, Matthias, author. | Maxim, Bruce
R., author.
Title: Software engineering for variability intensive systems : foundations
and applications / Ivan Mistrik, Matthias Galster, Bruce Maxim.
Description: Boca Raton : Taylor & Francis, a CRC title, part of the Taylor &
Francis imprint, a member of the Taylor & Francis Group, the academic
division of T&F Informa, plc, 2019. | Includes bibliographical references.
Identifiers: LCCN 2018045899| ISBN 9780815348054 (hb : acid-free paper) |
ISBN 9780429022067 (eISBN)
Subjects: LCSH: Software engineering. | Computer systems—Design and
construction. | Chaotic behavior in systems.
Classification: LCC QA76.758 .M58 2019 | DDC 005.1—dc23
LC record available at https://lccn.loc.gov/2018045899

Visit the Taylor & Francis Web site at
http://www.taylorandfrancis.com

and the CRC Press Web site at
http://www.crcpress.com

Printed in the United Kingdom
by Henry Ling Limited

Contents

Foreword by Paul Clements

Nothing endures but change.

— **Heraclitus, 544-483 BCE**

And they probably redesigned the whole sickbay, too. I know engineers; they love to change things.

— **Dr. McCoy to Admiral Kirk in Star Trek: The Motion Picture**

I was pleased to be asked to write a foreword to this book, which is about software for variability-intensive systems.

As a reader, you may be wondering if you've come to the right place, so I would like to begin by seeing if we can draw a line around "variability-intensive systems" and look at what we've corralled.

I believe that, for all practical purposes, we've captured everything. I believe that *all* software systems are variability-intensive systems. I am hard-pressed to think of a system that has not, does not, nor will not in the future have to deal with change. Software systems swim in a sea of variability. Their mission changes, either grossly or in fine detail or in between. The world around them changes. The other systems (hardware, software, mechanical, human) with which they much interact change. Their friends (in the form of a collaboration environment) and their enemies (in the form of a threat environment) change. On it goes.

Change happens. If we build our systems responsibly, we should be ready for it.

The key question is not whether a system is variability-intensive or not, but rather how well was that system endowed by its creators with the ability to deal with change.

Let's banish from our corral the ones that aren't so endowed, because this book is about techniques for building ones that are. We will wish the banished ones well as they wade into the sea of change for which they are totally unprepared. If they are ever fortunate enough to be re-habilitated in a way to make them amenable to variation, they will find themselves back in our corral.

What can we say about the systems that remain, the ones that we wish to study, the ones that have at least a passing familiarity with variability? Variability is the ability to deal with variation. It seems to me there are two major types of variation: Variation over time, and variation over the product space.

Variation over time is how a system evolves to do new things in new ways. I began my career investigating design approaches to making systems easy to change over time. It was a long time ago, when bytes of storage and microseconds of clock time were both expensive, and so programs were written to optimize the use of both. Assembly programmers would use tricks such as (when introducing a new numeric constant) scanning the program's binary to find the bit pattern they needed, slap a label on it, and voila! A new constant born with zero additional memory cost. Feel free to shudder—imagine maintaining a program like that—but such was the world once upon a time, a world sorely in need of ways to build variability-intensive systems.

Fast forward to a better world today. Software engineers have at their disposal a plethora of generalized techniques to create programs amenable to evolutionary change and, at least in certain domains, to create programs that have the ability to change *themselves* as they run and as the need arises.

For me and perhaps for at least some of you as well, a very interesting corner of variability-intensive systems deals with variability across the product function space. Put another way, this corner deals with variability not for a program, but for programs. Here we enter the world of product lines—a family of systems, similar to each other but different as well. Each member of the product line carries out a particular mission or provides a particular functionality for a particular customer or market segment. Thus, the family is created to be handle a variability-intensive setting. Product line engineering is the discipline that teaches us how to build these families as a single undertaking, not as a collection of separate things, because it pays handsomely to do so.

Product line engineering grew out of the software reuse and (more helpfully) the generative programming movements of the 1970s, but its roots go back centuries. In ancient Rome, the wealthy or semi-wealthy could commission marble statues of themselves to impress their friends and signal their station in society. Clever suppliers employed less skilled craftsmen to carve the same statue body over and over, and more skilled craftsmen to carve the customer's head to sit atop it. In 1103 A.D., Li Chieh, the state architect of Chinese emperor Hui-tsung wrote the *Ying tsao fa shih* (營造法式). A set of building codes for official buildings, it described the layout, materials, and practices for designing and building imperial structures. It listed standard parts and standard ways of connecting the parts, as well as parameterized variations of the parts. It allowed components based on the building's purpose, and gave options for various component choices. In short, it specified a product line of buildings.

Today product lines are everywhere. You probably drive a member of one, fly to meetings or vacations in a member of one, stay in a hotel that is a member of one, order a member of one at a fast food restaurant, listen to your music in a member of one, and you may even live in a member of one. Look around you right now and count the product lines you see, and don't stop until you've reached a dozen. It shouldn't take you more than a minute.

Beginning around 2000, commercially-available industrial-strength automation became available to support product line engineering in the software engineering, and then the systems engineering, fields. The tooling is the underpinning for a highly mature, repeatable, and well-defined methodology to replace the confusing jumble of ad hoc approaches that filled books and papers before. Known as Feature-based Systems and Software Product Line Engineering, or Feature-based PLE for short, it is the approach behind industrial successes by companies like General Motors, Lockheed Martin, and General Dynamics, who are all writing about PLE-engendered savings totaling many tens of millions of dollars each and every year.

Product line engineering does not occupy the whole space of variability-intensive systems, of course, and only some of the chapters in this book deal with it. But I like to think of it as a high-profile, highly-developed, high-payoff, industrially-pedigreed proof point of the importance of studying ways to build variability-intensive systems.

I hope you can put the ideas in this book to good use. Although great progress has been made, we still live in a world sorely in need of ways to build variability-intensive systems.

Paul Clements
Austin, Texas

References

1. Clements, P., Gregg, S., Krueger, C., Lanman, J., Rivera, J., Scharadin, R., Shepherd, J., and Winkler, A., "Second Generation Product Line Engineering Takes Hold in the DoD," *Crosstalk, The Journal of Defense Software Engineering*, USAF Software Technology Support Center, 2013.
2. Wozniak, L., Clements, P. "How Automotive Engineering Is Taking Product Line Engineering to the Extreme," *Proc. SPLC 2015*, Nashville, 2015.

Foreword by Ian Gorton

It's almost amusing to remember that 20 years ago, the software process movement was in full swing. Replete with maturity models, software process best practices, rigorous methods and hordes of process metrics, the industry strived to bake in the 'correct functionality' upfront through rigorous requirements identification and management.

This was waterfall-style development on the scale of Victoria Falls!

Some process models incorporated iterative and incremental approaches to enable some sensible handling of the inevitable changes in requirements that systems experience. Variability was carefully modeled and analyzed to attempt to maximize reuse and provide stable base platforms for system derivatives. Still, process, structure, documentation and metrics ruled the roost, as systems were mostly intellectually manageable in scale for individuals and small teams.

In some application domains, typically ones associated with tightly coupled software-hardware interactions (e.g. military, telecommunications, embedded systems, medical), or very stable business processes (typically found in government), these modeling and process-driven approaches made some sense and delivered many successes. Let's face it, if a software system is controlling a device that is keeping a patient alive, it's desirable that the software has been carefully designed and thoroughly tested and certified across different product variants so unexpected errors cannot impact a patient's life.

Such systems tend to evolve in controlled ways as hardware devices provide a stable set of characteristics to build on and evolve less frequently than software. In fact, the hardware platforms often defined the variability a system needed to exhibit, bringing some sense of stability to designs and evolutions. In contrast, the greatest advantage, and also disadvantage of software is that it is so easy to change.

When such devices must be customized to multiple different environments, approaches like software product lines provide sensible ways to manage variability across product variants. Product lines have successfully defined a rich set of processes and guidelines by which to engineer such product variability. Combined with the continued success of the CMMI Institute, this is a testament to the enduring success of these modeling and process-based approaches in a collection of application domains.

Still, not even rigor and process and models can always deliver success, as the continued failure of the F-35 fleet clearly demonstrates.

For example:

"The F-35 was built around the Autonomic Logistics Information System (ALIS). The software's final version has gone through 31 iterations but has yet to be rolled out because of 'key remaining deficiencies,' including vulnerability to cyberattacks.

Contributing to the "already overloaded" repair backlog is the fact that the diagnostic software often mistakenly flags parts for failure, requiring them to be sent back to Lockheed Martin for testing.

They then come back to the supply chain marked 'Re-Test OK' (RTOK), while the planes sit in hangars unable to fly."

The F-35 has been in development for approaching two decades. Sometimes, massive software systems are just hard to build. Period.

As the process movement was nearing its peak in the late 1990s, the seeds of its decline from the mainstream were being sown in two related areas.

First, in the mid-1990s, nascent "agile" methods were emerging, culminating in the Agile Manifesto in 2001. Agile methods were a reaction to rigor and process, and explicitly recognized variability and change as inevitable, intrinsic aspects of software engineering. Agile methods now dominate software development outside the domains where safety and hardware interactions are not relevant.

Second, the Internet boom was looming. Google was formed in 1998, the same year Yahoo added its Web portal. Organizations were starting to conduct business through their websites, a model pioneered by eBay.com and Amazon.com in this same timeframe. Exponential growth was inevitable, and today we see the ever-evolving results of this incredible, software-driven innovation. Hyperscalable systems [1] such as Facebook, YouTube, SalesForce, and Expedia are now woven into the fabric of society and business.

The complexity of these hyperscalable systems should not be underestimated. They comprise tens of millions of lines of code, execute on thousands of communicating and coordinated machines that are distributed globally, are written in tens of different languages, and build upon multiple layers of composed software libraries, both closed and open source. They process literally petabytes of data each day. Storing and managing exabytes of data is no longer uncommon. These are immense software systems, no doubt some of the most complex *machines* that humans have ever built.

As a concrete example, [2] describes the Google codebase:

"The Google codebase includes approximately one billion files and has a history of approximately 35 million commits spanning Google's entire 18-year existence. The repository contains 86TBs of data, including approximately two billion lines of code in nine million unique source files.

In 2014, approximately 15 million lines of code were changed in approximately 250,000 files in the Google repository on a weekly basis."

Building hyperscale systems throws a new light on the notion of variability and evolution in software systems. At scale, variability and change is inevitable.

Thousands of developers work concurrently on these systems, making tens of thousands of changes each day. Such systems are not static entities, evolving in controlled ways.

They are constantly in flux, changing every second in both minor (e.g., bug fixes) and major ways (e.g., A/B testing). No models exist of these systems, and no one overseas the evolution and change of the system as a whole.

This is a different world to the ones explored in this book. The chapters presented here describe the cutting-edge research results and directions based on system, architecture, and requirements models that can be created, managed, analyzed, and evolved in relatively slowly-changing systems. The techniques described give examples of current research directions and powerful results applicable to engineering when the pace and scale of variability and change can be controlled and comprehended.

However, variability in hyperscale systems is undoubtedly an area lacking in study and research. Current best practices in engineering hyperscale systems such as devops, infrastructure-as-code, microservice architectures, observability [3] and cloud platforms provide potential entry points into this area of study.

For example, can Software-as-a-Service platforms be effectively managed and evolved to exhibit variability for a huge range of customers using techniques from established product line engineering? How is the evolution of features supported by a widely used open source framework (e.g. messaging, database, security platforms) analyzed and managed at scale? Can observed performance monitoring data be used to direct efforts in to understanding, or even automatically transforming a system to provide differentiated quality of service for different classes of customers based on price? What aspects of variability can be specified through configuration variables rather than code changes at scale?

There are myriad open problems in hyperscalable systems that researchers in variability are perfectly positioned to work on. I hope this excellent book can act as a springboard for such research. It's needed both from a practical perspective, as the complexity of systems we engineer grows exponentially. And in reality, it is inevitable. In the not too distant future, all devices and systems will become ever more connected and woven into the Internet of Things. This will mean the dimensions of variability, the scope of changes, and most inevitably, the pace of change in all application domains will demand innovation in our knowledge and methods.

Ian Gorton
Seattle, Washington

References

1. Gorton, I. (2017). Hyperscalability–The Changing Face of Software Architecture, in *Software Architecture for Big Data and the Cloud* (1st ed.). Cambridge, MA, Morgan Kaufmann.
2. Rachel Potvin, Josh Levenberg, Why Google Stores Billions of Lines of Code in a Single Repository, *Communications of the ACM*, July 2016, Vol. 59, No. 7, pp. 78-87.
3. John Klein, Ian Gorton, Laila Alhmoud, Joel Gao, Caglayan Gemici, et al. Model-Driven Observability for Big Data Storage. *WICSA* 2016: 134-139

Foreword by John C. Grundy

Introduction

Once upon a time, computer systems were monolithic hardware and software beasts that had very limited end users, resided in one place, underwent limited change during maintenance, and were generally developed with top-down, waterfall-style approaches. As smaller, more diverse computing systems arose, and as end users and application domains became far more diverse, this approach failed to keep up with need. Computer systems needed to be deployed in ever more diverse environments. End users of a computer system—and their requirements and expectations of the system—may change greatly during its lifespan [1]. Very heterogeneous computing platforms, operating systems, programming languages, interaction technologies, integration approaches, and structuring and development of systems arose. These included diverse computing devices (cloud, HPC, desktop, laptop, tablet, phone, wearable, sensor, etc); dynamic programming languages; adaptive software architectures supporting runtime updates; Web, mobile, Internet of Things, Virtual and Augmented Reality, ubiquitous interfaces; AI-based software; product line, service-oriented, micro-services, edge and fog computing-based architectures; and various agile methods and end-user development support [1,3,4,5,6,7]. In all of these domains, the computing systems undergo sometimes very dramatic variability during their lifespan.

Building such systems is (very) hard [1,8]. They are inherently much more complex than traditional computing systems [9]. Development methods may need to include diverse stakeholders, including end users, who expect to be able to reconfigure their systems during use in various ways. Deployment environments, other applications to integrate with and all potential end users and their requirements might not even be known in advance. New architectures support greater variability but require improved modelling, development, implementation and testing practices. Systems don't operate in isolation and diverse interaction devices and deployment environments have resulted in much more complex scenarios of human-computer interaction and computer-computer interaction. Huge increases in compute and storage capacity, range of size and number of devices in a computer system, and concerns for energy efficiency, performance and reliability impact management of and capacity for variability. Increasing numbers of safety critical systems, including infrastructure, health, manufacturing, business, education, and personal usage make dependence on variability-intensive systems much more prevalent [3]. Systems are under almost constant threat from cybersecurity attacks of various sorts. Systems that are inherently meldable at runtime have significant advantages—but also significant disadvantages—over traditional systems.

Why Variability-Intensive Systems?

Given how hard such systems are to engineer, in general, why would we want to make use of such challenging things? Increasingly there is an expectation that computing systems will "vary" throughout their lifecycle [1,3,7,10]. This variability takes on various forms:

- Ability to modify a system at runtime e.g. patch code while it runs, integrate new services or make use of a different service;
- Ability to add new components to a system at run-time e.g. new sensors for a smart home, make use of new visualisations for a data analytics platform;
- Ability to tailor system to diverse application domains, users, integrations, etc e.g. product line templates instantiated to different using company contexts, different security solutions available depending on organisational deployment context;
- Deploying software systems on heterogeneous, unpredictable platforms e.g. deploying on different mobile devices, using different sensors and sensor networks, handling different interaction technologies (AR/VR, gesture, voice, movement, location, …);
- Handling evolution of organisation, team, software, environment e.g. run-time update of code to patch security bugs, adapting user interface to handle composition of different systems at runtime, architectural re-engineering due to change of organisational enterprise architecture, global software engineering across distributed teams using different agile processes and tools;
- Various combinations of all of the above software system variability.

In order to support these sorts of variability, software systems need to be conceived, designed, architected, implemented, tested, deployed, maintained and evolved with intensive, multi-faceted variability as a first-class characteristic [8,9,12].

Key Challenges to Engineering Variability-Intensive Systems

Complexity—Variability-intensive software systems are by their very nature more complex than traditional computing systems that do not undergo such variability at design, implementation and/or run-time. Engineers have to manage this additional complexity, which can take the form of complex configuration parameters, dynamic models-at-run-time updatability, additional abstractions to support domain-specific tailoring, and more challenging testing regimes and deployment infrastructure. Tools to support managing this complexity are also needed.

Development processes—Development methods differ from traditional software systems engineering where teams developing variability-intensive systems often need a greater range of technical skills than conventional systems. Highly variable requirements may need to be accounted for, dynamically reconfigurable architectures be used, a range of diverse stakeholders and including end users may need to be supported in configuring systems at runtime.

Deployment environments—One emergent theme of recent years has been the variability of deployment environments themselves, let alone the systems deployed in them. The other applications a system must integrate with and all of its potential end users and their requirements might not even be known in advance. New architectures support greater variability but require improved modelling, development, implementation and testing practices.

Integration and interaction—We have moved to engineering systems of systems and the use of diverse interaction devices and deployment environments have resulted in much more complex challenges for developers. A wider range of end-user input and output devices, and end-user expectations, has increased the issues of usability. This is especially challenging when user interfaces are composed from multiple sources and must be deployed on varying platforms.

Quality of service—QoS issues are challenging in many software systems but variability intensive systems introduce new dimensions to these. As the system may undergo significant change at runtime, handing diverse compute power, storage, networking, composition and deployment are all far more complicated—how do you meet energy and throughput targets when services change at runtime, potentially to slower, more power-hungry ones? How are constraints around composition and deployment—such as technology platform, user interface, security model and reliability—met under dynamic, runtime re-composition and re-deployment? Popular QoS areas for research and practice include performance, energy efficiency, reliability, robustness and self-healing capacity.

Safety-critical systems—Many safety critical domains have a need for variability-intense computing solutions. Particular ones of current and emerging interest are smart cities—smart transport, utilities, housing and health; defence, advanced manufacturing especially using robotics and mechatronics, and next-generation global business solutions requiring near real-time transaction processing at scale. In the later, the growth of distributed ledger-based systems (blockchains) are an increasingly popular and important approach to providing distributed contract management for a wide variety of domains.

Cybersecurity—Systems that are inherently variable in nature can be thought of as having significant advantages—but also significant disadvantages—over traditional systems. This includes the ability to self-heal and adapt on-the-fly while in use to mitigate emerging security threats and vulnerabilities. However, should the variability support in the software be compromised, then the application may be damaged in ways not feasible for less variable-intensive systems.

Current and Future Trends

Some key trends that are emerging and that will be important for software engineers to consider in engineering their next generation variability-intensive systems include:

- *Micro-services and DevOps practices*—These areas have become popular research topics and emerging SE practices. Their application to variability-intensive systems is still however under both research and practice exploration with many unanswered questions around how to (de)compose services, test, deploy, update, and maintain such complex systems.
- *Internet of Things*—Similarly, there is a burgeoning interest in IoT systems and many exhibit high variability. For example, a smart home may have new sensors added, multiple networks with mobile devices coming and going, various continuous and discrete data streams, and different users at different times with different tasks and preferences. How we design, build, compose and maintain highly diverse and dynamic IoT solutions is subject of much current and future investigation.
- *AI-based solutions*—Software engineering challenges of AI-based systems are increasingly popular areas for research and many new practical solutions are being deployed in practice. However, variability introduces many additional complexities, including how to adapt AI-based solutions to varying datasets, repeated re-training, addressing bias, and providing human-in-the-loop support.
- *Self-securing systems*—Variability-intensive software should provide a number of advantages over less meldable systems in terms of addressing emergent security threats and

vulnerabilities. However much further work is needed on designing, architecting, building, deploying and testing such systems.

■ *Augmented reality*—While AR-based systems are not necessarily variability-intensive, using AR interaction devices along with dynamic composition, AI, runtime emergent requirements, and IoT environments offers many new advances ion human-computer interaction. AR systems are also an example of context-aware systems where changing context—user, room, task, collaboration—often significantly perturb the interface, especially when using haptic and other direct feedback support.

■ *Combinations of the above*—One can see that a future generation variability-intensive system could easily exhibit most if not all of the above features.

This book contains many fine papers detailing the rationale and history for variability-intensive systems, different kinds of variability-intensive systems, key challenges in engineering such systems, and emerging future directions. These include more theoretic treatment of the subject providing a sound foundation for both practice and research, emerging technology trends and approaches, and case studies of successful development and deployment of such systems. I do hope that you find the book valuable in your own practice and research in this exciting domain.

John C. Grundy
Melbourne, Australia

References

1. Almorsy, M., Grundy, J., & Ibrahim, A. S. (2014). Adaptable, model-driven security engineering for SaaS cloud-based applications. *Automated Software Engineering, 21*(2), 187-224.
2. Boehm, B. (2002). Get ready for agile methods, with care. *Computer, 35*(1), 64-69.
3. Calinescu, R., Ghezzi, C., Kwiatkowska, M., & Mirandola, R. (2012). Self-adaptive software needs quantitative verification at runtime. *Communications of the ACM, 55*(9), 69-77.
4. Galster, M., Avgeriou, P., & Tofan, D. (2013). Constraints for the design of variability-intensive service-oriented reference architectures–An industrial case study. *Information and Software Technology, 55*(2), 428-441.
5. Galindo, J. A., Turner, H., Benavides, D., & White, J. (2016). Testing variability-intensive systems using automated analysis: An application to android. *Software Quality Journal, 24*(2), 365-405.
6. Grundy, J., & Hosking, J. (2002). Developing adaptable user interfaces for component-based systems. *Interacting with Computers, 14*(3), 175-194.
7. Hallsteinsen, S., Hinchey, M., Park, S., & Schmid, K. (2008). Dynamic software product lines. *Computer, 41*(4).
8. Liaskos, S., Yu, Y., Yu, E., & Mylopoulos, J. (2006, September). On goal-based variability acquisition and analysis. In *Requirements Engineering, 14th IEEE International Conference* (pp. 79-88). IEEE.
9. Metzger, A., & Pohl, K. (2014, May). Software product line engineering and variability management: achievements and challenges. In *Proceedings of the on Future of Software Engineering* (pp. 70-84). ACM.
10. Passos, L., Czarnecki, K., Apel, S., Wąsowski, A., Kästner, C., & Guo, J. (2013, January). Feature-oriented software evolution. In *Proceedings of the Seventh International Workshop on Variability Modelling of Software-intensive Systems* (p. 17). ACM.
11. Salehie, M., & Tahvildari, L. (2009). Self-adaptive software: Landscape and research challenges. *ACM Transactions on Autonomous and Adaptive Systems (TAAS), 4*(2), 14.
12. Zhang, J., & Cheng, B. H. (2006, May). Model-based development of dynamically adaptive software. In *Proceedings of the 28th International Conference on Software Engineering* (pp. 371-380). ACM.

Foreword by Rogério de Lemos

The ability of handling change has been an innate property of software systems. Although very brittle when dealing with some flaws, overall software has proven to be, within certain limits, sufficiently malleable towards human imperfections (related to the specification, implementation, evaluation and operation of systems). The reason for this is that software engineers have successfully dealt with a wide range of changes, mostly at development-time, by defining appropriate processes, techniques and tools target to emerging needs.

This has come at a cost by developing systems that are not able to account for variations that might be known during development-time. A source for these variations is the incorporation of changes that are expected to affect the system after its deployment. As a consequence, any changes that emerge at run-time that are not considered at development-time, need to be handled at the next maintenance cycle. This has proven to be a costly way of developing systems that is not sustainable at the long run since the software landscape is ever evolving, with increasing levels of system complexity regarding both system behaviour and structure.

New approaches are needed for handling changes since these cannot be dealt exclusively at development-time. For example, not all changes can be foreseen at development-time when disparate components (or component systems) interact, which may lead to emergent behaviours. Changes also need to be dealt at deployment-time and run-time, without interrupting the services provided by the system, and without any human involvement. This is particularly the case of variability-intensive systems. These are systems that can be derived from a single specification, and because of that they can be easily modified in order to handle change. Hence the demand to define new development processes that are able to produce, deploy, operate and maintain software that is effective, efficient and provable.

When dealing with variability-intensive systems, amongst the several promising approaches, dynamic software product lines (DSPL) and self-adaptation (based on an explicit feedback control loop) might provide the appropriate foundation for architecting resilient systems (i.e., systems that support the persistence of service delivery that can justifiably be trusted, when facing changes). Both DSPL and self-adaptation are able to deal with change at run-time, and architectures take a centre stage when reacting to change (at least for some classes of self-adaptive systems).

These two approaches should not be seen as competing in their usage, they are complementary. Moreover, complementarity is not restricted to which circumstances one or the other approach should be used, complementarity is also related to their combined usage. In other words, a feedback control loop (the basis of self-adaptive systems) should be able to manage effectively and efficiently the processes associated with dynamic software product lines. How this can be achieved, it is not clear if we consider the whole process starting from feature modelling.

In the context of resilience, depending on the criticality of the system, different degrees of assurances are required, and here dynamic software product lines might be useful in assisting the structuring of evidence. The latter is fundamental when building arguments that justify the level of trust that can be placed on the system—the 'provable' factor mentioned above. Based on this, we identify two key processes that should be related at system deployment-time: the process responsible for the provision of services and their quality, and the process responsible for the generation, collection and analysis of evidence to be used in the formulation of assurance arguments. These processes are related because of the decision whether to deploy or not a modified/adapted system. The formulation of assurance arguments, and their evolution as the system adapts, should also be supported by a dynamic process since small system variances may require a different line of assurance argumentation. Again, this is not the case for "one size fits all" since variations are expected between arguments. That is the reason why the motivation behind software product lines should also be inspirational when defining new approaches for formulating assurance arguments when building, deploying and operating resilient variability-intensive systems.

Rogério de Lemos
Kent, United Kingdom

Preface

Variability-Intensive Systems Defined

Modern software systems are not static constructs but flexible and adaptive systems where a single system or a platform needs to support a variety of usage scenarios. Supporting different usage scenarios means that software must be able to accommodate different (and maybe even unforeseen) features and qualities (for example, faster response for premium customers). These usage scenarios may be defined and implemented either during design time or dynamically "on the fly" while a system is running. From an implementation point of view, in the early days, variability has been enabled through generic programming, conditional compilation of source code and preprocessors in programming languages like C/C++, mostly for configurable and customizable single systems. Later, software product lines started to emerge and provided processes and practices to develop families of systems in a domain. Enabling variability has significantly impacted industrial software development practices. For example, today, open platforms, and context-aware, self-adaptive and dynamic mobile systems are common. However, modern software development practices (e.g., lean and flexible development; assembling complex systems from micro-services; building systems-of-systems and software ecosystems), unprecedented types of software (e.g., cyber-physical systems, smart homes, VR and AR systems in entertainment and health care, autonomous systems in military), dynamic and critical operating conditions of systems (e.g., disaster response and monitoring systems), fast-moving and highly competitive markets (e.g., mobile and web apps), and increasingly powerful and versatile computing equipment (e.g., mobile and "smart" devices) contribute to challenges when building variability-intensive systems. Comprehensive knowledge is needed to understand software engineering challenges involved in developing and maintaining these systems.

Goals of the Book

This book addresses new challenges arising with the software engineering of variability-intensive systems. These challenges concern requirements as well as architecture, detailed design, implementation and maintenance. Furthermore, the environment in which the software will operate is an important aspect to consider in developing high-quality software. That environment has to be taken into account explicitly. A software product may be appropriate (e.g., secure) in one environment, but inadequate (e.g., not sufficiently secure) in a different environment. While these considerations are important for every software development task, there are many challenges specific to variability-intensive systems. In this book, our goal is to collect chapters on software engineering of variability-intensive systems and more specifically, how to construct, deploy and maintain high quality software products.

The book covers the current state and future directions of software engineering of variability-intensive systems. The book features both academic and industrial contributions which discuss the role software engineering can play for addressing challenges that confront developing, maintaining and evolving systems, cloud and mobile services for variability-intensive software systems and the scalability requirements they imply. The book intends to feature software engineering approaches that can efficiently deal with variability-intensive systems and to learn more about applications and use cases benefiting from variability-intensive systems.

How This Book Differs from Other Books in This Area

Online media is filled with stories describing the promise and problems associated with the Internet of Things and autonomous vehicles. Context-aware computing practices have long been important to the creation of personalized mobile device user experience designs. The recent interest in augmented reality and virtual reality has raised the bar on how hard it is to engineer software which is truly adaptable to large number of users and diverse environments. Software engineers are being told to update their knowledge of both artificial intelligence and big data analytic techniques. Software products are being asked to control mission critical systems (such as vehicles and personal robot assistants) without any consideration of the complexities involved in adapting them to constantly changing real-world situations. Variability and the complexity of variability-intensive systems have had significant impact on industrial software development practices. Most practitioners are woefully uninformed about best practices which should be used in secure software engineering. All of these things are involved in software engineering for variability-intensive systems. Comprehensive knowledge is needed to understand software engineering challenges involved in developing and maintaining these systems. Systems and software variability has traditionally been addressed in product line engineering. Many books on variability focus on product line engineering, introduce specific product line techniques. This makes it difficult to gain a comprehensive understanding of the various dimensions and aspects of software variability in modern software development. Also, many of today's software systems are subject to variability even though they are not part of a product line. Here we address this gap by providing a comprehensive reference on the notion of variability from a technical and nontechnical perspective, including latest research and industry trends in engineering variability-intensive systems throughout the lifetime of systems. It focuses uniquely on the software engineering of variability-intensive systems. The book covers constructing (i.e., planning, designing, implementing, evaluating), deploying and maintaining high-quality software products and software engineering in and for dynamic and flexible environments. This book provides a holistic guide for those who need to understand the impact of variability on all aspects of the software life cycle, i.e., the problem space, design space, and solution space of variability-intensive systems. It leverages practical experience and evidence to look ahead at the challenges faced by organizations in a fast-moving world with increasingly fast-changing customer requirements and expectations, and explores the basis of future work in this area. Contributions from leading researchers and practitioners ensure scientific rigor and practical relevance of the content presented in the book.

Unique Features and Benefits for the Reader
- Familiarizes readers with essentials about variability and its benefits, drivers and impact
- Presents consolidated view of the state-of-the-art (techniques, methodologies, tools, best practices, guidelines), and state-of-practice from different domains and business contexts

■ Covers variability at all levels and stages of software engineering, including software design, implementation, and verification of variability-intensive systems
■ Provides useful leads for future research in established and emerging domains
■ Includes case studies, experiments, empirical validation, and systematic comparisons of approaches in research and practice

Chapter Overview

Part I reviews key concepts and models for variability-intensive systems. This includes modeling variability at the software architecture level, context modeling for variability-intensive systems during requirements engineering, and variability-aware simultaneous decomposition of models under structural and procedural views.

Part II focuses on the analysis and evaluation of variability-intensive systems. This includes the variability spectrum in self-securing software systems, the role of the ecosystems architect, features and how to find them; debt-aware software product lines engineering using portfolio theory and dynamic variability realization in dynamic software product line solutions.

Part III presents several experiments and studies in the field of variability-intensive systems. This includes a feature ontology to enable enterprise-level product line engineering, the design of variable big data architectures for e-government, refactoring support for variability-intensive systems, variability in library evolution and evolving variability requirements of IoT systems.

Chapter 1: Variability-intensive Software Systems: Concepts and Techniques

This chapter is authored by editors and discusses historical trends in variability-intensive systems and how variability evolved over time from conditional compilation to product lines to a characteristic (or even feature) of almost all modern software-intensive systems. The chapter also discusses different "notions" of variability and gives insights into how variability impacts different software development activities and software product life cycle stages, including fundamental challenges when designing and maintaining variability-intensive systems. Finally, the chapter provides concrete examples of variability-intensive systems.

Part I: Concepts and Models

Chapter 2: Observations from Variability Modelling Approaches at the Architecture Level

Ana Paula Allian, Rafael Capilla, and Elisa Yumi Nakagawa argue that modeling the variability of system families is still challenging as it has been investigated for years. Nevertheless, because the software architecture is the cornerstone of any design process the challenge to represent the variability of systems in architecture is still not properly addressed. The lack of specialized notations to describe the common and variable aspects in the design makes difficult to represent the variability of system at the architecture level, many times poorly described. In other cases, domain-specific variability languages are needed to describe in detail the variability before its realization. To date, a variety of techniques, languages and approaches have been proposed to represent software variability concerns in system families, but the challenges of modern systems demand now additional capabilities such as modeling context properties or runtime binding time requirements. In order to provide a comprehensive analysis on the evolution of variability modeling techniques, Allian, Nakagawa and Capilla provide an accurate analysis and discussion of variability modeling approaches and focused on the architecture issues. They also provide insights and trends about the variability modeling alternatives analyzed.

Chapter 3: Context Modelling for Variability-intensive Systems During Requirements Engineering

Nelufar Ulfat-Bunyadi and Maritta Heisel explain that context modeling defines how context (or environment) information for software systems is structured and maintained. Requirements for a system are defined based on assumptions about its context. Context modeling is an integral part of requirements engineering. In this chapter, Ulfat-Bunyadi and Heisel focus on context modeling for variability-intensive systems. Context modeling for such systems is a challenging task because of the presence of variability in both requirements and contextual knowledge required. This chapter provides an overview of several existing approaches to supporting engineers doing context modeling. Different approaches use different notions and concepts. This makes it difficult to compare approaches to one another. This chapter presents first a conceptual framework which establishes a clear-cut vocabulary that makes the interrelations between different concepts and notions used in context modeling understandable to the reader. Using this framework, they describe and compare existing modeling approaches. The authors illustrate the value of this framework by applying selected modeling approaches to a common example. This will help practitioners and academics in selecting an approach that best fits their application area.

Chapter 4: Variability Incorporated Simultaneous Decomposition of Models Under Structural and Procedural Views

In this chapter, Muhammed Cagri Kaya, Selma Suloglu, Gul Tokdemir, Bedir Tekinerdogan, and Ali H. Dogru present the use of decomposition during system specification as a tool to represent hierarchical variability in software. A mature domain-specific environment is a precondition for variability-centric engineering using compositional approaches as discussed in this chapter. Decomposition of the software's structure has been followed more recently by decomposition of the software's process. In this chapter, the role of variability management is demonstrated, starting with its high-level representation and advancing to lower-level decisions. Here, variability management considers the enhancements in the specification as well as the constraints. Previous work has associated elements of variability in the system model that correspond to the structure and also to its process. Decomposition, on the other hand, is a fundamental mechanism in many approaches for the specification of various dimensions of software modeling. Component-oriented approaches rely on the structural decomposition, whereas service-oriented development is supported by process decomposition. A vending machine case study is presented in this chapter to demonstrate the propagation of the variability specification as enhancements are made to both the component-oriented (structural) model and the process model.

Part II: Analyzing and Evaluating

Chapter 5: Towards Self-securing Software Systems: Variability Spectrum

Mohamed Abdelrazek, John C. Grundy, and Amani Ibrahim describe a new variability-intensive system idea, the "self-securing software system." They describe how such a system works using a multi-tenant cloud application as a motivating example. This supports runtime composition, detects emergent attacks and vulnerabilities, and supports runtime updating to mitigate problems. They describe recent work we have done in architecting and proof-of-concept prototypes for aspects of such systems. They then describe current limitations and future work plans to address these.

Chapter 6: The Emerging Role of the Ecosystems Architect

James Hedges and Andrei Furda claim that the business ecosystem model is increasingly pursued by today's organizations seeking higher flexibility, adaptability and scalability of offered software products and services. Supported by highly variable cloud-based software ecosystems, this modern business model has the potential of massive business value creation compared to the traditional pipeline model. In this chapter Hedges and Furda discuss the business aspects of variability-intensive systems in terms of their value, development stages, business strategies and risks, measures, architectural principles, and governance challenges. They explore the emerging role of the ecosystems architect and how it challenges the traditional enterprise architecture perspective of the organization as a closed system. By tracing the emergence of this role through the published literature, they identify the key tasks that an ecosystems architect performs using the lenses of strategy, measures, architecture and governance. These lenses are main aspects of the ecosystem architect role and may be used to uniquely characterize this role.

Chapter 7: Features and How to Find Them: A Survey of Manual Feature Location

Jacob Krüger, Thorsten Berger, and Thomas Leich assert that developers need to understand functionalities (referred to as features) that are implemented in a system to be able to maintain, extend, reuse, or reengineer it. However, the knowledge about features fades over time or is not available, due to missing documentation. In these cases, it is necessary to locate features in the source code. This is a costly process but nonetheless one of the most common tasks performed by developers. While several automated techniques have been proposed, they all require significant manual adaptations and often fall short in their accuracy. To improve this situation, it is necessary to understand how developers perform feature location manually. In this chapter, Krüger, Berger, and Leich provide an overview of existing studies on manual feature location. The few works that exist analyze four aspects of manual feature location in detail: search tools, performance, influencing factors, and distinct phases. Krüger and colleagues conclude that little is known about the actual efforts of performing feature location, how different factors influence these efforts, how automated techniques are scoped to the identified phases, and which additional information sources help developers to locate features. They also describe several open issues that still prevent the practical adoption of feature location techniques: missing knowledge about the required efforts and the influence of external factors, missing evaluations of approaches, and the exclusion of additional information sources

Chapter 8: A Debt-Aware Software Product Lines Engineering Using Portfolio Theory

Jasmine Lee and Rami Bahsoon claim that variability-intensive systems are now a common solution for organizations to respond to dynamic software requirements. Among different approaches, software product lines are an example that allows flexibility to support variable software products. The key factor that drives the success in software product line development is systematically managing commonalities and variability across the products of the product line. In order to maintain the sustainability of the product line to ensure organizations' profitability and productivity, there is a need to evaluate the optimality of different sets of features taking technical debt into account. Lee and Bahsoon describe a systematic approach to assess the optimality of different feature sets (portfolios) that could form a product. Modern portfolio theory is used to model and quantify the technical debt associated with each portfolio. A case study is used to demonstrate the applicability of the proposed method. This study shows that the optimality of a product line is affected by the risks associated with it, which could lead to technical debt in the future. This knowledge may help an organizations' decision-making on variability issues.

Chapter 9: Realising Variability in Dynamic Software Product Lines

Jane D. A. Sandim Eleutério, Breno B. N. de França, Cecilia M. F. Rubira, and Rogério de Lemos assert that modern software systems need to be able to self-adapt to changes in user needs and to changes affecting its environment. Dynamic software product lines (DSPL) are an engineering approach for developing self-adaptive systems based on commonalities and variabilities occurring in a family of similar systems. Currently, many DSPL approaches fail to meet all adaptability requirements because in many cases, they were developed in an unstructured manner. The trend in the development of newer DSPL approaches indicates the importance of combining the use self-adaptation with variability management. However, for that to achieve there is the need to define a clear taxonomy that allows the comparison of existing approaches from DSPL and self-adaptive software systems. Eleutério and her colleagues provide this taxonomy. They used their taxonomy to survey various DSPL approaches to evaluate and compare their various design strategies. They summarize practical issues, identify major trends in actual DSPL proposals, and suggest directions for future work.

Part III: Technologies, Experiments, and Studies

Chapter 10: A Feature Ontology to Power Enterprise-Level Product Line Engineering

Product line engineering (PLE) is an approach for engineering a portfolio of similar products in an efficient manner, taking full advantage of the products' similarities while respecting and managing the variation among them. PLE has long been used to manage and resolve the variation present across engineering assets, from requirements, to design, through implementation, verification, validation and documentation, in the software, mechanical and electrical realms. However, as PLE matures, we find enterprises seeking to adopt PLE at all levels of their organization, not just in the engineering departments. This includes areas such as product marketing, portfolio planning, manufacturing, supply chain management, product sales, product service and maintenance, the Internet-of-Things, resource planning, and much more. In some very large organizations, thousands of non-engineering users need different views of, and interaction scenarios with, the representation of a product line's commonality and variation. Each of these many stakeholders has a slightly different perspective on what a feature is. In this chapter, Charles Krueger and Paul Clements present an ontology for the concept of "feature" to help stakeholders at all levels of an organization communicate their PLE concerns with each other. This approach employs the venerable principles of abstraction and modularity to define concepts, views, relationships, and behaviors that are best suited to specific roles for stakeholders in both engineering and business operations. The result is a unified approach to variant management for all stakeholders across the enterprise.

Chapter 11: Design of Variable Big Data Architectures for E-Government Domain

Bedir Tekinerdogan and Burak Uzun claim that big data has become a very important driver for innovation and growth in various industries such as health, administration, agriculture, defense, and education. The term big data refers to data sets with sizes beyond the ability of commonly used software tools to capture, curate, manage, and process within a tolerable amount of time. The goal of e-government is to automate the public services to citizens. E-government systems are often characterized as big data systems in which data storage and processing are the crucial issues. However, different features and different big data architectures are required for different e-government systems. Even a single e-government system has to take multiples architectural concerns into account as it is designed. In this chapter, Tekinerdogan and Uzun present a systematic approach for the design of various big data architectures within the e-government domain. They adopt a big data reference architecture approach which includes a variability model for big data systems and is applicable to e-government systems. They use a case study approach to discuss the design decisions, the experiences and the lessons learned for deriving application architectures for different e-government systems.

Chapter 12: Refactoring Support for Variability-intensive Systems

Vahid Alizadeh, Marouane Kessentini, and Bruce Maxim assert that several studies show that programmers are postponing software-maintenance activities that improve software quality, even while seeking high-quality source code for themselves when updating existing projects. High-quality source code can be characterized using several quality attributes, but maintaining this high level of quality is expensive. One reason is that time and monetary pressures force programmers to neglect to enhance the quality of their source code while enhancing existing systems with new features or fixing bugs. Code bad smells represent symptoms of poor implementation choices. Previous studies found that these smells make source code more difficult to maintain, possibly also increasing its fault-proneness. There is a plethora of approaches that identify bad smells based on code-analysis techniques. In this chapter Alizadeh, Kessentini, and Maxim consider code-smells correction as a distributed problem. They combine different techniques during the optimization process to find a consensus regarding the correction of the code-smells. They use distributed evolutionary algorithms (D-EA). Many evolutionary algorithms with different adaptations (fitness functions, solution representation, and change operators) were executed in parallel to solve the common goal which was the correction of code-smells. The statistical analysis of the results obtained provide evidence to support the claim that a cooperative D-EA outperforms single-population evolution and random search based on a benchmark of eight large open-source systems where more than 86% of code smells are fixed using the refactoring suggestion.

Chapter 13: Variability in Library Evolution: An Exploratory Study on Open-Source Java Libraries

Mohamed Wiem Mkaouer, Hussein Alrubaye, and Anthony Peruma assert that variability can occur in different types of software artifacts. This chapter investigates variability in library evolution. As a means of reducing development time and increasing reusability, software systems rely more and more on the integration of third party (i.e., external) libraries or software frameworks. However, software systems evolution may require acquiring new libraries. Therefore, as part of software maintenance, developers may need to replace one existing library with another. This act of replacement may be categorized as either a library upgrade or library migration. An upgrade occurs when the developer replaces, an outdated library version with a more recent one. A migration occurs when the replacement library is one that was (most likely) developed by another development team, but still, performs the same (or similar) functionality as the library being replaced. This chapter explores existing studies on library migration with a special emphasis on variability aspects of libraries and exposes challenges still faced by developers. The chapter also analyzes more than 50,000 open-source projects to better understand how libraries of these systems evolve over time.

Chapter 14: Evolving Variability Requirements of IoT Systems

Luis Chumpitaz, Andrei Furda, and Seng Loke focus on delineating the requirements of variability intensive systems based on recent developments in Internet of Things (IoT) technologies and applications. IoT opens unprecedented possibilities for real-time information sharing between sensors, devices and systems, enabling intelligent decision-making, tracking, traceability and planning. IoT technologies, such as ubiquitous computing, radio-frequency identification (RFID), and wireless sensor networks (WSN), boost innovative applications for industrial manufacturing and enterprise systems, smart cities, smart driving and transportation, and smart environments. Current trends indicate a resurgence of interest in machine learning combined with IoT, but also new developments such as multi-access edge computing (MEC). These trends will ultimately lead to a new generation of variability intensive systems with complex, multi-perspective requirements that need to be accommodated. This chapter identifies the range of variability requirements of future IoT systems across multiple dimensions and provides guidance for practitioners on how to identify and realize variability requirements in IoT systems.

Part IV: Looking Ahead

Chapter 15: Outlook and Future Directions

This chapter by the editors revisits some of the reasons why this book was written and identifies some of the future work needed to address these concerns. Software variability is not widely understood, nor are the engineering practices required accommodate variability across multiple environments. Research is needed to better understand the impact of variability on software quality. New testing and verification techniques will need to be developed specifically with variability intensive systems in mind. This book includes some excellent chapters reviewing the literature on handling variability across the entire software engineering life cycle, but additional work is still needed. The use of tools and techniques developed for data science, machine learning, and program understanding are being applied to several software engineering tasks. Search-based and model-driven software engineering investigators have contributions from their work on software evolution and refactoring that may be useful to understanding software variability. The work done in the artificial intelligence community on handling knowledge modeling and feature interaction might be useful in understanding how to manage variability more effectively in complex software systems. Further research is required to develop disciplined approaches to handling variability in design and support of open service-based and context aware systems.

Readership of This Book

The book is primarily targeted at researchers, practitioners, and graduate students of software engineering, who would like to learn more about current and emerging trends in software engineering of variability-intensive systems and in the nature of these systems themselves. The book is especially useful for and who are interested in gaining deeper understanding, knowledge and skills of sound software engineering practices in developing variability-intensive systems and using variability-intensive systems to develop other software-intensive systems. The book is also interesting for people working in the field of software quality assurance and adaptable software architectures.

The book is secondarily targeted at upper/middle-level IT management, to learn more about trends and challenges in software engineering of variability-intensive systems.

Acknowledgements

The editors would like to sincerely thank the many authors who contributed their works to this collection. The international team of anonymous reviewers gave detailed feedback on early versions of chapters and helped us to improve both the presentation and accessibility of the work. Finally, we would like to thank the CRC Press management and editorial teams for the opportunity to produce this unique collection of articles covering the very wide range of areas related to software engineering for variability-intensive systems.

Ivan Mistrik
Heidelberg, Germany

Matthias Galster
Christchurch, New Zealand

Bruce Maxim
Dearborn, Michigan, United States

About the Editors

Ivan Mistrik is a researcher in software-intensive systems engineering. He is a computer scientist who is interested in system and software engineering and in system and software architecture, in particular: life-cycle system/software engineering, requirements engineering, relating software requirements and architectures, knowledge management in software development, rationale-based software development, aligning enterprise/system/software architectures, value-based software engineering, agile software architectures, and collaborative system/software engineering. He has more than forty years' experience in the field of computer systems engineering as an information systems developer, R&D leader, SE/SA research analyst, educator in computer sciences, and ICT management consultant. In the past 40 years, he has been primarily working at various R&D institutions in the United States and Germany and has done consulting on a variety of large international projects sponsored by ESA, EU, NASA, NATO, and UNESCO. He has also taught university-level computer sciences courses in software engineering, software architecture, distributed information systems, and human-computer interaction. He is the author or co-author of more than 90 articles and papers in international journals, conferences, books, and workshops. He has written a number of editorials, over 120 technical reports and presented over 70 scientific/technical talks. He has served on many program committees and panels of reputable international conferences and organized a number of scientific workshops. He has published the following scientific books: *Rationale Management in Software Engineering, Rationale-Based Software Engineering, Collaborative Software Engineering, Relating Software Requirements and Architectures, Aligning Enterprise, System, and Software Architectures, Agile Software Architecture, Economics-driven Software Architecture, Relating System Quality and Software Architecture, Software Quality Assurance in Large-Scale and Complex Software-Intensive Systems, Managing Trade-offs in Adaptable Software Architecture,* and *Software Architecture for Big Data and the Cloud.*

Matthias Galster is a senior lecturer (equivalent to tenured associate professor in the United States) in the Department of Computer Science and Software Engineering at the University of Canterbury, New Zealand. Previously he received a PhD in Software Engineering. His current work aims at improving the way we develop high quality software, with a focus on software requirements engineering, software architecture, software development processes and practices, and empirical software engineering. His research was published in some of the key journals in the field, including *IEEE Transactions on Software Engineering, IEEE Software,* the *Journal of Systems and Software,* and *Information and Software Technology.* Matthias Galster has organized various workshops at top-tier international software engineering conferences and has been member of organizing committees of leading international software engineering conferences. He has delivered numerous presentations at conferences, universities, research institutes and professional organizations in New Zealand and overseas. He has been involved in international research projects, most with strong industry collaboration. He is a frequent reviewer for journals, international conferences, and funding agencies.

Bruce Maxim has worked as a software engineer, project manager, professor, author, and consultant for more than 30 years. His research interests include software engineering, human computer interaction, game design, AR/VR, social media, artificial intelligence, and computer science education. Bruce Maxim is professor of computer and information science and collegiate professor of engineering at the University of Michigan—Dearborn. He established the GAME Lab in the College of Engineering and Computer Science. He has published more than 50 papers on computer algorithm animation, game development, and software engineering education. He is coauthor of both a best-selling introductory computer science text and a best-selling software engineering text. Bruce Maxim has supervised several hundred industry-based software development projects as part of his work at UM-Dearborn. Bruce Maxim's professional experience includes managing research information systems at a medical school, directing instructional computing for a medical campus, and working as a statistical programmer. Bruce Maxim served as the chief technology officer for a game development company. Bruce Maxim was the recipient of several distinguished teaching awards and a distinguished community service award. He is a member of Sigma Xi, Upsilon Pi Epsilon, Pi Mu Epsilon, Association of Computing Machinery, IEEE Computer Society, American Society for Engineering Education, Society of Women Engineers, and International Game Developers Association.

Contributors

Mohamed Abdelrazek
Deakin University
Geelong, Australia

Vahid Alizadeh
University of Michigan
Dearborn, Michigan, United States

Ana Paula Allian
University of São Paulo
São Carlos, Brazil

Hussein Alrubaye
Rochester Institute of Technology
Rochester, New York, United States

Rami Bahsoon
University of Birmingham
Birmingham, United Kingdom

Thorsten Berger
Chalmers University of Technology
Gothenburg, Sweden

Rafael Capilla
Rey Juan Carlos University
Madrid, Spain

Luis Chumpitaz
Queensland University of Technology
Brisbane, Australia

Paul Clements
BigLever Software, Inc.
Austin, Texas, United States

Ali H. Dogru
Middle East Technical University
Ankara, Turkey

Jane D. A. Sandim Eleutério
Federal University of Mato Grosso do Sul
Mato Grosso do Sul, Brazil

Breno B.N. de França
University of Campinas
São Paulo, Brazil

Andrei Furda
Queensland University of Technology
Brisbane, Australia

Matthias Galster
University of Canterbury
Christchurch, New Zealand

Ian Gorton
Northeastern University
Seattle, Washington, United States

John Grundy
Monash University
Melbourne, Australia

James Hedges
Queensland University of Technology
Brisbane, Australia

Maritta Heisel
University of Duisburg-Essen
Duisburg, Germany

Amani Ibrahim
Deakin University
Geelong, Australia

Muhammed Cargi Kaya
Middle East Technical University
Ankara, Turkey

Marouane Kessentini
University of Michigan
Dearborn, Michigan, United States

Charles Krueger
BigLever Software, Inc.
Austin, Texas, United States

Jacob Krüger
Otto-von-Guericke University
Magdeburg, Germany
and
Harz University of Applied Sciences
Wernigerode, Germany

Jasmine Lee
University of Birmingham
Birmingham, United Kingdom

Thomas Leich
Harz University of Applied Sciences
Wernigerode, Germany
and
METOP GmbH, Magdeburg, Germany

Rogério de Lemos
University of Kent
Kent, United Kingdom

Seng Loke
Deakin University
School of Information Technology
Victoria, Australia

Bruce Maxim
University of Michigan
Dearborn, Michigan United States

Ivan Mistrik
Computer Scientist & Software Researcher
Heidelberg, Germany

Mohamed Weim Mkaouer
Rochester Institute of Technology
Rochester, New York, United States

Elisa Yumi Nakagawa
University of São Paulo
São Carlos, Brazil

Anthony Peruma
Rochester Institute of Technology
Rochester, New York, United States

Cecilia M. F. Rubira
Institute of Computing
University of Campinas
São Paulo, Brazil

Selma Suloglu
Sosoft Information Technology
Ankara, Turkey

Bedir Tekinerdogan
Information Technology
Wageningen University
Wageningen, The Netherlands

Gul Tokdemir
Cankaya University
Ankara, Turkey

Nelufar Ulfat-Bunyadi
University of Duisburg-Essen
Duisburg, Germany

Burak Uzun
Information Technology
Wageningen University
Wageningen, The Netherlands

Chapter 1

Variability-intensive Software Systems

Concepts and Techniques

Matthias Galster[a], Ivan Mistrik[b], Bruce Maxim[c]

[a]*University of Canterbury, Christchurch, New Zealand*
[b]*Computer Scientist & Software Researcher, Heidelberg, Germany*
[c]*University of Michigan-Dearborn, United States*

1.1 Introduction

Modern software-intensive systems (i.e., systems "where software contributes essential influences to the design, construction, deployment, and evolution of the system as a whole to encompass individual applications" [1]) are flexible and adaptive products and services. Today's software users expect flexibility from software products and services in many dimensions, e.g., in features that can be easily updated or expanded, location and resource awareness of mobile apps, or fault tolerance and easy recovery of critical embedded systems. Therefore, to succeed in today's competitive and innovation-driven markets, modern software-intensive systems must support variability, i.e., must accommodate different deployment and usage scenarios (e.g., by delaying design decisions to the latest point that is economically feasible).

Supporting different usage scenarios means that software must accommodate changing and often unforeseen functional requirements and quality attributes. Intentional and unintentional variability in functionality and quality attributes of software contributes significantly to the complexity of the problem space and the design/solution space of those systems. Also, variability and the complexity of variability-intensive systems have had significant impact on industrial software development practices. Variability-intensive systems development differs from conventional software engineering in that conventional engineering does not address specifics of these systems, e.g., highly diverse stakeholders, extremely large design spaces, consistency checking among configurations/design options, etc. Therefore, variability needs to be addressed in a broader software engineering context and is not limited to "traditional" software product lines, the field in which variability has been discussed the most so far [2]. Many of today's software systems are subject to variability even though they are not part of a product line. Nowadays, variability is a "key fact of most, if not all, systems" [3]. As mentioned in an Future of Software Engineering talk at the International Conference on Software Engineering (ICSE) in 2014 [4], a trend and challenge in the next decade will be managing variability in a non-product line context and under open-world assumptions. Challenges that arise in the context of software engineering of variability-intensive systems concern requirements as well as architecture, detailed design, implementation and maintenance.

In some consumer domains of critical systems, e.g., autonomous and unmanned aerial vehicles (UAV), research is only slowly catching up with industry trends and needs [5]. Such systems may soon become an integral part of many industries, including construction, agriculture, emergency responder support, etc. Once this happens, practices need to be in place to help software engineers develop such systems. Therefore, a particularly complex aspect of the engineering of variability-intensive software systems is the provision of quality assurances with sufficient confidence. Furthermore, successful companies are innovative companies that target new market opportunities. On the other hand, the time to market can make the difference between product success and failure. This highlights the need for "light-weight" approaches to variability-intensive systems, which balance the need for innovation but also consider reducing development effort, even for innovative products. New development models for variability-intensive systems could help manage system growth over time and offer opportunities for innovation throughout development.

This introductory chapter presents an introduction to variability and an overview of basic concepts and techniques. We build on the above discussions and provide a more detailed definition of variability and variability-intensive software systems. In this chapter we also explore how variability impacts software development and provide an overview of generic variability-handling techniques and a brief discussion of historical trends in variability-intensive software systems.

1.2 Defining Variability and Variability-intensive Systems

In this section, we first provide a definition of variability and variability-intensive systems. Then, we discuss the vague notion of variability in software engineering based on the example of variability in software architecture. We reflect on software variability and hardware variability before discussing some of the drivers for variability.

1.2.1 Variability and Variability-intensive Systems

Variability is commonly understood as the ability of a software system or software artifacts (e.g., components, modules, libraries) to be adapted so that they fit a specific context [6]. Today's systems can be adapted in various system elements: hardware, software, data or processes. Therefore, variability is about adapting software functionality, behavior, qualities as well as the underlying structure and processes. These adaptations are enabled through a combination of variation points in software development artifacts and variants as options that can be chosen to resolve variability at variation points. Supporting variability in software systems is essential to manage commonalities and differences across software products and services, and to accommodate software reuse in different organizations and product versions. This is crucial to ensure that systems can adapt to changing needs, and to support reusability of software systems and artifacts. Systematically identifying and appropriately managing variability among different systems distinguishes variability from other approaches that support reuse [7].

Building on the definition of software-intensive systems given above, we define variability-intensive systems as systems where variability and related challenges contribute essential influences to the analysis, design, implementation, deployment, and evolution of the software-intensive system. Examples of variability-intensive systems include product lines and families, self-adaptive systems, configurable or customizable single systems, open platforms from which different products and versions can be derived, context-aware mobile apps, plug-ins of web browsers, service-based and cloud-based systems, Internet of Things, or cyber-physical systems. When designed and implemented properly, variability-intensive systems can achieve orders of magnitude of improvements in development costs, speed and quality, compared to developing and maintaining single products. In detail, systematically supporting variability provides several benefits:

- Helps manage commonalities and differences between software products and services
- Supports the development and evolution of different versions of software
- Enables the planned and systematic reuse of software artifacts (e.g., code, models, tests)
- Contributes to increased productivity and lower cost
- Supports efficient instantiation and assessment of product variants
- Supports runtime adaptations of deployed systems

Designing for, implementing and maintaining variability in software systems not only affects characteristics of the software product and variability in functionality and quality (i.e., what we build), e.g., systems with "continuous configuration management" from compile time and deployment time to runtime. It also affects the development process (i.e., how we build it), e.g., systematic quality assurance and validation despite a potentially large and highly complex design and solution space. As Bosch and colleagues argue, "industrial reality shows that for successful platforms, the number of variations points, variants (alternatives that can be selected for a variation point), and dependencies between variation points and variants easily reaches staggering levels" with systems that have tens of thousands of variation points [8]. This raises software engineering issues related to requirements, design, implementation, evaluation, deployment, runtime adaptation, and maintenance [2].

1.2.2 On the Vague Notion of Variability—The Example of Software Architecture

As found previously, variability is multifaceted [9] and has different notions in different fields of software engineering. In this section we pick one subfield of software engineering, software architecture, and discuss the notions of variability.

A study in 2011 investigated the principles and basic definitions of variability in software architecture. The study consisted of a questionnaire-based survey and a mini (pseudo) focus group with practitioners and researchers [10]. Details about the study can be found in Galster and Avgeriou [11]. The study found that none of the working definitions of variability from practitioners or researchers included the concepts of "variation points," or "version." On the other hand, most practitioners and researchers defined variability as a property or aspect of architectures related to differences in architectures and to changes in the architecture.

The study also aggregated all definitions from all participants to formulate one distinct definition of variability in software architecture. However, due to the different notions of researchers and practitioners, the study put forward four different definitions, each with a distinct focus:

- The first definition is similar to definitions that can be found in the product line domain [7, 12-14]: Variability in software architectures is the need of software to accommodate change and the ability to create architectures for different (but similar) products. This includes reconfiguring the architectural structure and behavior in an efficient and effective manner.
- The second definition is similar to the classification of variability that can be found in software product quality models that define variability as a subcategory of maintainability and changeability [15-17]: Variability in software architectures describes how well an architecture supports flexibility in a certain aspect, with an exact specification of the differences.
- The third definition describes variability in terms of how variability is achieved: Variability in software architectures is achieved through different variants that exhibit different behavior, and the determination of different features, while reusing common artifacts, without changing the scope of the architecture.
- The fourth definition treats variability as an architecture design time quality attribute [4]: Variability in software architectures is the ability of influential factors on design to vary. In other words, variability is a quality attribute whose solution impacts other quality attributes (causing tradeoffs between variability and other quality attributes).

In conclusion, the study found that there is no commonly-agreed-on definition of variability in the domain of software architecture. Furthermore, the definition of variability in software architecture seems to differ from the concept of variability in product lines.

1.2.3 Variability in Functionality Versus Variability in Quality Attributes

Variability usually refers to variability in features or functionality. However, variability also affects the quality of software systems [18]. Considering quality attributes throughout software development is crucial for producing systems that meet their desired quality attribute requirements. In this chapter we adapt the definition from the IEEE Standard Glossary for Software Engineering Terminology [19]: A quality attribute is a characteristic that affects the quality of software systems [19]. Furthermore, we refer to quality attributes as discussed in the SWEBOK (Software Engineering Body of Knowledge) guide [20]. The SWEBOK distinguishes quality attributes discernible at runtime (e.g., performance, security, availability), quality attributes not discernible at runtime (e.g., modifiability, portability, reusability), and quality attributes related to the architecture's intrinsic qualities (e.g., conceptual integrity, correctness). In addition, Bass et al. differentiate quality attributes of the system (e.g., availability, modifiability), business quality attributes (e.g., time to market) and quality attributes that are about the architecture (e.g., correctness, consistency, conceptual integrity) [21]. This means there are quality attributes which directly apply to a system and quality attributes in terms of business quality goals (e.g., time to market, cost and benefit, and targeted market) that shape a system's architecture [21].

Most current work on variability concerns functional variability while quality attribute variability has not been explored extensively [18, 22]. Some limited work has been conducted in the context of variability in quality attributes in product lines [23-30] or aspect-orientation [31], e.g., Myllarniemi et al., who discuss situations in which quality attributes vary in software product lines [32]; a tool to capture functional and quality variability in product lines has been proposed by Raatikainen et al. [33]. A systematic review on variability in quality attributes in product lines has been presented by Myllarniemi et al. and found that there are no empirical insights into variability in quality attributes in industry [18]. An informal survey of existing approaches for specifying and modeling variability in quality attributes has been presented by Etxeberria et al. [34]. A systematic review of variability of quality attributes of service-based systems has been presented by Mahdavi-Hezavehi et al. [35], while Montagud et al. provided a general overview of quality attributes in software product lines [36].

To better capture the context of variability in quality attributes of variability-intensive software systems, we define five scenarios for variability in quality attributes. Scenario 1 and Scenario 2 express "intentional" variability whereas Scenario 3, Scenario 4 and Scenario 5 express "unintentional" variability:

- Scenario 1 – Variability in quality attributes due to variations in the user and user needs, such as different market segments or customer profiles. Quality attributes (e.g., performance, security) and quality attribute requirements (e.g., level of performance or level of security) can differ between market segments or customer profiles. For example, the performance level for premium customers of a cloud-based service could be higher than the performance level for standard customers. Furthermore, premium customers may require additional security quality attributes that do not exist for standard customers. Additional examples for variations in users and user needs are listed in [18], such as different users and user preferences, different social and business contexts, different geographical market segments, high-end and low-end segments, different privacy legislations (e.g., in e-government), dynamic usage changes or evolution of data volumes and load over time.
- Scenario 2 – Variability in quality attributes in different phases of the software development process. For example, during different testing phases or integration phases, privacy may not be a concern, whereas for final delivery of a multi-tenant product, privacy is a concern. This idea also applies to different development iterations where one iteration may focus on achieving security and the next iteration may aim at meeting a privacy goal.
- Scenario 3 – Variability in quality attributes due to the impact of variability in functionality. For example, adding encryption functionality may reduce performance. In this scenario, quality attributes themselves are not the target of variability, but are affected by adaptations of functionality of a system. Quality attributes are affected because of new system configurations, adaptations or changes in the implementation. Even though the focus in this scenario would be on handling variability in functionality, it would still require that engineers anticipate changes in quality attributes and quality attribute requirements.
- Scenario 4 – Variability in quality attributes due to the impact of variability in other quality attributes. For example, a higher response rate (performance) may reduce security. Such variability is usually linked to tradeoffs between quality attributes. This type of variability also depends on the type of quality attribute. For instance, a quality attribute such as scalability may not be subject to changes as much as performance or availability.
- Scenario 5 – Variability in quality attributes due to variation in hardware resources [18]. Examples include different CPU or memory configurations that affect performance and memory consumption, variation in network capacity, batteries running low (e.g., for embedded portable systems) or devices running out of memory, variation in product hardware and chipsets (which may cause the need to tune software to achieve optimal performance). For example, low batteries or low memory means that processor load and/or disk load are reduced to save power, resulting in longer response time.

1.2.4 Software Variability Versus Hardware Variability

Variability not only occurs in the software part of variability-intensive systems but also in the hardware part. Many software-intensive systems control hardware or interact with hardware (e.g., embedded systems, systems that comprise mechanical parts). Traditionally, variability has been handled in the hardware part of systems (e.g., by adding or removing hardware components to support certain functionalities), but currently more responsibilities to handle variability in functionality are delegated to software. Here, additional challenges occur because hardware parts are also subject to variability. However, in contrast to software variability, variability in hardware is primarily concerned with a system's manufacturing stage and assembly than with system functionality [8]. Yet, as Bosch and colleagues argue, we need to define dependencies between mechanical and hardware variations and the software variations [8]. This becomes particularly challenging as the amount of software and the implemented functionality grow.

1.2.5 Drivers for Variability

In Figure 1.1, we list some drivers for variability and how they impacted the complexity of developing variability-intensive software systems over time. Given the increasing size and heterogeneity of software systems (e.g., software ecosystems, cyber-physical systems, systems of systems, ultra-large-scale systems), new and emerging application domains (e.g., unmanned aerial vehicles, smart health applications, large-scale surveillance systems, software-defined networking, social networking apps), dynamic operating conditions (e.g., availability of resources, variations in service availability, changing goals), fast moving and highly competitive markets (e.g., gaming, mobile apps), and increasingly powerful and versatile hardware (e.g., Raspberry Pi), the complexity caused by variability becomes more difficult to handle [2]. Similarly, diversity in data as well as the amounts of data that modern software systems need to process are increasing. For example, data needed to fulfill customer requests in modern enterprise information systems and to deliver a product to a customer vary.

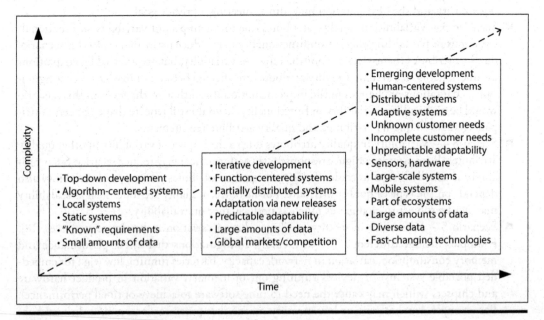

Figure 1.1 Drivers for variability.

1.3 Variability During the Software Product Life Cycle

1.3.1 Overview

Since variability is pervasive, software engineers need a proper understanding, suitable methods and tools for representing, managing and reasoning about variability [37]. Furthermore, variability needs to be considered by many different stakeholders (clients, acquirers, business analysts, requirements engineers, system and software architects, designers, technology experts, domain experts, service providers, subcontractors, end users who demand variability in requirements, coders who need to be aware where in the code variability appears, testers who need to test variants). Therefore, variability impacts software development practices for all types of software development activities and all phases of a software product life cycle. For example:

- Requirements engineering activities need to be able to help explore the problem space and to identify foreseeable and potentially unforeseeable features, capture these in an appropriate format and specification, and maintain these specifications throughout the lifetime of a system. Most conventional requirements engineering techniques are applicable to the analysis and design of variability-intensive systems.

- Software architecture needs to provide models and techniques to reason about variability and the implications of variants at design time and runtime of a system. In particular, care needs to be taken of ripple effects. For example, variability in business processes has ripple effects on implementation layers of systems (service layer, application layer, etc., in service-based systems). Therefore, Gomaa and Shin compared software product line approaches and explored what architecture views are supported by the different approaches [38]. Also, Gomaa and Shin presented a use case model view and a feature model view for product line requirements modeling, and a static model view, collaboration model view and a statechart model view for software product line analysis modeling. An evolution "perspective" (conceptually similar to a view) was introduced by Rozanski and Woods who define a perspective as a "collection of activities, tactics, and guidelines that are used to ensure that a system exhibits a particular set of related quality properties that require consideration across a number of the system's architectural views" [39]. Weyns et al. proposed a framework for updating software product lines [40]. This framework uses a dedicated "update viewpoint" that defines conventions for constructing and using architecture views to deal with multiple update concerns. The authors include variability as one of their concerns (besides traceability, versioning, availability and correctness). Questions answered by the model kinds related to the variability concern are about identifying core assets and product-specific assets, and if assets currently installed should be available after the update, and about the validity of a combination of assets [41].

- Implementation requires appropriate techniques and tools to implement variation points, but also to resolve variability when selecting variants, such as conditional compilation or "code switches" [42]. We discuss more implementation techniques later in this chapter.

- Testing variability-intensive systems requires awareness of the sets of combinations of variants which should be tested. Here, efficiency is key to test incrementally and to test based on equivalence classes of configurations, rather than for all possible configurations. Testing can combine off-line testing (where a more exhaustive test is performed using combinations determined up-front) with on-line testing performed using combinations detected at runtime [43]. Thum et al. provide a comprehensive overview of analysis techniques for variability-intensive systems [44]. For example, traditional analysis and testing techniques, such as type checking, static analysis and generic testing can analyze only one specific configuration at a time in an exponentially exploding space of possible configurations of a variability-intensive system. To address this problem, heuristics can be applied. For instance, Kaestner et al. [45] and Nguyen et al. [46] aimed at variability-aware analysis to analyze all configurations of a configurable system in a single run, while exploiting the similarities between configurations. In the large design spaces of variability-intensive systems, it is simply not possible to check each and every configuration.

■ Maintenance and evolution of variability-intensive systems needs to consider whether and how new variation points and variants may be added. Here, particular care needs to be taken to avoid introducing inconsistencies with existing variation points and variants. Furthermore, modern software systems often lack comprehensive and complete documentation since (in particular, small- and medium-sized) software development organizations often do not have resources (e.g., budget, staff and expertise) to document their processes and variability. Even though there is variability, organizations are not aware of the extent of variability or do not make it explicit. As a consequence, the documentation of processes and variability in different organizations becomes a burden. Also, updates to software systems become problematic in cases with a large number of potential end users (and separate instances of a system for each end user) and lots of variability between the needs of different end users. If each system instance is independently implemented to accommodate "local" specifics, we need to make "global" updates to each implementation of a system separately, rather than making updates to a core system and propagating the updates to all instances.

Figure 1.2 provides a simplified overview of how variability occurs in the previously mentioned generic types of software development activities and what stakeholders and development artifacts tend to be involved at different stages and how. Rows in the figure represent different types of roles or development artifacts, while columns represent different types of software development activities. Note that even though Figure 1.2 shows activities in a sequential order, phases may appear in nonlinear order. Also, stakeholders in Figure 1.2 refer to roles and responsibilities (including required skills and expertise), rather than individuals (e.g., in Scrum projects, one role or responsibility could be covered by one individual in a Scrum or development team). Furthermore, there is an overlap and collaboration between types of stakeholders and life cycle phases. For example, designing a software architecture usually requires negotiation with customers and communication among different stakeholders.

1.3.2 Variability and Software Life-cycle Processes

Going one step further from generic types of software development activities as previously discussed, ISO/IEC/IEEE 12207 defines software life-cycle processes [47]. Life cycles of systems vary according to the nature, purpose and prevailing circumstances of a software system. In Table 1.1, we list the types of processes for the software life cycle and highlight the processes impacted by variability (indicated by x in Table 1.1). We now discuss the most significant processes in more detail.

■ Agreement processes: Agreement processes are organizational processes about how acquirers and supplies realize value and support business strategies of their organizations [47]. Acquisition and supply are not particularly impacted in the development of variability-intensive software systems, since these processes are mostly about higher-level activities not related to the design, implementation and maintenance of software systems.

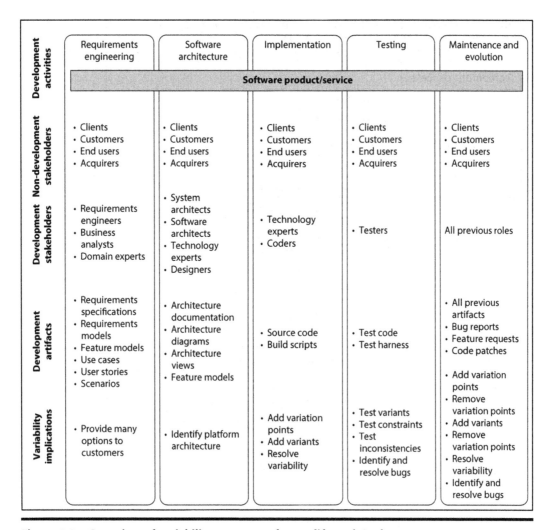

	Requirements engineering	Software architecture	Implementation	Testing	Maintenance and evolution
Development activities			**Software product/service**		
Non-development stakeholders	• Clients • Customers • End users • Acquirers	• Clients • Customers • End users • Acquirers	• Clients • Customers • End users • Acquirers	• Clients • Customers • End users • Acquirers	• Clients • Customers • End users • Acquirers
Development stakeholders	• Requirements engineers • Business analysts • Domain experts	• System architects • Software architects • Technology experts • Designers	• Technology experts • Coders	• Testers	All previous roles
Development artifacts	• Requirements specifications • Requirements models • Feature models • Use cases • User stories • Scenarios	• Architecture documentation • Architecture diagrams • Architecture views • Feature models	• Source code • Build scripts	• Test code • Test harness	• All previous artifacts • Bug reports • Feature requests • Code patches
Variability implications	• Provide many options to customers	• Identify platform architecture	• Add variation points • Add variants • Resolve variability	• Test variants • Test constraints • Test inconsistencies • Identify and resolve bugs	• Add variation points • Remove variation points • Add variants • Remove variation points • Resolve variability • Identify and resolve bugs

Figure 1.2 Overview of variability across a software life cycle's phases.

- Organizational project-enabling processes: Organizational project-enabling processes are about providing the resources to enable a project to meet the needs and expectations of the organization's stakeholders [47]. These are typically found at strategic levels of organizations.
  - The infrastructure management process is about establishing the infrastructure required to complete a project. In variability-intensive systems, this may require the identification of infrastructure elements, the development of infrastructure elements, and the maintenance of infrastructure elements. For example, software product lines require an infrastructure of processes (e.g., domain engineering, application engineering) and artifacts, such as core assets.
  - Portfolio management is also often referred to in the context of software product lines [47]. A portfolio may consist of assets, products and enabling systems (e.g., infrastructures).
- Technical management processes: Technical management processes are about managing the resources and assets allocated by organization management and applying them

Table 1.1   ISO/IEC/IEEE 12207 software life cycle processes and variability

Software life cycle processes in ISO/IEC/IEEE 12207		Variability
Agreement processes		
	Acquisition process	–
	Supply process	–
Organizational project-enabling processes		
	Life cycle model management process	–
	Infrastructure management process	x
	Portfolio management process	x
	Human resource management process	–
	Quality management process	–
	Knowledge management process	–
Technical management processes		
	Project planning process	–
	Project assessment and control process	–
	Decision management process	–
	Risk management process	–
	Configuration management process	x
	Information management process	x
	Measurement process	x
	Quality assurance process	–
Technical processes		
	Business or mission analysis process	x
	Stakeholder requirements definition process	x
	System/software requirements definition process	x
	Architecture definition process	x
	Design definition process	x
	System analysis process	x
	Implementation process	x
	Integration process	x
	Verification process	x
	Transition process	x
	Validation process	x
	Operation process	x
	Maintenance process	x
	Disposal process	x

to fulfill agreements to produce the desired outcome. These types of processes relate to the technical effort of projects [47].

- Configuration management processes manage and control system elements and configurations over the product life cycle [47]. They also manage consistency between a product and configuration definitions. Since there are usually many different configurations and configuration definitions in variability-intensive systems, their complexity becomes more difficult to handle. This is particularly true in fast-paced development where configurations change frequently with new releases of product or service versions. New business models (e.g., subscription-based payment models) are often based on turning features on or off.
- Information management processes: The complexity and the potentially large number of variation points leads to situations in which no one person in an organization has a comprehensive overview of the available variability [8]. This impacts maintenance in terms of removing obsolete variation points and changing binding times. This needs to be handled as part of the technical debt management since otherwise the cost of building new products from a platform would exceed the cost for building a product from scratch.
- Measurement processes are about collecting, analyzing and reporting data to support the effective management and demonstrate the quality of produces, services and processes [47]. The data to be collected and analyzed for variability-intensive software systems is usually more complex and more diverse than data in other types of systems.

■ Technical processes: Technical processes are about the actual technical actions throughout the life cycle of a software product or service. Technical processes apply at any level in the hierarchy of a software system structure [47]. Technical processes transform requirements into a product. All technical processes are impacted when developing variability-intensive software systems.

1.3.3 Crosscutting Impacts on Development Practices

There are also some "crosscutting" impacts on software development practices [42]. This is mostly because software development activities are not isolated from each other but require interaction and involvement of parties external to the software development organization. However, the degree to which a software product or service must be able to interact in an open-world setting is often unknown in advance, as external parties that interact with a large-scale software system may be different for each possible application and deployment scenario. Similarly, implementing a variability-intensive software system requires integration of a software with products from other vendors and third parties. However, knowledge about variability (e.g., in what processes or products variability occurs, what parts of a system are affected by variability) often resides with one software vendor and may lead to vendor lock-in. Finally, if variability occurs in the business processes of different customer organizations, we need to map processes to organizational units in organizations [42]. However, there is no concise mapping of processes to organizational units in different organizations.

1.4 Types of Variability

To further define and scope variability, we can consider different "types" of variability [9]. This also allows us to provide a more rigorous and holistic characterization of variability in contrast to the broad definition of variability given above ("ability of a software system to change and to adapt"). These types offer a framework to capture key aspects of variability in individual systems and to compare systems based on these key aspects. An overview of the types is shown in Table 1.2. We discuss the types in detail as follows.

Table 1.2 Types of variability in software systems (adapted from [9])

Category of types	Type of variability
Degree of anticipation	
	Anticipated
	Unanticipated
Intentional and unintentional	
	Intentional
	Unintentional
Incidental and structural	
	Incidental
	Structural
Requirements type	
	Functional
	Quality
Artifact type	
	Business process
	Architecture
	Component
	Code fragment
	Variable
Representation type	
	Feature models
	Rules/conditions
	Variant labels/annotations
	Change scenarios
	Profiles
Orthogonality	
	Separated
	Integrated
Trigger	
	Stakeholder
	Business process
	System
	Environment
Binding time	
	Design/construction/evolution
	Runtime

1.4.1 Degree of Anticipation

Anticipation refers to whether variability is anticipated (foreseen and potentially planned for) or not.

- Anticipated: Variability is anticipated, and the software is designed in a way to facilitate variability. We consider that variability-intensive software systems anticipate variability.
- Unanticipated: Variability is not anticipated during initial design and development stages but is explored at a later stage.

1.4.2 Intentional and Unintentional

Intentionality refers to whether or not variability is intentional.

- Intentional: Variability is a planned and conscious design decision and supports software project goals or business objectives for which a software product or service is developed. For example, variability in functionality is a typical case of intentional variability.
- Unintentional: Unintentional variability occurs because of forces and influences that are not controlled by project stakeholders. For example, variability in performance may impact other quality attributes as a side effect, therefore requiring systematic variability-handling techniques for these other quality attributes as well.

1.4.3 Incidental and Structural

Incidental and structural variability describe whether variability can be avoided (if undesired) [42].

- Incidental variability is relatively easy to anticipate. It occurs primarily in the technical architecture of software systems (e.g., different databases in different organizations or IT infrastructures). Incidental variability can be removed (or at least limited) by standardization (e.g., laws, regulations, software reference architectures, standardized IT infrastructures, standardized software services, data standards, and standardized services).
- Structural variability is often hidden and only poorly understood up-front. Structural variability occurs in the business architecture and focuses on product and process (e.g., business processes) issues. Structural variability will always exist and cannot be resolved by standardization initiatives.

1.4.4 Requirements Type

The requirements type defines what types of requirements are subject to variability.

- Functional: Variability occurs in the functionality of a software system (or parts of a software system), i.e., there is variability in the input, behavior and/or outputs of a software system. For example, a mobile app for live video streaming may offer the ability to fully record video streams for premium customers, but only offer 10-second snapshot recordings of video streams for basic customers.
- Quality: Variability occurs in the quality and in quality attributes (and quality attribute requirements) of a software system (or parts of a software system), i.e., variability in a

"nonfunctional" property of a software system that indicates how well the system delivers its functionality. For example, in a mobile app for live video streaming, the resolution of streamed videos might be offered in 4K for premium customers, but basic customers may receive video streams only in regular HD.

1.4.5 Artifact Type

Artifacts describe the types of elements of a software system (its documentation or implementation) that are subject to variability. The following artifact types are ordered from high-level and implementation-independent types of artifacts to lower-level implementation-related artifacts.

- Business process: There can be variability in a business process implemented by a software system, i.e., in a collection of related and structured activities or tasks that produce a specific output. For example, we could dynamically adapt and update workflows of a business process by selecting and replacing a new variant of a particular region in the workflow of a business process [48].
- Architecture: The subject of variability can be the software architecture of a system. For example, we may compare candidate architectures and select the optimal candidate for different change scenarios [49].
- Component: A component (including libraries, modules, etc.) within a software system's implementation can be the subject of variability. For example, as discussed by Chaari et al., a software service component can be dynamically adapted by selecting a replacement from a pool of services that fits best the current context [50].
- Code fragment: The subject of variability is a fragment of source code of a system. For example, Previtali and Gross suggest dynamic updates to applications by adding, removing, or replacing methods of classes based on the differences between variants of the classes [51].
- Variable: The most basic form of variability is when variability is controlled through setting variables to suitable values. For example, Floch et al. suggest parameterization of program variables to allow fine-grained adaptation at runtime [52]. Dhungana et al.'s work supports fine-grained variability in a steel plant automation system (among other types) with configuration variables for features such as colors and speed [53].

1.4.6 Representation Type

The representation type captures how variability is represented in the description and documentation of a software system.

- Feature models: Variability is represented as a compact, typically graphical description of all valid instances of a system. The feature model captures possible combinations of features (functional and quality) of a software system. A feature model typically includes mandatory and optional features as well as relationships between features (e.g., if optional features are exclusive).
- Rules/conditions: A set of rules and/or conditions can represent constraints on elements or artifacts in the documentation or implementation of a variability-intensive system. For example, we may use logical expressions and conditions that refer to elements of design patterns to express variants of the patterns [54]. Similarly, to describe variation points in a variability-intensive system, we can use decision templates which define a decision using a name, type, condition and additional attributes [53].

- Variant labels/annotations: Variant labels/annotations added to artifacts in the documentation or implementation of a software system can help represent variability. Labels and annotations can also complement other forms of representing variability. For example, we can annotate components with properties (e.g., required resources) to differentiate alternatives and to enable the dynamic selection of suitable variants with highest utility for a given context [52].
- Change scenarios: Change scenarios are textual or visual descriptions of events, sequences of events or options and how options affect a change to a system. For example, architects can map a set of strategic scenarios (i.e., possible future developments of the domain of a product) to a set of architecture scenarios, each specifying a specific set of potential future design choices [55].
- Profiles: Profiles represent variability as descriptive summaries of users or artifacts in the environment in which a system will be used/deployed. Profiles could be described in form of a table, models, etc. Profiles are typically combined with other types of representation. For example, we could describe meta data (or component policies) in profiles together with contextual information to dynamically select and add extensions for application components (e.g., to add authentication features) based on user needs [56].

1.4.7 Orthogonality

Orthogonality describes how the specification of variability is separated from other concerns of a software system.

- Separated: Variability is specified in distinct artifacts and separated from the artifacts that document and/or realize a system or a set of system instances. For example, we can describe variability with a decision model together with an asset model that describes the solution space to derive products in terms of assets, such as components, resources, etc. [53].
- Integrated: The specification of variability is interwoven within other artifacts that document and/or realize a system or a set of system instances. For example, we can associate variant labels to data elements of a database to capture the variants to which the elements apply [57]. Another example is the work of Batory and colleagues, who embed variability information in the implementation of classes by means of an inheritance refinement hierarchy and state machines [58].

1.4.8 Trigger

A trigger describes the source that initiates the binding of variants to variation points.

- Stakeholder: Variant binding is initiated by a stakeholder, i.e., a person or role with an interest in the system. For example, in Fritsch and Renz, user commands trigger the selection of variants of GUI forms that guide a user through a process of generating legal documents [59].
- Business process: A business process triggers variant binding. For example, Cicirelli et al. suggest firing conditions of a transition in a business process to trigger the execution of a variant of a region of the business process [48].
- System: Variant binding is triggered by a system itself. For example, a system may optimize its workflow by replacing services with services of better quality when the current quality of a service is not sufficient anymore. Ardagna and Pernici [60] propose a service system that optimizes its workflow by replacing services with services of better quality when the current quality of service differs from the prediction by more than a given threshold.

- Environment: An artifact in the environment triggers variant binding. For example, changes in the deployment context, (e.g., computing resources, the quality of a network, or the physical location in which an app is used or deployed) can trigger a system to replace components by variants that guarantee better utility [52].

1.4.9 Binding Time

Time of binding defines the time when a variant or variants are bound to variation points.

- Design/construction/evolution: Variants are bound to variation points during system construction (design, realization, instantiation) or evolution. For example, a designer may select alternatives and options specified in a design pattern to derive a pattern variant for the problem at hand [54]. Similarly, an analyst can select the best architecture among a set of variants during system development based on the impact analysis for a set of modifiability scenarios [49].
- Runtime: Variants are bound to variation points during system operation dynamically at runtime. For example, Forte et al. suggest dynamic content adaptations of mobile devices based on device profiles and user service-level agreements by selecting suitable services from a repository of variants [61].

1.5 Generic Activities and Techniques for Handling Variability

1.5.1 Overview

Handling variability requires explicitly representing variability in software artifacts throughout the life cycle of a software product or service [35]. We refer to "handling" variability rather than "managing" variability: As argued by Svahnberg et al. [62], managing variability is only one of several activities when dealing with variability. Additional activities include high-level activities such as variability governance, variability conceptualization and identification, variability implementation and variability evaluation [62]. Each activity can be considered a process by itself, with its own purpose, desired outcome and a list of detailed tasks that need to be completed to achieve the desired outcome. We now discuss in more detail these generic activities.

- Variability governance: Variability governance is about establishing and maintaining the variability goals and aligning them with enterprise goals and strategies of an organization, or the purpose of a product and service. For example, an organization may decide to target different market segments with different variants of one core product. Variability governance would ensure that this goal is maintained throughout the development of a software product or service.
- Variability management: For variability management, we adopt an existing definition from Svahnberg et al. [62], which considers variability management as tasks related to managing dependencies between variabilities, maintenance and continuous population of variant features with new variants, removing features, the distribution of new variants to customers, etc.
- Variability conceptualization: Variability conceptualization is about identifying solutions that address variability-related stakeholder concerns and to achieve relevant requirements. Variability could for example be implemented using "code switches" to activate or deactivate

variants at design time [63] or conditional compilation to activate or deactivate variants at compile time. We elaborate more on this in the following subsections.

■ Variability implementation: Variability implementation is about implementing (i.e., codifying and documenting) variability in a system, based on concepts defined during variability conceptualization activities. In general, implementing variability and binding variants can happen in different forms:

  – Manual: Variant binding is a manual effort. For example, America et al. suggest that architects select choices in the variability models of different architectural views for different change scenarios [55].

  – Semi-automatic: Variant binding is performed manually but supported by tools. For example, Breitman et al. provide automation support for managing scenario evolution by enabling users to define new scenarios and to select a scenario from available variants [64]. Buhne et al. propose a tool to help model requirements variability across a set of product lines [65].

  – Automatic: Variant binding is fully automated. Fully automated binding can happen at design time or dynamically at runtime. For example, Truyen et al. propose an approach where "interceptors" intercept component interactions and dynamically determine which services need to be selected and deployed based on a composition policy and context information of the current system state [56].

■ Variability evaluation: As with any property of software, we need to determine the extent to which systems meet their objectives and address variability. Traditional evaluation and analysis techniques such as type checking, model checking, and theorem proving have been challenged when designing variability-intensive systems [44]. This is because creating and analyzing all product variants is not feasible. Therefore, analysis techniques need to consider the distinguishing properties of variability-intensive systems, for example, by checking feature-related code in isolation or by exploiting variability information during analysis. Thum et al. propose a comprehensive classification of product line analysis approaches [44], which can also be utilized to evaluate other types of variability-intensive software systems.

In the following subsections, we discuss more detailed variability-handling techniques to support the above-mentioned generic activities.

1.5.2 Configuration

As Voelter writes [66], configuration is a simple technique since software engineers do not need to be familiar with complex formalisms for describing a variant. Rather, engineers can select from a predefined set of alternatives to resolve variability. Constraints between alternatives indicate invalid selections (e.g., requires, prohibits, recommends, discourages). Configuration is particularly suitable if end users are expected to configure a product [66].

The most basic way of achieving configuration is by providing configuration files with flags. Another way of achieving configuration is the use of configuration tables. For example, when using "function switching," all predefined functions for all system variants are delivered to all users (and are included in the source code). Customers then decide what functions to activate. Function switching does not require access to source code. Instead, configuration tables are selected when instantiating the software product or service. An example of systems that use configuration tables and function switching are enterprise resource planning (ERP) systems, where function switching defines functions that could be activated for a certain industry (e.g., functions only for organizations in the oil and gas industry) [63].

An example of configuration at the design level are design patterns like Bridge and Strategy, which support plugging in different implementations at variation points. However, unlike preprocessors (e.g., #ifdef in C), these implementations would be bound at runtime using polymorphism in object-oriented languages [66].

At high-level processes, configuration can be achieved by business rules. Business rules define the most common variants of a process flow to influence how a business process is executed. For example, a system may resolve variability through the configuration of rules for individual customers (e.g., minimum quantity of ordered items per order, or order lead time).

Finally, configuration at the level of end users can be achieved using wizards. Wizards guide users through a number of selections. In wizards, one selection may constrain other future selections.

1.5.3 Construction

As explained by Voelter [66], an example of construction are frameworks that define hooks into which engineers can plug code (as long as the code conforms to interface specifications of the frameworks). Furthermore, construction can be achieved by layering. Layering allows a high-level separation of concerns. For example, the lowest layer could contain core functionality, such as database access, while higher layers could contain generic functions that can be used in all instances of a system; the top layers could then include customer-specific or instance-specific functionality. Overall, construction is more powerful than configuration. This is because construction provides an unlimited space of variants. On the other hand, construction becomes more complex than configuration because of this potentially unlimited number of variants.

1.5.4 Add-ons and Add-ins

Add-ons allow customized extensions of an existing system. In contrast to add-ins, add-ons do not require changes in the source code as they are added "on top" of the system (e.g., through high-level API's) rather than "in" the system (i.e., the source code). Add-ins, on the other hand, allow users of software to enhance the system by modifying the source code, without the involvement of the original software developers. Updates would not overwrite modifications of the original source code. This is because add-ins provide specific points in the source code where designers anticipated customer-specific modifications (e.g., additional validity checks, or specific database access). These points are foreseen at design time and made explicit in the architecture. From a software development perspective, these points could be considered as empty subroutines (functions, procedures, methods, etc.). During customization, customers can fill these subroutines with their own code.

1.5.5 Selection

Selection means that variability is realized by selecting variants among a set of variants and by binding that variant to a variation point. For example, product line requirements can be specified using annotations that represent features. These annotations can then be used to select features for the product-specific requirements specifications [67].

Another example of selection are code switches. In contrast to function switching discussed previously, code switches do require access and manipulation of source code. Also, in contrast to add-ins, code switches do not require the implementation of code in terms of subroutines. Code switches can be enabled through programming language frameworks, e.g., the SPRING component plug-in framework for Java, or through a "Displaced Dispatcher" class inside the code that helps select an XML configuration.

Selection could be refined into removal and injection:

- Removal [66]: We can remove parts of a comprehensive whole. This would require that we mark various optional parts of the whole with conditions that determine when to remove that part. The whole needs to contain all the parts for all variants and maybe the parts for combinations of variants. This makes the whole very complex. Removal can be used with all kinds of development artifacts, e.g., code (using #ifdef in C/C++), models and documentation (e.g., some reference architecture standards support the annotation of model elements with conditions).

- Injection: Injection means that we add artifacts into a minimal core [66]. The advantage of this approach is that the core is usually small and only includes common elements. Any parts that are specific to a variant are kept external and are added when necessary. Accessing locations in the core where variable parts are added requires that "hotspots" or hooks are marked in the core. One example of implementing this strategy is aspect-oriented programming.

    Other examples of injection are the installation of optional packages and the Microkernel pattern. Microkernel architectures provide a minimal set of functionalities in the core together with a protocol for plugging in additional pieces of functionality.

1.5.6 Reorganization

Variability is realized by reorganizing the structure or behavior of the system artifacts. For example, a configuration manager may dynamically reconfigure a service chain according to an adaptation policy [68], or different variants of a "region" in a business process can be triggered for execution, each determining a different flow in the execution of the business process [48].

1.5.7 Parameterization

When using parameterization (also often referend to value assignment [9]), a variant is constructed by providing different values for parameters. Parameters are usually typed to limit the range of values [66]. The artifact that shall be parameterized needs to explicitly define the parameters as well as a way to specify values. Hence, variability is limited to the locations where parameters are defined. Parameterization makes it difficult to handle unexpected variability. In most cases, the values for the parameters are relatively simple, such as strings, integers, Booleans or regular expressions. However, in principle, they can be arbitrarily complex [66]. Examples of this approach include configurations files (which are read by an application) or the Strategy pattern (often in combination with the Factory pattern). Here, a variant is created by supplying an implementation of an interface defined by the configurable application. The application has to explicitly query the factory. The type of values is defined by the interface which strategy classes implement.

1.5.8 Summary

In practice, we would usually use a combination of types of activities. Today's systems are divided into different subsystems, where each subsystem implements variability differently.

Also, while there is a large set of variability-handling techniques, these techniques need to be supported by method and tools, as well as by proper training of software professionals. Developers in practice think in terms of development activities that they perform when describing their needs for new methods or tools [69], so tools need to support these needs. Training for variability can be separated into training for less-experienced developers and developers in general. For less-experienced developers, training should focus on the identifying varying functional features and identifying valid variation points. Training for developers in general should focus on identifying and characterizing dependencies between variation points and variants.

1.6 Historical Trends in Variability-intensive Software Systems

The idea of variability in software systems goes back very far into the past of software engineering. For example, the idea of generic programming emerged in the 1970s. Generic programming is a style of computer programming in which algorithms are written in terms of types to-be-specified-later and that are instantiated when needed for specific types provided as parameters. One example of generic programming is using templates in C++. In this section we list a couple of historical trends with an emphasis on more recent trends, such as product lines and reference architectures.

1.6.1 Conditional Compilation and Preprocessors

Conditional compilation is supported by preprocessors in languages like C. Preprocessor directives (e.g., #ifdef in C) enable programmers to include or exclude parts of the code by providing a corresponding configuration [70]. As argued by Hunsen and colleagues, preprocessors in C are widely used to implement highly configurable systems in industrial and open-source software systems [70]. For example, the Linux kernel uses the preprocessor to allow developers to choose among 12,000 distinct options at build time. Approaches have been proposed to check for bugs in preprocessor directives. For example, the TypeChef infrastructure [71] supports parsing and type-checking C code with #ifdef variability, targeted at finding bugs in highly configurable systems such as the Linux kernel.

1.6.2 Context-oriented Programming

Context-oriented programming allows behavioral variation in programs dependent on context [72]. Some mechanisms for context-oriented programming include features supported by current programming languages, such as exception handling. Similarly, Context L is a language extension that explicitly supports context-oriented programming and is integrated into Lisp on Lines, a web framework used in commercial applications [72].

1.6.3 Generative Programming

Generative programming is a style of computer programming that uses automated source code creation through generic frames, classes, prototypes, templates, aspects, and code generators to improve programmer productivity. It is often related to code-reuse topics such as component-based software engineering and product line engineering [73].

1.6.4 Software Product Lines and Families

The idea of product lines and families emerged because systems in certain domains share commonalities [12]. Instead of developing and maintaining each product individually, software product line engineering looks at these systems as a whole and develops them by maximizing the scale of reuse of platforms and mass customization [74]. Product lines assume the existence of a product line infrastructure, including related processes (such as core asset development, product development, management) [75].

The product line community also introduced the notion of "product line architecture" [76]. The product line architecture describes concepts and structures to achieve variation in features of different products, while sharing as many parts as possible in the implementation [77]. Thus, the product line architecture captures the central design of all products of the product line, including variability and commonalities of several product instances [78]. Product line architectures address variability explicitly and have a limited focus by emphasizing "features," "variation points," "variants," etc. [79].

While traditional product lines instantiate products at design times, a new trend is towards dynamic product lines. Dynamic product lines provide adaptability of systems during runtime. Many approaches utilize service-based computing to dynamically adapt systems, such as Shokry and Ali Babar [80] or Hallsteinsen and colleagues, who explored dynamic product lines [81], or Fiadeiro and Lopes who proposed dynamic reconfiguration of service-oriented architectures [82].

1.6.5 Reference Architectures

Reference architectures capture the essence of the architecture of a collection of similar systems. These systems usually belong to a certain technology domain (e.g., service-based systems), application domain (e.g., automotive systems), or problem domain (e.g., image processing). A reference architecture provides a common lexicon and taxonomy, a common architectural vision, and the modularization and the complementary context [83]. Reference architectures offer one way to systematically reuse existing architecture knowledge when developing new software systems, or new versions or extensions of similar products [74], see Figure 1.3.

The purpose of a reference architecture is to facilitate the development of concrete architectures for new systems, to help with the evolution of a set of systems that stem from the same reference architecture, and to ensure standardization and interoperability of different systems.

Reference architectures can occur at different levels of abstraction. For example, generic reference architectures for service-oriented architectures, such as IBM's foundation architecture [84] exist. A high-level service-based reference architecture has also been developed in the Nexof project [85]. On the other hand, more specific reference architectures can be found. For instance, reference architectures for e-contracting [86], security [87, 88] or web browsers [89] have been proposed. It was only recently that the notion of reference architecture has been brought to attention in the systems engineering community [90].

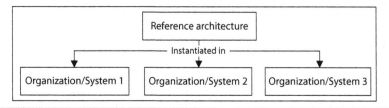

Figure 1.3   Instantiation of reference architectures.

Following Bass et al., we differentiate reference model and reference architecture [21]. A reference model is a "division of functionality together with data flow between the pieces," i.e., a decomposition of a problem into parts that cooperatively solve the problem. A reference architecture, on the other hand, is a reference model mapped onto software elements that cooperatively implement the functionality of the reference model. This means, whereas reference modeling divides functionality, a reference architecture is the mapping of that functionality onto system decompositions [91].

Reference architectures are sometimes considered the same as product line architectures [74]. However, according to Vogel et al., reference architectures can be categorized so that product line architectures are only one type of reference architecture (besides platform-specific architectures, industry-specific architectures, and industry-cross-cutting architectures) [92]. Moreover, according to Angelov et al., product line architectures are less abstract than reference architectures [93, 94], but more abstract than concrete architectures, i.e., product line architectures are one type of reference architecture [95]. In detail, we differentiate product line architecture and reference architecture as follows:

- A product line architecture represents a group of systems that are part of a product line, including processes and infrastructure required in product lines (e.g., core asset development, product development) [75]. A product line architecture is for products that are produced by a single organization. The product line architecture captures the central design of all products of the product line, including variability and commonalities.
- A reference architecture represent the spectrum of systems in a technology or application domain [89]. It must address business rules, architectural styles, best practices (e.g., decisions, standards). Reference architectures typically do not address variability in a systematic manner.

In general, a reference architecture is designed by capturing the essentials of existing architectures of a certain domain or a group of products, and by taking into account future needs and variability [96]. This involves three main problems: First, reference architectures are usually designed in an unsystematic manner; traceable and repeatable steps to design reference architectures are missing [97]. Second, in some situations (e.g., the development of reference architectures in the e-government domain), a reference architecture needs to be designed from scratch, without the ability to extensively mine existing software architectures. In such situation, people (e.g., architects, domain experts) and other types of documentation (e.g. domain or business models) might be the major source for designing a reference architecture. Third, there is usually no solid evidence about the validity of a reference architecture.

Cloutier et al. presented a high-level model for reference architecture development in systems engineering. This model covers the collection of information from existing systems, and the evolution of the reference architecture based on governing standards, emerging technology, changing stakeholder needs and maturing business [83]. High-level guidelines for reference architecture design are also provided by Pohl et al. as part of domain design during product line engineering [74]. Also in the context of software product lines, Bayer et al. proposed PuLSE-DSSA (Product Line Software Engineering – Domain Specific Software Architecture) [98]. In PuLSE-DSSA, reference architectures are created by capturing knowledge from existing architectures. Angelov et al. studied reference architectures in software engineering and developed a classification which could act as a starting point for designing reference architectures [93]. ProSA-RA is a process to design reference architectures outside the product line domain [99]. ProSA-RA focuses on aspect-oriented systems and neglects empirical validity of the reference architecture. Templates (but no guidelines) for reference architectures are often provided in industrial organizations to facilitate the creation of new reference architectures (e.g., the reference architecture template provided by the Swedish Defence Materiel Administration [100]). Despite these efforts, in software engineering, systematic approaches to define reference architectures are missing [97], or guidelines are usually not documented [101].

In domains outside software engineering, methods for reference modeling have been introduced to support the creation of reference models, processes, etc. For example, Karow et al. [102] introduced the empirical construction of reference process models in public administrations. Ahlemann and Gastl presented a more general approach for constructing empirically-grounded reference models for business processes [101]. These approaches can act as a starting point for developing methods that help construct valid reference architectures in the software engineering domain.

1.6.6 Service-oriented Architecture

Service-oriented architecture (SOA) has become a widely studied and used concept in software engineering research and practice [103]. SOA is a standard-based and technology-independent distributed computing paradigm for discovering, binding and assembling loosely-coupled software services. SOA aims at aligning business processes and IT. So far, variability in service-oriented systems has primarily been addressed at the business process level [104, 105]. However, SOA itself supports variability through dynamic service retrieval and binding [106]. Furthermore, the right level of service granularity can support variability. Coarse-grained services are distinguished from fine-grained services that offer less functionality [107]. If services are fine-grained, there are more possibilities to handle variability, which in turn increases the number of service orchestrations and complexity. More details on service granularity can be found in [107] and [108]. However, several reasons exist why SOA alone is not enough for handling variability [109]:

■ Variability occurs in different forms and at different levels of abstraction. For example, variability occurs at the level of individual services, in features and functionality, or in quality attributes (such as performance). However, in SOA, the focus of handling variability is on replacing services [110].

■ SOA does not support developing applications that fit individual customer needs [111]. Individual services may be reusable, but are not designed to be highly customizable. Service specifications and model are not designed for planned and enforced reuse [111]. Reusing SOAs is difficult because SOA a) do not treat several similar systems or services as a whole, but rather as multiple separate products, and b) do not keep generic components in a common base that is evolved and maintained.

■ When facilitating variability, we need to consider the integration of services, third-party applications, organization-specific systems and legacy systems. The integration of third-party applications happens in non-service-based systems as well, but this open-world assumption makes it a more difficult problem for variability [112].

■ Quality-related issues in SOA have been reported as a top challenge [113]. How to handle variability in quality attributes is still an unsolved problem in SOA.

Below we relate variability to a taxonomy of adaptation of service-based systems introduced by Kazhamiakin et al. [106] with three dimensions:

■ Why dimension: Variability in service-based systems enables adaptations to accommodate a particular environment, rather than as corrective, perfective, extending or preventive adaptation. Variability is caused by differences (rather than changes) in environments due to needs of particular customers.

■ What dimension: The entity that should be adapted is the business process instance as well as functionality of service-based systems. The adaptation is permanent when dealing with design time variability but can be temporary when implementing runtime (dynamic) variability in service-based systems.

■ How dimension: Variability in service-based systems does not prescribe any adaptation strategy, decision mechanism or adaptation implementation.

1.6.7 Systems of systems

Systems of systems (SoS) are large-scale systems composed of interacting systems that together meet a user's need. These systems are independently developed and provide functionality on their own that is different from when used as stand-alone applications. Examples include smart homes that integrate different hardware and software systems (where individual hardware and software systems are useful by themselves but provide new and enhanced functionality when integrated), air defense systems (that integrate radar, weapon and surveillance systems that are useful on their own, but offer a comprehensive and powerful defense network) and intelligent transportation systems that integrate sensor networks. Below we discuss criteria for SoS based on criteria defined by Maier [114]:

■ Operational independence of components: This criterion states that if the SoS is disassembled into its component systems, these systems must be able to usefully operate independently and in stand-alone applications [115]. Also, it states that instances of the same system may be used in many different systems of systems [116].

■ Managerial independence of components: This criterion states that components may be developed independently by a community of external developers.

■ Evolutionary development: According to this criterion, each of the systems integrated in the SoS should evolve. Thus, the composed SoS may be adjusted to remain operational [116].

■ Emergent behavior: SoS would exhibit behavior that is not about the behavior of one of the constituent systems.

1.6.8 Platforms and Software Ecosystems

Another type of large-scale variability-intensive software system that is comprised of other systems and components is a software ecosystem. Software ecosystems are software platforms and a community of external developers that provide functionality to extend the basic platform [117]. In contrast to SoS, ecosystems usually require a common platform.

Ecosystems tend to be "open" in the sense that their architecture enables added-value services by incorporating third-party contributions while retaining essential qualities [118]. These added-value services are typically not known in advance when designing the platform of the ecosystem. Examples of software ecosystems include Eclipse, Android, Firefox or Gnome [117]. Manikas and Hansen define three main elements in the definition of software ecosystems [117]:

■ Common software: Common software in ecosystems can either appear as common technological platforms or software platforms.

■ Business: Business refers to concepts that go beyond profit or revenue model, such as the benefits contributors would get from a free or open-source project.

■ Connecting relationships: Connections can exist in terms of sets of businesses, relationships among businesses, actors in social ecosystems related to the software ecosystem, communities, etc. Open-software ecosystems are often developed in a public and collaborative manner.

Similar to SoS, platforms and open ecosystems tend to be continuously modified to accommodate changing needs. In particular, the number of added-value services or systems may increase (perhaps more significantly in ecosystems). In ecosystems, this makes it difficult to track and analyze all extensions and components. Furthermore, different components or systems may be used and combined together to achieve a particular goal. In detail, software developers, maintainers and users of ecosystems face several problems:

■ Problem 1 – Unknown end users: In a large ecosystem, the actual end user of a component of an ecosystem may not be known to the developers(s) of that component. A component may be used in an application scenario that was not foreseen by the developer(s) of that component.
■ Problem 2 – Non-expert developers: Developers of software may not be experts in software development and not software engineering or domain professionals.
■ Problem 3 – Undefined development process: In large open-source and distributed cross-organizational ecosystems, there is no control over the software development process and quality assurance (e.g., the testing strategy). Open ecosystems do not follow standard governance strategies used in large organizations [119].
■ Problem 4 – Heterogeneous technologies: Large open-source and distributed cross-organizational ecosystems are often heterogeneous in terms of technologies and programming languages. Also, the types of available and usable software artifacts for components of an ecosystem differ. Components may or may not include compiled code, or source code. This makes it difficult to perform software and design analyses based on the source code only.
■ Problem 5 – Accessibility of artifacts: There are open systems whose source code, documentation, etc. are not available or easily accessible for analysis (e.g., open systems, legacy systems). Furthermore, how and where components are published is unclear since in open systems, there is not always a common repository from which the sources for all components and extensions of an ecosystem are available.

According to Berger et al., software ecosystems could be considered the conceptual successor of software product lines [120]. Berger et al. propose variability implementation techniques for software ecosystems based on analyzing five ecosystems (including the Linux kernel, Eclipse and Android, Debian and eCos). Berger et al. classify these techniques using the following criteria:

■ Variability representation: Variability representation includes the representation of the asset base (basic units, such as files, and composite units, such as packages and features) and variability models (such as feature models).
■ Decisions: Decisions include aspects related to the decision life cycle, decision binding and derivation/reconfiguration.
■ Encapsulation: Encapsulation includes aspects related to information hiding, interfaces, etc. For example, in the Linux kernel, interface mechanisms are captured in C header files.
■ Interactions: Interactions include information about how different artifacts interact. For example, in Android, interaction binding happens late and dynamically.

1.6.9 Self-adaptive Systems

Self-adaptation is an effective approach to deal with increasingly complex and dynamic software systems [121]. Self-adaptive software evaluates and changes its own behavior, whenever the evaluation shows that the software is not accomplishing what it was intended to do, or when better functionality or performance may be possible. System adaptability has been widely studied since the mid-1960s and has gained popularity over the past decade. A self-adaptive system usually comprises two parts: 1) the managed system that deals with domain functionality, and 2) the managing system that deals with adaptations of the managed system [122]. A popular approach to structure the managed system is MAPE-K [123]. A MAPE-K managed system consists of the following elements: a monitor component (M) to collect information from the managed system and the system's environment; an analysis component (A) to examine the information from the M component and to decide whether further actions are needed; a planning component (P) to perform a series of adaptation actions to resolve issues identified by the analysis component; an execution component (E) to carry out actions to the managed system; a knowledge repository (K), which contains models of the models. Oreizy et al. proposed an architecture-based approach for self-adaptive software [124].

1.6.10 Context-aware and Mobile Applications

Context-aware computing practices help create personalized mobile device designs. Mobile applications and operating systems are used in mobile consumer electronics and other industrial devices. For example, Android is a variability-intensive system that can be highly customized to support different customers' requirements and hardware environments. All code for all possible configurations would be included in all releases. A recent study investigated variability realization in Android [125]. The analysis focused on the usage of different variability realization mechanisms (e.g., conditional compilation) in the Android source code and build environment.

1.7 A Practical View on Variability

Several empirical works have investigated variability in practice. A study conducted by Chen and Babar investigated challenges related to variability management in industry (e.g., documentation or testing) [12]. Similarly, Ihme et al. studied what current variability challenges exist in small and medium enterprises and what practices exist in small- and medium-sized enterprises to manage variability [126]. The authors conducted a multiple case study using semi-structured interviews and identified technical challenges (e.g., decision making, change implementation) and non-technical challenges (e.g., resourcing, business models). Jaring and Bosch analyzed variability in an industrial software product line to identify variability-related issues (variability identification, variability dependencies and tools support) and to propose a representation of variability realization mechanisms based on introduction and binding of variability (e.g., at runtime, installation) [127]. An industrial survey with 25 software engineering practitioners described the current state of practice of variability management in 25 small- and medium-sized enterprises in Sweden [128]. This survey concludes that small enterprises can benefit from systematic variability management but that there is a lack of awareness for systematic variability management. In particular, little reuse and traceability activities are performed. Galster and Avgeriou [63] provided a snapshot of variability in large-scale enterprise software systems. Their study aimed at understanding the types of variability that occur in large industrial enterprise software systems and how variability is handled in such systems. Their exploratory case study in two large software organizations identified seven types of variability (e.g., functionality, infrastructure) and eight mechanisms to handle variability (e.g., add-ons, "code switches").

1.8 Variability and Agility

1.8.1 Overview

The agile paradigm is an umbrella concept for methods that are based on the manifesto of agile software development [129]. It values "individuals and interactions over processes and tools," "working software over comprehensive documentation," "customer collaboration over contract negotiation," and "responding to change over following a plan" [130]. Agile methods are defined in terms of values (or ideals), principles (i.e., the application of ideals to industry), and practices (i.e., principles applied to a specific type of project) [129]. All agile methods implement iterative, incremental activities. The agile paradigm accepts the reality of change instead of aiming for complete and rigid software requirements and software architectures. For most projects, accepting the existence of frequent changes can cost less than aiming for requirements or architectures that will never change. Furthermore, agile methods usually focus on delivering value to customers through early and continuous delivery [129]. Besides these common principles of agile methods, each agile method (e.g., XP, Scrum) defines its own practices (e.g., sprints in Scrum, pair-programming in XP). There are some common principles between agility and variability [130]:

- Agile methods and handling variability are about vague or changing (or adapting) requirements. Agility even encourages change and handles it when it happens, whereas variability is about anticipating change (or adaptations) during the design phase. Some of the changes handled in agile approaches will coincide with anticipated variation points [131].
- Agile development and handling variability require collaboration. Agile methods are based on the collaboration between stakeholders (e.g., customer, product users and developers) [131]. Similarly, to handle variability, there is a need for various stakeholder groups (e.g., architects, product users) to be involved in scoping variability. During both, agile development and handling variability, collaborations serve the purpose of a feedback circuit [131].
- Agile development and handling variability assume to operate within a scope. The scope of variability defines what the range of adaptation could be [131].
- Agility and variability aim at minimizing work to be done. Agility is about postponing work until it is needed, while variability is about systematically anticipating what will be needed in the future and then creating reusable common artifacts for specific purposes within the specific scope.

Furthermore, there are several benefits of combining agility and variability [130]:

- It helps achieve less heavy-weight variability handling as the agile paradigm claims to reduce the overhead introduced by many software development processes.
- It can obtain quick feedback from customers about required variability in the software product and the architecture.

■ It helps incorporate changing variability requirements in the architecture (e.g., new variation points or variants, or a new deployment context that a system must support). Thus, facilitating variability through agility can improve the evolution of variability.

On the other hand, work on combining the agile paradigm with variability handling is quite limited. Most work has been conducted in the context of agile product line engineering. In 2006, the First International Workshop on Agile Product Line Engineering [132] was held which concluded that it is feasible to combine agility and product line engineering. More recently, literature reviews on agile product line engineering have been published [129, 133]. These reviews discuss reasons for combining agility and product line engineering (e.g., to reduce costs during domain engineering, to deal with volatile business situations, or to handle situations in which a domain is not well understood up-front), what agile methods are used in product line engineering, and present open research challenges (e.g., that there is a need for more support for evolving variability). Most proposed approaches for agile product line engineering introduce agility in existing software product lines [134]. Other works suggest that the competing philosophies of agile software development (little up-front planning) and software product line engineering (heavy up-front planning) make their integration difficult [131]. Instead, agile development and product line engineering should be tailored so that both can "retain their basic characteristics" [134].

In contrast to these literature reviews, an industrial study on agile product line engineering has been presented by Hansen and Faegri [135]. This study concluded that introducing agile product lines involves multiple disciplines, e.g., product planning, knowledge management, organizational aspects, and innovation, and is thus a long-term effort. Similarly, Pohjalainen describes experiences on agile modeling of a product line [136], including a light-weight method for feature modeling. Additional examples of combining agility and product line engineering include agile product line planning that focuses on product line engineering as a highly collaborative process [137], and an agile process for building product lines using a light-weight feature model [138], similar to Pohjalainen. Furthermore, Ghanam et al. proposed reactive variability management in agile development [134] and using acceptance tests from test-driven development to elicit variability in requirements [139]. All these efforts show that combining agile development and product line engineering is feasible. However, thorough up-front planning is traded against faster development and more flexibility throughout the development process.

Not much work on combining variability and agility can be found outside the domain of product lines. One of the few examples includes recent work that explored the use of reference architectures with agile software development frameworks such as Scrum [140]. The work found that reference architectures support several agile software development principles (e.g., continuous delivery, constant development space), but that forcing the use of reference architectures on agile teams can pose a threat to self-organizing teams and motivated individuals in agile software development projects [140].

1.8.2 Challenges

We identified several challenges when integrating variability and the agile paradigm:

■ To identify variability (i.e., commonalities and variations) between software products and the variability needed, a comprehensive analysis is conducted up-front (e.g., to determine what requirements in a product may vary, including the sources of variation and the allowed options to resolve this variation). This also includes investigating how the architecture can facilitate the required variability. In agile development, however, the focus is on developing software systems that satisfy customers by minimizing up-front investment and process overhead [134]. This is, in fact, a direct conflict with handling variability as it requires up-front analysis to anticipate change.

■ Documentation of variability is essential to communicate architecture knowledge between stakeholders. Thus, the architecture must properly represent variability. When handling variability, designers usually plan and document extensively, and each designer has a specific responsibility [141]. In contrast, agile development tries to reduce overhead caused by excessive documentation but relies on implicit or light-weight documentation (e.g., through documentation in source code or story cards). As a result, in agile development designers use a lot of tacit knowledge and share responsibilities.

■ In agile development fast and frequent delivery is a key for quick customer satisfaction and feedback. This is difficult to achieve in variability-intensive systems: Variability is analyzed before delivering any product to provide a flexible infrastructure, which is later configured and deployed [138]. The agile principle of "simplicity" and implementing functionality that satisfies current instead of future requirements could contradict the need to support different variation points. In agile development, not a lot of effort is put into designing the architecture beyond the current iteration [141].

■ Agile methods focus on quick response to requirements changes with short iterations and small increments. This requires direct customer collaboration and participation in the whole software project life cycle [141]. When handling variability, communication between stakeholders is important. However, collaboration takes place not as extensively as in a typical agile development setting, and customers are rarely on-site.

■ One assumption of variability is that target application domains in which a system is deployed are stable and do not change much. In contrast, in agile environments, application domains are often assumed to be unstable and domain boundaries change. However, stable domains would reduce risks when pre-developing software assets for later (re-)use. Consequently, while there is no emphasis on reuse in agile development, variability puts special emphasis on maturity and reliability of reused artifacts [141].

With regard to tools, agile methods emphasize on simple and efficient tools (e.g., paper-based or virtual story cards, web-based tools for test-driven development), where technology only affects the current project [141]. To handle variability, on the other hand, practitioners often use robust, heavy-weight and powerful tools (e.g., Gears[1] or Pure::variants[2]).

1.9 Conclusions

Today's variability-intensive software systems vary widely in terms of purpose, application domain, complexity, size, novelty, adaptability, required qualities and life span. This chapter provided an overview of variability-intensive systems irrespective of any of these variations. The chapters in this book address these issues, and more. In doing so, they deepen our understanding of the foundations, concepts, techniques and applications of software engineering for variability-intensive

---

[1] www.biglever.com.
[2] www.pure-systems.com.

systems, and highlight the potential for new ways of designing, implementing and maintaining variability-intensive software, large and small. In particular, chapters in this book could:

- Help identify job roles and responsibilities in organizations and projects, along with required skills and competencies
- Ensure proper oversight and accountability and enable consistent governance and alignment of different artifacts and development/maintenance activities in variability-intensive software development projects
- Enable proper implementation of system governance directives and maintainability of systems

References

1. ISO/IEC/IEEE, "Systems and Software Engineering — Architecture Description," vol. ISO/IEC/IEEE 42010 Geneva, Switzerland, 2011.
2. M. Galster, D. Weyns, M. Goedicke, U. Zdun, R. Rabiser, G. Perrouin, and B. Zhang, "Variability and Complexity in Software Design — Towards a Research Agenda," *ACM Software Engineering Notes*, vol. 41, pp. 27-30, 2016.
3. R. Hilliard, "On Representing Variation," in *Workshop on Variability in Software Product Line Architectures* Copenhagen, Denmark: ACM, 2010, pp. 312-315.
4. A. Metzger and K. Pohl, "Software Product Line Engineering and Variability Management: Achievements and Challenges," in *Future of Software Engineering*, Hyderabad, India: ACM, 2014, pp. 70-84.
5. Backstory, "Boom Times for the New Camera Boom," *IEEE Spectrum*, vol. 52, p. 3, 2015.
6. J. van Gurp, J. Bosch, and M. Svahnberg, "On the Notion of Variability in Software Product Lines," in *Working IEEE/IFIP Conference on Software Architecture*, Amsterdam, The Netherlands: IEEE Computer Society, 2001, pp. 45-54.
7. J. Bosch, G. Florijn, D. Greefhorst, J. Kuusela, J. H. Obbink, and K. Pohl, "Variability Issues in Software Product Lines," in *4th International Workshop on Software Product Family Engineering*, Bilbao, Spain: Springer Verlag, 2002, pp. 303-338.
8. J. Bosch, R. Capilla, and R. Hilliard, "Trends in Systems and Software Variability (Guest editors' introduction)," *IEEE Software*, vol. 32, pp. 44-51, 2015.
9. M. Galster, D. Weyns, D. Tofan, B. Michalik, and P. Avgeriou, "Variability in Software Systems — A Systematic Literature Review," *IEEE Transactions on Software Engineering*, vol. 40, pp. 282-306, 2014.
10. J. Singer, S. E. Sim, and T. C. Lethbridge, "Software Engineering Data Collection for Field Studies," in *Guide to Advanced Empirical Software Engineering*, F. Shull, J. Singer, and D. Sjoberg, Eds. Berlin/Heidelberg: Springer Verlag, 2008, pp. 9-34.
11. M. Galster and P. Avgeriou, "The Notion of Variability in Software Architecture — Results from a Preliminary Exploratory Study," in *5th International Workshop on Variability Modelling in Software-intensive Systems (VaMoS)*, Namur, Belgium: ACM, 2011, pp. 59-67.
12. L. Chen and M. A. Babar, "Variability Management in Software Product Lines: An Investigation of Contemporary Industrial Challenges," in *14th International Software Product Line Conference*, Jeju Island, South Korea: Springer Verlag, 2010, pp. 1-15.
13. L. Chen, M. A. Babar, and N. Ali, "Variability Management in Software Product Lines: A Systematic Review," in *13th International Software Product Line Conference (SPLC)*, San Francisco, CA: Carnegie Mellon University, 2009, pp. 81-90.
14. L. Chen, M. A. Babar, and C. Cawley, "A Status Report on the Evaluation of Variability Management Approaches," in *13th International Conference on Evaluation and Assessment in Software Engineering (EASE)* Durham, UK: BCS, 2009, pp. 1-10.
15. ISO/IEC, "Software engineering — Product quality — Part 1: Quality model." ISO/IEC 9126-1, 2001.

16. S. Bode and M. Riebisch, "Impact Evaluation for Quality-Oriented Architectural Decisions Regarding Evolvability," in *4th European Conference on Software Architecture*, Copenhagen, Denmark: Springer Verlag, 2010, pp. 182-197.

17. M. Mari and N. Eila, "The Impact of Maintainability on Component-based Software Systems," in *29th Euromicro Conference*, Belek-Antalya, Turkey: IEEE Computer Society, 2003, pp. 25-32.

18. V. Myllärniemi, M. Raatikainen, and T. Mannisto, "A Systematically Conducted Literature Review: Quality Attribute Variability in Software Product Lines," in *16th International Software Product Line Conference*, Salvador, Brazil: ACM, 2012, pp. 41-45.

19. IEEE Computer Society Software Engineering Standards Committee, "IEEE Standard Glossary of Software Engineering Terminology," IEEE Std 610.12-1990, 1990.

20. A. Abran, J. W. Moore, P. Bourque and R. Dupuis, "Guide to the Software Engineering Body of Knowledge — 2004 Version," P. Bourque and R. Dupuis, Eds. Los Alamitos, CA: IEEE Computer Society, 2004.

21. L. Bass, P. Clements, and R. Kazman, *Software Architecture in Practice*. Boston, MA: Addison-Wesley, 2003.

22. L. Chen and M. A. Babar, "A Systematic Review of Evaluation of Variability Management Approaches in Software Product Lines," *Information and Software Technology*, vol. 53, pp. 344-362, 2011.

23. T. Dao, H. Lee, and K. C. Kang, "Problem Frames-Based Approach to Achieving Quality Attributes in Software Product Line Engineering," in *15th International Conference on Software Product Lines* Munich, Germany: IEEE Computer Society, 2011, pp. 175-180.

24. A. J. Nolan, S. Abrahao, P. Clements, J. D. McGregor, and S. Cohen, "Towards the Integration of Quality Attributes into a Software Product Line Cost Model," in *15th International Conference on Software Product Lines*, Munich, Germany: IEEE Computer Society, 2011, pp. 203-212.

25. R. de Oliveira Cavalcanti, E. S. de Almeida, and S. Meira, "Extending the RiPLE-DE Process with Quality Attribute Variability Realization," in *7th International ACM Sigsoft Conference on the Quality of Software Architectures (QoSA)*, Boulder, CO: ACM, 2011, pp. 159-163.

26. L. Etxeberria and G. Sagardui, "Variability Driven Quality Evaluation in Software Product Lines," in *12th International Software Product Line Conference*, Limerick, Ireland: IEEE Computer Society, 2008, pp. 243-252.

27. L. Etxeberria and G. Sagardui, "Evaluation of Quality Attribute Variability in Software Product Families," in *15th Annual IEEE International Conference on Engineering of Computer Based Systems (ECBS)*, Belfast, Northern Ireland: IEEE Computer Society, 2008, pp. 255-264.

28. L. Etxeberria, G. Sagardui, and L. Belategi, "Quality-aware Software Product Line Engineering," *Journal of the Brazilian Computer Society*, vol. 14, pp. 1-13, March 2006.

29. E. Niemela and A. Immonen, "Capturing Quality Requirements of Product Family Architecture," *Information and Software Technology*, vol. 49, pp. 1107-1120, November 2007.

30. M. Ortega, M. Perez, and T. Rojas, "Construction of a Systemic Quality Model for Evaluating a Software Product," *Software Quality Journal*, vol. 11, pp. 219-242, 2003.

31. R. Lence, L. Fuentes, and M. Pinto, "Quality Attributes and Variability in AO-ADL Software Architectures," in *1st International Workshop on Software Architecture Variability*, Essen, Germany: ACM, 2011, pp. 1-10.

32. V. Myllarniemi, T. Mannisto, and M. Raatikainen, "Quality Attribute Variability within a Software Product Family Architecture," in *2nd International Conference on the Quality of Software Architectures (QoSA)*, Vasteras, Sweden: Springer Verlag, 2006, pp. 1-5.

33. M. Raatikainen, E. Niemela, V. Myllarniemi, and T. Mannisto, "Svamp — An Integrated Approach for Modeling Functional and Quality Variability," in *2nd International Workshop on Variability Modeling of Software-intensive Systems (VaMoS)*, Duisburg, Germany: University of Duisburg-Essen, 2008, pp. 89-96.

34. L. Etxeberria, G. Sagardui, and L. Belategi, "Modelling Variation in Quality Attributes," in *First International Workshop on Variability Modelling of Software-intensive Systems (VaMoS)*, Limerick, Ireland: Lero, 2007, pp. 1-9.

35. S. Mahdavi-Hezavehi, M. Galster, and P. Avgeriou, "Variability in Quality Attributes of Service-based Software Systems: A Systematic Literature Review," *Information and Software Technology*, vol. 55, pp. 320-343, 2013.

36. S. Montagud, S. Abrahao, and E. Insfran, "A Systematic Review of Quality Attributes and Measures for Software Product Lines," *Software Quality Journal*, vol. 20, pp. 425-486, 2011.

37. M. Galster and P. Avgeriou, "Handling Variability in Software Architecture: Problems and Implications," in *9th IEEE/IFIP Working Conference on Software Architecture*, Boulder, CO: IEEE Computer Society, 2011, pp. 171-180.

38. H. Gomaa and M. E. Shin, "Multiple-view Modelling and Meta-Modelling of Software Product Lines," *IET Software*, vol. 2, pp. 94-122, 2008.

39. N. Rozanski and E. Woods, *Software Systems Architecture: Working With Stakeholders Using Viewpoints and Perspectives*. Reading, MA: Addison-Wesley, 2005.

40. D. Weyns, B. Michalik, A. Helleboogh, and N. Boucke, "An Architectural Approach to Support Online Updates of Software Product Lines," in *9th Working IEEE/IFIP Conference on Software Architecture (WICSA)*, Boulder, CO: IEEE Computer Society, 2011, pp. 204-213.

41. M. Galster and P. Avgeriou, "A Variability Viewpoint for Enterprise Software Systems," in *Joint 10th Working IEEE/IFIP Conference on Software Architecture (WICSA) & 6th European Conference on Software Architecture (ECSA)* Helsinki, Finland: IEEE Computer Society, 2012, pp. 267-271.

42. M. Galster, L. Lapre, and P. Avgeriou, "Service-Oriented Architecture in Variability-Intensive Environments: Pitfalls and Best Practices in the Example of Local E-Government," *IEEE Software*, vol. 31, pp. 77-84, 2014.

43. M. Galster, D. Weyns, M. Goedicke, U. Zdun, J. Cunha, and J. Chavariaga, "Variablity and Complexity in Software Design — Towards Quality through Modeling and Testing," *ACM SIGSOFT Software Engineering Notes*, vol. 42, pp. 35-37, 2017.

44. T. Thum, S. Apel, C. Kaestner, I. Schaefer, and G. Saake, "A Classification and Survey of Analysis Strategies for Software Product Lines," *ACM Computing Surveys*, vol. 47, pp. 6:1-6:45, 2014.

45. C. Kaestner, A. von Rhein, S. Erdweg, J. Pusch, S. Apel, T. Rendel, and K. Ostermann, "Toward Variability-aware Testing," in *4th International Workshop on Feature-oriented Software Development*, Dresden, Germany: ACM, 2012, pp. 1-8.

46. H. V. Nguyen, C. Kaestner, and T. Nguyen, "Exploring Variability-aware Execution for Testing Plugin-based Web Applications," in *36th International Conference on Software Engineering (ICSE)*, Hyderabad, India: ACM, 2014, pp. 907-918.

47. ISO/IEC/IEEE, "Systems and Software Engineering — Software Life Cycle Processes." vol. ISO/IEC/IEEE 12207, Geneva, Switzerland, 2015.

48. F. Cicirelli, A. Furfaro, and L. Nigro, "A Service-based Architecture for Dynamically Reconfigurable Worksflows," *Journal of Systems and Software*, vol. 83, pp. 1148-1164, 2010.

49. P. Bengtsson, N. Lassing, J. Bosch, and H. v. Vliet, "Architecture-level Modifiability Analysis (ALMA)," *Journal of Systems and Software*, vol. 69, pp. 129-147, January 2004.

50. T. Chaari, D. Ejigu, F. Laforest, and V.-M. Scuturici, "A Comprehensive Approach to Model and Use Context for Adapting Applications in Pervasive Environments," *Journal of Systems and Software*, vol. 80, pp. 1973-1992, 2007.

51. S. Previtali and T. Gross, "Dynamic Updating of Software Systems based on Aspects," in *22nd International Conference on Software Maintenance (ICSM)*, Philadelphia, PA: IEEE, 2006, pp. 83-92.

52. J. Floch, S. Hallsteinsen, E. Stav, F. Eliassen, K. Lund, and E. Gjarven, "Using Architecture Models for Runtime Adaptability," *IEEE Software*, vol. 23, pp. 62-70, 2005.

53. D. Dhungana, P. Gruenbacher, and R. Rabiser, "The DOPLER Meta-tool for Decision-oriented Variability Modeling: a Multiple Case Study," *Automated Software Engineering*, vol. 18, pp. 77-114, 2010.

54. I. Bayley and H. Zhu, "Formal Specification of the Variants and Behavioural Features of Design Patterns," *Journal of Systems and Software*, vol. 83, pp. 209-221, 2010.

55. P. America, D. Hammer, M. Ionita, H. Obbink, and E. Rommes, "Scenario-based Decision Making for Architectural Variability in Product Families," in *3rd International Conference on Software Product Lines (SPLC)*, Boston, MA: Springer, 2004, pp. 284-303.

56. E. Truyen, B. Vanhaute, W. Joosen, P. Verbaeten, and B. Jorgensen, "Dynamic and Selective Combination of extensions on Component-based Applications," in *23rd International Conference on Software Engineering (ICSE)* Toronto, Canada: IEEE, 2001, pp. 233-242.

57. F. Dordowsky and W. Hipp, "Adopting Software Product Line Principles to Manage Software Variants in a Complex Avionics System," in *13th International Software Product Line Conference (SPLC)*, San Francisco: ACM, 2009, pp. 265-274.

58. D. Batory, C. Johnson, B. MacDonaldvon, and D. von Heeder, "Achieving Extensibility trhough Product-lines and Domain-specific Languages: a Case Study," *ACM Transaction on Software Engineering and Methodology*, vol. 11, pp. 191-214, 2002.

59. C. Fritsch and B. Renz, "Four Mechanisms for Adaptable Systems," *Software Process: Improvement and Practice*, vol. 10, pp. 103-124, 2005.

60. D. Ardagna and B. Pernici, "Adaptive Service Composition in Flexible Processes," *IEEE Transactions on Software Engineering*, vol. 33, pp. 369-384, 2007.

61. M. Forte, W. L. de Souza, and A. F. do Prado, "Using Ontologies and Web Services for Content Adaptation in Ubiquitous Computing," *Journal of Systems and Software*, vol. 81, pp. 368-381, 2008.

62. M. Svahnberg, J. van Gurp, and J. Bosch, "A Taxonomy of Variability Realization Techniques," *Software — Practice and Experience*, vol. 35, pp. 705-754, April 2005.

63. M. Galster and P. Avgeriou, "An Industrial Case Study on Variability Handling in Large Enterprise Software Systems," *Information and Software Technology*, vol. 60, pp. 16-31, 2015.

64. K. Breitman, J. C. S. do Prado Leite, and D. M. Berry, "Supporting Scenario Evolution," *Requirements Engineering*, vol. 10, pp. 112-131, 2005.

65. S. Buhne, K. Lauenroth, and K. Pohl, "Modelling Requirements Variability across Product Lines," in *13th IEEE International Conference on Requirements Enginering*, Paris, France: IEEE, 2005, pp. 41-52.

66. M. Voelter, "Handling Variability," in *14th European Conference on Pattern Languages of Programs* Irsee, Germany, 2009, pp. 1-12.

67. M. Eriksson, J. Borstler, and K. Bjorg, "Managing Requirements Specifications for Product Lines - an Approach and Industry Case Study," *Journal of Systems and Software*, vol. 82, pp. 435-447, 2009.

68. A. Chan and S.-N. Chuang, "MobiPADS: A Reflective Middleware for Context-aware Mobile Computing," *IEEE Transactions on Software Engineering*, vol. 29, pp. 1072-1085, 2003.

69. T. B. C. Arias, P. America, and P. Avgeriou, "Defining and Documenting Execution Viewpoints for a Large and Complex Software-intensive System," *Journal of Systems and Software*, p. 15, 2010.

70. C. Hunsen, B. Zhang, J. Siegmund, C. Kaestner, O. Lessenich, M. Becker, and S. Apel, "Preprocessor-based Variability in Opten-source and Indistrual Software Systems: An Empirical Study," *Empirical Software Engineering*, vol. 21, pp. 449-482, 2016.

71. A. Kenner, C. Kaestner, S. Haase, and T. Leich, "TypeChef: Toward Type Checking #ifdef Variability in C," in *2nd International Workshop on Feature-Oriented Software Development (FOSD)*, Eindhoven, The Netherlands: ACM, 2010, pp. 25-32.

72. R. Hirschfeld, P. Costanza, and O. Nierstrasz, "Context-oriented Programming," *Journal of Object Technology*, vol. 7, pp. 125-151, 2008.

73. K. Czarnecki and U. Eisenecker, *Generative Programming — Methods, Tools, and Applications*. Boston, MA: Addison Wesley, 2000.

74. K. Pohl, G. Boeckle, and F. van der Linden, *Software Product Line Engineering — Foundations, Principles, and Techniques*. Berlin/Heidelberg: Springer Verlag, 2005.

75. P. Clements and L. Northrop, *Software Product Lines — Practices and Patterns*. Boston, MA: Addison-Wesley, 2001.

76. F. Ahmed and L. F. Capretz, "The Software Product Line Architecture: An Empirical Investigation of Key Process Activities," *Information and Software Technology*, vol. 50, pp. 1098-1113, October 2008.

77. M. Jazayeri, F. van der Linden, and A. Ran, *Software Architecture for Product Families: Principles and Practice*. Reading, MA: Addison-Wesley, 2000.

78. M. Verlage and T. Kiesgen, "Five Years of Product Line Engineering in a Small Company," in *27th International Conference on Software Engineering*, St. Louis, MO: ACM, 2005, pp. 534-543.

79. J. Bayer, O. Flege, P. Knauber, R. Laqua, D. Muthig, K. Schmid, T. Widen, and J.-M. DeBaud, "PuLSE: A Methodology to Develop Software Product Lines," in *Symposium on Software Reusability*, Los Angeles, CA: ACM, 1999, pp. 122-131.

80. H. Shokry and M. Ali Babar, "Dynamic Software Product Line Architectures Using Service-based Computing for Automotive Systems," in *2nd International Workshop on Dynamic Software Product Lines*, Limerick, Irleand: Lero International Science Centre, 2008, pp. 53-58.

81. S. Hallsteinsen, S. Jiang, and R. Sanders, "Dynamic Software Product Lines in Service-oriented Computing," in *3rd International Workshop on Dynamic Software Product Lines*, San Francisco, CA, 2009, pp. 28-34.

82. J. L. Fiadeiro and A. Lopes, "A Model for Dynamic Reconfiguration in Service-Oriented Architectures," in *4th European Conference on Software Architecture*, Copenhagen, Denmark: Springer Verlag, 2010, pp. 70-85.

83. R. Cloutier, G. Muller, D. Verma, R. Nilchiani, E. Hole, and M. Bone, "The Concept of Reference Architectures," *Systems Engineering*, vol. 13, pp. 14-27, March 2010.

84. R. High, S. Kinder, and S. Graham, "IBM's SOA Foundation — An Architectural Introduction and Overview," IBM, White Paper November 2005.

85. V. Stricker, K. Lauenroth, P. Corte, F. Gittler, S. D. Panfilis, and K. Pohl, "Creating a Reference Architecture for Service-based Systems — A Pattern-based Approach," in Towards the Future Internet, G. Tselentis, A. Galis, A. Gavras, S. Krco, E. Lotz, E. Simperl, B. Stiller, and T. Zahariadis, Eds. Amsterdam: IOS Press, 2010, pp. 149-160.

86. S. Angelov and P. Grefen, "An E-contracting Reference Architecture," *Journal of Systems and Software*, vol. 81, pp. 1816-1844, November 2008.

87. T. E. Faegri and S. Hallsteinsen, "A Software Product Line Reference Architecture for Security," in *Software Product Lines*, T. Kakola and J. C. Duenas, Eds. Berlin/Heidelberg: Springer Verlag, 2006, pp. 275-326.

88. M. Hafner, M. Memon, and R. Breu, "SeAAS — A Reference Architecture for Security Services in SOA," *Journal of Universal Computer Science*, vol. 15, pp. 2916-2936, 2009.

89. A. Grosskurth and M. Godfrey, "A Reference Architecture for Web Browsers," in *International Conference on Software Maintenance*, Budapest, Hungary: IEEE Computer Society, 2005, pp. 661-664.

90. G. Muller, "A Reference Architecture Primer," Embedded Systems Institute, Eindhoven, NL, May 22, 2010.

91. M. Galster and P. Avgeriou, "Empirically-grounded Reference Architectures: A Proposal," in *7th ACM Sigsoft International Conference on the Quality of Software Architectures (QoSA)*, Boulder, CO: ACM, 2011, pp. 153-157.

92. O. Vogel, I. Arnold, A. Chughtai, E. Ihler, T. Kehrer, U. Mehlig, and U. Zdun, Software-Architektur — Grundlagen — Konzepte Praxis. Berlin/Heidelberg: Spektrum Akademischer Verlag, 2009.

93. S. Angelov, P. Grefen, and D. Greefhorst, "A Classification of Software Reference Architectures: Analyzing Their Success and Effectiveness," in *Joint Working IEEE/IFIP Conference on Software Architecture & European Conference on Software Architecture (WICSA/ECSA)*, Cambridge, UK: IEEE Computer Society, 2009, pp. 141-150.

94. E. Y. Nakagawa, P. O. Antonino, and M. Becker, "Reference Architecture and Product Line Architecture: A Subtle but Critical Difference," in *5th European Conference on Software Architecture*, Essen, Germany: Springer Verlag, 2011, pp. 207-211.

95. S. Angelov, J. Trienekens, and P. Grefen, "Towards a Method for the Evaluation of Reference Architectures: Experiences from a Case," in *Second European Conference on Software Architecture*, Paphos, Cyprus: Springer, 2008, pp. 225-240.

96. P. Kruchten, *The Rational Unified Process: An Introduction*, 3rd ed. Boston, MA: Addison-Wesley, 2004.

97. U. Eklund, O. Askerdal, J. Granholm, A. Alminger, and J. Axelsson, "Experience of Introducing Reference Architectures in the Development of Automotive Electronic Systems," *ACM SIGSOFT Software Engineering Notes*, vol. 30, pp. 1-6, 2005.

98. J. Bayer, D. Ganesan, J.-F. Girard, J. Knodel, R. Kolb, and K. Schmid, "Definition of Reference Architectures Based on Existing Systems," Fraunhofer Institute for Experimental Software Engineering 085.03/E, 2003.

99. E. Y. Nakagawa, R. M. Martins, K. R. Felizardo, and J. C. Maldodano, "Towards a Process to Design Aspect-oriented Reference Architectures," in *XXXV Latin American Informatics Conference (CLEI'2009)*, Pelotas, Brazil, 2009, pp. 1-10.

100. O. Winberg, "Reference Architecture Template," Swedish Defence Materiel Administration, Stockholm, Sweden 33394/2006, 2007.

101. F. Ahlemann and H. Gastl, "Process Model for an Empirically Grounded Reference Model Construction," in *Reference Modeling for Business Systems Analysis*, P. Fettke and P. Loos, Eds., Hershey, PA: IGI Global, 2007, pp. 77-97.

102. M. Karow, D. Pfeiffer, and M. Raeckers, "Empirical-based Construction of Reference Models in Public Administrations," in *Multikonferenz Wirtschaftsinformatik*, Munich, Germany: Gito-Verlag, 2008, pp. 1613-1624.

103. M. H. Dodani, "SOA 2006: State Of The Art," *Journal of Object Technology*, vol. 5, pp. 41-48, November-December 2006.

104. C. Sun, R. Rossing, M. Sinnema, P. Bulanov, and M. Aiello, "Modeling and Managing the Variability of Web-Service-based Systems," *Journal of Systems and Software*, vol. 83, pp. 502-516, March 2010.

105. M. Aiello, P. Bulanov, and H. Groefsema, "Requirements and Tools for Variability Management," in *4th IEEE Workshop on Requirement Engineering for Services (REFS 2010)*, Seoul, South Korea: IEEE Computer Society, 2010, pp. 245-250.

106. R. Kazhamiakin, S. Benbernou, L. Baresi, P. Plebani, M. Uhlig, and O. Barais, "Adaptation of Service-Based Systems," in *Service Research Challenges and Solutions for the Future Internet*, M. P. Papazoglou, K. Pohl, M. Parkin, and A. Metzger, Eds. Berlin/Heidelberg: Springer Verlag, 2010, pp. 117-156.

107. M. Galster and E. Bucherer, "A Business-Goal-Service-Capability Graph for the Alignment of Requirements and Services," in *IEEE Congress on Services*, Honolulu, HI: IEEE Computer Society, 2008, pp. 399-406.

108. R. Haesen, M. Snoeck, W. Lemahieu, and S. Poelmans, "On the Definition of Service Granularity and its Architectural Impact," in *20th International Conference on Advanced Information Systems Engineering (CAiSE'08)* Montpellier, France: Springer, 2008, pp. 375-389.

109. M. Galster, P. Avgeriou, and D. Tofan, "Constraints for the Design of Variability-intensive Service-oriented Reference Architectures — An Industrial Case Study," *Information and Software Technology*, vol. 55, pp. 428-441, 2013.

110. Hadaytullah, K. Koskimies, and T. Systa, "Using Model Customization for Variability Management in Service Composition," in *IEEE International Conference on Web Services*, Los Angeles, CA: IEEE Computer Society, 2009, pp. 687-694.

111. F. M. Medeiros, E. S. de Almeida, and S. R. de Lemos Meira, "Towards an Approach for Service-Oriented Product Line Architectures," in *Workshop on Service-oriented Architectures and Software Product Lines*, San Francisco, CA: Software Engineering Institute, 2009, pp. 1-7.

112. Q. Gu and P. Lago, "On Service-Oriented Architectural Concerns and Viewpoints," in *Working IEEE/IFIP Conference on Software Architecture (WICSA)*, Cambridge, UK: IEEE Computer Society, 2009, pp. 289-292.

113. Q. Gu and P. Lago, "Exploring Service-oriented System Engineering Challenges: A systematic Literature Review," *Service Oriented Computing and Applications*, vol. 3, pp. 171-188, September 2009.

114. M. W. Maier, "Architecting Principles for Systems-of-systems," *Systems Engineering*, vol. 1, pp. 267-284, 1999.

115. D. Weyns and J. Andersson, "On the Challenges of Self-Adaptation in Systems of Systems," in *1st International Workshop on Software Engineering for Systems-of-Systems*, Montpellier, France: ACM, 2013, pp. 47-51.

116. S. d. S. Amorim, J. McGregor, E. de Almeida, and C. von Flach, "When Ecosystems Collide: Making Systems of Systems Work," in *2nd International Workshop on Software Engineering for Systems of Systems*, Vienna, Austria: ACM, 2014.

117. K. Manikas and K. M. Hansen, "Software Ecosystems - a Systematic Literature Review," *Journal of Systems and Software*, vol. 86, pp. 1294-1306, 2013.

118. J. Knodel, M. Naab, and D. Rost, "Supporting Architects in Mastering the Complexity of Open Software Ecosystems," in *2nd International Workshop on Software Engineering for Systems-of-Systems*, Vienna, Austria: ACM, 2014, pp. 1-6.

119. E. Eckhardt, E. Kaats, S. Jansen, and C. Alves, "The Merits of a Meritocracy in Open Source Software Ecosystems," in *2nd International Workshop on Software Engineering for Systems-of-Systems*, Vienna, Austria: ACM, 2014, pp. 1-6.

120. T. Berger, H. Pfeiffer, R. Tartler, S. Dienst, K. Czarnecki, A. Wasowski, and S. She, "Variability Mechanisms in Software Ecosystems," *Information and Software Technology*, vol. 56, pp. 1520-1535, 2014.

121. B. Cheng, R. Lemos, H. Giese, P. Inverardi, J. Magee, J. Andersson, B. Becker, N. Bencomo, Y. Brun, B. Cukic, G. Serugendo, S. Dustdar, A. Finkelstein, C. Gacek, K. Geihs, V. Grassi, G. Karsai, H. Kienle, J. Kramer, M. Litoiu, S. Mael, R. Mirandola, H. Mueller, S. Park, M. Shaw, M. Tichy, M. Tivoli, D. Weyns, and J. Whittle, "Software Engineering for Self-adaptive Systems: A Research Roadmap," in *Software Engineering for Self-adaptive Systems*, vol. 5525, B. Cheng, R. Lemos, H. Giese, P. Inverardi, and J. Magee, Eds. Berlin/Heidelberg: Springer Verlag, 2009, pp. 1-26.

122. D. Garlan, S.-W. Cheng, A.-C. Huang, B. Schmerl, and P. Steenkiste, "Architecture-based Self-adaptation with Reusable Infrastructure," *IEEE Computer*, vol. 37, pp. 46-54, 2004.

123. J. Kephart and D. Chess, "The Vision of Autonomic Computing," *IEEE Computer*, vol. 36, pp. 41-50, 2003.

124. P. Oreizy, M. M. Gorlick, R. N. Taylor, D. Heimbigner, G. Johnson, N. Medvidovic, A. Quilici, D. S. Rosenblum, and A. L. Wolf, "An Architecture-Based Approach to Self-Adaptive Software," *IEEE Intelligent Systems*, vol. 14, pp. 54-62, May 1999.

125. N. Fussberger, B. Zhang, and M. Becker, "A Deep Dive into Android's Variability Realizations," in *21st International Conference on Systems and Software Product Lines*, Sevilla, Spain: ACM, 2017, pp. 69-78.

126. T. Ihme, M. Pikkarainen, S. Teppola, J. Kaariainen, and O. Biot, "Challenges and Industry Practices for Managing Software Variability in Small and Medium Sized Enterprises," *Empirical Software Engineering*, vol. 19, pp. 1144-1168, 2014.

127. M. Jaring and J. Bosch, "Representing Variability in Software Product Lines: A Case Study," in *Second Software Product Line Conference*, San Diego, CA: Springer Verlag, 2002, pp. 15-36.

128. C. Thoern, "Current State and Potential of Variability Management Practices in Software-intensive SMEs: Results from a Regional Industrial Survey," *Information and Software Technology*, vol. 52, pp. 411-421, 2010.

129. J. Diaz, J. Perez, P. P. Alarcon, and J. Garbajosa, "Agile Product Line Engineering — A Systematic Literature Review," *Software — Practice and Experience*, vol. 41, pp. 921-941, 2011.

130. M. Galster and P. Avgeriou, "Supporting variability through agility to achieve adaptable architectures," in *Agile Software Architecture — Aligning Agile Processes and Software Architectures*, M. A. Babar, A. W. Brown, K. Koskimies, and I. Mistrik, Eds. Morgan-Kaufman, 2014, pp. 139-159.

131. J. D. McGregor, "Agile Software Product Lines, Deconstructed," *Journal of Object Technology*, vol. 7, pp. 7-19, 2008.

132. K. Cooper and X. Franch, "APLE — 1st International Workshop on Agile Product Line Engineering," in *10th International Conference on Software Product Lines* Baltimore, MD: IEEE Computer Society, 2006, pp. 205-206.

133. I. F. de Silva, P. A. da Mota Silveira Neto, P. O'Leary, E. S. de Almeida, and S. R. de Lemos Meira, "Agile Software Product Lines: A Systematic Mapping Study," *Software — Practice and Experience*, vol. 41, pp. 899-920, 2011.

134. Y. Ghanam, D. Andreychuk, and F. Maurer, "Reactive Variability Management in Agile Software Development," in *AGILE Conference* Orlando, FL: IEEE Computer Society, 2010, pp. 27-34.

135. G. Hanssen and T. E. Faegri, "Process Fusion: An Industrial Case Study on Agile Software Product Line Engineering," *Journal of Systems and Software*, vol. 81, pp. 843-854, 2008.

136. P. Pohjalainen, "Bottom-up Modeling for a Software Product Line: An Experience Report on Agile Modeling of Governmental Mobile Networks," in *15th International Software Product Line Conference* Munich, Germany: IEEE Computer Society, 2011, pp. 323-332.

137. M. A. Noor, R. Rabiser, and P. Gruenbacher, "Agile Product Line Planning: A Collaborative Approach and a Case Study," *Journal of Systems and Software*, vol. 81, pp. 868-882, 2008.

138. R. F. Paige, X. Wang, Z. Stephenson, and P. J. Brooke, "Towards an Agile Process for Building Software Product Lines," in *7th International Conference on eXtreme Programming and Agile Processes in Software Engineering (XP)*, Oulu, Finland: Springer Verlag, 2006, pp. 198-199.

139. Y. Ghanam and F. Maurer, "Using Acceptance Tests for Incremental Elicitation of Variability in Requriements: An Observational Study," in *AGILE Conference*, Salt Lake City, UT: IEEE Computer Society, 2011, pp. 139-142.

140. M. Galster, S. Angelov, S. Martinez-Fernandez, and D. Tofan, "Reference Architectures and Scrum: Friends or Foes?," in *11th Joint Meeting on Foundations of Software Engineering (FSE)*, Paderborn, Germany: ACM, 2017, pp. 896-901.

141. K. Tian and K. Cooper, "Agile and Software Product Line Methods: Are they so Different?," in *First International Workshop on Agile Software Product Line Engineering*, Baltimore, MD, 2006, pp. 1-8.

CONCEPTS
AND MODELS

Chapter 2

Observations from Variability Modelling Approaches at the Architecture Level

Ana Paula Allian[a1], Rafael Capilla[b], and Elisa Yumi Nakagawa[a]

[a]*Department of Computer Systems, University of São Paulo, São Carlos, Brazil*
[b]*Computer Science Department, Rey Juan Carlos University, Madrid, Spain*

2.1 Introduction

Versatile and configurable software systems must be built using software variability techniques to configure them for the variety of customer's needs and different scenarios. The ability of systems to represent this variability in software architecture models and views is still an open problem as stated in (Galster and Avgeriou 2011).

Moreover, recent challenges stated in (Bosch, Capilla and Hilliard 2015) refer to the inability of systems to predict unexpected variability when systems are reconfigured and redeployed at runtime, and this runtime variability is hard to represent in the software architecture through the binding time property. Conventional software variability approaches and techniques (Capilla, Bosch and Kang 2013) are unable to manage the runtime variability needs demanded by many modern systems (e.g., robots, unmanned vehicles, smart cities).

Over the last two decades, practitioners and researchers have witnessed a significant evolution from traditional feature-based models i.e., Feature-Oriented Domain Analysis (FODA) to more sophisticated languages aimed to represent and configure the variability of systems on behalf of a plethora of software variability management tools, and where system features are considered first-class entities. Recent surveys like (Galster, Weyns, et al. 2014) analyze the ongoing efforts, methods, and quality concerns using different software variability approaches. However, the authors fail to describe how existing software architecture approaches can represent variability concerns as they only provide the coarse numbers about how many studies deal with variability in design activities. Another recent study from (Bashroush, et al. 2017) nicely outlines the role of variability

---

[1] Corresponding author: ana.allian@usp.br

management tools in software product line approaches, but the authors neglect the architecture part of the problem, and they only show how features are represented by software variability management tools through architecture descriptions. However, they provide some discussion about existing domain-specific variability languages like the Orthogonal Variability Model (OVM), and they summarize the main approaches for representing variability, ranging from textual descriptions (most of them use XML) to UML-based ones. Consequently, due to the importance of software architecture for building software-intensive systems, as well as the lack of specific studies describing how variability can be represented in the software architecture and how they compare to other solutions based on domain-specific variability languages, we analyze in this chapter the evolution of both perspectives to distill new insight and show recent trends for describing and handling variability concerns.

This chapter is organized in four sections: Section 2.2 presents the research methodology we used to carry out a Systematic Mapping Study (SMS) on variability in software architecture. Section 2.3 presents an overview of variability modeling approaches in software architecture, while in Section 2.4 we summarize some findings and new insights, and we draw our conclusions in Section 2.5.

2.2 Research Methodology

As research methodology, we conducted a Systematic Mapping Study (SMS)[2] based on the guidelines proposed by (Kitchenham and Charters 2007) and (Petersen, Vakkalanka and Kuzniarz 2015). We used a predefined search strategy, which begins with defining a protocol to specify the research questions (RQs) aimed at investigating how software variability can be represented at the software architecture level. This search strategy is based on the following query we used to find the relevant primary studies:

(("software architecture" OR "system architecture" OR "reference architecture" OR "product line architecture" OR "product family architecture" OR "SPL architecture") AND (variability OR "variation point"))

The primary studies were selected conducting automatic search in the following digital libraries: Association for Computing Machinery Digital Library (ACM DL)[3], IEEEXplore Digital Library[4], EiCompendex[5], Scopus[6], and Science Direct[7]. The selection of primary studies was conducted according to the following inclusion and exclusion criteria:

Inclusion Criteria:
IC1: The primary study addresses variability in software architecture including product line architecture, software architecture, and reference architecture.

---

[2] The complete SMS protocol is available at https://sites.google.com/usp.br/varsasms.
[3] http://dl.acm.org.
[4] http://ieeexplore.ieee.org.
[5] https://www.engineeringvillage.com.
[6] https://www.scopus.com.
[7] http://www.sciencedirect.com.

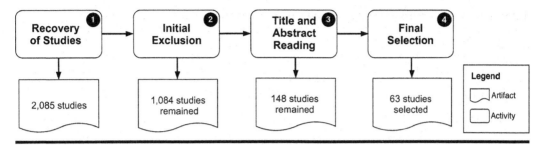

Figure 2.1   Steps of the SMS conducted to find out the primary studies.

Exclusion Criteria:
EC1: Short articles below four pages;
EC2: Duplicated studies;
EC3: Studies containing an editorial, abstract, or introduction; and
EC4: Studies not written in English.

As a summary, we found 2,085 studies from which we selected 63 according to our inclusion/exclusion criteria. The activities we conduct in our SMS are shown in Figure 2.1.

2.3 Overview of Variability Modeling Approaches in Software Architecture

From the 63 studies we selected, we focus in this chapter on the most recent approaches since 2010. We provide a more accurate analysis on recent trends describing those research works that represent variability concerns at the architecture level and apart from typical variability models. We organize the results according to the following categorization:

1. **UML-based:** As UML is widely used but too generic to provide specific constructions aimed to describe software variability, we are interested in those approaches that can extend UML notations and incorporate the notion of variants and variation points;
2. **Architecture Description Languages (ADLs):** As ADLs became popular years ago to formalize architectural descriptions, there are some approaches that attempt to introduce variability using these languages as opposed to graphical notations; and
3. **Domain-specific solutions:** When UML and ADLs are not enough to describe variability concerns, some research efforts suggest the use of textual variability languages and other techniques that complement UML and ADL notations.

The next two subsections summarize the older approaches and those recent ones from 2010.

2.3.1 Early Approaches to Model Variability in Software Architecture

Although software variability models begun in the 1990s, early approaches in the period 2000 to 2009 provide the initial attempts to introduce variability information in the software architecture. These approaches were classified, as shown in Table 2.1, according to the previous categorization.

Table 2.1 **Early approaches describing software variability in architecture**

Year	Approach Name/ based	Reference	Year	Approach Name/ based	Reference
UML-based			**ADL-based**		
2001	UML	(Bachmann and Bass 2001)	2000	Koala	(Ommering, et al. 2000)
2001	UML	(Clauß and Jena 2001)	2003	Koalish	(Asikainen, Soininen and Männistö 2003)
2002	QUASAR	(Thiel and Hein 2002)	2003	Ménage	(Garg, et al. 2003)
2003	UML	(Gotze 2003)	2004	Mae	(Roshandel, et al. 2004)
2003	UML	(Ziadi, Hélouët and Jézéquel 2003)	2005	ADLARS	(Bashroush, et al. 2005)
2004	UML	(Cerón, et al. 2004)	2007	Easel	(Hendrickson and Hoek 2007)
2005	SysML	(Ortiz, et al. 2005)	2008	vADL	(Zhang, et al. 2008)
2005	UML	(Kim, Chang and La 2005)	2009	ADL	(Mann and Rock 2009)
2005	UML	(Choi, et al. 2005)	**Specific Approaches**		
2006	Madam	(Hallsteinsen, et al. 2006)	2005	OVM	(Linden 2005)
2006	UML	(Moon, Chae and Yeom 2006)	2008	VML	(Loughran, et al. 2008)
2008	UML	(Razavian and Khosravi 2008)	2006	COVAMOF	(Sinnema, Ven and Deelstra 2006)
2008	UML	(Dobrica and Niemelä 2008b)	2009	PPC	(Pérez, et al. 2009)
2008	UML	(Dobrica and Niemelä 2008a)			
2009	UML	(Dai 2009)			

Most approaches found in the period 2000 to 2009 attempted to model the variability of systems in UML notations, using native UML constructs to represent variants (e.g., using stereotypes or tagged values), while other approaches introduced extended notations to increase the expressiveness of UML to better support variability concerns in the software architecture. Some on these approaches like Madam (Hallsteinsen, et al. 2006) model software variability in UML and are extended with aspect-oriented models. Although UML-based approaches facilitate the identification and modeling of variability through UML stereotypes, modeling variants and variation points is still not easy and not-well represented, which makes harder their identification by the relevant stakeholders. In addition, automation of derivation processes from UML models to implementation becomes challenging. For this reason, ADL-based approaches are considered other suitable ways to formalize variability in the software architecture.

In this period, many ADL-based approaches were essentially code-based and some of them included architecture visualization using graphical interfaces, such as the Koala component model (Ommering, et al. 2000) created by Philips Electronics to be used in the development of embedded software electronic devices. In Koala graphical notation, boxes are components and arrows attached to them are interfaces. The variability in Koala is usually represented by a design pattern defined by a switch connector that allows the association of one component through required interface with many alternatives of components through provided interfaces. These associations are based on some parameter values implemented inside each component. Architecture Description Language for Real-time Software Product Lines (ADLARS) (Bashroush, et al. 2005) is another approach designed with graphical tool support that allows the representation of feature model and architectural structures therefore acting like a bridge between the requirements space and the solution space. Koala and ADLARS share the same idea that Product Line Architecture (PLA) is a common architecture composed of interfaces and components. However, the main difference is the way that each approach represents variability. While Koala relies on many different interfaces controlled by a switch connector, ADLARS helps establish a relationship from the feature model to the architecture structure promoting a separation of concerns between solution space and problem space. This separation of concerns avoids stakeholders to be overloaded with a large amount of architecture models and abstractions.

Finally, specific languages developed to cope with the limitations of UML and ADL approaches attempt to provide textual variability description and reduce the inherent complexity of ADLs. In this light, the Orthogonal Variability Model (OVM) (Linden 2005) and ConIPF Variability Modeling Framework (COVAMOF) (Sinnema, Ven and Deelstra 2006) can represent variability concerns integrated with variability management tools. Moreover, the Variability Modeling Language (VML) from Loughran et al. (2008) and the Plastic Partial Component (PPC) approaches (Pérez, et al. 2009) enable variability as first-class elements in the architecture and provide explicit mechanisms to associate variation points with multiple architectural views.

2.3.2 Recent Efforts to Represent Variability in Software Architecture

In order to discuss the most recent approaches and solutions to represent variability in architecture, we found 35 relevant studies since 2010, as shown in Figure 2.2.

2.3.2.1 UML-based Approaches

UML-based approaches describing variability concerns are still very popular in those research works found in the period 2010 to 2017, such as Table 2.2 shows. The approaches combining variability and UML improve similar ones from the previous period. For instance, approaches developed and discussed by Xiao, et al. (2015) and Chakir, et al. (2012) use meta-models, and transformation rules to map variability information to architecture models. Other solutions, like those stated by Lin, Ye, and Li (2010) and Murwantara (2011), map feature models to UML component models to improve the traceability from features to components.

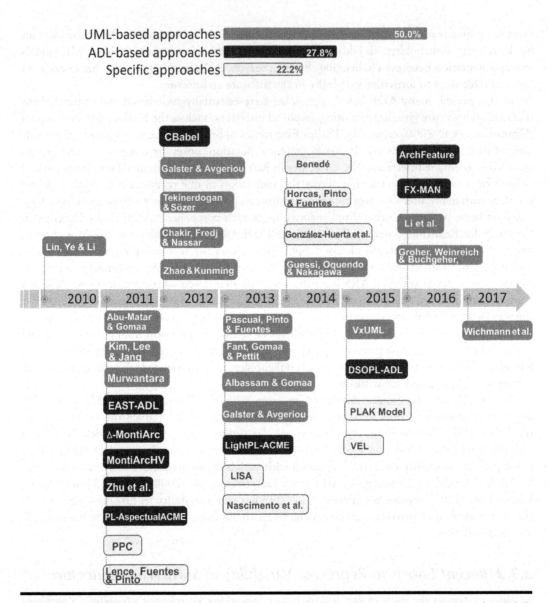

Figure 2.2 Timeline overview of approaches and techniques for the representation of variability in software architecture since 2010.

In addition, Tekinerdogan and Sözer (2012), Galster and Avgeriou (2012), Galster and Avgeriou (2013), and Guessi, et al. (2014) suggest a new variability viewpoint to introduce variability in the component model and represent variants and variation points explicitly compared with earlier techniques. Therefore, these approaches facilitate the recognition by software designers of variability elements in architecture models, but the major drawback is that traceability concerns are still described separately. Figure 2.3 shows an example of an UML-based approach where variability is modeled using stereotypes and cardinality properties to define minimum and maximum variants that can be selected, often not supported by native UML.

Table 2.2 List of UML-based approaches describing variability concerns

Study	Approach Name/ based	Architectural Views	Tools Support	Variability Representation Technique
(Lin, Ye and Li 2010)	UML-based	Component view		UML meta-model and transformation rules
(Murwantara 2011)	UML-based			Architecture style
(Kim, Lee and Jang 2011)	UML-based	Service Contract view, Business Process view, Service Interface view, Feature Modeling view		UML Stereotypes
(Abu-Matar and Gomaa 2011)	UML-based	Module view, Component and Connector view		UML Stereotypes
(Zhao and Kunming 2012)	UML-based			UML Stereotypes
(Chakir, Fredj and Nassar 2012)	UML-based	Business view, Service view, Functional view, Interaction view, Non-functional view		Meta-model and transformation rules
(Xiao, et al. 2015)	UML-based		✓	UML profile and transformation rules
(Fant, Gomaa and Pettit 2013)	UML-based	Collaboration diagrams, Interaction diagrams, and Component diagrams		UML Stereotypes
(Albassam and Gomaa 2013)	UML-based	Component view		UML Stereotypes
(Pascual, Pinto and Fuentes 2013)	UML-based			UML Stereotypes
(Li, et al. 2016)	UML-based	Physical view and Context view	✓	UML Meta-model and views
(Tekinerdogan and Sözer 2012)	UML Viewpoint			UML Meta-model and views
(Galster and Avgeriou 2012)	UML Viewpoint	Domain view, Business view		Architectural Viewpoint
(Galster and Avgeriou 2013)	UML Viewpoint			Architectural Viewpoint
(Wichmann, et al. 2017)	UML-based			UML Stereotypes
(Guessi, Oquendo and Nakagawa 2014)	UML Viewpoint			Architectural Viewpoint
(Groher, et al. 2016)	UML-based	Functional and Deployment view	✓	UML Stereotypes

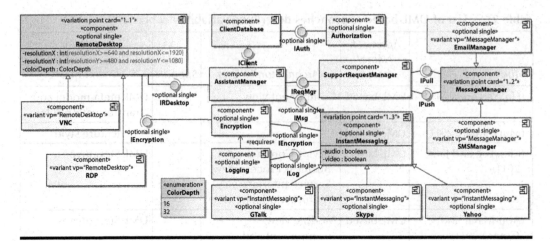

Figure 2.3   Example of UML-based approach. Extracted from (Pascual, Pinto and Fuentes 2013).

Benefits and Drawbacks

One of the main benefits of specifying variability in UML-based approaches is the ease with which it can be understood by stakeholders. Extending UML constructs to include variants and variation points facilitates software architects having two different representation techniques to describe the architecture and the variability concerns. One disadvantage is the poor scalability of UML models when the number of variants increases (Pascual, et al. 2013), and also the poor derivation process of variability models from UML notations to code in the case of no tool support. Besides that, maintaining the variability model embedded with UML constructs is hard when we add or remove variants and their corresponding constraints (Xiao, et al., 2015). Hence, UML notations prove useful to represent variability models when these are small.

2.3.2.2 *ADL-based Approaches*

Complementarily to UML approaches, a significant number of ADLs have been proposed, and used and many of them introduce techniques to incorporate variability concerns, such as we summarize in Table 2.3.

From the industry perspective, we can highlight EAST-ADL (Leitner, et al. 2011), an ADL-based approach developed for the automotive domain and to specifically support variability in the AUTOSAR (AUTomative Open System Architecture)[8]. It offers a complete feature-modeling technique (i.e., cloned features and parameterization of features) to represent variability in the architecture. EAST-ADL can describe variability concerns in a high level of abstractions, so this is why the level of penetration of the proposed solution is low.

Other solutions, such as PL-Aspectual-ACME (Barbosa, et al. 2011) and LightPL-ACME (Silva, et al. 2013), are examples of approaches that extend the ACME language (Garlan, Monroe and Wile 1997) to represent variability as crosscutting concerns. DSOPL-ADL (Adjoyan and Seriai 2017) combines ADL with XML languages to model variability and facilitates the analysis of architecture models by enhancing the interoperability between XML schemes and variability

---

[8] https://www.autosar.org/

Table 2.3   List of ADL-based approaches representing variability concerns

Study	Approach Name/ based	Tool Support	Variability Representation Technique
(Leitner, et al. 2011)	EAST-ADL	✓	Meta-model
(Cola, et al. 2016)	FX-MAN	✓	Component Model
(Zhu, et al. 2011)	ADL-based	✓	Meta-model
(Haber, et al. 2011a)	Δ-MontiArc	✓	Meta-model
(Carvalho, Murta and Loques 2012)	CBabel		Meta-model
(Haber, et al. 2011b)	MontiArcHV	✓	Meta-model
(Barbosa, et al. 2011)	PL-Aspectual ACME	✓	Crosscutting concerns
(Silva, et al. 2013)	LightPL-ACME	✓	Crosscutting concerns
(Adjoyan and Seriai 2015)	ADL-based		Variability Model
(Gharibi and Zheng 2016)	ArchFeature	✓	Variability Model

models. Figure 2.4 describes an example using an ADL to model the software of an electric window control system using MontiArcHV (Haber, et al. 2011). As we can observe, a variation point *MoreWindowsDog* is configured with the variant *WindowsSystem* (Haber, et al. 2011).

Benefits and Drawbacks

Unlike UML-based approaches, ADLs usually support the evolution and automatic formal analysis of the architecture. However, UML-based approaches are better to describe variability in different architecture views. Although ADL-based approaches still need to provide greater flexibility to describe variability constructs, they can extend graphical UML notations to increase the scalability of variability models. However, in many cases they lack more accurate constructs to describe other variability concerns like the runtime-binding property.

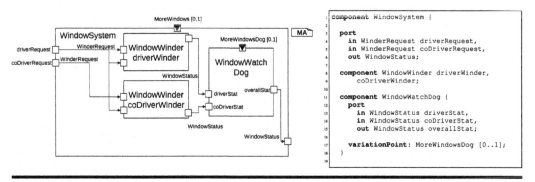

Figure 2.4   Example of an ADL-based approach to model variability in architecture. Extracted from (Haber, et al. 2011).

2.3.2.3 Specific-based Approaches

We finally discuss in this subsection a number of domain-specific approaches that complement both UML and ADL-based ones, as variability domain-specific languages are gaining popularity and offer additional capabilities compared with the other two sets of approaches analyzed. Table 2.4 summarizes these languages from the period 2010 to 2017. Among these languages, the Common Variability Language (CVL) was used in four studies to model variability in architecture through three different models: (i) a base model that is a meta-model that complies with the UML-MOF; (ii) a variability model defining variability constructs in CVL; and (iii) a resolution model that specifies how to resolve a variability model (Haugen, Wąsowski and Czarnecki 2013). CVL also encompasses a graphical editor to create CVL variability models.

Table 2.4   List of domain-specific approaches for representing variability concerns

Study	Approach Name/based	Architectural Views	Tool Support	Variability Representation Technique
(Nascimento, et al. 2013)	CVL-based	Component view	✓	CVL variability model
(Gonzalez-Huerta, et al. 2014)	CVL-based		✓	CVL variability model
(Horcas, Pinto and Fuentes 2014)	CVL-based		✓	CVL variability model
(Benedé 2014)	CVL-based	Variability viewpoint and Architectural viewpoint	✓	CVL variability model
(Lence, Fuentes and Pinto 2011)	VML		✓	Variability model
(Groher and Weinreich 2013)	LISA	Structural views, Component view, Configuration view, Behavioral views	✓	Meta-model
(Diaz, Pérez, et al. 2011)	PPC	Service view, Rationale view, Derivation view, Product view	✓	PPC components and Meta-model
(Diaz, Pérez, et al. 2015)	PLAK model	Component and Connector view	✓	PPC components and Meta-model
(Schulze and Hellebrand 2015)	Variability Exchange Language (VEL)			Meta-model

The Variability Modeling Language (VML) is another domain-specific language developed to represent variability (i.e., variation point, feature, constraints, and variants) as entities in a textual language format. VML links the features in the feature model to architectural elements (e.g., components and compositions), by allowing features to be selected for specific variation points (Loughran, et al. 2008). VML has mechanisms to specify variation points in different architectural views (e.g., deployment view and component-connector view) facilitating the architecture variability evolution (Loughran, et al. 2008). Both approaches attempt to define a link between the features and the architecture elements facilitating the resolution of the model into software products. However, while VML describes all these models and the variability model in a single textual file, CVL uses a graphical tool. Figure 2.5 illustrates an example of use of CVL, where the variability model shown in Figure 2.5a is transformed to a base model (Figure 2.5d), and resolved in Figure 2.5f via specific resolution rules. Variants are represented by rounded rectangles and a dashed arrow, while solid arrows between choices indicate that a child variant is resolved by its parent (Nascimento, et al. 2013). Therefore, after executing the transformations over CVL, an UML model is derived (Figure 2.5e).

Our last domain-specific language designed to represent variability concerns is a recent one from 2015 called the Variability Exchange Language (VEL), and specifically designed to exchange variability data between software artifacts through a standardized interface (Schulze and Hellebrand 2015). VEL provides a standard language and a common interface, which is supported by variant management tools such as pure::variants[9]. It provides a generic description of variation points and dependencies between variants and variation points. VEL uses serialized XML as format to facilitate interoperability issues. Some approaches, like CVL, VML, and EAST-ADL, define exchange formats similar to VEL to handle variability information among different tools. However, EAST-ADL is not generic enough to be used in different domains such as VEL. CVL and VML provide concepts to cope with variability in a generic way, but they lack a serialized representation approach required to exchange information between tools (Schulze and Hellebrand 2015).

Benefits and Drawbacks

From the domain-specific approaches previously described, CVL is the one that offers more capabilities and more flexibility to be used in different application domains. In addition, it also provides concepts to cope with the management of variability in a generic way, being a solution to exchange variability information between tools, similar to VEL approach. Moreover, VEL only specifies a communication interface and the data format to be exchanged, whereas CVL describes how to realize software products and variability description inside a tool support. Although CVL seems to be a good choice for describing variability in architecture, it only handles models defined by a meta-model that conforms to the Meta-object Facility (MOF). However, this is not always possible, as a further user could adopt no compatible MOF models.

---

[9] pure::variants;http://www.pure-systems.com.

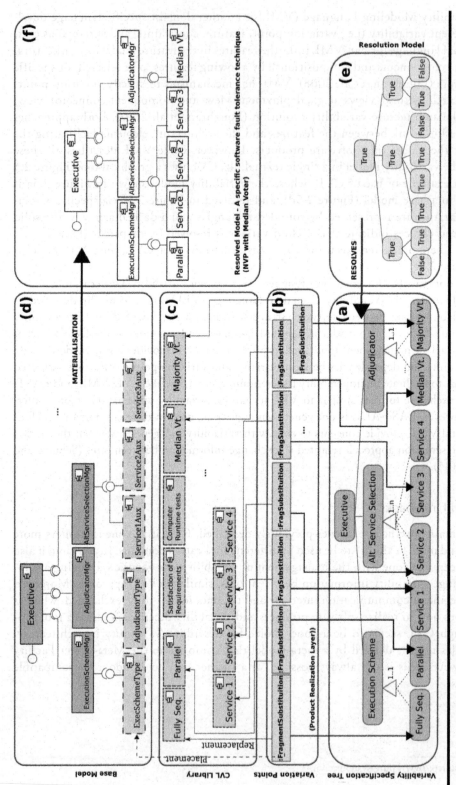

Figure 2.5 A CVL example to model and transform variability constructs. Extracted from (Nascimento, et al. 2013).

2.4 Findings

As an outcome from our SMS and analysis of the three different types of approaches to represent software variability concerns in architectural description, we derived the following findings:

Finding 1. Low product-derivation capabilities: Most UML-based approaches have difficulties to support product derivation from graphical models.

Finding 2. Interoperability of ADL approaches: The different semantics of different ADLs complicate interoperability of variability models. This may affect the use of a variability model by a tool not supporting a specific ADL. However, some variability domain-specific languages provide exchange formats that facilitate the integration with software variability management tools.

Finding 3. Low expressiveness of UML model: Graphical architecture descriptions using extensions to UML suffer from low expressiveness to represent detailed variability concerns.

Finding 4. High expressiveness of domain-specific languages: Variability domain-specific languages provide specific constructs that seem more suitable than ADL extensions to describe software variability. As these languages rely on textual descriptions, they are easy to use, but they need to be connected better with architecture descriptions.

Finding 5. Product derivation facilities: Many UML models describing variability do not have automated support for deriving features. This issue is partially improved by ADL-based approaches but not totally solved. However, domain-specific languages offer better capabilities to transform variability constructs into software artifacts through common interfaces, where system features can be selected.

2.5 Conclusion

This chapter reports a comprehensive study of the most important approaches to describe software variability in the software architecture. The evolution from UML and ADL approaches to more languages supporting variability concerns in software systems has facilitated the way to implement variability constructs. However, in many cases the transformation from models to variability constructs is not straightforward as the expressiveness of high level models is not enough and the gap between graphical and textual notations is still big in most cases. Also, the derivation process seems easier from variability management tools configuring the variants and from textual languages supporting variants and variation points.

Although graphical notations are easy to understand, their limitations in terms of visualization and scalability to describe large variability models are a major drawback, but today, there is still a lack of a more unique variability modeling solution that could be adopted by the variety of variability modeling tools.

Apart from this, the inability of graphical representations and most domain-specific languages to support runtime concerns or dynamic variability is another drawback of the approaches described, so new notations are needed to handle the changes in variability models at post-deployment time. For the next feature, we believe more effort must be put in interoperability concerns among the existing tools and languages to facilitate a smooth transition from variability models to implementation and from configuration to derivation process where the variability is realized.

Acknowledgment

This research was supported by the Brazilian funding agency FAPESP (Grant: 2016/05919-0 and Grant: 2017/06195-9).

References

Abu-Matar, M. and Gomaa, H. "Variability Modeling for Service Oriented Product Line Architectures." *SPLC.* Munich, Germany. 2011. 110-119.

Adjoyan, S. and Seriai, A. "Reconfigurable Service-based Architecture Based on Variability Description." *SAC.* Morocco, 2017. 1154-1161.

Albassam, E. and Gomaa, H. "Applying Software Product Lines to Multiplatform Video Games." *GAS.* San Francisco, CA, USA. 2013. 1-7.

Asikainen, T., Soininen, T. and Männistö, T. "A Koala-Based Approach for Modelling and Deploying Configurable Software Product Families". Vol. 3014, *LNCS*, 225-249. Siena, Italy, 2003.

Barbosa, E., Batista, T. V., Garcia, A. F., and Silva, E. "PL-Aspectual ACME: An Aspect-Oriented Architectural Description Language for SPL". *ECSA.* Essen, Germany. 2011. 139-146.

Bachmann, F. and Bass. J. L. "Managing Variability in Software Architectures." *SSR.* Toronto, Canada. 2001. 126-132.

Bashroush, R. A., Garba, M., Rabiser, R.,Groher, I., and Botterweck, G. "CASE Tool Support for Variability Management in SPL". *ACM Computer Survey*, 50(1) (2017): 14:1-14:45.

Bashroush, R., Brown, T. J., Spence, I. T. A., and Kilpatrick, P. "ADLARS: An Architecture Description Language for Software Product Lines". *SEW.* Maryland, USA, 2005. 163-173.

Benedé, J. "Towards the Automatic Resolution of Architectural Variability in Software Product Line Architectures through Model Transformations." *MODELS.* Valencia, Spain. 2014. 69-74.

Bosch, J., Capilla, R., and Hilliard, R. "Trends in Systems and Software Variability." *IEEE Software.*, 32 (2015): 44-51.

Capilla, R., Bosch, J., and Kang, K. C. "Systems and Software Variability Management: Concepts, Tools and Experiences". Springer, 2013.

Carvalho, S. T., Murta, L., and Loques, O. "Variabilities as First-Class Elements in Product Line Architectures of Homecare Systems." *SEHC.* Zurich, Switzerland, 2012. 33-39.

Cerón, R., Arciniegas, J. L., Ruiz, J. L., Dueñas, J. C., Muñoz, J. B., and Capilla, R. Architectural Modelling in Product Family Context. Vol. 3047, *LNCS*, 25-42, 2004.

Chakir, B., Fredj, M., and Nassar, M. "A Model Driven Method for Promoting Reuse in SOA-Solutions by Managing Variability." CoRR abs/1207.2742 (2012).

Choi, Y., Shin, G., Yang, Y., and Park, C. "An Approach to Extension of UML 2.0 for Representing Variabilities." *ICIS.* South Korea, 2005. 258-261.

Clauß, M. and Jena, I. "Modeling variability with UML." *GCSE.* Frankfurt, Germany, 2001. 1-5.

Cola, S. D., Tran, C. M., Lau, K., Qian, C., and Schulze, M. "A Component Model for Defining Software Product Families with Explicit Variation Points." *CBSE.* Venice, Italy, 2016. 79-84.

Dai, L. "Security Variability Design and Analysis in an Aspect Oriented Software Architecture." *SSIRI.* Shanghai, China, 2009. 275-280.

Diaz, J., Pérez, J., Garbajosa, J., and Wolf, A. L. "A Process for Documenting Variability Design Rationale of Flexible and Adaptive PLAs." *OTM.* Crete, Greece, 2011. 612-621.

Diaz, J., Pérez, J., Garbajosa, J., and Fernández-Sánchez, C. "Modeling Product-Line Architectural Knowledge." *HICSS.* Hawaii, 2015. 5383-5392.

Dobrica, L., and Niemelä, E. "A UML-Based Variability Specification for Product Line Architecture Views." *ICSOFT.* Porto, Portugal, 2008. 234-239.

Dobrica, L., and Niemelä, E. "An Approach to Reference Architecture Design for Different Domains of Embedded Systems." *SERP.* Las Vegas Nevada, USA, 2008. 287-293.

Fant, J. S., Gomaa, H., and Pettit, R. I. V. "A Pattern-Based Modeling Approach for Software Product Line Engineering." *HICSS.* Wailea, Hawaii, 2013. 4985-4994.

Galster, M. and Avgeriou, P. "Handling Variability in Software Architecture: Problems and Implications." *WICSA.* Colorado, USA (2011): 171-180.

Galster, M., Weyns, D., Tofan, D., Michalik, B., and Avgeriou, P. "Variability in Software Systems -A Systematic Literature Review." *IEEE Trans. Software Eng.*, 2014: 282-306.

Galster, M. and Avgeriou, P. "A Variability Viewpoint for Enterprise Software Systems." *WICSA/ECSA.* Helsinki, Finland, 2012. 267-271.

Galster, M. and Avgeriou, P. "Supporting Variability Through Agility to Achieve Adaptable Architectures." Vol. 1, *Agile Software Architectures*, 139-159. Massachusetts, 2013.

Garlan, D. "Software Architecture: A Travelogue." *FOSE*. Hyderabad, India, 2014. 29-39.

Garg, A., Critchlow, M., Chen, P., Westhuizen, C., Hoek, A. "An Environment for Managing Evolving Product Line Architectures." *ICSM*. Amsterdam, 2003. 358.

Gharibi, G., and Zheng, Y. "ArchFeature: A Modeling Environment Integrating Features into Product Line Architecture." *MoDELS*. Saint-Malo, France, 2016. 56-63.

Gonzalez-Huerta, J., Abrahão, S., Insfrán, E., and Lewis, B. "Automatic Derivation of AADL Product Architectures in Software Product Line Development." *MoDELS*. Valencia, Spain, 2014. 1-10.

Gotze, M. "A Flexible Object-Oriented Software Architecture For Smart Wireless Communication Devices." *DATE*. Grenoble, France, 2003. 126-131.

Groher, I., and Weinreich, R. "Supporting Variability Management in Architecture Design and Implementation." *HICSS*. Wailea, Hawaii, 2013. 4995-5004.

Groher, I., Weinreich, R., Buchgeher, G., and Schossleitner, R. "Reusable Architecture Variants For Customer-Specific Automation Solutions." *SPLC*. Beijing, China, 2016. 242-251.

Guessi, M., Oquendo, F., and Nakagawa, E. "Variability Viewpoint to Describe Reference Architectures." *WICSA*. Sydney, 2014. 14:1-14:6.

Haber, A., Kutz, T., Rendel, H., Rumpe, B., and Schaefer, I. "Delta-Oriented Architectural Variability Using MontiCore." *ECSA*. Essen, Germany, 2011a. 150-159.

Haber, A., Rendel, H., Rumpe, B., Schaefer, I., and Linden, F. "Hierarchical Variability Modeling for Software Architectures." *SPLC*. Munich, Germany, 2011b. 150-159.

Hallsteinsen, S. O., Stav, E., Solberg, A., and Floch, J. "Using Product Line Techniques to Build Adaptive Systems." *SPLC*. Baltimore, Maryland, 2006. 141-150.

Haugen, Ø.; Wąsowski, A.; Czarnecki, K. "CVL Common Variability Language." *SPLC*. Baltimore, Maryland, 2006. 141-150.

Hendrickson, S. A., and Hoek, A. "Modeling Product Line Architectures Through Change Sets and Relationships." *ICSE*. Minneapolis, USA, 2007. 189-198.

Kim, S. D., Chang, S. H., and La, H. J. "A Systematic Process to Design Product Line Architecture." *ICCSA*. Singapore, 2005. 46-56.

Kim, Y., Lee, S. K., and Jang, S. "Variability Management for Software Product-Line Architecture Development." *Int. Soft. Eng. Knowl. Eng.*, 2011, 931-956.

Kitchenham, B., and Charters, S. "Guidelines for Performing Systematic Literature Reviews in Software Engineering". Keele University Report, 2007.

Horcas, J., Pinto, M., and Fuentes, L. "Injecting Quality Attributes into Software Architectures With the Common Variability Language." *CBSE*. Lille, France, 2014. 35-44.

Lence, R., Fuentes, L., and Pinto, M. "Quality Attributes and Variability in AO-ADL Software Architectures." *ECSA*. Essen, Germany, 2011. 7.

Leitner, A., Mader, R., Kreiner, C., Steger, C., and Weiß, R. "A Development Methodology For Variant-Rich Automotive Software Architectures." *Elektrotechnik und Informationstechnik* 128 (2011): 222-227.

Li, M., Guan, L., Dickerson, C., and Grigg, A. "Model-Based Systems Product Line Engineering With Physical Design Variability For Aircraft Systems." *SoSE*. Kongsberg, Norway, 2016. 1-6.

Lin, Y., H. Ye, and G. Li. "An Approach for Modelling Software Product Line Architecture." *CiSE*. Wuhan, China, 2010. 1-4.

Linden, F. "Documenting Variability in Design Artefacts." In *Software Product Line Engineering*, 115-134. Springer, 2005.

Loughran, N., Sánchez, P., Garcia, A., and Fuentes, L. "Language Support for Managing Variability in Architectural Models." *SC*. Budapest, Hungary, 2008. 36-51.

Mann, S. and Rock, G. "Dealing with Variability in Architecture Descriptions to Support Automotive Product Lines." *EWEC*. Nuremberg, Germany, 2009. 3-5.

Moon, M., Chae, H. S., and Yeom, K. "A Metamodel Approach to Architecture Variability in a Product Line." *ICSR*. Turin, Italy, 2006. 115-126.

Murwantara, I. M. "Another Architecture Style For a Product Line Architecture." iiWAS. Vietnam, 2011. 443-446.

Nascimento, A. S., Rubira, C. M. F., Burrows, R., and Castor, F. "A Model-Driven Infrastructure for Developing Product Line Architectures Using CVL." *SBCARS*. Brasilia, Brazil, 2013. 119-128.

Ommering, R. C., Linden, F., Kramer, J., and Magee, J. "The Koala Component Model for Consumer Electronics Software." *IEEE*, Computer 33 (2000): 78-85.

Ortiz, F. J., Pastor J. A., Alonso, D., Losilla, F., and Jódar, E. "A Reference Architecture for Managing Variability Among Teleoperated Service Robots." *ICINCO*. Barcelona, Spain, 2005. 322-328.

Pascual, G. G., Pinto, M., and Fuentes, L. "Automatic Analysis of Software Architectures with Variability." *ICSR*. Pisa, Italy: Springer, 2013. 127-143.

Pérez, J., Diaz, J., Soria, C., and Garbajosa, J. "Plastic Partial Components: A Solution to Support Variability in Architectural Components." *WICSA/ECSA*. Cambridge, UK, 2009. 221-230.

Petersen, K., Vakkalanka, S., and Kuzniarz, L. "Guidelines for Conducting Systematic Mapping Studies in Software Engineering: An Update." *IST*, 2015. 1-18.

Razavian, M., and Khosravi, R. "Modeling Variability in the Component and Connector View of Architecture Using UML." *AICCSA*. Doha, Qatar, 2008. 801-809.

Roshandel, R., Hoek, A., Mikic-Rakic, M., and Medvidovic, N. "Mae - A System Model and Environment For Managing Architectural Evolution." *ACM Trans. Softw. Eng. Methodol.* 13 (2004): 240-276.

Silva, E., Medeiros, A. L., Cavalcante, E., and Batista, T. V. "A Lightweight Language for Software Product Lines Architecture Description." *ECSA*. Montpellier, France, 2013. 114-121.

Sinnema, M., Ven, J. S., and Deelstra, S. "Using Variability Modeling Principles to Capture Architectural Knowledge." ACM SIGSOFT Software Engineering Notes 31 (2006).

Schulze, M. and Hellebrand, R. "Variability Exchange Language– A Generic Exchange Format for Variability Data". *CEUR*. Dresden, Germany. 2015. 71-80.

Tekinerdogan, B. and Sözer, H. "Variability Viewpoint for Introducing Variability in Software Architecture Viewpoints." *WICSA/ECSA*. Finland, 2012. 163-166.

Thiel, S. and Hein, A. "Systematic Integration of Variability into Product Line Architecture Design." *SPLC*. San Diego, CA, USA, 2002. 130-153.

Wichmann, A.; Maschotta, R.; Bedini, F.; Jager, S.; Zimmermann, A. "A UML Profile for the Specification of System Architecture Variants Supporting Design Space Exploration and Optimization". *MODELSWARD*. Porto, Portugal, 2017. 418-426.

Xiao, H., Yanmei, F., Chang-ai, S., Zhiyi, M., and Weizhong, S. "Towards Model-Driven Variability-Based Flexible Service Compositions." *COMPSAC*. Taichung, Taiwan, 2015. 298-303.

Zhang, T., C. Ma, W. Jian, and D. Lei. "Formally Composing Components in Product Line Context." *SISE*. Shanghai, China, 2008. 271-275.

Zhao, L., and Kunming, N. "An Architecture Design Method For The Vessel Prognostics and Health Management domain." *ICCSNT*. Changchun, China, 2012. 1299-1304.

Zhu, J., Peng, X., Jarzabek, S., Xing, Z., Xue, Y., and Zhao, W. "Improving Product Line Architecture Design and Customization by Raising the Level of Variability Modeling." *ICSR*. Pohang, 2011. 151-166.

Ziadi, T., Hélouët, L. and Jézéquel, J. Towards a UML Profile for Software Product Lines. Vol. 3014, in *LNCS*, 129-139. Springer, 2003.

Chapter 3

Context Modelling for Variability-intensive Systems During Requirements Engineering

Nelufar Ulfat-Bunyadi and Maritta Heisel

University of Duisburg-Essen, Duisburg, Germany

3.1 Introduction

In general, context modelling refers to the activity of documenting knowledge about a system's context. Despite the word 'modelling', context modelling refers not only to the model-based documentation but also to the text-based documentation of context knowledge. However, in this chapter, we focus on the model-based documentation.

Context knowledge is knowledge about a system's context. In the literature, different definitions of the term *context* can be found. In requirements engineering, mainly two meanings are prevalent: first, in terms of a system's surrounding environment during operation and, second, in terms of the problem space which needs to be understood to develop a proper solution, i.e. the system (cf. [10], [14], [21], [30]). In this chapter, we consider both meanings.

Context modelling is performed during requirements engineering. Requirements engineering is the activity of eliciting, documenting, negotiating, validating, and managing requirements for a system [21]. Context modelling is an important activity during requirements engineering due to the following dependency. Each system is developed for a certain context. Requirements for the system are defined based on assumptions about this context. Satisfaction of the system requirements can only be guaranteed if the developed system is integrated into this context. If it is integrated into another context, it is possible that the set of system requirements is no longer satisfied. Due to this dependency between system and context, it is not sufficient to elicit and document only system requirements during requirements engineering. The underlying assumptions about the context, or more generally, the underlying knowledge about the context (i.e. facts and assumptions) needs to be documented as well during requirements engineering.

In this chapter, we consider context modelling for a specific type of system, namely variability-intensive systems. In general, a variability-intensive system is 'a system in which variability plays an important role' [7] and variability describes 'the ability of an artefact to vary, i.e. its ability to change' [21]. An artefact could be the entire software or a development artefact like a requirement, a component, or a test case.

Product line engineering is a prominent paradigm for developing variability-intensive systems. During product line engineering, a set of products (also called systems or applications) is developed based on a common set of core assets [8]. Typically, domain and application engineering are distinguished. During domain engineering, the core assets are developed which comprise common and variable development artefacts. Common artefacts become part of each product in the product line, while variable artefacts only become part of a product if they are selected. To this end, variation points with corresponding variants are provided. During application engineering, concrete products of the product line are derived by selecting certain variants and making application-specific extensions to the product, if necessary.

However, variability is not limited to product line engineering. It plays an important role in other types of systems as well, for example, in context-adaptive systems. A context-adaptive system monitors the context in which it is used to enable adaptation of its behaviour, structure, or realisation (cf. [9], [17], [23]). The adaptation decision is made autonomously by the system. These adaptation decisions are frequently modelled as variation points. Depending on the monitored data, the system decides by itself which variant to select at the variation point, i.e. how to adapt.

In case of variability-intensive systems, we distinguish between variability in the system and variability in the context. Variability in the system is designed into the system during its development, while variability in the context is simply given. For context modelling during requirements engineering this means that variability is inherent in requirements, since it is firstly introduced during requirements engineering. However, it may also be introduced in later development phases (e.g. architectural design, detailed design). Furthermore, variability is inherent in the knowledge about the context, if it is given in the context and has an impact on the system. Variants in the context may, for example, require or exclude variants within the system [11], [13]. Therefore, they need to be documented.

Variability in system requirements and in context knowledge increases the complexity of these two types of artefacts and makes context modelling a challenging task. In this chapter, we analyse existing approaches that provide support in performing this task. However, since different approaches use different notions and concepts, it is difficult to compare them and to select an approach for a certain application area. To solve this problem, we have developed a conceptual framework which introduces a clear-cut vocabulary. We use this framework for describing and comparing existing context-modelling approaches. This description and comparison will help practitioners and researchers in selecting an approach that fits best their needs.

In the following, we first introduce our conceptual framework (Section 3.2). Based on the framework, we derive evaluation criteria for comparing the approaches (Section 3.3). Using the terminology defined in the framework and the evaluation criteria, we describe and characterise the approaches (Section 3.4). In Section 3.5, we illustrate selected approaches by applying them to a common example from the automotive domain. Section 3.6 closes the chapter with a conclusion.

3.2 Conceptual Framework for Context Modelling

The framework was developed as follows. First, we performed a literature review to identify relevant work in the field of context modelling for variability-intensive systems. Our focus was specifically on approaches that are applied during requirements engineering. After having analysed the resulting approaches, we started creating our framework.

The framework is shown in Figure 3.1 as a UML class diagram. It contains the key concepts and the relationships between them. In the following subsections, we explain them in more detail.

3.2.1 Statement

As explained, we deal mainly with two types of statements during context modelling for variability-intensive systems: requirements and context knowledge. While requirements need to be satisfied by the system, context knowledge simply needs to be true/valid.

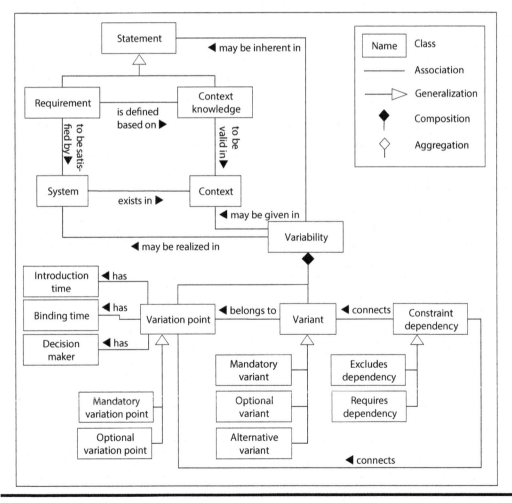

Figure 3.1   Conceptual framework for context modelling in requirements engineering.

3.2.2 Requirement

Generally, there are different types of requirements (e.g. functional requirements, quality requirements), and they can be defined on different levels of abstraction. A distinction, that is relevant for the context-modelling approaches that we consider in this chapter, is the differentiation between problem-oriented and solution-oriented requirements. In this book, Jackson [14] complains that many developers focus too much on the solution (the system) and therefore define right from the beginning requirements that are too much solution-oriented, without having understood the problem (in the context) properly. Instead, he suggests analysing and understanding the problem in the context thoroughly and defining, as a first step, requirements that will solve this problem—we call these requirements *problem-oriented requirements*. From these problem-oriented requirements, *solution-oriented requirements* should then be derived which are directly implementable. As we will show in Section 3.4, some context-modelling approaches focus solely on problem-oriented requirements, while others consider solution-oriented requirements as well.

3.2.3 Context Knowledge

Context knowledge is usually knowledge about context entities (i.e. material and immaterial objects in the environment which are relevant for the system) and their relationships to each other and to the system. Two types of context knowledge are frequently distinguished: facts and assumptions (cf. [12], [18]). Facts hold always regardless of the system (e.g. physical laws). Assumptions describe things that cannot always be guaranteed but which are needed to satisfy the requirements (e.g. rules for user behaviour).

3.2.4 Variability

Variability is expressed in the form of variation points and variants. A variation point represents a decision between variants that needs to be made. Each variation point is introduced (i.e. planned/modelled) at a certain point in time and bound at a certain point in time. Possible introduction times are: requirements engineering, architectural design, and detailed design (cf. [5], [28]). Possible binding times are: implementation, compilation, linking, installation/configuration, start-up, and runtime (cf. [5], [26]). The decision at a variation point is either made by a developer, the client, the user, or it can even be made autonomously by the system based on data it gathers during runtime. When variation points are permanently bound to variants, i.e. the variation point cannot be rebound to one or several of its other variants, then the variability is considered to be 'resolved'.

A variant may be mandatory (i.e. it must be selected), it may be optional (i.e. it can be selected), or it may be alternative (i.e. this variant is part of a set of variants from which at least one needs to be selected). Variation points may be mandatory or optional as well. Variants/variation points may generally require or exclude other variants/variation points.

Variability may be realised in a system. Then, it is frequently referred to as *system variability*. It may be given in the context. Then, it is referred to as *contextual variability*. It may also be inherent in requirements and context knowledge. Variability is inherent in requirements, if variation points and variants are introduced during requirements engineering. Variability is inherent in context knowledge, if variability is given in the context, impacts the system and therefore needs to be considered during requirements engineering.

3.3 Criteria for Comparing Context-Modelling Approaches

To facilitate a comparison of existing context-modelling approaches, we derived the following evaluation criteria based on our conceptual framework (Table 3.1). We apply these criteria to each modelling approach in Section 3.4.

Table 3.1   Evaluation criteria for comparing context modelling approaches

	Evaluation Criterion	*Possible Values*
Requirements	(1) How are requirements documented?	Kind of model that is created (e.g. goal model, feature model)
	(2) Does the approach consider problem- or solution-oriented requirements?	Problem-oriented, solution-oriented, or both
	(3) Which type of requirements is considered?	Requirements can be classified differently. We use here the most common differentiation between functional and quality requirements.
Context knowledge	(4) Which kind of context knowledge is documented?	Knowledge about context entities and relationships, or assumptions and/or conditions that need to be valid
	(5) How is context knowledge documented?	E.g. in a separate model, or in the requirements model
Relation	(6) How are relationships between requirements and context knowledge documented?	E.g. using specific relationship types, or by annotating the context knowledge right at the requirement
Variability	(7) How is variability in requirements documented?	E.g. using the variability concepts of the used requirements modelling language, or in a separate model
	(8) How is variability in context knowledge documented?	E.g. using the variability concepts of the used context-modelling language, or in a separate model
	(9) How are relationships between variability in requirements and in context knowledge documented?	E.g. using specific relationship types, or expressed as conditions
	(10) Is a specific binding time for variability in requirements considered?	E.g. implementation, compilation, linking, installation/configuration, start-up, runtime
	(11) Is a specific decision-maker w.r.t. variability in requirements considered?	E.g. developer, client, user, application/system

3.4 Context-Modelling Approaches

Context-modelling approaches can be classified into three categories: problem-based, goal-oriented, and feature-oriented approaches. We describe each approach in a category using the following structure: in the first step, we describe the approach using the terminology of the approach; in the second step, we apply the evaluation criteria defined in Table 3.1 to map the terminology of the approach to our terminology (defined in the conceptual framework) and to make the approaches comparable regarding the evaluation criteria. The result of this second step is presented in the form of a table. Note that all approaches that we consider in the following focus on requirements engineering. Therefore, it can be assumed that the introduction time of the considered variability is always requirements engineering.

3.4.1 Problem-Based Approaches

Problem-based approaches use Jackson's problem diagrams as described in [14] as a foundation. Jackson's problem diagrams are, in turn, based on a different understanding of system and context than the one that is traditionally used and that we use in this chapter (see Figure 3.2). Therefore, we explain first this different understanding and then explain problem diagrams.

As an example, we consider a typical control software Figure 3.2 which is connected to sensors and actuators for monitoring and controlling any properties in the environment. The items that are developed are the control software, the sensors, and the actuators. According to the traditional understanding (left-hand side of Figure 3.2), the developed items pertain to our system, while the context consists of the monitored and controlled environment. According to Zave and Jackson's understanding [30] (right-hand side of Figure 3.2), the system consists of the developed items *and* the context (namely the monitored and controlled environment). This understanding of system and context results obviously in a dependency between system and context which is expressed the best by means of Zave and Jackson's so-called satisfaction argument [30]. Since the context is part of the system, satisfaction of system requirements depends partially on the context. More precisely, the system is only able to satisfy its requirements, if the developed items each satisfy their own requirements and if the assumptions made about the context (i.e. hypotheses about and expectations regarding the monitored/controlled environment) are true/valid. Of course, traditional approaches are also aware of the fact that a system depends on its context and is developed having a certain context in mind, however, the dependency they consider is not as strong as the dependency considered by Zave and Jackson. The satisfaction of system requirements is mainly the task of the system.

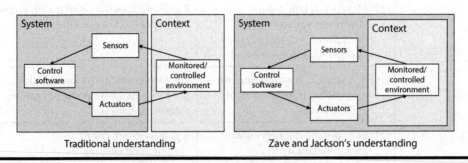

Figure 3.2 Different understanding of system and context.

Zave and Jackson [30] call the developed item(s) *machine* and the context *environment*. Thus, a system consists of a machine and its environment. Furthermore, they distinguish between three types of statements about the machine and the environment: requirements, domain knowledge, and specification. *Requirements* describe the effects/changes the customer wants to achieve in the environment by means of the machine. *Domain knowledge* consists of statements describing the environment as it is regardless or in spite of the machine. The *specification* describes how the machine will produce its output from the input it receives. The satisfaction argument is expressed as the following equation:

$$S, D \vdash R \tag{3.1}$$

R is the set of requirements, *D* is the domain knowledge, and *S* is the specification. The equation mainly says that if a machine is developed which satisfies *S* and is inserted into an environment as described by *D*, and *S* and *D* are consistent with each other, then *R* is satisfied.

All these concepts map to our conceptual framework (presented in Section 3.2) in the following way. Zave and Jackson's 'requirements' and 'specifications' map to our requirement concept. More precisely, 'requirements' represent problem-oriented requirements, while 'specifications' represent solution-oriented requirements due to the following reasons. The solution is the machine. Since specifications describe what the machine should do, they represent solution-oriented requirements. Requirements, on the other hand, describe the effects that shall be achieved in the real world by means of the machine. Thus, they describe how the problem in the environment can be solved. Therefore, they are rather problem-oriented. Finally, 'domain knowledge' maps to our context-knowledge concept.

An exemplary problem diagram and the notation of the modelling elements are shown in Figure 3.3. Generally, a problem diagram shows a machine domain, one or several problem domains, one requirement, and different kinds of connections between the domains and the requirement. The *machine domain* represents the machine. *Problem domains* are any material or immaterial objects in the environment that are relevant for the machine (e.g. people, other systems, physical representation of data). The *requirement* is to be satisfied by the machine domain together with the given problem domains. There are three types of connections. First, there are interfaces. An *interface* exists between two domains, either between the machine domain and

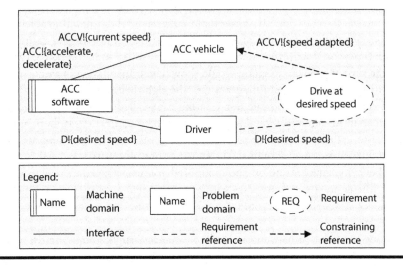

Figure 3.3 Example of a problem diagram.

a problem domain or between two problem domains. It represents an interface of shared phenomena (e.g. events, states, values). Sharing means that one domain observes the phenomena while the other (the one annotated at the interface with an abbreviation followed by an exclamation mark) controls them. Second, there are requirement references. A *requirement reference* connects the requirement and one or several problem domains. It expresses that the requirement refers to the annotated phenomena of the domain, i.e. for satisfying the requirement, information about these phenomena is necessary. Third, there are constraining references. A *constraining reference* also connects the requirement and one or several problem domains. Yet, it expresses that the requirement not only refers to but even constrains the domain phenomena, i.e. these phenomena shall result from requirements satisfaction.

In the example in Figure 3.3, the machine domain is an Adaptive Cruise Control (ACC) software. The (system) requirement to be satisfied is 'drive at desired speed'. Relevant problem domains in this example are the driver and the ACC vehicle, because the driver provides the desired speed to the ACC software (D! {desired speed}) and the ACC software adapts the current speed of the ACC vehicle to the desired speed by accelerating or decelerating it (ACC! {accelerate, decelerate}). The requirement refers to certain phenomena of the driver, namely D! {desired speed}, and it controls phenomena of the ACC vehicle, namely ACC! {speed adapted}.

3.4.1.1 Approach of Salifu et al.

Salifu et al. [24] focus on context-aware applications. A context-aware application monitors changes in the environment and switches its behaviour to continue satisfying its requirements. Salifu et al. suggest an approach that supports analysing changes that might occur in the environment and lead to the case that the set of requirements R is no longer satisfied. In order to ensure satisfaction of requirements, when such a change occurs, the authors suggest deriving variant specifications S which lead to restoring R in these cases. Thus, they identify variants in D, analyse their impact on the satisfaction of R, and introduce variants in S to restore R.

For each requirement, for which a variant exists, the variant is modelled in a so-called variant problem diagram. The concept of variant problem diagrams was already introduced by Jackson in [14]. A variant problem diagram differs from the original one, for example, with regard to an additional problem domain which is introduced, or with regard to the changed control characteristics of an interface. Yet, it has the same main concern as the original problem diagram. As an example, consider the requirement of transferring pictures from a digital camera to a mobile phone's storage. In the original problem diagram, data transmission in a secure location would be shown, while the variant problem diagram would show data transmission in a non-secure location.

To ensure that the right problem diagram (i.e. the right behaviour) is selected depending on the monitored context, the authors suggest creating a so-called composition problem diagram. Such a diagram contains one machine domain (the so-called context controller), at least one sensor domain (the so-called context sensor), and one or several controller domains. Beyond that, there might be further problem domains. The context controller (the machine) is responsible for switching the behaviour depending on the monitored context. The context is monitored by the context sensor. The context sensor assesses which environment applies. Depending on the information from the context sensor, the context controller ensures that the right controller domain is triggered.

For specifying the behaviour in more detail, Salifu et al. suggest creating, in addition to the problem diagrams, statecharts which show not only the behaviour of the machine and the controllers but also of the environment as concurrent state machines. (See Table 3.2.)

Table 3.2   Evaluation of the method of Salifu et al.

	Evaluation Criterion	*Values*
Requirements	(1) Problem- or solution-oriented requirements	Both. Set of requirements R corresponds to our problem-oriented requirements and the specification S corresponds to our solution-oriented requirements.
	(2) Functional or quality requirements	Functional and quality requirements.
	(3) Documentation of requirements	Two types of requirements are considered (R and S). R is documented in problem diagrams. Details regarding S are shown in statecharts.
Context knowledge	(4) Type of context knowledge	Structural information about context entities and relationships between them. In addition, information about the behaviour of context entities.
	(5) Documentation of context knowledge	Structural information is documented in problem diagrams. Behavioural information is documented in statecharts.
Relation	(6) Documentation of relationships between requirements and context knowledge	In problem diagrams, requirements are related to problem domains (i.e. context entities) by means of two types of relationships: requirement references and constraining references.
Variability	(7) Documentation of variability in requirements	Variability in R: documented using variant problem diagrams. Variability in S: documented as different states of the machine that can be entered depending on a condition in the environment (e.g. in secure location, in unsecure location).
	(8) Documentation of variability in context knowledge	Variability in D: documented as different states of a context entity (e.g. location).
	(9) Documentation of relationships between variability in requirements and in context knowledge	A change in environment (variant in D) necessitates creation of variant problem diagrams (i.e. variants in R), and in turn switch of behaviours (variants in S). Especially this relationship is shown in the composition problem diagram and its associated statechart.
	(10) Specific binding time	Runtime.
	(11) Decision maker	Machine, i.e. the application makes the decisions at the variation points.

3.4.1.2 Approach of Alebrahim et al.

Alebrahim et al. [1] extend Jackson's context and problem diagrams with variability. The goal is to support requirements engineering in product line engineering. Instead of Jackson's notation they use UML class diagrams, extended by means of a specific UML profile for problem frames, called UML4PF.

Alebrahim et al. introduce two types of context diagrams and two types of problem diagrams: variability context diagrams (for the entire product line), product context diagrams (for specific products of the product line), variability problem diagrams (for the entire product line), and product problem diagrams (for a specific product of the product line). Within these diagrams, the following modelling elements may vary: *requirements*, *problem domains*, and *phenomena*. Therefore, Alebrahim et al. suggest corresponding variability diagrams for each showing the selectable variants (i.e. requirement variability diagrams, domain variability diagrams, phenomenon variability diagrams). Whether a requirement, problem domain, or phenomenon represents a variation point or a variant, is made explicit by means of corresponding stereotypes. Stereotypes are also used to document whether a variation point is *mandatory* or *optional*. To express the relationships between variation points and variants (i.e. mandatory or optional variant) as well as *requires* and *excludes* relationships between variants, class diagram dependencies with corresponding stereotypes are used. *Requires* and *excludes* relationships are shown in a new type of diagram: the constraint variability diagram. It shows mainly the variants and the *requires* or *excludes* relationships between them.

When a concrete product of the product line is derived, an additional diagram is created: the configuration diagram. It shows the selections that have been made for the variants. (See Table 3.3.)

3.4.1.3 Approach of Ulfat-Bunyadi et al.

In contrast to Alebrahim et al. [1], Ulfat-Bunyadi et al. [29] do not integrate variability modelling into the problem diagram notation but combine orthogonal variability modelling [21] with problem diagrams. Ulfat-Bunyadi et al. use the same notation as Alebrahim et al. (UML class diagrams, extended by means of the UML4PF profile). However, they make other extensions to this profile.

The idea behind orthogonal variability modelling [21] is to have a separate variability model which is connected by means of so-called artefact dependencies to other development artefacts (e.g. requirement models or elements of them, design models, test cases, etc.). Therefore, Ulfat-Bunyadi et al. make the following extensions. They introduce a new type of diagram, namely the *variability diagram*, which shows variation points and variants, their type (i.e. whether they are mandatory or optional) as well as *requires* and *excludes* relationships between variants. Thus, all information about variability is in one diagram. Furthermore, they introduce the *artefact dependency* which is represented as a UML-class dependency with the corresponding stereotype. By means of this dependency relationship variants and variation points shown in the variability diagram can be connected to elements in the other context/problem diagrams or to entire context/problem diagrams. Similar to Alebrahim et al., Ulfat-Bunyadi et al. introduce separate context and problem diagrams for domain engineering (so-called essence diagram fragments and incarnation diagram fragments) and application engineering (product context diagrams and product problem diagrams). (See Table 3.4.)

Table 3.3 **Evaluation of the method of Alebrahim et al.**

	Evaluation Criterion	Values
Requirements	(1) Problem- or solution-oriented requirements	Focus is on requirements R, i.e. problem-oriented requirements.
	(2) Functional or quality requirements	Functional and quality requirements.
	(3) Documentation of requirements	R is documented in two types of problem diagrams: variability problem diagrams (containing variability) and product problem diagrams (without variability).
Context knowledge	(4) Type of context knowledge	Structural information about context entities and relationships between them.
	(5) Documentation of context knowledge	Context knowledge is documented in the different types of context and problem diagrams: variability context diagrams, product context diagrams, variability problem diagrams, and product problem diagrams.
Relation	(6) Documentation of relationships between requirements and context knowledge	Shown in the two types of problem diagrams: requirements are related to problem domains (i.e. context entities) by means of two types of relationships: requirement references and constraining references.
Variability	(7) Documentation of variability in requirements	Shown in requirement variability diagrams and in variability problem diagrams.
	(8) Documentation of variability in context knowledge	Shown in domain variability diagrams, variability context diagrams, and variability problem diagrams.
	(9) Documentation of relationships between variability in requirements and in context knowledge	Shown in the constraint variability diagram between as *requires* or *excludes* relationships between requirement variants, phenomena variants, and/or domain variants.
	(10) Specific binding time	Not defined.
	(11) Decision maker	Not defined.

3.4.2 Goal-Oriented Approaches

Goal-oriented approaches are based on the traditional understanding of system and context (as shown on the left-hand side of Figure 3.2).

The approaches that we present in this section use different goal modelling languages. However, they have in common that they start with defining high-level goals which are then analysed and

Table 3.4 Evaluation of the method of Ulfat-Bunyadi et al.

	Evaluation Criterion	*Values*
Requirements	(1) Problem- or solution-oriented requirements	Focus is mainly on requirements *R*, i.e. problem-oriented requirements. The term 'incarnation' is used to refer to concrete sensors or actuators that are used. These represent solutions in another sense than the ones that we mean by 'solution-oriented requirements'. The specification *S* is not considered. Therefore, solution-oriented requirements are not considered.
	(2) Functional or quality requirements	Mainly functional requirements are considered.
	(3) Documentation of requirements	During domain engineering, requirements are documented in essence and incarnation diagram fragments. During application engineering, requirements are documented in product problem diagrams.
Context knowledge	(4) Type of context knowledge	Structural information about context entities and relationships between them.
	(5) Documentation of context knowledge	Context knowledge is documented in essence diagram fragments, incarnation diagram fragments, product problem diagrams, product context diagrams.
Relation	(6) Documentation of relationships between requirements and context knowledge	Shown in essence diagram fragments, incarnation diagram fragments, and product problem diagrams.
Variability	(7) Documentation of variability in requirements	Shown in terms of artefact dependencies from variability diagram to essence diagram fragments and incarnation diagram fragments (which contain the requirements)
	(8) Documentation of variability in context knowledge	Shown in terms of artefact dependencies from variability diagram to essence diagram fragments and incarnation diagram fragments (which contain the context knowledge)
	(9) Documentation of relationships between variability in requirements and in context knowledge	Shown in the variability diagram.
	(10) Specific binding time	Not defined.
	(11) Decision maker	Not defined.

refined into low-level goals or tasks to be executed. The goal hierarchy is frequently represented as an AND/OR tree. An AND-refinement expresses that all subgoals must be satisfied to satisfy the parent goal, while an OR-refinement expresses that one of the subgoals must be satisfied to satisfy the parent goal. Furthermore, many approaches differentiate between (hard) goals and softgoals. While the satisfaction of (hard) goals can clearly be assessed, there are no clear-cut criteria to assess the satisfaction of softgoals. Therefore, soft goals can only be 'satisficed'.

These concepts map to our conceptual framework (Section 3.2) in the following way. Frequently, the high-level goals in a goal tree describe what should be achieved in the environment by means of the system, i.e. they describe what the problem in the environment is. Thus, they are rather problem-oriented. High-level goals are usually refined, until they can be assigned to individual components within the system or, for example, to the user (e.g. expectations regarding user behaviour). These low-level goals are more concrete than the high-level goals, and the responsibility for satisfying them is assigned to single components. Thus, they map to our solution-oriented requirements.

3.4.2.1 Approach of Ali et al.

Ali et al. [2] focus on a specific type of context-adaptive software (so-called self-contextualizable software), namely software which is able to monitor its context and to autonomously adapt its behaviour to it in order to keep its objectives (goals) satisfied. The satisfaction of the system goals is thus context-dependent.

Ali et al. suggest the creation of two types of models: Tropos goal models and separate context models. In a Tropos goal model, the following model elements might vary depending on the context:

- *OR-decomposition:* it might be necessary to specify in which context an alternative can be adopted.
- *Actors dependency:* in some contexts, an actor might attain a goal or get a task executed by delegating it to another actor.
- *Goal activation:* depending on the context, an actor might find it necessary or possible to trigger (or stop) the desire of satisfying a goal.
- *AND-decomposition:* a subgoal or subtask might only (or might not) be needed in certain contexts.
- *Means-end:* whether a task needs to be adopted or not, might depend on the context.
- *Contribution to soft goals:* contribution might vary form one context to another.

To make variation points referring to these elements of the goal model explicit, Ali et al. suggest creating separate context models. These context models represent mainly refinements of context statement into further statements and facts. A *statement* is a 'Boolean predicate specifying a current or previous context whose truth value cannot be computed objectively' [2]. In contrast, a *fact* is a 'Boolean predicate specifying a current or previous context whose truth value can be computed objectively' [2]. AND-/OR-decomposition relationships may exist among facts, among statements, and between facts and statements. Since the truth value of statements cannot be computed objectively, there might be facts which support the confirmation of these statements if they are true. In these cases, a *help* relation between the facts and the statement is modelled. In this way, the truth value of the root context statement can be assessed bottom up. An example of a context-dependent goal in a Tropos goal model is: 'Promote by cross-selling the product to customer'. The parameterized version of this goal is: 'Promote by cross-selling the product [p] to customer [c]'. The parameterized version of the goal represents a context statement which would be refined in a context model.

In [4], Ali et al. extend their approach by introducing so-called contextual goal models. Therein, they mainly add labels (so-called context tags) to the Tropos goal models to make explicit which goals are context-dependent.

In [3], Ali et al. suggest a framework that combines goal modelling, feature modelling, and problem diagrams. However, they describe mainly the idea but do not provide details on how to combine these three types of models. (See Table 3.5.)

3.4.2.2 Approach of Liaskos et al.

Liaskos et al. [20] present a method that supports elicitation and documentation of variability. They distinguish between two types of variability: intentional and non-intentional variability. Intentional variability refers to the variability in stakeholder intentions, i.e. goals. Non-intentional variability (also called background variability) refers to facts that unintentionally vary in the context, where the fulfilment of a goal is attempted (e.g. time, weather, stakeholder capabilities).

For the elicitation of intentional variability, Liaskos et al. suggest identifying variability concerns for each high-level goal in a goal model. They argue that, when a high-level goal is phrased, its generic activity is necessarily vague and incomplete. By answering questions like 'Who will perform the activity? When? Where? How fast?', alternative responses can be elicited which may result in alternative refinements of the goal (i.e. variants). In case of a patient-monitoring system, for example, notifying the nurse would be such a high-level goal. A question to be answered would be: 'Who will decide and fire the notification?' Possible answers are: the system, the nursing station's nurses. Another question would be: 'Who will receive the notification?' Possible answers would be: the closest nurse, the assigned nurse. To support this elicitation step, Liaskos et al. provide a generic set of variability concerns that can be used as a kind of template to elicit variability concerns for a high-level goal. This results in different alternatives for satisfying this goal.

For documentation of goals and their refinement, Liaskos et al. suggest using extended AND/OR trees. Therein, the following relationships types can be modelled (in addition to the typical AND/OR refinement relationships): *implies satisfaction of* (can be bidirectional), *implies denial of* (can be bidirectional), and *is precondition for*. Liaskos et al. extend this notation with a so-called *multi-faceted OR-decomposition* relationship. This means that the parent goal is decomposed according to different facets, each representing a separate variability concern.

During goal refinement, background facts that may unintentionally vary are elicited as well. Elicitation of these facts is supported by the method as well. The authors suppose that most background facts refer to agents, locations, and objects in the context. Therefore, they provide a list of attributes of these and relations among them (not shown here). This list may be used for eliciting varying background facts. These facts are then used for defining preconditions for the selection of an alternative subgoal in the AND/OR tree. The preconditions can be checked at runtime, i.e. these variation points are bound to variants and may be rebound at runtime. (See Table 3.6.)

3.4.2.3 Approach of Semmak et al.

Semmak et al. [25] extend the KAOS method with means for modelling variability in order to make KAOS applicable during product line engineering.

KAOS is a goal-oriented requirements engineering method which was originally developed by Lamsweerde [18]. KAOS provides four complementary submodels that describe a system and

Table 3.5   Evaluation of the method of Ali et al.

	Evaluation Criterion	*Values*
Requirements	(1) Problem- or solution-oriented requirements	Goals are rather abstract and focus on describing the effects that shall be achieved in the environment by means of the system. However, they are also refined to assign them to components within the system or to the user. Thus, high-level goals are problem-oriented and low-level goals are solution-oriented.
	(2) Functional or quality requirements	Both.
	(3) Documentation of requirements	As goals and tasks in Tropos goal model.
Context knowledge	(4) Type of context knowledge	Facts and assumptions (called statements).
	(5) Documentation of context knowledge	Shown in the context model (context statement hierarchies).
Relation	(6) Documentation of relationships between requirements and context knowledge	Dependence of goals (requirements) on context is shown using context tags in the goal model.
Variability	(7) Documentation of variability in requirements	Is implicit in Tropos goal models, for example, as OR-refinement of a goal into its subgoals. The subgoals may represent two variants of achieving the parent goal.
	(8) Documentation of variability in context knowledge	Shown in the context statement hierarchy. The hierarchy shows parameterized statements. If concrete values are set for the parameters, the statements represent variants in the context.
	(9) Documentation of relationships between variability in requirements and in context knowledge	Not modelled explicitly.
	(10) Specific binding time	Since the focus is on context-adaptive systems, mainly variability with binding-time runtime is considered.
	(11) Decision maker	Since 'self-contextualizable' software is considered, the software itself is the decision maker.

Table 3.6   Evaluation of the method of Liaskos et al.

	Evaluation Criterion	Values
Requirements	(1) Problem- or solution-oriented requirements	High-level goals map to our problem-oriented requirements and low-level goals map to our solution-oriented requirements.
	(2) Functional or quality requirements	Both.
	(3) Documentation of requirements	As goals in the AND/OR tree.
Context knowledge	(4) Type of context knowledge	Mainly conditions in the context are considered that represent preconditions for certain goals.
	(5) Documentation of context knowledge	As preconditions (rectangles) in the goal model.
Relation	(6) Documentation of relationships between requirements and context knowledge	Preconditions are related to the corresponding goals by means of the precondition relationship.
Variability	(7) Documentation of variability in requirements	Intentional variability (i.e. the variability in goals) is implicit in the AND/OR tree, i.e. variants are shown as alternatives in an OR-decomposition.
	(8) Documentation of variability in context knowledge	Variability in the context is mainly regarded as part of the non-intentional variability. Yet, a model of the variation points and variants in the context is not created. Only certain conditions (i.e. variants) are documented as preconditions in the AND/OR tree.
	(9) Documentation of relationships between variability in requirements and in context knowledge	Preconditions are related to the goals to which they refer. These goals can be variants—as mentioned above (evaluation criterion (7)), variants are not modelled explicitly as variants but as alternatives in an OR-decomposition.
	(10) Specific binding time	Mainly variability that is bound at runtime is considered.
	(11) Decision maker	Not defined. Yet, the information that is required for deciding, whether the preconditions annotated in the AND/OR tree hold or not, are monitorable, i.e. the system could possibly sense this information and decide itself.

its environment: a goal model, a responsibility model, an operation model, and an object model. Our focus is on the goal model. According to the KAOS method, multi-agent goals are refined into subgoals, until they can be assigned to single agents in the environment (then they are *expectations*) or to single agents in the system (then they are *requirements*). Leaf nodes in these AND/OR-refinement trees may also be *domain hypotheses* (i.e. general assumptions about the environment which cannot be assigned to single agents in the environment) or *domain properties* (i.e. facts that hold invariably regardless of the system like e.g. physical laws). Thus, KAOS not only allows for modelling requirements in terms of goals but also for modelling facts (domain properties) and assumptions about the context (expectations and domain hypotheses).

To support requirements engineering during product-line engineering, Semmak et al. suggest the creation of a so-called generic goal model and a so-called variant model during domain engineering. Based on these two models, specific requirements models for a concrete product of the product line can be derived during application engineering. The variant model simply shows which variation points, called facets, exist and which variants belong to them. The generic model is an extended KAOS goal model, i.e. it shows common and variable goals of the product line. To make the variable goals in the goal model explicit, Semmak et al. suggest using conditions like <F1, V1> (F1 stands for Facet 1 and V1 for Variant 1) at the edges in the goal model (i.e. at AND/OR-decomposition relationships and at responsibility assignments to agents). These edges are only considered if the condition is true, i.e. the referenced variant is selected. For example, a goal G0 may be decomposed into the three subgoals, G1, G2, and G3. The decomposition relationship between G0 and G3 is annotated with the condition <F2, V3>, the other two relationships between G0 and G1 and G2 have no conditions. G0 is decomposed into G1, G2, and G3, if Variant 3 is selected at Facet 2 in the variant model. If not, then G0 is only decomposed into G1 and G2.

The selection of a variant may have an impact on several parts of the goal model. In this case, the same condition can be annotated at several edges in the goal model. (See Table 3.7.)

3.4.3 Feature-Oriented Approaches

Feature-oriented approaches are based on the traditional understanding of system and context (as shown on the left-hand side of Figure 3.2).

The approaches that we present in this section all focus on product-line engineering, but they use different feature modelling notations. The original feature model, FODA (feature-oriented domain analysis), was developed by Kang et al. [15] in 1990 and was, since then, extended by many researchers. A feature is defined as 'a prominent or distinctive user-visible aspect, quality, or characteristic of a software system or systems' [15]. A feature model is an AND/OR graph in which features are organised using *composed-of* and *generalisation/specialisation* relationships [15]. There are three types of features: mandatory, optional, and alternative ones.

Meanwhile, several extensions of the FODA feature model have been suggested. Many approaches provide additional modelling elements for documenting feature cardinality (i.e. how many features can be selected at least and at most at a variation point) and XOR relationships (alternatives that exclude each other). According to the above-mentioned original definition (cf. [15]), a feature is user visible. However, later extensions of the FODA feature model (e.g. FORM [16]) allow for modelling any features, i.e. not only the user-visible ones.

These concepts map to our conceptual framework (Section 3.2) in the following way. Feature modelling is used during requirements engineering to model desired features of a system (or a

Table 3.7 Evaluation of the method of Semmak et al.

	Evaluation Criterion	*Values*
Requirements	(1) Problem- or solution-oriented requirements	High-level goals map to our problem-oriented requirements and low-level goals, assigned to system agents, map to our solution-oriented requirements.
	(2) Functional or quality requirements	Both.
	(3) Documentation of requirements	As goals in the generic goal model as well as the derived specific requirements model.
Context knowledge	(4) Type of context knowledge	Facts (domain properties) and assumptions about the context (domain hypotheses and expectations).
	(5) Documentation of context knowledge	Shown in the generic goal model and in the derived specific requirements model.
Relation	(6) Documentation of relationships between requirements and context knowledge	As refinement relationships in the generic and derived goal models. Domain properties, domain hypotheses, and expectations contribute to the satisfaction of higher level goals.
Variability	(7) Documentation of variability in requirements	Variability is documented in a separate variant model and is related to high-level goals and requirements in the goal model by means of annotations at refinement relationships and responsibility assignments.
	(8) Documentation of variability in context knowledge	Variability is documented in a separate variant model and is related to domain properties, domain hypotheses, and expectations in the goal model by means of annotations at refinement relationships and responsibility assignments.
	(9) Documentation of relationships between variability in requirements and in context knowledge	Not modelled explicitly. Results implicitly from the refinement relationships in the goal models and the related variability.
	(10) Specific binding time	Not defined.
	(11) Decision maker	Not defined.

product line) and their relationships to each other. The abstraction level of feature in a feature model is not predefined. Therefore, there may be rather abstract features as well as very detailed ones in a feature model. The mapping between features and requirements in our conceptual framework is as follows: a requirement describes one or several desired features of a system (or product line).

3.4.3.1 Approach of Hartmann and Trew

Hartmann and Trew [11] present an approach that supports modelling the commonality and variability of multiple product lines. However, the approach can also be applied for modelling commonality and variability of a single product line. Hartmann and Trew suggest creating two types of feature models: one showing the features of the range of products in the product line and the other one showing the features of the context. The notation that is used for both models is FODA [15]. Between context-feature model and the product-line (PL) feature model, the following types of dependencies can be modelled: *requires*, *excludes*, or *sets cardinality*. This means a feature in the context feature model may require or exclude a feature in the product-line feature model, and it may set the cardinality of features in the product-line feature model. (See Table 3.8.)

Table 3.8 Evaluation of the method of Hartmann and Trew

	Evaluation Criterion	*Values*
Requirements	(1) Problem- or solution-oriented requirements	Both.
	(2) Functional or quality requirements	Both.
	(3) Documentation of requirements	In the PL feature model.
Context knowledge	(4) Type of context knowledge	Mainly structural information about features of the context and their relationships.
	(5) Documentation of context knowledge	In the context model.
Relation	(6) Documentation of relationships between requirements and context knowledge	By means of three types of relationships: requires, excludes, sets cardinality. One directional, i.e. from context model to PL feature model.
Variability	(7) Documentation of variability in requirements	As mandatory, optional, or alternative features in the PL feature model.
	(8) Documentation of variability in context knowledge	As mandatory, optional, or alternative features in the context model.
	(9) Documentation of relationships between variability in requirements and in context knowledge	By means of three types of relationships: requires, excludes, sets cardinality. One directional, i.e. from context model to PL feature model.
	(10) Specific binding time	Not defined.
	(11) Decision maker	Not defined.

3.4.3.2 Approach of Tun et al.

The approach of Tun et al. [27] is based on Zave and Jackson's differentiation between requirements, domain knowledge, and specification, yet they do not use problem diagrams for modelling but feature models.

For modelling variability in requirements, domain knowledge, and the specification, they suggest creating separate feature models for each. The requirements-feature model (RFM) shows different sets of stakeholder requirements that need to be satisfied in different products of the product line. The world-feature model (WFM) is the context model. It shows the different contextual settings in which the software may be used. The specification-feature model (SFM) shows the different possible configurations of the software.

RFM, WFM, and SFM are translated into propositional formulae. Constraints between the RFM and the WFM as well as between the WFM and the SFM are also expressed in the form of propositional formulae, just as any other quantitative constraints that might exist in RFM, WFM, and SFM. (See Table 3.9.)

Table 3.9   Evaluation of the method of Tun et al.

	Evaluation Criterion	*Values*
Requirements	(1) Problem- or solution-oriented requirements	Both. Requirements are problem-oriented. The specification is solution-oriented.
	(2) Functional or quality requirements	Both.
	(3) Documentation of requirements	In the RFM (requirements-feature model) and SFM (specification-feature model).
Context knowledge	(4) Type of context knowledge	Mainly structural information about features of the context and their relationships.
	(5) Documentation of context knowledge	In the WFM (world-feature model).
Relation	(6) Documentation of relationships between requirements and context knowledge	Constraints between RFM and WFM as well as WFM and SFM documented as propositional formulae.
Variability	(7) Documentation of variability in requirements	As mandatory, optional, and alternative features in the RFM and SFM.
	(8) Documentation of variability in context knowledge	As mandatory, optional, and alternative features in the WFM.
	(9) Documentation of relationships between variability in requirements and in context knowledge	Constraints between variable features in the RFM and WFM as well as in the WFM and SFM documented as propositional formulae.
	(10) Specific binding time	Not defined.
	(11) Decision maker	Not defined.

3.4.3.3 Approach of Lee and Kang

Lee and Kang [19] state that the usage context of a system typically implies required quality attributes or constraints which in turn affect feature selection. By usage context they mean the user context (target user groups, usage patterns), physical context (physical environment or location where a product is deployed or used), social context (cultural traits and legal constraints), and business context (business factors like price, time-to-market, etc.). Therefore, it is necessary to create the following three types of models and to make the mapping between elements in the models explicit: a usage context-variability model, a quality attribute-variability model, and a product feature-variability model. The models and mappings between them can be used to derive an optimal product configuration during application engineering.

The *product feature-variability model* is a feature model describing the variability of the product line in terms of the product features. The *quality attribute-variability model* is a feature model showing the variability of the quality attributes that products of the product line must satisfy. The *usage context-variability model* is a feature model describing the variability in the contexts in which products of the product line are deployed or used. The notation that is used for all three types of feature models is FORM [16], an extension of FODA which allows for modelling additionally XOR relationships and *implemented-by* relationships.

The mappings between the features of the three types of models are documented using simple tables. First, there is a mapping between *usage context* and *product features* because a certain usage context may directly require or exclude the selection of a product feature or a set of features. Second, there is a mapping between *usage context* and *quality attributes* because a usage context may, for example, determine one or multiple quality attributes or a combination of different usage contexts may imply particular quality attributes. Third, there is a mapping between *quality attributes* and *product features* because some product features may work for or against a quality-attribute feature. (See Table 3.10.)

3.4.4 Comparison

All the approaches that we presented in Sections 3.4.1 to 3.4.3 focus on the documentation of requirements, context knowledge, and variability. However, they differ as regards the type of variability-intensive system they consider (mainly product lines vs. context-adaptive systems), the type of requirements that are considered (problem-oriented vs. solution-oriented), the type of context model that is created (partial models vs. preferably complete models), the way variability is documented (in a separate variability model or integrated into the models of requirements and context knowledge). An overview of the commonalities and differences among the approaches is given in Table 3.11. In the following, we discuss them in more detail.

All feature-oriented approaches that we considered focus on one type of variability-intensive systems: product lines. In product line engineering, feature models are predominant and are used very often. Their strength is that they allow for modelling different types of features on different abstraction levels. Furthermore, they allow for modelling common and variable features, and thus variability modelling is already integrated in the modelling language. Moreover, the definition of a feature is quite broad: 'a prominent or distinctive user-visible aspect, quality, or characteristic of a software system or systems' [15]. Therefore, there are only few rules that need to be observed by developers applying feature modelling approaches. Generally, feature-oriented modelling does not exhibit any restrictions that makes its use for the development of context-adaptive systems impossible.

Table 3.10   Evaluation of the method of Lee and Kang

	Evaluation Criterion	Values
Requirements	(1) Problem- or solution-oriented requirements	Product features are rather problem-oriented.
	(2) Functional or quality requirements	Both. Functional requirements are expressed in terms of product features. Quality requirements are expressed in terms of quality attributes features.
	(3) Documentation of requirements	As product features in the product feature variability model and as quality attribute features in the quality attribute variability model.
Context knowledge	(4) Type of context knowledge	Mainly structural information about features of the usage context and their relationships.
	(5) Documentation of context knowledge	As usage context features in the usage context variability model.
Relation	(6) Documentation of relationships between requirements and context knowledge	In the mappings of usage context and quality attributes, of quality attributes and product features, and of usage context and product features.
Variability	(7) Documentation of variability in requirements	As mandatory, optional, and alternative features in the product feature variability model and the quality attribute variability model.
	(8) Documentation of variability in context knowledge	As mandatory, optional, and alternative features in the usage context variability model.
	(9) Documentation of relationships between variability in requirements and in context knowledge	In the mappings of usage context and quality attributes, of quality attributes and product features, and of usage context and product features.
	(10) Specific binding time	Not defined.
	(11) Decision maker	Not defined.

In contrast to that, we found problem-based and goal-oriented approaches for both: context-adaptive systems and product lines. Problem diagrams are in general very helpful in modelling and analysing the context and creating a preferably complete structural model of the context. Alebrahim et al. [1] and Ulfat-Bunyadi et al. [29] show how problem diagrams can be used and extended to model the context of product lines. With the idea of having a separate context sensor (responsible for monitoring the context) and a context controller (responsible for switching the behaviour of the system based on monitored data), Salifu et al. [24] show that problem diagrams can even be used for modelling the context of context-adaptive systems. Goal models, on the other

Table 3.11 Support provided by the approaches

	Problem-based			Goal-oriented			Feature-oriented		
	Salifu et al. [24]	Alebrahim et al. [1]	Ulfat-Bunyadi et al. [29]	Ali et al. [2]	Liaskos et al. [20]	Semmak et al. [25]	Hartmann & Trew [11]	Tun et al. [27]	Lee & Kang [19]
Focus: Product lines	X	X	x			X	x	x	x
Focus: Context-adaptive systems	X			x	x				
Problem-oriented requirements	X	X	x	x	x	X	x	x	x
Solution-oriented requirements	X							x	
Partial context model				x	x	X	x	x	x
Complete context model	X		x			X			
Separate variability model			x			X			

hand, are very helpful in identifying, modelling, and refining system objectives, i.e. the effects that shall be achieved by means of the system in the context. In case of context-adaptive systems, the satisfaction of goals is frequently dependent on the context of the system. Ali et al. [2] and Liaskos et al. [20] show how this dependency can be made explicit. For this purpose, Ali et al. use Tropos goal models which are accompanied by partial context models, while Liaskos et al. use extended goal models. In contrast to these two goal-oriented approaches, Semmak et al. [25] focus on product lines. They extend the KAOS goal modelling language to enable variability modelling. The peculiarity of the KAOS goal modelling language is that it allows not only for modelling system goals (and their refinement) but also facts and assumptions that are made about the system's context (as well as their relationships to system goals, especially dependencies between goals and assumptions).

All approaches (problem-based, goal-oriented, and feature-oriented approaches) consider problem-oriented requirements, i.e. rather abstract requirements describing the effects that shall be achieved in the environment. By definition, problem diagrams focus on the problem space. Therefore, the system (i.e. the machine) is considered a black box, and the problem diagram shows how it is related to certain domains in the environment which are needed for satisfying the requirement. Thus, the requirements in problem diagrams are by definition problem-oriented. In goal models, the goals on higher levels are usually problem-oriented, because they describe either system objectives or intentions of stakeholders. These are then refined until they can be assigned to system components or to actors in the environment (e.g. the system user). In feature models, requirements are expressed in the form of required system features. As mentioned above, features can be modelled on different abstraction levels, i.e. requirements on different abstraction levels can be shown. Similar to goal models, features on higher levels are problem-oriented rather than solution-oriented.

Some approaches provide support for explicitly creating models of solution-oriented requirements, i.e. models that show more details about solution-oriented requirements. Salifu et al. [24], for example, suggest using statecharts for modelling not only the behaviour of the system (the solution) but also of the environment as concurrent state machines. Tun et al. [27] suggest creating a separate feature model for the solution-oriented requirements, the specification.

The three problem-oriented approaches aim at analysing the context and creating a preferably complete context model. The other approaches document some information about the context (e.g. assumptions or conditions in the context), but they do not have the objective of creating a complete model.

As shown in Table 3.11, only the problem-based approaches aim at creating a preferably complete context model. Problem diagrams represent structural models. Since Salifu et al. [24] also suggest creating statecharts in addition to problem diagrams, they create both: structural and behavioural models of the context. Goal-oriented and feature-oriented approaches do not aim at creating complete context models. However, they provide support in documenting context knowledge that is elicited.

As regards variability, only two approaches allow for creating a separate variability model (i.e. an orthogonal model). In all other approaches, variability is modelled in requirements or context models (i.e. it is integrated in these models). The advantage of the orthogonal model over the integrated one is that all the information about variability is documented in one model and not scattered across several models. This facilitates change integration as regards variability (i.e. adding, removing, modifying variants). However, the advantage of integrating variability into existing modelling languages is that tool support can be provided more easily because tools supporting the modelling language can be extended with the new variability concepts.

3.5 Applied Context Modelling

In this section, we illustrate the application of selected methods from the previous section using an example. We have selected a problem-based approach, a goal-oriented approach, and a feature-oriented approach. For each approach, we describe why we selected it, how we applied it, and which advantages and drawbacks we observed during application.

3.5.1 Example

We assume we are developing Adaptive Cruise Control (ACC) systems in a product-line engineering approach so that the systems will fit different types of vehicles. Generally, the task of an ACC system is to maintain the driver's desired speed while keeping the safety distance to vehicles ahead. To this end, the ACC system monitors the area in front of the ACC vehicle to identify vehicles ahead that are driving in the same lane. If there is a vehicle ahead in the same lane, the ACC system selects this object for tracking and adapts the speed of the ACC vehicle so that the safety distance to this object is kept. If there is no vehicle ahead in the same lane, the ACC system adapts to the driver's desired speed and maintains this speed.

In our product line, we develop the following three types of ACC systems (see Table 3.12): a simple version supporting only cruise control, an advanced version supporting cruise control as well as emergency braking, and a sophisticated version supporting cruise control, emergency braking, and stop-and-go in urban traffic. Our description of ACC systems is based on the technical information given in [6] and [22].

Table 3.12 Products in our ACC product line

	Simple ACC	*Advanced ACC*	*Sophisticated ACC*
Provided support	– cruise control	– cruise control – emergency brake assistant	– cruise control – emergency brake assistant – stop-and-go in urban traffic
Location of use	– motorway	– motorway – city	– motorway – city
Sensed area	– long range	– long range – mid-range	– long range – mid-range – short range
Sensors used	– long-range radar sensor (angle: ± 8°, range: 40–200 m) – ESP (Electronic Stability Program) sensors	– Long-range radar – ESP sensors – stereo video camera (angle: ± 22°, range: up to 80 m)	– long-range radar – ESP sensors – stereo video camera – short-range radar (angle: ± 50°, range: 25 cm to 20–50 m)
Speed	– 30–200 km/h	– 0–200 km/h	– 0–200 km/h
Braking support	– only deceleration – no full braking	– full braking support	– full braking support

3.5.1.1 Simple ACC

The simple ACC is intended to be used on motorways only. For identifying vehicles ahead that are driving in the same lane, the ACC software uses data provided by a long-range radar sensor and the ESP (Electronic Stability Program) sensors. The long-range radar sensor detects vehicles ahead and provides information about the speed, distance, and lateral offset of them. The ESP sensors provide information about the speed, steering wheel angle, lateral acceleration, and yaw rate of the ACC vehicle itself. Based on the data from the ESP sensors, the ACC software is able to predict the course of the ACC vehicle. Based on the predicted course and the lateral offset of vehicles ahead, the ACC software can, in turn, calculate the relative position of vehicles ahead and thus estimate whether they are driving in the same lane or not.

For adapting the speed of the ACC vehicle, the ACC software provides deceleration and acceleration instructions to two other systems in the ACC vehicle: the ESP and the engine-management system. The ESP is usually responsible for decelerating the ACC vehicle, while the engine-management system is responsible for accelerating it.

3.5.1.2 Advanced ACC

The advanced ACC differs from the simple ACC in an additional sensor that is uses: a stereo video camera. Thus, the ACC software does not need to estimate whether a vehicle ahead is driving on the same lane or not. The camera provides precise information about the number of lanes, the lane of the ACC vehicle itself, and the lane of vehicles ahead. Furthermore, it recognizes object dimensions and is thus able to differentiate between vehicles, bicycles, people, beverage cans, etc. on the road. Due to the more precise and more reliable information it receives, the ACC software is able to support emergency braking on stationary objects (at a speed of 0 to 60 km/h) and for moving objects (at a speed of 0 to 120 km/h).

3.5.1.3 Sophisticated ACC

The sophisticated ACC differs from the advanced ACC in two additional short-range radar sensors. They detect vehicles ahead in the short range (e.g. vehicles cutting in sharply). Due to this information, the ACC software is able to support additionally stop-and-go in urban traffic.

3.5.2 Applied Problem-Based Modelling

3.5.2.1 Selecting an Approach

We select the approach of Alebrahim et al. [1] for application for the following reasons. The approach of Ulfat-Bunyadi et al. [29] was developed by us. To avoid being biased, we exclude it from the selection here. The approach of Salifu et al. [24] is restricted to context-aware applications. The binding time of the variation points they consider is restricted to runtime and necessitates the existence of a context controller (which is making the decisions at the variation points). Our focus is broader: we consider also variation points whose binding times are during development.

3.5.2.2 Applying the Approach

The three products in our product line have some requirements in common (e.g. identification of vehicles ahead), while others only need to be satisfied by some products (e.g. perform emergency

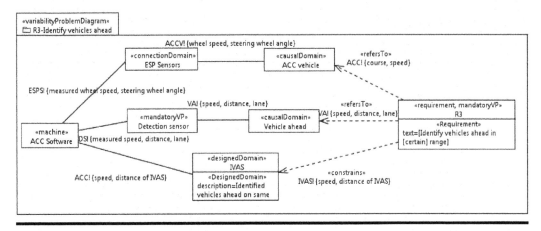

Figure 3.4   Problem diagram containing variation points.

braking). In the following, we focus on the common requirement R3: '*Identify vehicles ahead*'. This requirement is realised differently in the three products (using different sensors). So, it contains variability.

The variability problem diagram for R3 is shown in Figure 3.4. The ACC software uses ESP sensors and detection sensors to identify vehicles ahead that are driving in the same lane as the ACC vehicle. The speed and distance of identified vehicles ahead in the same lane are stored in the machine. This store is called IVAS and is shown as a designed domain, which means that it is part of the machine. R3 is reformulated as "*Identify vehicles ahead in [certain] range*" to express that there is a variation point in the requirement. Another variation point is the problem domain "detection sensor". Furthermore, the phenomena at the two interfaces from the detection sensor to vehicle ahead and ACC software represent variation points as well. However, this is not visible in Figure 3.4, because it was not possible to model that.

The variants for the variation point in the requirement as well as the variation point for the different types of detection sensors are shown in the two diagrams in Figure 3.5. There are three variants (R3-V1, R3-V2, R3-V3) for the requirement R3 which differ regarding the range that is monitored (see diagram on the left in Figure 3.5). The variants are optional, but one variant has to be selected at this variation point. Regarding the detection sensor, there are three variants as

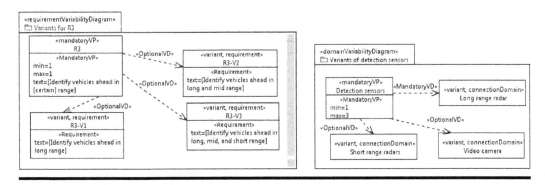

Figure 3.5   Selectable variants at two variation points.

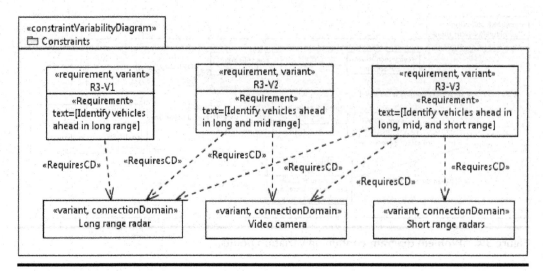

Figure 3.6   Constraints between requirement variants and sensor variants.

well: a long-range radar, a video camera, and two short range radars (see diagram on the right in Figure 3.5). The long-range radar is a mandatory variant, while the other two are optional. At least one detection sensor must be selected and at most three can be selected at this variation point. Between the requirements variants and the sensor variants, there are dependencies. These are documented in the constraint variability diagram in Figure 3.6.

The identification of vehicles ahead in the long range (R3-V1) requires a long-range radar sensor. The identification of vehicles ahead in the long and mid-range (R3-V2) requires a long-range radar sensor and a video camera. The identification of vehicles ahead in the long-, mid-, and short-range (R3-V3) requires a long-range radar sensor, a video camera, and short-range radar sensors.

As mentioned above, the phenomena at the two interfaces of detection sensor in Figure 3.4 represent two variation points as well. These variation points and their variants are shown in the two phenomenon variability diagrams in Figure 3.7. This variability results from the fact that the domain detection sensor represents a variation point. Each sensor variant results in different phenomena that are exchanged at the two interfaces. An interface might even be split into two or more

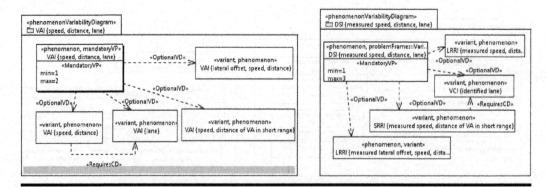

Figure 3.7   Phenomena variability.

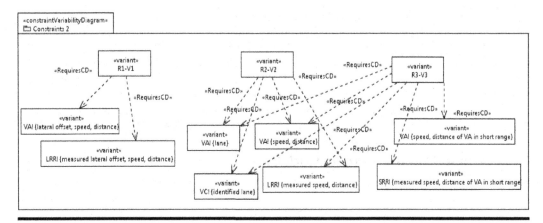

Figure 3.8   Constraints between phenomena variants.

interfaces depending on the number of sensor variants selected. The selection of R2-V2 would result in the selection of a long-range radar and a video camera as detection sensors. The phenomena "speed" and "distance" would then be monitored by the long-range radar and the "lane" would be identified by the video camera. Thus, there would be two interfaces realising the original interface between detection sensor and vehicles ahead (VA! {speed, distance, lane}). We tried to express this realisation relationship by using a 'requires' dependency between the phenomena "speed, distance" and "lane" in Figure 3.7 (left-hand side). However, this is insufficient for expressing the realisation relationship between interfaces.

Each requirement variant requires a certain combination of sensors as shown in Figure 3.6. And each combination of sensors results in a combination of phenomena variants. Thus, there is a dependency between requirement variants and phenomena variants. This is shown in Figure 3.8.

An exemplary problem diagram derived from the variability problem diagram in Figure 3.4 is shown Figure 3.9. R3-V1 was selected which requires a long-range radar as detection sensor and the corresponding phenomena at the two interfaces of it.

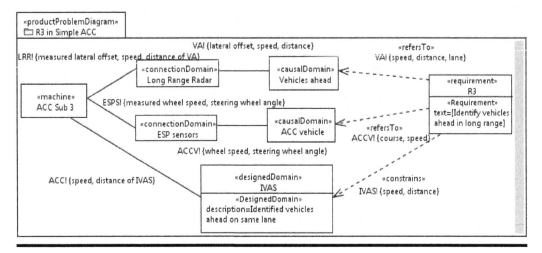

Figure 3.9   Derived problem diagram for Simple ACC.

3.5.2.3 Advantages and Drawbacks

The suggested modelling language provides powerful means for modelling variability: nearly each element of a context diagram and problem diagram can be made variable. However, this is, at the same time, also a drawback of the method. During application, we experienced that frequently several connected elements in a problem diagram are variable and not single ones (e.g. a problem domain together with the phenomena it observes/controls). In the example, this resulted in a large number of dependencies between variants and this in turn increases complexity unnecessarily.

3.5.3 Applied Goal-Oriented Modelling

3.5.3.1 Selecting an Approach

We select the approach of Semmak et al. [25] for application, since it is the only approach that is intended for product line engineering and our example is an ACC product line.

3.5.3.2 Applying the Approach

According to the approach of Semmak et al., a generic model and a variant model need to be created during domain engineering. The generic model shows common and variable goals of the system; the variant model shows the variation points and variants of the product line.

During application, we proceeded in the following way. First, we created the generic goal model without assigning any agent responsibilities. The focus was thus on refining the goals for the entire product line. Then, we created the variant model. Afterwards, we returned to the generic goal model and added the conditions (e.g. <F1, V1>) and responsibility assignments to agents. The generic model for our ACC product line is shown in Figure 3.10.

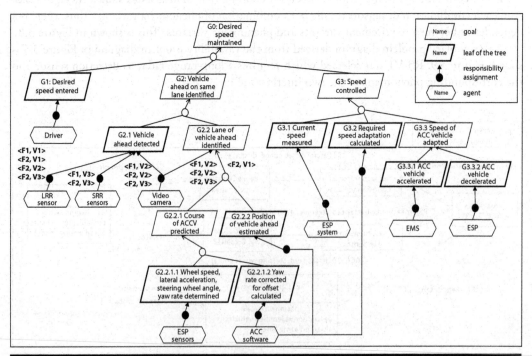

Figure 3.10   Generic goal model for ACC product line.

The overall goal of the systems in our product line is *G0: Maintain the driver's desired speed.* It is shown as the root of the tree. This goal is decomposed by an AND-refinement into the three subgoals: *G1: Desired speed entered*, *G2: Vehicle ahead on same lane identified*, and *G3: Speed controlled*. Note that G2 is actually an optional goal, but the modelling language did not provide any means for making that explicit. G2 only has to be satisfied, if there is a vehicle ahead in the same lane. If there is no vehicle ahead in the same lane, then the satisfaction of G1 and G3 is sufficient for satisfying G0.

G1 is not further decomposed and is assigned to the driver, an environmental agent who is responsible for satisfying this goal. Thus, it is an expectation. However, Semmak et al. do not explain whether expectations should be modelled as goals (i.e. parallelograms) or as assumptions (i.e. dashed parallelograms). Therefore, we decided ourselves to model it as a goal (more precisely, as a leaf of the tree). G2 is further decomposed by an AND-refinement into the two subgoals: *G2.1: Vehicle ahead detected* and *G2.2: Lane of vehicle ahead identified*. G3 is also further decomposed by an AND-refinement into three subgoals: *G3.1: Current speed measured*, *G3.2: Required speed adaptation calculated*, and *G3.3: Speed of ACC vehicle adapted*.

G2.2 and G3.3 are further decomposed. G2.2 is only decomposed for some products in our product line. This is expressed by means of the condition <F2, V1>. For the other products (<F2, V2> and <F2, V3>), it represents a leaf of the tree and is already assigned to an agent (the video camera). The corresponding facets and variants are shown in the variant model in Figure 3.11. There are two facets: *F1: Monitored area* and *F2: Extent of support*. F1 has three variants: *V1: Long range*, *V2: Mid-range*, and *V3: Short range*. F2 has also three variants: *V1: Cruise control*, *V2: Cruise control & emergency braking*, and *V3: Stop and go in urban traffic*. Actually, there are relationships between the variants of F1 and F2, but the modelling language did not provide any means for expressing them in the variant model. For example, V1 of F2 requires V1 of F1, while V2 of F2 requires V1 and V2 of F1, and finally V3 of F2 requires all three variants of F1. To model theses *requires* relationships, we needed to introduce corresponding conditions in the generic goal model. The result are the numerous conditions at the responsibility assignments of G2.1 and G2.2.

3.5.3.3 Advantages and Drawbacks

An advantage of the method is that the developer applying the method must reflect on goals, how they can be achieved and when they are satisfied. By decomposing goals, requirements and expectations can be derived systematically from high level goals (system objectives) and are thus backward traceable to them. However, when applying the method of Semmak et al., we noticed that some questions remain unanswered: 1) How should expectations be modelled?

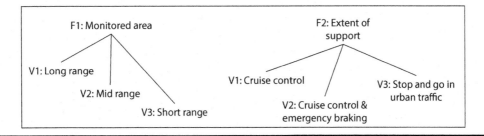

Figure 3.11 Variant model for ACC product line.

As goals or assumptions? 2) How should goals be modelled that are further refined, if certain variants are selected, and are not refined if other variants are selected? As goals (parallelogram) or leaves of the tree (parallelogram with bold lines)? Furthermore, we noticed the need for documenting optional goals. However, the method provided no means for modelling that. Finally, we noticed also the need for documenting *requires* relationships between variants in the variant model. Since this was not possible, we had to document these relationships in the form of several conditions in the generic goal model, which resulted in a high number of conditions at the edges of certain goals. This in turn has a negative impact on the readability of the generic goal model.

3.5.4 Applied Feature-Oriented Modelling

3.5.4.1 Selecting an Approach

The three feature-oriented approaches are quite similar. All focus on product line engineering and suggest modelling the features of the systems in the product line and the features of their context in separate feature models. As regards the relationships between these two models, Hartmann and Trew [11] suggest modelling *requires* and *excludes* relationships, while Tun et al. [27] suggest a documentation of such relationships as constraints using propositional formulae. Lee and Kang [19] suggest the documentation in separate tables and differentiate between different types of relationships that might exist between different types of features (product features, quality attribute features, and usage context features). Since the approach of Lee and Kang is the one that provides most insight into these relationships, we select their approach for application.

3.5.4.2 Applying the Approach

Following the approach of Lee and Kang, we created a product feature model (shown in Figure 3.12), a quality attribute feature model (at the top of Figure 3.13), and a usage context feature model (at the bottom of Figure 3.13) for our ACC product line.

The upper part of the product feature model shows the capabilities of the ACC software in our product line, while the lower part shows the operating environment. We neglected the domain-technology and implementation-technique parts which are usually also shown in a FORM feature model, because we apply the method during requirements engineering and thus these details are not yet determined.

The main capability supported by our ACC products is cruise control. This feature is decomposed into object identification, follow control (i.e. tracking), and speed control. Object identification is decomposed into the features long-range, mid-range, and short-range (i.e. object identification in the long/mid/short-range). Long-range is mandatory, while mid- and short-range are optional features. The long-range feature is related to sensors in the operating environment: the long-range radar sensor and ESP sensors. The mid-range feature is related to the video camera in the operating environment and the short-range feature is related to short-range radar sensors in the operating environment. Similarly, the speed-control feature is related to the ESP and engine management system features.

Emergency brake assistance (feature of our advanced and sophisticated ACCs) and support for stop-and-go in urban traffic (feature of our sophisticated ACC) are not shown as features in the feature diagram in Figure 3.13. The reason is that these are mainly realised by supporting cruise control at different speed. For example, to support emergency braking mainly precise information

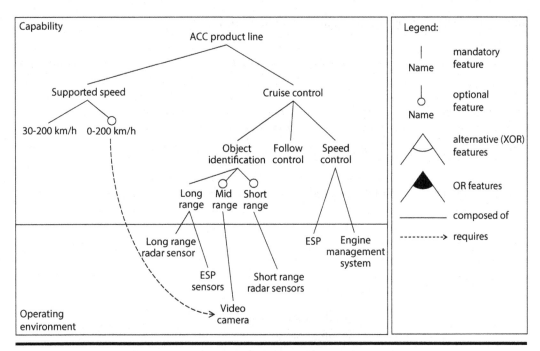

Figure 3.12   Product feature model (FM) for ACC product line.

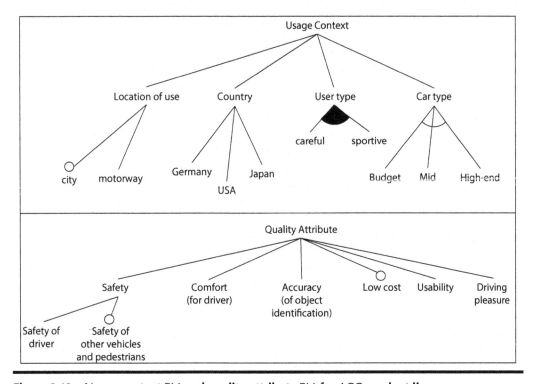

Figure 3.13   Usage context FM and quality attribute FM for ACC product line.

Table 3.13   Mapping between usage context and product features

Usage Contexts	Required Features	Excluded Features
Location of use = city	Mid-range AND short-range	
Car type = High-end	Long-range radar sensor AND ESP sensors AND video camera AND short-range radar sensors	
Car type = Mid	Long-range radar sensor AND ESP sensors AND video camera	
Car type = Budget	Long-range radar sensor AND ESP sensors	

about objects ahead is necessary (e.g. using a video camera). Then ESP may perform full braking, if necessary. Similarly, for supporting stop-and-go in urban traffic, not only objects in the long- and mid-range of the ACC vehicle must be detected but also objects in the short-range (e.g. vehicles ahead cutting in sharply). Then, the ACC software may control the speed of the ACC vehicle (i.e. stop and automatically restart) by means of the ESP system and the engine management system. Thus, in both cases, the capability is cruise control which is supported to a different extent.

However, we have modelled the supported speed as a feature of our ACC product line. If support shall be provided at a speed from 0 to 200 km/h, at least a video camera is required because precise and reliable information about objects ahead is necessary.

As regards quality attributes, for our product line, safety, comfort for driver, accuracy of object identification, low cost, usability, and driving pleasure are relevant quality attributes (top of Figure 3.13). Low cost is an optional feature because it is only relevant for some products in the product line. All other features are mandatory. Safety is decomposed into safety of the driver and safety of other vehicles and pedestrians. Safety of the driver is mandatory (relevant in all products) but safety of other vehicles and pedestrians is only relevant for some products of the product line (the ones supporting emergency braking).

The usage context comprises the location of use, the country, the user type, and the car type (bottom of Figure 3-13). The location of use may vary between city (optional) and motorways (mandatory). The ACC is used in cars driving in diverse countries: Germany, USA, and Japan. There are two types of users (car drivers): careful and sportive. Furthermore, the ACC is integrated into three different types of cars: budget, mid-, and high-end cars.

The different mappings between usage context, product features, and quality attributes are given in Table 3.13, Table 3.14, and Table 3.15. As shown in Table 3.13, if city is the location of

Table 3.14   Mapping between usage context and quality attributes

Usage Contexts	Quality Attributes
Location of use = city	Safety of other vehicles and pedestrians
Car type = budget	Low-cost
User type = sportive	Comfort, driving pleasure, accuracy, safety
User type = careful	Safety, usability

Table 3.15 Mapping between quality attributes (QA) and product features (PF)

QA / PF	Safety	Comfort	Accuracy	Low-cost	Usability	Driving pleasure
Mid-range	+	+	+	−		
Short-range	+	+	+	−		
Emergency brake assistant	++	++	++	−		

use, mid-range and short-range are required features, because for use in the city having only a long-range radar sensor is not sufficient. It would not detect objects in the mid- and short-range. If the car type is high-end, then long-range radar sensor, ESP sensors, video camera, and short-range radar sensors are required features. In case of the budget version, a long-range radar sensor and ESP sensors are required features.

There are the following relationships between usage context and quality attributes (Table 3.14). The location of use 'city' drives the quality attribute safety of other vehicles and pedestrians. In the city, we have shorter distances to objects on the road and the ACC software needs to react more rapidly. Therefore, the safety of other vehicles and pedestrians is an important quality attribute in the city. On motorways, on the other hand, there are no pedestrians and bicycles. The car type 'budget' drives the quality attribute 'low-cost'. For drivers of these cars, low cost is an important quality attribute. The user type 'sportive' drives quality attributes like 'comfort', 'accuracy of object identification', and 'driving pleasure', because sportive drivers may enjoy driving at high speed, but at the same time safety is very important to them. At high speed, precise information about objects ahead is necessary and objects ahead must be detected early on to enable a comfortable deceleration of the ACC vehicle. The user type 'careful' drives quality attributes like 'safety' and 'usability'.

There are the following relationships between product features and quality attributes (Table 3.15). The mid-range and short-range features have a positive influence on safety, comfort and accuracy due to the more reliable information about objects ahead (vehicles, bicycles, pedestrians). However, they impact the low-cost attribute negatively. The emergency brake assistant feature has a strong positive influence on safety, comfort, and accuracy. Yet, it has a negative impact on the low-cost attribute.

3.5.4.3 Advantages and Drawbacks

Lee and Kang perform a good separation of concerns: quality attributes are separately documented from product features and from usage context features. Furthermore, different types of relationships (*requires, excludes, drives,* and *influences positively/negatively*) between the three types of features are documented in the mappings. No other approach makes such a differentiation regarding the relationship types between feature model of the system(s) and feature model of the context.

However, a drawback of feature models in general is the broad definition of feature. Roughly speaking, everything can be documented as a feature. There are no rules to be observed or constraints to be considered and, thus, developers applying the method are not guided in documentation. Furthermore, the feature models and mappings can become quite complex.

3.6 Conclusion

Context modelling for variability-intensive systems is a challenging task due to the presence of variability in the system's requirements and context. There are several approaches that provide support in performing this task. In this chapter, we explained the key concepts of context modelling for variability-intensive systems and provided an overview and an evaluation of existing approaches. The application to a common example provided us with further insights into the approaches, which enable us to draw the following conclusions.

Goal-oriented approaches help identify the effects that shall be achieved in the environment. Thus, they support the developers applying these approaches in focussing on the problem in the real world and understanding it first, before defining a solution. During decomposition of high-level goals, the developers are forced to reflect, on the one hand, on different ways of satisfying a goal (OR-refinement). In this way, identifying different possible alternatives (variants) is supported. On the other hand, the developers have to answer the question of which subgoals need to be satisfied to ensure satisfaction of the parent goal (AND-refinement). This helps in ensuring completeness of identified goals. During decomposition, assumptions (e.g. expectations) about the context may be identified and documented as well. However, the focus of goal-oriented approaches is on the goals/requirements rather than on the context knowledge (assumptions). Therefore, only partial context models are created, and context knowledge is rather documented as a by-product.

The strength of problem-based approaches is that their main focus is on the context and, thus, they are very helpful in understanding and analysing the context. They bridge the gap between effects that shall be achieved in the real world (the problems to be solved) on the one hand and the system (the solution) on the other hand. Problem diagrams show the system as a black box, the problem-oriented requirements to be achieved, and the environmental domains to which the system needs to be connected to satisfy the requirements. Therefore, problem diagrams are also helpful for making expectations regarding these environmental domains explicit.

Feature models provide a good overview of system features and context features. They focus on commonality and variability among the features. Therefore, they are very useful for performing a commonality and variability analysis, i.e. reflecting on common and variable parts of a system and its context. Feature models can be created easily, and developers have a lot of freedom in modelling due to the broad definition of a feature. However, we made the experience that thinking in features and creating a model of context features is not as straightforward as creating a model of system features. It seems to depend on the type of context that is modelled. Feature models may, for example, be well suited for creating a model of the business context in terms of features of the market segment, customers, existing technologies, etc. Yet, for creating a model of the operating environment, problem diagrams might be more suitable.

References

1. A. Alebrahim, S. Fassbender, M. Filipczyk, M. Goedicke, M. Heisel, M. Konersmann: Towards a Computer-Aided Problem-Oriented Variability Requirements Engineering Method. In Proc. of CAiSE'14 Workshops, No. 178 in LNBIP, Springer, 2014, pp. 136-147.
2. R. Ali, F. Dalpiaz, P. Giorgini: Goal-Based Self-Contextualization. In: Proceedings of CAiSE'09 Forum, Amsterdam, 2009.

3. R. Ali, Y. Yu, R. Chitchyan, A. Nhlabatsi, P. Giorgini: Towards a Unified Framework for Contextual Variability in Requirements. In: Proceedings of the Third International Workshop on Software Product Management (IWSPM'09), IEEE, 2009.
4. R. Ali, F. Dalpiaz, P. Giorgini: A Goal-Based Framework for Contextual Requirements Modeling and Analysis. In: Requirements Engineering (2010) 15:439-458.
5. J. Bosch, R. Capilla: Variability Implementation. In: R. Capilla, J. Bosch, K. C. Kang (eds.): Systems and Software Variability Management – Concepts, Tools and Experiences, Springer, Berlin, Heidelberg, 2013, pp. 75-86.
6. Robert Bosch GmbH: ACC Adaptive Cruise Control. The Bosch Yellow Jackets, Edition 2003.
7. A. Classen: Modelling and Model Checking Variability-Intensive Systems. PhD thesis, University of Namur, Belgium, October 2011.
8. P. Clements, L. Northrop: Software Product Lines: Practices and Patterns. Addison-Wesley, 2001.
9. G. Chen, D. Kotz: A Survey of Context-Aware Mobile Computing Research. Dartmouth Computer Science Technical Report TR2000-381, 2000.
10. D. C. Gause: Why Context Matters – And What Can We Do About It. IEEE Software, Vol. 22, No. 5, 2005, pp. 13-15.
11. H. Hartmann, T. Trew: Using Feature Diagrams with Context Variability to Model Multiple Product Lines for Software Supply Chains. In: Proceedings of SPLC 2008, IEEE Computer Society, 2008.
12. M. Heisel, D. Hatebur, T. Santen, D. Seifert: Testing Against Requirements Using UML Environment Models. In: Software-Technik Trends, Volume 28, No. 3, 2008.
13. A. Heuer, K. Pohl: Structuring Variability in the Context of Embedded Systems during Software Engineering. In: Proceedings of VaMoS 2014, Article No. 21, ACM, New York, 2014.
14. M. Jackson: Problem Frames – Analysing and Structuring Software Development Problems. Addison-Wesley, 2001.
15. K. C. Kang, S. G. Cohen, J. A. Hess, W. E. Novak, A. S. Peterson: Feature-Oriented Domain Analysis (FODA) Feasibility Study. Technical Report, CMU/SEI-90-TR-21, November 1990.
16. K. C. Kang, S. Kima, J. Lee, K. Kim, E. Shin, M. Huh: FORM: A Feature-Oriented Reuse Method with Domain-Specific Reference Architectures. Annals of Software Engineering Volume 5, Issue 1, 1998, pp. 143-168.
17. C. Klein, R. Schmid, C. Leuxner, W. Sitou, B. Spanfelner: A Survey of Context Adaptation in Autonomic Computing. In: Proc. of Fourth International Conference on Autonomic and Autonomous Systems (ICAS'08), IEEE Computer Society, pp. 106-111, 2008.
18. A. van Lamsweerde, Requirements Engineering – From System Goals to UML Models to Software Specifications, John Wiley & Sons, West Sussex, 2009.
19. K. Lee, K. C. Kang: Usage Context as Key Driver for Feature Selection. In: Proc. of SPLC'10, LNCS 6287, Springer, Berlin, Heidelberg, 2010, pp. 32-46.
20. S. Liaskos, A. Lapouchnian, Y. Yu, E. Yu, J. Mylopoulos: On Goal-based Variability Acquisition and Analysis. In: Proc. 14th IEEE International Requirements Engineering Conference (RE'06), IEEE, 2006.
21. K. Pohl: Requirements Engineering – Fundamentals, Principles, and Techniques. Springer, 2010.
22. K. Reif (ed.): Fahrstabilisierungssysteme und Fahrerassistenzsysteme – Bosch Fachinformation Automobil (in German). Vieweg + Teubner, 2010.
23. M. Salehie, L. Tahvildari: Self-Adaptive Software: Landscape and Research Challenges. ACM Transactions on Autonomous and Adaptive Systems, Vol. 4, No. 2, 2009, pp. 14:1-14:42.
24. M. Salifu, Y. Yu, B. Nuseibeh: Specifying Monitoring and Switching Problems in Context. In: Proceedings of 15th IEEE International Requirements Engineering Conference (RE'07), Delhi, India, 2007.
25. F. Semmak, C. Gnaho, R. Laleau: Extended KAOS Method to Model Variability in Requirements. In: Proceedings of ENASE 2008/2009, CCIS 69, Springer, Berlin Heidelberg, 2010, pp. 193-205.
26. M. Svahnberg, J. van Gurp, J. Bosch: On the Notion of Variability in Software Product Lines. Proceedings of Working IEEE/IFIP Conference on Software Architecture, 2001.

27. T. T. Tun, Q. Boucher, A. Classen, A. Hubaux, P. Heymanns: Relating Requirements and Feature Configurations: A Systematic Approach. In: Proc. of SPLC'09, Carnegie Mellon University Pittsburgh, USA, 2009, pp. 201-210.
28. N. Ulfat-Bunyadi, E. Kamsties, K. Pohl: Considering Variability in a System Family's Architecture during COTS Evaluation. In: Proc. of ICCBSS 2005, LNCS 3412, Springer, 2005, pp. 223-235.
29. N. Ulfat-Bunyadi, R. Meis, N. Gol Mohammadi, M. Heisel: Introducing Product Line Engineering in a Bottom-up Approach. In: Proc. of ICSOFT-PT 2016, ScitePress, 2016, pp. 146-153.
30. P. Zave, M. Jackson: Four Dark Corners of Requirements Engineering. In: ACM Transactions on Software Engineering and Methodology, Vol. 6, No. 1, 1997, pp. 1-30.

Chapter 4

Variability Incorporated Simultaneous Decomposition of Models Under Structural and Procedural Views

Muhammed Cagri Kaya[a], Selma Suloglu[b], Gul Tokdemir[c], Bedir Tekinerdogan[d], and Ali H. Dogru[a]

[a]Department of Computer Engineering, Middle East Technical University, Ankara, Turkey
[b]SoSoft Information Technologies, Ankara, Turkey
[c]Department of Computer Engineering, Cankaya University, Ankara, Turkey
[d]Information Technology, Wageningen University, Wageningen, The Netherlands

4.1 Introduction

Our era is witnessing advances software engineering toward compositional approaches, while these approaches continue to inspire each other. However, none of them enjoy complete and widely-accepted methodologies. Observed from such a perspective, this work can be classified as a component-oriented approach, significantly influenced by Software Product Lines (SPL) and Service-Oriented Architecture (SOA) approaches. Actually, it is not only the compositional avenue but also generation based techniques are effective in modern software development environments. Transformational methods have also been considered in the more generalized studies related to this research, belonging to the latter group.

Component orientation was defined in (Dogru and Tanik, 2003) as a process targeting composition of software units. Actually, the decomposition view in software architecture was being addressed in those same days while the related software architecture notions were developing in parallel. Association among the terminology becomes more inclusive observing the strong connection between the software architecture and the compositional concepts. It is worth mentioning here that most of the approaches have been introduced with their "architecture" views preceding their "engineering" or "development" support. SPL Architecture (SPLA), for example, enables

SPL Engineering (SPLE) just like Model-Driven Architecture (MDA) supports Model-Driven Development (MDD) or Model-Driven Engineering (MDE).

Studies addressing software architecture in a limited fashion are mostly concentrated on the "structure" dimension of software-intensive systems, the Component-Oriented Software Engineering (COSE) therefore can be viewed as one of the earlier approaches defining this new trend. This work contributes to COSE in the form of addressing the other views of software architecture. This also coincides with addressing the data, function, and control dimensions besides the existing structure dimension despite the fact that such addressing is done in an implicit manner.

For summarizing the effects of SPLA and SOA to this work, feature modeling and especially variability management as a related activity have been utilized as fundamental constituents in the modeling and the development of systems. This perspective brings important consequences to the methodology for development. Also, process modeling has been imported from SOA, with its suggested role as the overall control model for the flow of executions. The commitment of web services to the tasks in a process model, constituting the next most important global contribution of SOA is not a very new idea for COSE, where packages were dispatched to components for the similar purpose.

It is worth mentioning the input from object orientation mostly through its modeling media—the Unified Modeling Language (UML). For development with UML, the goal is to "write" code after defining various cross sections of a software system through a set of graphical models. That is categorically different from the compositional approaches where locating and integration of "already written" code is desired. Nevertheless, UML has offered the component diagram, and even offers the usage of its diagrams for modeling the "architectural views." This is taken by the industry seriously and some tools do not even allow starting a UML diagram unless the architectural view is first determined. Similarly, some UML tools identify themselves as component-based as much as object-oriented. Of course, notions develop along with a chronology of influences. A fundamental concept in components and further, in the mentioned approaches is the "interface." Objects, after all, are supporting an explicit interface notion in the form of the public sub-sets of their class definitions.

Mentioning of UML brings an important issue when the bulk of the current development practices are considered. UML-based activities usually start with the use case model. That is where a set of process representing units are declared. These units are referred to as use cases. This is a logical model for the processes, without an expectation to be associated with solution units (structure). However, such a central model for UML is left alone without a methodical support for how to determine a good set of use cases—that is process decomposition. Of course, process decomposition has not been the goal of the use-case diagrams, hence they omit the flow specifications among the use cases: what is the order of their activations is not addressed, and intentionally left out. This model is not desired to include the control dimension. Documentation of use-case model descriptions is used to bridge the use-case specifications and control dimension. However, the documentation is not explicitly expressed and associated with related use cases in a defined manner in UML-based tools. Such association with the control dimension through documentation is left to analysts and developers.

Nevertheless, even the most prominent code development targeting tool—UML—addresses some limited form of process decomposition as the first step in modeling. Despite its intention to remain logical and to correspond to only requirements, a use-case model is used as a map for the rest of the development: Each use case is taken at a time, and its internals are defined using other UML diagrams. Such specification activity propagates to the solution space preserving the same guidance map. The developers are quite conscious of which use case they are currently implementing. Also, use case directed testing methods are quite common. Actually, the current trend has not been very far from the presented approach in this chapter except for some notions being addressed less and not utilizing the compositional power offered by the advancement of the development capabilities.

4.1.1 Variability in the Center of Development Activity

Most of the assumptions in optimizing the presented development approach are based on the existence of a mature domain (Togay et al., 2008). This is the hidden assumption behind any modern approach anyway. A mature domain can be characterized by the following properties:

1. Most of the domain requirements and reusable solutions have been developed,
2. A large community of developers are familiar with those domain repositories, and
3. Specific and effective tools are available.

SPLA, for example, is a domain-oriented technology. Also, the MDD would not be practically possible without a scoped domain. It is known that the success of automatic-code generation depends on the width of the boundary of its intended domain. Once the domain is known, the bulk of the necessary actions for the development of the "next product" is also known. This knowledge can be arranged in the form of the common features in any product and the variable ones that discriminate one product from another—all in the same domain. Modeling of the commonalities and the variabilities is the foundation of SPLE.

A mature domain suggests the existence of a critical mass of engineers who are well knowledgeable about the available assets for developing software in this specific domain. Components, for example, can be known by their names and functional and non-functional properties. This also implies that possible sub-problem definitions are known. The task of the developers now is to map the requirements to existing components and configure the components and their interconnection as guided by variability management. Actually, we are suggesting one additional layer between the requirements or selected features and the components: that is a process model. The top-level variability is first mapped to the process model, hence instantiating it for the required flow control of the system under development. Then the variability resolution ripples down the hierarchy, to the components level. Assuming the requirement that the domain model is sufficiently mature, the most important development effort will be consumed for the variability management.

The presented approach in this chapter corresponds to both "domain engineering" and "application engineering" tasks of the SPLE. There are few options for variability modeling for the domain. The developers make their choices starting with the highest-level, mostly by selecting variants for variation points. To enable the configuration of the final system, following these choices, a hierarchical variability representation is required. Also, constraints should propagate in general, from higher-level variability specifications to the lower-level ones. Such specifications should be enabled to set-up the configuration interfaces of components for example, for automated development. This research is supporting such mechanisms that are expected to leverage variability-centric development probably as a new paradigm for development methodologies.

4.1.2 Chapter Objectives

There are significant messages this chapter intends to convey to the reader. The presented approach supports the development of complex software intensive systems. Notions for efficiency are being utilized in modern environments such as reuse being systematized by SPL. Here, a further automation is suggested by exploiting some other notions that are explained below, while listing the targeted areas as the objectives to convey to the reader:

1. Variability can be the most important input for development, for the environments (such as for SPL) where certain capabilities have been established,
2. Hierarchical decomposition is an important notion in developing models and systems,
3. A system requires more than one model during development – their simultaneous development (especially through hierarchical decomposition) is very important for the efficiency of the process.

A combination of these principles establishes an efficient development paradigm.

4.2 Background

This section includes an introduction about the basic concepts that form the foundation for this chapter. The decomposition techniques for the structural and the procedural dimensions of software systems are discussed. However, those decompositions can be guided by variability. Also, hierarchical modeling of variability is crucial as it guides such decompositions. Hence, the hierarchical variability topic is introduced first.

4.2.1 Hierarchical Variability Specification

Variability modeling has been the target of many investigations since the usage of feature models (Kang et al., 1990). Soon after, explicit variability modeling alternatives were developed as more preferred alternatives that also suggested their association with hierarchy and constraints. Orthogonal Variability Model (OVM) (Pohl et al., 2005), Covamof (Sinnema et al., 2004), and CVL-Common Variability Language (Haugen et al., 2012) can be listed as the prominent and earlier work in this direction. The two important notions here that are hierarchy and constraints, need to be considered simultaneously. Hierarchy allows the automated configuration of lower-level variability specifications and eventually the software components because of the desire to support top-down development strategy. Constraints, on the other hand, assume the enabling of specific associations among the variabilities at different levels of the hierarchy.

Explicit variability modeling can be incorporated within the suggested approach in this chapter. It is considered as future work. However, the main view here is enabling variability, wherever it originates towards more automation for software development. That is why a mature domain is required and development is mostly through configuration. Variability should guide configuration.

Our previous work about propagating variability specifications (Suloglu, 2013) in that manner involved variant-to-variant associations from higher- to lower-level constituents (variation point regions in the models or configuration interfaces in the software components). Development experimentation conducted during the early work resulted in the suggestion to implement the variants as alternative flow paths in process models. At the component level, variability is generally resolved through component replacement or component configuration. Compliant components are expected to publish configuration interfaces that actually execute the external-to-internal variation propagation. This latter option was possible within the mentioned early work.

Propagation of variability resolution in a set of hierarchically represented variation points has been demonstrated in some examples that utilize COSE Modeling Language (COSEML)- and

Business Process Model and Notation (BPMN)-based representations for software components and process models, respectively. The component-related representations are introduced in the following section, where variability specifications and their propagation are also presented in examples.

The goal can be summarized as developing complex systems, mostly managing variability: Since commonality is more defined, to specify a new product it is mostly the variability that should be addressed. For complex systems, hierarchical modeling has been proposed earlier (Simon, 1996), complementing our variability emphasis for our goal.

4.2.2 COSEML/XCOSEML for Structural Decomposition

COSEML emerged as a graphical modeling language for component-oriented development. It can represent logical entities such as packages and their physical implementations such as components. Its aim is to meet the graphical representation of the structural decomposition approach of COSE. Dynamic constructs to represent procedural view are absent in this language. XCOSEML (Kaya et al., 2014) is an extended version of COSEML equipped with variability and dynamic constructs. Unlike its predecessor COSEML, it is a text-based language. In XCOSEML, language constructs and variability constructs are handled differently for easy management of models conforming to "separation of concerns." A graphical version of XCOSEML is under construction to ease especially the process modeling (Cetinkaya, 2017).

COSEML aims to develop systems by composing pre-built software components in a mature domain. Therefore, it did not use other concepts aside from components: such as objects, that are frequently used by the approaches that aim code writing. Connectors were also considered as abstract entities that define connections between two components. However, in (Cetinkaya et al., 2016), connectors became first-class entities like components by handling communication concerns in them and including some extra capabilities, such as data conversion.

Dynamic view is first defined by XCOSEML for component orientation. Initially, in the process model of the language (composition specification), plain messaging is shown explicitly. With the development of connectors, the messaging among components is allocated in the connectors, and connectors assume a bigger role in the development.

4.2.3 Process Decomposition for Software Composition

Usually, new processes leave the engineers with their creativity alone in creating new models. Earlier methodologies were more detailed in providing step-by-step instructions based on text-based user requirements. A considerable amount of detail is provided in the book of Pressman and Maxim (2015) for the hierarchical definition of structure models based on existing data-flow models. Data-flow models in return were also supported by methodological descriptions.

Most of our models should be organized in hierarchies that are naturally defined as a result of decomposition activities. That is a requirement for reducing the complexity: according to Miller (1956) due to cognitive limitations it is hard for our brains to concentrate on more than 7 ± 2 items at a time, especially if those items are interrelated. Those items can be lines of code or other constituents of software definition models. Grouping about seven items and encapsulating them under a new identifier reduces the total items significantly. However, this technique alone usually is not enough. A program of 700 lines, for example, can be reduced to 100 functions only for decomposition sake: every 7 lines can be organized as a function. However, the resulting 100 functions are still considerably above our 7 ± 2 limit, let alone the ignored cohesion principle in determination of the function boundaries.

So far, in the given example encapsulation reduced the cognition problem but not solved it completely. If those modules are also sorted in a hierarchy, almost like a tree diagram, we have far better chances to understand the model. As a result, looking at any locality in such a tree-based model, we can understand the whole by understanding its parts. In such a model, parts are positioned in a way that represents the relation of a module within the whole. Starting with the top module, we have better chances to keep the holistic view and orient ourselves in any navigation across the model. As a summary, complex models should be arranged by decomposition that corresponds to a hierarchy when conducted in a top-down manner.

One rare approach that suggests the hierarchy, hence the decomposition activity is the Axiomatic Design Theory (ADT) (Suh, 1998). Equipped with various techniques to support modularity, this approach offers tools for evaluating the coupling property of a given design. Although developed initially for mechanical engineering, the approach was quickly adapted to software development. Its methodological dimension offers simultaneous decomposition techniques for various development models. After the adaptation by the software industry, it was applied to component orientation (Togay et al., 2008). Finally, ADT was used for process decomposition, leveraging on its capability to decompose various models simultaneously (Togay et al., 2017). This is a methodology imported in this research for guiding the decomposition due to its compatibility with the process model and component model for simultaneous decomposition. However, a required condition is the persuasion for the use of decomposition in the definition of a model. Following the concerns about preserving the holistic view, this option is suitable. Also, ADT promotes this kind of orientation. As a summary, developing a model mainly based on decomposition is supported by this research.

In relevant literature, it is widely acknowledged that large (Mendling at al., 2007) and complex (Mendling et al., 2008) process models decrease the level of comprehension. They also create a setting which is unfavorable though further error generation in these models. To overcome this undesired result, decomposition is proposed as a supportive method.

Decomposition includes gradual dismantling of a system into smaller sub-systems (Dietz, 2006). It is argued that decomposing process models into sub-models will provide a solution for complexity (Dumas et al., 2013). This will also reverse the case of low understandability (Mendling et al., 2007). It is emphasized that decomposition will result in easier communication and improved maintainability of process models (Milani et al., 2016). It is also suggested that decomposition will promote reusability of the sub-models (Bass et al., 1998): decomposed systems will have less coupling and more cohesion as a consequence.

In the literature, various concepts have been utilized interchangeably in relation to the process of decomposition. Some of which are modularization, aggregation, generalization, and abstraction. Similarly, several approaches have been proposed for decomposition of process models including rules and criteria.

Dijkman et al. (2016) provide a detailed review on the comprehensive concept of decomposition. They explore studies on business process design approaches and furthermore classify studies based on how the processes and their relationships are defined. They group related approaches accordingly. These groups are namely goal-based, action-based, object-based and function-based approaches. The goal-based approaches (Anton et al., 1994) use structured goal definition which is used to derive the process architecture. Sub-goals can be defined at the lower levels which may be associated with sub-processes. Similarly, business actions/sub-actions and their relations can be designed and then mapped to processes/sub-processes in action based approaches (Dietz, 2006). On the other hand, object based approaches represent objects and their relations. The decomposition of objects can be associated with process decomposition. In function based approaches, a hierarchical relation between business functions is represented by a process/sub-process decomposition architecture.

Another recent review by (Milani et al, 2016) elaborates on methods of process model decomposition and classifies them based on heuristics that utilize breakpoints, data objects, roles, shared processes, repetition, and structuredness. Approaches that consider breakpoints are mainly grounded on the view that a process can be broken down into sub-processes based on specific interest points called breakpoints or milestones during the process lifespan which can be points where process properties are measurable (Milani et al., 2013). It is also suggested that decomposition can be performed based on how data objects are shared between the activities, hence yielding the activities using same objects placed in the same sub-process. Processes can be detached by means of the stakeholder views (Turetken and Demirors, 2011) where stakeholders model and improve their own processes individually which are then integrated to form the top level processes.

Another approach considered for decomposition is shared processes which combine process parts that are used in different parts of the process. Within this perspective, alternative approaches might be also suggested where behavioral aspects of process parts like sequential, parallel, or cyclical can be examined and the ones with similar behavior are combined. Similarly, in the block-structuring approach, "single entry single exit" blocks can be identified as process parts and through graph clustering related nodes can be combined as a sub-process (Reijers et al., 2011). This will also result in enriched understanding and improved nature of decomposition processes.

Similar ideas and propositions exist on concepts like vertical, horizontal and orthogonal modularization, and composition and merging as stated in La Rosa et al. (2011). Also on aggregation which specifies a top-level object being composed of lower-level fragments or being generalized that is a high-level abstraction of the lower level variants (Muehlen et al., 2010). Similarly, as another concept, though providing an alternative view, model abstraction describes aggregated activities of a process model in a more abstract view (Smirnov et al., 2011). Another approach uses separation of concerns that are involved in process activities by specifying roles played by activities for process decomposition (Caetano et al., 2010).

Methods for "how-to-decompose" are definitely not limited to the ones mentioned above. Within the last decade, especially in recent years, alternatives were proposed and discussed both in academia and in practice. For example, another basis for decomposition is through merging algorithms based on the graphs like EPCs (Event-driven Process Chains) and BPMN (La Rosa et al., 2013). For example, Huang et al. (2018) apply a graph mining algorithm to find out frequent subgraphs under the same process topic for merging processes, which is needed to be checked for semantic correctness of the merged parts.

Johannsen et al. (2014) apply decomposition conditions of Wand and Weber (1989)—minimality, determinism, losslessness, minimum coupling, and strong cohesion—to BPMN. They propose guidelines for a decomposition process and argue that these guidelines should be redefined for each modeling language.

To summarize the overall picture regarding the domain of process decomposition, there has been progress in terms of providing valuable insights and arguments into the practice. However, there is still need for a generalized guideline for widely accepted criteria for consistent decomposition (Johannsen and Leist, 2012), independent of the modeling context.

4.3 Variability-guided Decomposition

The advances in the compositional capabilities and the advantages of domain orientation can be leveraged in promoting variability management as the main development activity. The details of how variability models are developed is out of the scope of this work but can be found in several studies (Kang et al., 1990; Pohl, 2005; Sinnema et al., 2004).

The goal is to treat variability as a guide during procedural and structural modeling where variability affects process model first and then the process model shed light to structural decomposition along with its own variability specification. All these activities focus on mostly "domain design" and "domain realization" part of the "domain engineering." In a process-oriented decomposition, the flow of the activities leads the structural decomposition. The flow varies with respect to functionality and behavior also to cover the needs of different stakeholders. In this case, variability model is going to answer the questions:

- Why: the reasons for the process model to fork by representing variations;
- How: the way the flow forks and joins via pinpointing the variation points with respect to constraints; and
- What: the capabilities of the process model through an ability to resolve variations to produce the final product.

Therefore, corresponding variability model guides the process decomposition and establishes relations with hierarchical variability in structural decomposition. The modeling techniques and approaches employed in our approach are listed in Table 4.1.

Our approach is not limited to the models used for process decomposition and variability modeling. The modeling techniques and approaches are chosen for demonstration purposes as well as their popularity. Variability guided decomposition process is elaborated with a set of steps along with affected models in Table 4.2.

Concerning the "application engineering" part, mainly "application design and application realization," the goal is to conduct a top-down variability resolution while process and structure decomposition will accompany this effort where necessary. Also, variability-resolution actions are expected to automate related decompositions. Figure 4.1 depicts the variability decisions affecting the associated models.

Variability resolution first needs to consider the dependent variabilities at the feature level. If only feature models are used to represent variabilities, such consideration will be the observation of "include" and "exclude" constraints in the feature model. That way some further variability decisions will have to be made, preferably automatically.

Next, ramifications of a resolution at the feature level should be considered. For example, selecting an optional feature as a variability-resolution action will require further selections in some variability points in the process model, or in the structure model, or in both. These kind of consequences may be automatically handled based on the maturity of the domain and completeness in the domain models. Such a propagation can be from the feature model to both the process model and the structure model, from the process model to the structure model, and also can be

Table 4.1 Modeling techniques and tools

Modeling Type	Model Tool Type	Specific Tool
Variability modeling	Feature Model	FeatureIDE (2018)
Process decomposition	Business Process Modeling Notation (BPMN)	Signavio (2018)
Structural decomposition	Hierarchical Component Decomposition (XCOSEML HCD with its variability model—VM)	XCOSEML tool

Table 4.2 Variability-guided decomposition steps

Step	Affected Model
1. Start with appending an activity to the process model.	BPMN Model
2. Analyze the feature model with respect to the recently added activity whether any of the features are related to it and make the activity's behavior diverse.	None
3. If there will be more than one possible realization of the activity, then convert them to sub-processes to be decomposed further.	BPMN Model
4. Add a corresponding package to XCOSEML component decomposition model if there is no package that can be related to the activity/sub-process. Otherwise, use an existing package.	XCOSEML HCD – Package Specification
5. Define relevant components and their functions with respect to activity/sub-process if required.	XCOSEML HCD – Component Interface
6. Specify variation point and related variants with constraints for the newly introduced package and its parent package if exists. Define variation mappings among newly defined variation points and variants.	XCOSEML VM – Configuration Interface, XCOSEML HCD – Composition Specification
7. Define a new function or use an existing one in the package composition for the parent package. Specify or change the flow of the function with corresponding variation points and variants through "variation specification attachments." Append new function to parent package interface if added.	XCOSEML VM – Configuration Interface, XCOSEML HCD – Composition Specification
8. Apply 7th step to the newly introduced package.	XCOSEML VM – Configuration Interface, XCOSEML HCD – Composition Specification
9. Start from the 1st step and loop until process model is completed.	

internal to any model. By the way, the structure model in this work implies the COSEML representation of the logical and component levels altogether.

Propagation of variability decisions can be observed to be taking place inside any model, and from a higher-level model to a lower-level one. The structure level is considered as the lowest-level model, being below the process model: It is only after determining the flow of the operations that the operation instances can be connected.

A similar space of mutually-dependent models where the developers would be faced with the final status of all the models after one design decision was implied by Togay (2008). However, an explicit addressing of such methodological concerns was not incorporated. Also, variability was not employed. The interdependent actions in a set of models could be from any model constituent to any other, exploring the possibilities in a combinatorial complexity. Here, interventions are allowed only in the variant representations. This is both

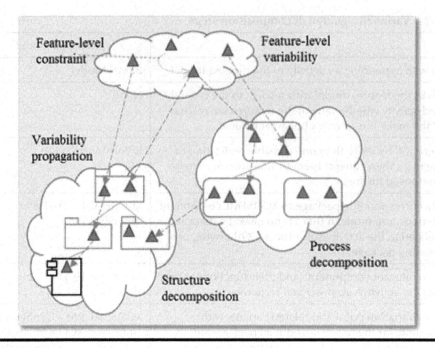

Figure 4.1 Propagation of variability in the decomposition environment.

a limitation to the complexity and the elevation of variability notion to the position where it becomes the primary development action.

4.4 A Case Study: Vending Machine

The vending machine as a case study is chosen to demonstrate variability-guided process decomposition. The variability information from the variability model is mapped in the process model and XCOSEML model. Variability propagation is achieved through selections and the end product is specified.

The vending machine is an automated machine invented in the late 1880s which provides a diverse set of items ranging from beverages, tickets, postcards, cigarettes, to hot pizzas. They accept payment by cash or, today, even by credit cards. The vending machine in our case study offers beverages, solid food, and soft drinks. Different items require different delivery processes for the vending machine. Solid food and soft drinks are placed in the dispenser directly. On the other hand, preparation of hot beverages such as tea or coffee includes a set of steps: placing cup and spoon, pouring tea or coffee, and adding sugar if requested.

A feature model for the vending machine has been created as shown in Figure 4.2. The feature model is the source of variability information. This, in turn, configures the XCOSEML variability model, leads to variability resolution, and propagation of resolution from upper levels to lower levels, all the way to components. In this way, variability binding of the process model is completed towards the configuring of an application.

For the domain design and realization part, process decomposition for vending machine starts with the initialization of corresponding models as shown in Table 4.3. Improvements in each stage

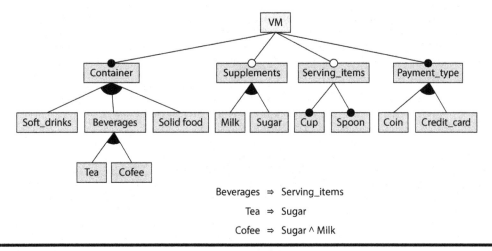

Beverages ⇒ Serving_items

Tea ⇒ Sugar

Cofee ⇒ Sugar ∧ Milk

Figure 4.2   Feature model of vending machine case study.

of the decomposition process are represented through a process model and an XCOSEML model conforming to the feature model.

Then, as shown in Table 4.4, the addition of the activities to the process model starts: Vending machine waits for the payment at first. After analyzing the feature model, it is observed that the machine supports two different payments: via cash or credit card. The feature "Payment_type" and its child features "Coin" and "Credit_card" point out that payment process will be diversified. Therefore, a sub-process is added to the process model with the name "Get Payment" to be decomposed further. The relation between "Coin" and "Credit_card" features are "optional" as the vending machine can support either one or both of them. As no package exists that can be related to payment associated activities, a new package "Payment" is added to the root of the XCOSEML component decomposition. A variation point "PaymentType" and its variants "Coin" and "CreditCard" are created with the "optional" relation, which is directly related to the newly introduced features. As our decomposition is hierarchical, there should be a related variation point and variants defined for "Payment" package which are "Type," "Coin," and "CreditCard," respectively. In order to represent and enable propagation from upper levels to lower levels of the hierarchy, variation mappings are defined. In this case, a one-to-one mapping is established in composition specification: the variant of "PaymentType" in vending machine package is mapped to "Coin," that is the variant of "Type" in the payment package.

To further decompose "Get Payment" sub-process shown in Table 4.5, a new process is created with the same name "Get Payment" and the flow of the activities are specified. In our case, for payment a coin can be deposited to the machine or a credit card can be used whose information is checked beforehand. There are two different paths for payment, so an XOR control item is placed after the "start," and two paths are forked and joined with this XOR.

Table 4.3   First stage of decomposition

Process Model	○ start
XCOSEML Structural Model	**Package** VendingMachine
XCOSEML Variability Related Models	None

Table 4.4 Second stage of decomposition

Process Model	
	start ○→ Get Payment ⊞

XCOSEML Structural Model	`Package VendingMachine`
	`  Configuration VendingMachine_conf`
	`  includes Payment`

	`Package Payment` `  Configuration Payment_conf`

XCOSEML Variability Related Models	`Configuration VendingMachine_conf of Package`
	`VendingMachine`
	`  externalVP PaymentType`
	`   optional`
	`     variant Coin`
	`     variant CreditCard`

	`Configuration Payment_conf of Package Payment`
	`   externalVP Type`
	`     optional`
	`       variant Coin`
	`       variant CreditCard`

	`Composition VendingMachine_cmps`
	`  import configuration VendingMachine_conf`
	`  variability mapping`
	`  VP PaymentType maps package Payment VP Type`
	`    variant Coin maps variant Coin`
	`    variant CreditCard maps variant CreditCard`

There is no need to add a new package in XCOSEML structural decomposition as "Payment" is an appropriate package for payment-related activities. Therefore, "Payment_comp" is introduced with two functions: "GetCoin" and "ConnectBank." There needs to be no change in the XCOSEML variation model. A function "Operate" is defined in the "VendingMachine" root package which calls "GetPayment" function from the "Payment" package. Therefore, a new function, "GetPayment" is specified in "Payment" composition specification with the corresponding variability attachments. "GetPayment" function includes coin-related activities (the "GetCoin" function) if only "Coin" is selected. This variability is represented by appending "#ifSelected(Coin)#" attachment at the beginning of the coin related activities (Payment_comp.GetCoin). The same holds for the "CreditCard" variation where the function call is surrounded with "#ifSelected(CreditCard)#" attachment. In this way, the activities will be added with respect to the selection of the variants, namely "Coin" and "CreditCard."

The decomposition process proceeds with applying the steps as exemplified with three stages in above until the process model is completed. After then, a family of vending machine applications can be constructed with its process model, and corresponding XCOSEML component decomposition along with its variation specifications. From this point on our domain design is ready to be configured with end-user choices which comprise activities of product design and realization. The finalized process model is shown in Figure 4.3 and the details of the sub-processes, "Get Payment," "Process Payment," "Prepare Item," and "Payback" are depicted in Figures 4.4, 4.5, 4.6, and 4.7.

Table 4.5   Third stage of decomposition

Process Model		

XCOSEML Structural Model	**Package** VendingMachine
	  Configuration
	    VendingMachine_conf
	    includes Payment
	
	Package Payment
	  Configuration
	    Payment_conf
		Composition VendingMachine_cmps
		  import configuration
		  VendingMachine_conf
		  Variability mapping
		  VP PaymentType **maps package**
		  Payment **VP** Type
		    variant Coin maps variant Coin
		    variant CreditCard maps
		    variant CreditCard
		
		  method Operate:
		    payment.getPayment

	Component Payment_comp **interface** Payment_int	

	Interface Payment_int
	  providedMethods
	    GetCoin
	    ConnectBank
		Composition Payment_cmps
		  import Payment_conf
		  has Payment_comp
		  ContextParameters
		    coinInserted
		    creditCardProvided

XCOSEML Variability Related Models	**Configuration**
	VendingMachine_conf **of**
	Package VendingMachine
	  externalVP PaymentType
	    optional
	      variant Coin
	      variant CreditCard
		Method GetPayment:
		  #vp Type **ifSelected**(Coin)**#**
		    guard(coinInserted)
		    Payment_comp.GetCoin
		  #vp Type **ifSelected**
		  (CreditCard)**#**
		    guard(creditCardProvided)
		    Payment_comp.ConnectBank

	Configuration Payment_conf
	of Package Payment
	  externalVP Type
	    optional
	      variant Coin
	      variant CreditCard	

For the "product realization" part of "product engineering," suppose the end user chooses "Beverages" from "Container" and "Coin" from "Payment_type" from the feature model in Figure 4.2. The final feature model includes all features that the final application covers, presented in Figure 4.8.

The propagation starts from the root package "VendingMachine" and is propagated to configure the interfaces and compositions, which in turn provides the final product with its process model. The process model of the application stays same as in Figure 4.1. However, the flow of the sub-processes is changed, which is shown in Figures 4.9, 4.10, 4.11, and 4.12.

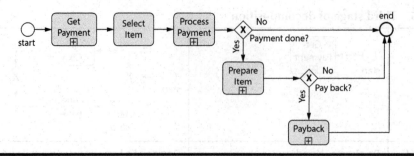

Figure 4.3   Finalized process model of vending machine.

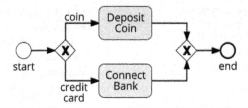

Figure 4.4   "Get Payment" sub-process.

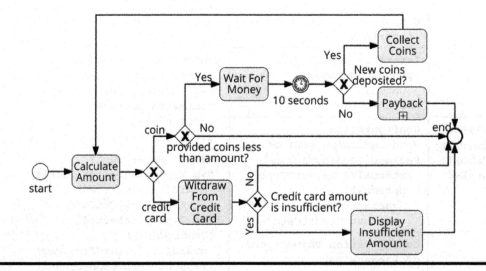

Figure 4.5   "Process Payment" sub-process.

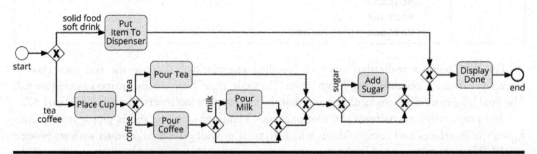

Figure 4.6   "Prepare Item" sub-process.

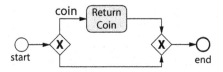

Figure 4.7 "Payback" sub-process.

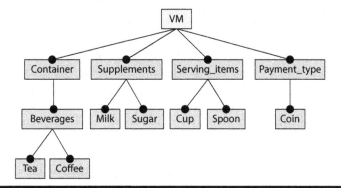

Figure 4.8 Configured feature model for the application.

Figure 4.9 "Get payment" sub-process for the application.

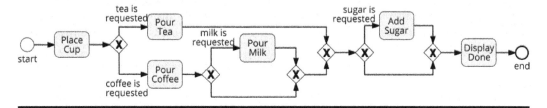

Figure 4.10 "Prepare Item" sub-process for the application.

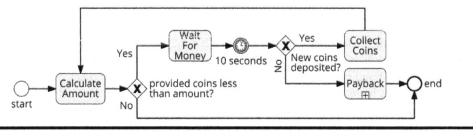

Figure 4.11 "Process Payment" sub-process for the application.

Figure 4.12 "Payback" sub-process for the application.

As "Coin" feature is selected, "Get Payment" includes only coin-related activities which are represented by the "Deposit Coin." Similarly, the activities related to the preparation of beverages are included in "Prepare Item" sub-process, represented in Figure 4.10.

The selection of "coin" feature also affects "Process Payment" and "Payback" sub-processes to include only coin related functionality, which is represented in Figures 4.11 and 4.12.

4.5 Discussion

Variability-guided decomposition may result in structural and procedural models that are very much related: there is usually a one-to-one relation in mapping the constructs between these models. A general difference is apparent here: flow connections are considered in processes and composition relations in structures.

It is assumed that the feature model–level variability should be the starting point and then reflected to the process model. Here, feature models are not claimed to be the indispensable source for variability. Any variability model can be used. Variability will be utilized starting from such a variability model and then following a hierarchical navigation. Based on the assessment that variability is the only high-level product-specific information that a set of models require, this work proposes a method to take variability as input and produce a system incorporating as much automation as possible. Also accepting variability as the highest abstraction-level information, Simon's (1996) findings support our approach as it supports a hierarchical decomposition.

This order also corresponds to the model-development order. As a result, the selected tasks in the process model will be implemented by corresponding components. Therefore, the next step after the definition of a process model is the configuration of the component-oriented/based solution with respect to the propagated variability constraints/specs. However, the feature model is not directly used in the configuration of the structural models, instead, the feature model is related to the variability model of XCOSEML which enables propagation of variability resolutions. Reasons for this choice are: XCOSEML works with its own variability model, and a feature model does not categorize its features as variation points and variants, however, these elements are important in the configuration of structural decomposition. Besides, from the end-user point of view, the contents of the feature model should be relevant and meaningful by representing available choices that the end user can select. In fact, the feature model constructed in the variability-guided decomposition process is developer-oriented which also includes functions of the system. Therefore, pruning of the feature model can be an additional step before it comes into use. The remaining features that are not selected by end users either are bound by the constraints or left to be chosen by developers of the system. In this way, variability resolution is ready to affect the structural decomposition.

Concerning variability propagation to process models, there have been various works, a detailed survey can be found in (La Rosa et al., 2017). Also, component models were addressed for variability. These separate efforts are consolidated in this research for a holistic modeling and development methodology by also devising further mechanisms for system composition. Here the important part is modeling variable parts of the process decomposition in a manageable way. A prospective approach is the definition of sub-processes in the presence of alternative or optional flows. The notion of sub-process also supports coherence, meaning that related flows are composed with each other. By following this approach, it can be a good practice to contemplate about the creation of a sub-process whenever the process model comes into a diversification point that serves different needs.

4.5.1 About the Architecture

The software architecture corresponding to the presented approach suggests three fundamental models, feature model, process model, and component model. The latter two will also be part of the run-time environment. If variability were not incorporated a similar architectural structure could be maintained. However, additional structures would be especially required for the development time. The existence of the feature model would be questioned without variability. The process and the set of components would need to be shaped up as a result of other models. Those models could include requirements and component based notations. Basically, the architecture would not include support for propagating variability over configuration interfaces that themselves would be excluded also. There would be bigger emphasis on a requirements model, guiding individually different component and process solutions.

4.5.2 Simultaneous Decomposition and Variability

The suggested process is based on two foundations. The first one is promoting top-down approaches in decomposition. Simon (1996) has suggested decomposition as the key tool for addressing complex engineering design. Moreover, this decomposition should be carried in a hierarchical manner, starting from top. Our approach accepts variability specifications as the highest-level information for software development. This is felt more in the product development activities than in the domain model development. Therefore, variability will be the reference point, guiding the development tasks that follow the abstraction levels after variability.

The other foundation is simultaneous decomposition. Since 1970s, the software industry has realized the problems with Waterfall-like processes: Models developed in isolation (usually in a predetermined sequence that does not allow revisiting the previous models much) will not render a consistent set of constituents to yield code. As a response, evolutionary and iterative processes were invented to allow for different models influencing each other. Suh (1998) specifically devised a method to develop a set of models simultaneously so that once one model is finalized, all are finalized that are in compliance to each other. Both Simon and Suh consent to the importance of building by decomposition as a starting point.

Various implementations of these ideas have been practiced. Here, variability-guided simultaneous decomposition is promoted, as a synthesis of these foundations in an effort to gain important efficiency increases in software development.

Similarly, variability in different models have been handled with different techniques. This should be continued, however, the expected mature domain suggests the constraints among different kinds and locations of variability being already defined. Also the necessary adaptations in different models should better be defined for all possible variants. One outcome of this approach would be a fast connection between the problem and the solution domains: Possible associations have already been set between the elements of these domains and product development will iron out the details in constraint propagation. Once the decisions are made about the variations, their repercussions in the requirements, design, or implementation will be followed by the constraint navigations. Also to mention, horizontal (peer-to-peer) constraints are also important. They should be dealt with as they would in any case. This research promotes top-down propagation as it is important in system definition. As the ripple effect of any constraint resolution, any resultant vertical or horizontal constraint requirements should be handled as intermediate steps. This may sometimes be painful.

Lastly, the decomposition is suggested to be carried top-down. In this perspective, the process is allocated in a higher-level of abstraction than the structure. However, not depending on a variation point being in any of these models, a top-down process should be carried out. This traversal, starting from the top, should advance until a variation point is found and process it and continue. Meaning, the higher-levels without variation points will not stop the process. Also the traversal will advance based on levels, not on models. Meaning, starting or ending at any model will not hamper the process.

4.5.3 Proactive/Reactive Variability

Here, a short discussion about what would happen if variability was omitted, is presented. In mature domains such as an established SPL infrastructure, variability is a pillar whose absence will nullify the SPL practice altogether. Still it is possible to contemplate a scenario where software development is carried out without the variability capability and tried to be applied after the case. First of all, variability considers a set of software products to be developed. Without it, the individual developments of a set of different products will be addressed albeit how related they may be. The result will materialize as a set of maintenance projects that take one product independent from the others, probably enduring difficulties due to the principle about the increased complexity when changes are applied late in the process. Here the changes will be applied after almost completion, hence very costly.

4.5.4 Disadvantages

One shortfall of the suggested approach is its dependence on advanced development environments, such as a well-established SPL infrastructure. Also, availability of additional tools in such an environment would be necessary. Since the idea is to increase the efficiency, this objective cannot be significantly achieved unless there are specific tools integrated to such an established environment. The existing stand-alone tools mentioned in this text have not been integrated to a full SPL infrastructure.

4.6 Conclusion

In this chapter, a variability-guided decomposition process defined that has been illustrated using a case study. Incorporating variability into system development eases management of change in requirements and adoption to change in a systematic way. It can be achieved proactively or reactively: constructing the system from the perspective of variability from scratch or reconstruct existing system with identification of variable parts respectively. The presented approach serves as guidance for the proactive attempt to variability. Decomposition of the system into smaller processes sheds light on structural decomposition along with variations. The hierarchical nature of process and structure enables propagation of variability specifications from upper levels to lower levels by establishing relations and constraints between them for variability resolution. In this way, variability binding is achieved in a systematic way by resolving variability in the upper levels and expecting configurations in the lower levels to reveal a complete system.

4.7 Lessons Learned and Future Work

There is an unresolved question that can define future work problems related to the presented approach. That is the question of how many isomorphism can be attainable in the various decomposition models for the modeling "domains" of the ADT. In software development, this question corresponds to the similarity between the requirements decomposition and the design decomposition. A ramification of this discussion would yield further efficiency in SPL approaches where the isomorphism between the feature model and the component decomposition would further automate the selection of components, once a product feature model is instantiated from the domain model. A research on ramifications for such isomorphism can be a good future work.

Actually, ADT offers design matrices and a method to evaluate them for the assessment of coupling: if functional requirements can map to design parameters in a one-to-one manner, the two models are uncoupled. However, this also implies a possible isomorphism—reducing the work for building the topology of the component network: Once the features are selected, so are the components and, further, their decomposition connections. What is still missing to convert this topology to an executable system is to incorporate a process model: define a set of connections for message sending and the ordering of the invocations for those messages. Yet, data needs to be saved and forwarded to be used as input and output parameters for the messages that stimulate methods. This is referred to as state management in the process modeling world.

ADT, allowing the coupling assessment through its "design matrices" would also allow two other coupling classifications for the less-preferred design choices. These correspond to one-to-many or many-to-many mappings between the functional requirements and design parameters. Usually the logical and physical parts of the decomposition in COSEML more or less correspond to requirements and design models. In the higher levels of a COSEML model, the diagram is suggested to preserve one-to-many relations from a parent node to its children.

COSEML suggests to start with a logical decomposition and at any level when the developers can associate a logical with a potential physical component, they stop the decomposition. Next, they link this logical module to the component. It is also possible to decompose components into smaller components. However, the goal is to reach a product practically and sooner; it is better to avoid composition or decomposition among the components. The related work suggests the two-level hierarchy (Togay et al., 2017) where a logical-level model is directly mapped to methods without a further structuring in the lower levels. That is reminiscent of the related SOA technologies consisting of an "orchestration" that is a process model and a set of web service method calls. However, it is possible to allow one-to-many as well as many-to-one relations from the logical level to the components: One logical module could correspond to more than one readily available component for its realization. An advanced COSEML engineer is supposed to decompose the logical level in an effort to convert this sub-section of the model to a one-to-one mapping alternative. On the other hand, the logical model could have been over decomposed where a component to be found in the industry could be implementing both of such requirements. Also if possible, the modification in the lower levels of the logical part is preferred for one-to-one mappings around such leaf-levels. However, the language does not impose any such restrictions.

References

Anton, A. I., McCracken, W. M., and Potts, C. 1994. Goal decomposition and scenario analysis in business process reengineering. In: Wijers G., Brinkkemper S., Wasserman T. (eds) Advanced Information Systems Engineering. CAiSE 1994. *Lecture Notes in Computer Science*, vol 811: 94-104. Springer, Berlin, Heidelberg.

Bass, L., Clements, P., and Kazman, R. 1998. *Software Architecture in Practice*. Addison-Wesley, Massachusetts.

Caetano, A., Silva, A. R., and Tribolet, J. 2010. Business Process Decomposition—An Approach Based on the Principle of Separation of Concerns, *Enterprise Modelling and Information Systems Architectures*, 5(1): 44-57.

Cetinkaya, A., Kaya, M. C., and Dogru, A. H. 2016. Enhancing XCOSEML with connector variability for component oriented development, In Proc SDPS 21st International Conference on Emerging Trends and Technologies in Designing Healthcare Systems, 120-125, Orlando, Florida, December 4-6.

Cetinkaya, A. 2017. Variable Connectors in Component Oriented Development. MSc Thesis, Middle East Techical University.

Dietz, J. L. G. 2006. The Deep Structure of Business Processes. *Communications of the ACM*, Vol. 49:59-64.

Dijkman, R., Vanderfeesten, I., and Reijers, H. A. 2016. Business process architectures: Overview, comparison and framework. *Enterprise Information Systems*, 10(2) 129-158, doi:10.1080/17517575.2014.928951.

Dogru, A. H., and Tanik M. M. 2003. A process model for component-oriented software engineering. *IEEE software*, 20(2), 34-41.

Dumas, M., La Rosa, M., Mendling, J., and Reijers, H.A. 2013. *Fundamentals of Business Process Management*, Springer, Berlin/Heidelberg.

FeatureIDE, 2018. http://www.featureide.com/ (accessed January 30, 2018).

Haugen, Ø., Wasowski, A., and Czarnecki, K. 2012. "CVL: common variability language." In SPLC, 266-267, Tokyo, Japan, Aug 26-30.

Huang, Y., Li, W., Liang, Z., Xue, Y., and Wang, X. 2018. Efficient business process consolidation: combining topic features with structure matching, *Soft Computing*, 22(2), 645-657.

Johannsen, F., and Leist, S. 2012. Wand and Weber's decomposition model in the context of business process modeling, *Business & Information Systems Engineering*, 54(5), 263-280.

Johannsen, F., Leist, S., and Tausch, R. 2014. Wand and Weber's good decomposition conditions for BPMN: An interpretation and differences to Event-Driven Process Chains, *Business Process Management Journal*, 20(5), 693-729, https://doi.org/10.1108/BPMJ-03-2013-0031.

Kang, K. C., Cohen, S. G., Hess, J. A., Novak, W. E., and Peterson, A. S. 1990. *Feature-oriented domain analysis (FODA) feasibility study*. No. CMU/SEI-90-TR-21. Carnegie-Mellon Univ Pittsburgh Pa Software Engineering Inst.

Kaya, M. C., Suloglu, S., and Dogru, A. H. 2014. Variability modeling in component oriented system engineering, Proc SDPS the 19th International Conference on Transformative Science and Engineering, Business and Social Innovation, 251-259, Kuching Sarawak, Malaysia, June15-19.

La Rosa, M., Wohed, P., J. Mendling, et al. 2011. Managing process model complexity via abstract syntax Modifications, *IEEE Transactions on Industrial Informatics*, 7(4), 614-629.

La Rosa, M., Dumas, M., Uba, R., and Dijkman R. 2013. Business process model merging: an approach to business process consolidation. *ACM Transactions on Software Engineering and Methodology (TOSEM)*, vol 22(2): 11:1-11:42.

La Rosa, M., Van Der Aalst, W. M. P., Dumas M., and Milani, F. P. 2017. Business process variability modeling: A survey, *ACM Computing Surveys*, 50(1):1-45.

Mendling, J., Reijers, H. A., and Cardoso, J. 2007. What makes process models understandable? In International Conference on Business Process Management, Lecture Notes in Computer Science, vol. 4714, pp. 48-63, Barcelona, Spain, Sept 10-15.

Mendling, J., Verbeek, H. M. W., van Dongen, B. F., van der Aalst, W. M. P., and Neumann, G. 2008. Detection and prediction of errors in EPCs of the SAP reference model, *Data & Knowledge Engineering*, 64(1), 312-329.

Milani, F., Dumas, M., and Matulevičius R. 2013. Decomposition driven consolidation of process models. In *International Conference on Advanced Information Systems Engineering*, 193–207, Essen, Germany, June 12-16.

Milani, F., Dumas, M., Matulevicius, R., Ahmed, N., and Kasela, S. 2016. Criteria and heuristics for business process model decomposition—Review and comparative evaluation, *Business & Information Systems Engineering*, 58(1), 7-17.

Miller, G. A. 1956. The magical number seven, plus or minus two: Some limits on our capacity for processing information, *Psychological Review*, 63(2), 81.

Muehlen M. Z., Wisnosky D., and Kindrick J. 2010. Primitives: design guidelines and architecture for BPMN models. In *21st Australasian Conference on Information Systems*, Brisbane, Australia, Dec 1-3.

Pohl, K., Bockle, G., and van der Linden F. 2005. *Software Product Line Engineering Foundations, Principles, and Techniques*, Springer-Verlag Berlin Heidelberg.

Pressman, R. S., and Maxim, B. R. 2015. *Software Engineering: A Practitioner's Approach*, 8th edition. McGraw-Hill Education. New York.

Reijers, H. A., Mendling, J., and Dijkman, R. M. 2011. Human and automatic modularizations of process models to enhance their comprehension, *Information Systems*, 36(5), 881-897.

Smirnov, S., Reijers, H. A., and Weske, M. 2011. A semantic approach for business process model abstraction, In *International Conference on Advanced Information Systems Engineering*, 497-511, London, June 20-24.

Suloglu S. 2013. Model-Driven Variability Management in Choreography Specification, PhD Thesis, Computer Engineering Department, Middle East Technical University (METU), Ankara, Turkey.

Retrieved from Signavio 2018. Signavio Process Manager, https://www.signavio.com/products/process-manager/, (accessed January 30, 2018).

Simon, H. A. 1996. *The sciences of the artificial*, 3rd edition. The MIT Press, Cambridge, MA.

Sinnema M., Deelstra S., Nijhuis J., and Bosch J. 2004. COVAMOF: A framework for modeling variability in software product families. In *International Conference on Software Product Lines*, 197–213, Boston, MA, Aug 30 – Sept 2.

Suh, N. P. 1998. Axiomatic design theory for systems. *Research in Engineering Design*, 10(4):189-209.

Togay, C. 2008. Systematic Component-Oriented Development with Axiomatic Design, PhD Thesis, Middle East Technical University, Ankara, Turkey.

Togay, C., Dogru, A. H., and Tanik, J. U. 2008. Systematic component-oriented development with axiomatic design. *Journal of Systems and Software* 81(11):1803-1815.

Togay, C., Tokdemir, G., and Dogru, A. H. 2017. Process decomposition using axiomatic design theory. In Proc SDPS the 22th International Conference on Emerging Trends and Technologies in Convergence Solutions, Birmingham, AL, USA, Nov 5-9.

Turetken, O., and Demirors, O. 2011. Plural: a decentralized business process modeling method. *Information Management* 48(6):235–247.

Wand, Y., and Weber, R. 1989. A model of systems decomposition. In DeGross, J. I., Henderson, J. C. and Konsynski, B. R. (Eds), *Proceedings 10th International Conference on Information Systems*, 41-51, Boston, MA.

ANALYZING AND EVALUATING

Chapter 5

Towards Self-securing Software Systems

Variability Spectrum

Mohamed Abdelrazek[a], John Grundy[b], and Amani Ibrahim[a]

[a]School of IT, Deakin University, Geelong, Australia
[b]Faculty of IT, Monash University, Melbourne, Australia

5.1 Introduction

What can go wrong when a software system is under a cyberattack? The system becomes malfunctional; this could happen in many ways—e.g. the system might become completely unavailable due to service disruption, systems could be compromised, or confidential data could be exfiltrated. Businesses economic conditions amplify the relentless challenge of staying ahead of security vulnerabilities in their computing systems and infrastructure [9,11,17]. Hence, the need to build smart, adaptive systems that are secure. *Self-securing*—also called self-protecting or self-defending—is the ability of the software system to identify security holes/bugs or detect current/potential attacks and automatically patch or stop to guarantee the availability, integrity and confidentiality aspects of the system and its data.

To enable self-securing systems, we need to: *(i)* package software security analysis and automated software security engineering in one ecosystem, and *(ii)* engineer systems to allow adaptability from the ground-up (architecture and design). Without adaptability, systems become hardwired and hard to respond to adaptation triggers including proactively self-secure [4,16]. Adaptiveness is achieved via engineering for variability points that allow for different system components—at different complexity levels from a class method to a system component—to be swapped in/out based on changes in the operational environment or customer needs and goals.

From a security point of view, variability is not always a good practice. From a security analysis perspective; it increases the potential of system vulnerabilities that might exist in these new modules, or in the connectors/interfaces between the modules [7,15]. From a security engineering perspective; variability is very useful, changes in user security requirements, risks, or new vulnerabilities detected can be mitigated/patched easily at either design-time (due to modularity nature of the system) as well as real-time adaptation [6,16].

In Software-as-a-Service (SaaS) applications—*e.g.* Salesforce.com—implementing a tenant-oriented security is a must. This is needed to enable the SaaS application to weave in security controls for different tenants depending on who is using the application/service—e.g. each tenant might need a different set of authentication/authorization controls. This adds a new dimension of SaaS application variability, which is SaaS application security variability [13,14]. Other quality-of-service attributes can add more variability aspects to the system such as reliability-specific modules and performance-critical modules that sacrifice resource efficiency for response time. This will eventually need to be managed through a SaaS variability management module.

In this short chapter, we present a proposal for the *self-securing software system* based on model-driven engineering using system-and-security description models for runtime configuration and weaving using an aspect-oriented programming and online security monitoring and analysis toolset. We also discuss how this model can be extended to SaaS applications where the same service/application needs to satisfy all tenants' security requirements.

5.2 Motivating Scenario

Imagine a software system—Galactic ERP, developed by the SwinSoft company, see Figure 5.1. GalacticERP is delivered as a SaaS application hosted on a cloud platform called Blue Cloud and uses external services delivered on Blue Cloud and another cloud provider called Green Cloud. Galactic ERP is currently used by three clients: Swin, Auck, and Super.

These three clients are operating in different domains, have different functional requirements, and have to comply to different security policies and requirements due to criticality

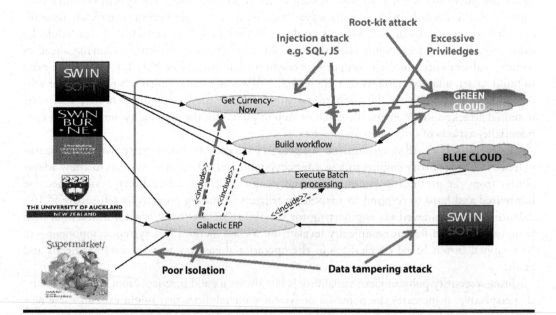

Figure 5.1   Example scenario of multi-tenant cloud application.

of their businesses. Furthermore, imagine that the below threats have come true and vulnerabilities have been detected:

- A root-kit attack on its infrastructure as a service, e.g. Green Cloud
- Injection attacks, from tainted requests to services, such as Get Currency or Build Workflow
- Poor isolation allowing compromise of one component to attack another e.g. between SwinSoft platform and GalacticERP
- Excessive privileges for one component allowing access to services of another e.g. between Green Cloud and Build Workflow

Each system vulnerability or cyberattack needs to be mitigated promptly to protect the underlying system. Currently, most systems require this to happen at design time—through major changes to the source code—with a patch and update of deployed services. This leaves systems vulnerable for a considerable period or requires them to be taken offline for fixing.

From example scenarios such as these, we have identified a set of key challenges in this domain:

- When we engineer cloud applications, we do not know what other applications and services will be deployed within the system, what hardware will be deployed on, what is the network underlying topology, etc.
- Stakeholder requirements change during deployment, especially for multi-tenant cloud apps, allowing for emergent requirements.
- New threats and vulnerabilities to attack are continually emerging and evolving.
- Design-time patching/re-deploying is a slow process that could leave a system vulnerable for a considerable period—even with the new DevOps practices, this still needs thorough testing.

Similarly, we have identified a set of key requirements to address these challenges, which include:

- Identify emergent threats—even as its environment changes.
- Identify mitigations to the threats, *i.e.* changes to the system configuration, code, deployment to mitigate the threat and protect it from attack.
- Self-adapt the application(s) using one (or more) mitigations while in use to counter the threat.

We describe several partial approaches to providing such a self-securing software solution in the following sections using runtime software variability-supporting approaches. We group these solutions as security analysis tools and capabilities including vulnerability analysis and security monitoring, and security engineering tools and capabilities including design time and runtime adaptations.

5.3 Static Vulnerability Detection

This work is a part of our larger "model-driven security engineering" platform body of work [4]. The idea is to develop semi-formal definition (signatures) of OWSAP and CAPEC databases of security vulnerabilities using a domain specific language; currently, this is done in Object

```
Public bool LogUser(string username, string password) {
    string query = "SELECT username FROM Users WHERE
UserID ='" username " ' AND Password = '" + password + "'";
```

(a)!Code vulnerable to SQL Injection attack.

```
if( Request.Cookies["Loggedin"] != true ) {
    if( !AuthenticateUser(Request.Params["username"],
                          Request.Params["password"] ) )
        throw new Exception("Invalid user");
}
DoAdministrativeTask();
```

(b) Code vulnerable to authentication bypass.

```
if( !AuthenticateUser( Request.Params["username"],
                       Request.Params["password"] ) )
    throw new Exception("Invalid user");
updateCustomerBalance(Request.QueryString["custID"], nBalance);
```

(c)!Code vulnerable to improper authorisation.

Figure 5.2   Examples of common attacks (© 2012 IEEE. Reprinted, with permission, from [2]).

Constraint Language (OCL) enriched with constructs from the traditional software architecture/ design/code concepts. Then we use these signatures to search for matches in code or in models associated with applications (e.g. configuration files and selection of application software). This approach can handle code vulnerability detection e.g. design and architecture vulnerability detection and several security "metrics" [2].

Figure 5.2 shows three different example code-level vulnerabilities: Figure 5.2(a) code that is vulnerable to SQL injection; Figure 5.2(b) code that is vulnerable to an authentication by-pass; and Figure 5.2 (c) code that is vulnerable to improper authorization threat. Figure 5.3 shows example semi-formal signatures written as OCL constraints. These signatures describe, using a model of the target software system, how such vulnerabilities in Figure 5.2 can be found in the code base using static analysis.

We have developed a toolset that can take source code, a signatures' database, and analyse the source code for code locations vulnerable to the specified attacks in the semi-formal signatures. Figure 5.4 shows the basic analysis process. We take a target program (left) and a set of signatures (right) and then search for matching code or model signatures in the target. This search is informed by the platform characteristics (top). We produce a set of vulnerabilities and their

Vul.	Vulnerability Signature
SQLI	Method.Contains(S : MethodCall	S.FnName = "ExecuteQuery" AND S.Arguments.Contains(X : IdentifierExpression	X.Contains(InputSource)))
XSS	Method.Contains(S : AssignmentStatement	S.RightPart.Contains(InputSource) AND S.LeftPart.Contains(OutputTarget))
Improper Authn.	Method.IsPublic == true AND Method.Contains(S : MethodCall	S.IsAuthenitcationFn == true AND S.Parent == IFEIseStmt AND S.Parent.Condition.Contains(InputSource))
Improper Authz.	Method.IsPublic == true AND Method.Contains(S : Expression	S.Contains (X: InputSource	X.IsSanitized == False OR X.IsAuthorized == False)

Figure 5.3   Example of formal vulnerability signatures (© 2012 IEEE. Reprinted, with permission, from [2]).

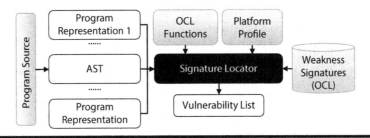

Figure 5.4 Vulnerability Analyzer (© 2012 IEEE. Reprinted, with permission, from [2]).

locations in the code base/model (bottom) as output. We have extended this approach to include design- and architecture-level model signatures, including configurations, architectural choices, and deployment platforms and associated application packages.

5.4 Dynamic Application Monitoring

To detect system vulnerabilities and threats, we need to implement dynamic analysis solutions, as well. One dynamic analysis approach is designed to better capture runtime metrics and analyse these for evidence of incorrect application behaviour or usage from a security perspective [3]. In an equivalent way to the static analysis discussed previously, we formalise a number of metrics and security constraints of interest—similar to vulnerability signatures—using OCL. Figure 5.5 illustrates some examples of such security-related metrics of interest [10,1]. Some of these metrics are architecture and design-related metrics. Others, are runtime metrics—e.g. how many requests have been authenticated, how many of these passed (valid) authentication check, mean time between failed authenticated request, etc. We chose these as examples of the kinds of metrics a security engineer would like to monitor in order to proactively judge the current security status of multi-tenant cloud applications[1,12].

We then process a deployed application's architecture and deployment model and code base to determine where to add "probes" to gather the required runtime monitoring data. Figure 5.6 provides an outline of this process. A set of services are "wrapped" to provide access to their runtime behaviour via a set of probes (top). A set of metrics specifications determine where these probes need to be injected into the application at runtime to monitor its behaviour (left). A probe generator takes the specifications, application model and configures and/or generates the probes (middle). The framework then captures the required runtime data, determines exceptions based on the metrics specifications, and then determines possible attack and vulnerability mitigations that can be actioned and reports these (right).

5.5 Runtime Vulnerability Mitigation

Finally, we must secure our vulnerable or under threat applications. Once we have found a vulnerability using one of the above techniques, we need to determine how to fix, mitigate or raise an alarm. We identify feasible modifications to the target application to address the vulnerability: these might be to inject code to fix an SQLI vulnerability, e.g. input sanitisation code; upgrade application software deployed with the services to ensure the latest version is being used with it; reconfigure service end points to apply more secure encryption, key management, auditing or

Metric	Signature
Information Disclosure	context Method inv InfoDisclosure: Let access : Request := self.Requests->last() in Let authorized : Response := self.**AuthorizationControl**.Responses-> select(R| R.IsValid = True AND access.UserID = R.UserID)->last() in IF (authorized) THEN true ENDIF
Chinese Wall	Let Subject := Classes->select(Name = 'Subj')->first() in Let Obj: Class := Classes->select(Name = 'Object')->first() Let mthdCall : Request := self.Requests->last() in Let mthdReturn: Response := self.Responses->last() in Let access : Request := self.Requests->last() in IF (access.RequestTime > mthdCall.RequestTime and access.RequestTime < mthdReturn.ResponseTime) THEN Not self.Conflictlist->exists(R| R = access.Target)
Restrict System Calls	Let SystemCalls : Request := Classes->select(Name = 'SystemHandler')->first().Requests()->last() in IF (SystemCalls <> null) THEN false ENDIF
Separation of Duties	Let xReq : Request:= Requests(Entity = 'MthdX') in Let yReq : Request:= >Requests(Entity = 'MthdY') in Let zReq : Request:= >Requests(Entity = 'MthdZ') in IF (xReq.UserID = yReq.UserID and xReq.Target = yReq.Target Or xReq.UserID = zReq.UserID and zReq.Target = zReq.Target Or yReq.UserID = zReq.UserID and xReq.Target = yReq.Target) THEN false ENDIF
Authenticated Requests	context System inv AuthenticatedRequests: self.AuthenticationControl.Requests->select()->count()/ self.Request->select()->count()
Authentic Requests	context System inv AuthenticRequests: self.AuthenticationControl.Response->select(R | R.IsValid = true)->count()/ self.AuthenticationControl.Request->select()->count()
Last(10) Authz. Reqs	context System inv Last10AuthzCtl: self.AuthorizationControl.Requests->select()->Last(10)
Top(10) admin Requests	context System inv Top10AuthnCtl: self.AuthenticationControl.Responses->select(R | R.UserID = 'Admin')->count()
Mean Time Between Unauthentic Request	context System inv MTBUnauthenticRequests: self.AuthenticationControl.Responses->select(R | R.IsValid = false)>differences('Measurementtime')-> sum() / self.AuthenticationControl.Responses->select(R | R.IsValid = false))->count()
Authenticated Requests Trend	context System inv Authenticated RequestsTrend: self.AuthenticatedRequests.Differences('AuthenticatedRequests')->sum() / self.AuthenticatedRequests-> count()
MTBUR Over Systems	context System inv MTBUROverSystems: self.MTBUnauthenticRequests->sum()/ self.MTBUnauthenticRequests->count()

Figure 5.5   Examples of security monitoring metrics formal signatures (© 2015 IEEE. Reprinted, with permission, from [1]).

other security services; make use of new, improved APIs, libraries and/or third party security solutions. Figure 5.7 shows examples of code updates to mitigate some of the code-level vulnerabilities illustrated earlier. In this example, we use an aspect-oriented toolset, "re-aspects," which describe code updates to make (add, remove, modify) using their own formal OCL signatures [3].

We then update the application to address the discovered vulnerability, security flaws or counter attack scenario. This may include making runtime code changes, making runtime configuration changes, redirecting requests to different third-party security solutions, or deploying different third-party security solutions. It may also in some cases mean restricting access to parts of the system that remain vulnerable, raising alarms, or worst-case scenario, taking a system or some services off-line. We validate that the originally identified vulnerability has been addressed using an appropriate testing framework e.g. by running attack scenarios on the vulnerable service, re-running vulnerability analysis on the updated code base, collecting new monitoring metrics etc.

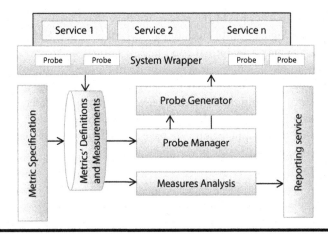

Figure 5.6 Runtime probe generation process (© 2015 IEEE. Reprinted, with permission, from [1]).

```
if( Request.Cookies["Loggedin"] != true ) {
    if( !AuthenticateUser(Request.Params["username"], Request.Params["password"]
                    ) );
        throw new Exception("Invalid user"); }
DoAdministration();
```

(a) Replacing authentication bypass vulnerable code

```
if( !AuthenticateUser( Request.Params["username"],
                    Request.Params["password"] ) )
throw new Exception("Invalid user"");
if( !AuthorizeUser( Thread.CurrentPrincipal,
        (new StakeFrame()).GetMethod().Name,
        (new StakeFrame()).GetMethod().GetParameters() ) )
    throw new Exception("User is not auhorized");
updateCustomerBalance(Request.QueryString["cID"], nBalance);
```

(b) Injecting code to fix improper authorization

```
bool updateCustomerBalance(string custID, decimal nBalance) {
    if(!AuthenitcateUser( username, password)) return false;
    if(!AuthorzUser(username, "updateCustBalance")) return false;
    LogTrx(username, dateTime.Now, "updateCustomerBalance");
    Customer customer = Customers.getCustomerByID(custID);
    customer.Balance = nBalance;
    Customers.SaveChanges();
    LogTrx(username, dateTime.Now, "updateCustBalance done");}
```

(c) Deleting obsolete security code

Figure 5.7 Code updates to mitigate vulnerabilities (© 2012 IEEE. Reprinted, with permission, from [3]).

Figure 5.8 (a) shows an example of the toolset we have developed to support these re-aspect runtime code update and Figure 5.8 (b) an example of the tool in use. (1) We first convert a target code base into Abstract Syntax Tree format (AST). (2,3) Formal signatures are constructed using a modelling tool, an example shown in the screen dump in Figure 5.8 (b). (4) We then use this set of re-aspect formal signatures to locate parts of the code base to modify. (5) We then determine the full impact analysis of making the code change, which may be at statement, method, class or caller (system-wide) levels, to determine the full set of code changes needed. (6) Finally we propagate changes to the code of the application. We have a .NET-based tool that is able to do this at runtime, modifying compiled CLI code of the application [3].

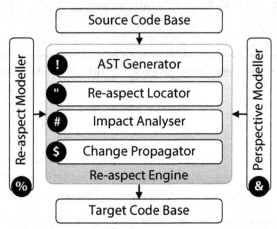

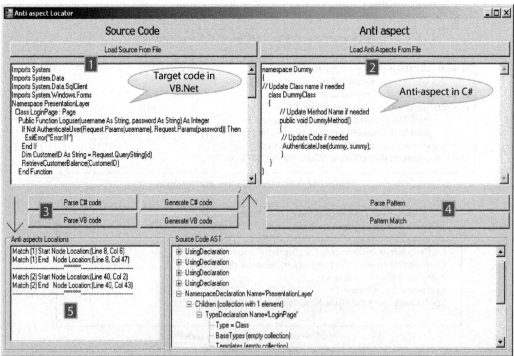

Figure 5.8 (a) code updating process; (b) SMART-code analysis and updating tool.

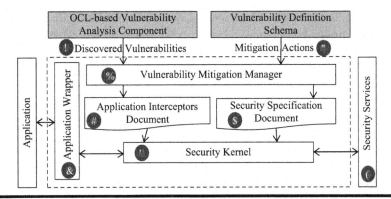

Figure 5.9 Runtime configuration updates to mitigate vulnerabilities (Reprinted by permission from Springer from [7] © 2012).

The other way to update an application is to use its built-in variability support features. Figure 5.9 shows our runtime reconfiguration framework, MDSE@R (Model-Driven Security Engineering @ Runtime), being used to modify configurations of a deployed system to mitigate discovered security flaws. (1) Vulnerabilities are discovered using static or dynamic analysis; (2) mitigation actions are identified to correct the discovered problem; (3, 4) a set of updates to our deployed application configuration are planned; (3, 5) a set of updates to our deployed application security-handling configurations are planned; (6, 7) these application and/or application security configuration updates are made; and (8) the reconfigured application makes use of appropriate security services as it is used.

5.6 Outstanding Challenges

To date we have built several proof-of-concept tools that implement the discussed aspects of variability-intensive self-securing software systems. We have found some interesting challenges as we try to adopt this approach. First, runtime updating of applications is inherently challenging. Running code/configured software applications must be modified with care to ensure no catastrophic failure occurs during update but also to handle partially completed processes in sensible ways. Even design-time modifications are very challenging when it comes to statement-level code modifications. Changes need to be thoroughly tested for both functionality as well as security defects.

Security analysis is a very complex task. It covers threat analysis, attack analysis, and vulnerability analysis. Many techniques have been developed to detect vulnerabilities using both static and/or dynamic analysis. The rule-based vulnerability analysis techniques are effective but not enough given that every vulnerability has many ways to be present and many ways to be detected. There is a trend to start using machine-learning techniques to try and detect security defects by learning what is best security practice and what is not.

Runtime security monitoring is always a necessary security capability recommended by most of the security standards. Although there is always a process to follow to develop security metrics, there is no recipe of a list of metrics to use, when to use these metrics, what to do when a metric is not within norm or what would be a norm. This gets even more complicated in a SaaS application where we have multiple tenants, each having their own security requirements and measures.

Comparing systems within the same domain across different security dimensions can be both deceiving and inaccurate. Vulnerability counts versus security metrics versus actual meaning for the vulnerability of the application varies greatly and the impact of the vulnerability on the application and its users can vary greatly. For example, a simple read of a highly confidential but improperly protected data element may be far more damaging than complex exploits or severe denial-of-service attacks. The scale of the system can also have major issues on the viability of some of our techniques where they are computationally expensive to run at runtime. This means some analyses are not real-time but can only detect vulnerabilities sometime after the fact. A minor change to the configuration of the application or its deployment environment, e.g. a new service or tenant, can have a major impact on the outcome of the security analysis. For example, a new tenant for the exact same multi-tenant cloud application may wish to make use of their own preferred security service, which introduces entirely new potential vulnerabilities or attack surfaces.

We have found runtime dynamic security analysis are still an emergent area with it being still unclear for many potential vulnerabilities what the "right" metrics are to capture, analyse, and determine threat. Security is a "cost," in that it introduces additional performance overhead and complexity to the application. Runtime adaptation to mitigate detected threats introduces further overheads and complexities into the system.

Finally, to implement runtime mitigation of emergent threats requires architectures, designs, code and deployments that support this in highly flexible ways and yet maintain high application performance and function. A highly variable system at runtime introduces its own risks in that compromise of the variability-supporting architecture components are their own major security vulnerabilities.

We are working on several areas to help us realise the concept of the self-securing software system. We are carrying out further formalisation of the OWSAP and CAPEC databases of security vulnerabilities to enable us to detect further security flaws and vulnerabilities in target applications. Similarly, we are working on further mitigations for these including formalised models of the mitigations that can be automatically actioned at runtime.

We are applying deep learning to static and dynamic vulnerability detection versus our current rule-based (DIGGER, SMART) approaches and are using statistical-based log analysis approaches to complement these. These will allow us to train vulnerability-detection models from examples and, we hope, to also allow us to update these trained models as new threats emerge. These approaches imply we have good training sets and vector-based models for our applications, both areas of our current work.

We believe that better supporting tenants to specify their security requirements is both essential for multi-tenant cloud applications, but very challenging [5]. We are working on improved tenant security modelling tools that will be used by the self-securing application to determine the actual security requirements to enforce. Finally, zero-day threat detection at the IaaS level is extremely hard, but we are working on how to apply this approach to IoT security analysis and mitigation. This is needed to self-secure new IoT-based systems.

5.7 Threats to Validity

To date we have built prototypes of our three approaches to static analysis, dynamic monitoring, and runtime adaptation frameworks [1,2,3]. We have evaluated these using a set of open-source cloud applications written in .NET. A major limitation of the static-checking approach is its use of rule-based signatures, requiring expert authoring, updating to new platforms and configurations, and fragility when applied to new code patterns and programming languages. We are exploring use of deep learning-based training of the vulnerability analyser where we train the learner on the vectorised code base, enabling us to retrain machine learning model on new examples and avoiding expert rule authoring [8]. Similarly our current dynamic monitoring approach may benefit from an approach of training a recongizer on examples of trace data rather than a rule based approach. Another limitation of the dynamic monitor is generating suitable probes and integrating probes into the runtime environment of existing cloud applications. Many are not architected to enable this level of monitoring nor runtime update of monitors. Overheads of monitoring are a classic problem of such approaches which we also need to address. Finally, our re-aspects framework has proven well suited to runtime adaptation of .NET platform multi-tenant cloud applications but such runtime update is fraught with challenges. Not least is handling update during processing of data by the target application, and efficient update is a further challenge. We are exploring use of micro-service-based architectures to allow more precise runtime modification of services and also because such architectures are designed for such small scale, runtime modifications.

5.8 Summary

We have described a concept of the "self-securing software system." This is a variability intensive system that *(i)* runs static and dynamic analysis techniques to determine if a running multi-tenant cloud application is vulnerable to attack; *(ii)* identifies potential runtime mitigations, or fix-ups to the application to counter the vulnerability; and *(iii)* carries out runtime code and/or configuration updates of the application to force these mitigations.

Acknowledgements

Support for this research from Swinburne University of Technology, Deakin University, Monash University and ARC Discovery projects DP170101932 and DP140102185 is gratefully acknowledged by the authors.

References

1. Abdelrazek, Mohamed Almorsy, John Grundy, and Amani S. Ibrahim. "Improving Tenants' Trust in SaaS Applications Using Dynamic Security Monitors." In *Proceedings of 2015 20th International Conference on Engineering of Complex Computer Systems (ICECCS)*, pp. 70-79. IEEE, 2015.
2. Almorsy, Mohamed, John Grundy, and Amani S. Ibrahim. "Supporting automated vulnerability analysis using formalized vulnerability signatures." In *Proceedings of the 27th IEEE/ACM International Conference on Automated Software Engineering (ASE), 2012*, pp. 100-109, IEEE, 2012.
3. Almorsy, Mohamed, John Grundy, and Amani S. Ibrahim. "Supporting automated software re-engineering using re-aspects." In *Proceedings of the 27th IEEE/ACM International Conference on Automated Software Engineering*, pp. 230-233. ACM, 2012.
4. Almorsy, Mohamed, John Grundy, and Amani S. Ibrahim. "Adaptable, model-driven security engineering for SaaS cloud-based applications." *Automated software engineering* 21, no. 2 (2014): 187-224.
5. Almorsy, Mohemed, John Grundy, and Amani S. Ibrahim. "Collaboration-based cloud computing security management framework." In Proceedings of *2011 IEEE International Conference on Cloud Computing (CLOUD)*, pp. 364-371. IEEE, 2011.

6. Almorsy, Mohamed, John Grundy, and Amani S. Ibrahim. "Smurf: Supporting multi-tenancy using re-aspects framework." In *Proceedings of 17th International Conference on Engineering of Complex Computer Systems (ICECCS)*, pp. 361-370. IEEE, 2012.
7. Almorsy, Mohamed, John Grundy, and Amani S. Ibrahim. "VAM-aaS: online cloud services security vulnerability analysis and mitigation-as-a-service." In *Proceedings of* 2012 *International Conference on Web Information Systems Engineering*, pp. 411-425. Springer, Berlin, Heidelberg, 2012.
8. Altekar, Gautam, Ilya Bagrak, Paul Burstein, and Andrew Schultz. "OPUS: Online Patches and Updates for Security." In *USENIX Security Symposium*, pp. 287-302. 2005.
9. Cetina, Carlos, Pau Giner, Joan Fons, and Vicente Pelechano. "Autonomic computing through reuse of variability models at runtime: The case of smart homes." *Computer* 42, no. 10 (2009).
10. Dam, Hoa Khanh, Truyen Tran, John Grundy, and Aditya Ghose. "DeepSoft: A vision for a deep model of software." In *Proceedings of the 2016 24th ACM SIGSOFT International Symposium on Foundations of Software Engineering*, pp. 944-947. ACM, 2016.
11. Devanbu, Premkumar T., and Stuart Stubblebine. "Software engineering for security: a roadmap." In *Proceedings of the Conference on the Future of Software Engineering*, pp. 227-239. ACM, 2000.
12. Hayden, Lance. *IT security metrics: A practical framework for measuring security & protecting data.* McGraw-Hill Education Group, 2010.
13. Krutz, Ronald L., and Russell Dean Vines. *Cloud security: A comprehensive guide to secure cloud computing.* Wiley Publishing, 2010.
14. Luna, Jesus, Hamza Ghani, Daniel Germanus, and Neeraj Suri. "A security metrics framework for the cloud." In *Proceedings of the 2011 International Conference on Security and Cryptography (SECRYPT)*, pp. 245-250. IEEE, 2011.
15. Mellado, Daniel, Eduardo Fernandez-Medina, and Mario Piattini. "Security requirements variability for software product lines." In *Proceedings of Third International Conference on Availability, Reliability and Security, 2008. ARES 08.*, pp. 1413-1420. IEEE, 2008.
16. Myllärniemi, Varvana, Mikko Raatikainen, and Tomi Männistö. "KumbangSec: An Approach for Modelling Functional and Security Variability in Software Architectures." In *VaMoS*, pp. 61-70. 2007.
17. Olaechea, Rafael, Steven Stewart, Krzysztof Czarnecki, and Derek Rayside. "Modelling and multi-objective optimization of quality attributes in variability-rich software." In *Proceedings of the Fourth International Workshop on Nonfunctional System Properties in Domain Specific Modeling Languages*, p. 2. ACM, 2012.
18. Petkac, Mike, and Lee Badger. "Security agility in response to intrusion detection." In *Computer Security Applications, 2000. ACSAC'00. 16th Annual Conference*, pp. 11-20. IEEE, 2000.
19. Zissis, Dimitrios, and Dimitrios Lekkas. "Addressing cloud computing security issues." *Future Generation computer systems* 28, no. 3 (2012): 583-592.

Chapter 6

The Emerging Role of the Ecosystems Architect

James Hedges and Andrei Furda

Science and Engineering Faculty, Information Systems, Services Science,
Queensland University of Technology, Brisbane, Australia

6.1 Introduction

Many of today's organisations have recognised the strategic value in participating in increasingly interconnected collaborative networks (Drews & Schirmer, 2014; Mäkinen & Dedehayir, 2012). Such organisations have begun to rely on ecosystems of partners, suppliers and customers to speed-up transformation, reduce innovation latency and to deliver greater value to their customers (Howard, 2016; Peyret et al., 2015).

In this chapter we explore the emerging role of the Ecosystems Architect and elaborate on how Enterprise Architects can equip themselves to become key enablers for organisations wishing to pursue digital Business Ecosystems strategies. We first elaborate a clear definition of the Business Ecosystem and Ecosystem Architecture, examine the emergence of this concept in the literature and explore the benefits, evolutionary stages, roles, and the transformation of organisations from the pipeline to the platform business model. We then elaborate on the strategy of Business Ecosystems, its implications and its risks. Available Business Ecosystem performance measures are discussed along with architectural and governance principles. We discuss motivations and give examples of organisations pursuing ecosystems strategies and clarify the role of the Ecosystems Architect by elaborating on the tasks that he or she performs. In understanding what an Ecosystems Architect does, the chapter assesses the available tools, techniques and methodologies and identifies constraints, limitations and gaps in the current research. Suggestions are made as to where and how the existing tools and methodologies could be developed to better support the role of the Ecosystems Architect.

The analysis and planning of the intertwinement between business and IT architecture—Enterprise Architecture—is well understood. However, the literature exposes a gap with respect to the way that Enterprise Architecture adequately handles the challenges of enterprises' interconnectedness (Drews & Schirmer, 2014). Enterprise Architects, experienced with conventional 'pipeline' businesses and conventional Architecture tools, often struggle with a lack of familiarity with complex platform business models (Parker, et al., 2016).

6.1.1 Origins of Business Ecosystems

The concept of the Business Ecosystems shares parallels with that of its biological counterpart. Biological Ecosystems consist of species that must interact and balance each other and an environment that supports the ecological needs of the species (Chang & West, 2006). Iansiti and Levien (2004) draw a closer comparison between the Business Ecosystem and the biological equivalent of a "community," given that it represents a large number of species with small population numbers that are divided into specialised niches (Stanley & Briscoe, 2010). According to Galateanu and Avasilcai (2013), there are four main types of ecosystems that are widely identified in the scientific world: biological, digital business, industrial and social ecosystems. This chapter focuses on digital Business Ecosystems and a related concept—the *platform*. While ecosystems focus on the economic interactions among participating organisations, the platform denotes the common technological basis on which stakeholders in the ecosystem rely (Schmid, 2013).

The early literature on Business Ecosystems first originates in the 1990s with Moore's (1993) seminal article introducing ecosystems and Baldwin and Clark's (1997) article on modularity. The literature timeline (Figure 6.1) pauses briefly and restarts in the mid-2000s with seminal articles on ecosystems strategy from Iansiti and Levien (2004) and Adner (2006). It is around this time that the ubiquitous social platforms of Facebook, Twitter and Instagram were introduced. The literature body then pauses until 2010 where topic of the platform ecosystem is first discussed. Platform tools and techniques start to be discussed in the literature from around 2012 onward. Figure 6.1 illustrates the timeline, linkages and influences between the seminal articles on ecosystems architecture from the late 1990s and early 2000s, and their relationships to current papers.

6.2 The Business Ecosystem and Ecosystems Architecture

A Business Ecosystem is a dynamic network of organisations, partners, suppliers and customers that collectively create and share value between participants (Drews & Schirmer, 2014; Iansiti & Levien, 2004; Mäkinen & Dedehayir, 2012).

At its highest level, architecture is a conceptual blueprint that describes the structure of a technology system (Tiwana, 2013). It describes the components within the system, their purpose and how they interact (Van Schewick, 2010). Ecosystems architecture also encompasses design principles and techniques such as *decomposition, modularity, interface design* and *openness*. Section 6.6 elaborates on these in detail.

Over the last ten years, we have seen a dramatic rise in organisations pursuing platform ecosystem strategies. Platform ecosystems are a sub-type of Business Ecosystems. They create value by leveraging technology and the massive scale of network effects between customers and producers. Platform architecture or a platform's "design" starts with the design of the *core interaction* that it enables between producers and customers (Van Alstyne, et al., 2016).

Ecosystems Architects approach ecosystems architecture from an end-to-end perspective that includes both the *customer* and *technology*. They consider not only the technical aspects of the ecosystem and the interactions on platforms, but also the relationships between ecosystems Strategy, Architecture and Governance.

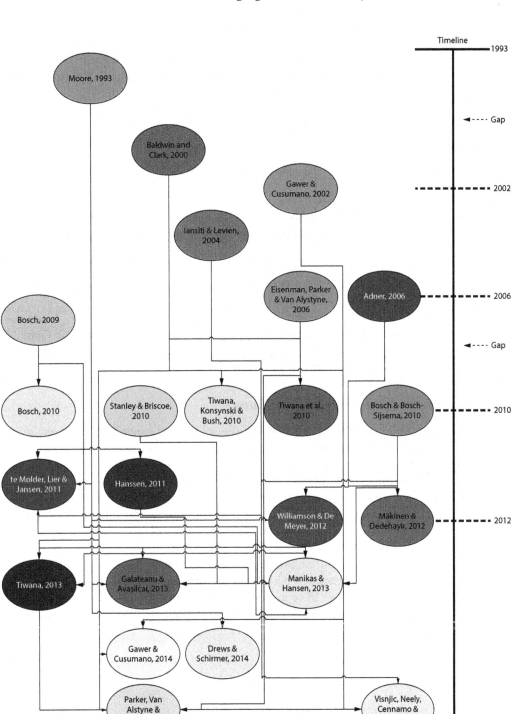

Figure 6.1 Ecosystem publications and influences.

Architecture, Strategy and Governance are three gears that must properly mesh in the evolutionary motor that drives a platform. Ecosystems Measures (Section 6.4) are essential tools for the Ecosystems Architect to know precisely how well the evolutionary motor is running so that tuning and re-design can occur when most appropriate.

6.2.1 Benefits of Ecosystems Strategies

There are many different reasons why organisations pursue an ecosystems strategy. Some examples of convincing arguments explaining the current trend are:

- Speed-up transformation and share the costs of innovation through collaboration with partners in the ecosystem (Eklund & Bosch, 2014; Iansiti & Levien, 2004).
- Unlock new sources of supply and demand by leveraging network effects (Van Alstyne, et al., 2016).
- Increase value of the core products and services to existing users (Bosch, 2009).
- Increase attractiveness for new users (Bosch, 2009).
- Increase customer "stickiness" and retention (Bosch, 2009).
- Decrease Total Cost of Ownership for commodity or standard platform functionality by sharing maintenance costs with ecosystem partners (Bosch, 2009, 2017; Gawer & Cusumano, 2014). This could, for example, include utilising OAuth access delegation from social media platforms like Facebook and Google.

6.2.2 Evolutionary Stages of Ecosystems

Moore (1993) first introduced the concept of the Business Ecosystem and defined four evolutionary stages (Figure 6.2): (1) Birth—the developing a value proposition around a new product or service; (2) Expansion—expand successful ideas to a wider market; (3) Leadership—encourage suppliers to work together to improve products or services; and (4) Self-Renewal—working with innovators to bring new products into the existing ecosystem.

The first evolutionary stage—the birth of a new product—begins with organisations working with customers and suppliers to develop a new value proposition around a product or innovation. Success at this stage is often defined by those organisations that best cooperate with partners to deliver the complete package of value for customers (Moore, 1993).

In the second stage, organisations reach a level of maturity that allows them to expand their successful ideas to a wider market. There are two conditions that are necessary for the second stage: *"A business concept that a large number of customers will value; and the potential to scale up to the concept to reach this broad market"* (Moore, 1993). During this stage, organisations can expand

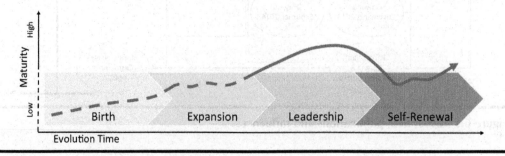

Figure 6.2 Evolutionary stages of an ecosystem.

significantly using a range of tactics. Walmart, for example, once it had established its chain of large regional discount stores, refocused on developing organisational capability that would allow it to scale effectively. This included building sophisticated hub-and-spoke distribution centres, a private satellite communications system to remotely monitor the stores' performance and the introduction of Electronic Data Interchange (EDI) with vendors (Wal-Mart Stores, 2017). Walmart was able to achieve massive growth in the late 1980s by leveraging the Business Ecosystems' strategy. Since the 'dot com' bubble in the 1990s, the platform-only business has allowed companies such as Amazon to achieve even bigger growth with far fewer employees.

In the third stage, organisations with a compelling product vision encourage other suppliers to continue to work together to improve the products being delivered to the customer (Moore, 1993; Moore, 1996). In this stage, organisations need to focus on standards, interfaces and modularity.

In the fourth stage, organisations consider working with other innovators to bring new ideas into the existing ecosystem (Moore, 1993). It is at this stage that organisations need to protect their ecosystem through high customer switching costs which could be monetary (such as the costs involved with breaking a mobile phone contract) or non-monetary (such as repurchasing your favourite smart phone apps on the Android ecosystems after migrating from Apple's iOS).

It is important to note that the third and fourth evolutionary stages have unique implications for the Ecosystems Architect. Depending on the organisation, it may make sense for the ecosystem to be as open as possible to encourage collaboration with other organisations. However, there is a danger in making the ecosystem too 'open' for other competitors to steal customers and offer a more compelling value proposition (Gawer & Cusumano, 2014; Mäkinen & Dedehayir, 2012). Ecosystems' openness and their relationship to architecture is discussed further in Section 6.5.

6.2.3 Roles within Ecosystems

A Business Ecosystem must be able to survive external shocks or disruptions from technological change or competing ecosystems (Iansiti & Levien, 2004). In a similar way to a Biological Ecosystem, a Business Ecosystem must increase diversity through the creation of valuable new functions or niches (Iansiti & Levien, 2004). For an organisation to be successful with its ecosystems strategy, it is important that it understands its function and role within the environment and that it tailors its strategy accordingly (Iansiti & Levien, 2004).

For the Ecosystems Architect, having the skills and tools to determine an organisation's place within an existing ecosystem is crucial. This is because organisations may wish to pursue very different strategies depending on their current and their ideal position within the environment. Iansiti and Levien (2004), in their model of an ecosystem, describe ecosystem participants as *niche providers, physical dominators, value dominators* and *keystones*.

Niche providers (also known as complementors) develop specialised capabilities and form the majority of most ecosystems.

Physical dominators[1] integrate horizontally and vertically to control the bulk of the innovation that occurs in the ecosystem, leaving little room for others to engage.

Value dominators,[2] on the other hand, have little direct control over an ecosystem. They create little, if any value, and instead extract as much as possible from the ecosystem. If left unchecked, this can ultimately lead to the ecosystem's collapse.

---

[1] An example of a physical dominator includes IBM during the pinnacle of mainframe computing.
[2] An example of a Value dominator includes the spectacular failure of Enron and its approach to exploit highly-fragmented energy markets.

The keystone organisation is arguably the most important member of an ecosystem (Iansiti & Levien, 2004). The keystone, the equivalent of the platform leader (Gawer & Cusumano, 2014) or ecosystems leader (Moore, 1993) plays a unique role in driving industry wide innovation and regulating the overall function and success of all ecosystems members (Gawer & Cusumano, 2014; Mäkinen & Dedehayir, 2012). The primary way keystone organisations create value for other members of the ecosystem is through creating and governing a platform (Iansiti & Levien, 2004). Keystones leverage the power platforms to allow the clear majority of value creation to be performed by others within the ecosystem (Iansiti & Levien, 2004).

6.2.4 From Pipeline to Platform Business Models

The emergence of platforms has allowed major industry segments to be conquered in a matter of months with none of the traditional resources required for survival or dominance (Van Alstyne, et al., 2016). Airbnb, Uber, Amazon, eBay and Alibaba are now all household names, synonymous for their disruptive effect on traditional industries and their stellar growth rates. Traditional pipeline organisations are taking notice.

Tiwana (2013) argues that the recent shift toward platform ecosystem business models is driven primarily by five factors: (1) Deepening specialisation within industries; (2) "Packetisation" of products, services and business processes; (3) Automation of routine business activities by software; (4) The emergence of the 'Internet of Things'; and (5) Ubiquitous fast, cheap and reliable internet connectivity.

A *platform* is a new business model that relies on a common technological platform to connect people, organisations, and resources in a Business Ecosystem where vast amounts of value can be generated and exchanged (Berger et al., 2014; Parker, et al., 2016). The term platform has become ever-present and appears in many fields. Gawer and Cusumano (2014) suggest that there are two predominate forms of platforms: internal or 'company-specific' platforms, and external industry-wide platforms. This chapter draws a clear distinction between the internal IT platforms that organisations use for their own product development and the external platforms that facilitate interactions between two or more groups. While internal platforms allow their owners to achieve gains by re-using or re-deploying assets across software product lines developed within the organisation, external platforms or 'platform ecosystems' facilitate the generation of complementary innovations by tapping into the diverse capabilities of a network of external developers (Eklund & Bosch, 2014; Gawer & Cusumano, 2014).

Platform ecosystems leverage the massive potential power of network effects to generate product innovations and value using resources that they do not control (Gawer & Cusumano, 2014; Van Alstyne, et al., 2016). As defined by Eisenmann, Parker and Van Alstyne (2006), a platform must have at least two sides: a buyer and a seller. A platform must also be governed by an individual or an organisation typically referred to as a keystone, a platform leader or a platform owner. The platform leader's goal in governing an ecosystem is to shape and influence, and to create value while avoiding any direct command or control (Williamson & Meyer, 2012).

Platform ecosystems are different from traditional pipeline businesses that typically create value through linear processes with producers at one end and consumers at the other (Parker, et al., 2016). In a platform ecosystem, the notion of only consuming value at the end of the line is replaced with a complex web of connections that allow value to be created, changed, exchanged and consumed in a variety of diverse ways and locations.

Parker, et al. (2016) suggest that there are four main reasons why platform businesses are superior to pipeline businesses: (1) Platforms can scale more efficiently by eliminating gate keepers;

(2) Platforms can unlock new sources of value and supply; (3) Platforms rely on data-based tools to inform community feedback loops; and (4) Platforms shift their focus from internal to external, relying on people, resources and functions outside the organisation to compliment those that exist inside a traditional pipeline business.

While the literature suggests several advantages of platform ecosystems, it is important for the Ecosystems Architect to be aware that the platform business model, by itself does not guarantee success. Almost all successful platforms began as standalone products or services that were extremely valuable to end users (Tiwana, 2013). EBay, Google, Facebook, Apple iOS, Salesforce and Dropbox are all examples of standalone products that first achieved wide adoption and popularity with consumers before a second side—app developers—was added (Tiwana, 2013).

For the Ecosystem Architect, it is essential to be familiar with the concept of the Business Ecosystem and the fundamental differences between platform and pipeline business models. Being able to pinpoint an organisation's current and desired position within its environment and to navigate the journey toward an ecosystem business model is the Ecosystems Architect's unique capability.

6.2.5 Variability in Software Ecosystems

Software ecosystems have generated significant attention due to their economic, strategic and technical advantages (Berger, et al., 2014). A software ecosystem is a set of software solutions that facilitate the interactions and transactions between actors in the associated Business Ecosystem and between the organisations that provide these solutions (Bosch, 2009). As opposed to the traditional practice of software product line engineering that aims to promote reuse and avoid variability without a clear advantage, software ecosystems encourage variability and focus on the reuse of the assets from a network of organisations and third-party contributors (Berger, 2012; Berger, et al., 2014; Eklund & Bosch, 2014; Schmid, 2013). While there has been significant research into variability mechanisms in software product lines, their role in supporting software ecosystems has not been extensively addressed (Jansen, Finkelstein, & Brinkkemper, 2009).

There are several reasons why an organisation may benefit from moving from software product lines towards a software ecosystem. First, an organisation may decide that the amount of functionality required by their customers is more than what can feasibly be built within a reasonable amount of time and investment budget (Bosch, 2009). Second, customers' demand for mass customisation requires significant investment for flexible and variable software applications, particularly in the web and mobile domains (Bosch, 2009). Customers now expect a significant degree of personalisation through being able to compose unique configurations of software assets that meet their specific needs and desires. By extending an internally developed software product line (including the platform) to external developers, it provides an effective mechanism to facilitate mass customisation (Bosch, 2009).

Software ecosystems such as Android and iOS successfully achieve high degree of customisation freedom for the intended users of the systems using *variability mechanisms* (Berger, et al., 2014). A variability mechanism is an implementation technique that delays the design decisions in order to flexibility adapt software to user requirements at a later stage such as build, start-up or runtime (Berger, et al., 2014). The Linux kernel and Android mobile platforms are excellent examples of two large, successful software ecosystems that implement variability using two different mechanisms (Berger, et al., 2014). The Linux kernel implements variability in the source code by conditionally compiling the desired functionality. The Android application platform uses a service-oriented architecture to encourage variability by allowing users to select, install and customise extensions (apps) to their own system (Berger, et al., 2014).

Software ecosystems can be differentiated into two types based on platform ownership and control: Vertical ecosystems and Horizontal ecosystems (Schmid, 2013). Vertical ecosystems consist of a single or small group of partners where one partner will build upon the work of another (e.g. Microsoft Windows) (Schmid, 2013). Horizontal ecosystems are created by combining software assets from participating organisations. Variability is highly important in both types of software ecosystems (Schmid, 2013).

6.3 Business Ecosystems as a Strategy

Organisations benefit from being part of a Business Ecosystem because cooperation has the potential to create value and opportunities that no single company could have reasonably created alone (Bosch, 2009; Mäkinen & Dedehayir, 2012). However, many ecosystems ventures will often fail to meet expectations unless every component in a family of complementary innovations also succeeds (Adner, 2006). Failure in an ecosystems strategy can be the result of technical failures or through difficulty in coordinating the innovations across the system (Adner, 2006). When planning to compete in a business or innovation ecosystem, the Ecosystems Architect must expect and plan for delays, compromises and setbacks.

There are two critical factors that have important strategic implications for the success of ecosystems strategies: investments and timing. The optimal amount of resources needs to be invested in both the firm's own innovation but also in the partners and complementary firms that reside outside the firm (Adner, 2006). The second factor is the timing of innovations. The firm must be aware of developing their innovation too far in advance of component and complementary technologies (Adner, 2006; Mäkinen & Dedehayir, 2012). Getting to market ahead of competitors is only of value if your partners are there, ready to support you (Adner, 2006).

In the formulation of an ecosystems strategy, Adner (2006) proposes an iterative approach that is designed to react to the many interconnected players and components of an ecosystem. Within this approach, Ecosystems Architects can work with business leaders and executives to understand their vision of what market to enter and with what offering, and then assist them on setting realistic performance expectations. Once the plan has been developed, the next step is to assess the risks associated with that plan and then modify performance expectations accordingly.

There are three types of risk that need to be considered when assessing an innovation strategy: *initiative, interdependence* and *integration risk*. Initiative risk refers to the feasibility of the innovation project and its success potential (Mäkinen & Dedehayir, 2012). For example, evaluating the competition, the relative benefits to customers, supply chain and the quality of the project team (Adner, 2006). Interdependence risk refers to the potential for success of the development, completion and deployment of all other components of the system. For example, Apple delayed the release of iTunes to allow digital rights management and online distribution to mature and become profitable (Van Alstyne, et al., 2016).

Integration risk refers to the likelihood of a given innovation being successfully integrated into down-stream sub-systems (Mäkinen & Dedehayir, 2012). Adner (2006) describes the example of Michelin's development of the run-flat tyre and the decade-long delay for it to be successfully integrated into cars, dealers and garages.

After the formulation of an ecosystem's strategy, we suggest that the Ecosystems Architect follows the risk assessment process to "acid test"[3] the strategy prior to execution. After performing

---

[3] The process of performing the process against the three categories of risk (e.g. initiative risk, interdependence risk, integration risk). In this context, an acid test is used to test the success or value of the proposed strategy.

a risk assessment, the resulting insights may lead organisations to shift funding and focus away from their own innovation to focus on that of a partner. They may also choose to alter their target market, lobby government and regulatory bodies, or delicately pursue horizontal or vertical integration within the ecosystem without removing all the opportunity and incentives for others to innovate (Gawer & Cusumano, 2014; Iansiti & Levien, 2004; Mäkinen & Dedehayir, 2012).

While it is important for all members of an ecosystem to properly assess their strategies, there are specific strategic considerations that relate more to particular members of an ecosystem (Mäkinen & Dedehayir, 2012). Platform leaders or keystone organisations (Section 6.2.3) face the challenges of preserving the compatibility of the platform through emerging technological innovations and the changing strategies of members, preserving backward compatibility of the platform and maintaining platform leadership within the ecosystem (Gawer & Cusumano, 2014; Mäkinen & Dedehayir, 2012).

Platform leaders can meet these challenges by influencing the direction of innovation in complementary products from third parties (Gawer & Cusumano, 2014). When done well, platform leaders can leverage the momentum gained from network effects between the platform and its complementary products to impose a barrier between potential competition (Gawer & Cusumano, 2014).

Niche providers (Section 6.2.3), also known as complementors, are able to leverage complementary resources such as platform extensions from other niche providers to expand the ecosystem (Angeren, 2013; Iansiti & Levien, 2004). It is vital for complementors within an ecosystem to invest resources in developing products that match the most viable platform (Mäkinen & Dedehayir, 2012). For example, mobile application developers should choose to target those smart mobile-phone platforms that are considered the most viable. A complementor may perform this assessment by considering the degree to which platform leaders share their vision and rally around ecosystem complementors, the level of openness of the interfaces and connectors made available, and the amount of sustained long-term investment the platform leader is making to ensure industry coordination (Gawer & Cusumano, 2014; Mäkinen & Dedehayir, 2012).

When competing in a Business Ecosystem, it is crucial to expect delays, compromises and setbacks, which are to a large degree outside the company's control. The Ecosystems Architect is in a unique position to work with Business Managers, Business Architects and Strategists to clarify product vision, assess ecosystem risk factors and know precisely which strategic considerations are relevant for the organisation. By following this approach, it is possible to establish more realistic expectations, develop a more refined set of contingencies and arrive at a more robust strategy (Adner, 2006).

One of the key distinctions that we make when discussing the ecosystem strategy is the differentiation between internal IT platforms used by organisations and "true" digital business platforms that support two-sided markets and facilitate interactions between customers and producers. We found that it is in the strategic business aspects of ecosystems and platforms where the Ecosystems Architect can deliver the most value. Enterprise Architects, Systems Engineers and Software Developers are typically well equipped to design and develop internal IT platforms.

Ecosystems Architects need to collaborate heavily with Business Managers, Product Managers, Strategists and Business Architects to clarify and refine the overall business strategy. We also found a significant link between the ecosystems' strategy adopted by an organisation and the ecosystems' architecture and its governance mechanisms. Consequently, it is essential that the Ecosystems Architect can identify these relationships and ensure that all three aspects complement and support each other. For example, a heavily decoupled platform will also require a decentralised approach to ecosystems governance.

6.4 Ecosystem Measures

Being able to correctly measure the performance and evolution of an ecosystem is an aspect of the Ecosystems Architect role that is as important as strategy development, technical systems architecture, interaction design and ecosystems governance.

Ecosystems measures are important tools for the Ecosystems Architect to identify the health and performance of an ecosystem. The Ecosystems Architect must be sensitive to any changes in the health of the ecosystem so that the ecosystem can continue to create value and opportunities for those who depend on it. It is also important for the Ecosystems Architect to be aware of conventional metrics that are suitable in the context of the pipeline businesses and those that are more appropriate for platform business models.

A wide range of metrics are available to Ecosystems Architects. The metrics vary between the specific growth stage of the ecosystem, the particular industry, the objectives of platform owners and characteristics of their users (Parker, et al., 2016). Tracking multiple metrics can be costly and time-consuming (Tiwana, 2013). For the Ecosystems Architect, it is critical to know which metrics to apply, when to apply them and which metrics to ignore.

Enterprise Architects, Executive Mangers and Business Strategists at conventional pipeline businesses are relatively familiar with typical metrics such as cash flow, operating income, inventory turnover, gross margin, overhead and return on investment. Parker, et al. (2016) note that conventional pipeline metrics are designed to gauge the efficiency of the value creation flowing through the pipeline. However, when applied to platform ecosystems, these conventional metrics are no longer effective (Parker, et al., 2016). Value creation on a platform is driven primarily through network effects and the positive interactions among users (Parker, et al., 2016).

Iansiti and Levien (2004) describe a set of measures for the health of an ecosystem that fit somewhere between conventional pipeline business metrics and those of a platform. The first measure of success defined by Iansiti and Levien (2004) is *Productivity*. Productivity is the network's ability to transform 'raw materials' such as technology innovation into new products or lower costs. Productivity is measured in terms of the conventional pipeline metric—Return on Investment (ROI). While some examples of sharply-declining ROI are provided for Internet companies leading up the 'dot com' crash of the early 2000s, it is unclear whether ROI is a successful measure in the context of the platform.

Measures of ecosystem health defined by Iansiti and Levien (2004) include *robustness* and *niche creation*. Robustness is the ecosystem's ability to survive unforeseen shocks and disruption. It is measured through the rate of survival of ecosystem members. Niche creation is the extent to which new 'niche' products and businesses are created within the ecosystem that apply emerging technologies. Niche creation as a measure of ecosystem health can also be used as a measure of the level of variability within an ecosystem (Section 6.2.5). That is, the extent to which niche assets developed by one organisation can be built-upon or combined by other organisations to deliver value.

The best measures of platform ecosystem health focus on the positive network effects of the platform and the activities that drive them (Parker, et al., 2016). Specifically, platform metrics must measure "the rate of interaction success and the factors that contribute to it" (Parker, et al., 2016, p. 185). The greater the rate of positive interactions on the platform, the more users will be drawn to the platform (Van Alstyne, et al., 2016). Through engaging in activities and interactions, new users create value for all existing users on the platform. Conversely, the rate of interaction failure is also an important concept given that negative feedback loops can significantly weaken a platform (Van Alstyne, et al., 2016). For example, passengers using the Lyft ride-sharing platform who are regularly unable to find a driver will too often stop using Lyft, leading to higher driver downtimes and drivers leaving the platform (Van Alstyne, et al., 2016). For the Ecosystems Architect, defining what constitutes interaction success throughout the various stages of the platform is an important task.

A broad range of metrics measure the performance of an ecosystem throughout its lifecycle. Tiwana (2013) defines a series of nine metrics that relate to the evolution of software platforms and reflect the reality of the business from the platform owner's perspective. Tiwana (2013) defines metrics for platform evolution including *resilience, scalability* and *composability* in the short-term; *stickiness, platform synergy* and *plasticity* in the medium term; and *envelopment, durability* and *mutation* in the long-term.

Parker, et al. (2016) describe a related set of eight metrics that are informed by the work of Eric Reis (2011), pioneer of the Lean Start-up Movement, and by the work of Amit Tiwana (2013) on software platforms. These metrics focus on interaction success and reflect the reality of the business from the users' perspective. They track similar evolutionary stages of a platform. These include *liquidity, matching quality* and *trust* during the start-up phase; *relative size of portions of the user base, lifetime value of producers/consumers* and *sales conversion rate* during the growth phase; and metrics that can drive innovation, and identify strategic threats from competitors during the maturity phase (Parker, et al., 2016).

The set of metrics defined by Tiwana (2013) reflect the reality of the business as perceived by the platform owner. On the other hand, the set of metrics defined by Parker, et al. (2016) reflect the reality of the business as perceived by the user. It is important for the Ecosystems Architect to consider both perspectives. For this reason, we have assembled in Table 6.1 a consolidated set of metrics that can be utilised by the Ecosystems Architect to track the evolutionary performance of an ecosystem. The metrics are general in nature so that they can be applied to various types of platforms. They have also been developed to have broad meaning to business stakeholders and are not solely limited in meaning to technical roles in Enterprise Architecture or Software Development.

Table 6.1 assembles a core set of metrics or "tools" that are readily deployable for most platforms and can be used for measuring ecosystem health and performance. Whichever metrics are agreed upon by the organisation, they must have relevance not just for Ecosystems Architects, but also for the roles with whom they will most regularly interact such as Business Strategists, Business Managers and Business Executives. After having compared the leading metrics for tracking platform ecosystem performance, we propose a consolidated list, readily deployable by the Ecosystems Architect, that meets the following requirements:

- Applicable to both the systems perspective of the ecosystem and users' perspective of the ecosystem;
- Generalisable to all platform ecosystems rather than specific variants such as software ecosystems;
- Meaningful for Business Managers, Business Strategists, Product Managers and Executives; and
- Meaningful for Enterprise Architects.

Our consolidated list of platform metrics (Table 6.1) is intended to act as a "toolbox" of metrics that Ecosystems Architects can apply to most platforms and in most situations. However, it is by no means an exhaustive list. For the Ecosystems Architect, there are many other examples of scenario-specific metrics discussed in the literature.

In the context of Software Ecosystems, some measures listed in Table 6.1 are directly affected by the degree of variability of the ecosystem. For example, the resilience measure is a direct result of variation points that manage partial failures in a software ecosystem. In a similar way, the plasticity measure is a result of existing variation points managing unforeseen changes and new features that were not part of the software requirements in the design stage.

Table 6.1   Ecosystems core measures

Metric	Definition and measurable proxy	References
Short-Term/Start-up Phase		
Liquidity	Liquidity is the capacity of a platform to successfully match consumers and producers within a reasonable time period. *Percentage of listings that lead to interactions within a given time period.*	Parker, Van Alstyne, and Choudary (2016)
Matching Quality	Matching quality is the platform's capacity to provide users with exactly what they are looking for as quickly as possible. *Percentage of searches that lead to interactions (Sales Conversion Rate).*	Parker, et al. (2016)
Trust	The degree to which users of a platform feel comfortable with the level of risk associated with interacting on it. *Reputation of a user as represented by the interactions of all other users that have interacted with it and their associated ratings.*	Isherwood and Coetzee (2011); Parker, et al. (2016)
Resilience	The capacity of an ecosystem to function acceptably even in the event of a failure inside or outside the ecosystem. *Recovery time of a platform or app after a failure outside it.*	Tiwana (2013)
Scalability	The capacity of an ecosystem to support larger (or smaller) numbers of users, apps or developers while maintaining performance and function without a corresponding increase in technical complexity. *Change in latency. Platform responsiveness. Net revenue per users or apps.*	De Weck, Roos, and Magee (2011); Tiwana (2013)
Composability	The degree to which changes can be made to a platform subsystem without breaking other interdependent subsystems, both inside and outside the ecosystem. Composability is also a useful measure for the ease at which the platform is able to support feature variability throughout. *Integration effort (man-hours) per number of internal changes.*	Tiwana (2013) and Schmid (2013)
Medium-Term/Growth Phase		
Relative size of portions of user base	The relative size of portions of the user base relates to a platform's ability to balance both sides of its market. *Producer-to-consumer ratio.*	Parker, et al. (2016)
Lifetime value of producers/consumers	Lifetime value is a measure of the revenue provided by repeat producers without the platform owner incurring any additional acquisition costs. Producer-side: *Expenses incurred by the platform in attracting and retaining producers.* Consumer-side: *Frequency of consumption, searches, rate of conversion to sale.*	Glady, Baesens, and Croux (2009); Parker, et al. (2016)

Table 6.1 (*Continued*)

Metric	Definition and measurable proxy	References
Stickiness	Stickiness is a measure of how much time a platform's users (e.g. end-users, developers) spend interacting with it. *Hours/Sessions Used over time. Change in API-calls per app over time.*	Tiwana (2013)
Plasticity	Plasticity reflects a platform's capacity to morph to meet new needs and possibilities (innovations) that were not available or possible at the time of its creation. *Major features added to a platform averaged per major release over its lifetime.*	De Weck, et al. (2011); Tiwana (2013)
Long-Term/Maturity Phase		
Envelopment	Envelopment is a mechanism whereby platform expands its core to provide new, innovative functionality offered by a different solution (such as an app or competing platform) that is also used by a large percentage of its own users. *Percentage of new adopters that actively use the enveloped functionality after an envelopment move is completed.*	Tiwana (2013); Van Alstyne, Parker, and Choudary (2016)
Durability	Durability is long-term metric for how well a platform or an app adapted to improve its fitness in a changing competitive environment and avoided strategic threats. *The change in initial adopters who remain active over an increasing timespan.*	Tiwana (2013); Parker, et al. (2016)

It is also necessary to identify potential limitations in our consolidated list of metrics. During the Growth phase of ecosystem development, Parker, et al. (2016) refer to the need to use metrics that identify strategic threats. We have proposed a measure of a platform's durability that is indirectly related to the platform's ability to avoid strategic threats. However, it is not a direct measure of a platform's strategic threats, and for this reason, we suggest that other measures may prove more effective.

6.5 Architectural Principles of Ecosystems

When designing a successful platform architecture, we suggest that the Ecosystems Architect considers Tiwana's (2013) four principles:

1. Simple: at its highest level of abstraction, the platform must be simple to understand.
2. Resilient: failures in isolated applications or components should not cause the entire ecosystem to malfunction.
3. Maintainable: it must be cost-effective to make changes within the platform without 'breaking' the applications that depend on it. This can be achieved through modular design, partitioning sub-system components and linking them using standardised interfaces.
4. Evolvable: it must have the capacity to do things in the future that were never originally designed. In other words, variability is one of the main principles of Ecosystems.

These four principles for platform success are broadly encapsulated by the following three perspectives: decomposition, modularity and design rules.

6.5.1 Decomposition

Decomposition is a platform's ability to break down form and function into its smallest components (Tiwana, Konsynski, & Bush, 2010). By decomposing a platform architecture, it is possible to minimise dependencies among evolving components of the ecosystem, supporting change and variability (Tiwana, 2013). However, Bosch and Bosch-Sijtsema (2010) note that decomposition often breaks down due to too many unnecessary dependencies between components and the delivery teams. As the number of dependencies grows, so does the overall effort required to manage the development – further reducing productivity (Bosch & Bosch-Sijtsema, 2010).

Reducing the overall number of "tight dependencies" through sufficient decoupling is an approach that can avoid the ripple effects of one team's delays spreading throughout the development effort (Bosch & Bosch-Sijtsema, 2010). For example, Application Programming Interfaces (APIs) must contain just the right amount of detail so that they do not expose the internal design of the component. APIs should also not be too detailed in order to avoid that every application scenario change requires an equivalent change in the API (Bosch & Bosch-Sijtsema, 2010). Techniques that contribute in part to balancing the right level of detail include *platform decoupling* and *interface standardisation*.

6.5.2 Modularity

To deliver a product or service to market quickly, an integral approach to design is often chosen. However, to be successful in the long term, a platform must be designed using a maintainable, modular approach (Cusumano & Gawer, 2002; Parker, et al., 2016; Tiwana, 2013).

Baldwin and Clark (1997, p. 86) provide the following definition for modularity:

> *Modularity is a strategy for organizing complex products and processes efficiently. A modular system is composed of units (or modules) that are designed independently but still function as an integrated whole. Designers achieve modularity by partitioning information into visible design rules and hidden design parameters.*

The design principle is to share information relating to interfaces but to hide any information relating to the proprietary function of the platform's core (Tiwana, 2013). The secrecy of a modular architecture is ensured through loose coupling. The openness of a modular architecture comes through interface standardisation (Tiwana, 2013). A detailed discussion around the trade-offs between integral and modular design approaches is beyond the scope of this chapter. However, it is extremely important for the Ecosystems Architect to be aware of the tools and principles available to perform decoupling of an ecosystem and effective interface standardisation.

Decoupling is achieved through a design process called encapsulation (Baldwin & Clark, 2000). The internal details of the platform should be well hidden. The external view is the platform's visible information that is accessible only through interfaces (Tiwana, 2013). A well-decoupled platform minimises an external application developers' need for any hidden information and reduces the coordination between development teams/parties as software can be deployed at any time (Eklund & Bosch, 2014; Tiwana, 2013).

We suggest that Ecosystems Architects, when deciding what functionality to include in the platform's core, follow Tiwana's (2013, p. 108) five rules: (1) High-reuse functionality resides inside the platform; (2) Generic functionality resides inside the platform; (3) Both the core codebase and interfaces should be treated as inseparable parts due to their long lifespan; (4) Stable

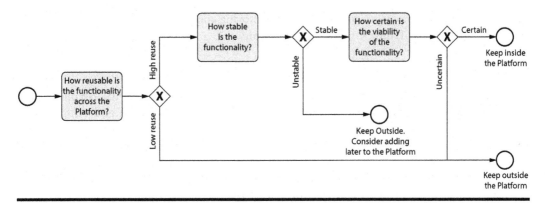

Figure 6.3   A process for identifying strategic distribution of platform functionality.

functionality resides inside platform; and (5) Experimental, unproven or functionality with high uncertainty resides outside the platform (Figure 6.3).

A second technique that the Ecosystems Architect can follow is to document the assumptions that a platform and an application make about each other. Explicitly defining the allowable assumptions weakens the dependencies between them (Tiwana, 2013). Neither the application nor the platform can make any assumptions about each other beyond what is visible in the interface. In this way, the platform's internals remain hidden, making changes to the platform less likely to break the application provided the interface specification remains frozen (Tiwana, 2013).

6.5.3 Interfaces

The architecture of the product or service including its interface to developers forms the visible design rules that are critical to the overall ecosystem (Baldwin & Clark, 1997; Bosch, 2010). The design of the new interface must balance providing enough functionality to the developer for it to be useful, while sufficiently decoupling it so that new versions of a product can be released without impacting externally developed applications (Bosch, 2010). Interfaces must therefore evolve predictably and must be backward compatible (Bosch, 2010). For this to be achieved, interface specifications should be narrow and allow for minimal interdependency, e.g. using Web Service or API interfaces (Bosch, 2009; Bosch & Bosch-Sijtsema, 2010). Both aspects are difficult to achieve in practice and require significant predictive abilities from the architect and the team (Bosch, 2010).

6.5.4 Evolution

All functionality starts off as highly differentiating. Over time, functionality commoditises and becomes less differentiating (Bosch, 2010). An example of this is Apple's incorporation of the wildly successful Google Maps app into their platform by developing their own Apple Maps app.

The Ecosystems Architect must work closely with the Product Management team to be aware of new commodity functionality emerging so that the scope of the platform can be regularly updated to envelop it, with new interfaces published significantly ahead of time for external developers (Bosch, 2010). Given that new functionality is regularly being added, proactively "slimming down" and simplifying the platform by removing unnecessarily complex code is a key concern of the Ecosystems Architect. For this reason, the Ecosystems Architect must be prepared to "walk away" from various components of the platform, removing complex proprietary code and replacing it with open source, industry-standard components.

6.5.5 Openness

A platform ecosystem consists of both rules and architecture (Parker, et al., 2016). An open architecture allows ecosystem members to access centralised platform resources (e.g. developer tools, APIs or frameworks for monetisation) to create value (Van Alstyne, et al., 2016). At its simplest, the openness or "closedness" of an ecosystem represents how easy it is for an actor to participate in it (Manikas & Hansen, 2013). However, closedness is not simply a matter of restricting participants' access. Being closed may also involve onerous rules governing participation that discourage potential future users such as excessive fees or rents (Parker, et al., 2016).

Within the literature, open and closed systems have been viewed as opposites. Te Molder, van Lier, and Jansen (2011) note that there is a continuum between open and closed which encompasses varying degrees of openness. Te Molder, et al. (2011) introduce the term "clopenness," a measure about the degree of openness on the continuum between open and closed. We are of the view that calibrating the degree of openness is a task that must be shared between the Ecosystems Architect, business strategists, product team and business executives. To assist with this task, the authors introduce the 'Clopenness Assessment Model' (CAM) that is used to describe the degree of openness of any context or situation in any kind of ecosystem (Te Molder, et al., 2011). The most essential part of this model includes the key attributes of availability, accessibility, transparency, reciprocity and licensing. The key attributes and description guidelines within the model are used to assess a narrative or story relating to the particular context and, in turn, calculate a score on the degree of openness.

In an evaluation of the CAM through four case studies in the transport and logistics sector, Te Molder, et al. (2011) conclude that their model has limitations and should not be regarded as the 'holy grail'. External factors such as trust, frankness and honesty are identified as potentially having an impact. However, it was not clear to the authors how these factors may impact the different elements in the model (Te Molder, et al., 2011).

6.6 Ecosystems Governance

This section provides an overview of the main types of ecosystems governance and the typical control measures that an Enterprise Architect must be familiar with.

Ecosystems Governance can be broadly defined as who makes what decisions within an ecosystem (Tiwana, 2013). For example, who is invited to participate in an ecosystem, how to divide the value and how to resolve conflicts (Parker, et al., 2016). Ecosystems governance is important and necessary because free markets are prone to failures (Parker, et al., 2016).

Ecosystems governance covers two broad types of ecosystems: traditional pipeline business operating in an "extended enterprise" ecosystem, and modern platform business operating in a "platform market" ecosystem (Van Alstyne, et al., 2016; Visnjic, Neely, Cennamo, & Visnjic, 2016). The structure of an ecosystem is determined by the role and position played by the "platform hub" or, by the organisation that directs the ecosystem (Iansiti & Levien, 2004).

The two main types of ecosystems lead to two distinct modes of governance: "extended enterprises" that are structured around an *integrator* and "platform markets" structured around a *platform hub* (Visnjic, et al., 2016). Research done by Visnjic, et al. (2016) suggests that neither approach is superior. For this reason, we note that it is essential for the Ecosystems Architect to be familiar with both approaches and the advantages and disadvantages of each.

6.6.1 Integrator Governance Approach

Within the extended enterprise model, the "integrator approach" to ecosystem governance can be effective. This is because the enterprise has full responsibility and control over integrating products and services from suppliers and other providers into a final product or service provided to the customer (Visnjic, et al., 2016). The interactions between the stakeholders, the integrator and final customers operate along a linear pipeline. Within the pipeline, the integrator is located between the complementors and customers to extract and bundle various products and services contributed by the ecosystems members in order to develop and sell its own product service offerings to customers (Visnjic, et al., 2016). Parker, et al. (2016) and Visnjic, et al. (2016) note that the disadvantages of this model include the high costs of coordination and complexity, and the limitations of the integrator acting as an inefficient "gatekeeper" that cannot scale as effectively as a platform marketplace.

6.6.2 Platform Market Governance Approach

Platform enterprises typically pursue 'platform market' governance models, where the structure and architecture of the ecosystem facilitates the interactions between third-party service providers, customers, developers and other companies (Visnjic, et al., 2016). In this model, the platform owner acts as the broker, facilitating direct interactions between parties on an ecosystem.

A challenge of platform governance is that the platform leader must retain enough control to be able to ensure the integrity and continued growth of the platform, while still devolving enough control to developers and other ecosystem participants to encourage continued innovation (Tiwana, et al., 2010; Williamson & Meyer, 2012). Ensuring that participants continue to create value for one another is another challenge for platform leaders. Where conflicts arise, governance rules must be put in place to resolve them as quickly as possible (Parker, et al., 2016).

6.6.3 Formal Control Mechanisms

Control mechanisms within a platform help to prevent market failures and increase the safety, transparency and quality of interactions within the market (Parker, et al., 2016). Control mechanisms include formal methods such as laws, gatekeeping and process control, and informal methods such as norms, architecture and markets (Parker, et al., 2016; Tiwana, 2013; Tiwana, et al., 2010).

The laws of a platform are formal, explicit rules governing a platform's use, for example, the terms of service or the rules of stakeholder behaviour (Parker, et al., 2016). Platform laws apply at both the user level and the platform level. For example, at the user level, Apple enforces rules about the sharing of digital content between six devices or family members (Apple Inc, 2017).

At the ecosystem level, 'Gatekeeping' represents the degree to which a platform owner uses pre-defined criteria to judge *who* and *what* is allowed into the platform (Tiwana, 2013). For example, Apple's tight control over developers, requiring them to submit all code for review prior to release on either their TestFlight Beta testing program or their public App Store (Apple Inc, 2018).

Process control is a formal method of control that refers to the degree to which platform owners reward or penalise app developers for following prescribed development rules, methods and procedures (Tiwana, 2013). The assumption behind process control is that if developers follow the tools and processes provided by the platform owner, the quality of the apps will increase (Tiwana, 2013). Examples of the tools that platform owners can provide include Integrated Development Environments such as Apple XCode, software tools such as the Android SDK, prototyping tools and integration protocols and test standards (Tiwana, 2013).

6.6.4 Informal Control Mechanisms

Norms and values are informal control mechanisms used to influence behaviour and generate lasting sources of value (Parker, et al., 2016). The control mechanism relies on the platform owner setting an overarching goal or vision for the platform and rallying app developers behind it (Tiwana, 2013). A good example of this is the Linux development community and their vision of openly sharing code for everyone to study, modify, repurpose and redistribute (Linux Australia, 2017).

The advantage of relational control is that it is the least expensive form of control, as it requires little enforcement. The disadvantage is that is it unlikely to be useful in platforms that have large amounts of new developers who do not share the history, the values or the norms of existing developers (Tiwana, 2013).

A platform's architecture should evolve together with its governance structure in order to encourage and reward good behaviour (Parker, et al., 2016). It is also necessary for a platform's governance structure to mirror its architecture. For example, decentralisation of platform architecture should reflect in the decentralisation of authority or decision rights (Tiwana, 2013). An example of this is the blockchain protocol in which public blockchain ownership allows self-enforcing, smart contracts that guarantee execution and payment once the contract terms have been triggered (Tapscott & Tapscott, 2017).

Markets are another information-control mechanism that governs through incentives. The incentives do not need to be purely financial, and in fact, on many platforms, money is far less important than social currency (Parker, et al., 2016). The idea of social currency is that by sharing information or knowledge, social benefits are received such as an achievement in status (Trudeau & Shobeiri, 2016). Examples for platforms driven by social currency are eBay, Reddit or StackOverflow. This mechanism is extremely useful for generating supply and demand on platforms and it is an important concept for the Ecosystems Architect.

When aligning a portfolio of platform control measures, the Ecosystems Architect should consider Tiwana's (2013) five simple rules: (1) simple; (2) transparent; (3) realistic; (4) reflect shared values; and (5) fair. It is also important that platform organisations consider how their governance structures and control mechanisms apply internally as well as externally.

We recommend that the Ecosystems Architect considers the practical, tangible example of a mandate issued by Amazon executive Steve Yegge to all employees aimed at improving internal transparency and breaking down "siloed behaviour". His mandate dictates that all teams must (1) expose data and functionality only through service interfaces; (2) enforce communication via service interfaces; and (3) design service interfaces to be used by external developers in the outside world (Parker, et al., 2016, p. 176).

Visnjic, et al. (2016) discuss two models for ecosystems governance: the Integrator approach and the Platform Market approach. We find that it is not clear which model is innately better than the other, or whether one model works better under certain circumstances. There seems to be a lack of published literature explaining at which point the Integrator approach fails to be successful due to difficulties in scaling effectively and managing the high costs of coordination.

We also find that within the Platform Market approach to ecosystems governance, there is a lack of suitable tools to determine the precise balance of control between a platform owner and the platform developers.

There are numerous formal and informal governance controls available for Business Ecosystems. Parker, et al. (2016) argue that because each platform can differ significantly from others already in the market, it is not beneficial to rely solely on other platforms for examples of appropriate governance controls. However, we find that the literature does not provide precise rules or heuristics to guide the Ecosystems Architect in knowing which controls to implement and when. Consequently, the Ecosystems Architect will need to experiment with a range of tools and carefully examine the effectiveness and performance of each.

6.7 Conclusion

Traditional pipeline organisations looking to reduce their innovation latency and their ability to generate value are increasingly pursuing Business Ecosystems strategies and, specifically, implementing platform business models. This chapter showed that the role of Ecosystems Architect is an essential new capability that has emerged as an extension of existing organisational roles including Enterprise Architecture, Business Architecture, Business Strategy, Product Management and general Business Management. The greatest amount of crossover of the Ecosystems Architect is between the conventional Business Strategy and Enterprise Architecture roles. Either conventional role could easily transition into ecosystems architecture.

The role of the Ecosystems Architect has emerged between existing, conventional business roles such as Enterprise Architecture, Business Architecture, Business Strategy, Product Management and Executive Management (Figure 6.4). Most importantly, the Ecosystems Architect shares aspects of several typical business roles. The general, strategic aspects of Business (Executive) Management including organisational strategy development, risk management and corporate performance indicators, are closely linked to the strategic and performance measurement components of ecosystems architecture.

The general Business Strategy roles within an organisation cross over into the Strategy, Governance and Measurement aspects of ecosystems architecture. Common activities between the Business Strategy role and Ecosystems Architecture include business model engineering, pricing and policy development, and the use of metrics to track progress against a strategy.

The role of the Business Architect typically focuses on activities such as capability-based planning, strategy development, business model development and working with Enterprise Architects to determine the level of openness that is required when integrating with other organisations.

On the other hand, the role of the Ecosystems Architect is typically focused on the internal aspects of how an organisation's systems, processes and technology integrate holistically to support an organisational strategy. An Enterprise Architect will typically use industry-standard tools such as Archimate[4] and UML[5] to perform activities such as systems decomposition, service and interface design. These activities share significant crossover with the Architecture of Ecosystems.

The role of the Product Manager typically focused on activities like requirements definition, feature mapping, customer journey mapping, design thinking and product pricing. These cross over into the Governance, Architecture and Measurement aspects of ecosystems architecture.

The motivations of organisations pursuing ecosystems strategies are centred around driving internal transformation efforts, targeting growth through new sources of supply and demand, increasing customer engagement and reducing costs of doing business. The emerging role of the Ecosystems Architect can add significant value in the early stages of ecosystems strategy development by analysing the key strategic implications and specific risks that ecosystems strategies typically present.

---

[4] Archimate is an Enterprise Architecture modelling language.
[5] Unified Modeling Language (UML) is a general-purpose modeling language often used in software engineering.

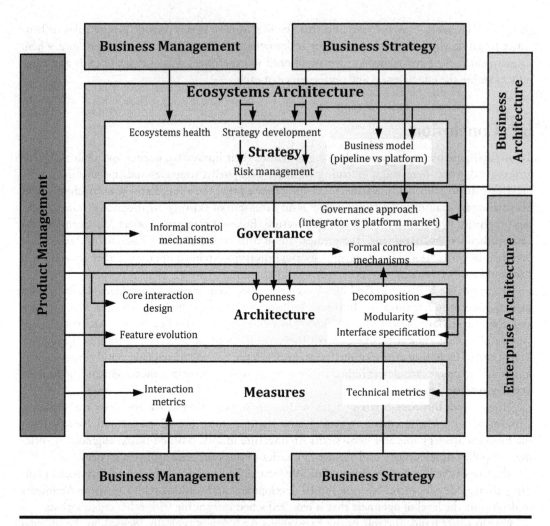

Figure 6.4 Relationships between Ecosystems Architecture and conventional organisational roles.

We examined the specific tasks performed by the Ecosystems Architects throughout the various components of Strategy, Measures, Governance and Architecture. In the area of Ecosystems strategy, we found that it is crucial for the Ecosystems Architect to be aware of the strong link between an organisation's ecosystems strategy and its architectural design and governance mechanisms.

Two broad categories of Ecosystems Measures can be identified: measures that focus on the technical aspects of an ecosystem and those that focus on customer interactions. Table 6.1 assembles a general list of metrics that can be used by Ecosystems Architects to meaningfully communicate ecosystem health and performance with a wide range of general organisational roles.

Ecosystems Architecture shares many principles, tools and techniques with complex systems architecture. This includes decoupling, modularity, interface design and system design rules. However, few published studies support the effectiveness of each of these techniques in ecosystems-specific scenarios.

Numerous governance and control mechanisms are available to Ecosystems Architects. These include formal methods such as laws, process control and gatekeeping, but also informal methods such as norms, architecture and markets. However, few tools exist that determine the precise balance of control required between a platform owner and its participants. We also found limited tools and heuristics available to Ecosystems Architects to determine which governance controls to implement under various scenarios.

References

Adner, R. (2006). Match your innovation strategy to your innovation ecosystem. *Harvard Business Review, 84*(4), 98.

van Angeren, J. (2013). Exploring Platform Ecosystems: A Comparison of Complementor Networks and their Characteristics Master thesis. Utrecht University.

Apple Inc. (2017). Apple Media Services Terms and Conditions. Retrieved 06/05/2018, from https://www.apple.com/legal/internet-services/itunes/au/terms.html

Apple Inc. (2018). Apple Developer Program License Agreement. Retrieved 06/05/2018, from https://developer.apple.com/services-account/download?path=/Documentation/License_Agreements__Apple_Developer_Program/Apple_Developer_Program_License_Agreement_20180402.pdf

Baldwin, C. Y., & Clark, K. B. (1997). Managing in an age of modularity. *Harvard Business Review, 75*, 84-93.

Baldwin, C. Y., & Clark, K. B. (2000). *Design rules: The power of modularity* (Vol. 1): MIT press.

Berger, T. (2012). Variability modeling in the wild. In *16th International Software Product Line Conference* (pp. 233-241).

Berger, T., Pfeiffer, R.-H., Tartler, R., Dienst, S., Czarnecki, K., Wąsowski, A., & She, S. (2014). Variability mechanisms in software ecosystems. *Information and Software Technology, 56*(11), 1520-1535.

Bosch, J. (2009). From software product lines to software ecosystems. In *Proceedings of the 13th international software product line conference* (pp. 111-119): Carnegie Mellon University.

Bosch, J. (2010). Architecture challenges for software ecosystems. In *Proceedings of the Fourth European Conference on Software Architecture: Companion Volume* (pp. 93-95): ACM.

Bosch, J. (2017). *Speed, Data, and Ecosystems: Excelling in a Software-Driven World*: CRC Press.

Bosch, J., & Bosch-Sijtsema, P. (2010). From integration to composition: On the impact of software product lines, global development and ecosystems. *Journal of Systems and Software, 83*(1), 67-76.

Chang, E., & West, M. (2006). Digital Ecosystems A Next Generation of the Collaborative Environment. In *iiWAS2006* (pp. 3-24).

Cusumano, M. A., & Gawer, A. (2002). The elements of platform leadership. *MIT Sloan Management Review, 43*(3), 51-58.

De Weck, O. L., Roos, D., & Magee, C. L. (2011). *Engineering systems: Meeting human needs in a complex technological world*: MIT Press.

Drews, P., & Schirmer, I. (2014). From Enterprise Architecture to Business Ecosystem Architecture. *Trends in Enterprise Architecture Research (TEAR), 2014*.

Eisenmann, T., Parker, G., & Van Alstyne, M. W. (2006). Strategies for two-sided markets. *Harvard Business Review, 84*(10), 92.

Eklund, U., & Bosch, J. (2014). Architecture for embedded open software ecosystems. *Journal of Systems and Software, 92*, 128-142. doi:https://doi.org/10.1016/j.jss.2014.01.009.

Galateanu, E., & Avasilcai, S. (2013). Business ecosystems architecture. *Fascicle of Management and Technological Engineering, 22*(1), 79-84.

Gawer, A., & Cusumano, M. A. (2014). Industry platforms and ecosystem innovation. *Journal of Product Innovation Management, 31*(3), 417-433.

Glady, N., Baesens, B., & Croux, C. (2009). Modeling churn using customer lifetime value. *European Journal of Operational Research, 197*(1), 402-411.

Howard, V. (2016). Business Ecosystems: A New Partnering Paradigm for High-Tech Supply Chains. Retrieved 06/05/2018, from Gartner Inc, https://www.gartner.com/doc/3454745/business-ecosystems-new-partnering-paradigm.

Iansiti, M., & Levien, R. (2004). Strategy as ecology. *Harvard Business Review*, vol. 82, pp. 68-78.

Isherwood, D., & Coetzee, M. (2011). Enhancing digital business ecosystem trust and reputation with centrality measures. In *Information Security South Africa (ISSA)* (pp. 1-8): IEEE.

Jansen, S., Finkelstein, A., & Brinkkemper, S. (2009). A sense of community: A research agenda for software ecosystems. In *Software Engineering-Companion Volume, 2009*. ICSE-Companion 2009. 31st International Conference on (pp. 187-190): IEEE.

Linux Australia. (2017). Linux Australia Statement of Values. Retrieved 06/05/2018, from https://linux.org. au/values.

Mäkinen, S. J., & Dedehayir, O. (2012). Business ecosystem evolution and strategic considerations: A literature review. In *18th International ICE Conference on Engineering, Technology and Innovation (ICE)*, 2012 (pp. 1-10): IEEE.

Manikas, K., & Hansen, K. M. (2013). Software ecosystems—A systematic literature review. *Journal of Systems and Software*, 86(5), 1294-1306.

Moore, J. F. (1993). *Predators and Prey: A New Ecology of Competition*. Harvard Business Review.

Moore, J. F. (1996). *The Death of Competition: Leadership and Strategy in the Age of Business Ecosystems*. Chichester: Wiley.

Parker, G., Van Alstyne, M., & Choudary, S. P. (2016). *Platform Revolution: How Networked Markets Are Transforming the Economy and How to Make Them Work For You* (Vol. 1). New York: W. W. Norton & Company.

Peyret, H., Cullen, A., Gill, M., Barnett, G., Warrier, S., & Izzi, M. (2015). Brief: Build An Ecosystem Architecture For Digital Business. Retrieved 06/05/2018, from Forrester Research Inc., https://www. forrester.com/report/Brief+Build+An+Ecosystem+Architecture+For+Digital+Business/-/E-RES115618.

Ries, E. (2011). *The lean startup: How today's entrepreneurs use continuous innovation to create radically successful businesses*. London: Penguin Group.

Schmid, K. (2013). Variability support for variability-rich software ecosystems. In 4th International Workshop on Product LinE Approaches in Software Engineering (PLEASE) (pp. 5-8).

Stanley, J., & Briscoe, G. (2010). The ABC of digital business ecosystems. *Communications Law*, 15(1), 12-25.

Tapscott, D., & Tapscott, A. (2017). How blockchain will change organizations. *MIT Sloan Management Review*, 58(2), 10.

Te Molder, J., van Lier, B., & Jansen, S. (2011). Clopenness of Systems: The Interwoven Nature of Ecosystems. In *Proceedings of the Workshop on Software Ecosystems* (pp. 52-64).

Tiwana, A. (2013). *Platform Ecosystems: Aligning Architecture, Governance, and Strategy*. Waltham, MA: Morgan Kaufmann.

Tiwana, A., Konsynski, B., & Bush, A. A. (2010). Research commentary—Platform evolution: Coevolution of platform architecture, governance, and environmental dynamics. *Information Systems Research*, 21(4), 675-687.

Trudeau, H. S., & Shobeiri, S. (2016). Does social currency matter in creation of enhanced brand experience? *Journal of Product & Brand Management*, 25(1), 98-114. doi:10.1108/JPBM-09-2014-0717.

Van Alstyne, M. W., Parker, G. G., & Choudary, S. P. (2016). Pipelines, platforms, and the new rules of strategy. *Harvard Business Review*, 94(4), 54-62.

Van Schewick, B. (2010). *Internet Architecture and Innovation* (Vol. 1). Cambridge, Mass: MIT Press.

Visnjic, I., Neely, A., Cennamo, C., & Visnjic, N. (2016). Governing the city: Unleashing the value from the business ecosystem. *California Management Review*, 59(1), 109-140. doi:10.1177/0008125616683955.

Wal-Mart Stores, I. (2017). Our History. Retrieved 06/05/2018, from http://corporate.walmart.com/ our-story/our-history.

Williamson, P. J., & Meyer, A. D. (2012). Ecosystem advantage: How to successfully harness the power of partners. *California Management Review*, 55(1), 24-46. doi:10.1525/cmr.2012.55.1.24.

Chapter 7

Features and How to Find Them

A Survey of Manual Feature Location

Jacob Krüger[a,b], Thorsten Berger[c], and Thomas Leich[b,d]

[a]Otto-von-Guericke University, Magdeburg, Germany
[b]Harz University of Applied Sciences, Wernigerode, Germany
[c]Chalmers University of Gothenburg, Gothenburg, Sweden
[d]METOP GmbH, Magdeburg, Germany

7.1 Introduction

Developers do not only implement software systems, but also maintain, extend, evolve, and re-engineer them (Standish 1984; Tiarks 2011). To this end, it is essential that developers understand the relevant source code (Siegmund 2016)—especially where the system's functionalities, or *features,* are located and what their relationships are among each other (von Mayrhauser, Vans, and Howe 1997). As such, feature location can arguably be seen as one of the most frequent tasks performed by developers (Biggerstaff, Mitbander, and Webster 1986; Poshyvanyk et al. 2007; Wang et al. 2013). Unfortunately, feature location can be costly and challenging—for instance, when features and their locations are not documented, when developers are newly assigned to a project, when previous developers retire, or when developers' knowledge about features fades over time (Kästner, Dreiling, and Ostermann 2014; Ji et al. 2015; Krüger et al. 2016; Krüger, Wiemann, et al. 2018). In these cases, developers have to re-obtain knowledge about features and recover their locations in the system's source code.

Several fully or semi-automated techniques have been proposed for identifying, locating, and documenting features (Rubin and Chechik 2013; Dit et al. 2013; Laguna and Crespo 2013; Assunção and Vergilio 2014). However, applying them in practice is challenging. First, automation of the feature-location process is difficult, since features are rather domain-specific entities and orthogonal to typical structures found in programs, such as components, classes or methods. This makes automated feature location—namely, deciding which source-code artifacts belong to a feature—a difficult problem that can hardly be solved by algorithms (Biggerstaff, Mitbander, and

Webster 1986; Kästner, Dreiling, and Ostermann 2014). Second, the proposed techniques lack in accuracy and require substantial effort from developers to adapt them to a specific system (Wilde et al. 2003; Ji et al. 2015; Krüger, Gu, et al. 2018). As a result, these techniques may be helpful, but developers still need to largely resort to manual feature location.

Unfortunately, little research exists on understanding how developers perform feature location manually. Thus, it is not clear if the proposed automated techniques actually do (or could) help developers performing feature location. This research gap calls for an analysis on manual feature location.

In this chapter, we survey the literature about studies of developers performing manual feature location. For this purpose, we conduct a systematic literature review (Kitchenham and Charters 2007) on the literature databases DBLP and SCOPUS, and extend our results with snowballing (Wohlin 2014). By relating synonymous and related terms, we consolidate the identified research into four topics that are primarily investigated. We also clarify the term feature location, summarize the findings of the identified literature, and identify open gaps that hamper our understanding of feature-location tasks and processes.

In summary, we:

- discuss different notions of features;
- identify and unify tasks that are considered as feature location;
- provide an overview of studies on manual feature location; and
- discuss open issues and problems identified in our review.

We describe feature location from a practitioners' perspective, hoping to provide actionable insights for developers. By consolidating existing knowledge on manual feature location, we also hope to foster the development of corresponding techniques, helping researchers to scope their work, and provide a starting point for further studies.

We proceed by discussing the notion of features in Section 7.2, since this notion differs among different communities and developers. Likewise, we show in Section 7.3 that different notions of feature location exist, comprising different kinds of tasks performed by developers. We discuss these tasks based on definitions provided in the literature, thereby illustrating the different notions of feature location and consolidating the distinct tasks into individual definitions. Thereafter, we provide a systematic review on studies about manual feature location, describing the review design in Section 7.4. We compare the studies' research approaches, their investigations of feature location, and their results. Within Section 7.5, we synthesize our observations and discuss them. Then, we discuss threats to validity in Section 7.6, related work in Section 7.7, and conclude in Section 7.8.

7.2 What is a Feature?

While not only most developers have their own notion of *feature*, the exact definitions provided by researchers also vary significantly (Apel et al. 2013; Berger et al. 2015). For example, there are more than ten definitions of the term *feature* (Classen, Heymans, and Schobbens 2008), ranging from rather abstract—"user-visible aspect, quality, or characteristic" (Kang et al. 1990)—to rather technical definitions—"an increment of program functionality" (Batory 2005). As a result, the concept of *feature* can be challenging to grasp, given the missing common definition. We rely on the definition of Apel et al. (2013, p. 18), who consolidate previous definitions:

> "A feature is a characteristic or end-user-visible behavior of a software system. Features
> are used in product-line engineering to specify and communicate commonalities and

differences of the products between stakeholders, and to guide structure, reuse, and variation across all phases of the software life cycle."

In this definition, features are foremost a means to communicate visible characteristics or observable behaviors of a system. This definition also explains the role of features in the context of a software product line (a portfolio of software variants) (Czarnecki and Eisenecker 2000; Clements and Northrop 2002; Apel et al. 2013), where features play an even more important role. There, features guide the structure of a system and can be reused among variants: A feature can be present in some variants of the software product line and absent in others, thereby reusing the feature. Enabling feature reuse requires implementing them in a specific way, for instance, as a component, which structures the software in a way that allows reuse. Such feature reuse also requires managing the variabilities represented by the features—commonly known as variability management, which comprises activities such as modeling features or managing feature dependencies.

For different contexts, different kinds of features are relevant, leading to different characteristics of the feature locations (Krüger, Gu, et al. 2018). In the context of product line engineering, the focus is primarily on managing (e.g., modeling) optional features, less on mandatory (i.e., common to all variants) features. The locations of such optional features are typically documented using preprocessor annotations (Apel et al. 2013; Medeiros et al. 2015), which allows switching features on and off when deriving individual variants from the product line. As such, the software-product-line engineering community is primarily concerned with optional features—as units of variability—and their locations. In contrast, other communities see features primarily as units of functionality, which is relevant for communities such as software maintenance. Here, a feature can be any visible characteristic or observable behavior of a system and is not necessarily configurable. This notion is broader and corresponds to the definition of Apel et al. (2013) that we rely on.

Features are a kind of software concern. While the latter term is more general, both terms are sometimes used synonymously (Wilde et al. 2003; Apel et al. 2013). A concern is defined as an area of interest in a system; in software-product-line engineering, features are the concerns of primary interest (Apel et al. 2013). However, the broad definition of concerns means that they comprise many kinds of entities in different contexts—for instance, studies on locating concerns include identifying code that causes a bug, corresponds to a requirement, or implements a feature (Wilde et al. 2003; Ko et al. 2006a). This results from the fact that an area of interest can be essentially anything. Thus, features are a specific kind of concern, but not all concerns are features (Wilde et al. 2003).

7.3 A Clarification of Feature Location

When developers analyze a system, they may investigate a specific concern according to the task at hand. In this chapter, we focus on locating features as such concerns, excluding bug localization (Hangal and Lam 2002) or requirements traceability recovery (Antoniol et al. 2002; Oliveto et al. 2010), among others. Still, feature location is a term, similar to feature, that developers have a notion of (or a vague idea about), but these notions often slightly differ among the developers. Our literature analysis in fact reveals different notions, for instance:

1. "Detection phase: initially, relevant information is extracted from the input artefacts, e.g. source code, to understand the existing structure, functionalities, data flow, relationships, existing features, etc. It is a discovery phase, often referred as feature location."

   (Assunção and Vergilio 2014, p.2)

2. "Feature location is the activity of identifying the source code elements (i.e., methods) that implement a feature."

(Revelle and Poshyvanyk 2005, p.1)

3. "Developers often have to identify where and how a feature is implemented in the source code in order to fix bugs, introduce new features, and adapt or enhance existing features. This activity is referred to as feature location in the context of software engineering."

(Wang et al. 2011, p. 1)

4. "Feature location is the activity of identifying an initial location in the source code that implements functionality in a software system."

(Dit et al. 2013, p. 1)

5. "While the set of available features in many cases is specified by the product documentation and reports, the relationship between the features and their corresponding implementation is rarely documented. Identification of such relationships is the main goal of feature location techniques."

(Rubin and Chechik 2013, p. 2)

6. "Concept location is a process that maps domain concepts to the software components."

(Chen and Rajlich 2000, p. 1)

Observe that each of these definitions comprises a slightly different meaning related to three tasks: Identifying, locating, and mapping features. Below, we will consolidate these definitions by distinguishing these three tasks from each other. The resulting definition will scope our literature analysis on manual feature location in this chapter.

7.3.1 Feature Identification

Most of the aforementioned definitions assume that the features to locate are already known and documented. However, this is rarely the case for software systems—except for optional features in software product lines—and can become a problem, especially in the context of variant-rich systems that are developed in an unsystematic clone-and-own approach (Dubinsky et al. 2013; Rubin, Czarnecki, and Chechik 2015; Krüger, Nell, et al. 2017; Krüger 2017). For example, it is questionable whether documentation (e.g., source code comments, models, or requirements) is regularly updated to reflect code changes (Jiang and Hassan 2006; Fluri, Wursch, and Gall 2007). Such inconsistencies can already cause problems in a single systems and may result in one clone developing divergently from the others, including features that are not documented and may be forgotten.

For these reasons, it is often necessary to first identify features that exist in a system, collect the corresponding information, and define their relationships. This is emphasized by definition (1), which describes feature location as the process of identifying existing features in a system. However, this task is more often referred to as feature identification and can utilize different input artifacts, such as documentation, models, and source code (Laguna and Crespo 2013). While the terms feature identification and feature location are often used synonymously, we clearly distinguish them. In feature identification, an exemplary output can be a variability model (Czarnecki et al. 2012; Berger et al. 2013) that describes the features of a system and their dependencies. We define feature identification as:

Feature identification is the task of determining the features that exist in a system based on a set of artifacts, revealing their dependencies and documenting the result.

There are several approaches that support feature identification (Laguna and Crespo 2013), such as the ones by Acher et al. (2012) and Davril et al. (2013). Most of these studies are related to recovering variability models from legacy systems. This emphasizes the importance of documenting the identified features and their dependencies in our definition, and distinguishes such tasks from feature location.

7.3.2 Feature Location

Feature location is solely concerned with finding the source code that implements a specific feature. Knowing these locations is necessary to update, reuse, and maintain a feature (von Mayrhauser, Vans, and Howe 1997; Krüger, Pinnecke, et al. 2017). In practice, feature locations are rarely documented explicitly, but depend on the knowledge of developers. When this knowledge fades or gets lost (Ji et al. 2015, Krüger, Wiemann, et al. 2018), developers need to recover these locations. The location of a feature can be seen as a traceability link, which is a broader term (Antoniol et al. 2002; Oliveto et al. 2010), referring to various kinds of relationships between any kind of code or non-code artifacts, such as requirements and code. The understanding of feature location as the recovery of implementation relationships between (known) features and source code is shared by most definitions above, specifically (2), (3), and (4). Consequently, we define feature location as:

> Feature location is the task of finding the source code in a system that implements a feature.

Many fully or semi-automated feature-location techniques have been proposed, as surveyed by Rubin and Chechik (2013), Dit et al. (2013), and Assunção and Vergilio (2014). Recall that automated feature location is problematic, given its adaptation needs and low accuracy (Duszynski, Knodel, and Becker 2011; Ji et al. 2015; Krüger, Nell, et al. 2017; Krüger, Gu, et al. 2018)—motivating our analysis of manual feature location.

7.3.3 Feature Mapping

Definitions (5) and (6) emphasize the declaration of relationships—the mapping—between features and their implementing source-code artifacts. Since this declaration can be done using different means, it is a task on its own, and we distinguish it from identifying features and locating features (Krüger, Nell, et al. 2017; Krüger, Gu, et al. 2018). For our purpose, we consider a specific task of this research area to which we refer to as feature mapping:

> Feature mapping is the task of documenting the connection between a feature and its implementation in a system's source code.

Feature mapping can be done with different complementary techniques. For example, annotation-based implementation techniques for software product lines require explicit annotations (e.g., preprocessor annotations such as #IFDEFs) for optional features (Apel et al. 2013). These annotations establish the mapping of parts of code artifacts to features defined in a variability model, which is the input to a configurator tool. Other authors, such as Revelle, Broadbent, and Coppit (2005), Ji et al. (2015), Seiler and Paech (2017), or Krüger, Gu et al. (2018) advocate also annotating the locations of mandatory features using annotations that are embedded into the source code, regardless of whether used in the context of a software product line or a single system. Other implementation techniques, such as feature-oriented programming (Prehofer 1997), physically separate features into different files (so-called modules) with a feature's name and achieve traceability this way.

7.3.4 Summary

In this section, we distinguished three different tasks that are sometimes synonymously described as feature location. We argued that the task of actual feature location differs from feature identification and feature mapping. However, these three tasks partly depend on each other and are tangled. For example, all three tasks can be performed in parallel when investigating source code, which may result in inconsistencies—for instance, when a feature is identified later on and all locations need to be reinvestigated to update the corresponding mappings. Also, without knowing about existing features and their locations in the source code, it is not possible to map both types of information. Overall, there are different approaches for each task and, especially for automation, a clear distinction is necessary to define input and output, or to measure the performance of a technique. In the remainder of this chapter, we will focus only on the task of feature location as we defined it above.

7.4 Methodology

Surveys show that a variety of automated feature-location techniques exist that utilize a variety of inputs and outputs (Dit et al. 2013; Rubin and Chechik 2013; Assunção and Vergilio 2014). However, little and mostly recent research investigates how developers actually perform feature location without automated techniques. Such research helps to understand the needs of practitioners, to identify challenges, and to design techniques based on real-world needs. In the following, we describe our review of manual feature location, roughly following the guidelines for systematic literature reviews described by Kitchenham and Charters (2007).

7.4.1 Research Questions

With our review, we aim to provide an overview on manual feature location to consolidate existing knowledge and to identify open issues. In particular, we are interested in the steps developers perform naturally when searching for a feature's code, without being supported by automated techniques. We formulate two research questions:

RQ$_1$ What topics are of primary interest in existing studies on manual feature location?
RQ$_2$ What topics are neglected in existing studies on manual feature location?

The first research question focuses on showing the state of the art of studies that report on developers performing manual feature location. In contrast, with the second research question, we aim to derive open issues based on the previous results.

To answer our research questions, we consolidate the research questions defined in each of the included studies into a topic. Such topics may be observing the search patterns of developers or measuring the effort it requires to manually locate a feature. For this purpose, we start with identifying those questions related solely to manual feature location, for example, excluding the comparison of automated techniques performed by Wilde et al. (2003). Then, we abstract more general topics by relating terms used in the research questions that are either identical or closely related.

7.4.2 Review Design

We start with an automated search in the dblp database—last updated on November 13, 2017. Our search string only contains the term *"feature location"* as a broad term, aiming to capture all indexed documents on this research area. This search string results in 271 documents that we check manually, starting with title and abstract, and continuing with the whole document if necessary. We exclude studies that are not explicitly investigating and reporting findings about manual feature location at least as a part of the study [e.g., Wilde et al. (2003) use manually derived locations as a baseline for two automated feature-location techniques], and those that are not written in English, or are not peer-reviewed. This way, we identify two relevant documents from the automated search.

For a more complete view, we apply backwards-snowballing on the selected papers' references and forward-snowballing (Wohlin 2014) using Google Scholar—last updated on November 15, 2017. For each newly identified document, we again apply snowballing and the same exclusion criteria as for our automated search. During this process, we find four additional, relevant studies. Additionally, we include one of our own studies (Krüger, Gu, et al. 2018) that is concerned with manual feature location, but not indexed at this time.

Finally, we check our search results by using the SCOPUS database—last updated on January 26, 2018. This time, we use the more specific search string *"manual AND feature locat*"* on abstracts, keywords, and titles. The resulting 37 documents contain no new relevant studies, wherefore we finally include seven studies in our review. The small number of mostly recent studies already indicates that more research on manual feature location may be necessary to improve our understanding of this task. We remark that DBLP as well as SCOPUS are databases that index publications from most important publishers in computer sciences, including ACM, IEEE, Springer, Elsevier, and Wiley.

7.5 Results

In this section, we provide an overview on the identified seven studies on manual feature location. Afterwards, we summarize and discuss the research topics addressed in these studies, as well as open issues.

7.5.1 Identified Studies

In the following, we briefly summarize the identified studies. We provide and overview on the used research method, considered systems, and participants to put the results into context. Moreover, we focus on the investigated research questions, based on which we derive the addressed research topics. In Table 7.1, we provide a brief overview on all studies included in this review. We remark, that study 3b is an extension of 3a, including an additional experiment, so we will consider these studies as a single one in the remaining chapter.

Wilde et al. (2003) report a case study that includes manual feature location. They focus on comparing two automated techniques to the results of a single developer who manually analyzes an industrial Fortran system containing 2,335 lines of code. The developer is allowed to use only simple search tools, like those that are integrated in most development environments and text editors. Overall, Wilde et al. investigate three research objectives:

■ Analyze the necessary effort to adopt any of the three techniques to the Fortran code;
■ Investigate the pros and cons of each technique; and
■ Identify inconsistencies between the results of all techniques.

Revelle, Broadbent, and Coppit (2005) describe a case study on concern location including two experienced developers. These developers analyze a C system with 2,100, and a Java system

Table 7.1 Overview on the documents included in this review

ID	Document
1	A Comparison of Methods for Locating Features in Legacy Software (Wilde et al. 2003) Journal of Systems and Software
2	Understanding Concerns in Software: Insights Gained from Two Case Studies (Revelle, Broadbent, and Coppit 2005) International Workshop on Program Comprehension
3a	An Exploratory Study of Feature Location Process: Distinct Phases, Recurring Patterns, and Elementary Actions (Wang et al. 2011) International Conference on Software Maintenance
3b	How Developers Perform Feature Location Tasks: A Human-Centric and Process-Oriented Exploratory Study (Wang et al. 2013) Journal of Software: Evolution and Process
4	Manually Locating Features in Industrial Source Code: The Search Actions of Software Nomads (Jordan et al. 2015) International Conference on Program Comprehension
5	A Field Study of How Developers Locate Features in Source Code (Damevski, Shepherd, and Pollock 2016) Empirical Software Engineering
6	Towards a Better Understanding of Software Features and Their Characteristics: A Case Study of Marlin (Krüger, Gu, et al. 2018) International Workshop on Variability Modelling of Software-Intensive Systems

with 3,000 lines of code. We remark that, in this study, feature location is mingled with feature identification and feature mapping (cf. our previous definitions in Section 7.3). The authors compare the findings of the two developers to compare different feature characteristics and derive guidelines to locate and map them, for example, the authors derive the guide that entire functions often refer to a concern or support one.

Wang et al. (2011, 2013) perform three controlled experiments. The first experiment includes 18 students and two full-time developers as participants, who analyze two Java systems with around 72,900 and 2,300 lines of code. For the other two experiments, two different Java systems with 43,950 and 18,750 lines of code are investigated by 18 students. Overall, the authors answer five research questions related to actions, search patterns, and phases of feature location. They also analyze the influence of knowing the phases and patterns of feature location on developers' performance as well as of external factors that may influence developers' choices.

Jordan et al. (2015) observe two professional developers while these locate features in an industrial system. The system is implemented in COBOL with various domain-specific languages (DSLs), adding up to around 3 million lines of code overall. The authors' focus is on the used search tools and how effective the developers locate features.

Table 7.2   Characteristics of the identified studies

ID	Identification	Location	Mapping	Method	Systems		Subjects
1	X	✓	✓	Case Study	1 FORTRAN	2,350 LOC	1
2	✓	✓	✓	Case Study	1 C 1 Java	2,100 LOC 3,000 LOC	2
3	✓	✓	X	Experiment	4 Java	72,900 LOC 2,300 LOC 43,950 LOC 18,750 LOC	20/18
4	X	✓	X	Field study	1 COBOL, DSLs	3 Mio. LOC	2
5	X	✓	X	Field study	/	/	67/~600
6	✓	✓	✓	Case Study	1 C	/	2

Damevski, Shepherd, and Pollock (2016) conduct a field study in which they analyze tracking data of developers that use an integrated development environment, Visual Studio, to locate features. The first part of the study is based on a dataset provided by the company ABB. The dataset contains data of 67 developers for who all interactions with Visual Studio have been tracked for an average of 25.6 days. Data for the second part of the study is derived with a plug-in that around 600 developers downloaded and that tracks search queries of the users. Again, the focus of this study is on the used search tools and queries but also on the patterns Wang et al. (2011, 2013) defined.

Finally, Krüger, Gu, et al. (2018) report a case study on the Marlin 3D-printer firmware that comprises over 10,000 lines of C code. In this study, two of the authors manually locate features in one variant of Marlin. The focus in this study is on possible entry points to identify and locate features, as well as comparing the characteristics of mandatory and optional features.

We summarize the characteristics of these studies in Table 7.2. We can see that most of the conducted research is focusing solely on feature location, relying on already identified features for the location task. Revelle, Broadbent, and Coppit (2005) and Krüger, Gu, et al. (2018) explicitly state and investigate the identification and mapping of features in the source code. Considering the remaining studies, Wilde et al. (2003) compare the located features of different techniques, which requires a mapping, and Wang et al. (2011, 2013) also investigate documenting located features, which in this case means to take notes about the features, but apparently not explicitly mapping them to the code. Considering the remaining characteristics, we see that different research methods have been applied, namely case studies, experiments, and field studies, that all observe the behavior of the participants. In addition, the used systems and artifacts differ in the programming languages, size, and number of subjects that performed the location tasks.

7.5.2 RQ₁: What Topics are of Primary Interest in Existing Studies on Manual Feature Location?

In order to answer this research question, we analyze the questions and objectives addressed in the identified studies. To this end, we identify common and related terms to generalize the investigated topics. For example, several research questions use the terms *search tools, actions, drawbacks,*

Table 7.3   Identified research topics

ID	Search Tools	Performance	Factors	Processes
1	✓	✓	X	X
2	X	X	✓	✓
3	X	✓	✓	✓
4	✓	✓	✓	X
5	✓	X	X	✓
6	X	X	✓	X

and *factors*. We show the results of this abstraction in Table 7.3. We will discuss each of these topics and the corresponding findings in the following.

7.5.2.1 Search Tools

Three of the identified studies particularly address how developers use standard *search tools*, as are included in most development environments and text editors, to locate the source code belonging to a feature. In general, these studies indicate that search tools are an important means for developers to search for terms that are related to a feature. The identified locations may correspond to the feature and can be used as starting points (a so-called seeds) to extend the search.

Jordan et al. (2015) as well as Damevski, Shepherd, and Pollock (2016) observe that their participants usually start with simple search queries, including single keywords that are later refined based on the results. For instance, a query may be specified by adding a term. Especially Jordan et al. (2015) also exhibit different triggers that result in a search and the origin of the used keywords. Their participants mainly use searches to browse the code, to refine a previous search, to inspect results, and to identify new seeds for a feature. To define their search queries, they rely on language syntax and conventions, terms in the source code, and the results of previous searches.

While Revelle, Broadbent, and Coppit (2005) find that such searches are fast and require no adaptation in contrast to automated techniques; they also remark a low accuracy of such searches. They argue that the reliance on keywords appearing in comments and source code reduces the success of simple search queries in contrast to more advanced techniques. In contrast, Jordan et al. (2015) find that searches performed by developers that are familiar with the system are likely to return relevant results, with only 29% of the investigated searches being unsuccessful. This not only contradicts the findings of Revelle, Broadbent, and Coppit (2005), but also other studies on search behavior, for example by Ko et al. (2006). Such studies are more generally interested in how developers search for information during software development tasks, namely for debugging and program enhancement in the study of Ko et al. (2006). Thus, they may also provide additional insights into this topic, but not with a focus on feature location.

7.5.2.2 Performance

The topic *performance* summarizes all findings related to the effectiveness of manual feature location, as well as its advantages and disadvantages in practice. While three studies address this topic, they always mingle it with another topic, making it problematic to draw isolated results about the topic *performance*. Specifically, Revelle, Broadbent, and Coppit (2005) find that manual location, focusing on simple search tools, is fast to set up and requires no adaptation effort—but is also not reliable. The same accounts for Jordan et al. (2015) who consider the performance of search tools themselves. Finally, Wang et al. (2011, 2013) compare the performance of their participants before and after the participants gain knowledge about feature-location patterns and processes, combining the topics *factors* (i.e., knowledge) as well as *processes* (i.e., feature-location patterns and processes) with *performance*. Overall, there are no reliable findings about the efforts and *performance* that are actually related to the feature-location task or parts of it, as the identified results are always intermingled with other topics.

7.5.2.3 Factors

The topic *factors* summarizes all influences (e.g., system characteristics, task at hand, developer characteristics) on the feature-location task, for example, how developers perform searches or how they conduct specific steps. A similar distinction is identified by Wang et al. (2013), who differentiate between three factors, listed from most to least important (regarding how searches are performed):

1. *Human factors* refer to knowledge, experiences, capabilities or preferences of a developer. Wang et al. (2013) find that such factors have the strongest impact on feature location, which is identical to the findings of Revelle, Broadbent, and Coppit (2005) as well as Jordan et al. (2015), stating program comprehension and knowledge as significant factors.
2. *Task properties* include factors that are connected to the task at hand, including characteristics of the system as well as the features under investigation. These findings are again identical to Revelle, Broadbent, and Coppit (2005), who identify the abstraction layer of features and the program context as further factors. Addressing the factors of the features of a system themselves, Krüger, Gu, et al. (2018) compare the characteristics of mandatory and optional features in a software product line. The findings indicate that locating the different kinds of features may require varying effort, as they are scattered differently among their subject system.
3. *In-process feedback* refers to any feedback the developer receives during the feature-location task, for example, the number of results a search query returns. This factor in particular seems to have less effect on the search behavior, as a search query can be reuse. However, the factors have more impact on the actual actions performed after receiving the results. An example of Wang et al. (2013) are searches with too many results being reduced by a refined search, not changing the search behavior but the developer's actions – repeating another search instead of investigating the results.

We see that several factors have been identified to influence feature-location tasks. These are reported repeatedly and, thus, to some extent verified by the other studies.

7.5.2.4 Processes

The actual processes and actions performed during manual feature location are intensively investigated by Wang et al. (2011, 2013). We also include the guidelines for feature location by Revelle, Broadbent, and Coppit (2005) and partly consolidate them into the processes for feature location, as they resemble similar steps. In Figure 7.1, we show an adapted version of the feature-location phases

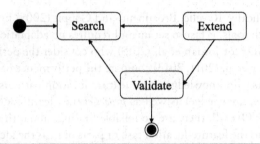

Figure 7.1   Feature-location phases adapted from Wang et al. (2013).

defined by Wang et al. (2013), which is also used by Damevski, Shepherd, and Pollock (2016), and reflected by the results of Revelle, Broadbent, and Coppit (2005)—for example, considering the recommendation that functions or class attributes can indicate feature seeds. We remark that we do not show the documentation phase, which we relate to feature identification and feature mapping according to our definitions (cf. Section 3). Consequently, for this survey the documentation phase is out of the scope of processes for feature location.

The search phase describes the initial step of feature location, in which the developers search for one or few initial seeds for a feature. Wang et al. (2013) identify three search patterns that developers commonly apply:

1. *Information retrieval-based* patterns are adaptations of information retrieval techniques but also include simple search tools. As identified in other studies, the developers identify key-words that relate to the feature they aim to locate and then derive a search query. Depending on the results, they change the queries to achieve better results.
2. *Execution-based* patterns require the developer to derive execution scenarios of the program in which the feature is active. They then set breakpoints (as for debugging) in the source code, wherever they assume the feature may be implemented. If the program stops at a breakpoint, the developers have to investigate the source code and refine these points to find seeds of a feature step-by-step.
3. *Exploration-based* patterns do not rely on keyword searches or program execution but on the static dependencies in the code. To this end, developers read the source code and aim to understand its behavior, for example, by investigating method calls or type hierarchies, to locate a feature.

After this phase, the developers are aware of seeds in the source code from which they continue to refine feature locations in the extension phase. During this extension phase, developers often rely on their own code comprehension and two types of search patterns described above: Execution-based and exploration-based extension patterns. However, the purpose of this phase is different, which also reflects on the actual actions performed in this phase: To locate all code belonging to a feature, developers extend the seeds identified previously. As a result, they often return to these seeds and restart their searches from there. In their study, Damevski, Shepherd, and Pollock (2016) find that almost all their participants rely on the exploration-based patterns (97%) to extend feature locations, while only few participants use execution-based patterns (3%). Finally, the developers need to validate whether the identified code belongs to the investigated feature. This can be done by analyzing the code, for example, based on its structure, comments, or further keywords. Wang et al. (2013) find that their participants often edit the code and then execute it to validate the output, or they rely on debugging.

7.5.2.6 Summary

In this section, we consolidated the findings of the seven included studies. With respect to RQ$_1$, we find that the studies investigate manual feature location in terms of search tools, performance, influencing factors, and occurring processes as well as patterns. Especially the studies of Wang et al. (2011, 2013) provide detailed insights into the behavior of practitioners and can help to better understand the feature-location task.

7.5.3 RQ$_2$: What Topics are Neglected in Existing Studies on Manual Feature Location?

As we described, the seven studies investigate the topics search tools, performance, factors, and processes in detail. Still, there are several important issues not yet analyzed, which we discuss in this section.

7.5.3.1 Studies on Efforts of Feature Location

Despite the extensive analyses, we find very little information about the actual efforts of locating features, for example, only as the number of recorded material or duration of a study. While several researchers find feature location to be the most expensive task in software maintenance, detailed analysis on the actual efforts are missing. This is problematic for several reasons: First, we do not understand what actions for feature location require what efforts. This knowledge would help to identify the actions that require most support to facilitate the whole feature-location task. For example, most automated techniques propose seeds for a feature, but if simple search tools are more accessible and provide comparable or even better results than automated techniques, this may not reduce efforts in practice. Second, we do not know whether physical actions or mental actions require more support. For example, if the effort is mainly connected to deriving suitable queries, automatically providing suggestions to the developer may be more helpful than fully automated searches. Third, missing understanding of efforts makes a comparable assessment of benefits and costs of feature-location techniques impossible. Without knowing the costs of performing the automated tasks manually, we cannot evaluate if the derived technique is helpful. Overall, we argue that the limited knowledge about the efforts of feature location prevents us from understanding its actual challenges and problems. Furthermore, this missing knowledge hampers cost estimations for software maintenance and reengineering; and is a threat to feature-location techniques, as they may try to facilitate actions that are already simple to perform.

7.5.3.2 Performance Studies and Factors

Several authors remark that different factors have positive impact on the feature-location task. However, detailed analyses or experiments in this regard are missing. For example, it is interesting to investigate if specified notions of features or programming patterns result in identical results. The studies by Wilde et al. (2003), Revelle, Broadbent, and Coppit (2005), Wang et al. (2013), and Jordan et al. (2015) find that the experience and knowledge of the developer is important, but do not reveal the actual positive or negative effects of these factors on the performance. Corresponding studies can help to identify and assess factors that considerably impact feature location. The results can help to scope automated techniques, to let developers focus on specific parts of the system based on their knowledge, and to avoid potential pitfalls.

7.5.3.3 Evaluating and Scoping Automated Techniques

A common problem of existing automated feature-location techniques is their low accuracy and that it is often unclear what steps they support to what extent. In this regards, it would be helpful to conduct more studies that compare such techniques to manual feature location. We only find the study of Wilde et al. (2003) addressing this issue. While they report a lower accuracy for the manual analysis compared to a reference study, this may only indicate that there are different notions of features. Thus, such studies can be helpful to not only compare, but also to scope techniques to the notions of developers. For this purpose, it seems also necessary to clearly define what tasks, phases, and actions are addressed by a feature-location technique. Such definitions are clearly missing, especially since the first feature-location techniques were already proposed, at least, in 1995 (Rubin and Chechik 2013). It seems curious that automation has been proposed long before the manual tasks that they support have been investigated. We argue that a comparison of existing, automated feature-location techniques with the already identified phases and patterns helps to scope the application scenarios of automated techniques.

7.5.3.4 Information Sources

While feature location is concerned with finding feature implementations in the source code, relevant information may be contained in artifacts beyond code. In fact, for feature identification, an increasing number of researchers proposes to rely on other information sources, for example, histories of modern code repositories and version control systems, such as GitHub or BitBucket (Krüger, Gu et al. 2018), or natural language processing of requirements documentations (Li et al. 2017). Repositories and version control systems, especially, already are common in software development, and have been for a long time, providing detailed information about code changes. Analyzing the additional data, such as the commit messages, and correlating changes in the same commit or among branches with each other may facilitate (automated) feature location. Still, also in this context, manual studies may provide detailed insights on analysis patterns that are different from the already identified ones.

7.5.3.5 Summary

With respect to RQ_2, we identify four open issues for further investigations. These include studies on the effort of feature location, factors that influence the performance, the scope and evaluation of automated techniques, and the used information sources. Additional studies are needed to address these open issues in feature-location research.

Recall the mapping study of Assunção and Vergílio (2014) on automated feature location (cf. Section 7.3). We find some similarities of their identified open research issues to ours above. Specifically, the authors also see the need to improve evaluations, combine information sources, and to conduct further studies to improve automation. These are open issues we share and that we emphasize can only be investigated by systematically observing actual developers performing feature location.

7.6 Threats to Validity

A threat to the external validity is that we focused on a specific research area and used narrow search terms. Thus, we may have missed some studies that are concerned with manual feature location or closely related areas that may include valuable insights. However, we mitigated these effects by applying snowballing on our search results to broaden the scope of our review. Consequently, we argue that we provide a detailed overview on research for manual feature location.

We discussed only four open issues that are derived from our own analysis of the included studies. However, we carefully derived these issues by analyzing gaps between the investigated topics in each study. Thus, while several other issues exist, we argue that they are a call for attention to improve our understanding on manual feature location. While these issues may be biased to our own opinions, other researchers can easily derive additional ones based on an analysis of our survey. Also, we focused on issues that hamper the practical adoption and support for feature location to support practitioners in understanding the problems connected to these. In this regard, we see that especially performances and costs are the most interesting topics.

Finally, we argue that any researcher can replicate and extend our review. We followed established guidelines for systematic literature reviews, described each step, and provided an overview on all included studies. Depending on future studies and the scope of a replication, the findings may slightly differ but should comprise the same results.

7.7 Related Work

There are some related works to our survey on manual feature location: Several surveys have been conducted on feature-location techniques (Dit et al. 2013; Rubin and Chechik 2013; Assunção and Vergilio 2014). These surveys compare different techniques, including, for instance, their underlying approach and potential application scenarios. These techniques support different aspects of the tasks we identified previously, mainly the processes to identify, locate, and map features in the source code. This is often done by identifying and extending feature seeds. Thus, these surveys extend the search tools we identified as a research topic and mostly evaluate their performance. Still, this is often done on single case studies and by comparing feature-location techniques. As we described above, there are some open issues in connecting the manual processes of feature location with such automated techniques.

Works on concept location investigate not only features, but also bugs or requirements (Wilde et al. 2003; Robillard and Murphy 2007). As a result, different approaches, for example on requirements traceability and recovery (Antoniol et al. 2002), also cover related techniques, but with a different scope compared to feature location. Similar to feature location, few studies actually are concerned with the manual processes in these domains. In this regard, especially studies on search processes and software maintenance activities provide detailed insights, as they often observe developers during their daily work (von Mayrhauser, Vans, and Howe 1997; Ko et al. 2006; Tiarks 2011). Thus, these studies can help to better understand how developers actually perform such maintenance tasks and processes, similar to the identified studies on feature location.

7.8 Conclusion

In this chapter, we reviewed studies on manual feature location. We provided an overview on the processes and steps connected to feature location, summarizing the state of the art to support practitioners in applying, and researchers in improving, automated and manual feature location. To this end, we identified that the most addressed topics are the used search tools, factors that influence feature location, performance measures, and unique phases. Moreover, we discussed open issues that still prevent the practical adoption of feature-location techniques: Missing knowledge about the required efforts and the influence of external factors, missing evaluations of techniques, and the exclusion of additional information sources. In summary, further studies on manual feature location are necessary to improve our understanding about such topics, to elicit empirical data, and to improve feature-location practices.

Acknowledgements

Supported by the German Research Foundation (DFG) grant number LE 3382/2-1, and the ITEA project REVaMP², funded by Vinnova Sweden (2016-02804) and the Swedish Research Council Vetenskapsrådet (257822902).

References

Acher, Mathieu, Anthony Cleve, Gilles Perrouin, Patrick Heymans, Charles Vanbeneden, Philippe Collet, and Philippe Lahire. 2012. "On Extracting Feature Models from Product Descriptions." In *International Workshop on Variability Modelling of Software-Intensive Systems (VaMoS)*, 45–54. ACM. doi:10.1145/2110147.2110153.

Antoniol, Giuliano, Gerardo Canfora, Gerardo Casazza, Andrea De Lucia, and Ettore Merlo. 2002. "Recovering Traceability Links Between Code and Documentation." *IEEE Transactions on Software Engineering* 28 (10): 970–83. doi:10.1109/TSE.2002.1041053.

Apel, Sven, Don Batory, Christian Kästner, and Gunter Saake. 2013. *Feature-Oriented Software Product Lines*. Springer. doi:10.1007/978-3-642-37521-7.

Assunção, Wesley Klewerton Guez, and Silvia Regina Vergilio. 2014. "Feature Location for Software Product Line Migration: A Mapping Study." In *International Systems and Software Product Line Conference (SPLC)*, 52–59. ACM. doi:10.1145/2647908.2655967.

Batory, Don. 2005. "Feature Models, Grammars, and Propositional Gormulas." In *International Systems and Software Product Line Conference (SPLC)*, 7–20. Springer. doi:10.1007/11554844_3.

Berger, Thorsten, Daniela Lettner, Julia Rubin, Paul Grünbacher, Adeline Silva, Martin Becker, Marsha Chechik, and Krzysztof Czarnecki. 2015. "What Is a Feature? A Qualitative Study of Features in Industrial Software Product Lines." In *International Conference on Software Product Line (SPLC)*, 16–25. ACM. doi:10.1145/2791060.2791108.

Berger, Thorsten, Ralf Rublack, Divya Nair, Joanne M. Atlee, Martin Becker, Krzysztof Czarnecki, and Andrzej Wąsowski. 2013. "A Survey of Variability Modeling in Industrial Practice." In *International Workshop on Variability Modelling of Software-Intensive Systems (VaMoS)*, 1–8. ACM. doi:10.1145/2430502.2430513.

Biggerstaff, Ted J., Bharat G. Mitbander, and Dallas Webster. 1986. "The Concept Assignment Problem in Program Understanding." In *International Conference on Software Engineering (ICSE)*, 482–98. IEEE. doi:10.1109/ICSE.1993.346017.

Chen, Kunrong, and Václav Rajlich. 2000. "Case Study of Feature Location Using Dependence Graph." In *International Workshop on Program Comprehension (IWPC)*, 241–47. IEEE. doi:10.1109/WPC.2000.852498.

Classen, Andreas, Patrick Heymans, and Pierre-Yves Schobbens. 2008. "What's in a Feature: A Requirements Engineering Perspective." In *International Conference on Fundamental Approaches to Software Engineering (FASE)*, 16–30. Springer. doi:10.1007/978-3-540-78743-3_2.

Clements, Paul, and Linda Northrop. 2002. *Software Product Lines: Practices and Patterns*. Addison-Wesley.

Czarnecki, Krzysztof and Ulrich W. Eisenecker. 2000. *Generative Programming: Methods, Tools, and Applications*. Addison-Wesley.

Czarnecki, Krzysztof, Paul Grünbacher, Rick Rabiser, Klaus Schmid, and Andrzej Wąsowski. 2012. "Cool Features and Tough Decisions: A Comparison of Variability Modeling Approaches." In *International Workshop on Variability Modelling of Software-Intensive Systems (VaMoS)*, 173–82. ACM. doi:10.1145/2110147.2110167.

Damevski, Kostadin, David Shepherd, and Lori Pollock. 2016. "A Field Study of How Developers Locate Features in Source Code." *Empirical Software Engineering* 21 (2): 724–47. doi:10.1007/s10664-015-9373-9.

Davril, Jean-Marc, Edouard Delfosse, Negar Hariri, Mathieu Acher, Jane Cleland-Huang, and Patrick Heymans. 2013. "Feature Model Extraction from Large Collections of Informal Product Descriptions." In *Joint Meeting on Foundations of Software Engineering (ESEC/FSE)*, 290–300. ACM. doi:10.1145/2491411.2491455.

Dit, Bogdan, Meghan Revelle, Malcom Gethers, and Denys Poshyvanyk. 2013. "Feature Location in Source Code: A Taxonomy and Survey." *Journal of Software: Evolution and Process* 25 (1): 53–95. doi:10.1002/smr.567.

Dubinsky, Yael, Julia Rubin, Thorsten Berger, Slawomir Duszynski, Martin Becker, and Krzysztof Czarnecki. 2013. "An Exploratory Study of Cloning in Industrial Software Product Lines." In *European Conference on Software Maintenance and Reengineering (CSMR)*, 25–34. IEEE. doi:10.1109/CSMR.2013.13.

Duszynski, Slawomir, Jens Knodel, and Martin Becker. 2011. "Analyzing the Source Code of Multiple Software Variants for Reuse Potential." In *Working Conference on Reverse Engineering (WCRE)*, 303–7. IEEE. doi:10.1109/WCRE.2011.44.

Fluri, Beat, Michael Wursch, and Harald C. Gall. 2007. "Do Code and Comments Co-Evolve? On the Relation between Source Code and Comment Changes." In *Working Conference on Reverse Engineering (WCRE)*, 70–79. IEEE. doi:10.1109/WCRE.2007.21.

Hangal, Sudheendra, and Monica S. Lam. 2002. "Tracking Down Software Bugs Using Automatic Anomaly Detection." In *International Conference on Software Engineering (ICSE)*, 291–301. ACM. doi:10.1145/581339.581377.

Ji, Wenbin, Thorsten Berger, Michal Antkiewicz, and Krzysztof Czarnecki. 2015. "Maintaining Feature Traceability with Embedded Annotations." In *International Systems and Software Product Line Conference (SPLC)*, 61–70. ACM. doi:10.1145/2791060.2791107.

Jiang, Zhen Ming, and Ahmed E. Hassan. 2006. "Examining the Evolution of Code Comments in PostgreSQL." In *International Workshop on Mining Software Repositories (MSR)*, 179–80. ACM. doi:10.1145/1137983.1138030.

Jordan, Howell, Jacek Rosik, Sebastian Herold, Goetz Botterweck, and Jim Buckley. 2015. "Manually Locating Features in Industrial Source Code: The Search Actions of Software Nomads." In *International Conference on Program Comprehension (ICPC)*, 174–77. IEEE. doi:10.1109/ICPC.2015.26.

Kang, Kyo Chul, Sholom G. Cohen, James A. Hess, William E. Novak, and A. Spencer Peterson. 1990. "Feature-Oriented Domain Analysis (FODA) Feasibility Study." Technical Report (CMU/SEI-90-TR-21). Carnegie-Mellon University. Pittsburgh.

Kästner, Christian, Alexander Dreiling, and Klaus Ostermann. 2014. "Variability Mining: Consistent Semi-Automatic Detection of Product-Line Features." *IEEE Transactions on Software Engineering* 40 (1): 67–82. doi:10.1109/TSE.2013.45.

Kitchenham, Barbara A., and Stuart Charters. 2007. "Guidelines for Performing Systematic Literature Reviews in Software Engineering." EBSE-2007-01.

Ko, Andrew J., Brad A. Myers, Michael J. Coblenz, and Htet Htet Aung. 2006a. "An Exploratory Study of How Developers Seek, Relate, and Collect Relevant Information during Software Maintenance Tasks." *IEEE Transactions on Software Engineering* 32 (12): 971–87. doi:10.1109/TSE.2006.116.

Krüger, Jacob, Jens Wiemann, Wolfram Fenske, Gunter Saake, and Thomas Leich. 2018. "Do You Remember This Source Code?" In *International Conference on Software Engineering (ICSE)*. ACM. doi:10.1145/3180155.3180215.

Krüger, Jacob. 2017. "Lost in Source Code: Physically Separating Features in Legacy Systems." In *International Conference on Software Engineering (ICSE)*, 461–62. IEEE. doi:10.1109/ICSE-C.2017.46.

Krüger, Jacob, Wolfram Fenske, Jens Meinicke, Thomas Leich, and Gunter Saake. 2016. "Extracting Software Product Lines: A Cost Estimation Perspective." In *International Systems and Software Product Line Conference (SPLC)*, 354–61. ACM. doi:10.1145/2934466.2962731.

Krüger, Jacob, Wanzi Gu, Hui Shen, Mukelabai Mukelabai, Regina Hebig, and Thorsten Berger. 2018. "Towards a Better Understanding of Software Features and Their Characteristics: A Case Study of Marlin." In *International Workshop on Variability Modelling of Software-Intensive Systems (VaMoS)*, 105–112. ACM. doi: 10.1145/3168365.3168371.

Krüger, Jacob, Louis Nell, Wolfram Fenske, Gunter Saake, and Thomas Leich. 2017. "Finding Lost Features in Cloned Systems." In *International Systems and Software Product Line Conference (SPLC)*, 65–72. ACM. doi:10.1145/3109729.3109736.

Krüger, Jacob, Marcus Pinnecke, Andy Kenner, Christopher Kruczek, Fabian Benduhn, Thomas Leich, and Gunter Saake. 2017. "Composing Annotations Without Regret? Practical Experiences Using FeatureC." *Software: Practice and Experience.* doi:10.1002/spe.2525.

Laguna, Miguel A., and Yania Crespo. 2013. "A Systematic Mapping Study on Software Product Line Evolution: From Legacy System Reengineering to Product Line Refactoring." *Science of Computer Programming* 78 (8). Elsevier: 1010–34. doi:10.1016/j.scico.2012.05.003.

Li, Yang, Sandro Schulze, and Gunter Saake. 2017. "Reverse Engineering Variability from Natural Language Documents: A Systematic Literature Review." In *International Systems and Software Product Line Conference (SPLC)*, 133-142. ACM. doi: 10.1145/3106195.3106207.

Medeiros, Flávio, Christian Kästner, Márcio Ribeiro, Sarah Nadi, and Rohit Gheyi. 2015. "The Love/Hate Relationship with the C Preprocessor: An Interview Study." In *European Conference on Object-Oriented Programming (ECOOP)*, edited by John Tang Boyland, 37:495–518. Schloss Dagstuhl - Leibniz-Zentrum fuer Informatik. doi:10.4230/LIPIcs.ECOOP.2015.495.

Oliveto, Rocco, Malcom Gethers, Denys Poshyvanyk, and Andrea De Lucia. 2010. "On the Equivalence of Information Retrieval Methods for Automated Traceability Link Recovery." In *International Conference on Program Comprehension (ICPC)*, 68–71. IEEE. doi:10.1109/ICPC.2010.20.

Poshyvanyk, Denys, Yann-Gael Gueheneuc, Andrian Marcus, Giuliano Antoniol, and Václav Rajlich. 2007. "Feature Location Using Probabilistic Ranking of Methods Based on Execution Scenarios and Information Retrieval." *IEEE Transactions on Software Engineering* 33 (6): 420–32. doi:10.1109/TSE.2007.1016.

Prehofer, Christian. 1997. "Feature-Oriented Programming: A Fresh Look at Objects." In *European Conference on Object-Oriented Programming (ECOOP)*, 1241:419–43. Springer. doi:10.1007/BFb0053389.

Revelle, Meghan, Tiffany Broadbent, and David Coppit. 2005. "Understanding Concerns in Software: Insights Gained from Two Case Studies." In *International Workshop on Program Comprehension (IWPC)*, 23–32. IEEE. doi:10.1109/WPC.2005.43.

Revelle, Meghan, and Denys Poshyvanyk. 2009. "An Exploratory Study on Assessing Feature Location Techniques." *International Conference on Program Comprehension (ICPC)*, 218–222. IEEE. doi: 10.1109/ICPC.2009.5090045.

Robillard, Martin P., and Murphy, Gail C. 2007. "Representing Concerns in Source Code." *ACM Transactions on Software Engineering Methodology* 16 (1): Article 3. doi:10.1145/1189748.1189751.

Rubin, Julia, and Marsha Chechik. 2013. "A Survey of Feature Location Techniques." In *Domain Engineering*, 29–58. Springer. doi:10.1007/978-3-642-36654-3_2.

Rubin, Julia, Krzysztof Czarnecki, and Marsha Chechik. 2015. "Cloned Product Variants: From Ad-Hoc to Managed Software Product Lines." *International Journal on Software Tools for Technology Transfer* 17 (5). Springer: 627–46. doi:10.1007/s10009-014-0347-9.

Seiler, Marcus and Barbara Paech. 2017. "Using Tags to Support Feature Management Across Issue Tracking Systems and Version Control Systems." In *International Working Conference on Requirements Engineering: Foundation for Software Quality (REFSQ)*, 174–180. Springer.

Siegmund, Janet. 2016. "Program Comprehension: Past, Present, and Future." In *International Conference on Software Analysis, Evolution, and Reengineering (SANER)*, 13–20. IEEE. doi:10.1109/SANER.2016.35.

Standish, Thomas A. 1984. "An Essay on Software Reuse." *IEEE Transactions on Software Engineering* SE-10 (5): 494–97. doi:10.1109/TSE.1984.5010272.

Tiarks, Rebecca. 2011. "What Maintenance Programmers Really Do: An Observational Study." In *Workshop Software Reengineering (WSR)*, 36–37.

von Mayrhauser, Anneliese, A. Marie Vans, and Adele E. Howe. 1997. "Program Understanding Behaviour During Enhancement of Large-Scale Software." *Journal of Software Maintenance: Research and Practice* 9 (5): 299–327. doi:10.1002/(SICI)1096-908X(199709/10)9:5<299::AID-SMR157>3.0.CO;2-S.

Wang, Jinshui, Xin Peng, Zhenchang Xing, and Wenyun Zhao. 2011. "An Exploratory Study of Feature Location Process: Distinct Phases, Recurring Patterns, and Elementary Actions." In *International Conference on Software Maintenance (ICSM)*, 213–22. IEEE. doi:10.1109/ICSM.2011.6080788.

———. 2013. "How Developers Perform Feature Location Tasks: A Human-Centric and Process-Oriented Exploratory Study." *Journal of Software: Evolution and Process* 25 (11): 1193–1224. doi:10.1002/smr.1593.

Wilde, Norman, Michelle Buckellew, Henry Page, Václav Rajlich, and La Treva Pounds. 2003. "A Comparison of Methods for Locating Features in Legacy Software." *Journal of Systems and Software* 65 (2): 105–14. doi:10.1016/S0164-1212(02)00052-3.

Wohlin, Claes. 2014. "Guidelines for Snowballing in Systematic Literature Studies and a Replication in Software Engineering." In *International Conference on Evaluation and Assessment in Software Engineering (EASE)*, 1–10. ACM. doi:10.1145/2601248.2601268.

Chapter 8

A Debt-Aware Software Product Lines Engineering Using Portfolio Theory

Jasmine Lee and Rami Bahsoon

University of Birmingham, Birmingham United Kingdom

8.1 Introduction

Software product line engineering helps businesses enhance the productivity and reduce the time-to-market by exploiting the benefit of reuse (Clements & Northrop, 2002). Where this is different from the typical development for individual software, a software product line is expected to be sustainable and needs to support the configurations of a range of products to bring long-term profitability. Therefore, the success is heavily reliant on the management of commonality and variability that allows various product variations and their value-added overtime. If a product line can capture the requirements from various potential markets and is able to provide the required pre-built core assets/components for the product configurations, it will assist the organisation to respond to the market demands efficiently. To achieve this, managers and developers need to rethink the way they can manage commonalities and variabilities of a given product line for value added and technical debt reduction. The configuration space for commonalities and variabilities can be vast, the decision is non-trivial one.

Engineering decisions for developing software product lines around commonalities and variabilities have been discussed by prior works, without explicit link of these decisions to value added and technical debt as acknowledged by (Schmid, Technical Debt in Product Lines, 2016). For example, Ensan et al. introduced a goal-oriented approach to select the most desirable features to form a product line by prioritising each of them according to the business goals (Ensan, Bagheri, Asadi, Gasevic, & Biletskiy, 2011). Mannion and Savolainen provided a management tool to aid decision making by mapping business strategy with reusable software development strategies (Mannion & Savolainen, 2016). Kishi, Noda, & Katayama developed a methodology for product line scoping based on a decision-making framework (Kishi, Noda, & Katayama, 2002). They evaluated multiple candidate architectures and selected the optimal one according to their individual optimality and the whole optimality within a product line. Nevertheless, these approaches have not taken technical debt into account, which can lead to significant technical and financial consequences.

According to Li, Avgeriou, and Liang, technical debt can be classified into 10 types corresponding to different software engineering activities such as; architecture TD, testing TD, and requirement TD, etc. (Li, Avgeriou, & Liang, 2015). The focus of this chapter is the management of requirement TD in software product line development since requirements are the basis of the product line scope. We provide a systematic approach to define the optimal set of features as a portfolio based on the modern portfolio theory taking relative requirement TD into account while achieving a sufficient level of generality when engineering commonalities in the view of supporting the incubation of multiple variants and unlocking potentials for new products. The applicability of the proposed method is demonstrated by applying it to the case study of Home Integrated System.

8.1.1 Software Product Lines

A software product line is "a set of software-intensive systems sharing a common, managed set of features that satisfies the specific needs of a particular market segment or mission and that are developed from a common set of core assets in a prescribed way" (Clements & Northrop, 2002). It is a new way of developing software products. The development of a SPL is based on the decisions on selecting commonalities and variabilities. Commonalities are the features that are shared across the product line and are developed as the core assets for the reuse in product configurations. On the other hand, variabilities are those product specific features, which required by different products within the product line according to the specific demands from different markets.

SPLs allow "higher productivity, reduced time-to-market, better product quality, higher customer satisfaction and easier maintenance of presence by reusing core assets in a strategic way" (Clements & Northrop, 2002). Hence, mining the commonality of a product family to maximize the level of reuse (Alves, Niu, Alves, & Valença, 2010), and identifying the necessary variations for each member product become the major goals that should be achieved in SPL development. However, the decisions on product line generality can lead to SPL specific technical debt, which requires careful management to maintain the sustainability of the product line and the potential exploitation of its common features to support new products.

8.1.2 Technical Debt (TD)

Technical debt is a metaphor that was first coined by Ward Cunningham in 1992. He argued that with partial understanding of the requirements due to the time constraints, "the shipping of the first time code is like going into debt. A little debt speed development so long as it is paid back promptly with a rewrite as the interest payment" (Cunningham, 1992). This metaphor was originally applied at the code level only but has now been expanded to different aspects of software engineering, such as architecture, detailed design, testing, and requirement (Alves, Niu, Alves, & Valença, 2010). Technical debt does not only raise the awareness of developers to understand the risks of taking shortcuts or sub-optimal decisions during the development process, but it also helps them to communicate design problems with non-technical people since the value of debt can be calculated and expressed in numerical terms to allow easy comparisons. Moreover, since technical debt cannot be avoided (Fowler, 2009), the management of it becomes crucial for developers to ensure that they understand the consequences of taking and accumulating debts.

TD can be classified according to intentionality (McConnell, 2007). Unintentional TD is incurred or accumulated without awareness, such as bad quality codes or insufficient requirement specification. On the other hand, Intentional TD is taken as a conscious strategic decision. It can be beneficial for organisations to gain recent business value as long as the accumulation of it is affordable for organisations to repay in the future. Therefore, it is essential for organisations to not only incur "right debts" and accumulate right level of it to maintain the balance between short-term benefits, and long-term expenditures and risks (McConnell, 2007).

8.1.3 Requirement Technical Debt in Software

8.1.3.1 Product Lines

As mentioned in the prior section, the success of a SPL depends on the decisions of commonalities and variabilities, which might lead to technical debt. Since these decisions are made dependant on the requirements specifications, the debt that arises from this stage is considered as the "requirement technical debt" (RTD). The RTD in SPLs is different from the traditional debt for a single product and can be significantly more expensive and severe due to the complexity of commonality and variability management. For example, a debt that is incurred in core assets can be copied and accumulated through the reuse of these assets. Without refactoring or repairing, the debt can lead to significant technical problems. Moreover, a product line may include thousands of variation points. Under such circumstance, a company may find it difficult to have a person who has complete overview about the product line, and hence, the management of technical debt becomes difficult. Such complexity also means that the evolution and maintenance of a product line become expensive (Bosch, Capilla, & Hilliard, 2015) (Nord, Ozkaya, Kruchten, & Gonzalez-rojas, 2012). Therefore, in order to avoid unaffordable financial and technical consequences, we require a sufficient way to manage commonalities and variabilities to hold an appropriate level of debt.

To calculate the debt level, we need to first understand the possible risks during the requirement engineering phase that could become the sources of RTD in SPL. A product line is expected to be sustainable and can provide long-term reuse, so the initial development phase should also consider the long-term risks that may arise in the future. An organisation can be in danger without the awareness of possible future trends (Clements & Northrop, 2002). Therefore, in this chapter, the author has identified some major product line specific risks that should be considered during the development process:

1. *Compatibility Risk*
   Recent business market trends tend to be dynamic since customers' requirements change at a rapid pace. The need to change/evolve a product line can be triggered by having a new requirement. When designing the commonality infrastructure, developers need to carefully assess the inherent flexibility. A flexible infrastructure of commonality may cost more in the development process, but with sufficient technology forecasting and market research, it can be reusable to allow wider range of product configurations that brings long-term saving in future redevelopment costs. In contrast, inflexible commonality infrastructure may save developing cost or time now but can also lead to high technical debt in the future from refactoring.

2. *Quality Risk*
   Each product within a product line requires a different quality level (Etxeberria, Sagardui, & Belategi, 2008). When determining the generality of a product line, developers need to consider what quality standard should be achieved. Usually, the ideal quality level cannot be achieved due to the development constraints. Therefore, there is a risk for developers to incur debt due to the need to enhance the real quality standard to the ideal quality standard in the future.

3. *Maintenance/Repairing Risk*

When choosing between commonality and variability, the costs on maintenance and repairing can be a key factor. The cost of maintaining a core asset component is a one-time-payment, which help organisations to gain significant economies of benefit (Clements & Northrop, 2002), while that for variability can be duplicated across products. However, this does not mean that it is always good to develop every possible feature as a commonality since some of them may not be required by so many products within the product line. This unnecessary development of commonality can have a negative impact on wider productivity.

In order to mitigate these risks to avoid unwanted debt, we need to understand the dependency between features within a product line using feature modelling.

8.1.4 Feature Modelling

A feature model is a tree-structured model that allows a graphical view of commonalities and variabilities of a SPL. A feature refers to a functionality or characteristic of a system and can occur at any level in the software engineering (De Vylder, 2010). In this chapter, we only focus on the features at the requirement level.

A basic feature model can represent four types of relationships between features, as shown in Figure 8.1 (Benavides, Trinidad, & Ruiz-Cortés, 2005).

The various types of relationships are explained as following:

1. *Mandatory:* A mandatory feature must be included in product configuration if its parent feature is included.

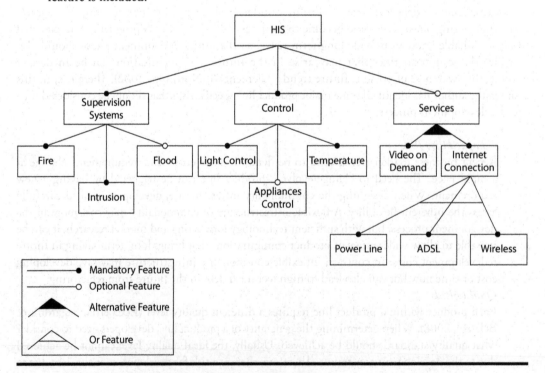

Figure 8.1   Basic feature model of the home integrated system.

2. *Optional:* An optional feature may or may not be included in product configuration if its parent feature is included.
3. *Alternative:* Alternative means that only one feature in a feature group can be included if their parent feature is included.
4. *Or-relationship:* The or-relationship means that one or more features in a feature group can be included in product configuration if their parent feature is included.

By visualizing the dependencies between features, a feature model provides flexibility to allow developers to add new features easily by expanding the tree or looking more closely into the detail of the product line by focusing on any sub-tree of it.

Before constructing a feature model, developers firstly need to consider what features that should be included in the product line. The main challenge in SPL development is how to select appropriate features to exploit commonality and variability with resource constraints (Li, Liu, Wang, & Guo, 2011). At this stage, a marketing and product plan (MPP) is a helpful methodology to reveal the real needs from markets (Kang & Lee, 2002).

MPP consists of two parts: the marketing plan and the product plan. A marketing plan "includes a marketing analysis and a strategy for realizing business opportunities in a market" (Kang & Lee, 2002). It is useful to identify the potential markets that can be penetrated, the relative user characteristics within each market, stakeholders' opinions, and the possible future technologies that may be required to help businesses realise their opportunities and setting up business goals. Once the marketing plan is defined, a product plan can be conducted. In this phase, product features, and quality attributes that are required by the potential markets are identified to form the initial feature models that correspond to the demands from each of the potential markets. In order to select the most beneficial model to the company, this chapter will adopt the modern portfolio theory to evaluate the value of each model, taking RTD into account, and identify the optimal feature model for the company.

8.1.5 Modern Portfolio Theory

The modern portfolio theory (Markowitz, 1952) was introduced by Harry Markowitz in 1952. It is a mathematical approach that attempts to calculate the value of a portfolio investment by assessing its risk and return relationship.

The theory shows that the real value of an investment does not only depend on its expected return, but also the risks associated with it. It argues that the general aim for investors is to maximise the return while minimising risks. This can be achieved by diversifying the investment into a portfolio, which consists of multiple assets, since the movement of these assets are related with each other. This means that the loss of one asset can be compensated by the return of other assets to mitigate the investment risks. The theory can be linked to our chapter where each feature model is considered as a candidate portfolio, each feature within the portfolio can contribute to some costs and benefits and is associated with some specific risks.

Based on the MPT, the risk-adjusted return: Shape ratio is developed by William F. Sharpe to represent "the reward provided to investors for bearing risks" (Sharpe, 1996). It is calculated using the following formula:

$$\text{Sharpe Ratio} = \frac{(E(r) - Rf)}{Risk\ Value}$$

E(r) is the expected return of an investment. *Rf* is the risk-free rate, which is the minimum acceptable return by investing in a risk-free investment. The *Risk Value* is the portfolio standard deviation. Usually a Sharpe ratio greater than 1 is considered a profitable investment, while a Sharpe ratio that is lower than one indicates that the rate of return is lower than the risk taken. In this chapter, the Sharpe ratio of each feature portfolio will be calculated for the evaluation of optimality.

8.2 Motivation and Related Works

There is much existing technical debt research focusing on traditional software engineering process.

Li, Avgeriou, & Liang attempted to "obtain a comprehensive understanding TD" by classifying TD into 10 types according to different software engineering activities and identifying 8 TD management activities (Li, Avgeriou, & Liang, 2015). They concluded that the definition of TD is ambiguous, which could lead to communication problems. Also, different types of technical debt receive unequal attention. There is a need to develop formal TD management processes and tools to manage various types of TD (Li, Avgeriou, & Liang, 2015).

One of the attempts to tackle this problem is made by (Guo & Seaman, 2011). They developed a portfolio approach to TD management in software development by adopting MPT to evaluate the optimal level of TD. Their work suggested that TD can be beneficial to organisations as long as it is at the optimal debt level. Debt items should be collected together as a whole. The optimal debt portfolio is chosen according to the risk level that an organisation is willing to take (Guo & Seaman, 2011).

Other research focuses on managing different types of TD. For example, Nord, Ozkaya, Kruchten, & Gonzalez-rojas introduced "an architecture-focused and measurement-based approach" to manage the architectural TD (Nord, Ozkaya, Kruchten, & Gonzalez-rojas, 2012). Ojameruaye and Bahsoon also developed a goal-oriented method and portfolio-based methodology to manage compliance debt systematically (Ojameruaye & Bahsoon, 2014).

However, Klaus Schmid argued that these researches and methodologies focus particularly on individual system and aim to support a single product development, but the complexity of SPL development will lead to different forms of TD and has not yet been addressed by existing tools (Schmid, 2016).

Inspired by the previous works that have been completed, this chapter is aiming at developing a systematic way to evaluate the optimality SPL and manage the related TD associated with it. As a product line consists of multiple features, we find that the portfolio theory, which is applied by the previous papers, can be a sufficient tool for SPL optimality evaluation, but we adopt it with different use. We view different combinations of feature models as portfolios and calculate their expected return and risk value to understand their real values. We then identify the optimal portfolio and compare others with it to get the value of TD for each of them.

8.3 The Problem

Insufficient decisions on product line generality and variation points will harm an organisation's profitability and productivity. Deficient generality in the requirements can make the product line inflexible to the market changes, while excessive generality can lead to unnecessary effort on core asset development and variation management (Clements & Northrop, 2002). Therefore, the problems this chapter addresses are:

1. How to determine the market segments that are considered profitable to an organisation?
2. How to construct appropriate feature sets to define the commonality and variability that correspond to the demands from each market?
3. What are the underlying risks behind each feature set that might incur technical debt?
4. Which is the optimal portfolio for the SPL? What is the value of technical debt for each portfolio?

8.4 Proposed Method

According to the motivation and the problems defined, this chapter provides a method as described below:

Step 1. Identify potential market segments, and realise business opportunities

The first step is to evaluate different market segments that the organisation can possibly penetrate in using the marketing and product plan (MPP). Since a product line is expected to be sustainable, we want to make sure that our research is conducted in a manner of understanding the markets' long-term needs. By analysing each market, organisations can realise the relative business opportunities, the user characteristics, and the future technology that might be required.

According to the marketing plan, organisations can define business goals, and decide on which are the potential markets that should be evaluated. Once the marketing strategies are developed, we can conduct the product plan to obtain the product features and quality attributes that are required by each market.

Step 2. Construct candidate portfolios

Based on the MPP, we can then construct feature models that reflect the needs from each potential market as the candidate portfolio for evaluations. MPP is also helpful to determine the selection of commonalities and variabilities and decide on the variation point that a product line should support. For example, suppose we have identified three market types and the required features from the conduction of MPP shown in Table 8.1. We can construct the initial feature models that meet the feature requirements for each market (see Figure 8.2).

From Figure 8.2, we can see that there is a so-called "risk-free portfolio." This is the portfolio that includes all the features that can be included in a product line as commonalities. We assume the risk-free portfolio can satisfy all the requirements from different markets. Hence, the return of it will be used as the risk-free rate to calculate the Sharpe ratio in the later stage.

Table 8.1　Potential markets and the features required

Market	Required Feature
Market 1	F1, F2, F3
Market 2	F1, F3, F4, F5
Market 3	F1, F2, F3, F4, F5

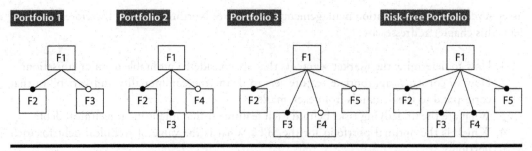

Figure 8.2 Candidate portfolios corresponding to each potential market and the risk-free portfolio.

Step 3. Estimate the costs and the benefits, and calculate the expected returns

Once the candidate portfolios are decided, we can now start to consider the costs and benefits. Since this is a qualitative process, in which the accuracy of estimations is based on the past experiences or professional knowledge, multiple stakeholders and relative experts should be involved to express their opinions and develop the estimations.

The costs can be both economical (e.g. procurement costs and personnel costs) and non-economical (e.g. productivity costs). The non-economical cost at this stage should be converted into economical terms, but the precise methods that are involved in doing this is beyond the scope of this chapter. The benefits, on the other hand, are the savings from future implementation. Instead of estimating the revenue generated, we want to understand the amount of savings that we could benefit from if a new feature is implemented now rather than in the future. After getting the values of costs and benefits for each portfolio, we can calculate the expected return ($E(r)$) of each portfolio using the following formula:

$$E(r) = \frac{(Total\ Benefits - Total\ Costs)}{Total\ Costs} \tag{1}$$

As mentioned in the previous step, the expected return for the risk-free portfolio will be used as the risk-free rate (see Table 8.2).

Table 8.2 The expected return of the risk-free portfolio (risk-free rate)

		Cost			
	Type	Procurement	Personnel	Benefit	E(r)
F1	C	10	20	50	N/A
F2	C	15	10	30	N/A
F3	C	10	15	30	N/A
F4	C	20	30	55	N/A
F5	C	10	16	24	N/A
Total		156		189	21%

Table 8.3 Consequence levels for risks

Level	Risk Consequence
0	None
1	Very low
2	Low
3	Medium
4	Severe
5	Very severe

Step 4. Evaluate the risk level of each portfolio

At this step, we should estimate the risk value for each portfolio according to the portfolio theory. Here we used what-if analysis as scenarios to consider; what are the consequences if certain anticipated situations occur, what are the risks that could be associated with such scenarios, and what is the likelihood that these scenarios would occur. In the chapter, we score the consequence from 0 to 5, where 0 means no consequence, and 5 means very severe consequence (details see Table 8.3). The likelihoods are expressed in percentages. The example calculation of risk level for portfolio 1 is shown in Table 8.4.

Similar to the cost-benefit estimation, the evaluation on risk levels is also qualitative. To make the final evaluation less biased and more accurate, we would like to involve different evaluators with relative experiences and knowledge to do the evaluations. The final risk value, therefore, is the weighted average of each evaluator's estimation according to their confidence levels on the figures that they provide.

Table 8.4 Calculation of the risk value for portfolio 1

Scenario	Associated Risks	Consequence	Likelihood	Confidence	Risk Value
Scenario 1 Flood Detection Feature Required	Compatibility Risk	3	40%	80%	19%
	Quality Risk	1	40%	80%	6%
Scenario 2 Remote Control of the System Required	Compatibility Risk	4	35%	60%	17%
	Quality Risk	4	35%	60%	17%
Scenario 3 Regular Maintenance and Repairing	Maintenance Risk	2	100%	95%	38%
Scenario 4 Raising Demand from Business Clients	Compatibility Risk	5	60%	70%	42%
	Quality Risk	5	60%	70%	42%
Total					26%

Step 5. Calculate the Sharpe ratios, identify the optimal portfolio, and calculate the technical debts
By having the expected return and the estimated risk value, we are now able to calculate the Sharpe ratio for each portfolio using the following formula:

$$\text{Sharpe Ratio} = \frac{(E(r) - Rf)}{Risk\ Value} \tag{2}$$

The risk-free rate (Rf) is the expected return that we got from the previous step for the risk-free portfolio. The Sharpe ratio greater than one is considered as a profitable portfolio. Here, we define the optimal portfolio as the one with the highest Sharpe Ratio.

Finally, we can calculate the technical debt by comparing the sub-optimal Sharpe ratios with the optimal one. The value of technical debt will be the loss in benefit that we sacrifice due to the non-optimal selection on the level of generality compared to the optimal portfolio. To obtain the value of debt, we should:

1. *Calculate the optimal E(r) using the optimal Sharpe ratio*

$$E(r)^* = \text{Optimal Sharpe Ratio} \times \text{Risk Value} + Rf \tag{3}$$

$E(r)^*$ is the optimal expected return that a sub-optimal portfolio should have to achieve the optimal Sharp ratio.

2. *Calculate the loss in benefit*

$$\text{Loss in Benefit} = E(r)^* \times Total\ Cost + Total\ Cost - Total\ Benefits \tag{4}$$

The value of loss in benefit is the technical debt value.

8.5 Evaluation

8.5.1 A Case Study: Home Integration System

In this section, we apply a case study of the Home Integration System (HIS) to evaluate the research. The case study is partially inspired by (Benavides, Trinidad, & Ruiz-Cortés, 2005) and (Kang & Lee, 2002) with some hypothetical data to estimate the expected returns and risk values over a five-year period to demonstrate the usability of the proposed method in the real-life context. For the simplicity of demonstration, we only focus on the development of some main functionalities in the HIS product line and show the major calculations in this section.

Step 1. Identify potential market segments, and realise business opportunities
The home integration system company aims to become a major player in providing the HIS system to budget-conscious customers. These customers will buy a small product, which consists of the core functionalities only, and will add on others according to their personal needs. Hence, the scalability and generality of the system becomes a key of the product line success. In order to exploit the market opportunities, the company decided to conduct the MPP to investigate three different markets: the basic family users, the advanced family

Table 8.5 Features required by each user group

	Fundamental Family Users	Advanced Family Users	Family & Business Users
Product Features	1. Services (fire, intrusion) 2. Facility Control (light, appliance, temperature) 3. Control (power line) 4. Emergency (call)	1. Services (fire, intrusion, flood) 2. Facility Control (light, appliance, temperature) Control (power line, remote) 3. Emergency (call, internet)	1. Services (fire, intrusion, flood, security) 2. Facility Control (light, appliance, temperature) 3. Control (power line, remote) 4. Emergency (call, internet)

users, or to sell to both family users and business clients. According to the market research, the user characteristics for each market are:

1. *Basic family users:* These are the users who do not have technical background and require only the basic functionalities from the systems.
2. *Advanced family users:* These users have special needs from the system due to the special condition of their houses.
3. *Family and business users:* Apart from the basic and advanced users, business clients require the system for the management of business building. This require a central control to the system and the ability to distribute real-time information over the network.

The features that are required by each group of users are shown in Table 8.5. According to this, we can generate the list of all the potential features (Table 8.6) that can be included in the SPL for the candidate feature models/portfolios construction.

Table 8.6 The list of all the potential features

1. Services	Fire
	Intrusion
	Flood
	Security
2. Facility Control	Light
	Appliance
	Temperature
3. Control	Power line
	Remote (internet)
4. Emergency Contact	Call
	Internet

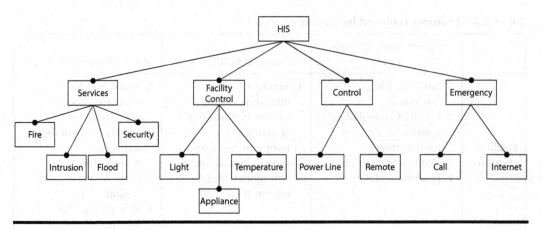

Figure 8.3   Risk-free model.

Step 2. Construct candidate portfolios

After generating the feature list, we are able to construct the risk-free portfolio, and the corresponding candidate portfolios for each market. Here, the initial feature models are constructed and shown from Figure 8.3 to Figure 8.6 As mentioned in the prior section, the decision on commonality or variability of each feature depends on the understanding of the real demands from the potential markets.

Step 3. Estimate the costs and the benefits, and calculate the expected returns

For each portfolio, we can now estimate the costs and benefits to calculate the expected return (Tables 8.7 to Table 8.10). As described in the prior section, costs can be both economical and non-economical. In the case study, we consider only the procurement and personnel costs for simplicity. In reality, costs and benefits in the five-year period are estimated by various experts and stakeholders. The calculations for each portfolio are shown in Table 8.11.

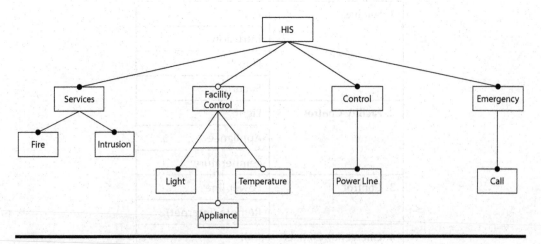

Figure 8.4   Portfolio 1 for the basic family users.

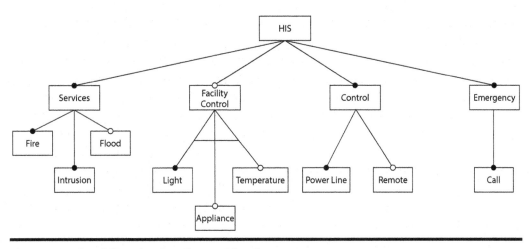

Figure 8.5   Portfolio 2 for the advanced family users.

The expected return for the risk-free portfolio is 7.57%, which will be used as the risk-free rate to calculate the Sharpe ratios at the later step.

Step 4. Evaluate the risk level for each portfolio

At this stage, scenarios are designed as the discussion results by experts and stakeholders. The scenarios for the case study are shown in Table 8.12. Suppose we have three evaluators, and their estimations on each portfolio are shown from Table 8.13 to 8.15. The final estimations on the portfolio risk values are calculated based on the estimations made by the evaluators and their confidence levels (see Table 8.16).

Step 5. Calculate the Sharpe ratios, identify the optimal portfolio, and calculate the technical debts

According to the figures that have been generated from the previous steps, we can calculate the Sharpe Ratio to rank the portfolios using Formula 2 and identify the optimal portfolio. In the case study, portfolio 3 (for the family and business users) received the highest ratio of 2.17, and hence, is the optimal portfolio for the product line.

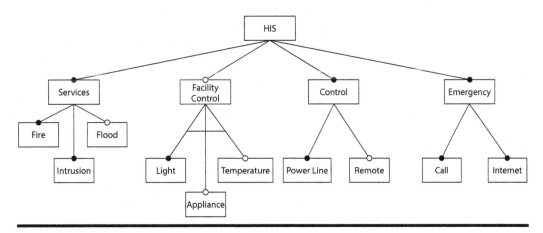

Figure 8.6   Portfolio 3 for family and business user.

Table 8.7 The estimated costs, benefits, and expected return of the Risk-free portfolio

		Commonality (c) or Variability (v)	Cost		Benefit (Saving from future implementation)
			Procurement Cost	Personnel Cost	
1. Services	Fire	c	1,300	1,650	6,000
	Intrusion	c	1,200	2,000	5,000
	Flood	c	1,800	2,100	2,050
	Security	c	2,500	2,500	3,000
2. Facility Control	Light	c	1,350	1,600	5,000
	Appliance	c	1,050	1,000	1,800
	Temperature	c	1,000	1,350	3,500
3. Control	Power line	c	1,200	1,500	2,500
	Remote (internet)	c	2,300	2,800	3,500
4. Emergency Contact	Call	c	900	1,250	3,000
	Internet	c	1,500	1,800	3,000
Total			**35,650**		**38,350**
Expected Return Rate					**7.57%**

Risk-free Portfolio

Table 8.8 The estimated costs, benefits, and expected return of the portfolio 1

		Commonality (c) or Variability (v)	Cost		Benefit (Saving from future implementation)
			Procurement Cost	Personnel Cost	
1. Services	Fire	c	1,300	1,650	6,000
	Intrusion	c	1,200	2,000	5,000
2. Facility Control	Light	c	1,350	1,600	5,000
	Appliance	v	500	750	1,350
3. Control	Power line	v	800	900	2,000
4. Emergency Contact	Call	c	900	1,250	3,000
Total			**14,200**		**22,350**
Expected Return Rate					**47.04%**

Portfolio 1. Basic Family Users

Table 8.9 The estimated costs, benefits, and expected return of portfolio 2

Portfolio 2. Advanced Family Users					
		Commonality (c) or Variability (v)	Cost		Benefit (Saving from future implementation)
			Procurement Cost	Personnel Cost	
1. Services	Fire	c	1,300	1,650	6,000
	Intrusion	c	1,200	2,000	5,000
	Flood	c	1,800	2,100	2,050
2. Facility Control	Light	c	1,350	1,600	5,000
	Appliance	v	500	750	1,350
	Temperature	v	1,000	1,350	3,500
3. Control	Power line	c	1,200	1,500	2,500
	Remote (internet)	v	1,000	1,800	3,500
4. Emergency Contact	Call	c	900	1,250	3,000
Total			24,250		31,900
Expected Return Rate					31.55%

Table 8.10 The estimated costs, benefits, and expected return of the portfolio 3

Portfolio 3. Family & Business Users					
		Commonality (c) or Variability (v)	Cost		Benefit (Saving from future implementation)
			Procurement Cost	Personnel Cost	
1. Services	Fire	c	1,300	1,650	6,000
	Intrusion	c	1,200	2,000	5,000
	Flood	v	900	1,000	1,200
	Security	v	1,200	1,000	2,400
2. Facility Control	Light	c	1,350	1,600	5,000
	Appliance	v	600	600	1,400
	Temperature	v	550	700	1,300
3. Control	Power line	c	1,200	1,500	2,500
	Remote (internet)	v	1,000	1,800	3,500
4. Emergency Contact	Call	c	900	1,250	3,000
	Internet	v	700	900	1,600
Total			24,900		32,900
Expected Return Rate					32.13%

Table 8.11 Summary of portfolio costs, benefits, and expected returns

	Cost	Benefit	E(r)
Risk-free Portfolio	35,650	38,350	7.57%
Portfolio 1	16,900	24,850	47.04%
Portfolio 2	24,250	31,900	31.55%
Portfolio 3	24,900	32,900	32.13%

Once the optimal portfolio is identified, we can compare the other two with its Sharpe ratio, and use Formula 3 to get the optimal expected return for the sub-optimal portfolios. Formula 4 can then be used to calculate the value of technical debt. The result of portfolio ranking, Sharpe ratio, and the technical debt values are shown in Table 8.17.

According to Table 8.17, the company can evaluate the appropriateness to investigate in different markets according to the budget and the risk level that they are willing to take. Note: the case study shows the optimality of the candidate portfolios after five years only. However, the ranking and the relative risk and debt level might vary as the expected life cycle of the product line is extended. A company needs to decide and evaluate on the time that they expect a product line to sustain in order to generate the appropriate data for the evaluation.

8.6 Quality of Estimations

In the previous section, we used hypothetical data to evaluate the proposed method for simplicity. However, as the method is qualitative and the accuracy of it heavily relies on the validity of the input data, organisations should carefully manage and generate the data from reliable sources. To achieve this, organisations should first critically review the historical data and assess that it is suitable to support the estimation. For example, if a company has the past experience in developing a software component that is required by the product line now, the company can make cost and benefit estimations according to the historical data. Second, the project manager should be able to identify who the qualified stakeholders are that are experienced and professional enough to be the evaluators. These evaluators have relative knowledge about the systems, so their estimations are more valuable to the

Table 8.12 Scenario list

Scenario	Description	Associated Risks
Scenario 1	Flood detection feature required	Compatibility Risk Quality Risk
Scenario 2	Remote control of the system required	Compatibility Risk Quality Risk
Scenario 3	Regular maintenance and repairing	Maintenance Risk
Scenario 4	Raising demand from business clients	Compatibility Risk Quality Risk

Table 8.13 Estimation 1

Portfolio	Scenario	Risk	Consequence	Likelihood	Confidence	Risk Value
Portfolio 1	Scenario 1	Compatibility Risk	3	40%	80%	19.20%
		Quality Risk	1	40%	80%	6.40%
	Scenario 2	Compatibility Risk	4	35%	60%	16.80%
		Quality Risk	4	35%	60%	16.80%
	Scenario 3	Maintenance Risk	2	100%	95%	38.00%
	Scenario 4	Compatibility Risk	5	60%	70%	42.00%
		Quality Risk	5	60%	70%	42.00%
	Total		N/A	N/A	N/A	25.89%
Portfolio 2	Scenario 1	Compatibility Risk	0	0%	100%	0.00%
		Quality Risk	0	0%	100%	0.00%
	Scenario 2	Compatibility Risk	1	70%	80%	11.20%
		Quality Risk	1	70%	80%	11.20%
	Scenario 3	Maintenance Risk	3	90%	90%	48.60%
	Scenario 4	Compatibility Risk	4	70%	60%	33.60%
		Quality Risk	4	70%	60%	33.60%
	Total		N/A	N/A	N/A	19.74%
Portfolio 3	Scenario 1	Compatibility Risk	0	0%	100%	0.00%
		Quality Risk	0	0%	100%	0.00%
	Scenario 2	Compatibility Risk	1	70%	80%	11.20%
		Quality Risk	1	70%	80%	11.20%
	Scenario 3	Maintenance Risk	4	80%	90%	57.60%
	Scenario 4	Compatibility Risk	1	80%	70%	11.20%
		Quality Risk	1	80%	70%	11.20%
	Total		N/A	N/A	N/A	14.63%

Table 8.14   Estimation 2

Portfolio	Scenario	Risk	Consequence	Likelihood	Confidence	Risk Value
Portfolio 1	Scenario 1	Compatibility Risk	4	70%	80%	44.80%
		Quality Risk	3	70%	80%	33.60%
	Scenario 2	Compatibility Risk	3	20%	70%	8.40%
		Quality Risk	3	20%	70%	8.40%
	Scenario 3	Maintenance Risk	1	100%	100%	20.00%
	Scenario 4	Compatibility Risk	5	70%	80%	56.00%
		Quality Risk	5	70%	80%	56.00%
	Total		N/A	N/A	N/A	32.46%
Portfolio 2	Scenario 1	Compatibility Risk	0	50%	100%	0.00%
		Quality Risk	0	50%	100%	0.00%
	Scenario 2	Compatibility Risk	0	50%	80%	0.00%
		Quality Risk	0	50%	80%	0.00%
	Scenario 3	Maintenance Risk	3	70%	70%	29.40%
	Scenario 4	Compatibility Risk	3	70%	80%	33.60%
		Quality Risk	3	70%	80%	33.60%
	Total		N/A	N/A	N/A	13.80%
Portfolio 3	Scenario 1	Compatibility Risk	0	50%	100%	0.00%
		Quality Risk	0	50%	100%	0.00%
	Scenario 2	Compatibility Risk	0	50%	80%	0.00%
		Quality Risk	0	50%	80%	0.00%
	Scenario 3	Maintenance Risk	4	100%	90%	72.00%
	Scenario 4	Compatibility Risk	1	20%	90%	3.60%
		Quality Risk	1	20%	90%	3.60%
	Total		N/A	N/A	N/A	11.31%

Table 8.15 Estimation 3

Portfolio	Scenario	Risk	Consequence	Likelihood	Confidence	Risk Value
Portfolio 1	Scenario 1	Compatibility Risk	4	50%	60%	24.00%
		Quality Risk	4	50%	60%	24.00%
	Scenario 2	Compatibility Risk	3	10%	60%	3.60%
		Quality Risk	3	10%	60%	3.60%
	Scenario 3	Maintenance Risk	1	100%	100%	20.00%
	Scenario 4	Compatibility Risk	5	70%	50%	35.00%
		Quality Risk	5	70%	50%	35.00%
	Total		N/A	N/A	N/A	20.74%
Portfolio 2	Scenario 1	Compatibility Risk	0	50%	100%	0.00%
		Quality Risk	0	50%	100%	0.00%
	Scenario 2	Compatibility Risk	0	10%	100%	0.00%
		Quality Risk	0	10%	100%	0.00%
	Scenario 3	Maintenance Risk	2	80%	80%	25.60%
	Scenario 4	Compatibility Risk	4	70%	50%	28.00%
		Quality Risk	4	70%	50%	28.00%
	Total		N/A	N/A	N/A	11.66%
Portfolio 3	Scenario 1	Compatibility Risk	0	50%	100%	0.00%
		Quality Risk	0	50%	100%	0.00%
	Scenario 2	Compatibility Risk	0	50%	80%	0.00%
		Quality Risk	0	50%	80%	0.00%
	Scenario 3	Maintenance Risk	3	100%	70%	42.00%
	Scenario 4	Compatibility Risk	1	70%	50%	7.00%
		Quality Risk	1	70%	50%	7.00%
	Total		N/A	N/A	N/A	8.00%

Table 8.16   Estimated risk value of each portfolio

	Estimation 1	*Estimation 2*	*Estimation 3*	*Total*
Portfolio 1	25.89%	32.46%	20.74%	**26.36%**
Portfolio 2	19.74%	13.80%	11.66%	**15.07%**
Portfolio 3	14.63%	11.31%	8.00%	**11.31%**

SPL development. As mentioned before, evaluators' estimations can be biased according to their personal preference. Hence, to eliminate the bias made from different evaluators, our proposed method rated the weight of each of the evaluations according to their confidence levels.

8.7 Discussion

The purpose of this chapter is to evaluate the optimal level of SPL generality by assessing costs, risks, and RTD of each candidate feature set. The study has developed a systematic evaluation process based on the modern portfolio theory and applied the proposed method to the case study of the Home Integrating System (HIS) to demonstrate its usefulness in the real-life situations.

The modern portfolio theory is well grounded for mitigating risks from diversification, however, when it is applied to our method some limitations still remain. The major limitation is the accuracy of estimations. Portfolio costs, benefits, and risk severities are estimated based on evaluators' experiences and confidence levels, which makes the whole process subjective. Although we have tried to eliminate the biased human factors as much as possible by involving various evaluators and emphasizing the importance of evaluators' professionalism, the degree of accuracy of estimations is still debatable. Consequently, this approach might only be able identify a "better portfolio," rather than an optimal portfolio.

According to (Ojameruaye & Bahsoon, 2014), we can score a methodology by its maturity stage. Our approach here is considered at the inception stage, which makes it hard to prove the generalisation of the proposed method. Therefore, in the future, more case studies and data should be tested in long-term to make the required refinements and to prove its applicability.

Furthermore, in order to improve the quality of estimations, there is a need to convert those non-economic costs and benefits into economic ones. With the realisation of the importance of requirement debt in SPL development, identifying various risks other than the ones that is realised in this chapter is also helpful to determine debt values.

Table 8.17   Portfolio ranking, Sharpe ratios, and technical debts

Portfolio	*E(r)*	*Risk Value*	*Sharpe Ratio*	*Optimal E(r)*	*Technical Debt*
Family & Business Users	32.13%	11.31%	2.17	32.13%	0.00
Advance Family Users	31.55%	15.07%	1.59	40.27%	2115.99
Basic Family Users	47.04%	26.36%	1.5	64.79%	2998.78

Conclusion

From this chapter, we realise the need of evaluating and managing commonality and variability in SPL development. The evaluation process is developed based on the marketing and product plan, modern portfolio theory and technical debt with specific focus at the requirement level. The main sources of TD were identified, which are compatibility risk, quality risk and maintenance risk. The proposed method is aimed at identifying the optimal market and feature set that is considered the most profitable with the awareness of the identified debt sources and the associated technical debt. The proposed method was illustrated using the HIS case study to prove the applicability. The result shows that the optimality of a product line is affected by the risks associated with it, which could lead to TD in the future. It was also proved that the approach was helpful in identifying the optimal selection of commonality and variability set for the product line development with the consideration of TD. Finally, we discussed the method limitations on the estimation and suggested the nature of future research work that can be done.

References

Alves, V., Niu, N., Alves, C., & Valença, G. (2010, August). Requirements engineering for software product lines: A systematic literature review. *ScienceDirect*, 52(8), 806-820.

Benavides, D., Trinidad, P., & Ruiz-Cortés, A. (2005). Automated Reasoning on Feature. Conference on Advanced Information Systems Engineering (CAISE), (491-503 July).

Bosch, J., Capilla, R., & Hilliard, R. (2015, April 23). Trends in Systems and Software Variability. *IEEE Software*, 32(3), 44-51.

Clements, P., & Northrop, L. (2002). *Software Product Lines: Practices and Patterns*. Addison-Wesley.

Cunningham, W. (1992). The WyCash Portfolio Management System. OOPSLA '92 Addendum to the proceedings on Object-oriented programming systems, languages, and applications (Addendum) (pp. 29-30). Vancouver, British Columbia, Canada: ACM.

De Vylder, T. (2010, November). Feature Modelling: A Survey, a Formalism and a Transformation for Analysis. Retrieved from Modelling, Simulation and Design Lab: http://msdl.cs.mcgill.ca/people/hv/teaching/MSBDesign/201011/projects/Thomas.DeVylder/

Ensan, A., Bagheri, E., Asadi, M., Gasevic, D., & Biletskiy, Y. (2011). Goal-Oriented Test Case Selection and Prioritization for Product Line Feature Models. *Information Technology: New Generations (ITNG)* (pp. 291-298). Las Vegas: IEEE.

Etxeberria, L., Sagardui, G., & Belategi, L. (2008, March). Quality aware software product line engineering. *Journal of the Brazilian Computer Society*, 14(1), 57-69.

Fowler, M. (2009, October 14). TechnicalDebtQuadrant. Retrieved from martinfowler.com: https://martinfowler.com/bliki/TechnicalDebtQuadrant.html.

Guo, Y., & Seaman, C. (2011). A Portfolio Approach to Technical Debt Management. Second International Workshop on Managing Technical Debt. Waikiki, Honolulu, Hawaii.

Kang, K., & Lee, J. (2002). Feature-oriented product line engineering. *IEEE Software*, 19(4), 58-65.

Kishi, T., Noda, N., & Katayama, T. (2002). A Method for Product Line Scoping Based on a Decision-Making Framework. International Conference on Software Product Lines (pp. 348-365). San Diego: Springer.

Li, J., Liu, X., Wang, Y., & Guo, J. (2011). Formalizing Feature Selection Problem in Software Product Lines Using 0-1 Programming. Proceedings of the Sixth International Conference on Intelligent Systems and Knowledge Engineering, (pp. 459-465). Shanghai.

Li, Z., Avgeriou, P., & Liang, P. (2015, March). A systematic mapping study on technical debt and its management. *Journal of Systems and Software*, 101, 193-220.

Mannion, M., & Savolainen, J. (2016). Choosing Reusable Software Strategies. Proceedings of the 20th International Systems and Software Product Line Conference (pp. 227-231). Beijing, China: ACM.

Markowitz, H. (1952, Mar.). Portfolio selection. *The Journal of Finance*, 7(1), 77-91.

McConnell, S. (2007, November 1). Technical Debt. Retrieved from Construx: http://www.construx.com/10x_Software_Development/Technical_Debt/

Nord, R., Ozkaya, I., Kruchten, P., & Gonzalez-rojas, M. (2012). In Search of a Metric for Managing Architectural Technical Debt. Software Architecture (WICSA) and European Conference on Software Architecture (ECSA) (pp. 20-24). Helsinki, Finland: IEEE.

Ojameruaye, B., & Bahsoon, R. (2014). Systematic Elaboration of Compliance Requirements Using Compliance Debt and Portfolio Theory. International Working Conference (pp. 152-167). Essen, Germany: Springer.

Portfolio Management. (2011). Modern Portfolio Theory (MPT). Retrieved from Portfolio Management: http://www.portfoliomanagement.in/author/Sushant.

Schmid, K. (2016). *Technical Debt in Product Lines*. Schloss Dagstuhl.

Sharpe, W. F. (1996). Mutual fund performance. *The Journal of Business*, 39(1), 119-138.

Chapter 9

Realising Variability in Dynamic Software Product Lines

Jane D. A. Sandim Eleutério[a], Breno B. N. de França[b],
Cecilia M. F. Rubira[b], and Rogério de Lemos[c]

[a]Faculty of Computing, Federal University of Mato Grosso do Sul, Mato Grosso do Sul, Brazil
[b]Institute of Computing, University of Campinas, São Paulo, Brazil
[c]School of Computing, University of Kent, Kent, United Kingdom

9.1 Introduction

Modern software systems need to adapt both at design time and runtime to heterogeneous environments and devices. Software product lines (SPLs) are related to emerging techniques where several artefacts are reused. Software product line (SPLs) deal with the modelling of commonalities and variabilities among a family of similar systems (Rosenmüller, et al. 2011). Commonality corresponds to similar parts among family products, while variability is defined as the ability of a product to be extended, modified, customised, or configured for a specific context (Svahnberg, van Gurp and Bosch 2005). In general, feature models (Kang and Lee 2013) are used to represent variability and commonality by means of features that can be classified as mandatory, optional or alternative (Kang, Cohen, et al. 1990). Mandatory features are present in all products derived from SPL. Optional features may or may not appear in derived products, while alternative features may be selected according to mutual exclusion constraints. While SPLs deal with static variability, which is defined at design time, and its decision is performed using binding, dynamic software product line (DSPLs) deal with both static and dynamic variability. Dynamic variability, also called late or runtime variability, is also defined at design time, however, its decision is performed using binding at deployment or runtime.

Systems able to adapt their behaviour and/or structure at runtime are called self-adaptive software systems (SASS) (Cheng, et al. 2009). These systems should be able to adapt in response to changes that occur to the system itself, its environment, or even its goals, with no human interference. Feedback control loops provide a generic mechanism of self-adaptation (Brun, et al. 2009), and they are often modelled as the MAPE-K loop (Kephart and Chess 2003). Software engineers could systematically reuse SASS good practices to develop DSPL approaches.

From the perspective of variability, software product lines (SPLs) deal with commonalities and variabilities in product families by performing binding during the design phase. Dynamic software product lines (DSPLs) are considered a subtype of SPLs, which handles variability by performing binding at runtime. From the perspective of dynamicity, self-adaptive software systems (SASS) are able to dynamically adapt their structure during runtime when responding to changes.

According to Bencomo et al. (2010), many DSPL approaches are not as dynamic as they should be, because they partially (or do not) implement self-adaptation activities. Bencomo et al. (2010) also conclude the research on DSPL variability is still heavily based on the specification of variability decisions during design time. In other words, variability and its decision options are defined at design time, and variability decision making occurs during execution. Ideally, a DSPL solution should allow new decision options to be incorporated at runtime, improving the dynamicity of such solution. Dynamicity can be understood as the system's ability to undergo changes and adapt at runtime, reacting to foreseen, foreseeable, and unanticipated changes in the most autonomous way as possible. Ideally, DSPL systems should be easy to understand, maintain and reuse. With such systems growing in size and complexity, employing self-adaptation and variability techniques while satisfying the software quality attributes, such as modifiability, reusability, and testability, are deep concerns to the DSPL systems engineers.

The goal of this chapter is to define a two-dimensional taxonomy that aims to identify how design issues related to variability and self-adaptation can affect the key quality attributes of DSPLs. In the context of self-adaptive system, variability design issues are related to the managed subsystem (or target system), the self-adaptation design issues are related to managing subsystem (or controller, or feedback control loop), and the quality attributes are related to the self-adaptive system that encapsulates both the managed and managing subsystems. Based on the above, the major contributions of this chapter are: (i) identifying design issues related to variability and self-adaptation that are relevant to DSPLs, and (ii) evaluating these design issues in the context of quality attributes that are pertinent to DSPLs. Based on our findings, we have also identified several research challenges when building DSPLs that make use of the SASS principles.

The remainder of this chapter is organised as follows. Section 9.2 gives a brief description of dynamic software product line (DSPL) and self-adaptive software systems (SASS). Section 9.3 describes a proposed taxonomy for classifying different design issues to DSPL, analysing set of investigated DSPL approaches. Section 9.4 presents an appropriate design criteria based on quality attributes for an ideal DSPL solution. Section 9.5 discusses some research challenges. Finally, Section 9.6 presents some concluding remarks and lessons learned.

9.2 Perspectives on Variability and Self-adaptation

Over the years, several contributions have emerged that apply variability modelling concepts, using features models, in the development of self-adaptive software systems, such as MoRE (Cetina and Pelechano 2013), MADAM (Hallsteinsen, et al. 2006), and DiVA (Morin, et al. 2009). From the viewpoint of runtime adaptation, variability modelling can include both system (*functional*) and context (*environmental*) information, and if well established, variability modelling promises to be a valuable basis for the definition of appropriate models in time of execution. Context information includes data related to the environment where the system is running, such as network, memory resources, battery level, and battery consumption, and other computing resources, while system information is obtained by specific sensors that monitor the system components at runtime.

On the other hand, research on DSPLs has increasingly been using SASS techniques to improve the management of runtime variability, such as ASPL (Abbas and Andersson 2013), ArCMAPE (Nascimento, Rubira and Castor 2014), and BSN-DSPL (Pessoa, et al. 2017). The MAPE-K feedback control loop (Section 9.2.2) can be applied to automate variability and product derivation management processes at runtime. Thus, we can infer that there is a synergy between these two areas of research, which encompasses both DSPLs that support dynamic variability using SASS techniques, and SASS that apply (D)SPL techniques to manage variability at runtime.

9.2.1 Dynamic Software Product Line

The Dynamic Software Product Line (DSPL) extends the concept of conventional SPL since the latter emphasises the variability analysis, decision making and product configuration at the design time. DSPL emphasises variability analysis at design time but postpones the decision of the variability and the application reconfiguration to be made at runtime.

In SPLs, the binding can occur at design time to generate a product using static binding. In the case of DSPLs, the binding should occur at runtime in order to support dynamic variability. Dynamic variability (also called *late* or *runtime variability*) can be represented using dynamic compositions, which is a set of features with dynamic binding (Rosenmüller, Siegmund and Saake, et al. 2008). In contrast, static variability can be represented using static compositions, which is a set of features with static binding (van Gurp, Bosch and Svahnberg 2001).

9.2.2 Self-adaptive Software Systems

Self-adaptive software systems are systems that are able to modify their behaviour and/or structure in response to changes that occur to the system itself, its environment or even its goals (Lemos, et al. 2013).

Self-adaptation enables a system to adjust itself in response to changes, and there is a wide range of approaches to engineering self-adaptive software systems through tried and tested reference models. For example, Weyns et al. (2010) formalise the self-adaptive system's environment as a collection of *processes* and *attributes* using their FOrmal Reference Model for self-adaptation (FORMS). Although there are several reference models for self-adaptive software systems (Kephart and Chess 2003) (Kramer and Magee 2007) (Oreizy, et al. 1999), most of them share the common use of a feedback loop (Brun, et al. 2009) (Dobson, et al. 2006) (Hellerstein, et al. 2004). In this chapter, we adopt as a feedback control loop, the Monitor, Analyse, Plan, Execute—Knowledge (MAPE-K) reference model (Kephart and Chess 2003), as shown in Figure 9.1.

The main feedback control loop in the *Managing Subsystem*, which embodies the stages of the MAPE-K reference model, observes (via probes) and adapts (via effectors) a *Managed Subsystem*. The *Monitor* stage enables to obtain the state of the target system and its environment. The *Analyse* stage analyses the state of the target system and its environment in order, first, to decide whether adaptation should be triggered, and second, to identify the appropriate courses of action in case adaptation is required. The *Plan* stage, first, selects among alternative course of action those that are the most appropriate, and second, generates the plans that will realise the selected course of action. The *Execute* stage executes the plans that deploy the course of action for adapting the system. Finally, *Knowledge* represents any information related to the perceived state of the target system and environment that enables the provision of self-adaptation.

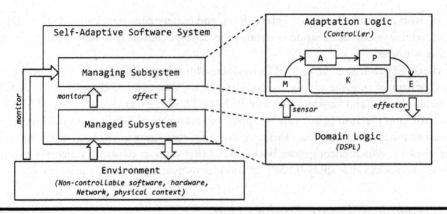

Figure 9.1   DSPL in the context of SASS.

9.2.3 DSPL versus SASS

Weyns et al. (2013) use the general terms manager subsystem and managed subsystem to indicate the constituent parts of a self-adaptive software system. The first part of Figure 9.1 (left side) represents this separation, where the managing subsystem manages the managed subsystem and is organised according to an autonomic control loop, and the managed subsystem consists of the application logic that provides the system's domain functionality.

The second part of Figure 9.1 (right side) illustrates a DSPL application represented as a self-adaptive system, in order to encompass managed and managing subsystems. The managed subsystem is a DSPL, which contains the application logic, according to its domain. This subsystem is unconscious of the rest of the system, and its components (parts) are isolated and do not access the rest of the system. The managing subsystem is a controller, which includes the adaptation logic and is independent of DSPL. So the logic can be reused in different domains. The managing subsystem is transparent to the DSPL and is responsible for monitoring, adaptation reasoning and acting on DSPL. Finally, the entire system interacts with an environment, which refers to the context in which the system is running, including hardware, operating system, other systems and networks access.

9.3 A Taxonomy for DSPL

There are several design issues for implementing DSPL approaches, and for each approach there are different associated alternative strategies, called design solutions. The proposed taxonomy identifies several common design issues for implementing DSPLs, and classifies their different design solutions. The taxonomy was developed based on previous studies that define taxonomies in the area of self-adaptation (Oreizy, et al. 1999) (Mckinley, Sadjadi, et al. 2004a) (Salehie and Tahvildari 2009) (Andersson, de Lemos, et al. 2009a) and DSPL (Galster, et al. 2014) (Bashari, Bagheri and Du 2017).

9.3.1 Dimensions of Taxonomy

Our proposed taxonomy classifies the design issues of a DSPL scheme into two dimensions: the first dimension is related to variability design issues, while the second dimension is related to self-adaptation design issues.

Variability dimension. This dimension was based on previous taxonomies (Bashari, Bagheri and Du 2017) (Galster, et al. 2014). Bashari *et al.* present a detailed adaptation taxonomy for DSPL, establishing an individual classification for each MAPE-K activity, that is: monitor, analyse, plan and execute. Galster et al. have provided a variability characterisation for software systems.

Using the taxonomies of Bashari et al. (2017) and Galster et al. (2014), we combine similar design issues and remove design solutions that are applicable only to SPL (static variability). Besides, design issues related to the self-adaptation process were reallocated to the self-adaptation dimension (Section 9.3.4), such as design issues and its design solutions for the MAPE-K loop.

After, the variability dimension was analysed using the DSPLs selected for validation (Section 9.3.2). This analysis also resulted in the refining of the set of design solutions and the addition of the design issue for feature modelling strategy and the platform to implement variability. Section 9.3.3 describes the variability dimension and applies it to the selected DSPLs.

Self-adaptation dimension. This dimension was based on previous taxonomies (Oreizy, et al. 1999) (Mckinley, Sadjadi, et al. 2004a) (Salehie and Tahvildari 2009) (Andersson, de Lemos, et al. 2009a). McKinley et al. (Mckinley, Sadjadi, et al. 2004a) have proposed a compositional adaptation taxonomy, comparing *how*, *when* and *where* the recomposition occurs. Later, Salehie and Tahvildari (2009) proposed a taxonomy for self-adaptation, that relies on the object to adapt (*what*), realisation issues (*how*), temporal characteristics (*when*), and interaction concerns of adaptation (*where*), extending the taxonomies of Oreizy et al. (1999) and McKinley et al. (2004a). Andersson et al. (2009a) have presented an adaptation taxonomy for self-adaptive software systems, focusing on modelling dimension.

Using these previous taxonomies, we combine similar design issues and remove design solutions that are not applicable to DSPLs, generating a first version of the self-adaptive dimension of our taxonomy. Besides, we have added design issues related to the feedback control loop MAPE-K.

After, our initial self-adaptation dimension was analysed using the DSPLs selected for validation (Section 9.3.2). This analysis also resulted in the refining of the set of design solutions and the addition of the design issue for the architectural pattern used. Section 9.3.4 describes the self-adaptation dimension and applies it to the selected DSPLs.

9.3.2 Selection of DSPL Approaches

We have selected relevant approaches in the intersection of DSPLs and SASS. In particular, we have selected two types of systems: (i) SPLs that support dynamic variability, and (ii) self-adaptive systems that apply SPL techniques to manage variability at runtime. The selected DSPL approaches that support some form of dynamic variability are: Abbas et al. (ASPL) (Abbas and Andersson 2013) (Abbas, et al 2010); Abotsi et al. (2011); Baresi et al. (2012); Bencomo et al. (Genie) (Bencomo, Blair, et al. 2008) (Bencomo, Grace, et al. 2008); Casquina et al. (Cosmapek) (Casquina, et al 2016); Cetina et al. (MoRE) (Cetina, Giner, et al. 2009) (Cetina, Fons and Pelechano 2008); Cubo et al. (Dynamic DAMASCo) (Cubo, et al. 2013) (Cubo, et al. 2015); Fuentes, et al 2009; Gomaa and Hashimoto (2011); Hallsteinsen et al. (MADAM) (Hallsteinsen, et al. 2006) (Floch, et al. 2006) (Geihs, et al. 2009); Lee et al. (Lee, Kotonya and Robinson 2012) (Lee and Kotonya 2010); Morin et al. (DiVA) (Morin, et al. 2009) (Morin, et al. 2009) (Morin, Fleurey, et al. 2008); Nascimento et al. (ArCMAPE) (Nascimento, Rubira and Castor 2014) (A. S. Nascimento, et al. 2013); Parra et al. (CAPucine) (Parra, Blanc and Duchien 2009) (Parra, et al. 2011); Pessoa et al. (2017); Rosenmüller et al. (Rosenmüller, et al. 2008) (Rosenmüller, et al. 2011). This list was defined based on two sources of information: (i) the systematic mapping study developed by the authors to identify approaches that include dependability attributes in DSPLs (Eleutério, et al. 2016), and (ii) two surveys (Bencomo, Lee and Hallsteinsen 2010) (Bashari, Bagheri and Du 2017) that identify DSPLs and analyse the use of the MAPE-K feedback control loop.

This previous systematic mapping study (Eleutério, et al. 2016) reviewed papers about Dependable DSPLs selecting nine primary studies. In addition, we made a comparison of the primary studies regarding the MAPE-K loop activities and the DSPL dimension. The survey developed by Bencomo et al. (Bencomo, Lee and Hallsteinsen 2010) questioned the dynamism level of DSPL approaches compared to MAPE-K loop. They selected nine DSPL approaches and analysed whether each DSPL meet phases of feedback control loop at runtime (dynamic) or design time (static). The survey presented by Bashari et al. (2017) proposed a conceptual framework for comparing adaptation realisation in DSPL based on MAPE-K loop. They also compared seven DSPL approaches using the proposed framework.

Table 9.1 and Table 9.2 summarize the main aspects of the DSPL approaches presented in this section, showing the different strategies for each design issue of our taxonomy (Section 9.3). In order to compare the DSPL approaches, we assign weights to each design strategy, which reflect the contribution (negative, neutral, positive and +positive) of that strategy in facilitating the construction of DSPL applications. A negative weight (−1) is attributed when a solution clarifies that it does not explicitly support a design issue or when the chosen design issue is a poor choice. However, in some situations, it is not possible to claim there is support or not a specific design issue, and in this case, we choose not to penalise the solution, indicating as 'Not specified' (−). A positive weight (+1) is attributed to the solution when a good design issue is chosen. And a +positive weight (+2) is attributed to the solution when it chooses the design issue considered the best choice. Adding up the weights of a DSPL approach produces a final score that is an indication of the suitability of that implementation developing well-structured DSPLs.

The reader should note that some design issues have mutually exclusive design strategies, while for others, the strategies have an additive character (these are marked with '+' in Table 9.1 and Table 9.2). Thus, the highest score attainable by a approach is 38, obtained by adding the maximum possible scores for each design issue. Section 9.3.3 evaluates the selected approaches (Section 9.3.2) for each design issue included in the variability dimension (D1). Section 9.3.4 evaluates the same approaches considering the design issues of the self-adaptation dimension (D2). Section 9.3.5 summarises our findings.

9.3.3 Variability Dimension

Table 9.1 presents the design issues and their respective design solutions of the variability dimension applied to the selected DSPLs, which are discussed in the following text.

D1-A1. Variability Type. Static variability is performed by the compiler while dynamic variability is performed by the system itself at runtime. A DSPL approach must support at least dynamic variability. We classify the design approaches for supporting DSPL variability in two types: (i) *only dynamic variability* and (ii) *both static and dynamic variabilities.* For the purpose of enhancing the structuring of DSPL systems, it is desirable to allow the support of both variability types. As a result, the support of both static and dynamic variability is assigned weight +2 while the support of only dynamic variability received +1.

D1-A2. Variability Conceptual Model. Although Kang and Lee (2013) present only two variability models for SPLs—feature model and decision model—we also consider other strategies for the variability modelling raised by Galster et al. (2014). Thus, the variability can be represented

Table 9.1 Summary of variability dimension

Variability Dimension	Design Issue	Abbas et al.	Abotsi et al.	Baresi et al.	Bencomo et al.	Casquina et al.	Cetina et al.	Cubo et al.	Fuentes & Gamez	Gomaa & Hashimoto	Hallsteinsen et al.	Lee et al.	Morin et al.	Nascimento et al.	Parra et al.	Pessoa et al.	Rosenmüller et al.
Variability Type	Dynamic	+1	+1	+1	+1		+1		+1	+1	+1		+1	+1	+1	+1	
	Static & Dynamic					+2		+2				+2					+2
Variability Conceptual Model	Feature model	+2	+2	+2	+2	+2	+2	+2	+2	+2		+2	+2	+2	+2	+2	+2
	Decision model																
	Change scenarios																
	Profiles																
	Rules/Conditions																
	Labels/Annotations									0							
Feature Modelling Strategy	FM only with dynamic features	0	0	0	0		0		0	0			0	0	0	0	
	Multiple models					+1		+1									+1
	Single model											+2					
Architectural Model	Unsupported		–							–						–	–1
	Customized lang.	+1		+1		+1	+1	+1			+1	+1		+1		+1	
	ADL			+1				+1				+1					
Architectural Style	Unsupported																–1
	Component-based	+1		+1					+1			+1				+1	
	Service-oriented		+1				+1					+1					
	Hybrid		+2		+2		+2			+2			+2	+2	+2		
Variability Managed Element	Code																+1
	Componente	+1	+1		+1	+1		+1	+1	+1	+1		+1	+1	+1	+1	
	Service		+1	+1			+1	+1		+1		+1	+1	+1	+1		
	Aspect		+1					+1					+1		+1		
	Architecture																
Variability Traceability	Direct link	+2	–	–	+2	+2			–		–	–	+2	+2	+2	–	+2
	Traceability matrix						+1	+1		+1							
	Transform. rules																
	Score	8	7	7	8	11	7	11	7	8	4	11	11	10	8	6	6

– Not specified.

Table 9.2 Summary of self-adaptation dimension

Self-Adaptation Dimension	Design Issue	Abbas et al.	Abotsi et al.	Baresi et al.	Bencomo et al.	Casquina et al.	Cetina et al.	Cubo et al.	Fuentes & Gamez	Comsa & Hashimoto	Hallsteinsen et al.	Lee et al.	Morin et al.	Nascimento et al.	Parra et al.	Pessoa et al.	Rosemüller et al.
Adaptation Cause	Context	+1	+1		+1		+1	+1	+1	+1	+1	+1	+1	+1		+1	+1
	System	+1	+1	+1		+1					+1	+1	+1	+1	+1		
	User			+1												+1	
Adaptation Automation	Assisted			0													
	Autonomous	+1	+1		+1	+1	+1	+1	+1	+1	+1	+1	+1	+1	+1	+1	+1
Adaptation Binding Time	Design					+1		+1	+1			+1					+1
	Load	+1									+1						
	Runtime	+1	+1	+1	+1	+1	+1	+1	+1	+1	+1	+1	+1	+1	+1	+1	+1
Adaptable Arquitetural Pattern	Not supported		-1	-1				-1				-1			-1	-1	
	Partly supported									0							
	Microkernel								+1								
	Reflection	+2			+2	+2	+2				+2		+2	+2			+2
Adaptation Realisation Type	Close		0	0		0	0		0	0				0	0	0	0
	Open	+1			+1			+1			+1	+1	+1				

Adaptation Realisation Technique	Replacement	+1	+1	+1		+1	+1	+1	+1	+1	+1	+1				+1	+1
	Reorganisation		+1	+1	+1			+1	+1	+1	+1	+1					
	Code generation					+1	+1						+1	+1	+1		
Monitor	Realisation	+1	+1	0	+1	+1	+1	+1	0	+1	+1	+1	+1	+1	+1	+1	+1
	How & When	+1	0	+1	0	0	+1	0		+1	+1	+1	+1	0	+1	+1	+1
Analyse	Realisation	+1	0	0	+1	+1	0	+1	+1	0	+1	+1	+1	+1	+1	+1	+1
	How & When	+1		+1	0	0		+1	0	+1	+1	+1	+1	0	0	0	0
Plan	Realisation	+1	0	0	+1	+1	+1	+1	+1	0	+1	+1	+1	+1	+1	+1	+1
	How & When	+1		+1	0	0	0	+1	0	+1	+1	0	+1	0	0	-1	0
Execute	Realisation	+1	+1	0	+1	+1	+1	+1	+1	0	+1	+1	+1	+1	+1	+1	+1
	How & When	+1	0	+1	0	0	0	+1	0	+1	+1	0	+1	+1	+1	+1	+1
Knowledge Model Support	Model-free		+1	+1			+1		+1	+1	+1						
	Model-based (static)				+2	+1								+1	+1		+1
	Model-based (dynamic)	+2						+2				+2	+2			+2	
MAPE-K Pattern	Not supported		-1	-1	-1		0	-1	-1	0		-1					
	Partly supported										0		0		0		0
	Fully supported	+1				+1	+1				0			+1		+1	
	Score	20	5	7	13	14	12	14	9	11	19	13	18	14	10	12	15

– Not specified.

as: (i) *feature model*, (ii) *decision model*, (iii) *change scenarios*, (iv) *profiles*, (v) *rules/conditions* and (vi) *variant labels/annotations*. The representation of variability as feature models is a classical approach used by most of the (D)SPL approaches. In the second scheme, the decision model represents the variability as a set of decisions, commonly in tabular notation or textual notation. In the third scheme, change scenarios are modelled to describe events or options that trigger changes in the system. In the fourth approach, profiles are created to represent descriptive summaries of artefacts in the environment (as a table, model or a set of expressions). In the fifth approach, a set of rules or conditions is defined referring to elements or artefacts that realise the system in order to support variability. In the sixth approach, variant labels or annotations are added to artefacts that represent the DSPL.

Kang and Lee (2013) consider the feature model as the most adequate variability representation because of its clearer semantics and graphical notation. Our choice of weights in Table 9.1 expresses this preference. The feature model technique is assigned weight +2 since it is a well-known technique for SPL development. Decision model and change scenarios techniques represent variability explicitly using textual notations, while profile and rules/condition definitions represent variability in a more implicitly manner. The variant label/annotation technique promotes variability to be scattered and tangled in the source code, which decreases the system's modularity. We consider the use of techniques, such as (i) decision model, (ii) change scenario, (iii) profile definition and (iv) rule/condition definition more robust than using the variant label technique. Correspondingly, these techniques have received weight +1 while the label/annotation technique received weight 0.

D1-A3. Feature Modelling Strategy. There are at least two design strategies for the DSPL feature representation: (i) *only dynamic feature modelling*, and (ii) *static and dynamic features modelling*. In the first case, the feature model represents only dynamic features with dynamic binding, encompassing FODA[1]-like feature models, orthogonal variability models (OVM) and common variability language (CVL). In the second case, the mechanism supports both static and dynamic features at the same time. Most of the traditional notations of feature models emphasise only *variability in space*, having no special representation to define whether a variation point should be bound at design time or runtime. Thus, there are at least two design strategies for combining static with dynamic features and representing *variability in time*: (i) use of *multiple models* with a feature model to represent all (static and dynamic) features and a separate model to differentiate static and dynamic features or to represent its binding times, and (ii) use of a *single feature model* based on an extended notation to represent both static and dynamic features. We have assigned weight 0 to approaches which support only dynamic features, whereas weight +1 was assigned to those which support both dynamic and static features using multiple models, and weight +2 to those which support dynamic and static features using a single model.

D1-A4. Architectural Model. There are at least three design techniques for representing PLA architectures: (i) using *customised languages*, and (ii) using *ADL*. In the first case, some DSPL approaches define customised languages or ad-hoc models to represent the architectural model. In the second case, architecture description languages (ADLs) are used to define the software architecture. ADL is any language used in an architecture description and it can be used by one or more viewpoints to represent identified system concerns within an architecture description (ISO/IEC/IEEE 2011). This design issue has mutually exclusive strategies. Adopting design strategies for representing architectural models produce well-structured software systems. This justifies the positive weight assigned to this design issue and the negative weight assigned to the approach that did not offer any support.

---

[1] Feature-Oriented Domain Analysis (Kang, Cohen, et al. 1990).

D1-A5. Architectural Style. It refers to the highly granular entities of the system and how they are connected to each other (Bashari, Bagheri and Du 2017). At least three different architectural styles are used by DSPL approaches: (i) *component-based style*, (ii) *service-oriented architecture style*, and (iii) *hybrid architectural style*. In the first approach, component-based architectures provide functionalities structured as architectural configurations composed of components and connectors. In the second approach, service-oriented architectures are based on services to provide systems' functionalities to service clients. In the third approach, hybrid architectural styles are based on components and services, using specifications such as Service Component-Architecture (SCA). We have assigned weight −1 to approaches which do not support any architectural style, whereas weight +1 was assigned to those which support some kind of architectural style; the hybrid approach was given weight +2.

D1-A6. Variability Managed Element. The variability-managed element is the part of the system that changes when the variability is carried out. The variability can be attached to different levels of abstraction, such as: (i) *code*, (ii) *component*, (iii) *service*, (iv) *aspect*, and (v) *software architecture*. In the first case, the variability promotes changes in the code, which is generated, compiled and deployed at runtime. In the second case, the variability is attached to components, allowing the connection and disconnection of components. In the third case, the variability promotes changes at service level by allowing the disconnection and connection of services. In the fourth case, the dynamic variability is performed by a dynamic aspect weaving. In the last case, two or more architectures are compared, and one is chosen to meet variability. For the purpose of enhancing the structuring and dynamicity of DSPL systems, it is desirable to allow changes to be applied to different kinds of managed elements as many as possible. This design issue has an additive character.

D1-A7. Variability Traceability. It refers to the mapping between the variability and architectural models. There are at least three strategies for supporting traceability: (i) *direct link*, (ii) *traceability matrix* or (iii) *transformation rules*. In the first approach, a direct link is defined between the variability elements and architectural elements, without the creation of a mapping element between both. For instance, using OVM to relate features to architectural elements. In the second approach, the traceability is performed by using a traceability matrix, such as a table or a mapping model, relating variability elements of variability to architectural elements. In the third approach, transformation rules define the mapping between variability elements and architectural elements. The direct link approach promotes well-structured DSPL that is easier to be changed and maintained since less complicated solutions can be developed. In order to reflect these qualities, we assigned a weight +2 to approaches which support direct link traceability, whereas weight +1 was assigned to those which support some traceability technique using two separated models; approaches that did not specify or declare the traceability used did not receive a weight.

9.3.4 Self-adaptation Dimension

Table 9.2 presents the design issues and their respective design solutions of the self-adaptation dimension applied to the selected DSPLs, which are discussed in the following text.

D2-A1. Adaptation Cause. It refers to the source that triggers/initiates the adaptation process. Such sources can be represented as: (i) *context*, (ii) *system* and (iii) *user*. Changes in *context* occur in the environment and are external to the system. The ability to react to context changes requires the capture of context information. Context information can be divided into the system context and user context (Hallsteinsen, et al. 2006) (Floch, et al. 2006). The system context information includes data related to the environment where the system is running, such as network, memory resources, battery level and consumption, and other computing resources. The user context information includes data such as position (based on GPS information in a smartphone, for instance), and environmental information in which the user is entered, such as light and noise. Changes in *system* occur internally, for instance, the failure of a component, the performance of a service, and exceptions. The ability to react to system changes requires specific sensors within the implemented system according to the change to be detected. The change can also be triggered by some *user* action while using the system and they refer to changes in user requirements or needs at runtime. This design issue has an additive character, and this approach could add up to 3 points.

D2-A2. Adaptation Automation. Automation refers to the degree of outside intervention during adaptation. Andersson et al. (2009a) define the automation as a degree, which can vary from (i) *assisted* to (ii) *autonomous*. In the first case, the adaptation is externally assisted, either by another system or by human intervention. In the second case, the adaptation process is fully automated with no external influence guiding how the system should adapt. Since autonomic computing promises that, increasingly, the adaptation processes should be completely autonomous, this justifies the neutral weight assigned to the assisted approach and the positive weight assigned to the autonomous adaptation technique.

D2-A3. Adaptation Binding Time. It defines the moment when the adaptation binding occurs. There are three different design solutions for the binding occurrence: (i) *at design time*, (ii) *at load time* and (iii) *at runtime*. In general, SPLs implement binding at design time, while DSPLs can support the three bindings types, although DSPLs should support at least the binding at runtime. In addition, each DSPL approach can optionally support design and/or load binding time mechanisms. This design issue also has an additive character, and an approach could add up 3 points.

D2-A4. Adaptable Architectural Pattern. Here, we consider the architectural patterns for adaptive systems presented by Buschmann et al. (1996), which are microkernel and reflection patterns. Hence, the use of an adaptable architectural pattern can be: (i) *not supported* when the approach does not follow an adaptable architectural pattern, (ii) *partly supported* when the approach follows another architectural pattern that is not specifically designed for self-adaptive applications, such as the layer architectural pattern, that brings several benefits such as separation of concerns, maintainability, and reusability (Buschmann, et al. 1996), (iii) *microkernel*, when the approaches follows the microkernel architectural pattern, or (iv) *reflection*, when the approaches follow the reflection architectural pattern.

Transparency refers to whether an application is aware of the "infrastructure" needed for adaptation. Different degrees of transparency (concerning application source, virtual machine, and so on) can be implemented. The reflection pattern supports a high degree of transparency, while the microkernel pattern supports a lower degree. In order to reflect these qualities, we have assigned weight −1 to approaches which have not used any architectural pattern; and weight 0 to approaches which support another architectural pattern not specific to adaptive systems, whereas weight +2 was assigned to those which support the reflection pattern, and weight +1 was given to those approaches which applied the microkernel pattern.

D2-A5. Adaptation Realisation Type. According to Salehie and Tahvildari (2009), there are two different types of adaptation: (i) *close adaptation* and (ii) *open adaptation*. In the first approach, the system has only a fixed number of adaptive options, and no new behaviours and alternatives can be introduced at runtime. In the second, the system can be extended, and new alternatives can be added at runtime. As a consequence, new behaviour and even new adaptable elements can be introduced into the system for use by adaptation mechanism. We have assigned a neutral weight when the approach implements close adaptation; and a positive weight when the approach supports open adaptation.

D2-A6. Adaptation Realisation Technique. It is related to the implementation approach to perform the adaptation. There are at least three different design solutions for implementing the adaptation: (i) *replacement,* (ii) *reorganisation of the architecture* and (iii) *code generation.* In the first approach, adaptation is achieved by replacing one element with another with a same interface, without affecting the rest of the system architecture. In the second approach, a reconfiguration of architecture is performed when the adaptation occurs, reorganising the architectural structure. In the third approach, the adaptation is performed by generating, compiling and deploying a new portion of source code in order to change or fix the system behaviour. This design issue also has an additive character and an approach could add up 3 points.

D2-A7. Use of the MAPE-K Pattern. This requirement should consider at least three design issues: (i) whether or not the four activities of the MAPE-K are present in the adaptation mechanism implementation as individual functionalities (*realisation of individual MAPE-K activities*), (ii) to what extent the knowledge base supports the representation of models (*knowledge model support*), and (iii) whether or not the approach adheres to *MAPE-K pattern,* as shown in Table 9.2.

The first aspect identifies whether or not the implementation of the monitor, analyse, plan and execute functionalities are supported. Each functionality can be classified as: (i) *not implemented,* or (ii) *implemented.* Moreover, when the activity is implemented, one should consider how the set of adaptation options is defined and when the option binding is performed. These options could be: (i) *statically defined + design-time binding:* statically defined at design time and it could not be changed during runtime execution, that is, the static binding is performed, (ii) *statically defined + runtime binding:* statically defined at design time but the option binding is performed at runtime, and (iii) *dynamically defined + runtime binding:* the set of options is dynamically defined, in the sense that new options could be included/removed during runtime, and the option binding is also performed at runtime. For each activity (monitor, analyse, plan and execute), we have assigned a neutral weight when the functionality was not implemented and a positive weight when it was implemented. When the activity is implemented, we have assigned a negative weight (−1) when the set of decisions is statically defined at design time, and their binding cannot be changed at runtime; a neutral weight (0) when the set of decisions is statically defined at design time but their binding is realised at runtime; and a positive weight (+1) when the set of decisions is dynamically defined and their binding is also realised at runtime.

For the second design issue, the knowledge base can be (i) *model-free,* or (ii) *model-based.* In the first approach, the knowledge base has no predefined model for the system or the environment. In the second approach, the knowledge base uses a model of the system and its context. Two kinds of models exist according to the adaptation realisation type: (i) *static models,* or (ii) *dynamic models.* We have assigned a neutral weight when the approach is model-free. When the approach supports the representation of knowledge models (model-based), we have assigned a +1 weight when the approach implements static models; and a +2 weight when the approach supports dynamic models.

On the one hand, static models are used by systems with close adaptation and model-based knowledge. Static models cannot be extended at runtime, that is, the set of adaptation options are defined at design time, and they cannot be changed at runtime. One of these options is chosen at runtime by the analyser and/or the planner components. On the other hand, dynamic models are used by systems with open adaptation and model-based knowledge. Dynamic models incorporate a set of adaptation options that can be changed at runtime by including new options or removing existing ones. The option to be executed is also chosen during runtime by the analyser and planner components.

The third aspect refers to whether or not a control loop pattern is supported. The control loop pattern can be: (i) *not supported* when the approach does not implement the feedback loop, (ii) *partly supported* when the control loop is structured in an ad-hoc manner, or (iii) *fully supported* when the approach explicitly applies the control loop pattern. We have assigned weight +1 for full support of control loops, weight 0 for partial support and weight −1 for no support.

Table 9.3 Summary of dimensions

DSPL Approach / Dimension	Abbas et al.	Abotsi et al.	Baresi et al.	Bencomo et al.	Casquina et al.	Cetina et al.	Cubo et al.	Fuentes & Gamez	Gomaa & Hashimoto	Hallsteinsen et al.	Lee et al.	Morin et al.	Nascimento et al.	Parra et al.	Pessoa et al.	Rosenmüller et al.
Variability	20	5	7	13	14	12	14	9	11	19	13	18	14	10	12	15
Self-Adaptation	8	7	7	8	11	7	11	7	8	4	11	11	10	8	6	6
Final score	28	12	14	21	25	19	25	16	19	23	24	29	24	18	18	21

9.3.5 Summary

As much as possible, DSPL approaches should be highly adaptable, dynamic, reliable and simple. In spite of these requirements, the previous discussions revealed that several decisions taken in the design of the studied DSPL approaches resulted in solutions which are too inflexible, static and complex. Ranking the studied approaches according to their final score (Table 9.3), out of the maximum of 38, we have: Morin et al. (29); Abbas et al. (28); Casquina et al., Cubo et al. and Nascimento et al. (25); Lee et al. (24); Hallsteinsen et al. (23); Bencomo et al. and Rosenmüller et al. (21); Cetina et al. and Gomaa and Hashimoto (19); Parra et al. (18); Fuentes and Gamez (16); Baresi et al. (14); and Abotsi et al. (12). Table 9.1 and Table 9.2 summarise both the positive and negative design issues of each approach, allowing the software engineer to compare different approaches and evaluate potential difficulties and the impact of a given choice in the construction of DSPLs. Therefore, Table 9.1 and Table 9.2 are meant primarily as a guide for decision making rather than an absolute measurement of the suitability of a given approach.

9.4 General Design Criteria

The taxonomy developed in Section 9.3 identifies several design issues, which should be taken into account while designing a DSPL. The design decisions should be taken according to the demanding quality attributes. This section outlines the main criteria that can be followed by software engineers to build effective DSPLs. Based on these criteria, we identify the choices for designing an ideal DSPL approach.

9.4.1 Quality Attributes

Q1. Dynamicity. Dynamicity is a system's ability to undergo changes and adapt at runtime. Dynamicity can be measured as the degree of a system to self-adapt to runtime, reacting to foreseen, foreseeable, and unanticipated changes in the most autonomous way possible.

Q2. Autonomy. Autonomy is the degree of external intervention during adaptation (Andersson, de Lemos, et al. 2009a). Autonomous systems operate without the direct intervention of humans or others systems, and have some kind of control over their actions and internal state (Huebscher and McCann 2008).

Q3. Flexibility. Flexibility is the degree to which a product or system can be used with effectiveness, efficiency, freedom from risk and satisfaction in contexts beyond those initially specified in the requirements (ISO/IEC 2014). Flexibility can be achieved by adapting a system for additional user groups, tasks and cultures (ISO/IEC 2014). Flexibility enables systems to take account of circumstances, opportunities and individual preferences that might not have been anticipated in advance (ISO/IEC 2014). If a system is not designed for flexibility, it might not be safe to use the product in unintended contexts (ISO/IEC 2014).

Q4. Performance. Performance is the degree of a system or component to accomplish its designated functions within given constraints, such as speed, accuracy, or memory usage (ISO/IEC/ IEEE 2010). Performance can be a measure of a system's ability to perform its functions, including response time, throughput, and number of transactions per second (IBM 2017). Performance is an indication of the system responsiveness to execute any action within a given time interval. It can be measured in terms of latency or throughput. Latency is the required time to respond to any event. Throughput is the number of events that occur in a period of time.

Q5. Complexity. Complexity establishes the degree to which a system's design or code is difficult to understand because of numerous components or relationships among components (ISO/IEC/ IEEE 2010). Complexity is a measurement of how many more computing resources the approach of a problem requires as the problem grows in number of variables (IBM 2017). Feedback control loop and adaptation pattern are examples of techniques to cope with and reign in the management complexity of dynamic systems (Müller, Kienle and Stege 2009).

Q6. Transparency. Transparency refers to whether an application or system is aware of the infrastructure needed for recomposition (Mckinley, Sadjadi, et al. 2004a). Different degrees of transparency determine both the proposed approach's portability across platforms and how easily it can add new adaptive behaviour to existing programs (Mckinley, Sadjadi, et al., 2004b).

Q7. Separation of Concerns. This principle is used to deal with the complexities that exist in the definition and use of software systems (van Zyl 2002). Separation of concerns can be understood as the principle of software design that the source code be separated into layers and components that each have distinct functionality with as little overlap as possible (Hursch and Lopes 1995).

Q8. Modularity. The modularity is related to the degree to which a system or computer program is composed of discrete components so that a change to one component has minimal impact on others (ISO/IEC/IEEE 2010). Modularity is the ability of a system to be composed of separate, interchangeable components, each of which accomplishes one function and contains everything necessary to accomplish this. Modularity increases cohesion and reduces coupling and makes it easier to extend the functionality (modifiability) and maintain the system (maintainability). Cohesion is the manner and degree to which the tasks performed by a single software module are related to one another (ISO/IEC/IEEE 2010). Coupling is the manner and degree of interdependence between software modules (ISO/IEC/IEEE 2010).

Q9. Modifiability. Software modifiability refers to a measure of how easy it may be to change an application to cater for new functional and nonfunctional requirements (Gorton 2011). The modifiability of a system is improved as system modularity improves. Modifiability can be understood as a design quality attribute that composes maintainability.

Q10. Reusability. The the reusability is the degree to which an software asset can be used in more than one software system, or in building other assets (ISO/IEC/IEEE 2010). Software reusability is the use of existing software assets in some form within the software product development process. Reusing the code of adaptation logic should be possible. Ideally, the adaptation logic should be defined independently of the application logic, so that adaptation logic components can be reused in distinct domains.

Q11. Testability. The effort required to test software is called testability (ISO/IEC/IEEE 2010). Software testability refers to the ease with which software can be made to demonstrate its faults through (typically execution-based) testing (Bass, Clements and Kazman 2003). In general, system testability relates to several structural issues (Bass, Clements and Kazman 2003): separation of concerns, the level of documentation and the degree to which the system uses information hiding. In the ideal world, it should not be difficult to test every adaptation scenario in a systematic manner. However, testability is affected by the dynamism of the self-adaptive system, as it increases the degree of unpredictability. Non-dynamic systems can be tested at design time to reduce the occurrence of unforeseen situations. Whereas dynamic systems are prepared to anticipate the changes that may occur at runtime, changes at runtime in self-adaptive systems may have different degrees of anticipation (Cheng, et al. 2009): foreseen (taken care of), foreseeable (planned for) and unforeseen (not planned for).

Q12. Reliability. Reliability is the capability of the software product to maintain a specified level of performance when used under specified conditions (ISO/IEC/IEEE 2010). Reliability is the ability of a system to remain operational over time, and how the system behaves in varying circumstances. Performing tests and correcting failures result in improved reliability.

9.4.2 An Ideal DSPL Approach

After describing the quality attributes in the previous section, we proceed by discussing each design issue and present an ideal model for developing DSPLs, considering both the self-adaptive dimension and the variability dimension. We discuss how each design choice can affect the quality attributes while designing the DSPL. Table 9.3 shows a summary of our findings. A '+' in the Table 9.4 indicates a positive relationship between a design alternative and a quality attribute, that is, the use of the design alternative helps in the achievement of the quality goal. A '−' indicated the opposite situation. Finally, a blank cell indicates that, depending on the context of use, it could have a negative or positive effect. Both design issues and quality attributes are abstract, and the scores are meant to guide developers in their choices among design alternatives and identify possible design conflicts. The interactions among design alternatives and quality attributes can be complex, and these design choices should be understood in the context of other design decisions. Trade-offs are also discussed in this section since the quality attributes can be conflicting to each other.

9.4.2.1 Variability Dimension (D1)

D1-A1. Variability Type. A DSPL approach should support at least dynamic variability. From the viewpoint of developing well-structured DSPLs, it seems to be a reasonable approach to provide support for both static and dynamic variability since part of the software variability could be decided during design time. Thus, an ideal DSPL approach should deal with static variability and dynamic variability.

D1-A2. Variability Conceptual Model. An ideal DSPL approach should represent the variability as feature model. Pohl et al. state that the explicit representation of the software variability has significant advantages as the improvement of modifiability, modularity and reusability (Pohl, Böckle and van der Linden 2005). The decision model, change scenario, profile definition and rule/condition techniques represent variability in a more implicitly manner when compared

Table 9.4 Taxonomy design issues versus quality attributes

Dimension	Design Issue	Q1	Q2	Q3	Q4	Q5	Q6	Q7	Q8	Q9	Q10	Q11	Q12
Variability Type	Dynamic												
	Static & Dynamic				+	+						+	+
Variability Conceptual Model	Feature models								+	+	+		
	Decision model								+	+			
	Change scenarios								+	+			
	Profiles								+	+			
	Rules/Conditions								+	+			
	Variant labels/ Annotations								−		−		
Feature Modelling Strategy	FM only with dynamic features												
	Multiple models					−				−			
	Single model					+				+	+		
Architectural Model	Unsupported					−			−	−	−	−	−
	Custom languages									+	+	+	
	ADL									+	+	+	
Architectural Style	Unsupported												
	Component-based												
	Service-oriented												
	Hybrid												
Variability Managed Element	Code			+						+			
	Component			+						+			
	Service			+						+			
	Aspect			+						+			
	Architecture			+						+			
Variability Traceability	Direct link					+				+	+		
	Traceability matrix					−				−	−		
	Transformation rules					−				−	−		

Variability Dimension

(*Continued*)

Table 9.4 Taxonomy design issues versus quality attributes *(Continued)*

Dimension		Design Issue	Q1	Q2	Q3	Q4	Q5	Q6	Q7	Q8	Q9	Q10	Q11	Q12
Self–Adaptation Dimension	Adaptation Cause	Context	+		+	−	−						−	−
		System	+		+	−	−						−	−
		User	+		+	−	−						−	−
	Adaptation Automation	Assisted		−										−
		Autonomous		+	+		−				−		−	−
	Adaptation Binding Time	Design			+		−							
		Load			+		−							
		Runtime			+		−							
	Adap Arquitetural Pattern	Not supported												
		Partly supported												
		Microkernel pattern			+	−		−	+	+	+			
		Reflection pattern			+	−		+	+	+	+	+		
	Adaptation	Close	−		−		+				+		+	+
Use of MAPE-K Pattern	Realisation Type	Open	+		+	−	−					−		
	Adaptation Realisation Technique	Replacement			−		+				+	+	+	
		Reorganisation			−	−				+	+	+	+	
		Code generation			+	−				−		−	−	−
	Activity Realisation	Not implemented												
		Statically + Design-time binding	−		−									
		Statically + Runtime binding	−		−									
		Dynamically + Runtime binding	+		+	−	−						−	−
	Knowledge Model Support	Model-free												
		Model-based (static)			−						+		+	+
		Model-based (dynamic)	+		+	−	−				+		+	+
	MAPE-K Pattern	Not supported												
		Partly supported												
		Fully supported	+							+	+	+	+	+

to the feature model scheme, as a consequence, their use can affect negatively the traceability quality attribute.

However, these techniques can support some variability modularity and modifiability since variability changes can be located in few places. We consider that performing changes to a single component is better than making a widespread change to the system. The variant label/annotation technique promotes variability to be scattered and tangled in the source code, which can decrease the system's modularity and variability traceability and reusability.

D1-A3. Feature Modelling Strategy. Considering that variability should be represented explicitly as feature models (*D1-A2* paragraph), and ideally DSPLs should support both static and dynamic variability (*D1-A1* paragraph), then the representation of both static and dynamic features is the design choice to be naturally taken. The single model scheme as a design alternative has some advantages by promoting the creation of simpler systems that are easier to be modified, traced and reused. On the other hand, the primary and secondary model strategy can promote the creation of more complex systems, it becomes more difficult to be maintained and more difficult to achieve variability traceability.

D1-A4. Architectural Model. An ideal approach for DSPL should adopt a design strategy for representing architectural models in order to benefit from all the advantages of a well-known architecture-centric approach (Bosch 2002), that is, yield systems easier to modify, reuse, test and trace. The non-use of architectural model is an design alternative that can have a negative effect on the system's complexity, modifiability, traceability, modularity, reusability, testability, and reliability.

D1-A5. Architectural Style. The three main styles considered in our study are: the component-based style, the SOA style, and the hybrid approach which combines both styles. An ideal DSPL approach should follow a specific architectural style, either component-based or SOA style, however, the use of the hybrid approach provides support to more flexible DSPLs.

D1-A6. Variability Managed Element. The variability managed element is the part of the system that changes when the variability is carried out. An ideal approach should provide a multi-level attachment of variability since it is important for DSPL developers/architects to be able to attach variability at different levels of system structure. This design alternative improves the system's flexibility and modifiability.

D1-A7. Variability Traceability. It refers to the mapping between the variability and architectural models. Ideally, a DSPL approach should use the direct link approach between variability elements and architectural elements, without the creation of a mapping artefact between both. This design choice improves modifiability, changes traceability, understanding, and readability since the system is less complex. Besides, direct links between the artefacts can facilitate systematic and consistent reuse (Pohl, Böckle and van der Linden 2005). The use of a traceability matrix or transformation rule implies in the creation of an extra artefact to define the mapping between variability and architectural elements, which can cause a negative effect on the system's complexity. Moreover, the traceability matrix technique represents more explicitly the mapping when compared to the transformation rule technique.

9.4.2.2 Self-adaptation Dimension (D2)

D2-A1. Adaptation Cause. Some of the required properties for DSPL, prescribed by Hallsteinsen et al. (2008), are: context and situation awareness, unexpected changes, and changes by users, such as functional or quality requirements. Ideally, a DSPL approach should react to the three kinds of adaptation causes (context, system and user). As a consequence, the approach would be more dynamic, complete and flexible. However, implementating the three strategies in the same system can cause a negative impact on the system's complexity, testability, performance and reliability. In order to support context and system changes, the system should support different kinds of sensors according to the information to be collected. Also, the volume of information could be very high, meaning that the performance of the system could be compromised. Moreover, since context, system and user changes occur at runtime when a system implements all strategies, this approach could also affect negatively the system's testability and reliability.

D2-A2. Adaptation Automation. According to Hallsteinsen et al. (2008), DSPLs should include autonomic capabilities. This design alternative improves system's flexibility, however, it can increase the system's complexity, and, as a consequence, the system can be more difficult to be tested, harder to be maintained and less reliable. Each of the predicted situations should be supported by the system, and unpredicted situations should be handled properly during runtime. When the adaptation process is assisted by humans or other systems, the approach can become less autonomous and less reliable since software adaptation, when performed by humans or other systems, becomes an onerous (regarding time, effort and money) and error-prone activity, mainly due to involuntary injection of uncertainties by developers (Andersson, de Lemos, et al. 2009b) (Salehie and Tahvildari 2009).

D2-A3. Adaptation Binding Time. Runtime binding is required for DSPLs. Hallsteinsen et al. (2008) also indicate the necessity of supporting other kinds of bindings in order to ease maintenance throughout their life cycle. So, an ideal approach should realise the three types of binding time (design time, load time and runtime). This design alternative can improve system's flexibility, however, it can increase system's complexity since a high number of variation points are going to be specified in the system.

D2-A4. Adap Architectural Pattern. Reflection and microkernel are well-known patterns recommended to build adaptive systems (Buschmann, et al. 1996). We consider that an ideal approach should apply the reflection architectural pattern since it supports transparency because the base level (managed subsystem) is unaware of the meta-level (managing subsystem). Changing a software system is easy since the metaobject protocol provides a safe and uniform mechanism for changing software (Buschmann, et al. 1996).

The use of the microkernel pattern also improves modifiability, and flexibility since additional adaptations only requires the addition or extension of internal elements (Buschmann, et al. 1996). Also, this pattern provides support for separation of concerns and modularity since external elements can implement their own policies. However, transparency is not fully satisfied since the use of a metaobject protocol is not required.

A disadvantage of using both patterns is a possible negative impact on the system's performance. Reflective software systems are usually slower than non-reflective systems, as a consequence of the complex relationship between the base level and the meta-level (Buschmann, et al. 1996). Microkernel systems can be slower when compared to monolithic systems due to their support for flexibility and modifiability.

D2-A5. Adaptation Realisation Type. The design decision of using open adaptation has a number of advantages since the system can be extended, and new alternatives and behaviours can be added at runtime. It leads to better dynamicity and flexibility; however, the runtime discovery mechanisms can be complex, and they can impact negatively on the system's performance and testability. On the other hand, the close adaptation strategy leads to more reliable and tes systems since the system has only a fixed number of adaptive options, and no new behaviours and/ or alternatives can be introduced at runtime. Moreover, it makes the system simpler and easier to maintain, although, it impacts dynamicity and flexibility negatively.

D2-A6. Adaptation Realisation Technique. An ideal model for DSPL should allow reconfigurations of the architecture structure when adaptations occur. This design alternative promotes an architecture-centric adaptation approach at a higher level of abstraction than code, based on coarse-grained architectural elements, realised by components and/or services. This design decision also promotes the construction of modular software systems, which in turn improves modifiability, reusability, and testability. However, it can lead to a worse performance and flexibility since on-the-fly adaptations can be complex and fine-grained modifications are not supported.

The replacement technique is simpler and less flexible than architecture reorganisation since the components can be changed individually at runtime, but no modifications to the architectural configuration are carried out. The use of this technique can make the system easier to reuse, test, trace and modify since it reduces the number of possible applications scenarios and limits customisability of DSPLs (Rosenmüller, et al. 2011). This strategy is also based on changes of coarse-grained elements when compared to the code generation technique, which promotes fine-grained modifications.

In this context, one can claim that the code generation technique can lead to more flexible systems, however, it becomes less reliable, less modular and less reusable. Moreover, this technique can also impact negatively on performance and testability since code generation, compilation, and loading are performed during runtime. However, a hybrid approach also could be adopted by the architect, combining coarse-grained and fine-grained adaptation realisation techniques.

D2-A7. Use of MAPE-K Pattern. Ideally, a DSPL should implement all four activities of the MAPE-K control loop. Moreover, it should be possible for the set of decisions to be dynamically defined and their binding be realised at runtime. This strategy can lead to more dynamic and flexible systems since options can be included/modified/removed during runtime. However, it can impact negatively the complexity, testability, reliability and performance. The design choice using the dynamically defined adaptation options with runtime binding is more dynamic and flexible when compared to the most commonly used design choice in DSPLs, which is the statically defined with runtime binding (Bencomo, Lee and Hallsteinsen 2010).

An ideal model should support a model-driven approach for representing knowledge models at runtime. Cheng et al. (2014) argue that models at runtime support the development of runtime assurance strategies. All studied approaches have realised model-based approaches for designing the knowledge base. It leads to approaches which are easier to test, more reliable and easier to modify. Moreover, ideally, dynamic models should be supported in order to improve the system's dynamicity and flexibility. However, this design alternative can impact negatively the complexity and performance since the execution of runtime adaptations is not a simple task and the correctness of the dynamically modified models should be validated. The use of static models solves part of these limitations during design time, however, the approach becomes less flexible, but more reliable.

Lemos et al. (2014) consider that the use of feedback control loop patterns is one of the cornerstones for developing self-adaptive software systems since they can be associated to different kinds of assurances at the conceptual level and at the code level. It leads to approaches which are more modular and reliable, and easier to modify, test and reuse.

9.5 Research Challenges

Despite many improvements in mechanisms to support runtime adaptation, the full potential of building dynamic software product line systems depends on advances in other research fields.

Testing and Assurance. Self-adaptive software systems (SASS) can take different configurations at runtime in response to changes in context, in the system itself or its goals. Considering scenario variations, decision making and binding at runtime, performing the test and validation tasks becomes very complex. This complexity is further extended in systems that perform open adaptation because they can introduce new behaviours and new options at runtime, such as systems that perform service discovery at runtime.

In the context of DSPLs, Metzger and Pohl (2014) claim that to address (context) situations unknown during design time, quality can be only partially assured and under certain assumptions. The authors raise the following issues as challenges: how to model such assumptions? How to check if the assumptions hold in the actual situation? How to ensure the quality of an application during runtime if not all potential adaptations of the application are known and predefined?

There are several researches in model-based testing for SPL as listed in Razak et al. (2017). However, these surveys only consider static variability, and may not be able to test situations that might occur at runtime. In the context of DSPLs, Santos et al. (2016) address the formal verification of DSPL, proposing a formal structure, which specifies the DSPL adaptive behaviour to reason about the adaptations that could be triggered at runtime; however, their approach is focused on DSPL verification at design time. Two other works, A-FTS (Cordy, et al. 2013) and DFPN (Muschevici, Clarke and Proenca 2010), were proposed for models supporting and model checking of DSPL, focusing on execution states ('*ready*', '*wait*'). Ongoing work is the Devasses project (DEVASSES 2017) which has as one of its objectives to deal with model-based online testing, aiming to research, define and implement a solution to employ model-based testing techniques to SOA orchestrations at runtime.

Fault Tolerance and Reliability. In a previous work (Eleutério, et al. 2016), we also compared DSPL approaches regarding dependability and fault tolerance. Most of the DSPLs analysed in this study did not have as one of their objectives the improvement of dependability or the ability to tolerate failures. However, Nascimento et al. (2014) deal with the highest amount of dependability attributes, exploring the different software fault tolerance techniques based on design diversity.

Besides, there are some approaches dealing with variability-aware reliability analysis techniques that can be applied in DSPLs, as (Nunes, et al. 2013) (Rodrigues, et al. 2015). For instance, Rodrigues et al. (2015) proposed a model for feature-aware discrete-time Markov chains, called FDTMC, for verifying probabilistic properties (e.g., reliability and availability) of product lines. Among the DSPL approaches analysed in our study (listed in Section 9.3.2), only Pessoa et al. (2017) deal with reliability. Pessoa et al. (2017) proposed a DSPL approach that is explored and evaluated in the medical area, in particular in the body sensor network domain, in which reliability and maintainability are key requirements. The proposed approach by Pessoa et al. (Pessoa, et al. 2017) is based on FDTMC (Rodrigues, et al. 2015).

A Uniform Solution for Modelling Static and Dynamic Variability. Bosch et al. (Bosch, Capilla and Hilliard 2015) list dynamic variability and runtime concerns as one of the trends of software variability area. According to Bosch et al. (Bosch, Capilla and Hilliard 2015), designing variation points such that the variability mechanism, which determines the binding time, can be easily replaced during system implementation is particularly important. In this context, we pose another challenge: How to represent dynamic variability efficiently?

Despite the numerous notations for modelling variability using a feature model, most of them deal only with static variability. The modelling of dynamic variability has been neglected, with few attempts to represent it, as showed in Table 9.1. Among sixteen analysed approaches

(Table 9.1) only four of them deal with both static and dynamic variabilities (Rosenmüller, et al. 2011) (Casquina, et al 2016) (Cubo, et al. 2015) (Lee, Kotonya and Robinson 2012), using their own notations, as Lee et al. (2012), or multiple models in order to complement the feature model. Thus, one of the challenges is the definition of a standard notation to represent both static and dynamic variabilities.

Reference Models, Reference Architectures, Implementation Frameworks and Automated Tools. In the context of DSPLs, there is no reference model to be followed on how to build a DSPL. Salehie and Tahvildari (Salehie and Tahvildari 2009) raised the following issues that are applicable to the DSPL project: Which architecture styles and design patterns are appropriate for this purpose? Which component model provides the best support for the sensing and effecting in vivo mechanisms? Which interfaces and contracts need to be considered?

On architectural styles, our taxonomy concluded that DSPLs use both hybrid, component-based, and service-oriented architectures. On architectural patterns, DSPLs are mostly based on the reflection architectural pattern. However, there is a gap between the definition of architectural styles and patterns and the concrete realisation of DSPLs. There is still a lack of models and processes that guide the development of DSPLs, applying these architectural styles and patterns.

Regarding the component model, at the level of the managing subsystem, it is necessary to build monitoring and adaptation components that are reusable in other DSPLs, that is, they are domain independent. At the managed subsystem level, a DSPL needs to be constructed in order to be "understood" by the controller, to expose important information through sensors, and expose its variation points to facilitate variability management by effectors.

Regarding interfaces and contracts, although numerous research efforts have investigated approaches to develop DSPLs, there is still a lack of reference models and reference architectures that could help realising in a systematic manner adaptation processes, variability management, and the instrumentation of probes/effectors.

Based on the sixteen DSPL approaches (Table 9.1) from our study, we identified the following challenges: how to facilitate the technologies selection that fits in a given purpose? Bashari et al. (2017) proposed a conceptual reference framework for DSPL, but they do not address practical issues for developing and realising DSPLs. There is still a gap in reference models and reference architectures that can serve as a basis or guide the design and construction of DSPLs. Similarly, implementation frameworks and automated tools are needed as means of supporting and instrumenting the process of building DSPL, and to make them widely usable by the industry.

Feedback Control Loops. Metzger and Pohl (2014) state that the use of the autonomic computing concepts is a challenge in the DSPL development—in particular, the application of feedback control loops when building well-structured DSPLs. Also, Capilla et al. (2014) discuss the need to explore mechanisms for compositional adaptation (Mckinley, Sadjadi, et al. 2004a) in order to implement runtime variability in DSPLs, in particular, the adoption of MAPE-K loop. Moreover, Lemos et al. (2014) discuss the importance of using the feedback control loops in order to obtain assurances (Schmerl, et al. 2017).

According to Table 9.2, few approaches have applied the MAPE-K loop, for example. More specifically, only four approaches (Abbas and Andersson 2013) (Nascimento, Rubira and Castor 2014) (Pessoa, et al. 2017) (Casquina, et al 2016) have used the MAPE-K feedback control loop for structuring the managing subsystems. The adoption of feedback control loops contributes to raising the maturity of DSPLs.

9.6 Conclusions

The trend in the development of new dynamic software product line (DSPL) approaches indicates the combined use of self-adaptation and variability management. However, for that to be achieved there is the need to define a clear taxonomy that allows comparing of existing approaches from dynamic software product line and self-adaptive software systems.

This chapter has provided a comprehensive taxonomy for comparing DSPL approaches regarding two key dimensions, namely, self-adaption and variability. Using our taxonomy, sixteen prominent DSPL approaches were compared and weighted to evaluate their design decisions, aiming better understand the research area. Then, these design decisions were analysed in the face of quality attributes. Thus, as key messages of this chapter we realise that: (i) there is no single way to design and develop DSPLs, and this chapter demonstrated, based on the taxonomy, that there are a variety of design decisions taken by the DSPL approaches, (ii) in the same way, each design decision has trade-offs when analysed concerning the quality criteria, and this analysis guides the architectural decisions of the engineers in the development of the DSPL, (iii) the taxonomy presented in this chapter supports the reuse of knowledge from the SASS research, which is a promising way to develop more dynamic DSPLs, and (iv) both the DSPL and SASS research areas can take advantage of the intersection of these two areas, providing more dynamicity and autonomy for the DSPLs and providing more means to represent the variability for adaptation in SASS.

References

Abbas, Nadeem, and Jesper Andersson. 2013. "Architectural Reasoning for Dynamic Software Product Lines." *SPLC '13 Workshops Proceedings of the 17th International Software Product Line Conference co-located workshops*. Tokyo, Japan: ACM Press. 117-124. doi:10.1145/2499777.2500718.

Abbas, Nadeem, Jesper Andersson, and Welf Löwe. 2010. "Autonomic Software Product Lines (ASPL)." *Proceedings of the Fourth European Conference on Software Architecture: Companion Volume*. Copenhagen, Denmark: ACM. 324-331. doi:10.1145/1842752.1842812.

Abotsi, Komi S., S. Tonny Kurniadi, Hamad I. Alsawalqah, and Danhyung Lee. 2011. "A Software Product Line-based Self-healing Strategy for Web-based Applications." *SPLC '11 Proceedings of the 15th International Software Product Line Conference, Volume 2*. Munich, Germany: ACM. 31:1-31:8. doi:10.1145/2019136.2019171.

Andersson, Jesper, Rogério de Lemos, Sam Malek, and Danny Weyns. 2009a. "Modeling Dimensions of Self-Adaptive Software Systems." Vol. LNCS 5525, in *Software Engineering for Self-Adaptive Systems*, edited by Betty H. C. Cheng, Rogério de Lemos, Holger Giese, Paola Inverardi and Jeff Magee, 27-47. Berlin, Heidelberg: Springer, Berlin, Heidelberg. doi:10.1007/978-3-642-02161-9_2.

———. 2009b. "Reflecting on Self-adaptive Software Systems." *2009 ICSE Workshop on Software Engineering for Adaptive and Self-Managing Systems*. Vancouver, BC, Canada: IEEE. 38-47. doi:10.1109/SEAMS.2009.5069072.

Baresi, L., S. Guinea, and L. Pasquale. 2012. "Service-Oriented Dynamic Software Product Lines." *Computer* (IEEE) 45 (10): 42-48. doi:10.1109/MC.2012.289.

Bashari, Mahdi, Ebrahim Bagheri, and Weichang Du. 2017. "Dynamic Software Product Line Engineering: A Reference Framework." *International Journal of Software Engineering and Knowledge Engineering* (World Scientific Publishing Company) 27 (2): 191-234. doi:10.1142/S0218194017500085.

Bass, Len, Paul Clements, and Rick Kazman. 2003. *Software Architecture in Practice*. 2nd ed. Addison Wesley.

Bencomo, Nelly, Gordon Blair, Carlos Flores, and Pete Sawyer. 2008. "Reflective Component-based Technologies to Support Dynamic Variability." *Second International Workshop on Variability Modelling of Software-Intensive Systems*. Essen, Germany. 141-150.

Bencomo, Nelly, Jaejoon Lee, and Svein Hallsteinsen. 2010. "How Dynamic is your Dynamic Software Product Line?" *4th International Workshop on Dynamic Software Product Lines (DSPL), 14th International Software Product Line Conference (SPLC 2011).* 61-68.

Bencomo, Nelly, Paul Grace, Carlos Flores, Danny Hughes, and Gordon Blair. 2008. "Genie: Supporting the Model-driven Development of Reflective, Component-based Adaptive Systems." *Proceedings of the 13th International Conference on Software engineering—ICSE '08.* Leipzig, Germany: ACM. 811-814. doi:10.1145/1368088.1368207.

Bosch, Jan. 2002. "Architecture-Centric Software Engineering." Edited by Cristina Gacek. In *Software Reuse: Methods, Techniques, and Tools. ICSR 2002.* Berlin, Heidelberg: Springer Berlin Heidelberg. 347-348. doi:10.1007/3-540-46020-9_36.

Bosch, Jan, Rafael Capilla, and Rich Hilliard. 2015. "Trends in Systems and Software Variability." *IEEE Software* (IEEE) 32 (3): 44-51. doi:10.1109/MS.2015.74.

Brun, Yuriy, Giovanna Di Marzo Serugendo, Cristina Gacek, Holger Giese, Holger Kienle, Marin Litoiu, Hausi Müller, Mauro Pezzè, and Mary Shaw. 2009. "Engineering Self-Adaptive Systems Through Feedback Loops." Vol. LNCS 5525, in *Software Engineering for Self-Adaptive Systems,* edited by Betty H. C. Cheng, Rogério de Lemos, Holger Giese, Paola Inverardi and Jeff Magee, 48-70. Berlin, Heidelberg: Springer Berlin Heidelberg. doi:10.1007/978-3-642-02161-9_3.

Buschmann, Frank, Regine Meunier, Hans Rohnert, Peter Sommerlad, and Michael Stal. 1996. *Pattern-Oriented Software Architecture—A System of Patterns.* Vol. 1. John Wiley & Sons.

Capilla, Rafael, Jan Bosch, Pablo Trinidad, Antonio Ruiz-Cortés, and Mike Hinchey. 2014. "An Overview of Dynamic Software Product Line Architectures and Techniques: Observations from research and industry." *Journal of Systems and Software,* 91: 3-23. doi:10.1016/j.jss.2013.12.038.

Casquina, Junior C., Jane D. A. S. Eleutério, and Cecília M. F. Rubira. 2016. "Adaptive Deployment Infrastructure for Android Applications." *12th European Dependable Computing Conference Adaptive.* Gothenburg, Sweden: IEEE. 218-228. doi:10.1109/EDCC.2016.25.

Cetina, Carlos, and Vicente Pelechano. 2013. "Variability in Autonomic Computing." Chap. 17 in *Systems and Software Variability Management: Concepts, Tools and Experiences.* Edited by Rafael Capilla, Jan Bosch and Kyo-Chul Kang, 261-267. Berlin, Heidelberg: Springer Berlin Heidelberg. doi:10.1007/978-3-642-36583-6_17.

Cetina, Carlos, Joan Fons, and Vicente Pelechano. 2008. "Applying Software Product Lines to Build Autonomic Pervasive Systems." *2008 12th International Software Product Line Conference.* Limerick, Ireland: IEEE. 117-126.

Cetina, Carlos, Pau Giner, Joan Fons, and Vicente Pelechano. 2009. "Autonomic Computing through Reuse of Variability Models at Runtime: The Case of Smart Homes." *Computer* (IEEE) 42 (10): 37-43. doi:10.1109/MC.2009.309.

Cheng, Betty H C, Kerstin I Eder, Martin Gogolla, Lars Grunske, Marin Litoiu, Hausi A. Müller, Patrizio Pelliccione, et al. 2014. "Using Models at Runtime to Address Assurance for Self-Adaptive Systems." Vol. LNCS 8378, in *Models@run.time: Foundations, Applications, and Roadmaps,* edited by Nelly Bencomo, Robert France, Betty H. C. Cheng and Uwe Aßmann, 101-136. Springer, Cham. doi:10.1007/978-3-319-08915-7_4.

Cheng, Betty H. C., Rogério de Lemos, Holger Giese, Paola Inverardi, Jeff Magee, Jesper Andersson, Basil Becker, et al. 2009. "Software Engineering for Self-Adaptive Systems: A Research Roadmap." Vols. LNCS, 5525, in *Software Engineering for Self-Adaptive Systems,* edited by Betty H. C. Cheng, Rogério de Lemos, Holger Giese, Paola Inverardi and Jeff Magee, 1-26. Berlin, Heidelberg: Springer, Berlin, Heidelberg. doi:10.1007/978-3-642-02161-9_1.

Cordy, Maxime, Andreas Classen, Patrick Heymans, Axel Legay, and Pierre-Yves Schobbens. 2013. "Model Checking Adaptive Software with Featured Transition Systems." Vol. LNCS 7740, in *Assurances for Self-Adaptive Systems: Principles, Models, and Techniques,* edited by Javier Cámara, Rogério de Lemos, Carlo Ghezzi and Antónia Lopes. Berlin, Heidelberg: Springer Berlin Heidelberg. doi:10.1007/978-3-642-36249-1_1.

Cubo, Javier, Nadia Gamez, Ernesto Pimentel, and Lidia Fuentes. 2015. "Reconfiguration of Service Failures in DAMASCo Using Dynamic Software Product Lines." *2015 IEEE International Conference on Services Computing.* New York, NY: IEEE. 114-121. doi:10.1109/SCC.2015.25.

Cubo, Javier, Nadia Gamez, Lidia Fuentes, and Ernesto Pimentel. 2013. "Composition and Self-Adaptation of Service-Based Systems with Feature Models." Edited by John Favaro and Maurizio Morisio. *Safe and Secure Software Reuse. ICSR 2013*. Springer Berlin Heidelberg. 326-342. doi:10.1007/978-3-642-38977-1_25.

de Lemos, Rogerio, David Garlan, Carlo Ghezzi, and Holger Giese. 2014. "Software Engineering for Self-Adaptive Systems: Assurances (Dagstuhl Seminar 13511)." *Dagsthul Reports*, 67-96. doi:10.4230/DagRep.3.12.67.

de Lemos, Rogério, Holger Giese, Hausi Müller, Mary Shaw, Jesper Andersson, Marin Litoiu, Bradley Schmerl, et al. 2013. "Software Engineering for Self-Adaptive Systems: A Second Research Roadmap." Vols. LNCS, 7475, in *Software Engineering for Self-Adaptive Systems II: International Seminar, Dagstuhl Castle, Germany, October 24-29, 2010 Revised Selected and Invited Papers*, edited by Rogério de Lemos, Holger Giese, Hausi Müller and Mary Shaw, 1-32. Berlin, Heidelberg: Springer, Berlin, Heidelberg. doi:10.1007/978-3-642-35813-5_1.

DEVASSES. 2017. *DEsign, Verification and VAlidation of large scale, dynamic Service SystEmS*. Accessed May 25, 2018. http://www.devasses.eu/.

Dobson, Simon, Spyros Denazis, Antonio Fernández, Dominique Gaïti, Erol Gelenbe, Fabio Massacci, Paddy Nixon, Fabrice Saffre, Nikita Schmidt, and Franco Zambonelli. 2006. "A Survey of Autonomic Communications." *ACM Transactions on Autonomous and Adaptive Systems (TAAS)* (ACM) 1 (2): 223-259. doi:10.1145/1186778.1186782.

Eleutério, Jane D. A. S., Felipe Nunes Gaia, Andrea Bondavalli, Paolo Lollini, Genaína N. Rodrigues, and Cecília Mary Fischer Rubira. 2016. "On the Dependability for Dynamic Software Product Lines A Comparative Systematic Mapping Study." *42th Euromicro Conference on Software Engineering and Advanced Applications (SEAA)*. Limassol, Cyprus: IEEE. 323-330. doi:10.1109/SEAA.2016.40.

Floch, Jacqueline, Svein Hallsteinsen, Erlend Stav, Frank Eliassen, Ketil Lund, and Eli Gjorven. 2006. "Using Architecture Models for Runtime Adaptability." *IEEE Software* (IEEE) 23 (2): 62-70. doi:10.1109/MS.2006.61.

Fuentes, Lidia, and Nadia Gámez. 2009. "Modeling the Context-Awareness Service in an Aspect-Oriented Middleware for AmI." *3rd Symposium of Ubiquitous Computing and Ambient Intelligence 2008*. Springer Berlin Heidelberg. 159-167. doi:10.1007/978-3-540-85867-6_19.

Fuentes, Lidia, and Nadia Gamez. 2008. "A Feature Model of an Aspect-oriented Middleware Family for Pervasive Systems." *Proceedings of the 2008 Workshop on Next Generation Aspect Oriented Middleware—NAOMI '08*. ACM. 11-16. doi:10.1145/1408620.1408623.

Galster, Matthias, Danny Weyns, Dan Tofan, Bartosz Michalik, and Paris Avgeriou. 2014. "Variability in Software Systems — A Systematic Literature Review." *IEEE Transactions on Software Engineering* (IEEE) 40 (3): 282-306. doi:10.1109/TSE.2013.56.

Geihs, Kurt, Paolo Barone, Frank Eliassen, Jacqueline Floch, R. Fricke, E. Gjorven, Svein Hallsteinsen, et al. 2009. "A Comprehensive Solution for Application-level Adaptation." *Software: Practice and Experience* (John Wiley & Sons) 39 (4): 385-422. doi:10.1002/spe.900.

Gomaa, Hassan, and Koji Hashimoto. 2011. "Dynamic Software Adaptation for Service-oriented Product Lines." *Proceedings of the 15th International Software Product Line Conference on - SPLC '11*. Munich, Germany: ACM. doi:10.1145/2019136.2019176.

Gorton, Ian. 2011. "Software Quality Attributes." *Essential Software Architecture* (Springer Berlin Heidelberg) 1: 23-38. doi:10.1007/978-3-642-19176-3_3.

Hallsteinsen, S., E. Stav, A. Solberg, and J. Floch. 2006. "Using Product Line Techniques to Build Adaptive Systems." *10th International Software Product Line Conference (SPLC'06)*. Baltimore, MD, USA: IEEE. 10. doi:10.1109/SPLINE.2006.1691586.

Hallsteinsen, Svein, Mike Hinchey, Sooyong Park, and Klaus Schmid. 2008. "Dynamic Software Product Lines." *Computer* (IEEE) 41 (4): 93-95. doi:10.1109/MC.2008.123.

Hellerstein, Joseph L., Yixin Diao, Sujay Parekh, and Dawn M. Tilbury. 2004. *Feedback Control of Computing Systems*. John Wiley & Sons. doi:10.1002/047166880X.

Huebscher, Markus C., and Julie A. McCann. 2008. "A survey of autonomic computing — degrees, models, and applications." *ACM Computing Surveys* (ACM) 40 (3): 7:1-7:28. doi:10.1145/1380584.1380585.

Hursch, Walter L, and Cristina Videira Lopes. 1995. *Separation of Concerns*. NU-CCS-5-03, Northeastern University, Boston, MA, USA: Northeastern University, 1-20.

IBM. 2017. *IBM Terminology*. Accessed May 25, 2018. https://www-01.ibm.com/software/globalization/terminology/.

ISO/IEC. 2014. *System and Software Engineering—System and Software Quality Requirements and Evaluation (SQuaRE)—System and Software Quality Models*. ISO/IEC 25000:2014, ISO/IEC.

ISO/IEC/IEEE. 2011. "Systems and Software Engineering—Architecture Description." ISO/IEC/IEEE 42010:2011, IEEE. doi:10.1109/IEEESTD.2011.6129467

ISO/IEC/IEEE. 2010. *Systems and software engineering—Vocabulary*. ISO/IEC/IEEE 24765:2010, IEEE, 418. doi:10.1109/IEEESTD.2010.5733835.

Kang, Kyo C., and Hyesun Lee. 2013. "Variability Modeling." Chap. 2 in *Systems and Software Variability Management: Concepts, Tools and Experience*. Edited by Rafael Capilla, Jan Bosch and Kyo-Chul Kang, 25-42. Berlin, Heidelberg: Springer Berlin Heidelberg. doi:10.1007/978-3-642-36583-6_2.

Kang, Kyo C., Sholom G. Cohen, James A. Hess, William E. Novak, and A. S. Peterson. 1990. *Feature-Oriented Domain Analysis (FODA) Feasibility Study*. CMU/SEI-90-TR-21, Software Engineering Institute, Carnegie Mellon University, Pittsburgh, PA: Software Engineering Institute, Carnegie Mellon University.

Kephart, Jeffrey O., and David M. Chess. 2003. "The Vision of Autonomic Computing." *Computer* (IEEE Computer Society Press) 36 (1): 41-50. doi:10.1109/MC.2003.1160055.

Kramer, Jeff, and Jeff Magee. 2007. "Self-Managed Systems: an Architectural Challenge." *Future of Software Engineering, 2007. FOSE '07*. Minneapolis, MN, USA: IEEE. 259-268. doi:10.1109/FOSE.2007.19.

Lee, Jaejoon, and Gerald Kotonya. 2010. "Combining Service-Orientation with Product Line Engineering." *IEEE Software* (IEEE) 27 (3): 35-41. doi:10.1109/MS.2010.30.

Lee, Jaejoon, Gerald Kotonya, and Daniel Robinson. 2012. "Engineering Service-Based Dynamic Software Product Lines." *Computer* (IEEE) 45 (10): 49-55. doi:10.1109/MC.2012.284.

Müller, Hausi A., Holger M. Kienle, and Ulrike Stege. 2009. *Autonomic Computing Now You See It, Now You Don't*. Vol. LNCS 5413, in *Software Engineering: International Summer Schools, ISSSE 2006-2008, Salerno, Italy, Revised Tutorial Lectures*, edited by Andrea De Lucia and Filomena Ferrucci, 32-54. Berlin, Heidelberg: Springer Berlin Heidelberg. doi:10.1007/978-3-540-95888-8_2.

Mckinley, Philip K., Seyed M. Sadjadi, Eric P. Kasten, and Betty H. C. Cheng. 2004a. "Composing Adaptive Software." *Computer* (IEEE) 37 (7): 56-64. doi:10.1109/MC.2004.48.

Mckinley, Philip K., Seyed M. Sadjadi, Eric P. Kasten, and Betty H. C. Cheng. 2004b. *A Taxonomy of Compositional Adaptation*. MSU-CSE-04-17, Michigan State University, East Lansing, Michigan: Michigan State University.

Metzger, Andreas, and Klaus Pohl. 2014. "Software Product Line Engineering and Variability Management: Achievements and Challenges." *Proceedings of the on Future of Software Engineering - FOSE 2014*. Hyderabad, India: ACM. 70-84. doi:10.1145/2593882.2593888.

Morin, Brice, Franck Fleurey, Nelly Bencomo, Jean-Marc Jézéquel, Arnor Solberg, Vegard Dehlen, and Gordon Blair. 2008. *An Aspect-Oriented and Model-Driven Approach for Managing Dynamic Variability*. Vol. LNCS 5301, in *Model Driven Engineering Languages and Systems*, edited by Krzysztof Czarnecki, Ileana Ober, Jean-Michel Bruel, Axel Uhl and Markus Völter, 782-796. Berlin, Heidelberg: Springer Berlin Heidelberg. doi:10.1007/978-3-540-87875-9_54.

Morin, Brice, Olivier Barais, Gregory Nain, and Jean-Marc Jezequel. 2009. "Taming Dynamically Adaptive Systems using Models and Aspects." *IEEE 31st International Conference on Software Engineering*. Vancouver, BC, Canada: IEEE. 122-132. doi:10.1109/ICSE.2009.5070514.

Morin, Brice, Olivier Barais, Jean-Marc Jezequel, Franck Fleurey, and Arnor Solberg. 2009. "Models@ Run.time to Support Dynamic Adaptation." *Computer* (IEEE) 42 (10): 44-51. doi:10.1109/MC.2009.327.

Muschevici, Radu, Dave Clarke, and Jose Proenca. 2010. "Feature Petri Nets." *Proceedings of the 14th International Software Product Line Conference (SPLC).*, 99-106. Jeju Island (South Korea).

Nascimento, Amanda S., Cecilia M. F. Rubira, Rachel Burrows, and Fernando Castor. 2013. "A Model-Driven Infrastructure for Developing Product Line Architectures Using CVL." *2013 VII Brazilian Symposium on Software Components, Architectures and Reuse*. Brasilia, Brazil: IEEE. 119-128. doi:10.1109/SBCARS.2013.23.

Nascimento, Amanda S., Cecilia M.F. Rubira, and Fernando Castor. 2014. "ArCMAPE: A Software Product Line Infrastructure to Support Fault-Tolerant Composite Services." *2014 IEEE 15th International Symposium on High-Assurance Systems Engineering*. Miami Beach, FL: IEEE. 41-48. doi:10.1109/HASE.2014.15.

Nunes, Vinícius, Danilo Mendonça, Genaína Rodrigues, and Vander Alves. 2013. "Towards Compositional Approach for Parametric Model Checking in Software Product Lines." *Workshop on Dependability in Adaptive and Self-Managing Systems—WDAS*. Rio de Janeiro, Brazil. 19-22.

Oreizy, Peyman, Michael M. Gorlick, Richard N. Taylor, Dennis Heimbigner, Gregory Johnson, Nenad Medvidovic, Alex Quilici, David S. Rosenblum, and Alexander L. Wolf. 1999. "An Architecture-Based Approach to Self-Adaptive Software." *IEEE Intelligent Systems and their Applications* (IEEE) 14 (3): 54-62. doi:10.1109/5254.769885.

Parra, Carlos, Xavier Blanc, and Laurence Duchien. 2009. "Context Awareness for Dynamic Service-Oriented Product Lines." *SPLC '09 Proceedings of the 13th International Software Product Line Conference*. San Francisco, CA: ACM. 131-140.

Parra, Carlos, Xavier Blanc, Anthony Cleve, and Laurence Duchien. 2011. "Unifying design and runtime software adaptation using aspect models." *Science of Computer Programming* (Elsevier B.V) 76 (12): 1247-1260. doi:10.1016/j.scico.2010.12.005.

Pessoa, Leonardo Monteiro. 2014. "Flexibilidade em Linhas de Produtos Dinâmicas Cientes de Qualidade: uma Abordagem Baseada em Linguagens Específicas de Domínio." Master thesis [in Portuguese], Universidade de Brasília, 87.

Pessoa, Leonardo, Paula Fernandes, Thiago Castro, Vander Alves, Genaína N. Rodrigues, and Hervaldo Carvalho. 2017. "Building Reliable and Maintainable Dynamic Software Product Lines: An Investigation in the Body Sensor Network Domain." *Information and Software Technology* (Elsevier B.V.) 86: 54-70. doi:10.1016/j.infsof.2017.02.002.

Pohl, Klaus, Günter Böckle, and Frank van der Linden. 2005. *Software Product Line Engineering—Foundations, Principles, and Techniques*. Berlin, Heidelberg: Springer Berlin Heidelberg.

Razak, Safwan Abd, Mohd Adham Isa, Dayang Norhayati Abang Jawawi, and Ong Liang Fuh. 2017. "Model-Based Testing for Software Product Line: A Systematic Literature Review." *International Journal of Software Engineering and Technology* 2 (2): 27-34.

Rodrigues, Genaina N., Vander Alves, Vinicius Nunes, Andre Lanna, Maxime Cordy, Pierre-Yves Schobbens, Amir Molzam Sharifloo, and Axel Legay. 2015. "Modeling and Verification for Probabilistic Properties in Software Product Lines." *2015 IEEE 16th International Symposium on High Assurance Systems Engineering*. Daytona Beach Shores, FL: IEEE. 173-180. doi:10.1109/HASE.2015.34.

Rosenmüller, Marko, Norbert Siegmund, Gunter Saake, and Sven Apel. 2008. "Code generation to support static and dynamic composition of software product lines." *Proceedings of the 7th international conference on Generative programming and component engineering—GPCE '08*. Nashville, TN: ACM Press. 3-12. doi:10.1145/1449913.1449917.

Rosenmüller, Marko, Norbert Siegmund, Sven Apel, and Gunter Saake. 2011. "Flexible Feature Binding in Software Product Lines." *Automated Software Engineering*, 18 (2): 163-197. doi:10.1007/s10515-011-0080-5.

Salehie, Mazeiar, and Ladan Tahvildari. 2009. "Self-adaptive Software: Landscape and Research Challenges." *ACM Transactions on Autonomous and Adaptive Systems* (ACM) 4 (2): 1-42. doi:10.1145/1516533.1516538.

Santos, Ismayle S., Lincoln S. Rocha, Pedro A. Santos Neto, and Rossana M. C. Andrade. 2016. "Model Verification of Dynamic Software Product Lines." *Proceedings of the 30th Brazilian Symposium on Software Engineering—SBES '16*. Maringá, Brazil: ACM. 113-122. doi:10.1145/2973839.2973852.

Schmerl, Bradley, Jesper Andersson, Thomas Vogel, Myra B. Cohen, Cecilia M. F. Rubira, Yuriy Brun, Alessandra Gorla, Franco Zambonelli, and Luciano Baresi. 2017. "Challenges in Composing and Decomposing Assurances for Self-Adaptive Systems." In *Software Engineering for Self-Adaptive Systems III. Assurances*. Edited by Rogério de Lemos, David Garlan, Carlo Ghezzi and Holger Giese (Springer International Publishing) LNCS 9640: 64-89. doi:10.1007/978-3-319-74183-3_3.

Svahnberg, Mikael, Jilles van Gurp, and Jan Bosch.2005. "A taxonomy of variability realization techniques." *Software: Practice and Experience* 35: 705-754. doi:10.1002/spe.652.

van Gurp, Jilles, Jan Bosch, and M. Svahnberg. 2001. "On the Notion of Variability in Software Product Lines." *Proceedings Working IEEE/IFIP Conference on Software Architecture*. IEEE. 45-54. doi:10.1109/WICSA.2001.948406.

van Zyl, Jay. 2002. "Product Line Architecture and the Separation of Concerns." In *Software Product Lines: Second International Conference.* Edited by Gary J. Chastek. *SPLC 2 San Diego, CA, August 19-22,* Berlin, Heidelberg: Springer Berlin Heidelberg. 90-109. doi:10.1007/3-540-45652-X_7.

Weyns, Danny, Bradley Schmerl, Vincenzo Grassi, Sam Malek, Raffaela Mirandola, Christian Prehofer, Jochen Wuttke, Jesper Andersson, Holger Giese, and Karl M. Göschka. 2013. "On Patterns for Decentralized Control in Self-Adaptive Systems." *Software Engineering for Self-Adaptive Systems II: International Seminar,* edited by Rogério de Lemos, Holger Giese, Hausi A. Müller and Mary Shaw. *Dagstuhl Castle, Germany, October 24-29, 2010 Revised Selected and Invited Papers* (Springer, Berlin, Heidelberg) LNCS 7475: 76-107. doi:10.1007/978-3-642-35813-5_4.

Weyns, Danny, Sam Malek, and Jesper Andersson. 2010. "FORMS: a FOrmal Reference Model for Self-adaptation." *Proceeding of the 7th International Conference on Autonomic Computing—ICAC '10.* Washington, DC: ACM Press. 205-214. doi:10.1145/1809049.1809078.

TECHNOLOGIES, EXPERIMENTS, AND STUDIES

III TECHNOLOGIES, EXPERIMENTS, AND STUDIES

Chapter 10

A Feature Ontology to Power Enterprise-Level Product Line Engineering

Charles Krueger and Paul Clements

BigLever Software, Inc., Austin, Texas, United States

10.1 Introduction

Product line engineering (PLE) is an approach for engineering a portfolio of similar products in an efficient manner, taking full advantage of the products' similarities while respecting and managing the variation among them. By "engineer," we mean all of the activities involved in planning, producing, delivering, deploying, sustaining, and retiring products. PLE gains advantages by building and evolving the product line as a single entity, not as a collection of separate systems. This "single system" is truly variability-intensive, and PLE is a longstanding discipline for managing that variability. PLE is in widespread use in industries as diverse as automotive, healthcare, aerospace, consumer goods, finance, and more.

PLE has long been used to manage and resolve the variation present across the engineering assets in the systems engineering "V"—from requirements, to design, through implementation, verification, validation, documentation, and more—in the software, mechanical, and electrical disciplines.

However, as PLE matures, we find enterprises seeking to adopt PLE at all levels of their organization, not just in the engineering departments. This includes areas such as product marketing, portfolio planning, manufacturing, supply chain management, product sales, product service and maintenance, Internet-of-Things, resource planning, and much more. In some very large organizations, thousands of *non*-engineering users need different views of and interaction scenarios with the representation of a product line's commonality and variation.

As this occurs, the concept of "feature" that has long held sway in the engineering realm may no longer be appropriate to these new and non-engineering-oriented stakeholders.

Starting in the early 2000s, a form of PLE known as *Feature-based Software and Systems Product Line Engineering* (Feature-based PLE) has emerged as a modern, repeatable, codified, and proven-in-practice specialization of generic PLE practice. Supported by industrial-strength automation and methodology, Feature-based PLE is the subject of an upcoming ISO standard that is in progress with involvement and support from INCOSE through its Product Line Engineering International Working Group [13]. Feature-based PLE involves automation-supported configuration of engineering artifacts to reflect the feature choices embodied by a product. Configuration of artifacts based on feature choices is a powerful paradigm, and there are many successful applications of Feature-based PLE in the literature [3][5][6][7].

Like PLE in general, Feature-based PLE got its start in the engineering realm. As implied by the name, the notion of *feature* lies at the conceptual heart of Feature-based PLE. We, along with many others, adopt the definition that a feature is a distinguishing characteristic that sets products in a product line apart from each other. We find this definition to be intuitive, easy to teach, and helpfully exclusionary: In Feature-based PLE, a capability common to all products in a product line is *not* considered a feature.

And, for small product lines built by small organizations, it has (in our experience) been quite sufficient. However, we find that for extremely large product lines (with thousands to millions of members) produced by extremely large enterprises (with thousands of engineers and large numbers of non-engineering stakeholders), a more textured and robust definition is needed.

Such organizations are in existence today. The automotive product line at General Motors, for instances, comprises 9 to 10 million vehicle instances in some 30,000 unique electrical/electronic configurations, all put together by some 5,000 product line engineers [18]. As we tour the ontology, this is the kind of organization to bear in mind.

What becomes immediately clear is that what constitutes a "distinguishing characteristic" depends on organizational roles. To a test engineer working to fully define a test procedure that can be used for one or more products in a product line, a distinguishing characteristic might be as fine-grained as whether or not to cycle the power on a subsystem before initiating a test. Such a distinction could not be further from the mind of, say, a vice president of portfolio planning in the same company, for whom a distinguishing characteristic might be which of her company's automotive vehicles are (and are not) going to offer fully autonomous driving three years from now. To compel her to swim in the ocean of all features, without shielding her from those that do not help her do her job, is out of the question to enable enterprise-wide PLE.

The PLE literature is rife with examples of feature models, typically shown in a notional box-and-line representation such as provided by FODA [11]. A car might have bucket seats or bench seats; a user interface might present in English or German; a smartphone might have a five-inch screen or a seven-inch screen; and so forth. Interestingly, *those* features correspond to *neither* the test engineer's notion of a distinguishing characteristic nor the vice president's. Rather, it would seem that they are somewhere "in between," and of (legitimate) interest to stakeholders somewhere "in between" the test engineer and the vice president.

Indeed, others have recognized that "feature" is a concept in need of elaboration for application to large multi-role organizations; a simple one-size-fits-all notion simply won't do [1][10][16].

So, then, if Feature-based PLE is to grow into its full potential of powering an enterprise, we need to ask: For each of the many stakeholders, what is a feature? And how can the various answers—the various kinds or "levels" of features—be related to each other in a unified way so that we can consistently describe *all* of the variation in a product line from top to bottom, while letting each individual stakeholder work at the right descriptive level for his or her job?

To answer that question, this chapter presents a unified approach to variant management for all stakeholders across the enterprise. It employs the venerable principles of abstraction and modularity to define concepts, views, relationships, and behaviors that are best suited for specific roles for stakeholders in engineering and business operations. In short, it presents an *ontology* for the concept of "feature."

10.2 Ontologies

An ontology is an "explicit formal specification of the terms in a domain and relations among them" [9], in order to "share common understanding of the structure of information among people or software agents" [14]. The people are those who will use the Feature-based PLE paradigm. The "software agents" to inform include the PLE tools that are the technological engines of the Feature-based PLE paradigm.

Our ontology will introduce terminology for features that recognize the kinds of levels to which the Introduction alluded. It will have the following characteristics:

- The levels fully partition the space of features. No feature can be in two levels.
- Features in each level can be described in terms of the choices they make available, and *instances* that reflect choices actually made.
- Features in each level can be described in terms of typical roles in a large organization that will find features at that level useful in doing their jobs.
- Each level incrementally constrains the complexity and combinatorics of the variation space. Variation possibilities are literally cosmological in scale at the bottom, but reduce to a number at the top able to be grasped by a human.
- The levels are connected to each other thus: The choices made at a particular level constitute the choices that are available at the next higher level.

Before we present our ontology, it is necessary to explore the form of PLE to which it applies, to see how features and feature choices lead to the production of products.

10.3 Feature-Based Product Line Engineering: An Overview

Feature-based PLE uses a reference model that is based on the metaphor of a factory. The PLE factory produces digital assets across the entire life cycle for products in a product family, analogous to a conventional factory producing physical assets and products. All development happens inside the factory; the output of the factory is for validation and delivery.

The components of the PLE factory (Figure 10.1) are as follows:

1. A product line's **feature catalog** is a model of the collection of all of the feature options and variants that are available across the entire product line. Feature owners and feature architects create their respective sections in the feature catalog.
2. A **bill-of-features** is a specification for a product in the product line portfolio, rendered in terms of the specific feature choices from the feature catalog that are included in the product. In other words, it is a feature-based product specification, defined as an instantiation

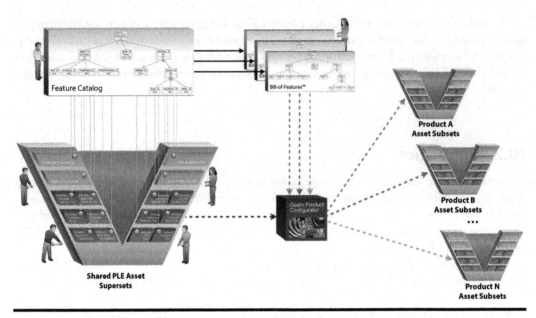

Figure 10.1   Overview of Feature-based product line engineering; the PLE factory.

of the available feature choices in the feature catalog. The bill-of-features portfolio is the collection of bills-of-features that, together, define the entire product line. Portfolio teams, typically working with product marketing teams, create bill-of-features for product families and "flavors," based on the features available in the feature catalog.

Whereas the feature catalog lays out the choices that are *available*, a bill-of-features is a set of choices <u>made</u> (i.e., selections) against the feature catalog.

3. **Shared assets** are the digital artifacts associated with the systems and software engineering life cycle of the product line. Shared assets can be whatever digital artifacts compose a part of a delivered product or support the engineering process to create and maintain a product.

Shared assets can include, but are not limited to, requirements, design specifications, design models, source code, build files, test plans and test cases, user documentation, repair manuals and installation guides, project budgets, schedules, and work plans, product calibration and configuration files, data models, manufacturing parts lists, engineering drawings, and more. Assets in PLE are engineered to be shared across the product line.

In Feature-based PLE, shared assets are maintained as *supersets*; that is, any content needed by any of the products can be found in the superset. The supersets include *variation points*, which are declarations that specify under what feature choice combinations a specific piece of content is needed and in what form it is needed. (Variation points are indicated by the gear symbols in Figure 10.1.) Variation point content will be included in a product's digital assets if that feature or feature combination has been chosen, and omitted otherwise. Asset engineers create variation points in their subsystem assets, based on the features available in the feature catalog. Asset engineers typically specialize into their own specific disciplines: requirements engineers, system modeling engineers, test engineers, BOM engineers, document engineers, and so forth.

4. The **PLE factory configurator** is the mechanism that automatically produces application assets for the digital twin of a specific product. In Feature-based PLE, the configurator is an automated tool, as opposed to a manual process. It performs its task by processing the bill-of-features for that product, and exercising the shared assets' variation points in light of the feature choices in that bill-of-features. The configurator provides the abstraction-driven automation that eliminates the labor-intensive and error-prone activity of manually assembling and modifying engineering assets for the digital twin for each product in the product line. An example is Gears [2], although there are others as well.

5. **System asset instances** are product-specific instances of the Shared Asset Supersets, automatically produced by the PLE factory configurator. System Asset Instances are validated and delivered to the next life cycle phase (e.g., manufacturing), to the customer, or to the market. Suppliers, testers, manufacturing, sales, and more use the generated assets, configured by the bill-of-features for a system or product family.

The factory operates as follows: Shared asset supersets are configured by the PLE factory configurator based on a bill-of-features in the bill-of-features portfolio, derived from the feature catalog, to produce system asset instances. The complete collection of digital engineering assets across the systems engineering and software engineering and operations life cycle for a single physical product is sometimes referred to as the "digital twin" of that product. Thus the Feature-based PLE factory in this reference model gives birth to the digital twin for each product in a product line portfolio.

10.4 PLE Evolves to PLE for the Enterprise

The complexity of managing the variability in a family of similar products or systems is not limited to engineering groups. Other organizations that can spend inordinate amounts of time and effort dealing with product feature diversity include manufacturing and supply chains in automotive, certification and compliance documentation in aerospace and defense, product marketing and product portfolio planning in highly competitive markets, web system deployments in e-commerce, sales automation for complex configurable systems, plus training, support, service, maintenance, disposal, and more in many industries.

Although it became clear to many successful PLE organizations that alignment of PLE with their existing business operations was crucial, the idea of consolidating the variant management disciplines across engineering and operations groups is an idea at the edge of the practice envelope. Some of the industry's most innovative product line enterprises are now leveraging or planning to leverage their PLE competence to create highly efficient product line operations. We refer to this convergence as product line engineering and operations, or PLE&O.

Prior to the Feature-based PLE methodology, individual stages of the systems and software engineering life cycle would typically invent their own solutions for managing product line variation. Requirements engineers might use attributes to annotate requirements variations in their database, designers might use supertypes and subtypes to model design variants, software developers might use IFDEFs to indicate source code variants, and testers might use file system directory naming conventions to sort out their test case variants. Of course, dissonance among the solutions across the life-cycle stages made it nearly impossible to manage the traceability among variants in the different life-cycle stages.

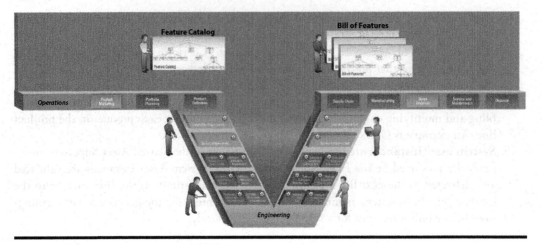

Figure 10.2   PLE for the enterprise.

Feature-based PLE consolidates variation management across the different stages of the systems and software engineering life cycle with a single source of the "feature truth" and sophisticated feature-based automation. Some of the most advanced PLE organizations are pushing towards a similar convergence between PLE and Product Line Operations. However, business operations (such as product marketing or customer training) are not part of the engineering "V." A good way to think of operations is that they are on the "wings" of the "V." That is, there are operations that are upstream of the engineering activities on the left of the "V," and there are operations that are downstream of the engineering activities on the right of the "V."

As shown in Figure 10.2, the single source of the "feature truth" has been elevated out of the middle of the "V," so that it can also be the single source of the "feature truth" for the operations on the wings of the "V" and thereby facilitate the PLE&O convergence.

PLE&O extends PLE with a fundamental new perspective and methodology for consolidated feature-based complexity management, variation management and automation across an enterprise's entire engineering and business operations for their family of product or system deliverables.

10.5 Tools for Building our Ontology: Abstraction, Aggregation, and Instantiation

As we build our ontology, we will appeal to three well-known engineering principles at each level. *Aggregation* and *instantiation* will let us build and consolidate the elements at each level, whereas *abstraction* will describe what each level offers as well as serve as the springboard to take us from one level to the level above.

■ **Abstraction** is how we describe the features – the choices available – at each level of the ontology. Our introductory thought experiment about the test engineer and the Vice President of Portfolio Planning almost cried out for the concept of abstraction to help us describe the different kinds of "distinguishing characteristics" meaningful to each.

An abstraction is a one-to-many mapping [17]. In classical software engineering, the counterpart to abstraction is implementation, and there the one-to-many mapping allows for any of a number of different implementations to provide the same abstraction to a construct's users. In our feature ontology, the higher we go, the more abstract the features will be. Our one-to-many mapping will mean an *available* choice represented as a feature at one level will correspond to a set of one or more choices *made* from among features at the next lower level. Put another way, choices made at one level will form a more abstract choice available at the next higher level. Each level of abstraction will be suitable for different stakeholders across the enterprise, ranging from detailed engineering variants to glossy marketing variants.

For example, a car's climate control system may be a feature in which the choices available include premium, mid-level, or economy-level. Each one of those choices corresponds to (and effectively abstracts from) a set of lower-level choices, such as whether the climate control system includes air conditioning or just a heater, is single-zone or dual-zone (meaning there are settings for both driver and front-seat passenger), whether is automatically maintains a set temperature or the driver has to make manual adjustments, and so forth. Choices *available* at the higher level each correspond to choices *made* at the lower level.

■ **Aggregation** is simply the formation of a number of things into a cluster. At each level in our ontology, we are going to find that we have a number (often a large number) of features that are made available. Having one undistinguished bag of choices will not help the stakeholders for that level find the choice they're looking for. So we use aggregation to cluster the choices into related sets. Again, we appeal to classical software engineering: In practice the clustering scheme will tend to reflect separation of concerns criteria, so that each cluster exhibits high conceptual cohesion. The result of aggregation should be a set of right-sized manageable clusters that make sense to someone familiar with the domain.

■ Within a level, **instantiation** will deliver us from the overwhelming and theoretical art of the *possible* to the practical craft of the *useful*. At any level, the features available may admit literally astronomical numbers of choice combinations, but in practice only a tiny fraction represent useful combinations. Instantiation is the definition and enumeration of those choices. If the feature choices at any level represent a wide-ranging restaurant menu, instantiation turns the countless possible meals (most of which we would never want to order) into a smaller set of appealing *prix-fixe* dinners. Every level in our feature ontology will define a space of *choices available*, against which individual products will be assigned a *choice made*. The job of instantiation is to enumerate a tractable list of desired offerings from the intractably combinatoric possibilities.

With these concepts in hand we are ready to introduce our feature ontology.

10.6 Feature Ontology for Enterprise PLE

10.6.1 Level 0: Asset Variation Points, the Ultimate "Distinguishing Characteristics"

Imagine performing a "diff" operation across all of the engineering artifacts that represent all of the product instances in a product line. It would sort through, for example, requirements specifications, design models, test cases, software, files mechanical parts listed in a bill-of-materials, sections or paragraphs or even individual words in a user's manual, slides in training courseware, and much more. What would the diff operation return? No doubt:

- Words, phrases, or lines of requirements
- Terms or lines of source code
- Words or lines or paragraphs of test procedures
- Model elements or attributes in design specs

And so on—in other words, all of the places where the digital engineering representations of any two products differ from each other.

In a product line comprising thousands to tens of thousands of instances such as in the automotive domain, for example, there may easily be *millions* of these differences, meaning that the variation space is roughly $2^{1,000,000}$ in size. While they are undeniably "distinguishing characteristics," albeit tiny ones, and undeniably important to manage correctly, it becomes immediately clear that they cannot be what we wish to consider as features: No organization could do business by creating and managing a bank of millions of features and nothing more. Nor do these tiny differences lend any insight into qualitative and interesting ways in which products differ from each other.

Nevertheless, these individual asset variation points represent the "base case" and launching point for our feature ontology. They are the ultimate "distinguishing characteristics" in a product line. Table 10.1 lists the relevant characteristics of Level 0.

10.6.2 Level 1: Component Feature Models

Level 1 is the level in our ontology where features we are most familiar with make their debut. Here and beyond, they serve as the *de facto* abstraction mechanism, offering choices that may be selected in ways to define a product.

Table 10.1 Characteristics of level 0, asset variation points

Abstraction	Variation points within assets implement differentiating characteristics for a product line
Aggregation	Naturally aggregated according to the asset type and specific artifact
Instantiation	Variation point semantics for an asset type define the possible instantiations. Example: A requirements paragraph is included or excluded; the value of a test parameter is −1, 0, or +1; a server rack in a bill-of-materials is 19″ wide but either 39″ or 41″ deep; etc.
Data structures	Each variation point is either optional (meaning included or excluded) or comes in mutually exclusive variants, possibly including parameterization of selected content
Roles	Asset engineers across the systems engineering 'V'
Example combinatorics	On the order of 1,000,000 variation points resulting in $2^{1,000,000}$ possible configurations

In order for a feature catalog to be tractable to represent and manage, a feature needs to be more powerful than a switch that turns a tiny bit of content on and off in a shared asset superset. Here on Level 1, features are abstractions of the asset variation points from Level 0; one feature can "drive" many artifact-level variations.[1]

This one-to-many mapping matches our engineering intuition about features: If a capability is included in a system, then requirements, design elements, source code, test cases, user documentation and more, *all* corresponding to that capability, should be included in the product's digital twin. If the capability is omitted, then all of that material should be omitted.

This also matches our practical intuition about features. To elicit the distinguishing characteristics among products, we would not expect our product portfolio experts to tell us about differences in lines of requirements, lines of source code, or lines of test procedures. Rather, we would expect to hear about more abstract differences expressed in terms of capability, function, usage environment, etc.

Therefore, in order to realize the Feature-based PLE narrative (feature choices are used to configure engineering artifacts), there must be a one-to-*many* correspondence between features and engineering artifact variation.

10.6.2.1 Abstraction

Following the previous discussion, the abstraction we make available at this level is called a *primitive standalone feature*. This is a single distinguishing characteristic that can "drive" the setting of one or more variation points in one or more assets. It is characterized not in terms of the specific variation point content but rather as a more abstract characterization of a product.

Each primitive standalone feature, by its very existence, constitutes and establishes a choice to be made on behalf of each product. A type may be introduced to constrain the choices; for example:

- A Boolean type limits the choice to whether the feature is selected or not.
- An enumeration type requires exactly one flavor to be chosen, effectively providing an exclusive-OR construct.
- A set type allows any number of flavors to be chosen, providing an inclusive-OR construct.
- Flavors themselves may have primitive data-carrying types such as "integer" or "string," which limit the values they may take on.

A primitive standalone feature is conveniently (but not necessarily) represented graphically, using a tree-shaped box-and-line structure. Figure 10.3 illustrates.

A "flavor"—one of the children in Figure 10.3—may itself be a primitive standalone feature, leading to the notion of a tree of features.

The point of a single primitive standalone feature is that it may configure multiple variation points in multiple shared asset supersets. If it configures on the order of 10 variation points, then our variation space of millions in the shared asset superset realm reduced to a variation space measured in the hundreds of thousands overall. An individual engineer is likely to be concerned with primitive standalone features numbering in the dozens.

---

[1] In practice, an asset variation point may depend on more than one feature, combined using familiar Boolean operators: (Feature 1 OR Feature 2) AND NOT Feature 3, and so forth. The one-to-many mapping means that one feature drives (but perhaps not exclusively drives) potentially many variation points.

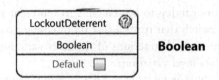

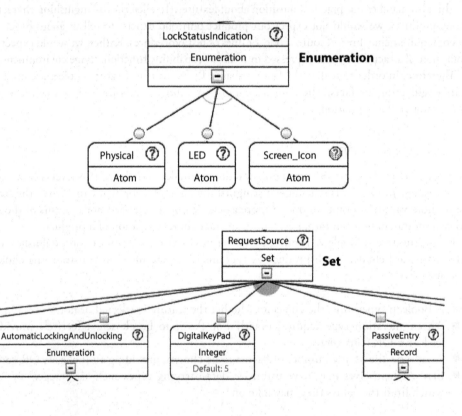

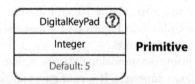

Figure 10.3 Four examples of primitive standalone features.

Making features abstract with respect to specific variation points in specific engineering artifacts reduces the number possibilities by orders of magnitude. A product line as large as the portfolio of a company like General Motors may comprise on the order of ten thousand features like the ones we are describing here [6]. For a company that large, with thousands of engineers working in the product line context, ten thousand is a manageable amount.

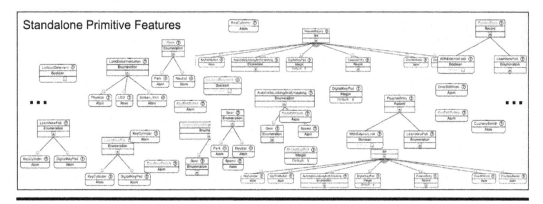

Figure 10.4   Unaggregated primitive standalone features.

At this point, we now have a collection, unsorted and unorganized, of primitive standalone features, something like that shown in Figure 10.4. That's our cue to introduce aggregation to impose some helpful organization.

10.6.2.2 Aggregation

Primitive standalone features are conceptually very helpful but in practice too fine-grained to be an ongoing focus of attention. In product lines of complex systems, product line engineers tend to be assigned to specific areas of knowledge and expertise, and the variation in these areas transcends individual features. A bundled construct is more helpful to let them capture variation in those broader areas.

Just as large software systems are composed into coherent modules, to facilitate ease of change and productive work by separate members of a large team [15], so then it is with features. This bundling provides a cleanly packaged and coherent set of features, to achieve ease of change and to enable productive work by members of a team. At this level, our unit of aggregation is called *a component feature model.*

Component feature models have names and, in practice, generally correspond to specific capabilities or other generally acknowledged unit of system decomposition. Just as dividing software into parts requires keen architectural insight and ability, defining the scope of a component feature model requires the same kind of architectural thinking. Just as a software module should have high cohesion, features in a component feature model should be similarly cohesive, and a feature model should be assigned to an appropriate subject matter expert (or team) to own and manage its content and evolution.

As an example of introduced modularity, component feature models may be used to distinguish between customer-facing features (for example, would you like a cruise control on your car that detects the car ahead of you and keeps you from running into it?) and inward-facing or implementation-oriented features (to detect a car in front of us, shall we use a camera on the front bumper, a LIDAR sensor, or a short-range radar?). Both kinds of decisions represent important and legitimate feature choices, but are meaningful to different audiences, and so it is convenient to put them in different feature models. Assuming any of the inward-facing choices would do the job, the actual decision there is based not on functionality, but typically on the achievement of quality attributes: *this* sensor costs less, but *that* sensor weighs less and produces less heat; however we happen to have a warehouse full of this *other* sensor, all ready to use.

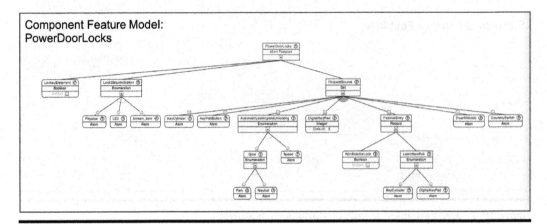

Figure 10.5   Component feature model for an automotive power doors locks system.

Figure 10.5 illustrates a component feature model for an automotive power door locks system. Nodes exhibit the primitive feature types, plus one at the root of the tree for non-variant composition.

A bundle of individual features also is a place where constraints on choices can be conveniently expressed and captured – for example, that two features are mutually exclusive (so at most one may be chosen) or mutually required (so that zero or both must be chosen).

We find that a typical component feature model combines on the order of ten primitive stand-alone features (each of which may have a number of flavors from which to choose, usually 10 or fewer). Smaller ones are certainly possible. Larger ones are certain possible as well, but we find that component feature models with many more than ten features become difficult to grasp.

10.6.2.3 Instantiation

A feature model such as one in Figure 10.5 only lays out choices that are available. Someone has to make choices from that model, and we need a way to record the choices.

We could let people browse through the feature model and choose any combination of features present. However, this quickly reveals itself to be an undesirable choice. Combinatorics of feature models are such that even quite modest feature models may lead to many thousands of possible choice combinations – too many to implement and too many to test.

Thus, we don't want to let people pick and choose among individual features. Rather, we want to offer only those sets of pre-packaged choices that (a) contribute to products that are technically and economically feasible to engineer and build; and (b) contribute to products that a customer or the market would actually want to buy. *Feature profiles* serve that role. Feature choices available in the component feature model are bound to create a feature profile.

A feature profile represents a unique and *supported* configuration of a component feature model. These, then, are the combinations we are willing to build and test and offer to the product line at large—not just any combination at random, but a set that has been identified with analysis and forethought. The list of feature profiles that should be offered are typically determined and defined by the subject matter experts collaborating with the business to determine which offerings are technologically feasible and provide the best economic return for the enterprise. Feature profiles are given names based on their differentiating characteristics.

Figure 10.6 illustrates.

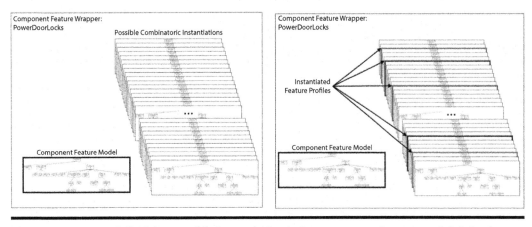

Figure 10.6 **Out of all of the possible instantiations of a component feature model (left), feature profiles are named and supported instances (right).**

We find that a typical component feature model offers on the order of ten or so feature profiles. Thus, overall, it is not unusual to see feature models with up to a hundred or so features offered with a dozen or less feature profiles, thus reducing the available choices by more orders of magnitude. Our complexity space is now around 2^{1000}.

Feature profiles define a set of choices available at this level. These turn out to be the primitive abstractions available at the next level.

10.6.2.4 Summary of Level 1

Table 10.2 lists the salient characteristics of Level 1.

10.6.3 Level 2: Subsystem Feature Models

After primitive standalone features are assembled into component feature models and their individual feature instances bundled into feature profiles, the result is a collection—possibly thousands of feature models (and tens of thousands of feature profiles) in a large product line. Also, our heuristic of not wanting feature models to be too large (and therefore difficult to comprehend, work with, and change) has led us to want multiple feature models that may belong to the same subject matter area. A construct to bundle those would be helpful. Level 2 provides that construct.

10.6.3.1 Abstraction

The component feature models of Level 1, each with its named feature profiles, together represent a higher order feature abstraction in our feature ontology. Each component feature model becomes a subsystem standalone feature at this level. The list of named feature profiles becomes a higher-order enumeration of mutually exclusive choices for that higher-order feature.

For example, Figure 10.5 wrapped many primitive features into a component feature called power door locks. Figure 10.6 whittled down the astronomical number of possible choice sets

Table 10.2 Characteristics of Level 1, component feature models

Abstraction	Essential root-cause functional and non-functional variation, for abstract differentiating characteristics applied to asset variation
Aggregation	A component feature model is formed when primitive standalone features are grouped into modular bundles based on an architectural concern, such as differentiating characteristics for a component.
Instantiation	Feature profiles represent a named, unique, and supported configuration of a component feature model. A feature profile binds all of the choices made available by the component feature model.
Data structures	For primitive standalone features, a feature plus its possible values (in accordance with its type). For an aggregation of primitive standalone features, a set of primitive standalone features plus a non-variant node designating the composition. Both primitive and aggregated features are conveniently represented graphically as a tree. Component feature model and instances are encapsulated in a named container.
Roles	Engineers concerned with specific product capabilities work with primitive standalone features. Feature catalog engineers, and subsystem and component engineers work with component feature models. Bill-of-features engineers and subsystem and component interface engineers are concerned with feature profiles.
Example combinatorics	On the order of 10,000 primitive features aggregated into an order of 1,000 component feature models

to five useful ones, defined as feature profiles for power door locks. Thus, a component feature model such as power door locks becomes a *subsystem standalone feature* at this level. It encapsulates and hides the details of the Level 1 primitive feature model tree (and, by extension, the Level 0 asset variation points they drive). Power door locks is a feature that comes with a fixed set of named atomic values, which correspond to the feature profiles of power door locks. Figure 10.7 illustrates.

10.6.3.2 Aggregation

Level 2 aggregation applies separation of concerns and modularity criteria to the set of all subsystem standalone features, in order to create cohesive bundles of features that correspond to a product line's domain areas.

Defining the scope of a subsystem feature model is, like scoping a component feature model, also an architectural activity. We find that, at this level, it will often represent a subsystem that is part of the products of the product line.

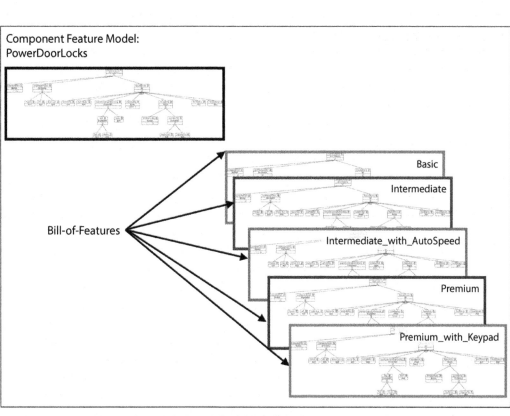

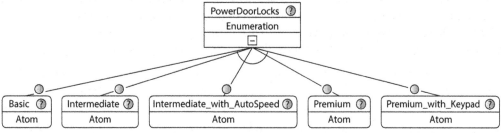

Figure 10.7   A Level 1 component feature model and its feature profiles (left) become a Level 2 feature with a fixed set of value choices (right).

Figure 10.8 illustrates the aggregation of a number of standalone subsystem features into a subsystem feature model.

Because every standalone subsystem feature offers a mutually exclusive set of atomic choices, it is convenient to represent a subsystem feature as a table. Each column holds the choices available from one standalone subsystem feature. Figure 10.9 illustrates.

10.6.3.3 Instantiation

Once again, instantiation provides a way to extract a tractable number of cases from an intractable number of possibilities. Even if comprising a modest number of standalone subsystem features, each with a modest number of atomic choices available, subsystem feature models may be

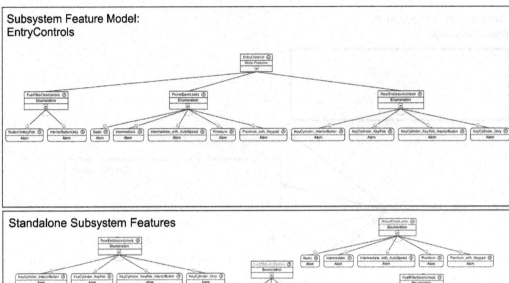

Figure 10.8 A set of standalone subsystem features (top) are aggregated into cohesive subsystem feature models (bottom). Here, Power Door Locks was aggregated with FuelFillerDoorUnlock and RearEnclosureUnlock to form the subsystem feature model EntryControls.

instantiated in many more ways than are helpful in practice. The solution is to identify a named set of packaged choices that are economically appealing: Feasible to build and deploy, and answering a customer need.

Figure 10.10 illustrates. At the top is the enumeration of all possible combinations of choices of each of the three standalone subsystem feature models that EntryControls comprises. At the

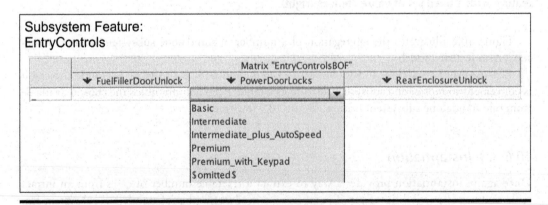

Figure 10.9 Representing a subsystem feature model as a table.

Possible Combinatoric Instantiations

Instances	Matrix "EntryControlsTemplate.EntryControlsProliferated"		
	▼ PowerDoorLocks	▼ FuelFillerDoorUnlock	▼ RearEnclosureUnlock
Product4	Basic	ButtonOnKeyFob	KeyCylinder_Only
Product5	Basic	ButtonOnKeyFob	$omitted$
Product6	Basic	InteriorButtonOnly	KeyCylinder_InteriorButton
Product8	Basic	InteriorButtonOnly	KeyCylinder_KeyFob_InteriorButton
Product9	Basic	InteriorButtonOnly	KeyCylinder_Only
Product10	Basic	InteriorButtonOnly	$omitted$
Product12	Basic	$omitted$	KeyCylinder_KeyFob
Product13	Basic	$omitted$	KeyCylinder_KeyFob_InteriorButton
Product15	Basic	$omitted$	$omitted$
Product16	Intermediate	ButtonOnKeyFob	KeyCylinder_InteriorButton
Product17	Intermediate	ButtonOnKeyFob	KeyCylinder_KeyFob
Product18	Intermediate	ButtonOnKeyFob	KeyCylinder_KeyFob_InteriorButton
Product19	Intermediate	ButtonOnKeyFob	KeyCylinder_Only
Product20	Intermediate	ButtonOnKeyFob	$omitted$
• • •			
Product2648656	Premium	$omitted$	KeyCylinder_InteriorButton
Product2648657	Premium	$omitted$	KeyCylinder_KeyFob
Product2648658	Premium	$omitted$	KeyCylinder_KeyFob_InteriorButton
Product2648659	Premium	$omitted$	KeyCylinder_Only
Product2648660	Premium	$omitted$	$omitted$
Product2648661	Premium_with_Keypad	ButtonOnKeyFob	KeyCylinder_InteriorButton
Product2648662	Premium_with_Keypad	ButtonOnKeyFob	KeyCylinder_KeyFob
Product2648663	Premium_with_Keypad	ButtonOnKeyFob	KeyCylinder_KeyFob_InteriorButton
Product2648664	Premium_with_Keypad	ButtonOnKeyFob	KeyCylinder_Only
Product2648665	Premium_with_Keypad	ButtonOnKeyFob	$omitted$
Product2648666	Premium_with_Keypad	InteriorButtonOnly	KeyCylinder_InteriorButton

Instantiated Bill-of-Features

Instances	Matrix "EntryControlsTemplate.EntryControlsProliferated"		
	▼ PowerDoorLocks	▼ FuelFillerDoorUnlock	▼ RearEnclosureUnlock
Product4	Basic	ButtonOnKeyFob	KeyCylinder_Only
Product5	Basic	ButtonOnKeyFob	$omitted$
Product6	Basic	InteriorButtonOnly	KeyCylinder_InteriorButton
Product8	Basic	InteriorButtonOnly	KeyCylinder_KeyFob_InteriorButton
Product9	Basic	InteriorButtonOnly	KeyCylinder_Only
Product10	Basic	InteriorButtonOnly	$omitted$
Product12	Basic	$omitted$	KeyCylinder_KeyFob
Product13	Basic	$omitted$	KeyCylinder_KeyFob_InteriorButton
Product15	Basic	$omitted$	$omitted$
Product16	Intermediate	ButtonOnKeyFob	KeyCylinder_InteriorButton
Product17	Intermediate	ButtonOnKeyFob	KeyCylinder_KeyFob
Product18	Intermediate	ButtonOnKeyFob	KeyCylinder_KeyFob_InteriorButton
Product19	Intermediate	ButtonOnKeyFob	KeyCylinder_Only
Product20	Intermediate	ButtonOnKeyFob	$omitted$
• • •			
Product2648656	Premium	$omitted$	KeyCylinder_InteriorButton
Product2648657	Premium	$omitted$	KeyCylinder_KeyFob
Product2648658	Premium	$omitted$	KeyCylinder_KeyFob_InteriorButton
Product2648659	Premium	$omitted$	KeyCylinder_Only
Product2648660	Premium	$omitted$	$omitted$
Product2648661	Premium_with_Keypad	ButtonOnKeyFob	KeyCylinder_InteriorButton
Product2648662	Premium_with_Keypad	ButtonOnKeyFob	KeyCylinder_KeyFob
Product2648663	Premium_with_Keypad	ButtonOnKeyFob	KeyCylinder_KeyFob_InteriorButton
Product2648664	Premium_with_Keypad	ButtonOnKeyFob	KeyCylinder_Only
Product2648665	Premium_with_Keypad	ButtonOnKeyFob	$omitted$
Product2648666	Premium_with_Keypad	InteriorButtonOnly	KeyCylinder_InteriorButton

Figure 10.10   Possible instances (top) vs. chosen instances (bottom).

bottom is a set of seven, chosen for their usefulness and suitability, that we will use going forward. We call each of these a bill-of-features.

At Level 2 of our ontology, then, there is a set of named subsystem feature models, each of which has a set of named instantiated profiles.

Table 10.3   Summary of Level 2

Abstraction	Level 1's component feature models become Level 2 features. The feature profiles available for a Level 1 component feature model become the atomic values available for the Level 2 feature.
Aggregation	A subsystem feature model is formed when standalone subsystem features are grouped into modular bundles based on an architectural concern, such as differentiating characteristics for a subsystem.
Instantiation	Subsystem feature models are instantiated into a manageable and useful set of instances, called a Bill-of-Features, each named according to the variation it presents.
Data structures	For subsystem feature models, an aggregation of subsystem standalone features plus a non-variant node designating the composition. A root list has one level of subsystem feature enumerations. Both primitive and aggregated features are conveniently represented graphically as a table.
Roles	Feature catalog engineers. System and subsystem engineers. Engineers may collaborate with the portfolio planning organization to determine which differentiating characteristics should be offered as higher-order feature choices. The list of profiles that should be offered are also determined and defined by the systems engineering experts collaborating with the business to determine which offerings provide the best economic return for the enterprise.
Example combinatorics	1,000 subsystem features consolidated in 250 subsystem feature models. Because subsystems typically combine ten or so feature models, our variation space is now roughly 2^{100}.

10.6.3.4 Summary of Level 2

Table 10.3 summarizes the key characteristics of Level 2.

10.6.4 Level 3: System Feature Models

Subsystem feature models tend, in practice, to capture the variation and shared assets associated with a subsystem. A subsystem may be clearly identified in a common architecture for the product line, or it may be informally identified by the presence of a dedicated group of people who work on it, and a collection of shared assets devoted to engineering it.

Clearly another level of scope beckons. We need to bundle subsystem production lines into product offerings at the system or whole-product level.

After all of the feature models are partitioned and aggregated into subsystem feature models, the result is a collection of feature models that can still encompass a quite large variation space— possibly hundreds or even thousands of features in a large product line, as may be found in the automotive industry [18]. There, subsystem production lines may exist for brakes, transmissions, lighting, infotainment, entry controls, climate control, and a whole host more.

Instances	Subsystem Feature Model		
	Matrix "EntryControls"		
	⬇ PowerDoorLocks	⬇ FuelFillerDoorUnlock	⬇ RearEnclosureUnlock
Basic	Basic	$omitted$	$omitted$
Basic_Plus	Basic_plus_KeyFob	$omitted$	KeyCylinder_Only
Intermediate_Low	Intermediate	$omitted$	KeyCylinder_KeyFob
Intermediate_Low_Plus_Speed	Intermediate_plus_AutoSpeed	InteriorButtonOnly	KeyCylinder_KeyFob
Intermediate_Plus	Intermediate_plus_AutoGearNeutral	InteriorButtonOnly	KeyCylinder_InteriorButton
Premium	Premium_with_KeyCylinder	ButtonOnKeyFob	KeyCylinder_KeyFob_InteriorButton
Premium_Plus	Premium_with_Keypad	ButtonOnKeyFob	KeyCylinder_KeyFob_InteriorButton

Instances

Figure 10.11   Subsystem feature models (Power Door Locks, Fuel Filler Door Unlock, and Rear Enclosure Unlock) aggregated into a system feature model (Entry Controls).

At Level 3 (and beyond) we will employ the same pattern as the one that took us from Level 1 to Level 2: Feature choices at the lower level are aggregated to form higher-level features at the higher level. So, here, a subsystem feature model is abstracted as a standalone system feature, whose flavors are related by the exclusive-OR operator. Subsystem profiles are abstracted as the atomic values for the system feature.

But Level 3 features can also be constructed from component-level feature choices also. So, a Level 3 feature model includes, as its choices, bills-of-features from subsystem and/or component feature models.

Figure 10.11 illustrates, using the table notation described earlier. It provides a system feature, Entry Controls, that offers seven flavors, shown as the titles of the rows: Basic, Basic_Plus, and so forth. Each flavor is defined as a set of choices made against each of three subsystem feature models: Power Door Locks, Fuel Filler Door Unlock, and Rear Enclosure Unlock. As in Level 2, each row is a bill-of-features.

Table 10.4 summarizes Level 3.

10.7   Completing the Ontology

10.7.1 Level 4 and Beyond: System of Systems Feature Model

Higher levels of the ontology, as many as needed, can be created by following the pattern of Level 3: Bills-of-features from lower levels form the feature values for higher-level feature models. Aggregation is applied to form logical groupings, and instantiation to create instances. For example, our system feature model "Entry Controls" can be combined with other components, subsystems, and/or system feature models (e.g., for climate control, engines, brakes, lighting, and many more) to produce a product line vehicle. Vehicle instances can be combined to create a product line of vehicle fleets, and so forth. This enables a hierarchical system-of-systems structure, to any number of levels needed (although in practice we seldom see levels beyond Level 4).

10.7.2 Feature Models and the Architecture of the Digital Assets: Production Lines

The end goal of features is to configure shared assets, as shown in Figure 10.1. PLE organizations, especially those who build systems of systems (or even just systems of subsystems, or systems

Table 10.4   Summary of Level 3

Abstraction	Level 2's subsystem feature models and/or Level 1's component feature models become Level 3's features. The feature profiles available for a Level 2 subsystem feature model or a Level 1 component feature model become the atomic values available for the Level 3 feature.
Aggregation	Modularize a collection of subsystem and system features based on an architectural concern
Instantiation	Each instance of a system production line is a bill-of-features, as illustrated in Figure 10.11. A bill-of-subsystem feature choices are the ultimate feature-based description for a whole product.
Data structures	Data structure: The same as for subsystem production lines.
Roles	Anyone concerned with the variation of systems at the highest level is concerned with the system production lines. This can include portfolio planners and managers, marketers and business development specialists, and the engineering and business leadership in a business area or the enterprise at large.
Example combinatorics	Each level in the production line hierarchy often provides a one- to two-orders of magnitude reduction in the combinatoric complexity by limiting the number of specified profiles relative to the number of possible profiles. A two- or three-level hierarchy (typical, in our experience) yields a complexity space of about 2^{50}.

of components) almost always have an architecture of assets that matches the structure of the decomposition architecture of their systems. For instance, they may have requirements documents, design models, and test suites that apply to each component, each subsystem, and the entire system, respectively.

Primitive standalone features (for example, "Lock Status Indication" in Figure 10.3) or logical combinations of primitive standalone features (expressions using AND, OR, NOT, etc.) are used to configure shared assets. We need a way to combine one or more feature models and the shared asset supersets that are configured using the primitive features that that feature model comprises, so that the PLE factory configurator can apply the former to the latter. We call this combination of feature models and configured shared assets a production line—an instance of the PLE factory scheme of Figure 10.1.

Each production line has in it the set of feature models that contain the features needed to configure the variation points in the production line's shared assets. If the feature model is defined to be part of the production line, it can be said to be *owned* by that production line. But sometimes a production line needs to refer to other feature models in order to configure an asset. In that case, it can *import* a feature model (by reference) from the owning production line. A feature model can be owned by one production line, but imported into multiple production lines if its features are crosscutting – a common occurrence. Imported feature models are used to manage feature dependencies and constraints on feature selections across subsystems.

Figure 10.12 illustrates.

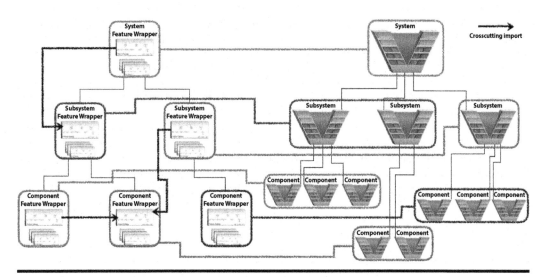

Figure 10.12   Product-line-of-product-lines architecture and asset architecture.

10.7.3 Overlay: System Family Trees

Large product lines often occur in clusters, where products in a cluster have more in common with each other than they do with products in other clusters. System family trees [4][12] allow bills-of-features at any ontological level to be grouped based on their features. This division helps manage the conceptual complexity of the entire product line by focusing on a group of related products. Groups can be further divided into subgroups, and so on.

Family trees are represented by a tree of bills-of-features. Choices made in a bill-of-features anywhere in the tree are inherited by its descendants in the tree. This ensures successive refinement of bills-of-features through the reduction of the configuration space at each level of the hierarchy.

There are two mechanisms for reducing the configuration space at each level in the bill-of-features hierarchy: bindings and downselections. Bindings are used to explicitly state that a choice *must* be the value provided. This decision is said to "bind" the feature. Once a profile has provided definitions for all features, it is said to be "fully bound." Downselections are used to explicitly state that a choice must *not* be any of the downselected values. Downselections partially bind a feature.

The opposite of a bound feature is a feature that may take on any value. Features that may take on any value are said to be "unbound." This assignment explicitly articulates the engineer's decision to not choose a value for this feature in this bill-of-features. The bill-of-features at the root of a bill-of-features tree specifies every feature choice that applies to the product cluster it is defining; it will have the most unbound features choices. Bills-of-features at the leaves of the tree will have all feature choices fully bound.

Family trees may be applied to Level 2 and higher in the ontology.

10.7.4 Overlay: Feature Bundles

Organizations that specify thousands or tens of thousands of products don't want to painstakingly fill out a bill-of-features for every one of them. Modern PLE factory configurators have a "proliferate" feature that can automatically produce a bill-of-features at the leaf of the hierarchy for every combination of profile choices that are still unbound. A proliferated matrix lays out all the choices for all the products that we can now, for example, take to manufacturing.

However, 50 or so choices still leave us with 2^{50} possible combinations of choices, which means we could define 2^{17} (about 131,000) absolutely unique products for every one of the 2^{33} people on Earth. Before we push the "proliferate" button, we need a way to further pare down the choices.

In the same way that feature profiles reduced the potential complexity inherent in primitive feature models, we will use *feature bundles* to whittle down the potential choices. The idea is to create meaningful bundles of the unbound selections to limit proliferation.

Figure 10.13 illustrates the concept. At the top is a template matrix with eight columns A-H. We have annotated the number of choices that remain available in each column: There are 16 choices available for A, 10 for C, 7 for E, and 8 for H. All other columns have fully bound selections. At this point we have the possibility of $16 \times 10 \times 7 \times 8 = 8,960$ unique products. This is too many; this wide variety would overwhelm our manufacturing capability.

We realize that we don't need or want the 70 combinations possible from columns C through F. Instead, we decide that we create a bundle called VX that offers 4 combinations instead. By defining that bundle and letting subsequent (descendant) matrices choose from its choices, we have slashed our possible number of products to 512.

These feature bundles, in which combinations of different features are limited and offered as packages, are common in the automotive industry. General Motors calls them "regular production options"; other automakers have their own terminology. These so-called "RPO codes" comprise feature bundles that are available to a customer, such as a sports package that combines a high-performance engine, a particular transmission, a tight suspension system, a prescribed steering wheel cover, external paint trim, and more.

Feature bundling may be applied to Level 2 and higher in the ontology.

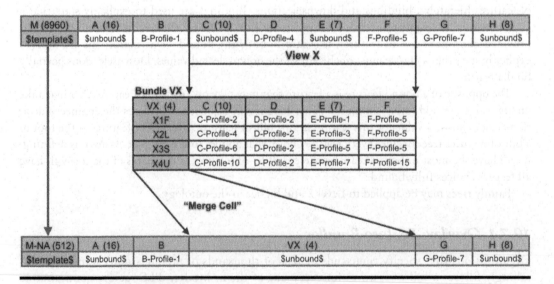

Figure 10.13 Feature bundles.

10.8 Summary and Conclusions

Table 10.5 summarizes our enterprise feature ontology, and shows the kinds of roles involved in decision-making and selection at each level. At each step along the way, the number of choices available to engineers and other enterprise stakeholders working at that level shrinks by many orders of magnitude. A decision space on the order of $2^{1,000,000}$ (at the shared asset variation point level) becomes a decision space on the order of 2^{10} to 2^{20}.

For smaller production lines with, say, dozens of product instances, the ontology will produce tractable decision spaces much earlier. In that case, a few of the ontology's lower levels (e.g., features, profiles, and feature models, packaged into a single production line) can suffice; however, in practice, we observe that most product lines in this size still avail themselves of the separation of concerns brought about by the production-line-of-production-lines structure.

We began with a question: How do you bridge the gap between potentially 1,000,000 variation points in a product line's shared assets down to a few dozen customer-facing decisions? Our feature ontology, which is in industrial use today, is the answer. This ontology came about through practice and experience (for example, from product lines described in [6][8]), not speculation or imagination.

Table 10.5 Enterprise feature ontology and complexity management

Level	Abstractions	Stakeholder Roles	Complexity Potential
0	Asset Variation Points	**Asset Engineers** create feature-based variation points to implement differentiating characteristics	$2^{1,000,000}$
1	Component Feature Model	**Feature Catalog and Bill-of-Features Engineers for Components** create feature abstractions for root-cause functional and non-functional variation, modularize primitive features into component feature models, and instantiate offerings	$2^{10,000}$
2	Subsystem Feature Model	**Feature Catalog and Bill-of-Features Engineers for Subsystems** create feature abstractions for root-cause functional and non-functional variation, modularize primitive features into component feature models, and instantiate offerings	2^{1000}
3	System Feature Model	**Feature Catalog and Bill-of-Features Engineers for Systems** create feature abstractions for root-cause functional and non-functional variation, modularize primitive features into component feature models, and instantiate offerings	2^{100}
4+	System-of-Systems Feature Model	PLE Factory and Product Line Architects create feature abstractions	2^{50}
Overlay: Product Family Trees		Feature Catalog Engineers, Portfolio Managers, and Manufacturing Engineers hierarchically structure Bills-of-Features into Product Family Trees	2^{25}
Overlay: Feature Bundles		Product Marketing, Sales Strategists, and Portfolio Designers define marketing or manufacturing Feature Bundles	2^{10}

As Feature-based PLE made larger and larger strides into larger and larger product lines, each level in the model was added on top of previous levels as a result of need. At each level, we combined large numbers of available choices into smaller numbers of pre-packaged selections. There is no reason the ontology could not be extensible in this way by adding still more levels to the top, should the need arise to work with product lines orders of magnitude larger than the largest ones today. We look forward to the day when we can see Feature-based PLE applied in those settings.

10.9 References

1. Acher, M., Collet, P., Lahire, P., France, R. "FAMILIAR: A domain-specific language for large scale management of feature models," *Sci. Comput. Program.* 78(6): 657-681 2013.
2. BigLever Software, "BigLever Software Gears," http://www.biglever.com/solution/product.html.
3. Clements, P., Gregg, S., Krueger, C., Lanman, J., Rivera, J., Scharadin, R., Shepherd, J., and Winkler, A., "Second Generation Product Line Engineering Takes Hold in the DoD," Crosstalk, *The Journal of Defense Software Engineering*, USAF Software Technology Support Center, 2013.
4. Czarnecki, K., Helsen, S., Eisenecker, U. "Staged Configuration Using Feature Models," International Conference on Software Product Lines, Boston, 2004. dx.doi.org/10.1007/978-3-540-28630-1_17.
5. Dillon, M., Rivera, J., Darbin, R., Clinger, B., "Maximizing U.S. Army Return on Investment Utilizing Software Product-Line Approach," Interservice/Industry Training, Simulation, and Education Conference (I/ITSEC), Orlando, Florida, 2012.
6. Flores, R., Krueger, C., Clements, P. "Mega-Scale Product Line Engineering at General Motors," Proceedings of the 2012 Software Product Line Conference (SPLC), Salvador Brazil, August 2012.
7. Gregg, S, Scharadin, R., Clements, P. "The More You Do, the More You Save: *The Superlinear Cost Avoidance Effect of Systems and Software Product Line Engineering*, Proceedings Software Product Line Conference, Nashville, 2015.
8. Gregg, S., Scharadin, R., LeGore, E., Clements, P. "Lessons from AEGIS: Organizational and Governance Aspects of a Major Product Line in a Multi-Program Environment," Proceedings, Software Product Line Conference 2014, Florence, Italy, 2014.
9. Gruber, T. R. (1993). A Translation Approach to Portable Ontology Specification. *Knowledge Acquisition* 5: 199-220.
10. Hubaux, A., Heymans, P., Schobbens, P., Deridder, D. "Towards Multi-view Feature-Based Configuration," International Working Conference on Requirements Engineering: Foundation for Software Quality, 2010. http://dx.doi.org/10.1007/978-3-642-14192-8_12.
11. Kang, K., Cohen, S., Hess, J., Novak, W., Peterson, A. "Feature-Oriented Domain Analysis (FODA) Feasibility Study" (CMU/SEI-90-TR-021, ADA235785). Pittsburgh, PA: Software Engineering Institute, Carnegie Mellon University, 1990.
12. Krueger, C., "Multistage Configuration Trees for Managing Product Family Trees," *Proceedings SPLC2013*, Tokyo, August 2013.
13. INCOSE Product Line Engineering International Working Group, http://www.incose.org/ChaptersGroups/WorkingGroups/analytic/product-lines, downloaded 09 November 2016.
14. Noy, Natalya F., and McGuinness, Deborah L., "Ontology Development 101: A Guide to Creating Your First Ontology," Stanford University, Stanford University, Stanford, CA, http://protege.stanford.edu/publications/ontology_development/ontology101-noy-mcguinness.html, downloaded 09 November 2016.
15. Parnas, D. L., "On the Criteria to be Used in Decomposing Systems into Modules," *Communications of the ACM*, 15, 12, 1053-1058, Dec. 1972.
16. Reiser, M., and Weber, M. "Managing Highly Complex Product Families with Multi-Level Feature Trees," 14th IEEE International Conference on Requirements Engineering, Minneapolis/St. Paul, Sept. 2006. https://doi.org/10.1109/RE.2006.39.
17. Saitta, Lorenza, and Zucker, Jean-Daniel, *Abstraction in Artificial Intelligence and Complex Systems*, Springer Science & Business Media, 2013.
18. Wozniak, L., Clements, P. "How Automotive Engineering Is Taking Product Line Engineering to the Extreme," *Proc. SPLC 2015*, Nashville, 2015.

Chapter 11

Design of Variable Big Data Architectures for E-Government Domain

Bedir Tekinerdogan and Burak Uzun

Information Technology, Wageningen University, Wageningen, The Netherlands

11.1 Introduction

Big Data has become a very important driver for innovation and growth for various industries such as health, administration, agriculture, defense, and education. The term *Big Data* usually refers to datasets with sizes beyond the ability of commonly used software tools to capture, curate, manage, and process data within a tolerable elapsed time. The realization of Big Data relies on several disruptive technologies such as cloud computing, Internet of Things and data analytics. Usually, big data systems represent major, long-term investments requiring considerable financial commitments and massive scale software and system deployments. Hence, it is important to identify the required features for developing the proper big data system. In practice, the characteristics of big data systems may vary in terms of the application domain and as such require different properties

One of the important domains in which big data is applied are e-government systems [1][8] [15][20]. E-government is a general term describing the use of Information and Communication Technology (ICT) to facilitate the operation of government to provide better public services to citizens and businesses. The target of the services can be different and as such e-government includes different models including *government-to-government (G2G)*, *government-to-business (G2B)*, and *government-to-citizen (G2C)*. E-government systems are often characterized as big data systems in which data storage and processing is one of the relevant issues. However, different features are required for different e-government systems, and likewise the corresponding big data architectures will need to be different as well. In general, designing big data systems for the specific requirements of the corresponding e-government system is not trivial.

In the literature we can identify several reference architectures for Big Data systems, but these are usually abstract and do not provide the required steps for deriving the specific big data architecture. Moreover, the features of e-government systems themselves are also not fixed and can

251

vary based on the different contexts. To support and guide the architect in deriving the proper big data architecture for e-government systems we present a systematic approach. The approach aims to develop the common and variant features of e-government systems and the required reference architecture. To this end, we have adopted a reference architecture for big data systems. Further, we discuss the design decisions for deriving the application architectures from this reference architecture, the experiences and the lessons learned. The results of our study can be of benefit for both practitioners who wish to develop big date e-government systems and researchers who are interested in challenges in these domains.

The remainder of the chapter is organized as follows. In Section 11.2 we present the background on reference architectures and related to this big data reference architecture. In Section 11.3 we present the overview of the method for deriving e-government systems from a reference architecture. Section 11.4 presents the steps for developing reference models. Section 11.5 presents the steps for deriving a concrete e-government big data architecture. Section 11.6 presents the discussion, Section 11.7 the related work, and finally Section 11.8 concludes the chapter.

11.2 Background

11.2.1 Reference Architecture

Every software system has a software architecture, whether it is complex or simple. A software architecture is an abstract representation that identifies the gross-level structure of the system and is important for supporting the communication among stakeholders, for guiding the design decisions, and for analysis of the overall system [24][26]. A stakeholder is defined as an individual, team, or organization with interests in, or concerns relative to, the system.

The architecture can be designed for a single system, but when we are dealing with a family or domain of systems we can define a reference architecture. One of the key motivations for adopting reference architectures is to support reuse and productivity. Several definitions of reference architecture exist in the literature. Angelov et al. [2] define a reference architecture as a generic architecture for a class of information systems that is used as a foundation for the design of concrete architectures from this class. Software Engineering Institute (SEI) defines the reference architecture as "a reference model mapped onto software elements that implements the functionality defined in the reference model"; and the reference model is described as "a division of functionality into elements together with the data flow among those elements"[6]. In general, a reference architecture presents the architectural best practices by various means such as standards, design patterns, and can be employed by software architects as a base from the beginning of the project to the end of it. While reference architectures are generic and focus on the family of systems, a concrete architecture or application architecture represents the architecture of a single system. Hereby, a concrete architecture is an instantiation of the reference architecture that defines the boundaries and constraints for the implementation and is used to analyze risks, balance trade-offs, plan the implementation project and allocate tasks [13].

Developing reference architectures is not trivial and requires a thorough understanding of the domain and the systems that it needs to cover. In general, a reference architecture can be developed either from scratch whereby no concrete system exists yet, or be derived from the knowledge and experiences accumulated in designing concrete architectures in the past. Each concrete architecture is specific and shaped based on the requirements of the stakeholder concerns and the related requirements.

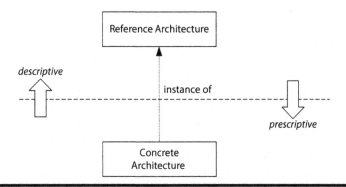

Figure 11.1   Relation between reference architecture and concrete architectures.

A reference architecture can have a descriptive role and/or prescriptive role. A reference architecture is descriptive in the sense that it captures the essence of existing architectures. It is prescriptive when it is used to guide the development of concrete architectures. Figure 11.1 depicts the relations between reference architecture and concrete architectures [13]. In this chapter we adopt both roles of the reference architecture. We will develop reference architectures for e-government systems and Big Data systems, and define the approach deriving concrete e-government architecture.

11.2.2 Big Data Reference Architecture

Obviously, an appropriate Big data architecture design will play a fundamental role to meet the big data processing needs. Several reference architectures are now being proposed to support the design of Big Data systems [3][4][5][10][11][14][16][19]. In this chapter, we adopt the functional architecture as described in [18] and as shown in Figure 11.2. The reference architecture

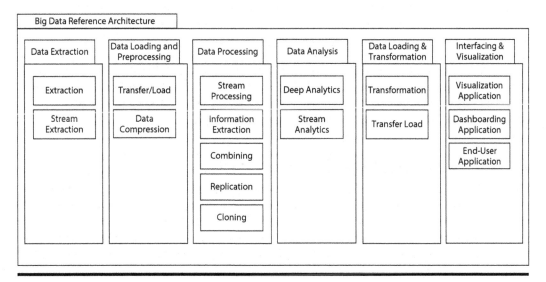

Figure 11.2   Big Data reference architecture (adapted from: [18]).

distinguishes six key modules including *Data Extraction, Data Loading and Preprocessing, Data Processing, Data Analysis, Data Loading & Transformation,* and *Interfacing & Visualization.* The reference architecture can be used to describe many different big data systems. We will use it to describe e-government big data systems.

11.3 Method for Deriving E-Government Systems

When developing e-government systems we must consider multiple different concerns. Although different e-government systems adopt different concerns and likewise will have a different architecture we can still identify a large part of commonality that can be reused. Hence, we describe a reuse-based approach in which we will make use of predefined reference architectures from which we will derive the concrete e-government architecture. Besides of e-government system concerns we will also explicitly distinguish big data concerns.

The method for deriving a concrete e-government big data system is shown in Figure 11.3. The method is represented using BPMN and consists of two key activities including the development of reference models, and the final concrete architecture from these reference models. In the top-level activity *Development of Reference Models* four different reference models are developed including the variability model for big data systems, the variability model for e-government systems, the reference business process models and the e-government big data reference architecture. During this activity, no particular e-government system is developed, but only reference models are developed that could be reused.

In the activity *Development of Concrete Application,* the four reference models are reused to develop the concrete models including the selection of concrete features for the required big data system, the selection of the e-government system, the development of the concrete business process model, and finally the development of the concrete e-government big data system.

11.4 Development of Reference Models

In this section we present the reference models that will be later reused to derive the e-government systems. Subsection 11.4.1 presents the variability model for big data systems, 11.4.2 the variability model for e-government systems, 11.4.3 the reference business process models and 11.4.4 the e-government big data reference architecture.

11.4.1 Variability Model for Big Data Systems

The variability model for big data systems is represented as a feature diagram [12] and is shown in Figure 11.4. This has been adopted from our earlier work on a feature-based analysis of big data systems [19].

The feature diagram includes a root node representing the domain or system that includes features representing the essential characteristics or externally visible properties of the system. Features may have subfeatures which as such can lead to a hierarchical tree. Features can be mandatory or variant. Variant features are usually represented as optional or alternative features. Optional features can be selected or not, whereby alternative features require the selection of one

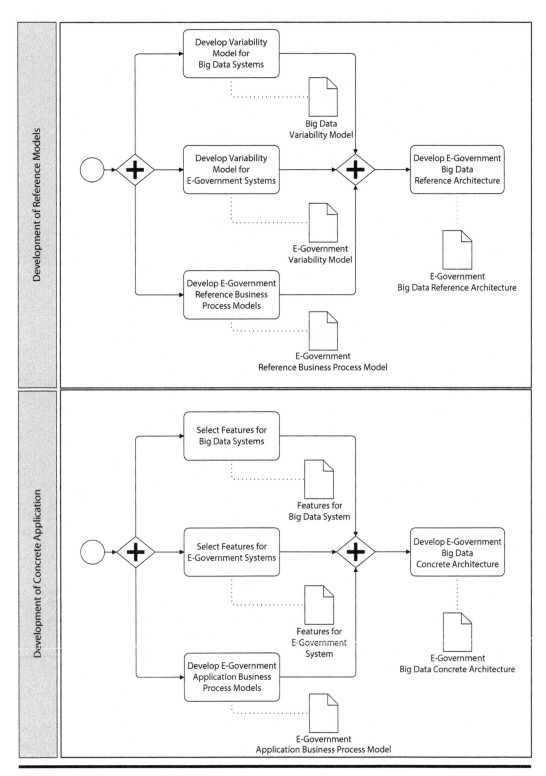

Figure 11.3 Method for developing e-government Big Data System.

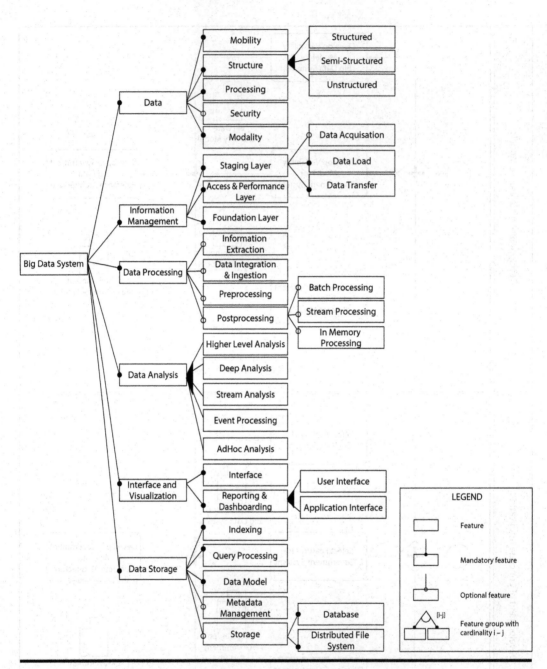

Figure 11.4   Top-level feature model for Big Data system (adapted from: [19]).

of the defined features. A feature configuration is a set of features which describes an alternative model. A feature constraint further restricts the possible selections of features to define configurations. Since the variability model represents the domain of big data systems we term this as a family feature diagram that can be used to derive concrete feature diagrams representing the required features for a concrete big data system.

11.4.2 Variability Model for E-Government Systems

Figure 11.5 represents the variability model for the e-government domain. The model has been derived from a set of selected chapters on e-government systems [1][8][15][20].

The variability model has been again represented as a feature diagram. Based on the sources that we have selected e-government systems are characterized using the top-level features style, security, fault management, network, data management and requirements. Each of these features have on their turn subfeatures which define the variability. E-government style feature consists of government-to-government (G2G), government-to-customer (G2C) and government-to-business (G2B) and all e-government systems must conform to one of these styles. Every e-government

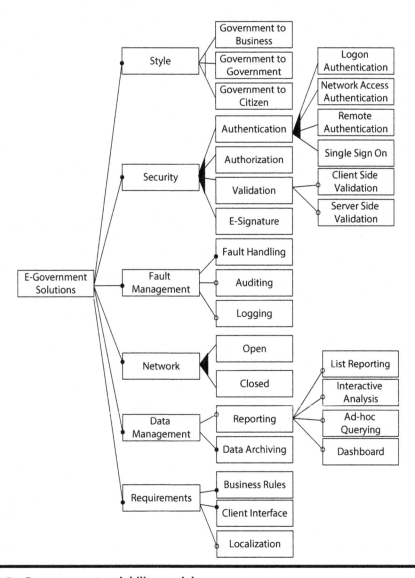

Figure 11.5   E-government variability model.

system must have security feature which includes the subfeatures logon authentication, authorization, validation and e-signature. Every e-government system must have at least one of these subfeatures. Likewise, authentication subfeature is decomposed into logon authentication, network access authentication, remote authentication and single sign. Any e-government system must be authenticated according to one of these authentication types. On the other hand, validation feature is decomposed into client-side and server-side validations but these two subfeature types are optional in an e-government system. Every e-government system must manage faults that occur during the operation of the system. Fault management is divided into three subfeatures which are fault handling, auditing and logging. It can be seen from the figure that fault handling is a mandatory feature, but auditing and logging features are optional in a e-government system. E-government network can be open network in which any computer connected to internet can have access or can be located in a closed network intranet) such as VPN (Virtual Private Network). Data management is a crucial feature for e-government systems as the data stored in these systems are often used for reporting. As the e-government systems are big data systems, the generated data of the system must be archived regularly so that no data loss can occur. E-government reporting consists of list reporting, interactive analysis, ad-hoc querying and dashboards. At last, e-government systems are built from requirements from different stakeholders in which each stakeholder concern is addressed. These concerns must consist business rules and visualization of the system. Moreover, localization of the system can represent a concern for stakeholders.

11.4.3 E-Government Reference Business Process Models

One of the aspects that differentiate e-government systems is the adoption of different workflows. Figure 11.6 shows the generic workflow for e-government domain using the business process modeling notation (BPMN). The model represents the workflows for different e-government styles including G2G (government to government), G2C (government to citizen) and G2B (government to business).

There are three participants in the figure including government clerk, e-government system, and requester which can be further divided into business, government clerk or citizen. In the overall process, first a requester fills the e-forms and sends it to the system to process the request. The system processes the request and it either completes its task or sends the request to government clerks for approval. System requests a service from the government clerk by sending a request for evaluation of request. Government clerk evaluates the request and sends the result back to system and completes its task. The workflow represents the generic steps and can be customized in different ways.

11.4.4 E-Government Big Data Reference Architecture

We provide the reference architecture for e-government big data system with respect to three viewpoints including decomposition viewpoint, layered viewpoint and deployment viewpoint [6].

The decomposition viewpoint defines the partitioning of the system into modules and submodules. Hereby, the only architectural relation that is used is the decomposition relation. In Figure 11.7 the decomposition view reference model for e-government big data system is presented. The figure shows that the system is decomposed into five main modules which are security, networking, fault management, functional requirements and data management modules. The security module is further divided into authentication, authorization, validation and e-signature modules. Furthermore, networking is another important aspect of the system as e-government system can have internal and external communications during the operation of the system. The networking module is decomposed into cooperability, communication and network security submodules in which the communication

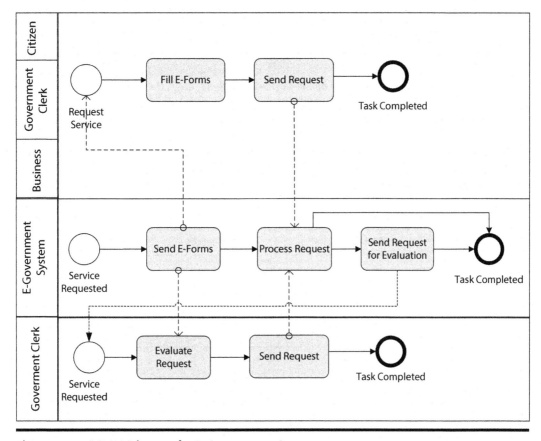

Figure 11.6   BPMN Diagram for E-Government Systems.

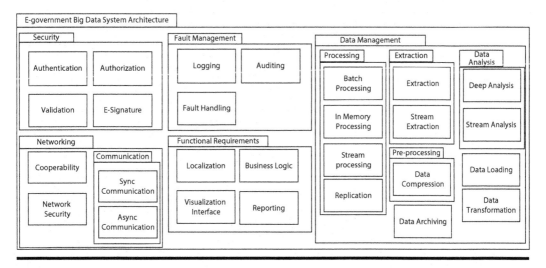

Figure 11.7   Decomposition View Reference Model for E-Government Big Data System.

submodule is further divided into sync and async communication modules. The fault management module is decomposed into three submodules which are logging, auditing and fault handling. Functional requirements address the concerns of stakeholders and as shown in the figure it consists of localization, business logic, visualization interface and reporting. As stated before, data is invaluable for any e-government system and must be managed delicately through the e-government system life cycle. Data management module is divided into seven submodules which are analysis, processing, extraction, pre-processing, archiving, loading and transformation. Processing, extraction, analysis and pre-processing is further divided into submodules as shown in the decomposition view.

Layered viewpoint reflects the decomposition of the system as a set of layers. Each layer offers a cohesive set of services that are provided to the upper layers. In a layered architecture every layer can access the next lower layer, and no callbacks are allowed, nor bridging of layers. Figure 11.8

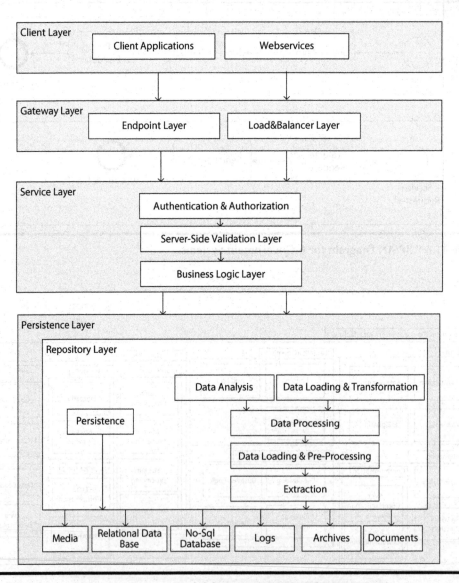

Figure 11.8   Layered view reference model for e-government Big Data System.

shows the layered view for the reference model of big data e-government systems. Hereby, the system is divided into four main layers which are client, gateway, service and persistence layer. Client layer represents interaction layer of the users of the system where it has two different types either client applications or webservices at the same level. Client layer uses gateway layer which does the load balancing and serves as endpoint for applications to communicate with. Gateway layer uses the service layer to send service requests from different applications at client layer. Service layer is decomposed into three layers: authentication authorization, validation and business logic layer. After processing of service requests, service layer can retrieve information from persistence layer or simply store the necessary information from the request. Persistence layer has different data sources to populate and retrieve from as media, relational databases, no-sql databases, logs, document and archives. Repository layer has different layers for persistence of data and retrieval of data. Data sent from the service layer to be persisted passed into respective data source according to data type. Data retrieval is divided into five layers which are data extraction, data loading and pre-processing, data processing, data analysis and data loading and transformation.

Deployment viewpoint defines the mapping of software modules to hardware nodes. Figure 11.9 shows the reference deployment view model for e-government big data systems. It has three main nodes which are clients of different types, server and data. Clients interacts only with server node and can be webservices integrated into these systems services or client applications that interacts regularly with system through services that are publicly defined. Server node holds seven main inner artifacts that can be deployed to server such as security, validation, service for downloading interface, logging, gateway, business logic and data management. Server artifacts interact with both client and data nodes. Data node holds different data sources to be serviced on demand to data management node. The data sources are shown as relational database, nosql database, logs, archives, documents and media.

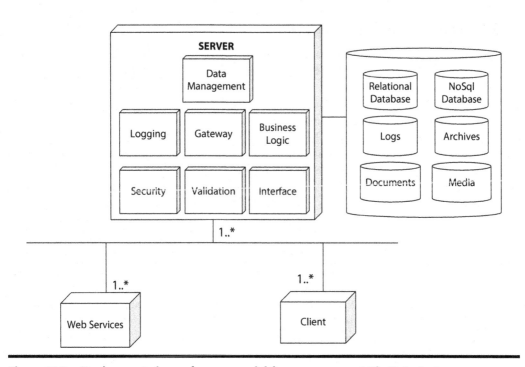

Figure 11.9 Deployment view reference model for e-government Big Data Systems.

Table 11.1 Features of the Big Data System

Feature	Selected Features of Big Data System
Data	Mobility; Structure: Structured, Semi-Structured, Unstructured; Security; Modality: Textual, Graphic, Media
Information Management	Data Load; Data Transfer
Data Processing	Batch Processing; Stream Processing; Pre-Processing: Compression
Interface and Visualization	Reporting and Dashboarding: User Interface, Application Interface
Security	Trusted: Data over VPN, data access control

11.5 Development of Concrete E-Government Architecture

In this section we will describe the concrete architecture for the case study. To this aim we will first select features from big data variability model and e-government variability model for our application. We will then develop the business process model and present the concrete architecture with respect to the earlier stated three viewpoints.

11.5.1 Select Features for Big Data

For instantiating the big data reference architectures, we first need to identify and describe the features of the system. This means in essence the selection of features in the earlier defined family feature diagram. The selected features are listed in Table 11.1. The left column represents the important features of big data systems based on the features as shown in Figure 11.4. The right column represents the features that are important for our example system. For the given case study, data can be of different types including structured, semi-structured and unstructured. The system adopts all the three types of data. The majority of the data is structured data which is stored in the relational database. Besides of these semi-structured data is also processed such as xml files. Finally, unstructured data comes in the form of graphics and media that is mainly used for visualization. Data loading and transfer methods are developed for different data types. To support the real-time statistics queries the system adopts batch processing of data which is updated periodically from day to weeks, and sometimes months depending on different requirements. Real-time stream processing is also adopted, for web service integrations. Streaming data from web services are processed and stored in the system for further operations. Due to the privacy issues, security is an important concern in the overall system. Several security protocols including data access mechanisms are adopted during both the storage, pre-processing, processing and visualization of the data. Reporting and dashboarding of the data are important for users to gather valuable data information in presentable format.

Table 11.2   Features of the e-government system

Feature	Features of E-Government System
Style	Government to Government
Security	Log-on Authentication, Network Access Authentication, Authorization, Client-Side Validation, Server-Side Validation, E-Signature
Fault Management	Fault Handling, Logging
Network	Closed
Data Management	Data Archiving, List Reporting, Dashboard, Interactive Analysis
Requirements	Client Interface, Business Rules

11.5.2 Select Features for System E-Government System

Besides of selecting the features for the required big data system we also need to select the features for the e-government concerns. These e-government features are listed in Table 11.2. The left columns present important features for e-government systems based on the feature diagram in Figure 11.5. The right column presents the features that are selected for the example e-government system. The selected e-government system style is G2G. The systems security is crucial as important operations are being held by the system and system data holds private information for different organizations. To this aim, we select network access authentication to control user who are able reach the systems network and also log-on authentication for entrance to the system. Moreover, authorization should be done both by data level and roles that the logged-in user have. Fault management is done by two features fault handling and logging. System network is closed, using a VPN. Data archiving is important as it is a big data system and data size can slow down real-time operation of the system, but archives are used in batch processing for different statistics to be taken from the system. Three types of reporting are selected: list reporting, dashboard and interactive analysis. The system must meet requirements of the organization for different business processes and must have client interface for users of different roles to interact with the system.

11.5.3 Develop E-Government Application Business Process Model

After selecting the big data and e-government system, we need to define the required workflow. Figure 11.10 shows the BPMN diagram for a government-to-citizen e-government system which is required for the selected case study. There are three actors which are requester government clerks, the e-government system and approver government clerks. A requester government clerk makes requests for retrieving client-side application from the system. The system sends a response which holds e-forms for client-side application, and the government clerk fills out e-forms and sends a request to the system. The system returns response for this request and it either completes the task directly or sends an evaluation request to the approver government clerk asking for service. The approver government clerk receives a request from the system and evaluates the request and sends the response to the system. As it can be seen in the figure, the business process model largely follows and reuses the earlier-defined reference business process model of Figure 11.6.

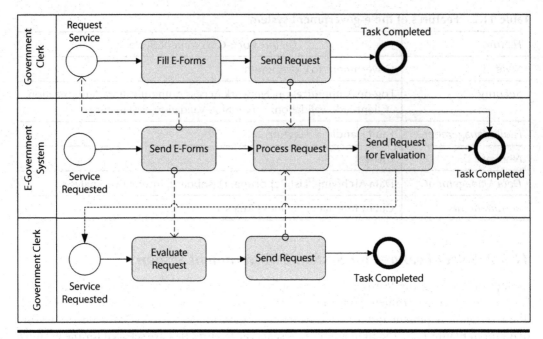

Figure 11.10 BPMN diagram for G2G application.

11.5.4 Develop E-Government Big Data Concrete Architecture

After selecting the required big data system features, the e-government features, and the workflow, we can derive the concrete architecture. For this we will reuse the earlier defined reference architecture that provided the decomposition view, the layered view, and the deployment view.

In our approach the selection of the features in the variability models implies a design decision for the selection of the modules in the architecture views. These design rules could be defined as follows:

IF feature <f> selected THEN select architecture component <c> in architecture view

We can also represent the design decisions in a table format. Likewise, in Table 11.3 and Table 11.4 we show the implied architecture design decisions for the selected features for each architecture view. Each selection of a feature represents thus an architecture design decision. The rationale for these design decisions, that is, the selection of the corresponding features is driven by the project requirements and constraints. Both the selection of the features for big data systems and the e-government system will have an impact on the eventual architecture. Features that do not have a direct implication on the architecture have been indicated as not applicable (NA).

As a result of the adopted design decisions, Figure 11.11 shows the decomposition view of the application architecture of example e-government system. It has five modules which are security, networking, functional requirements, fault management and data management. Security is decomposed into four more modules which are authentication, authorization, validation and e-signature. The networking module has only network security submodule. The fault management module is decomposed into logging and fault-handling modules. Functional requirements module

Table 11.3   Features of the Big Data System and the implied architecture design decisions

Feature	Features of Big Data System	Architecture Design Decision		
		Decomposition	Layered	Deployment
Data	Mobility; Structure: Structured, Semi-Structured, Unstructured; Security; Modality: Textual, Graphic, Media	Select modules Extraction, Data Archiving	Select Media, Relational DB, Logs, Archives, Documents layers	Select Media, Relational DB, Logs, Archives, Documents at Server Node
Information Management	Data Load; Data Transfer	Select modules Data Loading, Data Transformation	Select Data Loading, Data Transformation layers	Select Data Management at Server Node
Data Processing	Batch Processing; Stream Processing; Pre-Processing: Compression	Select Batch Processing, Stream Processing, Data Compression modules	Select Data Processing, Data Loading, Data Preprocessing Layers.	Select Data Management at Server Node
Interface and Visualization	Reporting and Dashboarding: User Interface, Application Interface	Select Visualization and Reporting Modules	Select Client Layer together with its Client Applications, Web Services Layers	Select Web Services and Client Nodes
Security	Trusted: Data over VPN, Data Access Control	Select Network Security Module	NA	NA

Table 11.4 Features of the e-government system and the implied architecture design decisions

Feature	Features of Big Data System	Architecture Design Decision		
		Decomposition	*Layered*	*Deployment*
Style	Government-to-Government	NA	NA	NA
Security	Log-on Authentication, Network Access Authentication, Authorization, Client-Side Validation, Server-Side Validation, E-Signature	Select modules Authentication, Authorization, Validation, E-Signature	Select layers Authentication, Authorization, Validation in the Service Layer	Select Security and Validation Modules at the Server Node
Fault Management	Fault Handling, Logging	Select modules Fault Management module with Fault Handling and Logging modules	NA	Select Logging to Server Node
Network	Closed	Select module Network Security	NA	NA
Data Management	Data Archiving, List Reporting, Dashboard, Interactive Analysis	Select modules Data Archiving, Visualization Interface, Reporting	Select layers Client Applications, Persistence, Webservice	Select Client Node
Requirements	Client Interface, Business Rules	Select modules Functional Requirements Module, Business Logic, Reporting	Select Business Logic Layer	Select Business Logic module to Server Node. Select Interface module to Server Node. Select Client Node

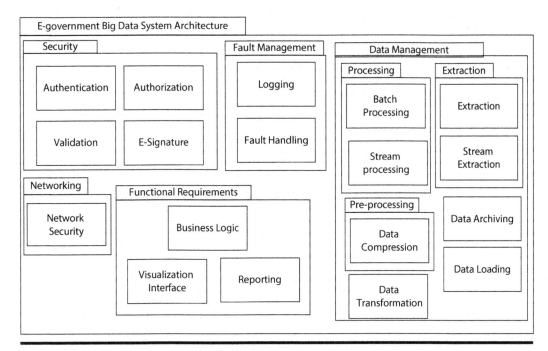

Figure 11.11 Decomposition view of the application architecture of example e-government system.

is decomposed into business logic, visualization interface and reporting submodules. At last data management module is decomposed into pre-processing, processing, extraction, archiving, data loading and transformation.

Figure 11.12 shows the layered view of the application architecture of example e-government system. The first layer is the client layer where it consists of client applications and webservices. It interacts with the service layer which consists of authentication, authorization, validation and the business logic layer. The service layer than unidirectionally interacts with repository to use the services offered by the persistence layer. The persistence layer is decomposed of different data sources such as relational database, media, logs, documents and archives. Data is persisted into these data sources by the service layer or different systems. Data is also queried from this layer by service layer. In this process data is first extracted and pre-processing is applied which is followed up by loading the data. Loaded data is then processed and transformed into structure recognizable by the service layer.

Figure 11.13 shows the deployment view of the application architecture of example e-government system. There are three main artifacts shown in figure client applications, server application and data sources. Client applications that interact with the server application can be web services or client-side interfaces. Server application has data management, logging, business logic, security, validation and interface artifacts deployed on it. The deployed artifacts operate with each internally while data management also operates with data sources to manage the differently structured data. There are structured, semi-structured and unstructured data sources available which are relational database, logs, archives, documents and media.

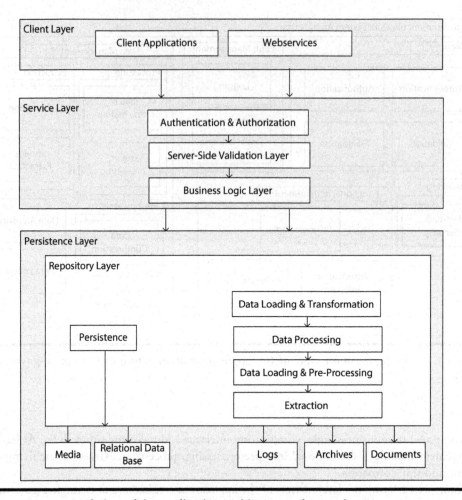

Figure 11.12 Layered view of the application architecture of example e-government system.

11.6 Discussion

We have provided a reuse-based approach for developing big data architectures of e-government systems. For this we have adopted a reference architecture based on the functional architecture as described in [18]. This reference architecture appeared to be quite useful together with the feature diagrams for big data systems and e-government systems that we have developed. In the literature several different reference architectures can be identified. One of the popular reference architecture is the so-called Lambda architecture, which is a big data architecture that is designed to satisfy the needs for a robust system that is fault-tolerant, both against hardware failures and human mistakes [14]. Hereby it takes advantage of both batch- and stream-processing methods. In essence, the architecture consists of three layers including the batch processing layer, speed (or real-time) processing layer, and serving layer. The batch processing layer has two functions: (1) managing the master dataset (an immutable, append-only set of raw data), and (2) to pre-compute the batch views. The master dataset is stored using a distributed processing system that can handle very large quantities of data. The batch views are generated by processing all available data. As such, any errors can be fixed by recomputing based on the complete dataset, and subsequently

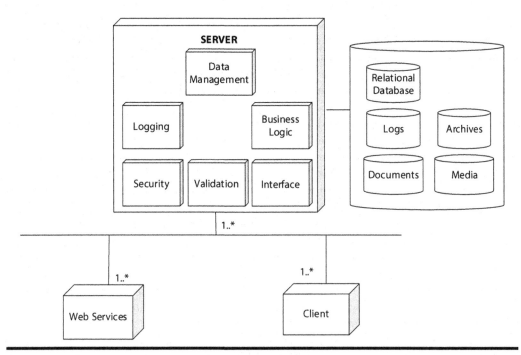

Figure 11.13 Deployment view of the application architecture of example e-government system.

updating existing views. The speed layer processes data streams in real time and deals with recent data only. In essence, there are two basic functions of the speed layer: (1) storing the real-time views and (2) processing the incoming data stream so as to update those views. It compensates for the high latency of the batch layer to enable up-to-date results for queries. The speed layer's view is not as accurate and complete as the ones eventually produced by the batch layer, but they are available almost immediately after data is received. The serving layer indexes the batch views so that they can be queried in low-latency, ad-hoc way. The query merges result from the batch and speed layers to respond to ad-hoc queries by returning precomputed views or building views from the processed data. If we would have adopted the Lambda architecture instead of the functional architecture, the overall process would not differ but the feature diagrams for big data systems had to be aligned for this.

Architecture design is critical for the success of a project and it is therefore important to evaluate the architecture with respect to the stakeholders' concerns [6][24]. A proper architecture evaluation will help predict the quality of the system before it is built, thereby reducing unnecessary maintenance costs. Different architecture evaluation approaches have been proposed in the literature. In essence, each architecture evaluation approach takes as input the stakeholder concerns, the environment issues and the architecture description. Based on these inputs, the evaluation results in an architecture evaluation report, which is used to adapt the architecture. In the method that we have provided feature models are used to capture the required features. The focus hereby was on functional features and less on non-functional or quality concerns. The approach is however agnostic to any architecture evaluation method and can be easily integrated with existing architecture evaluation approaches.

The method that is proposed in this chapter can be categorized as a reuse-based approach in which we focus on a family of systems or products. In this context the method borrows the ideas of software product line engineering that distinguishes between the activities of domain engineering and application engineering. A software product line is a set of software-intensive systems sharing a common, managed set of features that satisfy the specific needs of a particular market segment or mission and that are developed from a common set of core assets in a prescribed way [7][27]. Software product line engineering (SPLE) is a systematic and comprehensive process that aims to develop and maintain product lines. SPLE aims to provide proactive, pre-planned reuse at a large granularity (domain and product level) to develop applications from a core asset base. In the domain engineering activity core assets are developed for reuse purposes. Core assets can include any work product in the development life cycle. We have focused on the architecture design. In principle we could elaborate the approach and define a product line engineering approach for e-government systems. The results in this chapter pave the way for this idea since the architecture design is also the core asset of SPLE that defines the scope of the products in the product family.

Several mitigation strategies have been carried out to cope with the potential threats to this study. Construct validity refers to what extent the operational measures that are studied really represent what the researchers have in mind and what is investigated according to the research questions [28]. Our key focus was on developing models that could be reused to derive concrete models and in particular the architecture. For developing the reference models, we have applied a thorough domain analysis. The domain scope could be further broadened by selecting additional papers, which would further shape the models. Internal validity relates to a causal relationship between treatment and the outcome. In our study there is a causal relationship between the selected features and the architecture design decisions. We have shortly discussed the implication of the selection of features to the architecture design decisions. External validity concerns the ability to generalize the results of the study. Although the reference models could be further refined in case the corresponding domain evolves, the overall approach is generic and will be persistent. Hence, we believe that from this perspective the result of the study, a reusable and generic method has been provided.

11.7 Related Work

In the literature, we can identify different approaches for defining reference architectures. Galster and Avgeriou [9] propose a methodology to define empirically-grounded reference architectures. The approach consists of the following steps: Decision on type of reference architecture, selection of design strategy, empirical acquisition of data, construction of reference architecture, enabling the reference architecture variability and finally evaluation of the reference architecture.

Design rationale has been studied in different disciplines including engineering design in AI, human computer interaction and software engineering. Various surveys have been published that compare different systems that capture and use design rationale [25][17]. These studies have shown that design rationale is considered important by practitioners, but it is rarely captured in practice. In our earlier work, we have provided a systematic approach for feature-based approach for adapting architectures. and the corresponding tool environment ArchiRationale for supporting software architecture adaptation [25]. The approach takes as input an existing architecture and captures the design rationale for adapting the architecture for a given quality concern. For this we define a feature model that includes the possible set of architectural tactics to realize the quality concern. The presented approach captures the rationale for deciding on feature selections and for selecting the corresponding architecture design alternatives. ArchiRationale customizes and integrates the Eclipse plugin tools XFeature, ArchStudio and XQuery to provide tool support for capturing, storing and accessing the design rationale. We illustrate the approach for adapting a software architecture for fault tolerance.

In our earlier work we have defined an approach for supporting the decision making on the selection of platforms within the context of model-driven architecture [21]. Hereby, we have adopted the notion of platform independent model (PIM) and Platform Specific Model (PSM) and stated that although the MDA approach provides a conceptual framework for separating the two models and as such adapting the platforms, it does not provide the decision support for selecting the proper platform. The similar problem applies to the adoption of big data systems in e-government systems. In fact, e-government can be considered as a platform independent model whereas the big data system can be considered as the platform specific model and infrastructure. In case of multiple different big data systems, we could integrate our earlier approach with the approach for deriving application architecture that we have discussed in this chapter.

Quality assurance is one of the important issues when developing e-government systems [23]. For supporting quality early on, several software architecture analysis approaches have been introduced. The goal of these approaches is to assess whether or not a given architecture design satisfies desired concerns including quality requirements. We were able to derive the architecture based on the reference architectures. For further detailed analysis we could use the existing architecture analysis approaches. We consider this as part of our future work in which we will investigate the impact of quality concerns on big data architectures.

In our recent work we have provided a feature driven survey of big data systems [19]. To this end, we proposed a domain engineering approach in which a family feature model, a reference architecture and the corresponding design rules are identified. The family feature model is derived based on a domain analysis of big data systems and represents the common and variant features. The reference architecture represents the generic structure for various application architectures of big data systems. Finally, the design rules define the reusable design heuristics for designing an application architecture based on the selection of features of the family feature model and the reference architecture. We have illustrated our approach for deriving the big data architectures of different well-known big data systems [19].

11.8 Conclusion

In this chapter we have focused on supporting the software architecture design of e-government systems. For this we have adopted reference architectures and variability modeling. The adoption of reference architecture for deriving architectures is well-known in the literature [13][22]. In fact, for the design of an architecture either an existing reference architecture can be used, or a reference architecture can be designed first. For our study, we used the reference architecture for big data systems and developed the reference architecture for e-government systems. The approach that we have provided is generic, and the study could be replicated by using different reference architectures for both big data systems and e-government systems.

For deriving the application architecture, we first analyzed the stakeholders, the workflow models and the required features for e-government systems using big data. Based on the selected features we instantiated the reference architecture. Hereby, we implicitly made design decisions to derive the architecture that meets the selected features. One of the key issues in architecture design is the design rationale management, that is, the reasons why and how design decisions are made and applied. In this chapter we have guided the decision making through the reference models. The particular design decisions are dependent on the required e-government systems.

In our approach we have adopted architecture views to model the architecture for different stakeholder concerns [6]. We have used the decomposition view, layered view and deployment. These viewpoints appeared to be essential in designing e-government systems. If needed other viewpoints could be integrated in the approach. The overall process that is developing a reference architecture for e-government system together with the commonality and variability modeling, and the workflow models will however be the same.

An e-government system must consider multiple different concerns. We have adopted a reuse-based approach in which we modeled the common and variant features of an e-government system together with its big data and workflow properties. This supported not only the quick development of the required e-government architecture, but in this way we also ensured that all the required properties were identified. As stated before the approach itself is generic. The reference models could be further enhanced to broaden the scope of the domain and herewith the architecture.

References

1. T. Almarabeh & A. AbuAli. A general framework for e-government: Definition maturity challenges, opportunities, and success, *European Journal of Scientific Research,* Vol. 39 No.1, pp.29-42, 2010.
2. S. Angelov, P. Grefen, & D. Greefhorst. A classification of software reference architectures: Analyzing their success and effectiveness. *In Software Architecture, 2009 & European Conference on Software Architecture.* WICSA/ECSA, pp. 141-150, 2009.
3. C. Ballard, C. Compert, T. Jesionowski, I. Milman, B. Plants, B. Rosen, & H. Smith. *Information Governance Principles and Practices for a Big Data Landscape*, IBM Redbooks, 2014.
4. E. Begoli, & J. Horey. Design principles for effective knowledge discovery from big data. In *Software Architecture (WICSA) and European Conference on Software Architecture (ECSA)*, pp. 215-218, IEEE, 2012.
5. D. Chapelle. 2013. Big Data & Analytics Reference Architecture, An Oracle White Chapter.
6. P. Clements, F. Bachmann, L. Bass, D. Garlan, J. Ivers, R. Little, P. Merson, R. Nord, & J. Stafford. *Documenting Software Architectures: Views and Beyond,* 2nd. Edition. Addison-Wesley, 2010.
7. P. Clements & L. Northrop. *Software Product Lines: Practices and Patterns.* Addison-Wesley Longman Publishing Co., Inc., 2001.
8. N. Debnath, L. Felice, G. Montejano, & D. Riesco. A Feature Model of E-Government Systems Integrated with Formal Specifications. Information Technology: New Generations, *Fifth International Conference on Information Technology: New Generations,* pp. 27-31, 2008.
9. M. Galster & P. Avgeriou. Empirically-grounded reference architectures: A proposal. In Proceedings of the joint ACM SIGSOFT conference—QoSA and ACM SIGSOFT symposium—ISARCS on Quality of software architectures—QoSA and architecting critical systems—ISARCS (pp. 153-158). ACM, 2011.
10. B. Geerdink. A reference architecture for big data solutions introducing a model to perform predictive analytics using big data technology. In *Internet Technology and Secured Transactions (ICITST),* 2013 8th International Conference for (pp. 71-76). IEEE, 2013.
11. I. Gorton & J. Klein. Distribution, data, deployment: Software architecture convergence in big data systems. *Software, IEEE,* 32(3), 78-85, 2015.
12. K.C. Kang, S. Cohen, J. Hess, W.E. Novak, & A. Peterson. Feature-oriented domain analysis (FODA) feasibility study (No. CMU/SEI-90-TR-21). Carnegie-Mellon Univ. Pittsburgh Pa. Software Engineering Inst, 1990.
13. A. Kassahun, R. Hartog, B. Tekinerdogan. Realizing chain-wide transparency in meat supply chains based on global standards and a reference architecture, *Elsevier Computers and Electronics in Agriculture Journal,* Vol. 123, pp. 275-291, 2016.

14. N. Marz, & J. Warren. *Big Data: Principles and Best Practices of Scalable Realtime Data Systems*. Manning Publications Co., 2015.
15. B. Medjahed, A. Rezgui, A. Bouguettaya & M. Ouzzani, Infrastructure for e-government Web services. In *IEEE Internet Computing*, vol. 7, no. 1, pp. 58-65, Jan/Feb 2003.
16. Oracle, 2013. Information Management and Big Data A Reference Architecture, An Oracle White Chapter.
17. K. Öztürk & B. Tekinerdogan. Feature Modeling of Software as a Service Domain to Support Application Architecture Design, in the *Proc. of the Sixth International Conference on Software Engineering Advances* (ICSEA 2011), Barcelona, Spain, October, 2011.
18. P. Pääkkönen & D. Pakkala. Reference Architecture and Classification of Technologies, Products and Services for Big Data Systems. Big Data Research, 2015.
19. A. Salma, B. Tekinerdogan, I. Athanassiadis. Feature Driven Survey of Big Data Systems, in *Proceedings.of International Conference on Internet of Things and Big Data (IoTBD)*, April 2016.
20. Sang M. Lee, X. Tan, and S. Trimi. Current practices of leading e-government countries. Communications.ACM48,10(October2005),99-104.DOI=http://dx.doi.org/10.1145/1089107.1089112, 2005.
21. B. Tekinerdogan, S. Bilir, & C. Abatlevi. Integrating platform selection rules in the model driven architecture approach. In *Model Driven Architecture* (pp. 159-173). Springer Berlin Heidelberg, 2005.
22. B. Tekinerdogan, K. Ozturk. Feature-driven design of SaaS architectures. In: Z. Mahmood & S. Saeed (Eds.), *Software Engineering Frameworks for Cloud Computing Paradigm*, Springer-Verlag, London, pp. 189-212, 2013.
23. B. Tekinerdogan, N. Ali, J. Grundy, I. Mistrik, R. Soley. Quality Concerns in large scale and complex software-intensive systems. In: I. Mistrik, R. Soley, N. Ali, J. Grundy, B. Tekinerdogan. *Software Quality Assurance in Large Scale and Complex Software-Intensive Systems*. Elsevier, pp.1-17, 2015.
24. B. Tekinerdogan. Software Architecture, chapter in: T. Gonzalez and J.L. Díaz-Herrera, *Computer Science Handbook*, 2nd. ed., vol. I: Computer Science and Software Engineering, Taylor and Francis, 2014.
25. B. Tekinerdogan, H. Sözer, & M. Aksit. Feature-based rationale management system for supporting software architecture adaptation, *International Journal of Software Engineering and Knowledge Engineering*, Vol. 22, No. 7, pp. 945-964, 2012.
26. B. Tekinerdogan & M. Akşit. Classifying and evaluating architecture design methods. In: *Software Architectures and Component Technology: The State of the Art in Research and Practice*. M. Aksit (Ed.), Boston: Kluwer Academic Publishers, pp. 3-27, 2001.
27. E. Tuzun, B. Tekinerdogan, ME Kalender, S. Bilgen. Empirical evaluation of a decision support model for adopting software product line engineering. *Elsevier Information and Software Technology*, Vol 60, pp. 77-101, 2015.
28. R.K. Yin. *Case Study Research: Design and Methods*. Sage Publications, 2003.

Chapter 12

Refactoring Support for Variability-intensive Systems

Vahid Alizadeh, Marouane Kessentini, and Bruce Maxim

Department of Computer and Information Science,
University of Michigan, Dearborn, Michigan, United States

12.1 Introduction

Today, maintenance and evolution are critical software development activities that might comprise up to 80% of the overall cost and effort throughout a software's lifetime [13]. Maintenance costs often can be inflated through poor software design called code smells and defined as design situations that adversely affect the software maintenance [12]. These code smells, such as Blob and functional decomposition, decrease the cohesion in the classes and increase coupling leading to a poor modularity. In fact, code smells appear, in general, extensively in systems where requirements change quickly over time due to the customers need since developers have limited time to release a new version of the system [27][28]. Thus, the quality of variability-intensive system is lower than regular systems with lower requirements or code changes, so it is important to consider automated tools for the correction of code smells in similar situations. One of the widely used techniques to fix code smells is refactoring defined as the process of changing a software system in such a way that it does not alter the external behavior of the code yet improves its internal structure [20].

An example of refactoring is moving methods between classes to increase cohesion and reduce coupling. Some work proposes "standard" refactoring solutions that can be applied by hand for each kind of code smell (e.g. Blobs, large methods, etc.). However, there is no consensus to define these standard solutions since the same type of code smell can be fixed by many alternatives. In fact, developers can propose different refactoring solutions to fix the same code fragment and these solutions have different adaptability/calibration effort. Thus, the question is how to identify the best refactorings solution? Some researchers start from the hypothesis that useful refactorings are those which improve the metrics [20][21]. Some limitations can be drawn from studying these metric-based approaches:

- First, how to determine the useful metrics for a given system?
- Second, how best to combine multiple metrics such as coupling, cohesion and average number of methods per class?

■ Third, improving the metric values does not mean that specific defects are corrected. Furthermore, it is difficult to find a consensus regarding the definition of threshold values for the used quality metrics.

To address these issues and mainly due to the absence of consensus to find the best set of refactorings that fix code smells, we propose in this chapter to consider code smells correction as a distributed problem. The idea is that different techniques are combined during an optimization process to find a consensus regarding the correction of code smells. To this end, we used distributed evolutionary algorithms (D-EA) [2][8] where many evolutionary algorithms with different adaptations (fitness functions, solution representation and change operators) are executed in parallel to solve a common goal which is the correction of code smells. We believe that a D-EA approach is suitable to our problem because it combines different expertises (algorithms) to correct code smells. We show how this combination can be formulated in a cooperative search. In D-EA, many refactoring algorithms evolve simultaneously where the goal is to maximize the intersection between the refactoring solutions proposed by different evolutionary algorithms (with different adaptations) while satisfying also their own fitness functions. We executed in parallel two algorithms that we proposed in our previous work [16][23]. We implemented our approach and evaluated it on eight open-source systems using an existing benchmark. We report the results on the efficiency and effectiveness of our approach, compared to a random search in addition to two different existing single population approaches of our previous work [16][23]. Our results indicate that the D-EA approach has great promise. Over 51 runs for each approach, D-EA significantly outperforms both random and single population approaches in terms of the percentage of fixed code smells by the suggested refactoring. The first algorithm is based on genetic algorithm to find the best sequence of refactorings that can minimize the number of code smells detected using metrics-based rules [16]. The second algorithm is based also on genetic algorithm to find the best sequence of refactorings that can minimize the distance between the code-fragments to refactor (code smells) and a base for good examples [23]. The primary contributions of this chapter can be summarized as follows: (1) the chapter introduces a novel formulation of the code smells' fixing problems as a distributed problem, to the best of our knowledge, this is the first chapter in the literature to use distributed evolutionary algorithms to software refactorings; (2) the chapter reports the results of an empirical study with an implementation of our D-EA approach, compared to random search and two existing single population approaches [16][23] (the two used GA algorithms executed separately). The statistical analysis of the obtained results over 51 runs shows that D-EA is more efficient and effective than single population evolution and random search based on a benchmark of eight large open-source systems.

12.2 Background and Problem Statement

In this section, we first provide the necessary background of fixing code smells and discuss the challenges and open problems that are addressed by our proposal.

12.2.1 Background

12.2.1.1 Code smells

A code smell is defined as bad design choices that can have a negative impact on the code quality such as maintainability, changeability and comprehensibility which could introduce bugs [12]. Code smells classify shortcomings in software that can decrease software maintainability. They are also defined as structural characteristics of software that may indicate a code or design problem that makes software hard to evolve and maintain, and trigger refactoring of code [15]. Code smells are not limited to design flaws since most of them occur in code and are not related to the original design. In fact, most of code smells can emerge during the evolution of a system and represent patterns or aspects of software design that may cause problems in the further development and maintenance of the system. As stated by [26], code smells are unlikely to cause failures directly, but may do it indirectly. In general, they make a system difficult to change, which may in turn introduce bugs. It is easier to interpret and evaluate the quality of systems by identifying code smells than the use of traditional software quality metrics. In fact, most of the definitions of code smells are based on situations that are daily faced by developers. The 22 code smells identified and defined informally by Fowler et al. [30] aim to indicate software refactoring opportunities and 'give you indications that there is trouble that can be solved by a refactoring'.

We defined, in the following, the most important code-smell types:

■ Blob: It is found in designs where one large class monopolizes the behavior of a system (or part of it), and the other classes primarily encapsulate data.
■ Feature Envy (FE): It occurs when a method is more interested in the features of other classes than its own. In general, it is a method that invokes several times accessor methods of another class.
■ Data Class (DC): It is a class with all data and no behavior. It is a class that passively stores data.
■ Spaghetti Code (SC): It is a code with a complex and tangled control structure.
■ Functional Decomposition (FD): It occurs when a class is designed with the intent of performing a single function. This is found in a code produced by non-experienced object-oriented developers.
■ Lazy Class (LC): A class that is not doing enough to pay for itself.
■ Long Parameter List (LPL): Methods with numerous parameters are a challenge to maintain, especially if most of them share the same data-type.

12.2.1.2 Refactoring

The detected defects can be fixed by applying some refactoring operations. For example, to correct the Blob code-smell (large class containing most of the features of the system) many operations can be used to reduce the number of functionalities in a specific class: move methods, extract class, etc. Fowler [12] defines refactoring as the process of improving a code after it has been written by changing the internal structure of the code without changing the external behavior. The idea is to reorganize variables, classes and methods in order to facilitate future extensions. This reorganization is used to improve different aspects of software-quality: reusability, maintainability, complexity, etc. [13]. Some examples of refactoring operations include: (1) push down field: moves a field from some class to those subclasses that require it; (2) add parameter: adds a new parameter to a method, (3) push-down method: moves a method from some class to those subclasses that require it; and (4) move method: moves a method from one class to another. Overall, the refactoring process consists of three main steps [12]: (1) identify where the software should be refactored (e.g. bad smells detections); (2) select which refactorings should be applied to the identified code fragments; and (3) ensure that the applied refactoring preserves the program behavior.

12.2.1.3 Search-Based Software Engineering

Software engineering is by nature a search problem, where the goal is to find an optimal or near-optimal solution [21]. This search is often complex with several competing constraints, and conflicting functional and non-functional objectives. The situation can be worse since nowadays successful software are more complex, more critical and more dynamic leading to an increasing need to automate or semi-automate the search process for acceptable refactoring solutions by software engineers. As a result, an emerging software engineering area, called Search-Based Software Engineering (SBSE) [22], is rapidly growing. SBSE is a software development practice that focuses on couching software engineering problems as optimization problems and utilizing metaheuristic techniques to discover and automate the search for near optimal solutions to those problems.

The aim of SBSE research is to move software engineering problems from human-based search to machine-based search, using a variety of techniques from the fields of metaheuristic search, operations research and evolutionary computation paradigms. SBSE has proved to be a widely applicable and successful approach, with many applications right across the full spectrum of activities in software engineering, from initial requirements, project planning, and cost estimation to regression testing and onward evolution. There is also an increasing interest in search based optimization from the industrial sector, as illustrated by work on testing involving Berner, Mattner and Daimler [34], Google [35] and Microsoft [36], work on requirements analysis and optimization involving Motorola [37] and NASA [38], and work on refactoring involving Ford [31][32]. The increasing maturity of the field has led to a number of tools for SBSE applications.

12.2.2 Problem Statement

Some issues need to be addressed when automating code smells correction using refactoring. In many situations, code quality can be improved without fixing code smells. We need to identify if the code modification corrects or not some specific code smells. In addition, the code quality is estimated using quality metrics, but different problems are related to how to determine the useful metrics for a given system and how to combine in the best way multiple metrics to detect or correct code smells. As mentioned previously, it is difficult to find a consensus to define thresholds values for metrics. In addition, specifying manually a 'standard' refactoring solution for each type of code-smell can be a difficult task due to the large list of possible defects and possible fixing solutions. Indeed, these 'standard' solutions can remove all symptoms for each defect. However, removing the symptoms does not mean that the code smell is corrected. Moreover, the process of defining rules manually for detection or correction is complex (absence of consensus to define 'standard' refactoring solutions), time-consuming and error-prone. Another important issue is that there is no consensus to define these standard solutions since the same type of code-smell can be fixed by many alternatives. In fact, developers can propose different refactoring solutions to fix the same code fragment, and these solutions have different adaptability/calibration efforts. Thus, the question is how to find a consensus between all these possible solutions? To answer this question, we believe that it is important to take the best from different refactoring techniques that can be applied to fix code smells using a distributed approach that is described in the next section.

12.3 Code Smells Correction using Cooperative Parallel Evolutionary Algorithms

We first present an overview of the used distributed evolutionary (D-EA) algorithms and, subsequently, provide the details of the approach and our adaptation of the D-EA to fix code smells.

12.3.1 Parallel Evolutionary Algorithms

Today, real-life optimization problems are increasingly complex. Consequently, their resource requirements are ever increasing. Optimization problems are often hard and expensive from a CPU time and/or memory viewpoint [1]. The use of metaheuristics, such as evolutionary algorithms (EAs) and particle swarm optimization (PSO), allows reducing the computational complexity of the search process. However, the latter remains computationally costly in different application domains where the objective functions and the constraints are resource intensive and the size of the search space is huge. In addition, to the problem of complexity, we find today resource-expensive search methods such as hybrid metaheuristics and multi-objective ones. The rapid technology development in terms of processors, networks and data storage tools renders parallel distributed computing very interesting to use. This fact has motivated researchers to more focus on designing and implementing parallel metaheuristics in order to solve more complex optimization problems [2].

There are several motivations behind the use of parallel and distributed computing for the design and implementation of parallel metaheuristics. Firstly, parallelization permits to speed up the search process by reducing the search time. This is very interesting in time-dependent and interactive resolution methods. Secondly, the quality of the obtained solutions may be significantly improved. In fact, cooperative metaheuristics has been demonstrated to explore the fitness landscape more efficiently on different problems such as the code smell identification problem [3]. This is realized by portioning the search space and then exchanging information between the different search methods which allows examining the search space efficiently. Thirdly, the use of different metaheuristics simultaneously in solving a particular problem reduces the sensitivity to the parameter values. Indeed, each search method would be launched with a particular parameter value set which is different from the other ones. Hence, the search process would work according to different parameter value sets which may augment the *robustness* of the obtained results. Finally, parallel distributed metaheuristics allows tackling the problematic of scalability. Several problems actually involves a very large number of decision variables (called large-scale problems [4]), a high number of objectives (called many-objective problems [5]), a large number of constraints (called highly constrained problems [6]), etc. These types of problems are very computationally costly. Parallel distributed metaheuristics can represent one possible remedy to tackle such problems.

Different models exist for designing parallel metaheuristics. According to [7], these models follow the following three hierarchical levels:

- *Algorithmic level:* In this parallel model, independent or cooperating self-contained metaheuristics are used. It can be seen as a *problem-independent inter-algorithm parallelization*. If the different metaheuristics are independent, the search will be equivalent to the sequential execution of the metaheuristics in terms of the quality of solutions. However, the cooperative model will alter the behavior of the metaheuristics and enable the improvement of the quality of solutions.
- *Iteration level:* In this model, metaheuristic iterations are parallelized. It is a *problem-independent intra-algorithm parallelization*. The metaheuristic behavior is not altered. The main goal is to speed up the algorithm by reducing the search time. In fact, the iteration cycle of metaheuristics on large neighborhoods for trajectory-based metaheuristics or large populations for population-based metaheuristics requires a large amount of computational resources.

■ *Solution level:* In this model, the parallelization process handles a single solution from the search space. It is a *problem-dependent intra-algorithm parallelization*. In general, evaluating the objective function(s) or constraints for a particular generated solution is almost always the *most costly* operation in metaheuristics. In this model, the metaheuristic behavior is not altered. The goal is mainly the speed up of the search.

Although parallel distributed EAs is still a challenging research field, several contributions are mature enough today be exploited within the SBSE framework. Since the most studied and known models are based on EAs [9], the scope of this chapter is to illustrate one of the first attempts of using D-EAs to solve software engineering problems, and particularly the code smells correction one. Indeed, to the best of our knowledge and based on an existing survey [22], D-EAs are applied in software engineering only to the test cases' generation problem by Alba and Chicano [24]. Thus, this work represents the first research contribution to solve the code smells detection problem using D-EAs.

The parallelization proposed in this work intervenes in the solution level since it affects the solution-evaluation module. Consequently, it could be seen as a *problem-dependent intra-algorithm* parallelization. In fact, in each generation of the parallel process, the top 5% elite solutions, i.e., those with the highest fitness values, are updated according to a *parallel fitness function*. The update operation role is to penalize solutions that do not perform well according to the parallel model and to favour good solutions w.r.t. the parallelization. For the problem considered in this work, code smells correction, we use a simple *bi-algorithm parallel* model illustrated by Figure 12.1. We see, from this figure, that the fitness of elite solutions of EA1 is updated based on the fitness values of elite solutions of EA2 and vice versa. The main goal of the parallel fitness-update operation is alleviating the encountered challenges of the code-smell correction, which are discussed in the previous section. From a semantic viewpoint, the parallel model goal is *to circumvent the absence* of a well-defined consensus concerning the correction of code smells (symptoms, thresholds value, adaptability effort, semantic, etc.) where the goal is to maximize the intersection between the different refactoring solutions. The next section describes in detail our adaptation of D-EA.

12.3.2 Distributed Code Smells Correction: Overview

We propose a framework based on the use of two evolutionary algorithms in parallel with completely different adaptations [16][23]. The two algorithms interact during the optimization process by maximizing the intersection (in terms of number of common refactorings) between the best refactoring solutions provided by both algorithms for the system to evaluate/improve.

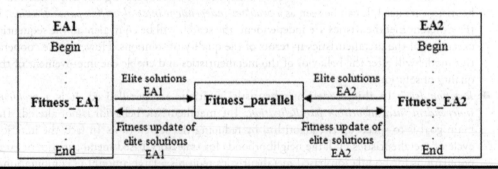

Figure 12.1   The proposed cooperative parallel model scheme.

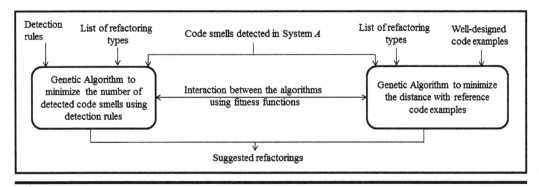

Figure 12.2   Distributed evolutionary algorithms for code smells correction.

The general structure of our approach is introduced in Figure 12.2. We are using two different evolutionary algorithms from our previous work [16][23] to find a consensus to correct code smells.

The first algorithm is based on genetic algorithm [16] to find the best sequence of refactorings that can minimize the number of code smells detected using metrics-based detection rules generated by a genetic programming algorithm. It takes as controlling parameters, the detection rules, and a set of refactoring operations that were defined and discussed in the related literature [12]. It takes as input a the source code of a system (A) containing code smells to be fixed. As output, this step recommends a refactoring solution, which suggests a set of refactoring operations that should be applied in order to correct the input code. The algorithm start by using the detection rules to detect code smells in the input code (A). Then the process of generating a correction solution can be viewed as the mechanism that finds the best way to combine some subset (to be fixed during the search) among all available refactoring operations, in such a way to best reduce the number of detected code smells. More details about this algorithm can be found in [16].

The second algorithm is based on genetic algorithm [23] also to find the best sequence of refactorings that can minimize the distance between the well-designed code examples and the system (A) (after applying the refactorings solution) using alignment techniques [23]. This algorithm takes as controlling parameters examples of well-designed (reference) code, and a set of refactoring types. It takes as input the list of code smells detected on system (A) to correct, and the well-designed code examples. As output, this algorithm recommends a refactoring solution, which suggests a set of refactoring operations that should be applied to improve the quality of the input code. The process of generating a correction solution is the mechanism that finds the best way to combine some subset (to be fixed during the search) among all available refactoring operations, in such a way as to best minimizes the similarity between the reference code and code fragments containing bad smells. The similarity distance is also based on the use of global and local alignment techniques. A detailed description of this algorithm can be found in [23].

In our D-EA framework, both algorithms are executed in parallel and during the optimization process (each iteration) they interact by maximizing the intersection between the best solutions of suggested refactorings, by both algorithms, to correct the system (A). In fact, at each iteration, our D-EA selects the best solutions from both algorithms using a selection operator. Then, the intersection score between the suggested refactorings is to maximize. This score is used to penalize or favor the best solutions of both algorithms.

12.3.3 Distributed Code Smells Correction: Problem Formulation

This subsection is devoted to describing the formal formulation of the code smells correction problem using D-EA. In order to ease the understanding of this formulation, we first describe the pseudo-code of our adaptation. Then, we present the solution structure, the objective functions to optimize and finally the used change operators.

A high-level view of our D-EA approach to the code smells correction problem is introduced by Figure 12.3 where both GA algorithms are executed in parallel and interact using a fitness function in each generation.

Lines 1 to 3 construct initial GA populations, which are sets of individuals that stand for possible solutions representing a random combination of refactoring operations. Lines 4 to 15 encode the main loops for both algorithms, which explores the search space and constructs new

```
Input:  List of refactoring types RT.
Input:  Detection rules DR.
Input:  System A containing a list of code-smells.
Output: refactoring sequence RS.
1: I1 := refactorings(RT);
2: P1 := set_of(I1);
3: initial_populationGA(P1, Max_size) ;
4: repeat
5:          for all I1 ∈ P 1 do
6:                  detected_codesmells _GA(A) := execute_rules(I1, A);
7:                  fitness(I1) := number_of_code_smells(detected_codesmells_GA(A) );
8:          end for
9:          best_sol_P1 := select(P1, number_best_solutions);
10:         send (best_sol_P1);
11:         best_sol_P2 := receive(best_sol_P2);
12:         for all I1 ∈best_sol_P1 do
13:                 fitness_intersection (I1) := := Max_intersection(refactoring(I1) ∩ refactoring(best_sol_P2))/(Max_number_refactoring(I1, best_sol_P2));
14:                 fitness(I1) := updatefitness (I1, fitness_intersection);
15:         end for
16:         best_solution_P1 := best_fitness(P1);
17:         P1 := generate_new_population(P1);
18:         it:=it+1;
19: until it=max_it
20: return best_solution_refactorings
```

(a)

```
Input:  Set of well-designed code examples GE.
Input:  System A containing a list of code-smells.
Input:  List of refactoring types RT.
Output: refactoring sequence RS.
1: I2 := refactorings(RT);
2: P2 = set_of(I2);
3: initial_populationGA(P2, Max_size) ;
4: repeat
5:          for all I2 ∈P2 do
6:                  A := ApplyRefactoring(I2, A);
7:                  fitness(I2) := distance(A, GE);
8:          end for
9:          best_sol_P2 := select(P2, number_solutions);
10:         send(best_sol_P2);
11:         best_sol_P1 := receive(best_sol_P1);
12:         for all I2 ∈best_sol_P2 do
13:                 fitness_intersection (I2) := Max_intersection(refactoring(I2) ∩ refactoring(best_sol_P1))/(Max_number_refactoring(I2, best_sol_P1)) ;
14:                 fitness(I2) := updatefitness (I2, fitness_intersection);
15:         end for
16:         best_solution_P2 := best_fitness(P2);
17:         P2 := generate_new_population(P2);
18:         it:=it+1;
19: until it=max_it
20: return best_solution_refactorings
```

(b)

Figure 12.3 High-level pseudo-code of our D-EA adaptation. Both algorithms interact with each other using *"fitness_intersection"* function in each interaction.

individuals by combining refactorings. At each iteration, we evaluate the quality of each individual in the population for each algorithm (lines 6 and 13). The first algorithm evaluates the refactoring solutions on the number of detected code smells using detection rules and the second algorithm evaluates solutions based on the deviance from well-designed code (input) using global and local alignment techniques. Then, a set of best solutions are selected from both algorithms in each iteration. Both algorithms interact with each other using *intersection_fitness* where the goal is to maximize the *intersection* between the sets of suggested refactoring operations by each solution. Thus, some solutions will be *penalized* due to the absence of consensus and others will be favored (lines 11 to 16). Then, the best solution for each algorithm is saved and a new population of individuals is generated by iteratively selecting pairs of parent individuals from population *p* and applying the crossover operator to them. We include both the parent and child variants in the new population *pop*. Then, we apply the mutation operator, with a probability score, for both parent and child to ensure the solution diversity; this produces the population for the next generation. Both algorithms terminate when the termination criterion (maximum iteration number) is met, and returns the best set of refactorings solutions from both algorithms. In the following, we describe the three main steps of adaptation for both algorithms GP and GA to our problem.

We used the same solution representation and change operators used in our previous work [16][23]. Thus, the solutions of both algorithms are represented as a vector where each dimension is a refactoring operation (e.g. move method, add attribute, etc.) applied to some code elements of system *A* to fix. For instance, the solution represented in Figure 12.4 is composed of three steps corresponding to three refactoring operations to apply in some code fragments.

For both algorithms, after selecting parents using the roulette wheel selection mechanism, the mutation operator consists of randomly replacing some dimensions in the vector (refactoring) with new ones. The crossover operation creates two offspring $I'1$ and $I'2$ from the two selected parents $I1$ and $I2$. It is defined as follows: A random position, k, is selected. The first k refactorings of $I1$ become the first k elements of $I'1$. Similarly, the first k refactorings of $I2$ become the first k refactorings of $I'2$.

One of the unique aspects of our distributed evolutionary algorithm is the use of an intersection fitness function. In fact, a set of best solutions are selected (5% of the population) from both algorithms, in each iteration, and then executed on a new system *A* to fix. A matrix is constructed where rows are composed by best solutions of the first GA $\{SR_i\}$, columns are composed by best solution of second GA $\{SD_j\}$ and each case (SR_i, SD_j) is defined as:

$$f_{\text{intersection}}\left(SR_i,\ SD_j\right) = \frac{\left|\left\{\text{refactoring of } SR_i\right\} \cap \left\{\text{refactoring of } SD_j\right\}\right|}{\text{Max}\left(|\ SR_i\ |, |\ SD_j\ |\right)}$$

Then, the intersection score for each solution is defined as:

$$f_{\text{intersection}}\left(SR_i\right) = Max\left(f_{\text{intersection}}\left(SR_i,\ SD_{\forall j}\right)\right)$$

and

$$f_{\text{intersection}}\left(SD_j\right) = Max\left(f_{\text{intersection}}\left(SR_{\forall i},\ SD_j\right)\right).$$

MoveMethod(division, Department, University)	AddParameter(x, int, average, Student)	PushDownMethod(average, Student, Person)

Figure 12.4 Individual representation for both algorithms.

In this case, the fitness function, to maximize, used by the first algorithm is defined as

$$f_1 = f_{\text{intersction}} - n,$$

where n is the number of code smells detected by the detection rules after applying the solution (refactorings) on the system A to fix. $f_{\text{intersection}}$ takes the value 0 if the solution is not selected for intersection. The fitness function, to maximize, of the second GA algorithm is defined as

$$f_2 = AlignmentSimilarity\ (A,GE) + f_{\text{intersection}},$$

where *AlignmentSimiliarty* score is obtained from the global alignment algorithm executed on the system A (after applying refactoring) and the set of reference systems (*GE*). More details can be found about this similarity function in our previous work [23].

12.4 Evaluation

In this section, we start by presenting our research questions. Then, we describe and discuss the obtained results.

12.4.1 Goals

The goal of the study is to evaluate the effectiveness of our approach for correction of bad smells from the perspective of a software maintainer conducting a quality audit. We present the results of the experiment aimed at answering the following research questions: *RQ1*: To what extent can the proposed approach generate valid refactoring sequences?; *RQ2*: To what extent can the proposed approach correct bad smells?; *RQ3:* To what extent can D-EAs perform compared to single-population approaches [16][23](both algorithms executed separately) and random search?

To answer *RQ1*, we manually verified the feasibility of the different proposed refactoring sequences for each system. To this end, we asked a group of experts composed of seven PhD students from University of Michigan to perform a manual validation of the suggested refactoring. All these PhD students are expert in refactoring and familiar with the used open source systems, and they have a minimum experience in industry as programmers of four years. We considered the majority of votes between the participants to decide if a recommended refactoring is correct or not. We report the percentage of proposed refactorings that were semantically correct (did not violate the behavior of the programs): *SP* is defined as

$$Semantic - precision = \frac{\text{number of valid refactoring}}{\text{number of refactoring}}$$

To answer RQ2, we used an existing corpus of known bad smells [26], and we validated manually whether the proposed corrections were useful to fix bad smells found in the corpus. The precision denotes the fraction of fixed code smells among the set of all code smells: *RP* is defined as

$$refactoring - precision = \frac{\text{number of fixed code - smells}}{\text{number of code - smells}}$$

Table 12.1 The systems studied

Systems	Number of classes	Number of code smells
ArgoUML v0.26	1358	138
ArgoUML v0.3	1409	129
Xerces v2.7	991	82
Ant-Apache v1.5	1024	103
Ant-Apache v1.7.0	1839	124
Gantt v1.10.2	245	51
Azureus v2.3.0.6	1449	108

For the remaining question, we compared our results to those produced, over 51 runs, by existing single-population approaches [16][23] in addition to random search. We selected 51 runs based on the existing guidelines for comparing metaheursitics algorithm [29]. Further details about our experimental setting are discussed in the next subsection.

12.4.2 Studied Systems and Setting

Our study considers the extensive evolution of different open-source Java analyzed in the literature [25][26]. The corpus [25][26] used includes the releases of Apache Ant, ArgoUML, Gantt, Azureus and Xerces-J. Table 12.1 reports the size in terms of classes of the analyzed systems. The considered existing corpus contains the three well-known code smells (Blob, Spaghetti Code, and Functional Decomposition).

We choose the above-mentioned open source systems because they are medium/large-sized open-source projects and were analyzed in the related work. JHotdraw was chosen as an example of reference code because it contains very few known code smells. After executing our D-EA technique, we select the best refactoring solutions of both algorithms to analyze (having the better fitness score which is normalized for our experiments between 0 and 1). We used the above-described measures (*SP* and *RP*) for all these comparisons over 51 runs. Since the used algorithms are metaheuristics, they produce different results on every run when applied to the same problem instance. To cope with this stochastic nature, the use of rigorous statistical testing is then essential to provide support to the conclusions derived from analyzing such data. Thus, we used the Wilcoxon rank sum test in the comparative study. For the single population algorithms (GA) and random search, population size is fixed at 100 and the number of generations at 1000. For D-EA, the population size is 100 and number of generations 500. In this way, all algorithms perform 100,000 evaluations (fair comparison).

12.4.3 Results and Discussions

As showed in Table 12.2, the majority of proposed refactoring are feasible (preserve the behavior) and improve the code quality. For instance, for Azureus, 84% of refactoring suggestions are valid and fix 88% of design defects. Around 92% of suggested refactorings are correct for Gantt. The best results were obtained for Xerces-J. The main reason is that this system is smaller than the

Table 12.2 Precision (SP an RP) median values of D-EA, GA1, GA2 and RS over 51 independent simulation runs

Systems	D-EA		GA1 [16]		GA2 [23]		RS	
	SP	RP	SP	RP	SP	RP	SP	RP
Azureus v2.3.0.6	84	88	77	82	74	71	37	19
Gantt	92	90	84	76	71	73	31	22
Argo UML (V 0.26)	81	86	73	79	68	77	27	17
Argo UML (V 0.3)	84	91	78	84	82	71	24	24
Xerces (V 2.3)	93	86	82	81	84	82	27	17
Xerces (V 2.7)	86	92	74	78	79	72	29	19
AntApache (V 1.5)	91	84	82	77	83	78	31	23
AntApache (V 1.7.0)	87	94	79	81	81	81	33	21

others. In addition, Xerces-J contains fewer bad smells than the remaining systems. The average of our D-EA approach is more than 85% of SP and RP on the different eight systems. We found that the unfeasible (invalid) refactorings are mainly related to some semantic incoherence (for example when moving some methods between classes) or conflicts between the suggested refactoring. Other suggestions represent some bad recommendations. These bad recommendations correspond to different proposed code changes related to classes that are not classified as bad smells in the corpus. To conclude, after manually applying the feasible refactoring operations for all systems, we found that on average are better than both single population algorithms executed separately (GA1 is based on minimizing the number of code smells [16] and GA2 is based on maximizing similarity with reference code [25]). The majority of unfixed bad smells are Blobs. In fact, this type of bad smell needs a large number of refactoring operations and is very difficult to correct.

We note that the SP and RP median values of D-EA, GA1, GA2 and RS over 51 independent simulation runs. The p-values of the Wolcoxon rank sum test indicate whether the median of the algorithm of the corresponding column (GA1/GA2/RS) is statistically different from the PEA one with a 99% confidence level ($\alpha = 0.01$). A statistical difference, in terms of the obtained recall values, is detected when the p-value is less than or equal to 0.01.

Figure 12.5 shows that the performance of our approach improves as we increase the percentage of best solutions (from each population of detectors and rules) for intersection at each iteration. However, the results become stable after 5%. For this reason, we considered this threshold in our experiments. Our D-EA technique requires a number of comparisons between the selected solutions, thus the execution time need to be considered (number of comparison). Indeed, we believe that 5% is a good threshold value for a population of 100 individuals to keep reasonable execution time.

All the algorithms under comparison were executed on machines with Intel Xeon 3 GHz processors and 8 GB RAM. We note that each of GA1 and GA2 were run on a single machine. However, our D-EA was executed on two nodes (machines) following the previously described parallel model. We recall that all algorithms were run for 100,000 evaluations. This allows us to

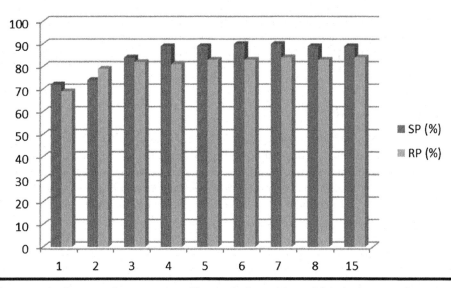

Figure 12.5 **The impact of percentage of best solutions selected for the intersection process on detection results (average precision scores on all systems to evaluate).**

make a fair comparison between CPU times. Figure 12.6 illustrates the obtained CPU times of all algorithms on each of the considered systems. We note that the results presented in this figure were analyzed by using the same previously described statistical analysis methodology. In fact, based on the obtained p-values regarding CPU times, the D-EA is demonstrated to be faster than GA1 and GA2 as highlighted through Figure 12.6. The D-EA spends approximately the half amount of time required for GA1 or GA2. This observation could be explained by the fact that the performed 100,000 evaluations are distributed between the two machines (50,000 for each). In this way, the D-EA is able to evaluate 200 individuals at each iteration, which is not the case for GA1 or GA2 which evaluates only 100 individuals at each iteration. We can see that parallelization seems to be

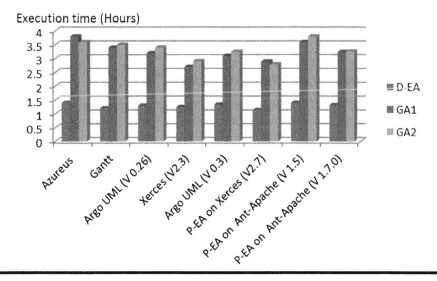

Figure 12.6 **Average execution time on the different systems.**

an interesting approach to tackle software engineering problems where the individual evaluations are expensive like refactoring problem. However, refactoring is not a real-time problem, thus we did not use parallel-EA to improve the execution time but the accuracy of the results (precision, manual correctness, etc.).

12.4.4 Threats to Validity

Some threats need to be considered when interpreting our study results.

The first threat concerns the conclusion validity. We used the Wilcoxon rank sum test with a 95% confidence level to test if significant differences existed between the measurements for different treatments. This test makes no assumption that the data is normally distributed and is suitable for ordinal data, so we can be confident that the statistical relationships we observed are significant.

For the internal validity, we used techniques to detect code-smell instances that can lead to some false positives that have an impact on the results of our experiments. However, the used detection rules have high precision based on our previous work but some of the incorrect refactorings could be probably explained by the false positive in the detected code smells.

External validity refers to the generalizability of our findings. In this study, we performed our experiments on several different widely used open-source systems belonging to different domains and with different sizes. However, we cannot assert that our results can be generalized to industrial Java applications, other programming languages, and to other practitioners. Another threat can be the limited number of subjects and studied systems, which externally threatens the generalizability of our results. Future replications of this study are necessary to confirm our findings.

Construct validity is concerned with the relationship between theory and what is observed. The manual evaluation of suggested refactorings depends on the expertise of the subjects involved in our experiments.

12.5 Related Work

A large number of research works have addressed the problem of code smells correction and software refactoring in recent years. We start by surveying those works that can be classified mainly into two broad categories: manual and semi-automated approaches, and search-based approaches.

12.5.1 Manual and Semi-automated Approaches

We start by summarizing existing manual and semi-automated approaches for software refactoring. In Fowler's book [30], a non-exhaustive list of low-level design problems in source code has been defined. For each design problem (i.e., code smell), a particular list of possible refactorings is suggested to be applied by software maintainers manually. Indeed, in the literature, most of the existing approaches are based on quality metrics improvement to deal with refactoring. In [39], Sahraoui et al. have proposed an approach to detect opportunities of code transformations (i.e., refactorings) based on the study of the correlation between some quality metrics and refactoring changes. To this end, different rules are defined as a combination of metrics/thresholds to be used as indicators for detecting code smells and refactoring opportunities. For each code-smell a pre-defined and standard list of transformations should be applied in order to improve the quality of the code. Another similar work is proposed by Du Bois et al. [40] who start from the hypothesis that refactoring opportunities corresponds of those which improve cohesion and coupling metrics to perform an optimal distribution of features over classes. Du Bois et al. analyze how refactorings manipulate coupling and cohesion metrics, and how to identify refactoring opportunities that improve these metrics. However, these two approaches are limited to only some possible refactoring operations with a small set of quality metrics. In addition, improving some quality metrics does not mean that existing code smells are fixed.

Moha et al. [26] proposed an approach that suggests refactorings using formal concept analysis (FCA) to correct detected code smells. This work combines the efficiency of cohesion/coupling metrics with FCA to suggest refactoring opportunities. However, the link between code smells detection and correction is not obvious, which make the inspection difficult for the maintainers. Similarly, Joshi et al. [41] have presented an approach based on concept analysis aimed at identifying less-cohesive classes. It also helps identify less-cohesive methods, attributes and classes in one go. Further, the approach guides refactoring opportunity identification such as extract class, move method, localize attributes and remove unused attributes.

Other contributions are based on rules that can be expressed as assertions (invariants, pre and post-condition). The use of invariants has been proposed to detect parts of a that require refactoring by [42]. In addition, Opdyke [12] have proposed the definition and the use of pre- and post-condition with invariants to preserve the behavior of the software when applying refactoring. Hence, behavior preservation is based on the verification/satisfaction of a set of pre and post-condition. All these conditions are expressed in terms of rules.

The major limitation of these manual and semi-automated approaches is that they try to apply refactorings separately without considering the whole program to be refactored and its impact on the other artifacts. Indeed, these approaches are limited to only some possible refactoring operations and a few quality metrics to assess quality improvement. In addition, improving some quality metrics does mean necessary that actual code smells are fixed.

12.5.2 Search-based Approaches

Search-based approaches can be classified into two main categories: mono-objective and multi-objective optimization approaches.

In the first category, the majority of the existing work combines several metrics in a single fitness function to find the best sequence of refactorings. Seng et al. [43] have proposed a single-objective optimization-based approach using genetic algorithm to suggest a list of refactorings to improve software quality. The search process uses a single fitness function to maximize a weighted sum of several quality metrics. The used metrics are mainly related to various class level properties such as coupling, cohesion, complexity and stability. Indeed, the authors have used some preconditions for each refactoring. These conditions serve at preserving the program behavior (refactoring feasibility). However, in this approach, the semantic coherence of the refactored program is not considered. In addition, the approach was limited only on the refactoring operation *move method*. Furthermore, there is another similar work of O'Keeffe et al. [20] that have used different local search-based techniques such as hill climbing and simulated annealing to provide an automated refactoring support. Eleven object-oriented design metrics have been used to evaluate the quality improvement. One of the earliest works on search-based approaches is the work by Qayum et al. [47] who considered the problem of refactoring scheduling as a graph transformation problem. They expressed refactorings as a search for an optimal path, using ant colony optimization, in the graph where nodes and edges represent respectively refactoring candidates and dependencies between them. However, the use of graphs is limited only on structural and syntactical information and therefore does not consider the domain semantics of the program neither its runtime behavior. Furthermore, Fatiregun et al. [18] showed how search-based transformations could be used to reduce code size and construct amorphous program slices. They have used small atomic level transformations in their approach. In addition, their aim was to reduce program size rather than to improve its structure/quality. Recently, Kessentini et al. [16] have proposed a single-objective combinatorial optimization using genetic algorithm to find the best sequence of refactoring operations that improve the quality of the code by minimizing as much as possible the number of code smells detected on the source code. Also, Otero et al. [46] use a new search-based refactoring. The main idea behind this work is to explore the addition of a refactoring step into the genetic programming iteration. There will be an additional loop in which refactoring steps drawn from a catalogue of such steps will be applied to individuals of the population. Jensen et al. [45] have proposed an approach that supports composition of design changes and makes the introduction of design patterns a primary goal of the refactoring process. They used genetic programming and software metrics to identify the most suitable set of refactorings to apply to a software design. Furthermore, Kilic et al. [44] explore the use of a variety of population-based approaches to search-based parallel refactoring, finding that local beam search could find the best solutions.

In the second category of work, Harman et al. [33] have proposed a search-based approach using Pareto optimality that combines two quality metrics, CBO (coupling between objects) and SDMPC (standard deviation of methods per class), in two separate objective functions. The authors start from the assumption that good design quality results from a good distribution of features (methods) among classes. Their Pareto optimality-based algorithm succeeded in finding a good sequence of 'move method' refactorings that should provide the best compromise between CBO and SDMPC to improve code quality. However, one of the limitations of this approach is that it is limited to unique refactoring operation (move method) to improve software quality and only two metrics to evaluate the preformed improvements. Recently, Ó Cinnéide et al. [20] have proposed a multi-objective search-based refactoring to conduct an empirical investigation to assess some structural metrics and to explore relationships between them. To this end, they have used a variety of search techniques (Pareto-optimal search, semi-random search) guided by a set of cohesion metrics. One of the earliest works on multi-objective search-based refactoring is the work by Ouni et al. [25], who proposed a multi-objective optimization approach to find the best sequence of refactorings using NSGA-II. The proposed approach is based on two objective functions, quality (proportion of corrected code smells) and code modification effort, to recommend a sequence of refactorings that provide the best trade-off between quality and effort.

12.6 Conclusion

In this chapter, we proposed software refactoring as a distributed problem. In our cooperative distributed metaheuristic adaptation, two populations evolve simultaneously with the objective of each depending upon the current population of the other in a cooperative manner. Both populations are executed, on the same system to fix code smells, and the solutions are penalized based on the consensus found, i.e.: intersection between the refactoring solution of both algorithms. The statistical analysis of the obtained results provide evidence to support the claim that cooperative D-EA outperforms single-population evolution and random search based on a benchmark of eight large open-source systems that frequently change over time. Future work should validate our distributed metaheuristic approach with new software engineering problems such as project management, software evolution, etc. We are planning also to provide a distributed search-based framework that can be used in all life-cycle activities.

References

1. Patrick Siarry, Zbigniew Michalewicz (2008) *Advances in Metaheuristics for Hard Optimization.* Natural Computing Series, Springer, ISBN: 978-3-540-72959-4.
2. Enrique Alba (2005) *Parallel Metaheuristics: New Class of Algorithms.* John Wiley & Sons, ISBN: 0-471-67806-6.
3. Tadeusz Burczyńskia, Wacław Kuśa, Adam Długosza, Piotr Oranteka (2004) Optimization and defect identification using distributed evolutionary algorithms. *Engineering Applications of Artificial Intelligence,* 4(17): 337-344.
4. Xiaodong Li, Xin Yao (2012) Cooperatively coevolving particle swarms for large scale optimization. *IEEE Transactions on Evolutionary Computation,* 16(2): 210-224.
5. Evan J. Hughes (2005) Evolutionary many-objective optimization: Many once or one many? In: *Proceedings of IEEE Congress Evolutionary Computation* (CEC'05), pp. 222-227.
6. Yong Wang, Zixing Cai, Guanqi Guo, Yuren Zhou (2007) Multiobjective optimization and hybrid evolutionary algorithm to solve constrained optimization problems. *IEEE Transactions on Systems, Man, and Cybernetics, Part B: Cybernetics,* 37(3): 560-575.
7. El-Ghazali Talbi (2009) *Metaheuristics—From Design to Implementation.* John Wiley & Sons, ISBN: 978-0-470-27858-1.
8. Carolina Salto, Enrique Alba (2012) Designing heterogeneous distributed GAs by efficiently self-adapting the migration period. *Applied Intelligence,* 36(4): 800-808.
9. Marco Tomassini, Leonardo Vanneschi (2010) Guest editorial: special issue on parallel and distributed evolutionary algorithms, part two. *Genetic Programming and Evolvable Machines,* 11(2): 129-130.
10. David E. Goldberg (1989) *Genetic Algorithms in Search, Optimization and Machine Learning.* Addison Wesley, ISBN 0-201-15767-5.
11. Y. Kataoka, M. D. Ernst, W. G. Griswold, D. Notkin (2001) Automated support for program refactoring using invariants, in *Proc. ICSM.* pp. 736-743.
12. W. F. Opdyke (1992) Refactoring: A Program Restructuring Aid in Designing Object-Oriented Application Frameworks, Ph.D. thesis, University of Illinois at Urbana-Champaign.
13. Reiko Heckel (1995) Algebraic Graph Transformations with Application Conditions, M.S. thesis, TU Berlin.
14. Terry Van Belle, David H. Ackley (2002) Code factoring and the evolution of evolvability. In *Proceedings of the Genetic and Evolutionary Computation* Conference (GECCO '02). Morgan Kaufmann Publishers Inc., San Francisco, CA, pp. 1383-1390.
15. Kessentini, M., Vaucher, S., Sahraoui, H. (2010) Deviance from perfection is a better criterion than closeness to evil when identifying risky code, in *Proc. of the International Conference on Automated Software Engineering.* ASE'10 pp. 1-10.
16. M. Kessentini, W. Kessentini, H. Sahraoui, M. Boukadoum, A. Ouni (2011) Design defects detection and correction by example. In *Proc. ICPC,* pp. 81-90.
17. Houari A. Sahraoui, Robert Godin, Thierry Miceli (2000) Can metrics help to bridge the gap between the improvement of oo design quality and its automation? In *ICSM '00:* 154.
18. Ladan Tahvildari, Kostas Kontogiannis (2004). Improving design quality using meta-pattern transformations: A metric-based approach. *Journal of Software Maintenance,* 331-361.
19. Scott Grant, James R. Cordy (2003) An interactive interface for refactoring using source transformation. In *Proceedings of the First International Workshop on Refactoring: Achievements, Challenges, Effects (REFACE'03),* pp. 30-33, November.
20. M. O'Keeffe, M. Cinnéide (2008) Search-based refactoring: An empirical study, *Journal of Software Maintenance,* vol. 20, no. 5, pp. 345-364.
21. M. Harman, J. A. Clark (2004) Metrics are fitness functions too. In *IEEE Metrics.* IEEE Computer Society, pp. 58-69.
22. Mark Harman, S. Afshin Mansouri, Yuanyuan Zhang (2012) Search-based software engineering: Trends, techniques and applications. *ACM Comput. Surv.* 45.
23. M. Kessentini, R. Mahouachi, K. Ghedira (2013) What you like in design use to correct defects, *Software Quality Journal,* 21(4), pp. 551-571 (DOI=http://link.springer.com/content/pdf/10.1007%2Fs11219-012-9187-6).

24. Enrique Alba, J. Francisco Chicano (2008) Observations in using parallel and sequential evolutionary algorithms for automatic software testing. *Computers & OR* 35, 3161–3183.

25. Ouni, A., Kessentini, M., Sahraoui, H., Boukadoum, M. (2013) Maintainability defects detection and correction: A multi-objective approach, in *Journal of Automated Software Engineering (JASE)*, Springer. vol. 20, no. 1, pp. 47-49.

26. N. Moha, Y.-G. Guéhéneuc, L. Duchien, A.-F. Le Meur: DECOR: A Method for the Specification and Detection of Code and Design Smells. TSE, 36, 20-36, 2010.

27. Wolfram Fenske, Sandro Schulze, Daniel Meyer, Gunter Saake (2015) When code smells twice as much: Metric-based detection of variability-aware code smells. In *International Working Conference on Source Code Analysis and Manipulation (SCAM)*, pp. 171-180.

28. Wolfram Fenske, Sandro Schulze (2015) Code smells revisited: A variability perspective. In *International Workshop on Variability Modelling of Software-intensive Systems (VaMoS)*, pp. 3-10.

29. Arcuri, A., Briand, L. C. (2011) A practical guide for using statistical tests to assess randomized algorithms in software engineering. In *Proceedings of the 33rd International Conference on Software Engineering.* ACM, pp. 1-10.

30. Fowler, M., Beck, K., Brant, J., Opdyke, W., Roberts, D. (1999) *Refactoring–Improving the Design of Existing Code*, Addison-Wesley.

31. Sahin, Dilan, Marouane Kessentini, Slim Bechikh, Kalyanmoy Deb (2014) Code-smell detection as a bilevel problem. *ACM Transactions on Software Engineering and Methodology (TOSEM)* 24 (1): 6.

32. Mkaouer, W., Kessentini, M., Bechikh, S., Deb, K., Ouni, A. (2015). Many-objective software remodularization using NSGA-III. *ACM Transactions on Software Engineering and Methodology (TOSEM)*, 24(3): 17.

33. K. Lakhotia, M. Harman, H. Gross (2010) AUSTIN: A tool for search based software testing for the C language and its evaluation on deployed automotive systems. In *2nd International Symposium on Search Based Software Engineering (SSBSE)* pp. 101-110, Benevento, Italy, September.

34. J. Wegener, O. Buhler. (2004) Evaluation of different fitness functions for the evolutionary testing of an autonomous parking system. In *Genetic and Evolutionary Computation Conference (GECCO)*, pp. 1400-1412, Seattle, Washington, June, LNCS 3103.

35. S. Yoo, R. Nilsson, M. Harman (2011) Faster fault finding at Google using multi objective regression test optimisation. In *8th European Software Engineering Conference and the ACM SIGSOFT Symposium on the Foundations of Software Engineering (ESEC/FSE '11)*, Szeged, Hungary, September 5th-9th. Industry Track.

36. C. Cadar, P. Godefroid, S. Khurshid, C. S. Psreanu, K. Sen, N. Tillmann, W. Visser (2011) Symbolic execution for software testing in practice: preliminary assessment. In *33rd International Conference on Software Engineering (ICSE'11)*, pp. 1066-1071, ACM.

37. P. Baker, M. Harman, K. Steinhofel, A. Skaliotis (2006) Search-based approaches to component selection and prioritization for the next release problem. In *22nd International Conference on Software Maintenance (ICSM06)*, pp. 176-185, Philadelphia, Pennsylvania, Sept.

38. S. L. Cornford, M. S. Feather, J. R. Dunphy, J. Salcedo, T. Menzies (2003) Optimizing spacecraft design—Optimization engine development: Progress and plans. In *Proceedings of the IEEE Aerospace Conference*, pp. 3681-3690, Big Sky, Montana, March.

39. Sahraoui, H., Godin, R., Miceli, T. (2000) Can metrics help to bridge the gap between the improvement of OO design quality and its automation? *International Conference on Software Maintenance*, San Jose, California, pp. 154-162.

40. Du Bois, B., Demeyer, S., Verelst, J. (2004) Refactoring—Improving coupling and cohesion of existing code. In: *Proc. 11th Working Conference on Reverse Engineering.* Tampere, Finland, pp. 144-151.

41. Joshi, P., Joshi, R. K. (2009) Concept analysis for class cohesion. In: *Proceedings of the 13th European Conference on Software Maintenance and Reengineering*, Kaiserslautern, Germany, pp. 237-240.

42. Kataoka, Y., Ernst, M. D., Griswold, W. G., Notkin, D. (2001) Automated support for program refactoring using invariants. In: the *International Conference on Software Maintenance*, Florence, Italy, pp. 736-743.

43. Seng, O., Stammel, J., Burkhart, D. (2006) Search-based determination of refactorings for improving the class structure of object-oriented systems. In: *Proceedings of the Genetic and Evolutionary Computation Conference*, Seattle, Washington, pp. 1909-1916.

44. Kilic, H., Koc, E., Cereci, I. (2011) Search-based parallel refactoring using population-based direct approaches. In: *Proceedings of the 3rd international Symposium on Search Based Software Engineering*, Szeged, Hungary, pp. 271-272.

45. Jensen, A., Cheng, B. (2010). On the use of genetic programming for automated refactoring and the introduction of design patterns. In: *Proceedings of the 12th Annual Conference on Genetic and Evolutionary Computation*. Portland, Oregon, pp. 1341-1348.

46. Otero, F. E. B., Johnson, C. G., Freitas, A. A., Thompson, S. J. (2010). Refactoring in automatically generated programs. *International Symposium on Search Based Software Engineering*, Benevento, Italy., pp. 1-2.

47. Qayum, F., and Heckel, R. (2009) Local search-based refactoring as graph transformation. *Proceedings of 1st International Symposium on Search Based Software Engineering*. Cumberland Lodge, Windsor, UK, pp. 43–46.

Chapter 13

Variability in Library Evolution

An Exploratory Study on Open-Source Java Libraries

Hussein Alrubaye, Mohamed Wiem
Mkaouer, and Anthony Peruma

Rochester Institute of Technology, Rochester, New York, United States

13.1 Introduction

Software systems are evolving through the composition and maintenance of various components, under one architecture, designed to serve the purpose of the client's needs. These components are either created in-house by project developers or outsourced from third-party open-source or commercial libraries. Recently, an increasing number of software systems rely on the use of third-party libraries by means of cutting the implementation time and effort and increase the quality of the end-product. These libraries offer services that can be (re)used as part of the core program functionalities. Thus, reusability is one of the main reasons why developers opt for libraries, and from that perspective, libraries can be seen as software artifacts that ensure variability. Variability is known as the ability of a software artifact to adjust with respect to a given context (Van Gurp, Bosch et al. 2001). With the large number of heterogeneous environments that a software artifact can be exposed to, its variability is measured by the degree of its immunity to manual adjustments and configurations (Galster, Weyns et al. 2014). So, the more a software artifact is variability friendly, the more it is reusable in various contexts through its adaptations, these adaptations are also known as variants. From this perspective, libraries are variants that software architects must choose wisely to increase the reusability of their system and to reduce the development and to tune overhead. However, localizing the right variant, i.e., library, may not be straightforward. A a wide variety of libraries offer similar functionalities, and developers are not necessarily aware of all of them to decide on which library better fits the given project requirement(s) (Yu and Woodard 2008).

Moreover, the primary key challenge that faces the choice of libraries as variants is the evolution of software systems requirements. When dealing with feature requests, developers may be forced to acquire richer APIs, i.e., as part of maintenance practices, developers need to replace an existing library with another. This act of replacement can be categorized as either a library upgrade or migration. An upgrade occurs when the developer replaces, an outdated library version with a more recent one (Cossette and Walker 2012). A migration, on the other hand, is the replacement of the library with one that was (most likely) developed by another development team, but still, performs the same (or similar) functionality as the replaced library (Teyton, Falleri et al. 2013). Although the automation of library upgrades has been advancing especially with the rise of continuous integration and dynamic component frameworks (Wu, et al. 2016), library migrations' automation is challenging for developers due to the high risk of introducing malfunctions into an already-stable software system. Thus, from variability perspective, it is crucial for a variant, i.e., library, to be chosen based on how well-maintained it is, in a way to keep its services up-to-date, to be agnostic to deprecation, and to provide services that are compatible with environmental changes.

Prior research on software variants has been framed in the area of software variability (Coplien, Hoffman et al. 1998). Although variability was widespread in the area of software product lines, it still applies to all aspect of the software lifecycles (Galster, Weyns et al. 2014). In particular, there is a need for software systems to accommodate potential changes in their third-party libraries especially since recent studies have shown that third-party libraries can constitute up to 38% of the software source code (Wu, et al. 2016).

Our research goal in this chapter is to raise the awareness of libraries' role, as an important variant, in the software life cycle, by investigating their evolution on a wide variety of Java projects and inspecting their impact from a maintainability perspective. In this context, we analyze the relationship between libraries and software systems from two perspectives: (1) the client software using several libraries, and (2) libraries hosted on various client software systems. From the software's perspective, developers are constantly searching for the most appropriate library that better satisfies the requirements. The search process can result in including new libraries as well as replacing existing libraries with different ones. Developers are also required to update their libraries into more reliable and stable releases constantly. Thus, developers need automated tools that allow them to maintain and evolve their external libraries. From the library's perspective, its maintainers, are also required to update the libraries' functionalities to be compatible with newly appearing environments and to stay competitive with other libraries offering similar services. The update process tends to be challenging as developers must guarantee that their new releases do not introduce any breaking changes in the client systems, already deploying their old releases.

This chapter presents the results of the study which: 1) gives an overview of libraries' evolution in a large set of software systems; 2) demonstrates the degree of variability among libraries' researchers in the field with the main challenges and limitations that require further investigation; and 3) enumerates the current challenges of maintaining libraries and how to support their variability.

The remainder of this is as follows: The next section gives the necessary background information to understand the terminology related to library upgrade and migration. Section 13.3 contains the related studies underlying the challenges that developers face when upgrading libraries. It also enumerates studies related to automating the process of migration and recommendation. In Section 13.4, we explain our research methodology accompanied by the research questions. It also explores the process of mining projects under study and the algorithms used to identify library upgrades and migrations. The research questions are then addressed and discussed in Section 13.5. Section 13.6 identifies threats to validity and limitations faced in this work. Section 13.7 finalizes the chapter with a conclusion and our future research directions.

13.2 Background

This section reviews the necessary background for library evolution. We start by giving a set of formal definitions for the used keywords throughout this chapter:

Library. Consider L the set of libraries, each library $l \in L$ is a standalone library with multiple versions, each version is implemented and made available for use through function(s). These functions are publicly available in the form of an API. Let F be the set of functions provided by the interface. i.e., for $l \in L$, there exist a set of functions $f \in F$ such that $api(l) = f$. In the context of Apache Maven, we are restricted to one interface (set of publicly available functions embedded in the JAR file) per library. Maven also defines a clear naming scheme for all Java libraries to follow.

Naming Scheme. It serves the purpose of providing unique identifiers to libraries. Apache Maven adopts the following naming scheme:

$$< GroupID > . < ArtifactID > . < Version >$$

GroupID. It identifies the developer of the library. It is required to follow the package-naming convention, and thus it is unique as it represents the domain or subdomain the library provider owns, e.g., *org.apache.maven*.

ArtifactID. It is the name of the library. It must be unique within the set of libraries belonging to the same provider, i.e., two libraries belonging to two different providers can have the same ArtifactID since they can be distinguished by the GroupID.

Version. Consider Each library $l \in L$ has multiples releases throughout its lifecycle i.e., we consider a chronologically ordered list of version numbers v such that $v \in \mathbb{R} \mid l_v \in L$. There are several version numbering schemes recommended by the development communities, for instance, the Apache Maven project recommends the use of the following versioning strategy:

$$< major > . < minor > . < patch > [- < type > - < attempt >]$$

Where *major* represents a significant release of the library, such as adding new functionalities. *Minor* indicates few changes, usually related nonfunctional requirements such as performance optimization, etc. *Patch* refers to bug fixes and security patches etc. *type-attempt* refers to the maturity level of the released version, e.g., alpha, beta, stable, etc.

Note that classes and interfaces offered by the library's API can also be packaged for organizational purposes. From variability perspective, it is important for libraries to explicitly announce their changes for client systems since some of these changes may have consequences on the functions offered by the libraries, and thus the client software behavior. These changes are usually announced through the library's changelog and the API documentation. As an example, *Barcode4J* is a flexible generator for barcodes written in Java, its GroupID is identified by the *net.sf.barcode4j* domain, while its ArtifactID is labeled *barcode4j-fop-ext-0.20.5-complete*. So, the library is known as *net.sf.barcode4j.barcode4j-fop-ext-0.20.5-complete*.

Dependency. Let D be the set of dependencies and invocations of all functions belonging to F and linking L to the software S. Formally, for $l \in L$, we define a set of functions $f \in F$ such that, if l_p is used by s_q (p and q are arbitrary numbers representing respectively the library and software versions) then we define a set of dependencies $d \in D \mid D \subset F \mid dep(l_p, s_q) = d$ containing all function in $api(l_p)$ that are used in s_q xis. For example, in Figure 13.5, the *ps2-parser* project is invoking multiple instances of the function *assertThat()* belonging to the library *fest-assert-code*. *ps2-parser is then* dependent to *fest-assert-code* since it utilizes at least on its API functions.

Library Upgrade. For a given software S, let $l_p \in L$ be a library belonging to the version s_q. The upgrade process is defined as the enhancement of existing libraries functionalities by either updating its existing functions or/and by adding new functions. The upgrade process is denoted $l_p \rightarrow l_{p+1}$ if all functions of l_p are located l_{p+1} unless deprecated. Formally: if f_p (respectively f_{p+1}) the functions offered by l_p (respectively l_{p+1}) then $f_p, f_{p+1} \in F \mid f_p \subset f_{p+1}$, expect for when some functions from f_p might be deprecated or merged. For example, *dox4j* is an *OpenXML* editor that is dependent on the *log4j* library. As shown in Figure 13.2, *log4j* was automatically updated from 1.2.13 to 2.15.0. Unlike migration (to be seen in the next definition) this update has not triggered in further changes in the client source code.

Library Migration. For a given software S, let $l_p \in L$ be a library belonging to the software version s_q to be replaced by another library $l'_r \in L$ in the next version s_{q+1}. The migration process, denoted $l_p \rightarrow l'_r$, is defined by the following condition: $dep(l_p, s_q) \neq \varnothing \wedge dep(l'_r, s_q) = \varnothing \wedge dep(l_p, s_q) \neq \varnothing \wedge dep(l'_r, s_q) = \varnothing$. Let F be the set of services and functions provided by APIs. for $l_1 \in L$ and $l_2 \in L$, unlike the upgrade process, l_p and l'_r are independent so for f_p (respectively f_r) the set of functions provided by l_p (respectively l'_r) we assume that there are no common functions provided by both libraries, i. e., $f_p \cap f_r = \varnothing$. Note that this definition does not enforce replacing one library with exactly one other, i.e., one library is considered retired if none of its dependencies exist in the new version of the software. A function change is considered a candidate migration if there is a least one function from the retired library that has been replaced by another function from the newly added library. This definition is also loose in the sense of not requiring a retired library to be physically removed from the project, it just enforces that none of its functions are being actually invoked in the project's source code. As an illustrative example, the developers of *ps2-parser* project have decided to utilize *testng* coupled with *fest-assert-core* instead of *junit* for their unit tests. As shown in Figure 13.4 and Figure 13.5, each function of *junit* was replaced with function(s) issued from *testng* and/or *fest-assert-core*. *Junit* was no longer referenced as a dependency in the next release of the *ps2-parser* project.

Library Degree of Variability. A library is considered variability friendly if and only if its set of changes does not affect the client software systems that are dependent on it. In fact, developers want their software to be dependent on most up to date libraries that offer stable functionalities while being less prone to errors and vulnerabilities, etc. At the same time, they do not want these library changes to become a significant overhead on their maintenance tasks.

For example, the upgrade of the *org.springframework*, in the Hudson project,[1] from version *2.5* to *2.5.6* has not triggered any changes in the classes that are already using some of the library's functions. Such a process is considered variability friendly. On the other hand, the migration of the library labeled *httpunit* to *htmlunit* [2] has triggered code changes that were spread over 22 java files, including the addition of 460 lines of codes and the deletion of 258 lines of code. This manual process represents a maintenance overhead for software developers and thus reduces its variability degree.

One of the primary objectives of this chapter is to identify which of the library evolution practices are variability friendly. In this context, to better understand the implications of lack variability in the evolution of libraries, several studies have focused on their side effects on maintenance tasks, e.g., the identification of breaking changes due to library upgrades. Other studies focused on helping developers with recommending better library alternatives and automating their migration process. All these studies are enumerated in the next section of this chapter.

---

[1] https://github.com/hudson/hudson-2.x/commit/606af32cad07e0040d53f7bfc3957b7b79792477.
[2] https://github.com/apache/archiva/commit/4825f8eb88ef35ca265903515ae715014bb4d597.

13.3 Related Work

There has been much research focusing on analyzing the impact of libraries' evolution on existing software systems. This section briefly describes the past research work in the area of external API usage under three categories: (1) library breaking changes, (2) library migration and (3) library recommendation.

13.3.1 Library Breaking Changes

By definition, any API change between two versions of a library, which would trigger the client software to experience syntactic errors when performing library upgrade, is known as a breaking change. Breaking changes are thus a real challenge for library variability as they lock client software systems to (a) specific version(s) and prevent their automatic upgrade. Past research around breaking changes has been in the form of both human-based and empirical studies which were primarily focused on Java-based open-source systems.

Surveys by Bogart et al. (Bogart, Kästner et al. 2015) indicate that the policies and principles of the development community, to which an ecosystem belongs to, has an important role to play with regards to the introduction of breaking changes. Xavier et al. (Xavier, Brito et al. 2017) not only formulated the five primary reasons as to why developers to introduce breaking changes but also claimed that developers understand the repercussions caused by introducing breaking changes. A study of Android SDK-related posts on StackOverflow by Linares-Vasquez et al. (Linares-Vásquez, Bavota et al. 2014) shows that as the number of changes in an API method increase, the number of questions posed by users also increases.

An empirical study on backward compatibility of API's by Xavier et al. (Xavier, Brito et al. 2017) indicates that the percentage of breaking changes increase over time and that almost 30% of APIs are not backward compatible. Kula et al. (Kula, German et al. 2015) found that systems are likely to adopt latest library releases. Work by Zhou and Walker (Zhou and Walker 2016) have shown that use of API deprecation is sporadic and inconsistent, and emphasize the need for library developers to pay careful attention to this concept. Dig and Johnson proposed an approach to detecting code refactoring that is liable to cause breaking changes in client/dependent systems (Dig and Johnson 2006). In their study of Android apps, McDonnell et al. (McDonnell, Ray et al. 2013) indicate that developers are reluctant to use APIs introduced in new versions of the SDK. Linares Vasquez (Linares-Vásquez, Bavota et al. 2013), analyzed fault-and-change proneness of over 7,000 Android apps, and claim that successful apps are less fault-prone and change-prone than apps with low user ratings. An exploratory study by Linares-Vasquez (Linares-Vásquez 2014) resulted in a classification mechanism for the different types of changes. These studies show that developers experience, in general, difficulties in updating their libraries. To ensure variability, these studies offer several classifications for non-functional changes and refactorings to expose those preventing backward compatibility of libraries.

13.3.2 Library Migration

From variability perspective, automating the library migration process is recommended to reduce the maintenance overhead caused by in case of deprecation. In this context, several studies focused on automatically generating migration rules. Teyton et al. (Teyton, Falleri et al. 2013) proposed function-level mapping rules, relying on analyzing previous transitions, gathered in a dataset, to recommend similar migrations. The study performed by the authors is limited by the number of considered projects, thus, as stated by the authors, the algorithm cannot be generalized due to the need of a base of previous migrations between the two given libraries. Kabinna et al. (Kabinna, Bezemer et al. 2016) performed a study on the migration of logging libraries in Apache software foundation projects. The authors found that the majority of the 49 detected migrations were successful, but the process was error-prone with an average of two post-migration bugs and involved experienced developers performing the migration task. The authors also indicate that flexibility and performance are critical drivers for logging library migrations. In their study on library migration, Teyton et al. (Teyton, Falleri et al. 2014) indicate that the larger the software project is, the higher is its dependency on libraries. The authors also found that libraries can be recommended based on analysis of migration trends. Another very relevant work was proposed by Pandita, Jetley et al. (2015), which detects mapping rules between the source and target libraries by automatically discovering likely method mappings across their APIs using text mining on functions textual descriptions. Their work was extended to include temporal constraints (Pandita, Taneja et al. 2016) and to compare text mining between various IR techniques (Pandita, Jetley et al. 2017). A dynamic analysis was also used by Gokhale, Ganapathy et al. (2013) who have developed a technique to infer likely mappings between the APIs of Java2 Mobile Edition and Android graphics.

13.3.3 Library Recommendation

Since a wide variety of libraries offer similar services, it is essential to choose a library which not only provides the needed functionality but also guarantees variability, i.e., automated upgrades, ease of use and cross-platform compatibility. The choice of the library can rely on recommendations that are extracted from similar projects. The review of previous studies in recommending code enumerates how they have approached detecting and extracting similar code. API recommendations based on results returned by web search engines and crowdsourcing was the focus of multiple studies (Thung, Lo et al. 2013, Thung, Oentaryo et al. 2017). Recommendation of relevant functions was also the focus of many studies. In (Ishio, Kula et al. 2016) the comparison relies on signature-based similarity. McMillan et al. (McMillan, Grechanik et al. 2011) proposed Portfolio, a search engine that models the developer's behavior then looks for relevant functions based on call graph similarity and based querying open-source projects using natural language processing. Zhong et al. (Zhong, Xie et al. 2009) built MAPO to select API usage patterns then extracts common sequences that can be used to transform code snippets and recommend it automatically. CLAN (McMillan, Grechanik et al. 2012) calculates behavioral similarity by comparing API call-graphs. Recommending libraries has been recently approached as an optimization problem where Ouni et al. (Ouni, et al. 2017) used NSGA-II (Deb, Pratap et al. 2002) to find the best tradeoff between maximizing the coverage and similarity between libraries while reducing the number of recommended libraries.

13.4 Study Design

13.4.1 Motivation

Since Java libraries are widely available for reusability, software developers are provided with opportunities to include them in the core functionalities of their systems. So, measuring the existence and frequency of library usage helps in detecting upgrade and migration trends. To this end, we defined the following research questions.

RQ1. (Existence of Libraries). To what extent do developers rely on libraries in their software systems?

To answer this research question, we perform a quantitative analysis by designing a mining algorithm to detect the libraries dependencies on any given software. Mining existing dependencies allows us to uncover the spectrum of library usage regarding frequency, type of invocations and the ratio of API functions' calls in client libraries.

RQ2. (Evolution of Libraries). How often libraries evolve within client software systems?

We monitor the evolution of libraries offered functions throughout various releases to quantify libraries upgrades and migration trends. We identify the topmost-performed library upgrades and migrations along with their count. This research question complements the first research question in quantifying the developer-performed, library-related tasks. It also provides the background for the following research question that distinguishes the tasks that included changes to the client java files.

RQ3. (Variability Degree of Libraries). Does the migration process ensure better libraries from variability standpoint?

The purpose of this research question is to investigate whether the newly migrated-to libraries are considered better variants (less triggering to code changes) in comparison with 'retired' libraries. In order compare them, we need to formally quantify the variability of artifacts, i.e., their ability to evolve through changes without altering the client software system's code base from syntactic and behavioral perspective. To answer this research question, we propose the variability degree (VD) defined as follows:

$$VD\left(l_p, l_{p+1}\right) = 1 - \frac{1}{occ}\sum_{i=1}^{occ} CC\left(s_i\right)$$

$$\text{With}\left(\begin{array}{ll} CC\left(s_i\right) = 1 & \textit{if there exists at least one code change related to } f_{p+1} \\ CC\left(s_i\right) = 0 & \textit{if there is no code change related to } f_{p+1} \end{array}\right)$$

Where the library version l_p has been updated to $l_{p+1}\left(l_p \rightarrow l_{p+1}\right)$ in the software S's version s_i.

$CC(s_i)$ (Code Change) represents a function that takes as input the code base of S with the newly updated library version l_{p+1} and returns 1 if there exist at least one code change in the source files i.e., java classes related to the functions of library and 0 otherwise. It is important to note that configuration files changes are not considered as part of the code changes as we aim to measure whether the upgrade process has triggered developers to manually change their source classes to reflect the library update. Although changing configuration files may be also considered as a manual process, there are a lot of development frameworks that can automate the process of updating dependencies when newer version of libraries are available. The automation of software configurations has been well studied in the area of variability (Cetina, Giner et al. 2009, La Rosa, et al. 2009, Shatnawi, Seriai et al. 2015).

To calculate the VD between l_p and l_{p+1}, we gather all upgrades occurrences (*occ*), we calculate the sum of CC(), computed for each occurrence, then the sum is normalized by the total number of occurrences and then inversed. Thus, the higher the VD is, the less 'explicit' is the upgrade between the two versions of the library. This metric helps in measuring the effect of library evolution activities on client software systems.

As an illustrative example, Figure 13.2 shows the upgrade of *log4j* from version *1.2.13* to *1.2.15*. Since this upgrade is reflected in the project library configuration file without altering any class files, then their variability degree according to one occurrence is as follows: $VD(log4j.1.2.13, log4j.1.2.15)= 1$. As shown in Figure 13.3, the upgrade of *jetty* from *8* to *9* has triggered various changes in 5 class files, so their variability degree according to one occurrence is as follows: $VD(jetty.8.0.0, jetty.9.0.0)= 0$.

To answer the research questions mentioned above, we have examined the evolution of several libraries in open-source projects, the details of the retrieval and analysis are detailed in the next subsection.

13.4.2 Retrieval Phase

Previous studies on library evolution (Teyton, Falleri et al. 2013) (Wu, et al. 2016) (De Roover, Lammel et al. 2013) have conducted their experiments on known datasets of Java and Android projects (Tempero, Anslow et al. 2010) (Allix, Bissyandé et al. 2016). They also analyzed a limited set of libraries within projects (Teyton, Falleri et al. 2014). We have decided to extend these studies, and we have decided to consider all third-party libraries that we encounter on the projects under study and to restrict our study to projects using Maven. Maven is the Apache foundation project management tool. We have chosen Maven projects because they encapsulate their dependencies to libraries on a specific file labeled Project Object Model (POM), which facilitates the identification of libraries used by any project. To collect the projects depending on Maven libraries, we used GHTorrent (Gousios and Spinellis 2012) to scan projects' metadata initially. Since the preliminary results have shown a very high number of candidate projects, and since we want to make sure we include projects that had enough cycles to include library evolution, we have decided to only select well-engineered projects using criteria extracted from a study by (Munaiah, Kroh et al. 2017). Our inclusion criteria were mainly chosen to guarantee the feasibility of our study by reducing the search space among projects and by extracting more significant results by only considering well-maintained and engineered projects. This filtering process has been applied to approximately 312,137 Java projects (Allamanis and Sutton 2013), of which 53,703 projects were selected for the study. The following Figure 13.1 describes our data collection process.

As shown in Figure 13.1, we start with cloning every Java project to perform the static analysis. We scan only projects containing a POM file (step 1). Along with the cloned source code, we collect all its commits as well. For every commit, we record its information including the *commitID*, *commitDate*, *developerUsername*, *commitText*. We also keep track, for each commit, of all updated files. All this extracted data is saved on a database to facilitate its querying. After saving all projects information in the database, we chronologically scan, for each project, all its commits while comparing between the two POM files of two consecutive commits if a POM-related change is detected (step 2). Once an update on the POM file is detected, all associated libraries are shortlisted and then compared against the set of libraries in the previous POM file. It allows us to identify any added/removed library (step 3). For example, in Figure 13.4, when we compare libraries' changes between two commits, we find that *Junit* was removed and *testng* and *fest-assert-core* were added.

13.4.3 Detection of Library Evolution

By definition, a library is being used by a project if it is (1) recognized by the project as an external resource, and (2) there is at least one function of the library being used by one of the code elements belonging to the project. In order to collect the set of libraries used by any project, we rely on first

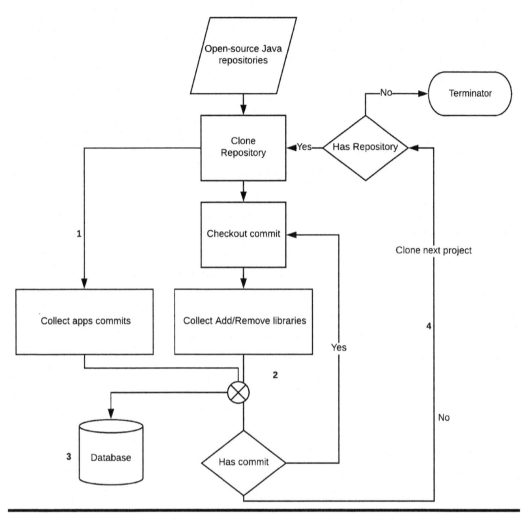

Figure 13.1 **Bird's-eye view of our data extraction process.**

analyzing each project POM file to identify all its dependencies to libraries. Second, we need to guarantee that at least one function belonging to the library is invoked in the project (through method calls, reflection, etc.). For this purpose, we parse the project source code while searching for any Java file (1) importing on its header at least one of libraries' API packages, and (2) at least inheriting one of its types or invoking one of its object's functions. Once a library is identified in the project, we scan all its commits and monitor library-related changes. These changes are then classified into the following categories that we have defined:

13.4.3.1 Library Upgrade

Just like any typical Java project, upgrading a library undergoes various possible forms of updates going from adding new classes and methods, updating existing functions, repackaging existing or newly added classes into new packages, remodularizing packages, etc. All these changes should first be reflected in the libraries name, and second, it typically should not affect, without notice,

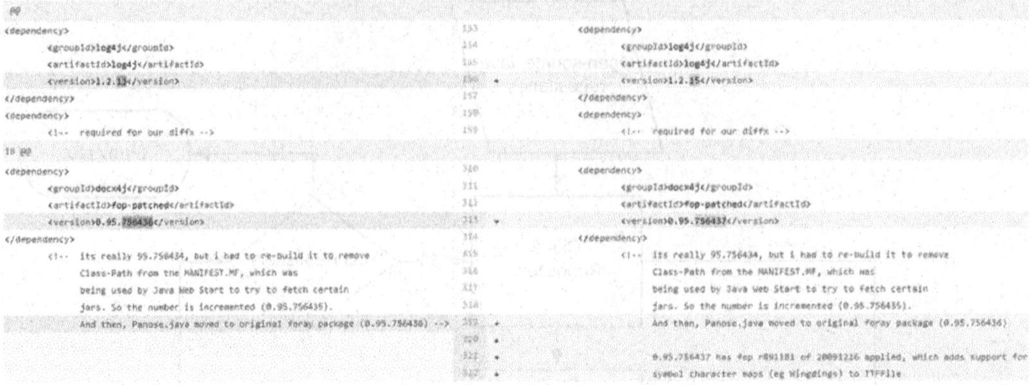

Figure 13.2 Upgrading log4j from 1.2.13 to 1.2.15 in the docx4j project.[3]

how the library is being utilized at the client software side. In this context, we have distinguished two possible main upgrades:

13.4.3.1.1 Incremental Version

The library's upgrade is reflected by incrementing its version. For example, in Figure 13.2, *docx4j*, a library for creating and managing *OpenXML* packages, has upgraded *log4j* from 1.2.13 to the newly patched 1.2.15. This change is usually reflected in the POM file of *docx4j* and has no impact on the class files using *log4j*.

13.4.3.1.2 Repackaging

Just like any regular Java project, libraries are subject to design improvement. This process includes restructuring class files into multiple packages based on various criteria including their coupling and cohesion, semantic similarity, collaboration in the functionality, etc. This process is known as software remodularization (Wiggerts 1997).

As shown in Figure 13.3, in the *Apache hive* project, the *jetty-all* library has been remodularized. The developers of *hive* have removed the dependency to the library's old ArtifactID labeled *jetty-all*, and they have included the newly repackaged version by including needed packages, e.g., *jetty-rewrite*, *jetty-server*, and *jetty-servlet*. The remodularization process is reflected in the library's artifactID, but the GroupID usually remains intact. Unlike incremental version upgrade, developers are required to update the headers of class files referencing the old library to reference any used package; this process requires searching, in each class file, for the suitable packages that contain used the library's classes and functions to include.

13.4.3.2 *Library Migration*

By definition, a library migration requires the replacement of one library by at least another one. Similar to the upgrade process, we distinguish two types of migrations:

---

[3] https://github.com/plutext/docx4j/commit/d1e28e6fbb3b5ed8974572920c0899254abbd49b.

```
71          <dependency>                                      71          <dependency>
72   -        <groupId>org.eclipse.jetty.aggregate</groupId>   72   +        <groupId>javax.servlet</groupId>
73   -        <artifactId>jetty-all</artifactId>               73   +        <artifactId>javax.servlet-api</artifactId>
74   -        <version>${jetty.version}</version>              74   +      </dependency>
75   -        <exclusions>                                     75   +      <dependency>
76   -          <exclusion>                                    76   +        <groupId>org.eclipse.jetty</groupId>
77   -            <groupId>javax.servlet</groupId>             77   +        <artifactId>jetty-rewrite</artifactId>
78   -            <artifactId>servlet-api</artifactId>         78   +      </dependency>
79   -          </exclusion>                                   79   +      <dependency>
80   -        </exclusions>                                    80   +        <groupId>org.eclipse.jetty</groupId>
                                                               81   +        <artifactId>jetty-server</artifactId>
                                                               82   +      </dependency>
                                                               83   +      <dependency>
                                                               84   +        <groupId>org.eclipse.jetty</groupId>
                                                               85   +        <artifactId>jetty-servlet</artifactId>
81          </dependency>                                     86          </dependency>
```

Figure 13.3   Upgrading jetty-all library in the Apache hive project.[4]

13.4.3.2.1 Instant Migration

The migration process is considered instant if the replacing library is added and replaced library is removed simultaneously. More practically, developers may perform the migration process on multiple files sequentially. This induces the existence of one or many commits containing code changes related to swapping dependencies between libraries. Once no dependency on the retired library exists, developers merely remove it from the POM file. In the following example exacted from *ps2-parser* project, we detected a migration from, i.e., the *junit* library to two replacing libraries labeled *testng* and *fest-assert-core*.

As illustrated in Figure 13.4, the project's dependency on *junit* has been completely removed, and instead, the developers introduced two new libraries, *testng* and *fest-assert-core* in the POM file. It is explained by the developers' intention of replacing the functionalities of *junit* by including introducing new objects and functions at the source code level, which explains the removal of all *junit* objects and functions from the project test files.

```
9            <dependency>                             9            <dependency>
10   -         <groupId>junit</groupId>               10   +         <groupId>org.testng</groupId>
11   -         <artifactId>junit</artifactId>         11   +         <artifactId>testng</artifactId>
12   -         <version>4.11</version>                12   +         <version>6.8</version>
13           </dependency>                            13          </dependency>
                                                      14   +       <dependency>
                                                      15   +         <groupId>org.easytesting</groupId>
                                                      16   +         <artifactId>fest-assert-core</artifactId>
                                                      17   +         <version>2.0M10</version>
                                                      18   +       </dependency>
```

Figure 13.4   Migrating from junit to testng and fest-assert-core in the ps2-parser project.[5]

---

[4] https://github.com/apache/hive/commit/191302cf4f9eae5ef51964bdab8d8e859292aa17.
[5] https://github.com/ssindelar/ps2-parser/commit/4e76b35f32011159db321e8a1540d03e004d25e8

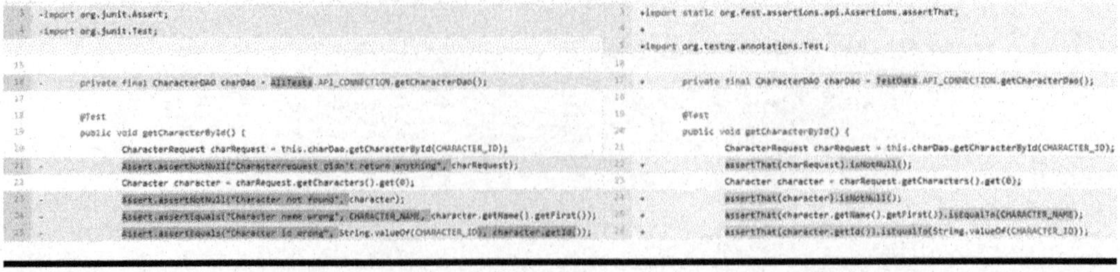

Figure 13.5   Replacing junit functions by fest-assert-core functions in the ps2-parser project.[5]

For example, Figure 13.5 shows how developers updated the class file *CharacterDaoTest.java* by removing the imported *junit* packages and replacing them with both *testng* and *fest-assert-core* imports. The *junit* invoked functions *Assert.assertNotNull()* and *Assert.assertEqual()* have been replaced, respectively, by *assertThat().isNotNull()* and *assertThat().isEqualTo()*, functions belonging to *fest-assert-core*. This example is interesting. It demonstrates that one or many functions can replace one or many functions. Such n-to-m possible migrations stand against the ease of automation of the migration process as it requires the developer's deep understanding of both source and target APIs. More precisely, the developer is required to correctly map each function from the replaced API to a possible candidate function(s), if they exist, in the replacing API. Coming back to the illustrative example in Figure 13.5, the *CurrencyDaoTest.java* class file reflects the migration changes. In this file, *junit*'s *Assert* object has been replaced by *testng*'s *AssertJUnit* object.

As shown in Figure 13.6, the migration process was more straightforward compared to the previous example shown in Figure 13.5; *testng* has provided a package that contains objects and functions that can immediately replace any *junit* objects and functions. It is explained by the *testng* developers' intention of encouraging developers to migrate to their library by providing them with a richer API package that contains means of easily replacing famous and popular competitor libraries like *junit*.

13.4.3.2.2 Delayed Migration

The migration is considered delayed if, in contrast with the instant migration, the retired library remains in the project POM file even if it no longer contributes to the project.

In the example shown in Figure 13.7, the developers included the new library *json* whose exception-handling object *JSONException* has replaced *JsonFormatException*, the default exception handler previously used. Even if the retired library was removed from the files' headers, the developers did not remove it from the project's POM file. The detection of such a situation tends

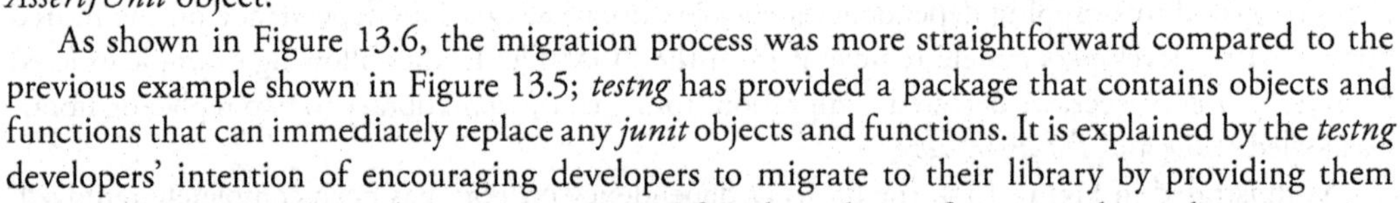

Figure 13.6   Replacing junit functions by to testng functions in the ps2-parser project.[5]

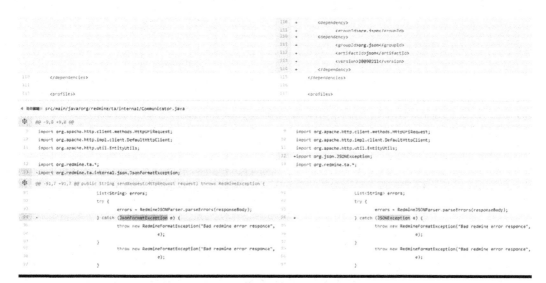

Figure 13.7 Replacing org.redmine.ta.internal.json functions by to org.jason:jason functions in the redmine-java-api project.

to be very tricky because it can be similar to simply adding a new library with new functionalities. We spot such situations only if the newly included library replaces at least one other library at the function level.

13.4.4 Detection of Candidate Library Migration

Unlike the detection of upgrades, the detection of migration process cannot be straightforward. As shown in Figure 13.7, one or multiple libraries can be replaced by one or multiple libraries. It sophisticates the identification of the exact library replacement(s), especially that multiple migrations may also occur at the same time (same set of commits) or in a delayed fashion. For this purpose, we rely on the heuristic of Teyton et al. (Teyton, Falleri et al. 2014), as shown in Figure 13.8, for the approximation of possible migrations.

Figure 13.8 gives the steps used to apply to heuristic to candidate migrations between libraries. A reminder that a candidate migration (1) should contain evidence of added and possibly removed libraries at the POM file, (2) and it should trace at least one function from the removed library that has been replaced by another function from the added library. Any pair of libraries satisfying these two conditions automatically qualifies for a potential match for migration.

Since multiples libraries can be added and removed simultaneously, we apply the following heuristic: *Every added library can be a candidate of a replacement for any removed library as long as there is at least one swap at the function level.* This allows us to detect migrations pairs as follows: We apply the Cartesian product (CP) between the set of added libraries and the set of removed libraries to generate every possible migration pair. It creates a potential link starting from a deleted library to all added libraries. Then, to verify which of these links is valid, we search the entire database for similar identified links. It allows us to calculate the number of occurrence of each link in similar migration contexts. Then we use this frequency as a voting system to champion one link over the remaining links and thus generate a final migration pair. Note that, in case of a tie between two links, they are both considered valid links, and so the migration pair will contain

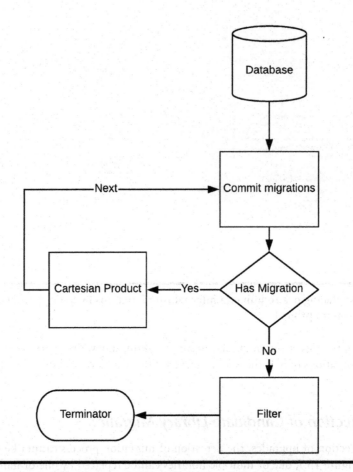

Figure 13.8 Overview of the library migration-detection heuristic.

one removed library and two or more added libraries. This voting system utilizes the knowledge extracted from similar migration scenarios (the same candidate added and removed libraries) to help in distinguishing pairs. Therefore, using a broader set of projects is strongly recommended to increase the accuracy of the voting system.

To illustrate the voting process, we consider the following sets: removedLibraries = [org.json, jmock, testing] and addedLibraries = [mockito, gson, junit]. We build an indirect graph between the two sets using the CP where the starting nodes are the removed libraries and the ending nodes are the added libraries. Figure 13.9, illustrates the resulting graph.

The weight of every edge is calculated based on the frequency of occurrence of such link in the entire set. In the example above, the occurrence of *org.json* moving to *gson* is equal to 12. After determining the weights, we normalize them by dividing each weight by the maximum weight initiated from one source library to all target libraries. For example, the maximum weight of an edge leaving from *org.json* is 12. Thus, the normalized values between of edges linking *org.json* to *Mockito*, *gson*, and *junit* are, respectively, $\frac{5}{12} = 0.4$, $\frac{12}{12} = 1$, and $\frac{12}{12} = 1$. After applying this process, we filter out all links not equal to 1. In case of a tie between two or more links, we consider all of them as a migration set. For example, the detection of the migration of *junit* to both *testng* and *fest-assert-core* in Figure 13.4 shows the tie between both edges of the graph containing *junit* as a starting node and *testng* and *fest-assert-core* as part of candidate ending nodes.

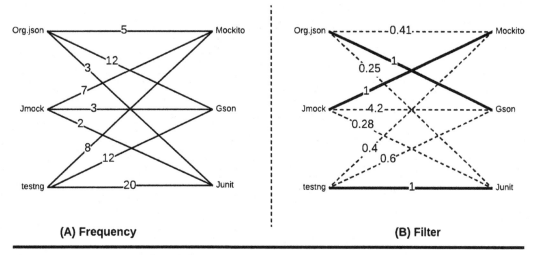

(A) Frequency   **(B) Filter**

Figure 13.9   Detection of candidate migration pairs.

13.5   Experimental Results

13.5.1 Studied Projects

This section presents the set of quantitative and comparative experiments related to answering the existence and evolution of Maven libraries in Java software systems. Our experiments were conducted on a set of libraries detected in the selected Java projects from (Allamanis and Sutton 2013). We did not focus on a limited set of popular libraries as it may give a biased view since these libraries are well-maintained by their developers. The data collection scripts along with the dataset that was part of our study are available for replication and extension purposes.[6]

13.5.2 RQ1. Existence of Libraries

We highlight the existence of libraries in the studied Java projects by exploring their usage throughout the history of the software maintenance. Once a library is detected on a given project, it is difficult to distinguish whether it is newly introduced or an existing library. Another challenge consists of distinguishing external libraries and internal software functions that are invoked as a library. In these situations, we applied a heuristic that clusters libraries first by their GroupID, then by their ArtifactID; we ignored all subgroups and version information, and only kept GroupID and ArtifactID as the main identifiers of the library. The limitation of this heuristic is its incapability to distinguish two versions of the same library in case they are identified by different GroupID and ArtifactID. However, this case is rare because subdomain changes are hardly occurring unless the library's ownership changes. Table 13.1 first gives an overview of the highlights of our findings in numbers.

Table 13.1 shows that the selected projects in this study are heavily dependent on third-party libraries. Also, the high number of detected upgrades and migrations show an extensive history of evolution. It was not surprising to observe that the number of upgrades, in general, is higher than the number of migrations, since developers tend to update their libraries more often, and the incremental version upgrade can sometimes be automated in contrast with repackaging upgrades

---

[6] http://sevis2017-replication.alruabye.net/

Table 13.1 Projects overview

Item	Count
Cloned Repositories	57,516
Scanned POM files	53,703
Libraries with unique ArtifactID	74,575
Libraries with unique control version	280,631
Commits Retrieved	9,583,718
Incremental version upgrades	8,879
Repackaging upgrades	298
Unique upgrades combined	9,177
Unique migrations combined	2,249
All upgrade instances	345,541
All migration instances	28,509

and migrations that tend to be manual. Roughly we found that, on average, the ratio commits of involving libraries is around 16% of the overall commits in all projects combined. Regardless of whether this ratio is considered low or high, it represents evidence of library-related maintenance activities that software engineers are responsible for. So, it is critical to account for such variants as they affect both software's functionalities from the user's perspective as well as requiring maintenance from the developer's perspective.

Figure 13.10 shows the top libraries mostly involved in all the commits involving library changes. These commits can be linked to any library-related activity such as adding a new one to including new library functions in the source code etc.

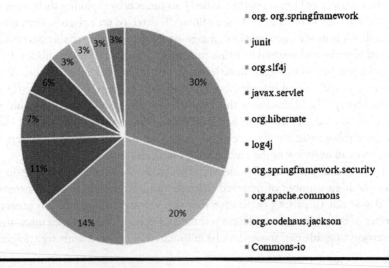

Figure 13.10 Top actively updated libraries.

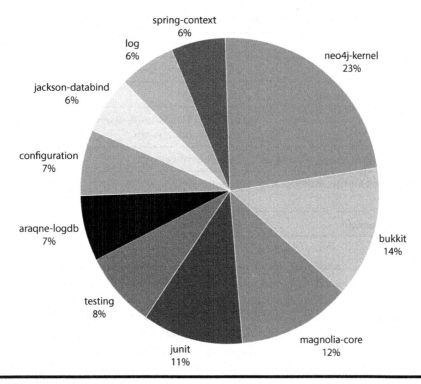

Figure 13.11   Topmost version-upgraded libraries.

We did expect testing related libraries such as *junit* or *testng* to be the highest in this ranking since they are heavily involved in various testing practices. Therefore, developers tend to pay more attention to keeping their APIs up to date and quickly move to any testing library that shows promise in helping them with building better test suites. Instead, *springframework* was found with the highest number of commits in client software systems. This library is demanded in J2EE-based projects, offering a wide variety of spring patterns that are useful for several architectures and frameworks.

Figure 13.11 enumerates the libraries with the highest update frequency. An actively updated library may be interpreted as a sign of a healthy service that is up to date from a compatibility perspective and lesser prone to bugs. On the other hand, with every update, besides the overhead of performing the physical update and any regression testing required on the source code afterward, there is always the chance of introducing behavioral or syntactic breaking changes. Developers need better strategies to quantify the pros and cons of evolving a library to better analyze the tradeoff and make a better decision; this explains why developers are sometimes reluctant towards library changes (Kula, German et al. 2015) (Kula, German et al. 2017).

13.5.3 RQ2. Evolution of Libraries

Table 13.2, contains the five most frequent remodularization instances detected, e.g., *pax-url-mvn* has been split into two packages namely *pax-logging-service, pax-logging-api*. This transformation has been spotted in 72 POM files. The remodularization process may also include merging existing packages, e.g., we detected that tomcat-tribes, *tomcat-el-api* and *tomcat-api,* had been replaced by *tomcat-embed-core.*

Table 13.2 Topmost-remodularized libraries

Library Name	Remodularized Library Name	Count
pax-url-mvn,	pax-logging-service, pax-logging-api	72
websocket-server, fcgi-server	jetty-home	49
Cditest	openwebbeans-impl, openwebbeans-jsf, openwebbeans-spi	30
tomcat-tribes, tomcat-el-api, tomcat-api	tomcat-embed-core	25
gshell-network, gshell-file, gshell-pref, gshell-artifact,	gshell-core	12
openwebbeans-openejb	test:cditest, cditest-owb	11

Table 13.3 has the cumulative count of all detected migration instances between two given libraries. We have conducted a manual analysis of the top-10 detected migrations; we observed that the highest-detected migration was a false positive. In fact, *jackson-mapper-asl* has been renamed to *jackson-databind*. Its detection as a migration was due to the simultaneous change of their GroupID from *org.codehaus.jackson* to *com.fasterxml.jackson.core*. In a similar context, it is difficult to detect such a false positive without an extensive manual validation, that is why previous studies have conducted qualitative analysis of all their findings to filter out any inconsistent migration (Teyton, Falleri et al. 2014). We also compared the results of our migration with Teyton et al. (Teyton, Falleri et al. 2014). The purpose of this comparison is to verify whether the results of Teyton et al. were specific to the set of projects under study or can be generalized across a larger set which proves the existence of migration trends. The comparison results are shown in Figure 13.12.

Based on Figure 13.12, we identified the same migration rules expect for (*org.json* moving to *gson*). This can be explained by the fact that we are using a larger set of both libraries and projects.

Table 13.3 Topmost-performed migrations

Source Library	Target Library	Count
jackson-mapper-asl	jackson-databind	344
log4j	slf4j	202
Junit	Testng	167
commons-logging	slf4j-api	144
commons-httpclient	Httpclient	132
Easymock	Mockito	115
xqj-api	Tagsoup	109
org.json	Gson	102
jersey-server	pax-logging-api, pax-logging-service	101
Contextmenu, refresher, confirmdialog	rxtx	98

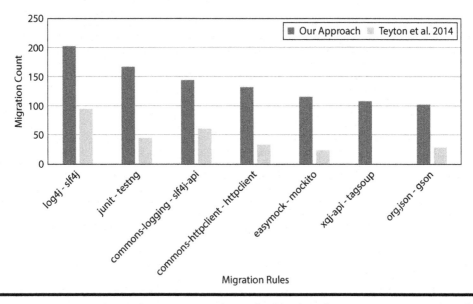

Figure 13.12 Comparison of top most performed migrations between Teyton et al. and our study.

However, both studies have identified *log4j* to *slf4j* as the most popular migration pair while they disagreed on the second-most popular pair. *Junit* to *testng* was ranked second in our study, while it was third in Teyton et al.'s ranking, whereas *commons-logging* to *slf4j-api* was second but in our study, it was third. The regency of our study gives a more recent snapshot of the all occurring migrations in general, but it does not still reflect the upcoming migration of trends. Since the migration process is symmetric, then it is hard to detect which libraries are gaining popularity and which libraries are losing developers' interest without considering the time factor. In general, we were able to, through this comparison, show that migration trends exist between a set of libraries, which are similar from a functional perspective. From a variability perspective, it is crucial to choose libraries that are being migrated to, rather than using a library that tends to be migrated away from. Although we have not investigated the motivation behind these migrations, since they are recorded in several independent projects, we empirically show the existence of a general agreement among developers, who made these migrations, on their decisions.

13.5.4 RQ3. Variability Degree of Libraries

The goal of measuring the variability degree is to show that library evolution, in general, involves various changes to the code using the functions offered by their APIs. In this context, while existing studies try to predict the types of changes accompanied with library evolution, our study aims to use the large set of detected upgrades/migrations to quantify the degree of these changes based on real-world scenarios. Such information can be valuable for developers who are seeking to upgrade libraries while reducing the change effort. Answering the third research question investigates whether the recorded migrations improve, in general, the variability of libraries. Therefore, we selected the topmost-performed migrations, and for each project that belongs to any migration rule, we calculate its VD. Then we create two sets of VD values that we plot, in Figure 13.13, to verify if the values of the target libraries are better than the source libraries.

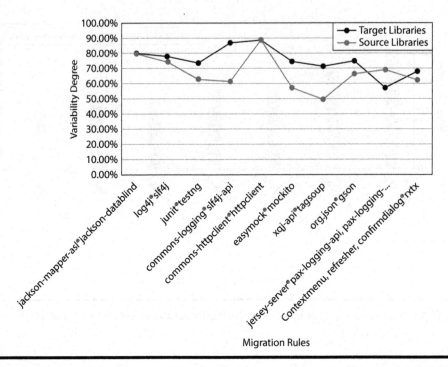

Figure 13.13 Comparison between VD values of source and target libraries involved in the topmost-performed migrations.

We notice in Figure 13.13 that the target libraries have a relatively higher VD value compared to source libraries. This applies to the majority of migrations such as *log4j* to *slf4j* and *junit* to *testng*. We noticed for two migration rules that the VD values, for both source and target libraries, were similar. This is explained by the fact that the source and target library are historically identical; they are being seen as different libraries since they are identified by a different GroupID and ArtifactID, as discussed in Section 5.3. Another outlying rule was the swapping of *jersey-server* by *pax-logging-api, pax-logging-service*. We applied the Mann-Whitney U test with *p*-value = 0.05, for the migrations rules we identified, and we could not find the difference between the values of two sets to be statistically significant. Thus, we plan to qualitatively analyze the detected migrations and filter out the false-positives since they negatively impact the statistical analysis by introducing identical values in both groups under comparison.

13.5.5 Discussion and Future Directions

Our quantitative study proves the existence of third-party libraries is an essential factor in the life cycle of the project. We have shown that libraries are subject to evolution by their own developers, which represents an extra maintenance effort from the perspective of client project developers. To reduce the overhead of maintaining libraries, it is important to account for their change. Thus, there is a need for identifying metrics that help rank libraries not only from the functional and nonfunctional perspective but also based on their impact on client-code changes. From that perspective, we developed a metric to measure the variability degree of previously evolved projects; such information is valuable for studies focusing on library recommendation (Thung, Lo et al. 2013) (Ouni, et al. 2017). Yet, the migration process is responsible for around 20% of the libraries' evolution, and it is challenging to automate. Our initial manual classification for the commits has revealed that feature enhancement stands as the primary motivation for developers to switch to a new library. Such decisions are hard to predict and so making the right library choice early in the software design remains minimal and the necessity to account for library migration remains valid. Therefore, we plan to automate the classification of evolved libraries' commits to reveal the reasons behind these changes. Understanding the developer's perspective when evolving libraries helps automate it.

13.6 Threats to Validity

In this section, we report the threats to the validity of our methodology (Wohlin, Runeson et al. 2012):

Internal Validity. The tools we build to collect commits and detect candidate upgrades and migrations may not be accurate and may exhibit false positives (wrong upgrades, incorrect migrations, detecting a migration as an upgrade) and false negatives (miss some upgrades, migrations). To mitigate this problem, we manually selected random commits from both upgrades and migrations, and we validated their correctness. We also confirmed that we were able to reproduce the same migrations found by previous existing studies (Teyton, Falleri et al. 2013). We only manually checked the most frequent migrations detected, and so, we will continue reviewing the remaining migrations and removing any identified false positives. Another way to mitigate this threat is to check if upgrades/migrations are explicitly-admitted by developers manually, but this approach, while guarantees correctness, cannot be scaled to the whole set of collected commits.

Another key limitation of this work is our assumption, when measuring the degree of variability, that developers make an effort to accommodate new functions only through code changes. Moreover, so, if there is any other type of effort that is not reflected in the source code, such as updating the software documentation, etc. it will not be considered by our metric. At the same time, our metric captures any library upgrade that prevents the client system from being syntactic-error free. Thus, any changes external to the source code may not necessarily introduce syntactic errors unless they are linked to the project configuration files. Furthermore, as part of our future work, we plan on conducting a qualitative analysis to understand better developers' perceptions of the changes they performed while upgrading their project libraries.

Another threat is related to detecting the functions of the libraries in the client code. We use a combination of syntactic and lexical analysis to identify functions belonging to the library's API. We assume that all functions are being called through libraries' APIs. If a function is being copy/pasted in the client code, we will not be able to consider it as part of the library.

We rely on Maven for detecting the evolution of libraries in general. This represents a limitation to our work, and we plan on analyzing other possible ways to automatically identify libraries in existing projects. In our study, we have not considered the intention of developers when evolving libraries, so it is hard to justify their choices regarding choosing an outdated library or replacing a known library with an unknown one (in terms of popularity). In our future investigation, we want to focus on developers' perceptions of changes. This will help us analyze how developers perceive variability in their choices by better understanding their motives when migrating between libraries.

Construct Validity. We report in this section the factors that may impact the measurements and metrics in reflecting real-world scenarios. When we have manually analyzed GitHub projects, we have noticed that few developers incorporate more than one project in the same repository, and with only one POM file that existing in a multi-project repository. This may interfere with our segment-detection algorithm since it may be searching for a migration that does not necessarily exist. Still, this does not affect our results, but we did discard these repositories from our analysis. Another principal threat to our work is the human validation of our results, mainly to verify the correctness of the found migrations, in general, and more particularly the function mappings. We plan, in the future, to implement many state-of-the-art, mining algorithms and perform a comparative analysis of their findings regarding function-level changes between libraries.

External Validity. In this study, we considered a broad set of projects that we believe represents a good spectrum of open-source Java projects. Although it may not represent commercial and closed-box projects, we expect our study to provide similar results if these projects do use the libraries we studied. To help in reproducing and extending this study, we carefully selected the set of Java projects to analyze. They were all available on GitHub; we also analyzed public libraries. We also publicly provided the dataset we collected in the form of a database that is easily queried to reproduce the results. Our approach can also be applied to closed-box and commercial tools as long as they maintain their libraries dependencies using Maven.

13.7 Conclusion and Future Work

In this chapter, we conducted an exploratory study of the existence and evolution of libraries as variants in a broad set of open-source Java projects. We identified the automation challenges linked to library upgrade and migration. Library upgrade is mainly triggered by library maintainers while library migration is a design choice performed by client software developers. To estimate the frequency of these changes, we have developed several collection tools, and we examined 53,703 projects to extract all their library-related changes. We classified these changes based on how they were performed in the project source files. We extended existing studies to detect candidate library migrations. We reported all our findings, and we compared some of them with results from previous studies.

Our main findings indicate the vast existence of library changes in software systems; these changes tend to be manual, requiring several interventions in multiple source files. This existence seems to be problematic for library variability, this explains the rapid growth of research in automating all aspects of library management starting from analyzing its evolution (Dig and Johnson 2006) (Xing and Stroulia 2007) (Qiu, Li et al. 2016), detecting API breaking changes (McDonnell, Ray et al. 2013) (Linares-Vásquez, Bavota et al. 2013), recommending API migrations (Nguyen, Nguyen et al. 2010) (Jezek, Dietrich et al. 2015) (Pandita, Taneja et al. 2016) (Ouni, et al. 2017), going to automating library migration (Teyton, Falleri et al. 2013) (Teyton, Falleri et al. 2014) (Pandita, Jetley et al. 2015). We want to contribute to all this ongoing research by providing this dataset of all detected library changes and their location in the project files. We plan to continue the refinement of our findings to build a coherent dataset that allows automation solutions to learn from it. Moreover, we plan on expanding our dataset with including more projects. We also plan (1) on using information-retrieval techniques to automatically classify commits, relevant to migration sets, in order to understand developers' perception and motivation, (2) analyzing the impact of these migrations on class files' proneness to bugs, and (3) comparing the various state-of-the-art existing recommendation approaches in terms of their ability to replicate existing decisions of manually performed migrations. Since our current study indicates the substantial existence of library migrations, we can quickly identify the actual developers who performed them. As part of our future directions, we will also survey Java developers to gauge their opinions about how they account for variability when choosing libraries for their projects.

References

Allamanis, M. and C. Sutton (2013). Mining source code repositories at massive scale using language modeling. Proceedings of the 10th Working Conference on Mining Software Repositories, San Francisco, CA, USA, IEEE Press: 207-216.

Allix, K., T. F. Bissyandé, J. Klein and Y. Le Traon (2016). Androzoo: Collecting millions of android apps for the research community. Mining Software Repositories (MSR), 2016 IEEE/ACM 13th Working Conference on, Austin, TX, USA, IEEE: 468-471.

Bogart, C., C. Kästner and J. Herbsleb (2015). When it breaks, it breaks: How ecosystem developers reason about the stability of dependencies. Automated Software Engineering Workshop (ASEW), 2015 30th IEEE/ACM International Conference on, Lincoln, NE, USA, IEEE: 86-89.

Cetina, C., P. Giner, J. Fons and V. Pelechano (2009). "Autonomic computing through reuse of variability models at runtime: The case of smart homes." *Computer* 42(10).

Coplien, J., D. Hoffman and D. Weiss (1998). "Commonality and variability in software engineering." *IEEE software* 15(6): 37-45.

Cossette, B. E. and R. J. Walker (2012). Seeking the ground truth: a retroactive study on the evolution and migration of software libraries. Proceedings of the ACM SIGSOFT 20th International Symposium on the Foundations of Software Engineering, Cary, North Carolina, ACM: 1-11.

De Roover, C., R. Lammel and E. Pek (2013). Multi-dimensional exploration of api usage. Program Comprehension (ICPC), 2013 IEEE 21st International Conference on, San Francisco, CA, USA, IEEE: 152-161.

Deb, K., A. Pratap, S. Agarwal and T. Meyarivan (2002). "A fast and elitist multiobjective genetic algorithm: NSGA-II." *IEEE Transactions on Evolutionary Computation* 6(2): 182-197.

Dig, D. and R. Johnson (2006). "How do APIs evolve? A story of refactoring." *Journal of Software: Evolution and Process* 18(2): 83-107.

Galster, M., D. Weyns, D. Tofan, B. Michalik and P. Avgeriou (2014). "Variability in software systems—a systematic literature review." *IEEE Transactions on Software Engineering* 40(3): 282-306.

Gokhale, A., V. Ganapathy and Y. Padmanaban (2013). Inferring likely mappings between APIs. Software Engineering (ICSE), 2013 35th International Conference on, IEEE: 82-91.

Gousios, G. and D. Spinellis (2012). GHTorrent: GitHub's data from a firehose. Proceedings of the 9th IEEE Working Conference on Mining Software Repositories, Zurich, Switzerland, IEEE Press: 12-21.

Ishio, T., R. G. Kula, T. Kanda, D. M. German and K. Inoue (2016). Software ingredients: Detection of third-party component reuse in Java software release. Mining Software Repositories (MSR), 2016 IEEE/ACM 13th Working Conference on, Austin, TX, USA, IEEE: 339-350.

Jezek, K., J. Dietrich and P. Brada (2015). "How Java APIs break—an empirical study." *Information and Software Technology* 65: 129-146.

Kabinna, S., C.-P. Bezemer, W. Shang and A. E. Hassan (2016). Logging library migrations: a case study for the apache software foundation projects. Proceedings of the 13th International Conference on Mining Software Repositories, Austin, Texas, ACM: 154-164.

Kula, R. G., D. M. German, T. Ishio and K. Inoue (2015). Trusting a library: A study of the latency to adopt the latest maven release. Software Analysis, Evolution and Reengineering (SANER), 2015 IEEE 22nd International Conference on, IEEE: 520-524.

Kula, R. G., D. M. German, A. Ouni, T. Ishio and K. Inoue (2017). "Do developers update their library dependencies?" *Empirical Software Engineering* 23(1): 1-34.

La Rosa, M., W. M. van der Aalst, M. Dumas and A. H. Ter Hofstede (2009). "Questionnaire-based variability modeling for system configuration." *Software and Systems Modeling* 8(2): 251-274.

Linares-Vásquez, M. (2014). Supporting evolution and maintenance of android apps. Companion Proceedings of the 36th International Conference on Software Engineering, Hyderabad, India, ACM: 714-717.

Linares-Vásquez, M., G. Bavota, C. Bernal-Cárdenas, M. Di Penta, R. Oliveto and D. Poshyvanyk (2013). Api change and fault proneness: A threat to the success of android apps. Proceedings of the 2013 9th joint meeting on foundations of software engineering, Saint Petersburg, Russia, ACM: 477-487.

Linares-Vásquez, M., G. Bavota, M. Di Penta, R. Oliveto and D. Poshyvanyk (2014). How do api changes trigger stack overflow discussions? a study on the android sdk. proceedings of the 22nd International Conference on Program Comprehension, Hyderabad, India, ACM: 83-94.

McDonnell, T., B. Ray and M. Kim (2013). An empirical study of api stability and adoption in the android ecosystem. Software Maintenance (ICSM), 2013 29th IEEE International Conference on, Eindhoven, Netherlands, IEEE: 70-79.

McMillan, C., M. Grechanik and D. Poshyvanyk (2012). Detecting similar software applications. Software Engineering (ICSE), 2012 34th International Conference on, Zurich, Switzerland, IEEE: 364-374.

McMillan, C., M. Grechanik, D. Poshyvanyk, Q. Xie and C. Fu (2011). Portfolio: finding relevant functions and their usage. Proceedings of the 33rd International Conference on Software Engineering, New York, NY, USA, ACM: 111-120.

Munaiah, N., S. Kroh, C. Cabrey and M. Nagappan (2017). "Curating GitHub for engineered software projects." *Empirical Software Engineering* 22(6): 3219-3253.

Nguyen, H. A., T. T. Nguyen, G. Wilson Jr, A. T. Nguyen, M. Kim and T. N. Nguyen (2010). A graph-based approach to API usage adaptation. ACM Sigplan Notices, New York, NY, USA, ACM: 302-321.

Ouni, A., R. G. Kula, M. Kessentini, T. Ishio, D. M. German and K. Inoue (2017). "Search-based software library recommendation using multi-objective optimization." *Information and Software Technology* 83: 55-75.

Pandita, R., R. Jetley, S. Sudarsan, T. Menzies and L. Williams (2017). "TMAP: Discovering relevant API methods through text mining of API documentation." *Journal of Software: Evolution and Process* 29(12): 18-45.

Pandita, R., R. P. Jetley, S. D. Sudarsan and L. Williams (2015). Discovering likely mappings between APIs using text mining. Source Code Analysis and Manipulation (SCAM), 2015 IEEE 15th International Working Conference on, Bremen, Germany, IEEE: 231-240.

Pandita, R., K. Taneja, L. Williams and T. Tung (2016). ICON: inferring temporal constraints from natural language API descriptions. Software Maintenance and Evolution (ICSME), 2016 IEEE International Conference on, Raleigh, NC, USA, IEEE: 378-388.

Qiu, D., B. Li and H. Leung (2016). "Understanding the API usage in Java." *Information and Software Technology* 73: 81-100.

Shatnawi, A., A. Seriai and H. Sahraoui (2015). Recovering architectural variability of a family of product variants. International Conference on Software Reuse, Springer: 17-33.

Tempero, E., C. Anslow, J. Dietrich, T. Han, J. Li, M. Lumpe, H. Melton and J. Noble (2010). The Qualitas Corpus: A curated collection of Java code for empirical studies. Software Engineering Conference (APSEC), 2010 17th Asia Pacific, Sydney, NSW, Australia, IEEE: 336-345.

Teyton, C., J.-R. Falleri and X. Blanc (2013). Automatic discovery of function mappings between similar libraries. Reverse Engineering (WCRE), 2013 20th Working Conference on, Koblenz, Germany, IEEE: 192-201.

Teyton, C., J.-R. Falleri, M. Palyart and X. Blanc (2014). "A study of library migrations in Java." *Journal of Software: Evolution and Process* 26(11): 1030-1052.

Thung, F., D. Lo and J. Lawall (2013). Automated library recommendation. Reverse Engineering (WCRE), 2013 20th Working Conference on, Koblenz, Germany, IEEE: 182-191.

Thung, F., R. J. Oentaryo, D. Lo and Y. Tian (2017). "WebAPIRec: Recommending Web APIs to Software Projects via Personalized Ranking." *IEEE Transactions on Emerging Topics in Computational Intelligence* 1(3): 145-156.

Van Gurp, J., J. Bosch and M. Svahnberg (2001). On the notion of variability in software product lines. Software Architecture, 2001. Proceedings. Working IEEE/IFIP Conference on, Amsterdam, Netherlands, IEEE: 45-54.

Wiggerts, T. A. (1997). Using clustering algorithms in legacy systems remodularization. Reverse Engineering, 1997. Proceedings of the Fourth Working Conference on, Amsterdam, Netherlands, Netherlands, IEEE: 33-43.

Wohlin, C., P. Runeson, M. Höst, M. C. Ohlsson, B. Regnell and A. Wesslén (2012). Experimentation in software engineering, Springer Science & Business Media.

Wu, W., F. Khomh, B. Adams, Y.-G. Guéhéneuc and G. Antoniol (2016). "An exploratory study of api changes and usages based on apache and eclipse ecosystems." *Empirical Software Engineering* 21(6): 2366-2412.

Xavier, L., A. Brito, A. Hora and M. T. Valente (2017). "Historical and impact analysis of API breaking changes: A large-scale study". Software Analysis, Evolution and Reengineering (SANER), 2017 IEEE 24th International Conference on, Klagenfurt, Austria, IEEE: 138-147.

Xing, Z. and E. Stroulia (2007). "API-evolution support with Diff-CatchUp." *IEEE Transactions on Software Engineering* 33(12): 818-836.

Yu, S. and C. J. Woodard (2008). Innovation in the programmable web: Characterizing the mashup ecosystem. International Conference on Service-Oriented Computing, Berlin, Heidelberg, Springer: 136-147.

Zhong, H., T. Xie, L. Zhang, J. Pei and H. Mei (2009). MAPO: Mining and recommending API usage patterns. European Conference on Object-Oriented Programming, Berlin, Heidelberg, Springer: 318-343.

Zhou, J. and R. J. Walker (2016). API deprecation: a retrospective analysis and detection method for code examples on the web. Proceedings of the 2016 24th ACM SIGSOFT International Symposium on Foundations of Software Engineering, ACM: 266-277.

Chapter 14

Evolving Variability Requirements of IoT Systems

Luis Chumpitaz[a], Andrei Furda[a], and Seng Loke[b]

[a]Science and Engineering Faculty, Information Systems, Services Science, Queensland University of Technology, Brisbane, Australia
[b]Deakin University, School of Information Technology, Victoria, Australia

14.1 Introduction

The Internet of Things (IoT) is the network of globally interconnected smart devices, sensors and machines that enables them to communicate and operate with real-time information. The IoT integration of devices, systems, services and networks provides the means to overcome the limitations of local systems, leading to a new generation of variability-intensive systems and ecosystems with unlimited application opportunities and emerging new requirements. It is interesting to note that the term IoT was first introduced by Kevin Ashton in 1999 in the context of supply chain management (SCM) [30], and it has been extended to a variety of applications. For example, in the near future, road sensors will measure traffic flow, air pollution sensors will measure the air quality, and traffic management systems will guide vehicles accordingly to optimize traffic flow and minimize air pollution in smart cities.

In this chapter, we first provide an overview of IoT definitions and state-of-the-art technologies and applications of IoT systems. We then introduce the notion of variability as it has been traditionally considered in the context of software engineering, software product line engineering and more recently software architecture. The motivations for analysing, modelling and managing variability in software systems—minimising deployment timeframe and cost, controlling system complexity, maximising component reuse and genericity—apply equally well to IoT systems, however the scale and complexity of such implementations requires a more thorough understanding of the potential range of variation points and deployment alternatives. With this aim in mind, we analyse the variability requirements of both current and future IoT systems at multiple levels based on the underpinning technology stack. We consider this "stack" to comprise five major elements, all of which are required to deploy a candidate IoT system: (1) the coordinating application, (2) the Cloud platform on which it is hosted, (3) the connectivity gateway interlinks the various system components, (4) the software which operates individual IoT devices, and (5) the hardware on which individual IoT devices are deployed.

To better understand the potential range of variation points and configuration considerations at each level in the IoT stack, we analyse each level from a range of distinct perspectives based on the viewpoints adopted by the Zachman Framework [69, 56], a widely utilised enterprise ontology that supports the capture and analysis of the structure and operation of organisations in terms of their core architectures and constituent applications, resources and artifacts. There are six orthogonal viewpoints embodied in the Zachman Framework: What (Data), How (Function), Who (People), When (Time) and Why (Motivation). In the context of variability, we apply the "What" dimension in terms of variability required to manage the different formats, types, and sample rates of data that is collected, analysed, and shared between the IoT system components. The "How" dimension is applied in terms of the required variability of functional interfaces between the IoT system components. The "Where" dimension covers the variability in terms of network characteristics, while the "Who" dimension addresses variability in terms of trusted devices, trusted user roles, and trusted applications that provide safety-critical data. The "When" dimension addresses temporal variability characteristics such as real-time constraints, sample rates of sensors, and network clocking. Finally, the "Why" dimension addresses variability in terms of the application domain, quality of service, service-level agreements and hardware options that allow an IoT system to be integrated in a variety of application scenarios.

This analysis and discussion are aimed at helping and guiding practitioners during the design and realization of future-oriented IoT-based variability-intensive systems.

The remainder of this chapter is structured as follows. Section 14.2 presents the three views of IoT and an overview of state-of-the-art IoT technologies, applications and trends. Section 14.3 discusses related work and the range and impact of variability requirements of future IoT systems, under the dimensions of the Zachman Framework. Section 14.4 concludes discussing the increasing impact of future IoT systems and the emerging requirements of privacy, security and ethics.

14.2 State-of-the-Art IoT Technologies and Applications

This section explains the term IoT, the three views of IoT (things-oriented, Internet-oriented, semantic-oriented) and presents an overview of significant state-of-the-art IoT technologies, applications and future trends that will lead to unprecedented requirements of the future systems with respect to variability.

14.2.1 Internet of Things (IoT)

IoT interconnects devices that share data in real time. These devices are equipped with sensors, actuators, displays or any computational element that can be embedded in the everyday objects that people interact with. These devices share sensed environment information that can be used for real-time decision making [30]. The purpose of collecting this data is to enable intelligent decision making, to predict future events and to improve the efficiency and productivity of systems [14]. Atzori et al. [7] note that three visions define IoT: things-oriented vision, Internet-oriented vision and semantic-oriented vision. It is expected that the highest potential of IoT is likely to be achieved in domains at the intersection of the three visions [30].

Things-oriented vision regards IoT systems as a group of objects that belong to a network and can be identified using, for example, radio-frequency identification (RFID) [7]. Xia et al. [66] define IoT as the "networked interconnection of everyday objects, which are often equipped with ubiquitous intelligence" [66]. The things-oriented IoT vision divides the IoT components into assets and devices. An asset is a property or piece of equipment that generates revenue or improves the company's operations, whereas an IoT device is a sensor or an actuator that is typically deployed on the assets [13]. The Internet-oriented vision is the Smart Objects Alliance's view of IoT, based on the Internet Protocol stack [7]. Zanella et al. [70] define IoT as a set of communicating objects that are an integral part of the Internet. Gubbi et al. [30] include elements from both things-oriented and Internet-oriented visions. They define IoT as an "interconnection of sensing and actuating devices providing the ability to share information across platforms through a unified framework, developing a common operating picture for enabling innovative applications" [30].

The *semantic-oriented vision* emphasizes the increasing number of inter-connected devices and the semantic technologies that will play a key role to appropriately manage the resulting complexity [7]. Semantic technologies are defined as "the encoding of meaning separately from data files, content files, and application codes to enable machines as well as people to understand, share, and reason with them at execution time" [39]. Examples of semantic technologies include data mining, natural language processing, semantic search technologies and ontologies [43].

The semantic-oriented IoT vision leads to big data, due to the high amount of data the devices collect and share. IoT devices with embedded sensors and actuators are the source of large volumes of data, delivered at high speed, and therefore exceeding the capacities and bandwidths of typical legacy systems [42, 5]. Cai et al. [15] note that big data is characterised by: (1) heterogeneous data sources; (2) large and increasing numbers of connected sensors; (3) low-level, semantically weak data; (4) low accuracy of data [15].

14.2.2 IoT Technologies

In this section, we present some of the most relevant technologies used to implement IoT systems.

Radio-frequency identification (RFID) is a technology for identifying physical objects using wireless communication capable computer chips (so-called 'tags') that allow automatic identification of the objects they are attached to [36, 30]. Two types of tags are common: active and passive tags. Passive tags use the power of a reading device's signal, while active tags can actively initiate communication [30]. The low cost of RFID makes it attractive for business and industrial applications, for example for optimizing processes through accurate inventory data [7, 68].

Wireless sensor networks (WSN) consist of intelligent sensors used to collect, process and communicate data in a variety of environments [30]. WSN can be integrated with RFID, enabling the development of powerful IoT applications for industrial environments [68].

Ubiquitous computing integrates technology into everyday life [30]. Weiser et al. [65] define ubiquitous computing as a "physical world richly and invisibly interwoven with sensors, actuators, displays, and computational elements, embedded seamlessly in the everyday objects of our lives and connected through a continuous network" [65]. Ubiquitous computing is enabled by smart devices that are capable of analysing data for decision making. It is based on communication and integration of different information systems for real-time data management [14]. Examples of such smart devices are smart phones, smart wristwatches and health-monitoring devices (e.g., Fitbit).

Multi-access edge computing (MEC) is an ecosystem that enables information technology and cloud-computing capabilities at the edge of a radio access network (RAN). RAN is defined as the section of the network that is shared by all devices in an IoT network and that is closest to the end-user [35]. It provides an environment with low-latency, high-bandwidth and real-time access to radio and network analytics [59]. MEC is based on the idea of hosting applications on the network edge, assuming that this is the closest possible location to service consumers [18].

One of the main advantages of MEC is computation offloading, allowing devices with limited computation resources to offload a certain intensive task to a Cloud environment [59, 50]. MEC can be considered as one of the key enablers of IoT, providing scalable storage and processing resources, fast response times to user requests, or delivering new services [59]. For example, in a smart environment, such as a smart city, it is possible to locate wanted or missing people by analysing the information from the CCTV or police patrol cameras. With the use of MEC, a face-recognition algorithm can be run at the edge of the network which will avoid overloading the main server [59].

AWS Greengrass is an Amazon Web Services offering for building applications that integrate edge devices. These are simplified devices typically used in an IoT system that are usually designed to perform a single function [16]. AWS collects and analyses data from the closest source of information and connects them to the Cloud, allowing devices to securely communicate with each other. AWS Greengrass allows local (on-device) code execution, secure messaging, data caching and synchronization capabilities for all interconnected devices, including not-always-connected mode [2].

14.2.3 IoT Applications

The application of IoT is revolutionizing industries by connecting machines, allowing collaborative automation between machines, and optimizing industrial processes [46]. Watteyne et al. [64] note that this revolution takes place through ubiquitous devices with low-cost sensors and actuators that operate autonomously and connect to the Internet through low-power wireless technologies.

Supply chain management (SCM) was the first application domain of IoT, as originally introduced by Kevin Ashton in 1999 [30]. One of the main effects of integrating a supply chain with IoT is the constant information sharing between every entity that is part of it: people, machines and products [45]. The objective of information sharing in the supply chain is to improve products, services and consumer experience, without affecting security [5]. IoT supports SCM processes in sourcing, production and distribution, which enables suppliers and manufacturers to share real-time information and make decisions based on real up-to-date inventory levels [45]. Manufacturers receive accurate and up-to-date information on stock levels, which enables them to avoid over- or under-production, saving potentially estimated $1 trillion per year [10, 45].

RFID is used in supply-chain management to identify objects and to improve tracking and traceability throughout the supply chain [67]. Tracking is the ability to follow a specific product or group of products from the upstream to the downstream of the supply chain. On the other hand, traceability is the ability to identify the path of a specific unit or group of products from the downstream to the upstream of the supply chain. The information flow in a supply chain is enhanced by real-time monitoring and control [67]. Tracking the quality of the products during transportation can only be achieved through IoT. Machines involved in this process and those that are part of the production process can be tracked to predict failure rates and to perform preventative maintenance before they break [45].

MEC is suitable to connect vehicles and moving IoT devices, through broadband mobile networks. MEC is therefore used in supply chain management to track goods during transportation. Smart transportation applications can be supported through IoT, by collecting information about road vehicles to optimize road traffic, and to monitor the transportation of freight containers and goods [7, 10, 30, 53]. In the near future, IoT will be used in autonomous vehicle systems to detect pedestrians, obstacles, traffic lanes, other vehicles and to make real-time driving decisions [68, 3, 25, 27].

Industrial IoT supports the optimization of industrial manufacturing and production processes by allowing to monitor parts and products throughout the entire lifecycle, from production to disposal, from engineering, over sales, to after-market services [10, 13]. This development will lead to innovative applications for industrial systems, such as cyber-physical production systems with optimised equipment and operations, remote control and management of equipment, prediction of service activities, remote diagnostics, optimised field service and provision of information and data-driven services [32]. Industrial IoT (IIoT) has the following characteristics: (1) interconnected smart devices are pervasive with unpredictable inputs, requiring human intervention if critical processes depend on them [34]; (2) IIoT smart services allow a vertical and horizontal integration of value chains [44]; (3) IIoT systems resemble open and distributed systems that concurrently process a high amount of information [34]; (4) due to the distributed nature of IIoT, such systems are susceptible to security threats, for example by exposing the entire system to security threats if the security of only one device is breached [34, 44].

Smart environments integrate IoT in houses and offices to save energy, improve security, and connect and control home devices [7, 53, 30]. Smart cities rely on IoT to improve the quality of services for citizens and to reduce the cost of public administration [70]. Such applications include, for example, the monitoring of structural health of buildings, the optimization of waste collection and recycling processes; control of smart lighting; air quality information systems, noise monitoring, traffic monitoring and optimization of vehicle parking [70]. In Europe, the FP7 Smart Santander project aims to deploy an IoT infrastructure in several cities [53]. China has announced IoT-based water monitoring, smart traffic and building management in Beijing and Shanghai [53]. U.S. and Canadian cities are building smart grid and water pipeline infrastructures [53].

14.3 Variability Requirements of IoT Systems

This section presents a holistic multidimensional view of variability requirements for future IoT systems. By applying the Zachman Framework [69, 56], we elaborate a comprehensive analysis of the range of potential variation points in IoT systems. It is important to note that concrete implementations of IoT systems might only require a subset of the variability dimensions identified here.

In the following subsections, we first present an overview of related work, followed by our analysis, classification and guidance for practitioners.

14.3.1 Related Work

The concepts of *variability* and *commonality* in software [20] have long been recognised as key contributors to the development of scalable and configurable software systems [17]. Commonalities across software artifacts provide the basis for reuse and replication in multiple distinct contexts [22]. Variation points in software systems identify areas of software functionality or behaviour, where alternative possible realisations are possible, and a specific approach must be selected and implemented [31]. Such variation points provide the basis for software configuration enabling common system functionality to be tailored to specific operational needs [8]. The concept of configurable functionality triggered the emergence of the software product-family engineering domain [52, 58, 9, 1, 63] which sought to leverage the potential opportunity through the development and evolution of large-scale commercial software products. To support these efforts, a range of variability modelling and management techniques were developed [38, 12, 21, 62, 55, 54, 51]. There has also been foundational work developing a theoretical basis for variability [40, 28, 17] and cataloguing the range of alternate realisation strategies [58, 6, 19]. More recently, the impact of this work has extended beyond the software product-family domain, and variability concepts have been harnessed in a range of related areas including ambient intelligent middleware [24], web service-based systems [57], legacy software assets [41], Software-as-a-Service (SaaS) applications [4], mobile services [37], and enterprise architecture [49].

Galster et al. [29] present a systematic literature review on software variability. Heymans et al. [33] observe that variability is present in every modern system, allowing systems to meet new customer requirements or to change the usage context without redeveloping entirely new systems. However, certain requirements need to be considered as a concept or as methods in order to make changes in IoT-based variability-intensive systems. These include, for example, dynamic software product lines, FCORE, machine learning and a regulatory algorithm.

Dynamic software product lines (DSPLs) realise runtime adaptation in cases when changes can be anticipated [47]. This means that certain changes in the code of different software products will enable the activation or deactivation of certain features in changing contexts.

FCORE is a model-based approach that extends DSPLs and allows the coordination between different variability-intensive systems [47]. FCORE's objective is to find the correct configuration for each system to achieve optimal satisfaction. This is very useful since IoT systems operate in Cloud environments and consist of various sub-systems, where each sub-system has its own adaptability rules. These systems can be successfully coordinated using FCORE models [47].

Machine learning can be applied to infer constraints to change the configuration of variability-intensive systems, especially in product lines. This is achieved by randomly generating different products maintaining their resolution model, classifying them and using these models to discover combinations that make the current configuration invalid or unviable [60].

Methods for managing the variability of feature selection are also required. Meyer et al. [48] propose a regulatory algorithm, called RGA. It consists of two components: a regulatory vector and a structural vector. Regulatory vectors include genes that will control structural genes by determining their position in the vector, by switching them on and off or by defining a specific weight for their connections [48].

Tomlein and Gronbaek [61] propose a model for IoT application deployment, that includes semantic annotations and semantic reasoning. The proposed model is capable of handling deployment variability, application context variability, and functionality variability.

14.3.2 Dimensions of Variability in IoT Systems

For the purposes of characterising the scope of an IoT system, we consider the five main elements in its operational "stack" (Figure 14.1): coordinating application, cloud platform, connectivity gateway, device software and device hardware. This is analogous to the major operational elements proposed in the IoT system context by reference architectures such as IoT-A [11] and ETSI M2M standard [23].

The purpose of these elements is as follows. The overall *coordinating application* or *service* dictates the overall system operation and value delivery. The *cloud platform* on which the application is deployed may itself be comprised of a number of distinct server platforms. The *connectivity gateway* facilitates the communication between the coordinating application and the various IoT *devices*.

There are two distinct areas of interest in the individual device: *device software* which controls the operation of individual IoT devices (and indeed may vary in scope and capability accordance

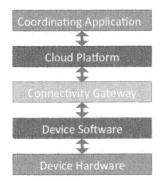

Figure 14.1 Elements of the IoT 'stack', arrows indicating dependencies.

with the needs of specific devices) and *device hardware* which supports the requirements of individual IoT nodes and may include elements such as sensors (e.g., air pollution sensor), actuators (e.g., traffic light controller), tags, etc.

To characterise the spectrum of static and dynamic variation points that are relevant in the context of IoT Systems, we delineate the range of potential variation points across two dimensions (Table 14.1): (1) the range of domain elements that comprise an IoT-based information system and (2) the relevant perspective or viewpoint to which they apply (i.e., the variability dimensions).

We characterise each variation dimension of IoT systems from six distinct viewpoints in accordance with the architectural perspectives identified by the Zachman Framework [69, 56]. By considering individual elements of the IoT stack (Figure 14.1) from a specific viewpoint, a range of orthogonal variation points can be identified.

Table 14.1 summarizes the range of variation points in terms of IoT stack elements: Coordinating Application, Cloud Platform, Connectivity Gateway, Device software and hardware. The colours denote the logical processing layers (i.e., row 1 and 2 denote server-side processing aspects, row 3 the communication layer, and row 4 and 5 denote IoT device aspects). By applying the Zachman Framework, each of these leads to a range of finer-grained considerations in terms of data, function, network, people, time and motivation. The following subsections elaborate on the variability requirements for each element of the IoT stack.

14.3.2.1 Coordinating Application Variability

The coordinating application variability (Row 1 in Table 14.1) needs to be addressed in terms of data, for example by integrating multiple supported data formats through message transformation patterns. Furthermore, this includes implementing different data persistence models, for example considering IoT devices with and without persistent storage. Data persistence affects the statefulness of application components running on such devices. Variable data security measures need to consider data that could be provided by untrusted sources. The aggregation of data from trusted and untrusted sources needs to be considered through security policies. Finally, the CAP theorem aspects (i.e., consistency, availability, network partitioning) should be considered with respect to data.

Functional variability is typically addressed through process and software configurations, such as enabling or disabling of specific functions or features, and context-specific process flow (re-)configuration. This can be done statically, or dynamically at runtime.

Network variability enables an IoT application to adapt to location-specific requirements, for example to enable or disable features depending on the user's location. This can be implemented

Table 14.1   IoT variability points in the context of the Zachman Framework [69]

IoT stack Element / Variability Dimension	What? (Data)	How? (Function)	Where? (Network)	Who? (People)	When? (Time)	Why (Motivation)
Coordinating Application	App-level data format persistence aggregation security	Process configuration Software configuration	User Interface Client software	User privileges User profile	Device interaction timing & protocol	Application goals
Cloud Platform	OS configuration	OS processes	Network interface configuration Firewall configuration	Security profiles	Program and service execution calendar (cron)	Platform SLAs
Connectivity Gateway	Data transport format	Interface format Supported bindings	Network configuration	Network subnet configuration & recognized devices	Network clocking	Network QoS
Device Software	Device software config.	Device OS firmware software configuration	Network interface configuation	Software privileges	Program & service execution calendar (cron)	Device SLAs
Device Hardware	Device OS system configuration	Device hardware configuration	Network settings	Security hardware profiles	Device clocking & synchronization	Device hardware choice

through server-side or client-side variation points in the configurations of the user interface and client software (e.g., multi-tenancy requirements [26]).

In the "People" dimension, user privileges, roles and profiles affect the variability in terms of security, privacy and ethics. Device interaction timing and interaction protocol variability needs to be addressed for example by the system's real-time constraints, for example by rejecting obsolete sensor data. Finally, the application variability in terms of motivation goals allows its usage in different domains, for example by allowing an IoT application to be deployed in a school or in a hospital environment.

14.3.2.2 Cloud Platform Variability

The Cloud platform variability (Row 2 in Table 14.1) needs to be addressed in terms of data and function by the operating system configuration that defines which operating system processes are executed with which priority level. The network interface configurations and firewall configurations are variation points of the "Where" dimension, while security profiles define platform variation points in the "Who" dimension.

Timing variability, such as real-time constraints, is addressed through configuration mechanisms of program and service execution calendar (e.g., alternate timing and triggering functions for safety-critical systems). Platform service-level agreements (SLAs) address the system's motivation or goal variability.

14.3.2.3 Communication Gateway Variability

The communication gateway variability (Row 3 in Table 14.1) needs to be addressed in the data dimension through configurable data transport formats, for example by implementing flexible network communication protocols.

The function variability can be supported by flexible communication interfaces and different supported bindings and thorough the network configuration (in the "Where" dimension). For example, an application can restrict the access to IoT actuators that open a door, if the requesting user is not in the immediate proximity.

The "Who" dimension variability is addressed through configurations of subnets and the types of supported IoT devices. Network clocking settings can be used to implement variation points in the timing dimension, while the network quality of service (QoS) addresses variability of the system's motivation or goal. For example, if the application is deployed for a safety-critical goals, it will require access to a high-availability cloud platform.

14.3.2.4 Software Variability

The software variability (Row 4 in Table 14.1) needs to be addressed in the data dimension through device software configurations, for example by enabling or disabling data formats that are not supported by certain devices. In the functionality dimension, variability is achieved through firmware and software configuration mechanisms. In the network dimension, variation points specify supported network interface configurations. In the "Who" dimension, variability is achieved through software privilege configurations (e.g., restricting access to a file system or sensors), in the "When" dimension through program and service execution calendars, and in the motivation dimension through service-level agreements (SLAs).

Typical software variation points should support both static and dynamic changes of the IoT environment, caused for example by failing IoT devices, device updates or addition of new IoT components.

14.3.2.5 Hardware Variability

The IoT hardware variability (Row 5 in Table 14.1) needs to be addressed in the data variability dimension through configurations of device operating systems.

Variability in the functional dimension is implemented through hardware configurations (e.g., enabling or disabling of IoT sensors). In the "Where" dimension, it is implemented through network configurations (e.g., location and availability of sensors), in the "Who" dimension through security hardware profiles, for example by checking and restricting hardware access depending on the trust level of registered IoT devices. In the "When" dimension, variability can be implemented using device clocking and synchronization settings, such as the maximum acceptable response times of IoT devices for real-time applications. Static variability in the motivation dimension can be achieved through device hardware choices, or dynamically through selection of available and suitable IoT sensors and data sources.

14.3.2.6 Socio-Technical Variability

Variability requirements on IoT devices will also need to evolve according to socio-technical policy changes. Such evolving requirements will have an impact on multiple variability dimensions (Table 14.1). For example, it is expected that IoT devices will be deployed to continuously operate over relatively long periods of time, such as IoT devices embedded in buildings, operating in factories and industrial environments, in utilities, vehicles, as well as in homes and city infrastructure. During their time of operation, such IoT systems will require variability on multiple dimensions, for example due to changes of legislation, security, privacy and ethical norms.

Security policies will change the requirements for the hardware capabilities, for example in terms of computational capability for encryption and decryption of data at rest, in transit and in use. Certain devices may have hardware-based security modules, whereas less powerful devices might support only basic security functions. Hence, upgrades to device hardware will require software updates, which in turn require the reconfiguration of the cloud platform. Changes of security requirements, such as additional encryption needs, will affect the IoT hardware and even the Cloud platform requirements.

Privacy policies will affect, for example, where IoT devices are available and allowed to send data to the cloud directly, or only through a local privacy mediator for filtering. New privacy policies could require devices to record data or operations, or a privacy policy might require a device to prompt users for authorization before displaying or transmitting certain types of data.

Ethical policies will also affect the motivation and function dimensions of IoT devices. For example, some ethical policies might require human approval for transmitting user data or require IoT devices in certain environments to log all operations for future auditing.

14.4 Conclusion

The fast developments of IoT technologies lead to new application domains that have the potential to revolutionize our lives and massively impact society in unprecedented ways. IoT technologies not only bring enormous benefits to industrial applications but will also affect our daily lives through smart environments, smart cities, smart transportation, and potentially many more applications that are yet to be invented.

These IoT systems will form in the near future a new generation of variability-intensive systems with unparalleled requirements. In this chapter, we have discussed the emerging variability requirements of future IoT application stacks, consisting of: (1) coordinating application, (2) Cloud platform, (3) connectivity gateway, (4) IoT device software and (5) IoT device hardware. A holistic multidimensional view of the variation points in an IoT application stack was given in line with the dimensions of the Zachman Framework: What (Data), How (Function), Where (Network), Who (People), When (Time) and Why (Motivation).

While an exhaustive discussion of all variation points is not feasible in the scope of a book chapter, we hope that this holistic discussion provides valuable support for practitioners designing the variability-intensive IoT systems of the future. Security, privacy and ethical considerations will play an increasingly important role in the near future, when such systems take their place in our daily lives. We hope that our discussion on these aspects motivates practitioners to incorporate these variability points in future IoT systems.

Also, there is an impact on future software engineering methodologies for developing (and continually updating of) IoT systems. These will need to support variability at the design, development and even at post-deployment stages, not only to cope with changes in hardware and computer network technology, but also changes in physical environments, societal values, QoS needs, real-time requirements, policy, regulations and standards.

References

1. *Software Product-Family Engineering: 4th International Workshop* (PFE 2001). F. van der Linden, Ed.
2. AWS Greengrass. https://aws.amazon.com/greengrass/, 2017. Accessed: April 25, 2018.
3. Waymo. https://waymo.com/, 2017. Accessed: April 25, 2018.
4. A. Shahin, A. Variability Modeling for Customizable SaaS Applications. *International Journal of Computer Science and Information Technology 6*, 5 (2014), 39-49.
5. Addo-Tenkorang, R., and Helo, P. T. Big data applications in operations/supply-chain management: A literature review. *Computers & Industrial Engineering 101* (2016), 528-543.
6. Asikainen, T., Männistö, T., and Soininen, T. Kumbang. A domain ontology for modelling variability in software product families. *Advanced Engineering Informatics 21*, 1 (2007), 23-40.
7. Atzori, L., Iera, A., and Morabito, G. The Internet of Things: A survey. *Computer Networks 54*, 15 (2010), 2787-2805.
8. Bachmann, F., and Bass, L. Managing variability in software architectures. *ACM SIGSOFT Software Engineering Notes 26*, 3 (2001), 126-132.
9. Bachmann, F., and Clements, P. Variability in Software Product Lines. Tech. Rep. Technical Report CMU/SEI-2005-TR-012, Software Engineering Institute; Pittsburgh; USA, 2005.
10. Bandyopadhyay, D., and Sen, J. Internet of Things: Applications and challenges in technology and standardization. *Wireless Personal Communications 58*, 1 (2011), 49-69.
11. Bauer, M., Boussard, M., Bui, N., Carrez, F., Jardak, C., De Loof, J., Magerkurth, C., Meissner, S., Nettsträter, A., Olivereau, A., Thoma, M., Joachim, W., Stefa, J., and Salinas, A. Internet of things – architecture IoT-A deliverable d1.5 –final architectural reference model for the iot v3.0. Tech. rep., 07 2013.
12. Becker, M. Towards a general model of variability in product families. *Workshop on Software Variability Management*. Editors Jilles van Gurp and Jan Bosch. Groningen, The Netherlands (2003), 19-27.
13. Bhatnagar, R., Morrish, J., Puhlmann, F., and Slama, D. *Enterprise IoT*. O'Reilly Media, Inc., 2015.
14. Bi, Z., Xu, L. D., and Wang, C. Internet of Things for Enterprise Systems of Modern Manufacturing. *IEEE Transactions on Industrial Informatics 10*, 2 (2014), 1537-1546.

15. Cai, H., Xu, B., Jiang, L., and Vasilakos, A. V. IoT-based Big Data storage systems in Cloud computing: Perspectives and challenges. *IEEE Internet of Things Journal 4*, 1 (2017), 75-87.

16. Canedo, J., and Skjellum, A. Adding scalability to Internet of Things gateways using parallel computation of edge device data. *IEEE*, pp. 1-5.

17. Capilla, R., Bosch, J., and Kang, K.-C. *Systems and Software Variability Management.* Springer-Verlag, Berlin Heidelberg, 2013.

18. Carella, G. A., Pauls, M., Magedanz, T., Cilloni, M., Bellavista, P., and Foschini, L. Prototyping nfv-based multi- access edge computing in 5G ready networks with open baton. In *2017 IEEE Conference on Network Softwarization (NetSoft)*, pp. 1-4.

19. Chen, L., and Ali Babar, M. A systematic review of evaluation of variability management approaches in software product lines. *Information and Software Technology 53*, 4 (2011), 344-362.

20. Coplien, J., Hoffman, D., and Weiss, D. Commonality and variability in software engineering. *IEEE Software 15*, 6 (1998), 37-45.

21. Deelstra, S., Deelstra, S., Sinnema, M., Sinnema, M., Gurp, J. V., Gurp, J. V., Bosch, J., and Bosch, J. Model Driven Architecture as Approach to Manage Variability in Software Product Families. *Workshop on Model Driven Architecture: Foundations and Applications, MDAFA 2003, CTIT Technical Report TR-CTIT-03-27*, May 2014 (2003), 1-6.

22. Estublier, J., and Vega, G. Reuse and variability in large software applications. *ACM SIGSOFT Software Engineering Notes 30*, 5 (2005), 316.

23. ETSI. Machine-to-machine communications (M2M); functional architecture (ETSI TS 102 690 V2.1.1). Tech. rep., 10 2013.

24. Fuentes, L., Gámez, N., and Sanchez, P. Managing variability of ambient intelligence middleware. *International Journal of Ambient Computing and Intelligence 1*, 1 (2009), 64-74.

25. Furda, A., Bouraoui, L., Parent, M., and Vlacic, L. The role and future challenges of wireless communication networks for co-operative autonomous city vehicles. *IFIP Advances in Information and Communication Technology 327* (2010), 241-251.

26. Furda, A., Fidge, C., Zimmermann, O., Kelly, W., and Barros, A. Migrating enterprise legacy source code to microservices: On multi-tenancy, statefulness and data consistency. *IEEE Software* (2017).

27. Furda, A., and Vlacic, L. Real-time decision making for autonomous city vehicles. *Journal of Robotics and Mechatronics 22*, 6 (2010), 694-701.

28. Galster, M., Avgeriou, P., Weyns, D., and Männistö, T. Variability in software architecture: Current practices and challenges. *ACM SIGSOFT Software Engineering Notes 36*, 5 (2011), 30-32.

29. Galster, M., Weyns, D., Tofan, D., Michalik, B., and Avgeriou, P. Variability in software systems: A systematic literature review. *IEEE Transactions on Software Engineering 40*, 3 (2014), 282-306.

30. Gubbi, J., Buyya, R., Marusic, S., and Palaniswami, M. Internet of Things (IoT): A vision, architectural elements, and future directions. *Future Generation Computer Systems 29*, 7 (2013), 1645-1660.

31. Gurp, J. V., Bosch, J., and Svahnberg, M. On the Notion of Variability in Software Product Lines In *Proceedings of the Working IEEE/IFIP Conference on Software Architecture (WICSA'01)*, 02 (2001), 45-54.

32. Herterich, M. M., Uebernickel, F., and Brenner, W. The impact of cyber-physical systems on industrial services in manufacturing. *Procedia CIRP 30*, Supplement C (2015), 323-328.

33. Heymans, P., Legay, A., and Cordy, M. Efficient quality assurance of variability-intensive systems. In *Proceedings of the 2013 International Conference on Software Engineering* (2013), IEEE Press, pp. 1496-1498.

34. Huberman, B. Ensuring trust and security in the industrial IoT: The Internet of Things (Ubiquity symposium). *Ubiquity 2016*, January (2016), 1-7.

35. Johnson, C. *Radio access networks for UMTS: Principles and practice.* John Wiley & Sons, Hoboken, NJ; Chichester, England, 2008.

36. Kamigaki, T. Object-oriented RFID with IoT: A design concept of information systems in manufacturing. *Electronics (Switzerland) 6*, 1 (2017), 14.

37. Kang, D. A Classification Method of Commonality and Variability for Mobile Services. *International Journal of Software Engineering and Its Applications 10*, 3 (2016), 119-130.

38. Keepence, B., and Mannion, M. Using patterns to model variability in product families. *IEEE Software 16*, 4 (1999), 102-108.

39. Khosrow-Pour, M. *Dictionary of Information Science and Technology* (2nd ed.), Information Science Reference (Isr), 2013.
40. Kim, S. D., Her, J. S., and Chang, S. H. A theoretical foundation of variability in component-based development. *Information and Software Technology 47*, 10 (2005), 663-673.
41. Kumaki, K., Tsuchiya, R., Washizaki, H., and Fukazawa, Y. Supporting commonality and variability analysis of requirements and structural models. *Proceedings of the 16th International Software Product Line Conference on SPLC '12—volume 1* (2012), 115.
42. Lee, I. An exploratory study of the impact of the Internet of Things (IoT) on business model innovation: Building smart enterprises at Fortune 500 Companies. *International Journal of Information Systems and Social Change (IJISSC) 7*, 3 (2016), 1-15.
43. Leenen, L., and Meyer, T. Semantic technologies and Big Data analytics for cyber defence. *International Journal of Cyber Warfare and Terrorism (IJCWT) 6*, 3 (2016), 53-64.
44. Lesjak, C., Druml, N., Matischek, R., Ruprechter, T., and Holweg, G. Security in industrial IoT quo vadis? *e & i Elektrotechnik und Informationstechnik 133*, 7 (2016), 324-329.
45. Li, B., and Li, Y. Internet of Things drives supply chain innovation: A research framework. *International Journal of Organizational Innovation (Online) U6 9*, 3 (2017), 71B.
46. Meng, Z., Wu, Z., Muvianto, C., and Gray, J. A data-oriented M2M messaging mechanism for Industrial IoT applications. *IEEE Internet of Things Journal 4*, 1 (2017), 236-246.
47. Metzger, A., Bayer, A., Doyle, D., Sharifloo, A. M., Pohl, K., and Wessling, F. Coordinated runtime adaptation of variability- intensive systems: An application in cloud computing. In *Variability and Complexity in Software Design (VACE), IEEE/ACM International Workshop on* (2016), IEEE, pp. 5-11.
48. Meyer, O., Wessling, F., and Klüver, C. Finding optimized configurations for variability-intensive systems without constraint violations using a regulatory algorithm (rga). In *Evolutionary Computation (CEC), 2017 IEEE Congress on* (2017), IEEE, pp. 1908-1915.
49. Rurua, N., Eshuis, R., and Razavian, M. Representing Variability in Enterprise Architecture. *Business & Information Systems Engineering 3* (2017), 1-13.
50. Sabella, D., Vaillant, A., Kuure, P., Rauschenbach, U., and Giust, F. Mobile-Edge Computing Architecture: The role of MEC in the Internet of Things. *IEEE Consumer Electronics Magazine 5*, 4 (2016), 84-91.
51. Schaefer, I. Variability Modelling for Model-Driven Development of Software Product Lines. *VaMoS* (2010), 85-92.
52. Schmid, K., and Geppert, B. The Early Steps: Planning, Modeling and Managing. *Proceedings of the PLEES'02 International Workshop on Product Line Engineering, 056* (2002).
53. Sheng, Z., Mahapatra, C., Zhu, C., and Leung, V. C. M. Recent Advances in Industrial Wireless Sensor Networks Toward Efficient Management in IoT. *IEEE Access 3* (2015), 622-637.
54. Sinnema, M., and Deelstra, S. Classifying variability modeling techniques. *Information and Software Technology 49*, 7 (2007), 717-739.
55. Sinnema, M., Deelstra, S., Nijhuis, J., Bosch, J., Sinnema, M., Bosch, J., Nijhuis, J., Deelstra, S., Nijhuis, J., and Bosch, J. COVAMOF: A framework for modeling variability in software product families. *Software Product Lines 3154* (2004), 197-213.
56. Sowa, J. F., and Zachman, J. A. Extending and formalizing the framework for information systems architecture. *IBM Syst. J. 31*, 3 (June 1992), 590-616.
57. Sun, C.-A., Rossing, R., Sinnema, M., Bulanov, P., and Aiello, M. Modeling and managing the variability of Web service-based systems. *Journal of Systems and Software 83*, 3 (2010), 502-516.
58. Svahnberg, M., Van Gurp, J., and Bosch, J. A taxonomy of variability realization techniques. *Software—Practice and Experience 35*, 8 (2005), 705-754.
59. Taleb, T., Samdanis, K., Mada, B., Flinck, H., Dutta, S., and Sabella, D. On multi-access edge computing: A survey of the emerging 5G network edge cloud architecture and orchestration. IEEE *Communications Surveys & Tutorials 19*, 3 (2017), 1657-1681.
60. Temple, P., Galindo, J. A., Acher, M., and Jézéquel, J.-M. Using machine learning to infer constraints for product lines. In *Proceedings of the 20th International Systems and Software Product Line Conference* (2016), ACM, pp. 209-218.

61. Tomlein, M., and Gronbaek, K. Semantic model of variability and capabilities of iot applications for embedded software ecosystems. In *2016 13th Working IEEE/IFIP Conference on Software Architecture (WICSA)* (2016), pp. 247-252.

62. Van Der Hoek, A. Design-time product line architectures for anytime variability. *Science of Computer Programming 53*, 3 (2004), 285-304.

63. van der Linden, F., Ed. *Software Product-Family Engineering, 5th International Workshop (PFE 2003)*. 2010.

64. Watteyne, T., Tuset-Peiro, P., Vilajosana, X., Pollin, S., and Krishnamachari, B. Teaching Communication Technologies and Standards for the Industrial IoT? Use 6TiSCH! *IEEE Communications Magazine 55*, 5 (2017), 132-137.

65. Weiser, M., Gold, R., and Brown, J. S. Origins of ubiquitous computing research at PARC in the late 1980s. *IBM Systems Journal 38*, 4 (1999), 693-695.

66. Xia, F., Yang, L. T., Wang, L., and Vinel, A. Internet of Things. *International Journal of Communication Systems 25*, 9 (2012), 1101-1102.

67. Xu, L. D. Information architecture for supply chain quality management. *International Journal of Production Research 49*, 1 (2011), 183-198.

68. Xu, L. D., He, W., and Li, S. Internet of Things in Industries: A Survey. *IEEE Transactions on Industrial Informatics 10*, 4 (2014), 2233-2243.

69. Zachman, J. A. A framework for information systems architecture. *IBM Systems Journal 26*, 3 (1987), 276-292.

70. Zanella, A., Bui, N., Castellani, A., Vangelista, L., and Zorzi, M. Internet of Things for smart cities. *IEEE Internet of Things Journal 1*, 1 (2014), 22-32.

LOOKING AHEAD

IV LOOKING AHEAD

Chapter 15

Outlook and Future Directions

Bruce Maxim[a], Matthias Galster[b], and Ivan Mistrik[c]

[a]Department of Computer and Information Science,
University of Michigan, Dearborn, Michigan, United States
[b]University of Canterbury, Christchurch, New Zealand
[c]Computer Scientist & Software Researcher, Germany

15.1 Introduction

Our goal for this book was to collect chapters on software engineering for variability-intensive systems and activities related to their construction (i.e., planning, designing, implementing, evaluating), deployment, and maintenance as high-quality software products in dynamic and flexible environments. The chapter authors discussed the practical application of the system variability through case studies, experiments, empirical validation, and systematic comparisons with approaches already in use. To this end it is our hope that the chapters appearing in this book provide a comprehensive reference on variability from both a technical and non-technical perspective. The authors focus the latest research and industry trends in the engineering of variability-intensive systems throughout the lifetime of software products. This final chapter presents an overview of some the challenges faced by organizations in a fast-moving world filled with frequently changing customer expectations and explores the basis of future work in this area.

In Section 15.2 we highlight some of the new concepts and models required to understand the software engineering of variability-intensive systems. Section 15.3 discusses the current state of the art and science of working with variability-intensive software systems. The results of several experiments and literature reviews provided suggestions for the summary of the trends discusses in Section 15.4. Some of the challenges that that will face software engineers working of variability-intensive systems in the future are presented in Section 15.5. Of course, a chapter like this is highly speculative and cannot completely cover all the software engineering trends, challenges, and opportunities. Section 15.6 provides readers with suggestions for further reading.

15.2 New Concepts and Models

We have seen variability-intensive systems evolve from discussions on conditional compilation of source code to the creation of product line software and context ware systems. Many people would say that variability is now a needed feature in many if not all software products. The cost of involving human programmers in the development of software products demands that project managers use their staff wisely and not allow every product to be built from scratch as a custom application. Variability impacts many software development activities and software life-cycle phases in any engineering process model. Variability-intensive systems provide fundamental challenges that must be addressed when they designed or maintained. Several new concepts and models were addressed in Part I of this book.

15.2.1 Software Architecture Variability

Variability in software intensive systems is often described as the ability of the software to change to meet the needs of different stakeholders, environments, or purposes. Software architecture changes are often very costly. Explicitly managing variability within a given software architecture is considerably more complex if the intention is to use the same software architecture to support changes being made to a system to support a family of related software products over a long-time period. It is important to reduce the effort required to introduce variability in software architecture and improve the reusability of the software components.

Software architectural design is highly dependent on modeling. Modeling variability in architectures requires support allowing for architectural variability, managing multiple architectural views, requirements traceability to views, and runtime support in context aware systems. Most studies of this topic lack formal evaluation of the approaches being described. Empirical work examining the management of variability during the evolution of software architectures over time is needed (see Chapter 2).

15.2.2 Context Modeling

Context modeling defines how a system's context data are structured and represented. Context data is the presentation of the information used by a system to allow it to behave differently for different users and different application environments. The aim of context modeling is to produce a formal description of the data needed by a context-aware system. Context modeling must to be considered during the requirements engineering of highly variable systems if it is to be affective. It is important for context variability and its impact of system variability to be documented using multiple perspectives. Each perspective will have its own set of advantages and disadvantages.

Feature oriented approaches provide a lot of freedom in modeling but require the discovery of a means to manage the complexity of the models and the relationships among models. Documenting knowledge the assumptions made about the real world is important even when the developer cannot control it. Variability in the real world and its impact on the software may place constraints on the system being developed. These constraints need to be represented in a form that allows the developers to take them into account as the system is evolved (see Chapter 3).

15.2.3 Decomposition

The purpose of decomposition in software development is to break a complex problem into smaller parts that are easier to understand, construct, and maintain. The use of decomposition can be an important tool for helping to represent the architecture of software product in a manner that may expose the places where changes are planned or allowed. Incorporating variability into the system development can ease the management of requirements changes and allow for their adoption in a systematic way.

Constructing a system from scratch using the perspective of variability is one way to use decomposition to proactively allow for system evolution. Reconstructing an existing system from previously identified variable parts is a way of reactively evolving a system. Proactive approaches are generally preferred in software engineering because they require less rework. Decomposition of a system into smaller processes may help to identify on structural decompositions and potential variations. The hierarchical nature of process and structure allows for the propagation of variability specifications from higher levels to lower levels. The act of decomposition exposes the variability relationships and constraints that will need to be taken account and resolved at the upper levels before they are passed to the lower levels (see Chapter 4).

15.3 Analyzing System Variability

Software variability has been studied for several years now often in the context of software product line engineering. Devising approaches for analyzing system variability is dependent on creating techniques for measuring the impact of variability on system evolution.

15.3.1 Self-Securing Software Systems

As cyberattacks become widespread and more devastating many organizations are looking at creating systems capable of defending themselves from threats. Self-securing systems will need to be context aware and self-adapting real-time systems if they are to monitor and mitigate threats. Design and testing of self-securing systems will be very difficult since system security requirements are hard to define because the attack surface is so large. Machine-learning techniques may be required to recognize attack signatures and suggest security patterns that may be useful in mitigating the damage. An important part of this work is to be able to get the system to focus on mitigating the threats that have the potential to cause the greatest losses (Chapter 5).

15.3.2 Ecosystems Architecture

Organizations are making use of highly variable cloud-based software ecosystems to gain greater flexibility, adaptability, and scalability than is possible closed software ecosystems. Developers realize that this calls for rethinking development processes and architectural principles. This also forces software engineers to consider the business aspects of variability-intensive systems such as: value, business strategies, risks, measures, and governance challenges.

This suggests that a more holistic view may be needed to take these variability concerns into account. This is where an ecosystems architect can provide values to an organization by focusing on the internal aspects of how to integrate the systems, processes, and technologies to better support an organization's long-term strategies. This work needs to be done early in the early stages of ecostrategy development if the goal is increasing customer involvement and reducing the cost of doing business. This should be done by analyzing the implications and risks associated with the sources of business variability driving evolution of the system being developed (see Chapter 6).

15.3.3 Manual Feature Location

Knowledge of a system's implemented features is essential to be able to maintain, extend, reuse, or reengineer the system or its components. This knowledge fades over time or is simply not available due to missing documentation. Frequently developers are forced to locate features in the source code manually because automated processes are lacking in their precision or accuracy. Yet automating this process would make it easier of manage the variability found in creating systems using component-based engineering techniques.

Some work being done on program comprehension and automatic source code documentation may be useful in the future. Studies involving manual feature extraction are both necessary and costly. We need more information on the effort required to locate features and the influence of external factors on automating the process. We need better ways of evaluating the costs and benefits of manual feature extraction techniques (see Chapter 7).

15.3.4 Software Product Lines

Many people equate the study of variability-intensive systems with the study of software product line engineering. Development of software product lines requires sufficient understanding of component commonality to manage system variability effectively. However, to sustain an organization's profitability and the corresponding level of productivity there is a need to take technical debt into account when assessing value combining different sets of features that may become a new software variant. Technical debt should reflect the implied cost of additional rework caused by making a poor design choice early in development (see Section 15.5 for further discussion).

Portfolio theory is financial engineering technique which develops products and procedures using mathematical techniques to advise investors on means to maximize expected investment returns based on acceptable levels of market risks. There are dangers in blindly applying portfolio theory to the evolving software variants using the product line engineering approach. Portfolio theory depends heavily of having accurate estimations of the costs and risks associated with each proposed portfolio of features. Estimations of portfolio costs, benefits, and severity of risks are often a function of the developer's experience and level of confidence, making the whole process highly subjective. This means that portfolio theory might be useful in helping engineers develop better feature portfolios. Portfolio theory may not help always help engineers to develop the single best portfolio of features. More work with case studies will be needed to obtain data needed to make better estimates. The recommendations offered by portfolio theory/technical debt approach will need to be validated by human developers evolving systems over many years. It will be important to find a way to quantify non-economic costs and benefits when making these estimations. It will also be important to identify additional sources of technical debt beyond those posed by compatibility risks, quality risks, and maintenance risks (see Chapter 8).

15.3.5 Self-Adaptive Systems

A self-adaptive software system (SASS) evaluates its own performance and makes changes to its behavior when this evaluation indicates that it is not accomplishing what the software is intended to do or when better performance is possible. Modern software systems need to be designed with the ability to adapt at runtime to heterogeneous environments and devices. Systems need to be able to self-adapt to changes in user needs and to changes in their deployment environments. Software product lines may be able to accommodate static variability which can be described at design time, but they are not adequate to dealing with dynamic changes that are not known till runtime. Newer dynamic software product line (DSPL) techniques could be helpful to accommodate both static and runtime variability. However, most DSPL approaches were developed in an unstructured manner and do not always include the enough provisions for runtime changes that can be accommodated using SASS approaches.

The current trend in the development and evolution of variability-intensive systems indicates that the combined use of DSPL and SASS approaches may be beneficial. To accomplish this will require the creation of taxonomy for comparing system design using two key dimensions: variability management and self-adaption characteristics. This taxonomy would allow design decisions to evaluate with regards to their projected impact on system quality attributes. While there will never be a single right way to design and maintain variability-intensive systems, it is important to provide software engineers with the quality attribute trade-offs that will take place as each architectural design decision is made. This may necessitate the creation of an architecture reference model as an important starting point to increasing the integration and reuse of variability-intensive system components (see Chapter 9).

15.4 Emerging Work

The case studies, literature reviews, and empirical studies discussed in the previous chapters of this book have far-reaching consequences for advancing the state for the art on software engineering of variability-intensive systems. In Chapter 1 of this book we discussed various notions of variability and described how variability impacts both software development activities and software life-cycle process models. Requirements engineering needs to take a longer view and the importance of planning for reuse in software product line work is especially important. Accommodating system variability during the design and construction process as stakeholder needs vary from the original design and trying to make systems more context-aware when the runtime environments change after deployment added to the complexity of these systems. Of course, when system complexity goes up system quality (non-functional requirements) is threatened. This is especially true when these changes call for fundamental changes to the software architecture of the system. In this section, we highlight some of research being done to better support the software engineering of variability-intensive systems.

15.4.1 Feature Ontology

Product line engineering is a strategy that takes advantage of similarities among software products and to resolve the variability that need to be in place to make the products unique. In some very large organizations thousands of non-engineering users need different views of the way the system will manage the commonalities and similarities among the many interaction scenarios needed to accommodate the needs of all stakeholders. To manage all these features in these software variants requires a unified approach that relies on the principle of abstraction and modularity to define concepts, views, relationships, and behaviors best suited for specific stakeholders. Creating a feature model based on these similarities and transforming it into a feature ontology is one way to move away from reliance on developer intuition when trying to build reusable system components.

An engineering ontology assists software engineers in defining information for the exchange of semantic project information and is used as a communication framework with all stakeholders. A feature ontology can serve as a communication vehicle among stakholders when creating and evolving variabilty intensive systems. This would allow develpers construct a high-quality feature model based on common understanding of a feature before attempting its implementation in software. Making use of a well-designed feature ontology can help developers helps developers to reduce the number of choices that must be considered at each architectural decisison point. The feature ontology assists developers in formulating a method of extracting the commonality and variability from features based on semantic similarity mapping and whcih can enhance the reusability of feature model. It may be the case that product line engineers may still need to make us of separtion of concerns as a tool to manage the variability in the evolving systems. It is possible that feature ontologies may be extended by adding new top levels to accomodate larger and larger product lines (see Chapter 10).

15.4.2 Big Data

The term *big data* usually refers to datasets with sizes beyond the ability of most software tools to capture, curate, manage, and process data within reasonable time elapsed time. Big data systems require major financial commitments and massive scale software system deployments. Managing variability during the creation and maintenance is important when developing big data systems. It is important to identify the required features early and make plans to accommodate changes in stakeholder needs and managing the context data used to affect runtime behaviors of the of a variability-intensive system.

E-government systems are examples of big data systems in which data storage and processing are crucial issues. Designing e-government systems requires taking multiple architectural concerns into account. One way to derive a working e-government system architecture is to analyze stakeholder concerns, workflow models, and required features using big data. A reference architecture can be derived using implicit design decisions based on the required features selected. One of the key issues in architectural design is design rationale management. The design rationale documents the reasons design decisions were made and applied.

An architecture view is a representation of the set of system elements and relations associated with a single concern. Architectural views model the architecture from different stakeholder concerns. Having multiple views helps to separate concerns and supports modeling, understanding, and communication of the software architecture to different stakeholders. Developing the reference architecture for a big data system along with variability modeling could be application domains besides e-government. An architectural analysis process that evaluates the architecture for fitness with respect to stakeholder requirement still needs to be defined (see Chapter 11).

15.4.3 Refactoring Support

Studies of programmer behavior show that software developers often postpone software maintenance activities that improve software quality of existing source code. One reason for this is that time and monetary pressure force programmers to enhance existing systems with new features or by repairing bugs. Bad code smells make programs hard to maintain and increase its fault-proneness. These code smells often indicate poor design and implementation designs. Sadly, code smells do not always predict the needed architectural changes required to refactor the code. Sometimes code quality can be improved without fixing code smells. Code quality can be estimated using quality metrics, but it may be hard to formulate consensus among developers as to which combinations of metric are useful to detect code smells which need to be corrected. Code smells can help predict places where refactoring opportunities may exist which may be helpful in managing some types of system variability. It is difficult to manually specify a standard refactoring solution for each type of code smell due to the large number of defects and the large number of possible fixes for them.

One approach to detecting and correcting code smells makes use of distributed evolutionary algorithms (D-EA) with different adaptations being proposed and executed in parallel. It may be desirable to have two evolutionary algorithms (using different adaptations) execute in parallel and allow them to interact with each other during the optimization process. The two evolutionary algorithms work towards the common goal of maximizing the intersection of the solution space made up of the refactoring solutions proposed by each. Mutation and crossover operations are used to mitigate problems of elitism (over-specialization) caused by only focusing on the best solutions found in a single generation. Future work needs to be done to see if this type of evolutionary framework can be used to predict and mange variability in all life-cycle activities (see Chapter 12).

15.4.4 Library Evolution

Software systems are often evolved through the composition and maintenance of various components designed initially to meet the needs of a specific stakeholder using that software architecture. To reduce implementation time and effort developers may rely on the use of third-party libraries of components or design and architecture pattern. The use of libraries may also improve the quality of the system since the developers and making use of previously validated components. If the details of the application programming interface (API) do not change it may be deceptively easy to exchange one library for another.

If the goal is to replace an outdated version of a library with a newer version (an upgrade operation) developers are likely to be able to do so with very little risk of introducing defects. If the goal is to replace one library with a similar library created for different software system (a library migration) the risk of introducing defects increases as the variability in the new libraries increases. Often migrating from one library to another requires many manual changes to either the new library of the program making of it and this introduces the likelihood of introducing defects if the library functions are not very well understood.

This suggests importance of creating a dataset containing detected library changes and their locations in the project files. Information retrieval techniques might be used to automatically classify commits to better understand the developer's intentions. The dataset might be analyzed to understand the impact of these commits on the project in terms of likely defect injections. This dataset might also be compared to existing recommendation approaches to see if it is possible to replicate manual decisions performed found in existing library migrations. This type of information might help create a better understanding of the variability involved in library migration (see Chapter 13).

15.4.5 The Internet of Things

The Internet of Things (IoT) is characterized by the fact that sensor networks connect incredible numbers of small devices to the Internet. These devices send their data in regular intervals. Based on the sensor data the variability-intensive system will need to initiate appropriate actions. These actions depend on the context in which the sensor data is received. For example, in a context-aware system the traffic lights in a city can be controlled in a manner to reroute traffic to reduce congestion when it seems inevitable. The variability that will need to be accommodated in such a system is great since the number of events that require detection is almost unlimited. This seems to suggest that some level of self-modification be designed into the system before it is deployed.

Machine learning will play a major role in aggregating variability data to some form that humans can interpret when the system needs evolve due to changes in implied stakeholder requirements. Machine learning may also help context-aware system make (and document) software changes after deployment. The challenge here is that the learning process must take place in a dynamic runtime environment (see Chapter 14).

15.5 Needed Work

The chapters in this book have described the scope of software engineering for variability-intensive systems, what we know about their creation and management, and some of the research which is helping to extend our understanding of the challenges they pose to practitioners. There are several areas of variability-intensive systems that need further work: the decision-making process, managing technical debt, representation, and analysis, testing and assurance, and multi-access edge computing.

15.5.1 Decision-Making Process

Falessi et. al (2011) state that software-intensive system architecture can be defined by the set of relevant design decisions that affect the system quality and functionality. These architectural decisions are crucial to the success of the software project. The software engineering literature describes several techniques to choose among architectural alternatives, but it gives no clear guidance on which technique is best suited to a specific set of circumstances. Software engineers need a systematic to make decisions when trying to resolve tradeoffs in architectural design. Software architects need a reliable and rigorous process for selecting architectural alternatives and ensuring that the decisions made mitigate risks and maximize profit.

A good decision-making technique is one that guides the user towards better design alternatives and is easy to use. There is no perfect decision-making technique that dominates all the others. The value of a technique may depend on which difficulties the decision-makers want to avoid. However, there are techniques that are more susceptible than others to some difficulties. Currently, there is a lack of empirical evidence in understanding under which predicts the type of difficulties you will run into when using some decision-making techniques. The approach used to select a decision-making technique needs to be both adaptable and tunable.

15.5.2 Technical Debt

Technical debt is a software engineering concept used to describe the implied cost of additional rework caused from having chosen an easy solution now rather than looking for a better approach that would take longer. The cause of technical debt is often attributed to scheduling pressures. Using iterative or agile software development processes does not allow developers to ignore technical debt. Working with variability-intensive systems such as product line software can cause technical debt to grow even more rapidly unless time is taken for proper software design and planning for component reuse.

Kruchten, Nord, and Ozkaya (2012) made several suggestions on dealing with technical debt that are relevant to work on variability-intensive systems. We need to get a better understanding of how to identify the elements of technical debt and their causes. This debt can then be managed as a list of debt-related tasks in a common backlog during iteration planning. We also need quantitative evidence that these practices can reduce production costs and increase product quality.

Code analysis tools by themselves will not be able to predict technical debt. Technical debt is often caused by poor architectural choices or gaps in selected technologies. To mitigate this, software organizations need information on how to determine the direction for evolution and refactoring of current products and the order to sequence these planned changes. Ultimately these will need to be determined by balancing the short-term costs with long-term value to the stakeholders. We need data to understand this balance better.

15.5.3 Representation and Analysis

Modern software systems may exploit knowledge about user preferences and changes in the environment to trigger runtime adaptations in the software features. This variability must happen dynamically and after the software is deployed. The number of possible runtime scenarios can be enormous. Developing techniques for modeling and managing dynamic variability based on context knowledge would be a powerful tool for managing runtime reconfiguration challenges according to Mens et. al (2017).

The growing number of context-aware software systems (e.g. Internet of Things) requires appropriate techniques for modeling and handling context-aware software variability. Runtime variability models can be extended with new features after design to support software evolution. The complexity and diversity of runtime can be challenging for critical systems as features are activated, deactivated, updated, and reconfigured to adapt to changing scenarios. This requires the creation of dedicated runtime managers capable of analyzing the state of the context properties and providing smart systems reactions to them. This calls for a greater use of big data analytics and machine learning in software engineering.

15.5.4 Testing and Assurance

Software product lines and self-adaptive software products be exceeding difficult to test even using automated testing procedures because of their variability-intensive nature. The number of product variants grows exponentially with the size of the feature model and the number of possible scenario variations. This increases the cost of testing dramatically even if assisted by automated tools according to Galindo et. al (2016). Research is needed to determine ways to model assumptions made about the dynamically changing feature space along with techniques to reduce it. It is also important to figure out ways to manage the quality of product that will be changing at run-time that cannot be predicted in advance (e.g. modified product may become less secure or less reliable).

Software testing will remain a large task in any software project [Brooks, 1995]. However, before these tools and techniques developed for data science, machine learning, and program understanding are applied to several variability-intensive software engineering tasks they should be tested extensively prior to release to the developer community.

15.5.5 Multi-Access Edge Computing

Software solutions such as the Internet of Things have resulted in billions of users and devices exchanging trillions of gigabytes of data. This data exchange can be highly inefficient in its use of communications bandwidth and computing resources when it is transferred through centralized datacenters. Multi-access edge computing is a cloud framework whose goal is increasing capabilities and responsibilities of resources at the edge of the network rather than placing all services in centralized cloud architectures. Edge computing can help reduce latency and response times of these cloud applications. Many of these applications need to take an adaptive approach to better utilize the communications capacity of the network. Monitoring an adaptive edge network can be extremely challenging (Taherizadeh, et. al 2018).

Self-adaptation of edge network applications is not well understood. We will need the creation of new monitoring tools and testing strategies. End-to-end monitoring is important to ensure quality of service (QoS) for edge application and quality of experience (QoE) for end users of these variability-intensive systems. A better means of handling the creation of changing feature sets needs to be devised.

15.6 Further Reading

Several publications discussing future trends and software engineering challenges presented by variability-intensive systems have appeared recently. The topics discussed in these papers complement the material discussed in this book. We briefly summarize some of these papers to provide suggestions to the interested reader for further information on this topic.

S. Biffl, A. Aurum, B. Boehm, H. Erdogmus, and P. Grunbacher (2006) published a book of edited papers discussing value-based software engineering. Value-based software engineering provides a framework which allows all stakeholders to bring their values to bear when making software engineering decisions, rather than basing this decision solely on technical issues. Boehm contributed several chapters related to the concept of value-based variability in software engineering. Boehm writes that most of the critical success factors for software practices lie in the value domain such as lack of user input, changing requirements, lack of resources, unrealistic expectations, and unrealistic time lines. Value-based software engineering provides principles for dealing with emergent requirements, rapid and unpredictable change, and global software development by providing a unifying framework for stakeholders to reason about software investments in terms of value created. These many of the same concerns that need to be addressed when evolving software in product line software engineering.

J. Bosch, R. Capilla, and R. Hilliard (2015) discuss trends and future directions in systems and software variability in the lead article to a special issue of *IEEE Software*. They summarize the evolution of variability models as feature-oriented domain analysis extensions. They describe five practice areas suitable for the study of variability management: requirements variability, architecture variability, component development variability, run-time variability, and the evolution of variability. Lastly, they list four topics for future research: variability representation techniques, visualization and management of large variability models, constraint management, and post-deployment reconfiguration of software systems.

Casale et. al (2016) discuss the software design challenges present in the move from application development approaches to application composition approaches. Supporting software reuse through the development of software through the composition of microservices is one way to accomplish this. These deployed microservices need to be validated with regards to their characteristics and interconnection interfaces. Support must be provided for software evolution by design, which makes use reusable design patterns, separation of concerns, and high-level modeling. During software design the emerging system requirements need to consider the variability found in highly distributed applications and heterogeneous environments.

Czarnecki (2013) discusses the impact of variability on the software life cycle focusing on requirements, architecture, verification, and validation. He argues that the study of variability is relevant to software ecosystems and context-aware systems, as well as its use in engineering software product lines. Engineering any variable system amounts to engineering a set of systems simultaneously. Variability-aware methods and tools should be developed to leverage the commonalities among the system variants while managing their differences effectively.

Galster et al. (2016) summarizes several papers which discuss variability and complexity in software design. The complexity caused by variability becomes more difficult to handle due to increasing system sizes, dynamic operating conditions, highly competitive markets, and versatile hardware. Intentional variability in functional or non-functional system requirements significantly increases the complexity of the software engineering challenges of creating and managing these systems. The authors discuss the following topics as open research topics: lean processes and agile practices, continuous delivery/deployment and DevOps, impact of technology advances, variability in context, value-based variability, correctness of configurations, functional and quality variability, variability realization mechanisms, and training and tools.

Harman et al. (2014) presents survey work done which examines the applicability of search-based software engineering (SBSE) to work being done on software product lines (SPL). This paper contains an excellent list of 164 references examined during this survey. The authors highlight some directions for future work which focus on the use of genetic improvement by SPL researchers and practitioners. They suggest that genetic improvement might be used to grow software products with new functional and non-functional features that may be grafted on to evolving software product lines. This suggest that this technique might also be used to merge and parameterize multiple branches of the evolving software product to reduce impact of feature creep.

Metzger and Pohl et al. (2014) focuses on product line engineering as a means of empowering organizations to develop a variety of similar software-intensive software systems with lower cost, shorter delivery times, and higher quality than would be possible using if these systems were developed individually. They summarize the results presented in over 600 research and experience papers published over a seven-year period. This summary is structured using a standardized software product line framework. This paper includes their perceptions of the current and future software engineering research challenges based on trends discovered in their study.

References

S. Biffl, A. Aurum, B. Boehm, H. Erdogmus, and P. Grunbacher (eds.) (2006) *Value-Based Software Engineering*, Springer, Berlin, Heidelberg.

J. Bosch, R. Capilla, R. Hilliard (2015) Trends in Systems and Software Variability, *IEEE Software* Vol. 32, Issue 3, May-June 2015: 41-51.

F. Brooks (1995) *The Mythical Man-Month: Essays on Software Engineering, Anniversary Edition* (2nd Edition), Addison-Wesley, Reading, MA.

G. Casale, C. Chesta, P. Deussen, E. DiNitto, P. Gouvas, S. Koussourris, V. Stankowski, A, Symeonidasm V. Vlassuou, A. Zafeiropoulos, Z. Zhao (2016) Current and Future Challenges for Services and Applications, *Procedia Computer Science CF2016*, Madrid, Spain, Vol. 97, October 2016: 34-42.

K. Czarnecki (2013) Variability in Software: State of the Art and Future Directions, *Proceedings of Fundamental Approaches to Software Engineering: 16th International Conference, FASE 2013*, Rome, Italy, March 2013: 1-5.

D. Falessi, G. Catone, R. Kazman, P. Kruchten (2011) Decision-making techniques for software architecture design: A comparative survey, *ACM Computing Surveys*, Vol. 43, Issue 4, October 2011, Article No, 33.

J. Galindo, H. Turner, D. Benavides, et al. (2016) Testing variability intensive systems using automated analysis. An application to Android, *Software Quality Journal*, 24: 365. https://doi.org/10.1007/s11219-014-9258-y

M. Galster, D. Weyns, M. Goedicke, U. Zdun, R. Rabiser, G. Perrouin, B. Zhang (2016) Variability and complexity in software design, *ACM SIGSOFT Software Engineering Notes* Vol. 41, No. 6, November 2016: 27-30.

M. Harman, Y. Jia, J. Krinke, W. Langdon, J. Petke, Y. Zhang (2014) Search Based Software Engineering for Product Line Engineering: A Survey and Directions for Future Work, *Proceedings of 18th International Software Product Line Conference, SPL14,* Florence, Italy, Vol. 1, September 2014: 5-18.

P. Kruchten, R. Nord, I. Ozkaya (2012) Technical debt: From metaphor to theory and practice, *IEEE Software* Vol. 29, Issue 6, November-December 2012: 18-21.

K. Mens, R. Capilla, H. Hartmann, T. Kropf (2017) Modeling and managing context-aware systems' variability, *IEEE Software* Vol. 34, Issue 6, November-December 2017: 58-63.

A. Metzger, K. Pohl (2014) Software Product Line Engineering and Variability Management: Achievements and Challenges. *Proceedings of the Future of Software Engineering, FASE 2014,* Hyderabad, India, May-June 2014: 70-84.

S. Taherizadeh, A. Jones, I. Taylor, Z. Zhao, V. Stankovski (2018) Monitoring self-adaptive applications within edge computing frameworks. *Journal of Systems and Software,* 136 (February 2018): 19-38.

Glossary

Adaptation: the modification of an executed software application by a human operator or an automated routine, often focused on modifications in component deployment and allocation of computation resources.

Adaptive Maintenance: changing a program to accommodate changes in stakeholder needs or computing environments.

Adaptive Systems: a software product that changes its behaviour in response to its environment.

Agile Software Development: software creation that relies on iterative processes that are highly responsive to requirements changes through the collaborative effort of self-organizing cross-functional teams.

Application Programming Interface (API): a collection of code features (e.g. methods, properties, events, and URLs) that developers can use in their applications to interact with components of a software infrastructure.

Architecture Decision (AD): describes a concrete, architecturally significant design issue for which several potential alternative solutions exist.

Architecture Pattern: a general, reusable solution to a commonly occurring software architecture problem within a given context.

Architecture Refactoring (AR): a coordinated set of activities intended to remove a particular architecture smell (defect) to improve at least one quality attribute without changing the scope and functionality of the system.

Architecture Smell: a suspicion (or indicator) that something in the architecture is no longer adequate under the current requirements and constraints, which may differ from the originally specified ones.

Augmented Reality (AR): a real-time direct or indirect view of a real-world environment enhanced by computer-generated sensory input (e.g. sound, video, graphics).

Autonomous Systems (AS): a software product capable of sensing its environment and managing its interactions and survival within this environment.

Bill of Features: a way to define a product in terms of its features rather than its parts; it is a useful communication vehicle between business, product marketing, and engineering units for describing a product or portfolio of products. It represents a selection made from a product line's feature catalog.

Binding Time: The decision at a variation point must be made at some point in time. Possible binding times are implementation time, compilation time, linking time, installation/configuration time, start-up, and runtime.

Business Ecosystem: a business network, or business community, including suppliers, distributors, producers, and customers that facilitates the production and delivery of products and services through cooperation and competition.

Cloning: practice of creating code fragment by copying similar code fragments from other parts of the codebase.

Cloud Computing: a subscription-based service that relies on the practice of using a network of remote Internet servers to store, manage, or process data.

Code Generation: process by which a compiler's code generator converts some intermediate representation of source program into another form that can be readily executed by some machine.

Code Refactoring: process of restructuring existing computer code without changing its external behavior.

Code Smell: a bad design choice that can have a negative impact on the code quality which could introduce defects.

Cohesion: degree to which the elements of a module belong together given the purpose of the module.

Conditional Compilation: process which allows a compiler to produce different executable programs controlled by adjusting the parameters during execution.

Configuration Management: task of tracking and controlling changes made to an evolving software product.

Context: A software/system is always developed to solve a problem in the real world. This part of the real world is the context of the software/system. A synonym for context is environment.

Context-aware System: a software product able to modify its behavior based on characteristics of its user or the environment in which it is used.

Continuous Delivery: practices which provide the ability to get all types of changes (e.g. new features, configuration changes, bug fixes) into the hands of the users safely and quickly in a sustainable manner.

Corrective Maintenance: the processes changing a program to repair defects uncovered during operation.

Coupling: degree of interdependence between two software modules, systems, or environments.

Customizable Systems: software applications that allow developers or users to tailor its functionality to better meet their own needs.

Cyber-Physical Systems: a mechanism controlled by computer-based algorithms that monitor and control physical processes placed in a feedback which may in turn affect the nature of these computations.

Defect: any deviation of a system component from its intended functionality.

Design Pattern: a general, reusable solution to a commonly occurring software design problem within a given context.

Design Rules: design heuristics for creating software emphasizing the selection of software features which support selected quality attributes.

DevOps: software engineering practice whose aim is to unify software development and software operations.

Domain Models: conceptual models of all the topics related to a specific problem.

Dynamic System Development Method (DSDM): agile, iterative, incremental prototyping approach to software application development.

Ecosystems Architecture: an architectural paradigm that considers not only the technical aspects of the ecosystem and the interactions on platforms, but also the relationships between ecosystems strategy, architecture, and governance, as well as the end-to-end perspective that includes both the customer and technology.

Enterprise Applications: software products that are designed to meet the business needs of large organizations.

Evolution: modification of a software application to implement new features, migrate the application to a new environment, or correct defects.

Failure: inability of a software system to perform its required functions within specified performance requirements.

Fault-Tolerance: the ability of a system to provide correct and continuous operation even when faulty components are present.

Feature-based Product Line Engineering: the engineering of a portfolio of related products (i.e. a product line) using a common set of shared assets, a managed set of features, and an efficient and automated means of production.

Feature Catalog: a model of the collection of all feature options and variants that are available across the entire product line. It is the full set of available feature choices from which a Bill of Features is constructed.

Feature Model: a key approach to capture and manage the common and variable features in a system family or a product line.

Flexible Development: software practices that allow the ability to make changes in a product or the manner in which it is being created even late in the development process.

Hazard: a risk that if realized can lead to the failure of a software system to satisfy its safety requirements.

Hierarchical Variability: top-down variability specification through hierarchically represented variation points where constraints define specific associations among the variability at different levels of the hierarchy.

Intelligent Software Engineering: application of artificial intelligence (AI) techniques to the development of computing applications or the creation of software that incorporates AI techniques to achieve its functionality.

Internet of Things (IOT): inter-networking of physical devices, vehicles, buildings, or other artefacts containing embedded electronics which enable these objects to exchange to collect and exchanges data.

Intentional Variability: making planned changes to a software product to accommodate changing customer profiles or usage scenarios.

Lean Software Development (LSD): translation of lean manufacturing principles (eliminate waste, build in quality, create knowledge, defer commitment, deliver quickly, respect people, optimize the wholes) and practices to software creation.

Legacy Software: software applications that are maintained because they are critical to the business needs of an organization.

Machine Learning: a subfield of computer science with the goal of giving computers the ability to use knowledge without being explicitly programmed.

Maintenance: process of modifying existing software while preserving its integrity.

Microservices: architectural style that structures an application as a collection of loosely-coupled services that implement business capabilities.

Mobile Apps: computer program designed to run on mobile devices such as smart phones or tablets.

Model-Driven Engineering (MDE): a software development methodology that focuses on creating and exploiting domain models, which are conceptual *models* of all the topics related to a specific problem.

Module Replacement: practice of replacing a separable component in software system with another with similar interface,

Non-functional Requirements (NFR): quality attributes (e.g. usability, reliability, security) or general system constraints.

Ontology: an explicit formal specification of the terms in a domain and relations among them in order to share common understanding of the structure of information among people or software agents.

Open Platform: software system based on non-proprietary standards which allows developers to reimplement, replace, or extend the functionality provided by the system.

Perfective Maintenance: process of improving a program's structure without changing its functionality.

Platform Business Model: a business model that leverages network effects to generate product innovations and value using resources from outside the organizational boundary.

Platform Ecosystem: a digital marketplace, coordinated by an organization or individual, that relies on a common technological platform to connect people, organizations, and resources.

PLE Factory Configurator: the mechanism that automatically produces application assets for the digital twin of a specific product.

Preventative Maintenance: improving the quality of a program without changing its functionality.

Polymorphism: the provision of a single interface to entities of differing data types to provide variable program functionality at runtime.

Product Line: a family of products that populate a portfolio to serve target market segments and are built and maintained in a way that specifically takes advantage of the commonality shared across the family while efficiently and systematically managing the variation among subfamilies and individual products.

Product Line Architecture (PLA): It is a reuse-oriented architecture for the core assets in the software product line.

Product Line Engineering: Development paradigm for software product lines. Product line engineering is typically decomposed into domain and application engineering. During domain engineering, reusable artefacts exhibiting variability are created. During application engineering, concrete products of the product line are derived from the reusable artefacts.

Reactive System: software systems capable of detecting problems quickly and dealing with them effectively.

Real-time Processing Systems: guaranteed response within specified time constraints, referred to as deadlines.

Reconfigurable Systems: software designed at the outset for rapid change in its structure in order to quickly adjust its functionality within a software product line in response to sudden market changes or intrinsic requirements changes.

Reengineering: process of restructuring or rewriting part of all of a system without changing its functionality.

Reference Architecture: a reference model mapped onto software elements (that cooperatively implement the functionality defined in the reference model) and the data flows between them.

Reference Model: refers to a standard decomposition of a known problem into parts that cooperatively solve the problem.

Reliability: the extent to which software completes its intended task without failure in a specified environment.

Resilience: an inherent property of reactive systems that is concerned with the responsiveness of the software product under failure conditions.

Requirements Engineering (RE): process of defining, documenting, and maintaining the requirement or specifications for a software system.

Reusability: extent to which software components can be used in new applications.

Risk: is an expectation of loss caused by a potential problem that may or may not occur in the future.

Runtime Model: reflects the current state of a software application as it is being executed.

Safety: degree to which potential hazards that may affect software negatively and cause an entire system to fail are prevented or mitigated.

Security: degree to which assets (data, bandwidth, processor use) of value are protected from attacks that will result in their loss.

Self-Adaptive Systems: a software product that changes its own behaviour in response to its environment and when the evaluation indicates that it is not accomplishing what the software is intended to do, or when better functionality or performance is possible.

Service-Based System: set of software functionalities based on the composition of services with a purpose that can be reused by different clients for different purposes than originally specified.

Service Composition: is a paradigm where software services are combined to form a higher-level service to meet end-user needs.

Shared Asset: "soft" artifacts associated with engineering life cycle of the products, the building blocks of the products in the product line, they can be represented with software, they are used to either create a product or support the engineering process used to create a product.

Simultaneous Decomposition: concurrent decomposition of process model and structural model that facilitates linking the activities in the process model with the component structures

Smart Devices: electronic device connected to other devices via different wireless protocols (e.g. Bluetooth, NFC, Wi-Fi, 34G, etc.) that can operate interactively with these devices.

Smart Home: building whose devices (lighting, heating, electronic devices) that can be controlled by a mobile device or computer.

Software-as-a-Service (SaaS): a software distribution model in which applications are hosted on the Internet and made available to customers on a subscription basis.

Software Complexity: attempts to combine measure of the coupling cohesion among the modules and within the modules in a product codebase.

Software Design: the process of creating and implement software solutions to one or more set of customer problems.

Software Development Life Cycle (SDLC): the process used to sequence the activities used for planning, engineering, implementing, testing, and deploying a software product.

Software Ecosystems: a set of software components functioning as a unit and interacting with a shared market to provide services and their interrelationships.

Software Engineering: the application of a systematic, disciplined, adaptable, quantifiable approach to the development, operation, and maintenance of software.

Software Product Line (SPL): a set of software-intensive systems that share a common set of features and are developed from a common set of core assets to satisfy the needs of a particular market segment.

Software Quality: degree to which a software product conforms to its functional and non-functional requirements and how well it satisfies user expectations.

Testing: process of executing a software product with the intent of finding software defects.

Threat: conditions or events that may be used to damage system resources or render them in accessible to authorized users

Traditional (Pipeline) Business Model: a business model in which value flows from a producer to a consumer.

Trust: indicates the level of confidence that one entity (system, organization, person) can rely on another.

Unintentional Variability: unplanned changes to software products or side effects that may result from modifying software architectures or existing design solutions.

Usability: the degree to which a software product is easy to learn and easy to operate to accomplish a user's task.

Usage Scenarios: describes a real-world example of how one or more people or organizations interact with a software application describing the steps, events, or actions which occur during the interaction.

Validation: process that ensures that the product meets the user's needs and that the specification was correct in the first place.

Value-based Software Engineering: considers the value delivered to stakeholders by each software engineering process activity.

Variability: ability of artifacts to be adjusted for different uses in different contexts.

Variability-intensive Systems: software system in which variability plays an important role.

Variability Realization Mechanism: technique for accommodating rapids changes in systems under development or in production (e.g. cloning, conditional, compilation, conditional execution, polymorphism, module replacement, runtime reconfiguration).

Variant: a variant belongs to exactly one variation point and represents an alternative for the decision to be made at the variation point.

Variation-guided Decomposition: decomposition activity where a variability model guides the decomposition of a process with its structural models and establishes relations with hierarchical variability.

Variation Point: a variation point represents a delayed design decision. Usually, several variants are provided for selection at a variation point.

Variability Modelling: supports the development of detailed variability models using variability related information from domain and application engineering.

Variability Modelling Language: the concrete syntax of the language, which may be a graphical or textual syntax or a combination of both to express variation points, variants, and variability concerns.

Verification: process of ensuring that a product has been built according its requirements and design specifications.

Version Control System (VCS): an automated system that provides the ability to track and control the changes made to the data over time.

Virtual Reality (VR): an artificial computing environment experienced through sensory stimuli (such as sights and sounds) to simulate the user's physical presence in the environment.

Web Apps: client-server software application where client component requires a web browser to manage the user interface.

Workflow: a sequence of engineering processes through which an artifact passes from initiation to completion.

XCOSEML: text-based modeling language for the component-oriented development methodology, that covers static constructs of COSEML and extends it by including dynamic constructs and variability.

Index